Praise for *The Kingdom Among Us*

"This book is a striking work of original theology, effortlessly synthesizing philosophical phenomenology, spirituality, and doctrinal theology. Although it is more readable than most contemporary academic theology, it is simultaneously more profound and more intellectually challenging. It teaches readers what Jesus means by 'the kingdom of God.' It was a wonderful experience to hear anew the voice of Dallas Willard in this book, but also a great experience to discover a new, young, and vibrant theologian—the author."

Francesca Aran Murphy, professor of systematic theology at the University of Notre Dame

"*The Kingdom Among Us* explores theological foundations of Dallas Willard's wide-ranging work. A reliable and engaging guide to one of the most influential 'spiritual' writers of the late twentieth century."

Miroslav Volf, Henry B. Wright Professor of Systematic Theology, Yale Divinity School

"Dallas Willard was one of the most important and influential Christian philosophers of our time. The beauty of Willard's work is not only revealed in his intellectual acuity, but also in his deep love for Jesus and his desire to help people come to know Jesus more fully. In this book, Michael Stewart Robb sets out to capture something of the power, beauty, and Christ-centeredness of Willard's work and to offer it as a gift both to those who know Willard's work well and to those who may be beginning to move into the rhythm of his words. In providing a deep and thoughtful outline and interpretation of Willard's thinking, Robb takes us on a journey that touches and moves both the head and the heart. This is a fascinating book that deserves to be read widely."

John Swinton, professor in practical theology and pastoral care, University of Aberdeen

"To my knowledge, Michael Robb's *The Kingdom Among Us* is the first book-length academic study of the thought of Dallas Willard. Robb has rigorously and sympathetically entered Willard's mind and heart. Scholars will find Robb's book interesting and thorough. Lay readers will discover a helpful roadmap into the depths of Willard's thoughts on God and a host of related issues and concerns. Highly recommended."

Christopher Hall, distinguished professor of theology emeritus, Eastern University

"I pastored one of those early churches where Dallas Willard taught Sunday school. I mean, when I taught, folks might come, but when Dallas taught, they brought their tape recorders! Me too. It was astonishing. It didn't matter which passage Dallas was teaching from—he always ended up presenting us with a rich biblical *Weltanschauung*, as the Germans like to say. I marveled to see parishioners studying fifteen, maybe twenty hours to prepare for the next Willard Sunday school class. These were life-transforming sessions. And now with *The Kingdom Among Us* Michael Stewart Robb gives us insight into the theological foundation of the Willard corpus. I'm delighted."

Richard J. Foster, author of *Celebration of Discipline* and *Sanctuary of the Soul*

"Dallas Willard is more often quoted than grasped; Willard is read but his overall thought is rarely mined to its depths. Robb has gone to these depths to unveil the logic of Willard's approach to Scripture, revealing Willard's long-standing interest in discipleship and life in the kingdom. For anyone looking to understand Willard's thought, this is a necessary and important contribution."

Kyle Strobel, associate professor of spiritual theology, Biola University

"Michael Stewart Robb may be the leading theologian on the planet when it comes to understanding the ideas of Dallas Willard."

Gary W. Moon, author of *Becoming Dallas Willard*

The Kingdom Among Us

Michael Stewart Robb

The Kingdom Among Us

The Gospel According to Dallas Willard

Fortress Press
Minneapolis

THE KINGDOM AMONG US
The Gospel According to Dallas Willard

Cover design: Kristin Miller
Cover image: iStock/ivan-96

Paperback ISBN: 979-8-8898-3414-4
Hardcover ISBN: 978-1-5064-8073-2
eBook ISBN: 978-1-5064-8074-9

To Thomas Merrill Robb
who gave me confidence

CONTENTS

ACKNOWLEDGMENTS

FOR THEIR ACTS of kindness and thus their role in a book that took ten years to write, I have many relatively unknown persons to thank, some of whom I regret to have forgotten. Thank you to Anne Hilborn, Bill Young, and Scotty Williams, who listened and prayed for me for many years. Thank you to Ben Rhodes, Trevor Hudson, and Daniel Napier, who read and commented on previous drafts. Thank you to all of you who said that you wanted to read my book about Willard, though you knew virtually nothing about it. Thank you to everyone who dug out cassettes from closets or located MP3s on old hard drives. Thank you to the "sound guys" and cassette ministry volunteers who recorded Willard over the years. Thanks to you all, Willard survives with a fullness with which he never would have otherwise.

Thank you to Jane Willard for making possible that crucial week of rummaging through Dallas's office and library. Thank you to the Martin Institute for sponsoring the Dallas Willard Collection at Westmont, making research like this possible. Thank you to Gary Moon for opening doors I could never have opened. Thank you for your unobtrusive friendship and genuine partnership over the years. Thank you to Philip Ziegler for believing in this project but most of all in me. Thank you for all of the extremely helpful conversations about Willard and theology. Thank you to John Webster for your, I believe, providential seminar on Aquinas. Thank you to Christoph Schwöbel for always pushing me as a theologian and philosopher. Thank you to James Catford, whose wisdom helped me navigate the treacherous waters of authorship. Thank you to Chris Hall, who walked with me through the darkness (mostly by telling me stories of playing basketball). Thank you to Ryan, Bethany, and all at Fortress who have sharpened this book and guided it into print.

Without exaggeration, most of all, thank you to my wife, Katharina, who is also my partner in this work. Thank you for buying all those books for me, letting me put them in our house, and giving me the years needed to finish a book like this. May it now be the blessing to others that it was to me.

INTRODUCTION

As a proclaimer and teacher of the gospel of his kingdom, I do not cease to announce a gospel *about* Jesus. That remains forever foundational. But I also recognize the need and opportunity to announce the gospel *of* Jesus (Mark 1:1)—the gospel of the present availability to every human being of a life in The Kingdom Among Us. Without that, the gospel about Jesus remains destructively incomplete.

—Dallas Willard, *The Divine Conspiracy*

THE ODD DUCK OF TWENTIETH-CENTURY THEOLOGY

> By insisting on the unavoidability of theology, however, I do not in the least mean to downplay the hard, deep work of special theological training and thought. I only want to insist that theology must eventually be in the service of the ordinary life of ordinary persons, and will invariably have a great impact upon their lives. Therefore we must strive in our theological studies to arrive at beliefs about God which faithfully reflect the way He is and how He relates to man, so that we may know how to live intelligently before Him in His world.
>
> —Dallas Willard, "Draft of 'The Spirit of the Disciplines'"

> We all live at the mercy of our ideas.
>
> —Dallas Willard, *In Search of Guidance*

"IT WAS JUST Sunday school," she said.

I had asked about her husband's ministry in Madison, Wisconsin, where he was a graduate student in the 1960s. With two small children and her own work outside the home, Jane did not have the ability to attend all that her husband did for the little Christian and Missionary Alliance church plant they had joined. But she remembers well the original setting in which her twentysomething husband first made public his theology.

The setting was modest, the traditional adult Sunday school hour of an American church, a time when ministers had the opportunity to teach their people in longer, less-polished messages that bore often greater depth than the Sunday sermon. Here, often outside the main sanctuary, where audiences were smaller than in worship but also more diligent and freer to ask questions, Jane's husband taught through key sections of Scripture, fundamental doctrines, and existential issues. And he would continue doing this kind of theology until he died fifty years later. But it was only after about twenty-five years of being a church-basement theologian that anybody who had not run into him in the foyer of a local Los Angeles church or in the halls of a certain West Coast university would know the name of Dallas Willard.

Theology from Church Basements

WILLARD SAYS THAT he never intended to publish anything of what he was teaching in the churches.[1] Since he was an avid reader and intent on publishing in philosophy, the thought to publish in theology probably went through his mind. However, he never acted upon it. He thought the world was already filled with too many Christian books of too low quality. Another book to rehearse tired themes and then collect dust on shelves was the last thing the world needed. So with great confidence in the word spoken under the influence of the Spirit, he kept his focus on the people in front of him, the small audiences that attended his free classes.

In time, he learned from the Hebrew prophets not to despise the day of small things nor to seek great things for himself.[2] He later counseled pastors, "One of the banes of the ministry is worrying about people who aren't here, and you just don't do that. You just pour the life into the people who are there."[3] And they who were there in those early

---

1. Dallas Willard, "Transcript of 'My Journey to and beyond Tenure in a Secular University,'" C. S. Lewis Foundation Summer Conference (C. S. Lewis Foundation, San Diego, CA, June 21, 2003).

2. Dallas Willard, "The Kingdom of God and the Word of God," *Becoming Transmitters of God's Life and Power* (Kempton Park Methodist Church, Kempton Park, South Africa, August 8, 1987), MP3/cassette, 50:00.

3. Dallas Willard, "Kingdom Living 5," *Kingdom Living: Walking in the Character and Power of God* (Southside Vineyard, Grand Rapids, MI, April 13, 2002), MP3, 14:30.

days were not there because they would receive a degree or would listen to somebody famous. They were there because they were searching for light for their everyday lives. And this former Missouri farm boy seemed to have what they were searching for.

If one studies the surviving records of Willard's oldest classes (handouts, recordings, flyers), they have a quality beyond what is expected of Sunday school teaching. Considering that Christian education was not his day job, he put an inordinate amount of preparation into one informal class. Much of that preparation came out of his personal study of the Scriptures and of Christian classics—with no thought of teaching the material to others. Some of it spilled out of his formal educations in psychology and in religion and out of his professional work in philosophy. But when a church's Christian education director asked Willard to teach, the director in no way was expecting Willard to prepare *this much*.

Neither were they expecting that Willard would deliver fresh theological content. Most Sunday school teachers work from books that their audiences do not have the leisure or discipline to read themselves. But every early example of Willard's classes bears an *original* theological quality in both design and insight. True, he did tend to repeat themes from church to church. Still, to approach every new topic he taught in the posture of "constructive theology," as it is called these days, is not the most efficient way to conduct a one-off class for twenty laypeople.

It took a long time before Willard was even able to make it to twenty laypeople. While a student at Baylor, he could not find a group that wanted to hear him, and in his desperation, he heard God say, "Never seek to have a place to preach; seek to have something to say."[4] It would be about fifteen years between hearing this and delivering the first lectures, which survive for our examination. Certainly, Willard had found "something to say" in that time. He probably did not expect it would be something his twentieth-century contemporaries were *not* saying. But it was.

And it was *just* Sunday school.

---

4. Dallas Willard, "Ministering the Kingdom Today," *The Soul's Eternal Anchor* (Rolling Hills Covenant Church, Rolling Estates, CA, 1988), MP3/cassette, 34:00.

The Accidental Philosopher

The Spirit of the Disciplines was Willard's breakout book. It was published after Willard celebrated his fifty-second birthday. It was not long after that this University of Southern California (USC) professor's calendar started filling up with appointments to speak at seminaries, colleges, conferences, and churches where somebody had read this unusual book.

In the year of its publication, 1988, Dallas Willard was, to the world, a philosopher. But getting there was something of an accident in his life. Willard's main interest in higher education had been in further training for his calling as a Baptist preacher. He attended two Baptist schools to complete a bachelor's degree in psychology. He was ordained with the Southern Baptist Convention in 1956 while pastoring his first church near his home in the Missouri Ozarks. Then, upon returning to school at Baylor University the next year, he began taking philosophy classes. Thus it was that, when serving as an assistant pastor in Georgia and feeling the need for yet more education, he decided to go to the University of Wisconsin–Madison to attend *yet more* philosophy classes.

As a newly minted pastor responsible for the spiritual lives of others, he had come to the conclusion that he was dangerously ignorant of God and the soul and that he had better get some help before becoming a public hazard.[5] It is uncanny how nearly his self-assessment echoes Augustine's own words at age thirty-three: "God and the soul, that is what I desire to know."[6] But having already taken numerous classes in religion and psychology, Willard thought his prospects for illuminating research into these two inescapable realities in pastoral work were not good in psychology departments. Neither were they much better in seminaries. His best prospects to study God and the soul, he thought, were among those we today call philosophers. Thus, in 1959, Willard made a fateful decision to enter a modern research university, the University

5. Dallas Willard, "Dialogue with Dallas Willard," *Scripture and Ministry* (Trinity Evangelical Divinity Seminary, Deerfield, IL, October 26, 2010), MP3, 1:30.
6. Augustine, *Soliloquies* 1.2.7.

of Wisconsin–Madison, seeking a minor in the nascent discipline of the history of science and a major in philosophy.

Hoping to only benefit from the discussion in classes with Marcus Singer and William H. Hay, Willard originally did not even intend to graduate. However, through a key seminar with Hay, Willard discovered a writer who, as he later says of himself, "saved me from Kant": Edmund Husserl.[7] And in his three-year attempt to make sense of the first German edition of Husserl's landmark *Logical Investigations*, Willard wrote a dissertation and was awarded a PhD. Still, in his mind, he was a pastor, albeit one now with considerable philosophical muscle. So it was with reluctance that he gave up shepherding a couple of country churches to accept an unsolicited position to teach philosophy at USC in 1965.

In those early years in Los Angeles, he likely felt more confident as a gospel minister than as a professor of philosophy.[8] For years he labored on a book on the epistemology of logic, which he set aside in the 1970s to complete a book on Husserl's early philosophy (including *Logical Investigations*) that he titled *Logic and the Objectivity of Knowledge*.[9] But for the most part, he spent his days teaching courses in "Introduction to Philosophy" and "Metaphysics," writing articles and academic reviews for publication, and supervising doctoral research. A campus pastor who knew Willard in those early days described Willard's attitude toward being a professor as "tent-making," but it is hard to know exactly how Willard viewed his calling at that time. It is plain that he volunteered an astonishing amount of time to preach, teach Sunday school, and counsel pastors and numerous laypeople.

Initially, perhaps due to his continuing aspirations for a clerical career, Willard continued to discipline himself in prayer and the study of theology. He spent countless secret hours examining both the Scriptures

---

7. Dallas Willard, "On Discovering the Difference between Husserl and Frege," in *American Phenomenology: Origins and Developments*, ed. Calvin O. Schrag and Eugene F. Kaelin (Dordrecht, Netherlands: Kluwer Academic, 1989), 394.

8. Dallas Willard, "Dallas Willard Intro" (Fuller Theological Seminary, Los Angeles, CA, 2010), video/MP3, 1:00.

9. Dallas Willard, *Logic and the Objectivity of Knowledge: A Study in Husserl's Early Philosophy* (Athens: Ohio University Press, 1984).

and numerous classic and modern theological books.[10] What he brought to the study—namely, (1) his proficiency in a number of ancient and modern languages in reading philosophical texts and in recounting intellectual history; (2) his ongoing interests in psychology, philosophical realism, and formal logic; and finally, (3) his determination to live the Christian life amid his life experiences—meant that he could penetratingly understand all theological texts he laid hands on. Thus when *The Spirit of the Disciplines* was published in 1988, three decades after choosing to study philosophy, Willard not only had left very few theological rocks unturned but had, more importantly, become confident in all aspects of gospel ministry. This, if anywhere, is where young Dallas intended to be after he turned fifty.

But in getting there, he had unintentionally become a philosopher. There is no other way to describe him at fifty. He was a full professor in USC's Philosophy Department. He could teach and had taught almost every class the department offered and had served as department head from 1982 to 1985. He had a major thesis, a major book, and a slew of articles on his résumé and was known internationally for his work. John Herrmann, his old teacher at Tennessee Temple, used to tell his students, "You are who you are becoming." This was Dallas Willard. A man who had become a philosopher. The rest was *just* Sunday school.

Most people would see it that way, which may explain why most people's Sunday school lessons cannot be turned into books that, as Willard's did, catch the attention of ministers and Christian intellectuals around the world. But Willard seems to have thought differently about informal teaching assignments and their place in his vocation. They were a place to do very high-quality work with very real people. He was there not to write his next book but to teach. And to teach in a way that affected people's whole lives.

His disposition was the same at USC. In 1968, three years after arriving on campus, Willard spoke to the USC campus newspaper about the "publish or perish" attitude in higher education. In his clever way

10. Dallas Willard, "Finding Satisfaction in Christ," *Preaching Today* (Christianity Today International, 2005), MP3, 1:00.

with words, he said, "I think that too many teachers are 'publishing *and* perishing.' That is, most of the students do not know and do not care whether the professor is dead or alive." He went on to say, "The professor must answer the question, 'What good am I doing the student as a total person with this course?'"[11]

In the churches where he worked, the general attitude was not "publish or perish." Most ministers in Willard's day were quite intent on teaching their people in a way that affected their whole lives. But few ministers were willing to do what Willard *did* in order to be *able* to do it. Most ministers were not ready to order their lives in a way that might *accidentally* make them a philosopher.

And not just a philosopher. When *The Spirit of the Disciplines* put on paper what Willard had been teaching in the churches, it was the work of somebody who could competently straddle *a few* disciplines. In his attempt to be competent concerning God and the soul, Willard, it seems, had also *accidentally* become a theologian. None of his books were the work of *just a Baptist preacher*. They were the work of one who could now carefully weigh the church's past teachings and make reasoned judgments about what it should teach today.

Agree with him or not, Willard wrote as a disciplined constructive theologian. This too was *not* his intent for his life. As a young thoughtful minister desiring to be effective, he would have been satisfied, it seems, to have found one theologian or one movement whose teachings he could study and share with others. In philosophy, he found Husserl and *never tired* of teaching his seminal insights to others. But in theology, he never found such a person or movement. Weaving together many things, he felt compelled to make his own way and inevitably created constructive theology.

Theological Amateur or Genius?

HIS INDEPENDENCE CAN be the most confusing and even frustrating thing about Willard as a theologian. On one hand, he did not work as

---

11. Ivan Browning, "Professor Plans Progressive Policy," *Daily Trojan*, May 21, 1968 (emphasis mine).

a *professional* theologian. He did not get a PhD in theology or publish with academic publishers or reveal his competencies in the history of the discipline or thoroughly footnote his work. Other than teaching as an adjunct for Fuller Theological Seminary over the years, he never held an academic appointment in theology. On the other hand, he did not hold back in making major and purportedly seminal claims about exegesis or dogma or ministerial practice. Within the professional's domain of knowledge, he claimed to know. And to know better.

As I will argue in this book, some of this confidence came from his competence in the neighboring fields of philosophy and psychology. He became persuaded that professional theologians were often too engrossed in "their own field" to understand the interdisciplinary issues that inevitably affected their work. What's more, Willard knew he had discovered an obscure but substantial philosopher who could "save *us* from Kant."

But some of his confidence came from genuine competence typical of any theologian who is more than just a well-read minister. This competence was gained not through an earned PhD or through teaching seminary classes or through attending scholarly conferences. It was, oddly enough, competence Willard sought out for himself in order to be *just a minister* who affected people's whole lives. In seeking this competence, two things happened to him. The first is that he gradually became dissatisfied with the theological system he grew up in. The second is that despite being a voracious, ecumenical reader, he never found another system that largely satisfied him intellectually.

In terms of his church tradition, he ceased being an *exclusive* Baptist. Though always involved in a local fellowship, his view in ecclesiology was that the "local church" was *all of the churches* in an area.[12] Therefore, though he and his family switched their default fellowship a few times over his lifetime, his membership (at least in his mind) was in all of the Los Angeles churches that welcomed him.

12. Dallas Willard, "Q & A 2," *Leadership in the Kingdom* (First Church of the Nazarene of Pasadena, Pasadena, CA, 1997), MP3/cassette, 18:45.

This mindset makes it difficult for one to name Willard's confession with much precision. According to Rev. Gary Smith, the minister of Woodland Hills Presbyterian Church, where Willard and his family attended from about 1976 to 1980, he called himself a "King James Baptist with a Quaker twist."[13] He never handed in his Southern Baptist ordination papers (and never intended to), but it is misleading to call him a "Baptist theologian" without being very specific about what "Baptist" refers to in his theology. In a quite verifiable sense, he was a theological mutt. Though there are traditions with which he had very little direct contact—for example, the Orthodox—he read "anything that had the slightest smell of Christian on it," and something from everything made it into his theology.[14]

This is why Willard's claim to *know better* than professional theologians can be particularly confusing. He does not even appear to be working out of any recognizable confession or under the banner of any particular great theologian! This is usually the sign of an amateur. Even the masters have their master.

This puzzled me about Willard in the early years after I had first read his main theological books. *Where did he get all this stuff from?* I thought. By that time, I had studied the history of theology and many contemporary schools of thought. But Willard's teachings, delivered with such directness, did not seem to fit into any major or minor tradition I was aware of. In my concern to understand better, I wrote to Willard in 2004 and received a simple reply:

> *Nearly all of my "influences" are from people long dead. I have arrived at my views by studying the Bible philosophically, if*

---

13. Gary Smith, personal correspondence with Donald E. Pugh, review of *In Search of Guidance: Developing a Conversational Relationship with God*, by Dallas Willard, January 26, 1984. Available in the Dallas Willard Collection at Westmont College, Santa Barbara, California.

14. Dallas Willard, "Interview with Dallas Willard," *Navigators International Council 2003* (Navigators, May 2003), MP3, 3:45. See also Dallas Willard, "Study and Meditation," *The Disciples, the Discipline and the Triumphant Life* (Rolling Hills Covenant Church, Rolling Estates, CA, February 25, 1981), MP3/cassette, 49:45.

> *you wish, and by reading widely through the ages, and trying to put it all into practice. It is presumptuous to say, but I believe that God has guided my thinking. Certainly nothing I have is really new or "my own."*[15]

Though I never had the chance to get to know Willard personally, this sagely answer to my question, I confess, marks the historical beginning of this book and my research into his thought. From that point on, I began actively sniffing out those "people long dead" who made this man think "nothing I have is really new."

As a first step, I began to read the books he mentioned in his footnotes, including the bibliography from *Disciplines*.[16] Though I never enrolled, I received a copy of the syllabus he used for his Fuller "Spirituality and Ministry" class, on which Willard listed over four thousand pages of reading from major works in Christian history. For two years, I used that list to educate myself in historical theology, always with an eye for the building blocks of Willard's theology. After that list was exhausted, I used other clues to locate the books that might have provided the sources, norms, and methods for his theology.

In the meantime, I began formally studying historical and systematic theology, apprenticing myself to professional theologians and forming my own convictions about the nature of God and of his works. I gained a fairly comprehensive grasp of the history of theology and had read all of its weightiest teachers.

I eventually realized that with Willard, this exercise was futile. Between 2004 and 2011, I had successfully located and studied many of Willard's favorite authors. He was not popularizing *them*. I came to the conclusion that *if* he was popularizing anything, he was popularizing *his own* complex thought. Though there were discernable influences, these influences had been carefully and creatively pieced together, often

15. Dallas Willard, email correspondence with the author, July 3, 2004.

16. Dallas Willard, *The Spirit of the Disciplines* (San Francisco, CA: Harper & Row, 1988), 266–70.

twenty years prior to publication, and infused with fresh biblical exegesis and critiqued by Willard's own life experience.

The tipping point for deciding that I, an aspiring professional theologian, should formally study a theological maverick came in 2011, when I finally began reading Willard's philosophical articles. I thought I should know what this "weighty" author spent his day job doing. As I persevered through paragraphs on "the ontology of number" and "the phenomenology of mental acts," a different picture of Willard gradually emerged.

This was a man whose theology was not just a romantic throwback to simpler times, a so-called premodern theologian. This was a man who, after having worked through the centuries of intellectual history, took the modern questions seriously. And had found a way forward! Not in a way that justified everything the older theologians were doing but in a way that kept their research relevant and likewise called into question the research of many contemporary professional theologians.

What's more, this was a man whose theology was not a self-selected bouquet of inspiring doctrines. Having found a way through modern questions, this was a man with a very intentional, very disciplined approach to "the knowledge of Christ today," as he called it. And this lent his theology a great amount of coherence and precision. It was constructive theology, but it was not constructed theology. This was highly disciplined *realist theology*.

If I can bring it to a point, the theological genius of Dallas Willard was that *he studied the Bible philosophically*. In fact, he read the whole Christian tradition, everything he laid hands on, *philosophically*. And the best of philosophy, he thought, was realism. On this point, he was fond of quoting L. T. Hobhouse: "All that religion requires of philosophy is a fair field and no quarter given."[17] Thus, it was not his ingenuity or inclinations that selected his doctrines and pieced them together. His "scissors and glue" was *good*, *cutting-edge*, and ultimately, *realist*

17. Dallas Willard, "The Redemption of Reason and the University in the Next Millennium," *The Christian University for the Next Millennium: A Symposium Celebrating Biola's 90th Anniversary* (Biola University, La Mirada, CA, February 28, 1998), MP3/cassette, 42:30.

philosophy. This freed him from the need to be dogmatic or to seek safety in some professional guild. He simply studied God and the soul, armed, as it were, with the best philosophy he could find.

The Divine Conspiracy Begins

AS MENTIONED, THE *Spirit of the Disciplines*, published in 1988, was Willard's breakout book. It made him a "spirituality guru," but it was neither the material with which he began nor that around which his thought ultimately revolved.

Long ago, while working as an associate pastor and a high school teacher in Macon, Georgia, Willard started doing something he should not have been doing. He started to read the four Gospels as if they had something to do with how he should be living. This went against his dispensationalist Baptist professors and his Scofield Bible, who had told him that the Gospels were "for another age." But what Willard had been told was *for this age* was working neither for him nor for the people he was ministering to. In his desperation, he turned to Matthew, Mark, Luke, and John and began—in his mind, at least—to write *The Divine Conspiracy*. These were the years 1958 and 1959. In 1991, his wife, Jane, finally convinced him to put pen to paper and share more widely what he had been learning from the Gospels and teaching in the churches. He was already the author of *In Search of Guidance* (1984) and *The Spirit of the Disciplines* (1988). But this new book—which he called *The Kingdom among Us* until his editor unwaveringly rejected the title to make it *The Divine Conspiracy*—was to be something special: "This book . . . from the systematic point of view should have been written first and I've actually been teaching this material longer than I've been teaching any of the other. I write more in philosophy than I do in religion. I've never sought to publish a book, period. And so I tend to write books when I get asked to write books. And I got asked to write this one last."[18] From the moment he sat down at his typewriter in 1991, Willard knew he was

18. Dallas Willard, "Case Studies from the Sermon on the Mount," *The Spirit of the Disciplines* (Gordon-Conwell Theological Seminary, Hamilton, MA, March 14, 1998), MP3/cassette, 1:15.

writing something that mattered. He would add two more books to his trilogy to form what I call Willard's pentalogy, the sum of what he published in theology. These books include *In Search of Guidance* (1984), *The Spirit of the Disciplines* (1988), *The Divine Conspiracy* (1998), *Renovation of the Heart* (2002), and *Knowing Christ Today* (2009). The third book was the jewel in the crown.

In his original book proposal, he wrote, "For thirty years I have taught what this book will contain, to many types of church and non-church groups. The message and faith of Jesus himself had moved to the center of my work as a teacher long before the material on spiritual disciplines, and was the foundation and driving force for the later. It is still what I mainly cover in conferences, seminars and courses—with the material on spiritual disciplines as a logical development of it."[19] This would be a book absolutely central to his theology, written with material almost as old as his work as a minister. After thirty years of teaching its themes, it would be the hardest book for him to write. It *had* to be right. Both *In Search of Guidance* and *The Spirit of the Disciplines* contained isolated and cryptic references to Jesus's gospel. But *The Divine Conspiracy* would let out the secret.

Willard kept no journal, and we will likely never know exactly what was happening in his mind between 1958 and 1972. But these years were when *The Divine Conspiracy* first took shape. Parts of chapter 1, he says, date from some teaching he did while active with InterVarsity Christian Fellowship in Madison, Wisconsin.[20] With encouraging effects, but without really knowing what he was doing, he says he started preaching on the kingdom of God in a couple Wisconsin churches he was pastoring in 1964–65.[21]

19. Dallas Willard, "Book Prospectus for *The Kingdom Next Door: Sharing Jesus' Faith in the Kingdom of the Heavens*," 1991, Dallas Willard Collection, p. 4. This is the original proposal for the book later renamed *The Divine Conspiracy*.

20. Jan Johnson, Keith J. Matthews, and Dallas Willard, *Dallas Willard's Study Guide to "The Divine Conspiracy"* (San Francisco: HarperSanFrancisco, 2001), 1.

21. Dallas Willard and Jack Hayford, "Wide Awake," *Leadership*, no. 4 (Fall 1994): 18–24.

Coming to his famous but nontraditional interpretation of the Beatitudes in *Conspiracy*'s chapter 4 (what he later called the book's "deepest layer") was about as revolutionary for him as the decision to read the Gospels at all.[22] In 1966, after a year in Los Angeles, he began attending a small Friends church. This is where fellow church member Stephen Graves—and, I think, some personal experience with mourning and persons truly "poor in spirit"—tipped him off to a more grace-based interpretation of the famous lines. Of his teaching during the first five years in Los Angeles, we know almost nothing, but in the early 1970s, we know he began teaching systematically through Matthew's Gospel and the Sermon on the Mount.[23] His new eyes for the Beatitudes are evident in 1972 and would become a mainstay of his theology and gospel ministry.[24]

Though Willard insisted that his views on the gospel of the kingdom finally published in *Conspiracy* were arrived at without the help of anyone in particular, we can make some educated guesses about the voices that surrounded him in the 1960s. One of Willard's favorite authors in those early days was the Presbyterian/Congregationalist philosopher of revival Charles Finney, who wrote extensively about God's moral government.[25] We also know that, while at Baylor, Willard was required to read John Bright's *The Kingdom of God*.[26] And as a budding

---

22. Dallas Willard, "What a Discipline for Spiritual (Eternal) Living Is: Why You and I Must Do Something," *Living the Eternal Life Now* (Church of the Apostles, Fairfax, VA, February 20, 2010), MP3, 1:08:15.

23. Dallas Willard, *Jesus' Good News of God's Kingdom* (Woodlake Avenue Friends Church, Canoga Park, CA, June 18–September 10, 1972), MP3/cassette.

24. Dallas Willard, "Handout for 'Jesus' Good News of God's Kingdom,'" (Woodlake Avenue Friends Church, Canoga Park, CA, June 18–September 10, 1972), Dallas Willard Collection; cf. also Willard, "Discipline for Spiritual (Eternal) Living," 1:08:15.

25. Willard, "Finding Satisfaction in Christ," 1:45.

26. At the end of Willard's life, Gary Moon interviewed Willard multiple times for the research purposes of the newly established Dallas Willard Center. In these interviews, Willard told Moon that *The Kingdom of God* was assigned for a class with Kyle Yates on the Old Testament prophets during his years at Baylor (Gary W. Moon, email correspondence with the author concerning *Eternal Living*, January 9, 2014). I have not been able to listen to the recordings of these interviews. See Gary W. Moon, *Becoming Dallas Willard: The Formation of a Philosopher, Teacher, and Christ Follower* (Downers Grove, IL: InterVarsity, 2018), 85–86.

young philosopher, he also studied Augustine of Hippo's main books and even remarks on the similarity of "the city of God" to the kingdom.[27]

As for evangelists, he read George Fox's *Journal* early on. Fox's gospel as preached in seventeenth-century England, though somewhat elusive and lacking in theological description in his *Journal*, is remarkably similar to aspects of Willard's. Another evangelist he was reading was the world-famous missionary E. Stanley Jones. Jones was still traveling and speaking in the 1960s, and we know Willard went out to hear him at least once.[28] Since Jones was almost the only prominent Christian in the early twentieth century who insisted that the church preach a gospel of the kingdom, Willard must have felt some comradery with him.[29]

Finally, though the metaphysical element is less obvious in Willard's earliest view of the kingdom, we must note, in light of how important metaphysics would become in his mature view of the kingdom, that Willard repeatedly taught a metaphysics course at USC in those early years.

Marketing Willard: Philosophical Evangelist or Spiritual Guru?

ODD AS IT may seem, Willard arrived late to the topics on which he first published books and for which he was best known: disciples, discipleship, and disciplines. *Conspiracy*'s chapters on discipleship and on the church as a fellowship of disciples—that is, students of Jesus—were some of the last to form in his mind. He says it was "almost two decades" after beginning to preach until he even asked himself, "What do we

27. Dallas Willard, "Morning Session," *The Kingdom of God and Ministry Today* (Kempton Park Methodist Church / Bedfordview Methodist Church, Bedfordview, South Africa, August 4, 1987), MP3/cassette, 1:06:15.

28. Dallas Willard, "Who You Are and Why You Are Here (Redux)," *Learning to Live an Eternal Life Now* (Ojai Valley Community Church, Ojai, CA, after May 1994), MP3/cassette, 1:03:30.

29. Stanley Jones's *Is the Kingdom of God Realism?* (Nashville: Abingdon-Cokesbury, 1940) is one of the only books Willard quotes from in his first teachings on the kingdom that survive (Willard, "Handout for 'Jesus' Good News'").

make our hearers?"[30] Only then did he realize that he ought to be making his hearers into *disciples*.

The artifacts of Willard's messages before the mid-1970s make little to no mention of discipleship and even then only of "discipline." In the late '70s, thanks to a series he gave on discipleship, he was asked to write for *Christianity Today* his gauntlet article "Discipleship: For Super-Christians Only?" which would be his debut as a religious writer. Other teaching series on topics related to discipleship led to him being asked to write his first books, *Guidance* in 1984 and then *Disciplines* in 1988.

This chronology has led to a popular misconception of Willard, one I hope to dispel in this book—namely, that his thought revolves around that for which he was initially famous: disciples, discipleship, and disciplines. His publishing history certainly invites this classification, but I believe it is to put the cart before the horse in more ways than one. The publishers who first discovered Willard clearly wished to market him to a late twentieth-century Protestant movement known best as *spiritual formation* and more generally as *spirituality*. Many readers were certainly surprised when they took in their hands what they thought was going to be "a devotional book" and found themselves reading philosophical theology—albeit with a gentle touch.

Now, spiritual formation as a movement or as a theory has not turned as many heads in Protestant theology as it has in Protestant pastoral practice. Willard himself thought the spiritual formation movement emerged in Protestant churches as a response to the failure of the earlier Christian counseling movement of the 1960s and '70s to solve the real existential and moral problems.[31] In 1977, Willard's friend and former pastor Richard J. Foster's book *Celebration of Discipline* came out and met a general Protestant interest in and hunger for partially forgotten practices of the Christian tradition. The practices detailed in the book were looked to in the hope that they would provide better solutions to real-life problems than Christian counseling had. By the 1980s and

30. Willard, "Morning Session," 13:00.
31. See Dallas Willard, "Need, Vision and Strategy for Spiritual Formation," *Spiritual Formation Track* (European Leadership Forum, Eger, Hungary, May 2006), MP3.

'90s, *spirituality* and *spiritual formation* were becoming catchall terms for solutions in Protestant pastoral practice that were (1) *not* preaching and teaching, (2) *not* licensed counseling, and (3) *not* social action.

It was in this context of seeking a different way that Willard came to the attention of publishers and editors who tried their best to repackage his thought in a way that would capture this "spirituality" audience. For example, three of the pentalogy were labeled as "spirituality," one as "spiritual formation," and one as "religion." This certainly contributed to Willard's commercial success, but it led to the characterization of Willard as someone mainly interested in better methods and not primarily in better theories. We can imagine, I believe, a different public profile for Willard if we postulate what would have happened had his core ideas been published under the auspices of "theology." That, as I hope this book will show, would have, at a minimum, pointed readers to the knowledge base out of which Willard attempted to speak. Theories, ideas, and doctrines would have been in the forefront, as they were for him.

But Willard's passive, backward way of publishing his theological teachings meant that this important ordering was often missed, even by some of his closest associates. Publishers are often too market driven, but I think Willard is mostly to blame for this. He, after all, knew the difference. The books themselves did not move on the sublevel of pastoral practice and personal spirituality. They each worked through some new understanding of the basic concepts of Christian doctrine. If one was not willing to reorder one's mind theologically, their practical elements—be it guidance, spiritual disciplines, discipleship, or formation—would be misunderstood and misapplied.

And even this he knew. That is, he knew he was not saying things that anybody who has received one of the standard theological formations of the late twentieth century would think of as "routine." The theology of *Conspiracy* or of *Guidance* was not familiar to anyone alive and, if true, was not insignificant. He knew this. Why, then, did he not make a *scholarly* project of it? Why did he not put his ideas into a format that let them be readily weighed and complemented by minds well disciplined in theological subjects?

Generally, I am thankful that Dallas Willard was a professor and intellectual who was not too haughty to become a popular speaker and one-on-one counselor to laypeople. Nevertheless, I disagree with how he managed his writing and speaking once he knew he had "something to say"—that is, his backward way of publishing—for it mitigated the effect he was able to have on the seminaries, universities, and intellectuals. It left his scholarship buried on old cassettes, often oversimplified for the uninitiated or tucked into pithy quotables. This genre, while appropriate for laypeople, is for scholars—those who have the responsibility to listen to those with "something to say"—difficult to handle.

One can give many reasons for why Willard worked this way. I have yet to find one that fully satisfies me. Nevertheless, I will give Willard the last word on the matter. In his initial proposal for the book that became *The Divine Conspiracy*, he wrote, "This is not an academic book, but one for common people—which of course includes academics, though they often do not know it. My experience with this material is that it will carry its own weight of evidence if it is made intelligible to people in terms of their own lives."[32]

Curricular Theology for the Twenty-First Century, or A Word of Warning for the Theologically Astute

UNLIKE *THE DIVINE Conspiracy*, this is an academic book. But it is also for common people who are lifelong learners and who wish to know how what Dallas Willard taught fits in, or does not, with what else is being taught as knowledge.

Let us, in the spirit of academia, look first at what Willard has to say about the nature of theology as an academic discipline:

> *It seems to me that we might best understand* theology as inquiry into the existence and nature of God and of his

32. Willard, "Book Prospectus."

> relations to creation, with special reference to the purposes of human life and salvation.
>
> *It could be pursued simply as an intellectual exercise, driven by the will to know, or as an exercise in being right, driven by the need to control. But the description I have just offered emphasizes the primary need of human beings to know how to live. The general human problem is practical: to find an adequate knowledge-base for practice.*[33]

There are three things that one might say about this characterization. First, this is, for the twentieth century, a very tame if not dangerously quaint definition of theology. Willard's century was the era of naturalized, historicized, contextualized, immanentized, Christologized, and eschatologized theology. Speaking of the discipline as a sober inquiry into the ontology of God, his properties and relations, sounds as if Willard had been left in the nineteenth century or earlier.

But here is a place where his "day job" as a tenured professor of philosophy has its advantages for his "night job" as a theologian. Willard advances this view of the discipline of theology with the *knowledge*, not complete but adequate, that the lofty heights of this inquiry can be reached. In Willard's extensive philosophical oeuvre, he will patiently and thoroughly, if not also convincingly, walk anyone through the issues. And though we will not do so in this book, skeptics of Willard's "quaint" view of theology can consult this oeuvre.

Second, it is also clear from this definition that Willard had his doubts about "academic theology," which is driven by what the modern university calls "research." Next to none of Willard's theological books could be labeled as research or as a treatise—that is, a demonstration of one's grasp of a particular topic—because nearly everything he wrote has a pastoral tone to it. This tone does not affect the content of his writing (which, when relevant, could be quite abstract) so much as it affects the selection of topics and the form.

---

33. Dallas Willard, "Handout for 'Spiritual Formation Track' at *European Leadership Forum*," 2006, Dallas Willard Collection (emphasis mine).

Though theology on the university has some contemporary exceptions, Willard's combination of a standard ontological approach with a practical telos makes him more at home in the theology of past ages. Willard knew this and, therefore, called for the theologians of the church to once again develop "curricula of Christlikeness."[34] To his discredit, I think, Willard never wrote up one comprehensive curriculum of Christlikeness. But everything he did write was *curricular*. It was, in other words, theology that kept the educational needs of the people of God foremost in mind. In that respect, it had everything in common with the writing of Augustine, Aquinas, Bonaventure, John Calvin, John Wesley, and Charles Finney. What all these theologians held in common with Willard is that theology's form should be heavily informed by its telos—namely, its aim to edify *and* its success in edifying.[35] Treatises can be written from curricular theology or for it, but the construction of treatises is not theology's raison d'être.

Third, it may not be obvious—because Willard was disinterested in treatises and never issued any comprehensive curriculum of theology—how *systematically* he approached the subject matter. Though the occasional and improvised nature of some of his oeuvre may suggest differently, Willard aimed for and achieved a remarkable *logical coherence* in his thought. This logical coherence is in large part due to his work and conclusions in professional philosophy, where he was constantly engaged in weighing various strategies for knowledge and claims to knowledge and became a vigorous defender of traditional formal logic. Willard was convinced that he ought to let his mind be informed by the ideal, mind-independent connections that exist between objects as well as their causes and effects. This will be painfully obvious to those familiar with his philosophy.

---

34. Willard, *The Divine Conspiracy: Rediscovering Our Hidden Life in God* (San Francisco, CA: HarperSanFrancisco, 1998), 313–14.

35. Though *pedagogical* or *catechetical* are also good descriptors, *curricular* continues Willard's own idiom in his call for curricula for Christlikeness. He names Wesley's *Sermons* and Calvin's *Institutes* as examples of such curricula (Willard, 371–72).

Another meaning of systematic theology, however, refers to the holistic or *comprehensive scope* of one's thought. That is, a systematic theologian is one who has thought of all of the relevant pieces so as to let them influence the details. In this respect, many theologians who reject the former logical approach to theology will still appreciate a "full circle" approach. That Willard was also systematic in this latter respect is harder to recognize. But the extent of his teaching career (sixty years of formal ministry!) meant that, *if* one knows where to look, one can find an espoused and often well-refined view of all major and many minor topics in theology.

That said, Willard did have a passive, backward way of publishing his theological insights and system. And when it came to the selection of topics for speaking or writing, he believed one must "judge the lay of the land for your times and shoot where the enemy is."[36] That means that the systematic ideal Willard's theology lacks most is proportion. While some topics are overrepresented (e.g., the Sermon on the Mount), others are underrepresented (e.g., the sacraments) and, because they may only survive on an obscure cassette tape, very hard to locate.

Hence, even though Willard thought systematically about theology, if we wish to know the system, we are presented with considerable challenge. And we will only succeed if we exercise good discipline in historical theology.[37]

Knowing Willard Today

IF WILLARD ONLY backed his way into publishing, it is imperative that we, who wish to know his mind the right way around, exercise good discipline as biographers and historians. For those who, like I, wish to find Willard's mind without the "simplicity filter" on, there are four sources that need to be studied.

---

36. Dallas Willard, "Kingdom Living," *Christianity + Renewal*, May 2002, 18.

37. Though more could be written about Willard's view of the unity of truth and of how he thought the traditional loci ought to come together into a *curricular* whole, space forces me to show rather than tell.

The first is, of course, Willard's pentalogy, the five theological books he wrote in his spare time: *In Search of Guidance* (1984), *The Spirit of the Disciplines* (1988), *The Divine Conspiracy* (1998), *Renovation of the Heart* (2002), and *Knowing Christ Today* (2009).[38] Outside of working on these five, Willard was not averse, when asked, to producing short occasional pieces or to giving interviews for magazines and popular books. A few of these articles, no more than twenty, were produced for educated audiences, and these evidence the same level of care that Willard put into his books. The majority of his short pieces were produced for lay audiences and, with a few exceptions, were written very quickly. These are Willard's most accessible writings but, as a result, the least illuminating for the complexity of his thought.

Outside of the pentalogy, all other books with Willard's name on them fall into two categories: (1) collections of articles, conceptualized and edited by others, and (2) lectures, transcribed and edited by others. The only such book that is not posthumous is *The Great Omission* (2006).[39] Compared with the pentalogy, which Willard edited heavily before their final drafts, none of these other books bears his characteristic gravity and maturity. In the case of the transcribed books, Willard's *unedited* extant recordings are much more valuable for the scholar and layperson. In addition to being free from editorial intrusion, they have

38. The last four books of the pentalogy have one standard edition. Willard's first book, *Guidance*, however, went through four editions (1984, 1993, 1999, 2012). The second edition (*In Search of Guidance: Developing a Conversational Relationship with God* [San Francisco, CA: HarperSanFrancisco, 1993]) added the epilogue and received minimal editing in the body. Neither edition sold well for the first two publishers, and a third US publisher sold a third edition under the title *Hearing God: Developing a Conversational Relationship with God* (Downers Grove, IL: InterVarsity, 1999). But significant cuts were made to the book that were unsatisfactory to Willard. Positively, the third edition was able to stay in print, being minimally expanded and updated for a fourth edition, *Hearing God: Developing a Conversational Relationship with God* (Downers Grove, IL: InterVarsity, 2012). Because the second edition (1993) is the longest and most represents Willard's intentions for the book, it is the most useful to scholarship, and I will almost exclusively refer to it here.

39. Dallas Willard, *The Great Omission: Reclaiming Jesus' Essential Teachings on Discipleship* (San Francisco, CA: HarperSanFrancisco, 2006).

the advantage of preserving Willard's intonations and emphases, which cannot be transcribed.

The second source is Willard's philosophical oeuvre. Willard told audiences more than once that he wrote more in philosophy than he did in religion, adding wryly, "but nobody reads that."[40] Indeed, Willard was a careful philosopher with an aversion to publishing for a promotion. In fifty years, he wrote only three philosophical monographs: his PhD dissertation, *Meaning and Universals* (1964) published in 1967; *Logic and the Objectivity of Knowledge* (1984); and *The Disappearance of Moral Knowledge* (2018).[41] Alongside these, Willard's writing energy went into publishing over sixty articles and over twenty critical reviews for books and journals.[42] The articles cover a wide range of traditional philosophical topics, but many coincide with his two unfinished book projects: an abandoned untitled book on "the epistemology of logic" and a metaphysics book he started in 1992 and called *Rage against Identity*.[43] Beyond these published articles, he wrote a long list of shorter pieces that he never published, more often than not because they were for occasional audiences or for his own benefit. A lot of the material he was using in his USC classes, including recordings of the very classes, is also preserved, and these show how comprehensive Willard was as a philosopher.

The best scholarly analyses of Willard will be thoroughly familiar with his philosophical output. These writings *cannot* be bracketed. Because of "the cacophony of twentieth century thought," as Willard called it, theologians today cannot assume but must know specifically

---

40. Willard, "Dialogue with Dallas Willard," 6:30.

41. Dallas Willard, *Meaning and Universals in Husserl's Logische Untersuchungen* (Ann Arbor, MI: University Microfilms, 1967); Dallas Willard, "Meaning and Universals in Husserl's Logische Untersuchungen" (PhD diss., University of Wisconsin, 1964); Willard, *Logic*; Dallas Willard, *The Disappearance of Moral Knowledge* (New York: Routledge, 2018).

42. Willard's unpublished presentations and papers, of which there are many, are available in the Dallas Willard Collection.

43. Dallas Willard, "Proposed Project for Sabbatical Leave for Fall 1992," 1992, Dallas Willard Collection.

what Willard himself thought as a philosopher.[44] So let me add this for anyone who looks at Willard's philosophical oeuvre with a concern that the time and effort of reading it is not worth the benefit: I have read it all, and I believe, though I am a theologian more than anything else, that *Willard's greatest legacy is his philosophy.* If I were in an awkward lifeboat situation with Willard's philosophy and his churchly writings and needed to sacrifice one or the other, I would select to save his philosophy. Willard not only mastered the history of his discipline from the pre-Socratics to his American Philosophical Association colleagues; he discovered some ideas that, if more widely known and more seriously studied, would transform not only philosophy but theology and the whole academy. These ideas were not particularly new, but they were inherently weak when the modern era took off and entered its twentieth-century form. Willard's primary legacy to us in the twenty-first century is that realism—"super-sophisticated realism," as he once called it—is the only viable philosophical option.[45]

The third source I have already mentioned: Willard's footnotes and references to the books he was reading. The introduction to *Conspiracy* lists eleven theologians and spiritual writers Willard looked up to, and he expected, perhaps idealistically, that his readers would simply read them and compare what they said to what he said and, especially, to what reality "says." Willard's grasp of phenomenology meant that unlike Aquinas or, perhaps, Calvin, he did not tend to quote an authority, even a biblical authority, and rest his case. As a phenomenologist, he wanted his listeners to go "to the things themselves," for he believed that knowledge is most secure when persons see for themselves, if possible. This means that he exercised restraint as a teacher in naming the people who agreed with him on a particular point or from whom he learned a concept. If Willard was allergic to something in theology, it was secondhand

44. Dallas Willard, "The Bible, the University and the God Who Hides," in *The Bible and the University*, ed. David Jeffery and Stephen Evans (Bletchley, UK: Paternoster, 2007), 30.

45. Dallas Willard, "Transcript of USC Course Metaphysics, Phil 460," 1993, Dallas Willard Collection.

theologizing. This explains why he was fearful that he might only create Willardians, people who only believed something because "Willard said it."

These three sources were roughly all that was available to me in the year Willard died. But around that same time, I was making a discovery that would change how Willard's mind could be known and lays at the foundation of this book. It began by chronologically organizing recordings of Willard that I had in my own possession or could quickly find on the internet. Some of these addressed topics Willard never wrote on, which was helpful to me, but they also contained clues to a long history of speaking in the church, as I have recounted. Beginning with less than one hundred recordings in my possession, I started hunting for more and curating them for my own use in researching Willard.

What I noticed is that Willard's primary mental corpus was not his pentalogy or his other published works but his speaking, or the vast sea of recordings over four decades. As I argued previously, this was Willard's intention. He reminds us that "the first book I published and all of the books in religion that I publish basically come out of series of talks that I give. I never really sought to publish a book in religion, but I talk an awful lot."[46] Never to my knowledge did Willard bring his own tape recorder. But he rarely spoke without one in the room.

Eventually, I began collaborating with the newly formed Dallas Willard Center of Westmont College to create a permanent collection preserved for future listeners. The oldest extant recordings known to me are Sunday school lessons on Acts from 1971. To date, I have found more than twelve hundred recordings, and I surmise that the complete collection will easily surpass fourteen hundred assets. These are the single most valuable resources for studying Willard. They, not the books, are where Willard is Willard.

The majority of these recordings (more than six hundred) come from after the year 2000, when the revolution of digital recording and duplication coincided with Willard's highest level of public visibility.

46. Willard, "Dialogue with Dallas Willard," 7:30.

But these also coincide with a period when Willard had very little spare time. There are many gems from that period, but rarely are they so because Willard is presenting something that he himself was working on with fresh eyes. The high level of preparation that characterized his earlier teaching engagements, the search for "something to say," drops away. Up until his last address in 2013, Willard *never* gave the same lecture twice. With each address, he made a fresh outline and improvised the details on the spot. But what happens in the latter messages is that Willard becomes, if one listens long enough, repetitive.

Everything before 2000, about 600 recordings at present, was recorded on cassette tape, and almost every recording is unique. There are five reasons why these older recordings are special. First, since Willard did not keep a journal, keep much correspondence going, or work out his own theology in heuristic prose writing, recordings are the best vantage point we have on Willard's early thought.[47] Second, in many of these lectures, Willard is teaching on a subject or sharing his exegesis of a text de novo. This means that the "roots" of his thought—that is, their connection to his life and to other ideas—are often more visible. Third, though Willard always improvised while speaking, he gave more preparatory time to the topic and to scripting handouts in his early years, which means that many of the messages are weightier. Fourth, in them are many themes on which Willard spoke in his early years but never repeated when his audiences were bigger. Fifth, Willard was not speaking as frequently in those days, and the smaller quantity of recordings spread over more years make every asset count.

Though recordings are much more awkward to navigate than published print material, the fact is that the primary genre for Willard's theology was the spoken word. In preparation for this book, I have listened to more than 1,100 of these lectures, and this book would have

---

47. Willard did most of his note-taking and drafting on yellow legal pad, much of which is preserved in the Dallas Willard Collection. However, Willard usually did not date his papers or keep his notes in any easily discernable system of organization. What's more, others have moved around his papers, so the archivists at the Dallas Willard Collection do not have his papers in the (dis)order Willard left them.

been impossible to write without them. They are the only place where the whole scope of Willard's thought and some of his most profound theological insights can be found. Providentially, much of this has been preserved, thanks to those faithful twentieth-century scribes who ran their church's "cassette ministry."

For readers who wish to go further, let me point to *Something to Say: A Comprehensive Bibliography of Dallas Willard* (2022).[48] This book contains, as the title suggests, all the gritty details of Willard's oeuvre, which is still expanding as new primary sources are discovered and curated. It also contains information about how Willard's audio and video recordings as well as many of his articles may be found for free online.

A Road Map for What Lies Ahead

AS I INDICATED, this book is the result of my study that began after that day in 2004 when I received that email from Willard. Let me take a moment to orient you to what it contains.

The Kingdom among Us is not a short book. At the most general level, this work is an attempt to show theologically educated persons that Dallas Willard's theology is worth worrying about. When I discuss Willard among such persons, I find is that there is a basic lack of familiarity with his main teachings, not to mention his more obscure ones. I *also* find that theologically educated persons, when they do hear what Willard has to say, tend to ask for more rather than less detail. This is because what Willard has to say *is* strange. He is not following, as I have emphasized in this chapter and will underscore with the rest of the book, any recognizable theological tradition of the twentieth century. Familiarity will only be won by hearing Willard out. And it turns out that Willard had a lot to say.

I have chosen, for a number of reasons, space notwithstanding, to interpret Willard uncritically—that is, engaging exclusively in

48. Michael Stewart Robb, *Something to Say: A Comprehensive Bibliography of Dallas Willard* (Munich: Sanctus, 2022). This book is exclusively available as a free gift to donors of Sanctus: A European Institute for Theology and Spirituality. For more details, visit https://sanctus.institute.

reconstruction and analysis of his main theological themes. I am aware that an absence of criticism and a rhetoric lacking constant reminders of my objectivity may make me appear, in some academic circles, starstruck or *unwissenschaftlich* (a fancy German word for "stupid"). I can criticize Willard, but I believe that at this point in time, we are in more need of understanding rather than distance.

In that spirit of seeking understanding, especially historical, contextual understanding of Willard, I have also chosen to compare Willard mainly to authors I know he read and interacted with. Given Willard's intellectual range, this restriction leaves open a huge analytical task, and I did not come anywhere close to completing it. However, I do hope that it helps with the historical task of uncovering more in terms of sources for Willard's thought.

More specifically, the reader should come away with a greater understanding of how Dallas Willard conceives of the Christ event—that is, God's coming into history in the person of Jesus and how he accomplished through it something that had never been done before. Without discounting all that might have been going on behind the scenes, what God mainly gets out of the historical life of Jesus, says Willard, is the whole life transformation of a gathered group of fewer than one hundred Jews. I understand that may not be the result of the Christ event that any of us were expecting. If it is any consolation, it was not what the Jews of Jesus's day were expecting either. Nevertheless, Willard is remarkably consistent in the way that he reads the Bible on this matter.

Apropos reading the Bible, it will be important, before we launch into the Christ event, to get some understanding (in part 1) of how Willard does this. The first step—that is, the next chapter—is to explain Willard's theory of the diversity of the Bible and especially of the New Testament. For example, he does not go for the ancient "fourfold interpretation of Scripture," with its heavy emphasis on typology, nor does he follow the seventeenth century's "covenant theology" or the nineteenth century's "dispensational theology," which was present in his childhood. Rather, Willard thinks of the Bible as an inspired product of the progression through which God's people passed as they gradually came to better understand God and his kingdom. When Jesus comes, his first listeners pass through a number of stages before they embrace all of what Jesus's gospel of the kingdom means for them and the kingdom and also for Jesus.

Now, *kingdom* is one of those biblical words that has never had a stable interpretation in Christian history. In the twentieth century, renewed interest has been poured into discerning its meaning in the Scriptures, especially in light of the fact that the concept seems so incredibly important to Jesus. But Willard appears to ignore mainstream exegetical research and to discover in the Scriptures an *eternal* concept of the kingdom of God. This is a significant parting of ways and has to do, as we will see in the third chapter, with Willard's realist hermeneutics and his overall interest in discovering the Scriptures' inherent metaphysics, what I call *biblical ontology*. Though Jesus's listeners' *knowledge* of this ontology will be a perennial theme of this book, Willard's epistemology will be passed over quickly to discuss, in chapter 4, Willard's view of faith, or his pisteology.[49] As important as their knowledge is, salvation for Jesus's people is, in the end, *by faith*.

In chapters 5 through 12, the book is divided into three cumulative stages (parts 2, 3, and 4). This is the heart of the book. Each part corresponds to one historical stage of Jesus's first listeners' understanding of Jesus and his gospel. Along with the main chapters explaining each level of understanding, I have included a few chapters on theological topics, the ignorance of which may hinder the twenty-first-century reader from rightly understanding what is happening at that particular level. The first of these theological topics, chapter 5, deals with important concepts in the Old Testament–informed worldview of Jesus's first listeners. The second, chapter 7, deals with the work of God before the advent of Jesus and how this intersects with what happened in and after

---

49. In as large a book as this, I must assume that most readers are roughly familiar with Willard's account of knowledge because of its accessibility in his philosophical publications and in *Knowing Christ Today* (New York: HarperOne, 2009). Considering his epistemology, it is important to note Willard's interest in particularism: "One must accept the fact that there is no such thing as *the* method of knowledge" (*Knowing*, 60). Cf. Roderick M. Chisholm, *The Problem of the Criterion* (Milwaukee, WI: Marquette University Press, 1973).

the time of Jesus. The last two inserted chapters, chapters 10 and 11, deal with the transition to an ascended view of Jesus, who is recognized, by some, as the Christ.

The main chapters on the three stages, chapters 6, 8–9, and 12, have a certain cadence to guide the reader. Each has an initial section on the topography of the gospel as understood by listeners at that stage. This section is followed by one on Christology and one on soteriology. The last section in each stage is on faith. The reader would do well to think of the first sections as comprising the first listeners' *knowledge* at that particular stage. The last section, by contrast, is about the first listeners' *faith* at that particular stage. One of the things that led to popular misunderstandings of Willard in soteriology and in theological prolegomena is that Willard never made his view of faith abundantly clear.

After all these years of working on *The Kingdom among Us: The Gospel according to Dallas Willard*, I am still pleased with the stadial path it recommends for scaling the Willard mountain that is his conception of the Christ event. However, I think the real pleasure and amazement for me, the author, and for you, the reader, is had when one sees how it works in the details. The beauty and potency of the details are what I invite you to explore here.

Part I
IN SEARCH OF BIBLICAL ONTOLOGY

You need to develop a theory of knowledge about the Bible. You need to develop it in detail. And this involves the metaphysical questions. You can't avoid them. So you can't just say, "Well, I'm an authority on the text." You really do have to face questions like, What is a text? What is reading? What is interpretation? And so on. And now if you have to go at that—and this is a key point, folks, forgive me for saying so. . . . You see, one of the afflictions of higher criticism is it is environed in the subjective and skeptical theory of knowledge that characterizes the modern mind as a result of its failure to deal adequately with consciousness and its world. And you don't have to dig deep, especially if you read the standard sources on criticism, to see that what you're dealing with is skepticism, subjectivism. And by the time you get down to the current period and you read people who try to do something with this now, often well-meaning people, it's just, you know, it's just "flow." That's all it is . . . just "flow," and there isn't any possibility of anything else because the whole idea of objectivity is totally lost.

—Dallas Willard, Biola University, June 13, 1997

THE FIRST LISTENERS' EYE VIEW

> The purpose of God with human history is nothing less than to bring out of it—small and insignificant as it seems from the biological and naturalistic point of view—an eternal community of those who were once thought to be just "ordinary human beings." Because of God's purposes for it, this community will, in its way, pervade the entire created realm and share in the government of it. God's precreation intention to have that community as a special dwelling place or home will be realized. He will be its prime sustainer and most glorious inhabitant.
>
> —Dallas Willard, *The Divine Conspiracy*

ONE OF THE perennial questions of any attempt to pull together Christian theology to teach it to others is the question of order. What ideas should be presented first and what second? Should there be one idea around which everything else revolves? Should there be a climactic idea to which everything else builds? These questions matter because order affects not only how readers engage the teachings but also how the teacher sees the realities themselves. Describing a mountain from the pinnacle may result in a different relationship to the mountain than if it is described from the base or from its core. Describing Christ from all of eternity may result in a different relationship to him than if he is described from the perspectives of those who met him in the fields and streets of Galilee.

Since the early modern period, there has been increasing awareness that the Bible itself complicates the question of teaching order even further. Though Augustine was less aware of it, it is a settled belief now that the earlier books in the Bible were not written with the same theological understanding as later books. Take, again, the understanding of Christ. Hebrews has a different Christology than Deuteronomy—if the latter even has one. This may seem obvious to us now, but it was not always obvious to ancient exegetes who used a variety of hermeneutical techniques to smooth over the differences in the text. We now recognize that the unity of the Bible is not because of its homogeneous theology—one constant understanding of Christ and other topics—but because the Bible is part of a long historical process that took place in the people of God, both Israel and the church. Christians agree that this process is not merely human and haphazard; rather, the unifying principle is God's relationship with this people over time.

That is all fair and good for reading the Bible. We can read Deuteronomy in its place in the history of God with this people, and we can read Hebrews in its place. But it complicates the question of teaching Christian theology to others. Again, the understanding of Christ is a good example. Christians agree that the most mature, most robust view of Christ the Bible presents is the one that should ultimately be taught. So teachers ask questions about whether one should introduce Christ as a first topic, as a central topic, or even as a climactic, punchline-type topic. And how, teachers wonder, should one teach *the history* leading up to this mature view and teach *the books*, such as Deuteronomy, which were produced further back in the process? Since Christ will be highly important in any Christian attempt to teach others, need a teacher even refer to those earlier books and that earlier history?

Fortunately, these are the questions the writers of the Bible wrestled with as well, though we today seem less aware of the struggle. There is good evidence that the authors of the Gospels all, not just John, have a very mature view of Christ as their theological backdrop. But despite this, they persist in telling the story of people who do not hold a mature view and who are only fumbling along toward it (or away from it). In their efforts to teach the early Christian community and those outside it, they made a decision of order, deciding against teaching Christ and his gospel from an exclusively "God's eye view" of it all but for presenting the same concepts from the grassroots level, from the trenches, from the first listeners' eye view. Why did they do this? What were they hoping to accomplish?

Regardless of why they did it, their honesty about the real story, the unorthodox beginnings of Jesus's first listeners, raises the important question of why Christ came as he did. Why he did not come with his full glory on display—true God, true man? And this points to an even bigger question, that of what *God* was doing in all those years before Christ came. Both questions ask about the meaning of God's extremely, almost painfully patient relationship with his people in history. If Christ is so important to God's purposes, why did Christ not come right at the beginning of human history? And since he patently did not, what is the aim of God's having waited?

God's March through Human History

IN DECEMBER 1971, Dallas Willard was on sabbatical from the University of Southern California (USC) and had agreed, as he usually did, to teach Sunday school for his local church. Willard had been a child of both dispensationalism and revivalism, and the book he chose to teach on this quarter was a favorite of both movements. In his second lecture, he had this to say about the special way he was reading and teaching it: "I was attempting to place the events and the book of Acts in the context of the work of God throughout the ages." He then says to the participants, "Do your own thinking about this. Try to understand the sweep of history as the field in which God is working to bring something about."[1] This is an astoundingly early instance of themes that would occupy Willard for the rest of his life, such as human history—human history not as "one damned thing after another" but as caught up in the cumulative work of God in time. As he taught later in his life, human history only exists because God, in his wisdom, has set up the world in such a way as to get a *certain* result. So while humans are vital to the progress of the

1. Dallas Willard, "The Kingdom Comes in Power," *Studies in the Book of Apostolic Acts: Journey in the Spiritual Unknown* (Woodlake Avenue Friends Church, Canoga Park, CA, November 28, 1971), MP3/cassette, 2:00.

world to its end, it is above all important that God is involved, "working to bring something about."

Readers of Willard should be familiar from *The Spirit of the Disciplines* with what he called the *psychology of redemption*.[2] Taken from Oswald Chambers's book of the same title, this phrase denoted for Willard *the theory* of the "progressive sequence of real human and divine actions and events that resulted in the transformation of the body and the mind."[3] In other words, it is the theology of the process by which the Triune God saves the individual soul and saves it "to the uttermost" (Heb 7:25). As a member of the Western church in the late twentieth century, Willard felt a special burden to remind the church that this process will not happen if individuals are passive. "Grace," Willard insisted, "is opposed to *earning*, not to effort."[4] And much in Willard's pentalogy, including two whole books, *Disciplines* and *Renovation*, deal with the theology of this process.

Readers of Willard, however, will be less familiar with Willard's interest in what he called the *history of redemption*. Taken from Jonathan Edwards, this phrase refers to the *theory* of ordered steps God took and is taking in human history to accomplish his plans for salvation in the cosmos. "God's March through Human History," as Willard once called it, is the process in which God is gradually bringing about something that either has been lost or has never quite existed in his universe.[5] The history of redemption is the cosmic flow into which Willard was trying

2. Dallas Willard, "The Secret of the Easy Yoke," *Deliverance from the Law of Sin and Death* (Eastern Mennonite College, Harrisonburg, VA, January 14, 1985), MP3/cassette, 14:30: "One of the things we lack today is an adequate psychology of redemption." See also Dallas Willard, "Breaking the Bondages of Life—Part 2," *Essentials of Kingdom Living* (Valley Vista Christian Community, Sepulveda, CA, 1986), MP3/cassette, 1:30. In an early series on Romans, he says he learned to read the book as a manual on the human soul (Dallas Willard, "Reigning in Life through One, Christ Jesus," *Romans* [Faith Evangelical Church, Chatsworth, CA, September 18, 1977], MP3/cassette, 29:00).

3. Willard, *Disciplines*, 111.

4. Dallas Willard, "The Spirit Is Willing: The Body as a Tool for Spiritual Growth," in *Christian Educator's Handbook on Spiritual Formation*, ed. Kenneth O. Gangel and James C. Wilhoit (Grand Rapids, MI: Baker, 1994), 225.

5. Dallas Willard, "Plain People Lifted into God's March through Human History: The With-God Life under the Hebrew Covenant," *The With-God Life: The Dynamics of*

to set the acts, divine and human, that are recounted in Luke's second book.

As a cradle dispensationalist, Willard's earliest teachers had taught him one way of conceiving of this history.[6] But by the time Willard taught on Acts in 1971, he had clearly been reading an earlier treatment of the issue, Augustine's monumental *City of God*. And from Augustine and elsewhere, Willard was learning that there are ways other than dispensationalism of conceiving the theory, the central acts, and the final target of redemption.

In fact, Augustine's theology was probably more in his mind in those early days than he lets on to. His first attempts to describe the kingdom of God speak of it as a cosmic fellowship in which God's will is done and into which Jesus is inviting new members. This sounds remarkably like Augustine's city of God, likewise a fellowship composed of the unfallen angels, saints in glory, and faithful pilgrims on earth. Because its first members were the immortal angels, the city of God is very old, much older than the earth and the human race. And though it did not have any need of being "founded" by Jesus through his coming, Augustine thinks of the city of God as the sort of fellowship that seeks a certain completion in the consummation of human history, when the full number of God's elect are gathered in.[7]

Scripture for Christian Spiritual TransFormation (Renovaré International Conference / Spiritual Formation Forum, Denver, CO, June 20, 2005), MP3.

6. At present, Willard's earliest years in Missouri and at Tennessee Temple are too obscure to know the precise books or persons that were representative of his earliest theology, though one prominent name is Baptist pastor J. Harold Smith. Willard says that he was raised "without knowing the word" in dispensationalism and in a view that what Jesus taught is irrelevant to Christian life because it was for another age and that what is relevant about Jesus is what he did on the cross (Dallas Willard, "The Kingdom of God and the Person of the Psychotherapist Part 1," *The Care of the Soul* [Christian Association for Psychological Studies, Virginia Beach, VA, April 1995], MP3/cassette, 6:15).

7. Cf. Willard, *Disciplines*, 127. He continues, "As a result of Paul's experience with Christ's Kingdom, Paul recaptured the ancient, prophetic vision of the world being governed by the people of God—governing through the light and power resident in them *as* God's earthly dwelling place" (127).

With Augustine in mind, one may wonder what exactly Willard was talking about in his now famous statement of biblical teleology that he first expressed in those Acts lectures in 1971:

> *God's aim in human history is the creation of an all-inclusive community of loving persons with himself included in that community as its primary sustainer and most glorious inhabitant.*[8]

Is this a statement about the church? Or a statement about the kingdom of God? Or about both? If the kingdom of God *is* a fellowship of created beings gathered around their God, it would seem that Willard, at least in 1971, believed that God's *aim* in human history was the kingdom of God or, at least, its completion. If so, this kingdom is not a metaphysical reality that is transcendent and fundamentally immune to human history so much as the immanent and gradual goal of redemption.

Much more can be said about the development of Willard's mind than I am at liberty to do here. Suffice it to say, this is *not* how Willard spoke of the kingdom in his mature years. As the Augustinianism gradually falls away from his account, a more eternal, metaphysical, and Trinitarian view of the kingdom takes its place, and in the end, Willard comes to sound more like Bonaventure or Aquinas. The kingdom of God forms, along with God himself, a part of that which is blessedly eternal in biblical ontology.[9] Theologians will notice how Willard's mature view of the kingdom fits hand in glove with his interest in the psychology of redemption or, as Bonaventure called it, "the soul's journey into God."[10] For the medieval scholastics were far less concerned with the history of redemption and far more with their present participation in the redemptive ontology that is now at hand.

---

8. Dallas Willard, "Handout for 'Studies in the Book of Apostolic Acts,'" (Woodlake Avenue Friends Church, Canoga Park, CA, November 28, 1971–January 30, 1972), Dallas Willard Collection, 35.

9. Ontology is the study of what is and of what fundamentally is. Biblical ontology is the Bible's overall teaching about what is and what fundamentally is.

10. See Bonaventure's *Itinerarium Mentis in Deum.*

But as the kingdom of God migrates to a more ahistorical place in his overall theology, Willard does not abandon his interest in the history of redemption. He, after all, still has to account for the diversity in the biblical writings and for the fact that certain key events, like the coming of Christ, are *not* at the beginning of biblical history. He, unlike the medieval theologian, can no longer make use of patristic hermeneutical techniques to smooth out the Bible's message. Willard, as all who would presume to teach Christian theology today, must find an adequate theory of history, especially biblical history.

Key #1: Teleology

THIS IS WHERE Willard's ongoing interest in God's purposes and the history of redemption comes in. For Willard was not in the habit of repeating his famous 1971 statement of teleology. He kept tweaking it, and in 1989, he expresses it this way: "God is going to create a community of loving, creative, intelligent, loyal, faithful, powerful human beings. And they are going to rule the earth."[11] In this statement, there is still mention of fellowship, but there is more emphasis on the character of that fellowship. More significantly, this statement includes the vocation of that fellowship—namely, ruling the earth. In the 1971 formulation, the emphasis is entirely on the togetherness of the community. But here, the community has a responsibility. And the character that they instance is not just for keeping the community together but for guiding them as they rule.

Most of Willard's readers, even if they have never heard a statement like this, should recognize how Willard framed the work of God—creation and redemption—in terms of God's purposes. Even the possibility and fact of human rebellion against God is interpreted by Willard in terms of God's loving and most wise purposes for his creation. God made human rebellion possible so that he, at the end of history, could inhabit a people who lived and reigned with him by means of their freely chosen character. Perhaps it fit better with what he wanted to

---

11. Dallas Willard, "Why There Are People on Earth," *Life without Lack* (Valley Vista Christian Community, Sepulveda, CA, February 19, 1989), MP3/cassette, 35:45.

say about the fall and its remedy, but *reigning*, rather than mere fellowship, becomes for Willard the dominant activity of the people of God in eternity. This too, we may note, indicates his movement away from the Augustinian vision.

This is where theology comes in for Willard, not as an occupation for tenure-seeking academics, but as a part of a practical solution for humanity. For part and parcel of the depravity that came as a result of their rebellion was humanity's inability to know God. Good theology, though essential for human flourishing and cosmic reigning, is outright impossible in a depraved human state. Thus, the salvation of such beings would necessarily involve a process by which they could once again know their God. And so, before its foundation, God conceived of the world and his involvement in it in the most perfect and loving way *so that* human beings could, by his grace, know him as well as overthrow all other consequences of the fall.

But not only is knowledge intrinsic to the restoration of humanity to its *former* glory; the *future* glory of humanity is likewise a state and a vocation that depends on knowledge. God's grand intent for humanity is that we should creatively reign with him. And this vocation is not possible without much more knowledge than even Adam and Eve might have had in their so-called integral state.

Getting all this knowledge into human beings is easier said than done. But God, according to Willard, is so loving and so wise in the way that he providentially orders the world and his major acts in history. And *nothing* will stop him from accomplishing his purposes. With this God at the helm, this world, exactly as it is, is the best possible that could have been created, for it alone can be a stepping-stone to God's future plans.

Willard would sometimes ask skeptics if they could think of a better way for the world to exist than the one that does exist.[12] Needless to

---

12. See Dallas Willard, "History and Personality: Why a Good God Permits Sin and Suffering," *Prospects for an Evangelical Apologetics in the 1980s* (Bethel College, North Newton, KS, September 20, 1982), MP3/cassette, 43:45, where he cites Bishop Joseph Butler as inspiration for this question.

say, he never heard anything profound. The great evil and suffering in human history are all necessary and inescapable in order that humanity can take its honored place in the cosmic order. Everything is teleological. Everything that God does has been done so that the greatest number of people will inherit this glorious future of eternally reigning with their glorious God.

This, his teleology, is the first key to Willard's theory of the history of redemption. The second is found in a concept, virtually unknown to all his audiences, that he called *progressive apprehension*.

Key #2: Progressive Apprehension

IT WAS THROUGH digging around in the cassettes and yellowed handouts from Willard's speaking ministry that I first happened upon the term *progressive apprehension*. It was printed on a handout for a Sunday school series in 1975.[13] In the last lesson of the class, Willard planned to speak in general terms about Jesus's coming and preaching. The outline for his sixth main point reads thus:

> *6. The triumph of Christ in the life of mankind is not one of force. Ambiguity of the old testament vision of God's way. Indicates a progressive apprehension of God. The "bloody" eschatology current today is not in the spirit of Christ. We are simply to "be ready" and "be doing" (Matt. 24:44–46).*

Since recordings of the class are missing, we must infer some of the context. One may remember that Hal Lindsey's *The Late Great Planet Earth* was published in 1970 and created such a stir that it became one of the best-selling nonfiction books of the twentieth century. With this discussion in everyone's ears, Willard was teaching, we can infer, that the "old testament vision of God's way" was one in which Israel's God

---

13. Dallas Willard, "Handout for 'Studies in the Gospel of Jesus Christ'" (Shepherd of the Valley Lutheran Church, Canoga Park, CA, 1975), Dallas Willard Collection. Only the notes of these talks have, as of yet, been found.

triumphed on the earth by force.[14] Willard's point, a familiar feature of his mature theology, is that God and Christ's eternal way, expressed in the New Testament, is one of *gentleness.* But this point aside, it is the subpoint, how he accounts for the change from Old to New, that gives us an important angle on Willard's mind.

Progressive apprehension, the concept Willard purportedly will teach the class, is possibly his own construction.[15] It refers, for him, to the fact that biblical ontology—unchanging knowledge of God and his ways—was only gradually ascertained by God's people over the course of their history. So, for example, *gentle* was not how the biblical people thought of their God from the beginning. But gradually, they apprehend that he, in sharp contrast to them, is fundamentally and eternally gentle. An immediate advantage of Willard's theory when it is applied to the real history of God's people is that it can account for much of the historical diversity in the biblical texts. Deuteronomy does not have the same theology as Hebrews because the biblical people had not yet understood God as they would. And yet the theory does not solve all theological problems. It leaves unanswered the question of why God, who is certainly willing and able to speak to his people, did not reveal his eternal character to them sooner.

Now, not only were these 1975 class notes the first time I encountered Willard's concept; it seems to be the first time he did as well. On the first page of his personal copy of the handout, one finds the following handwritten note:

> *in the Bible not progressive revelation but a revelation of progressive ~~application~~ apprehension.*

14. Willard, probably not implicating the Old Testament literature specifically, is certainly implicating the covenant people during the time of the Old Testament events. Hal Lindsey, *The Late Great Planet Earth* (Grand Rapids, MI: Zondervan, 1970).

15. Possibly not. Augustine writes in *The City of God* X, 14, "The right education of humanity, so far as the people of God is concerned, like the right education of a single individual, advances through certain eras of time" (Augustine, *The City of God*, trans. William Babcock [Hyde Park, NY: New City, 2012], 321).

This scribble is important not only because his own thought process is visible but because Willard clearly names the more familiar view he is distancing himself from. Progressive revelation, an important theory to covenant and dispensationalist theology, is the theory that God guards but gradually lets out important information about himself over time.[16] His Trinitarian nature or certain elements of his character, for example, were intentionally kept secret until God decided to let them loose in the New Testament writings.

Sadly, Willard left us with no longer treatment to follow his line of thought here, and as with many finer points in his theology, some topics must be studied from bits and pieces that fall from his ad hoc teaching. But I think we can responsibly speculate that progressive revelation is distasteful to Willard as a theory because of how it directly implicates God for the "shoddy theology," which in earlier times guided God's people. Shoddy theology, such as claiming divine sanction in the improper use of force to bring about good, has resulted over the past millennia in vast moral evils, as Willard well knows. If God is directly responsible for suboptimal views of himself, he is responsible for the application of those views in suboptimal living, to put it mildly. As an alternative, Willard conceives of the Bible as divinely inspired *revelation*, yes, but one rooted in a people's *progressive apprehension* of their God and his kingdom.

Now the decade in which this note was written represents years in Willard's life when he was still forming the theology that would operate largely *in the background* of his books and teaching. In 1975, Willard was not yet asking about the knowledge and character that God's people would need to rule the earth for eternity. But he did know that some general account needed to be given for the divergence evident in the inspired Scriptures. And in questioning the neat but forced epochal categories in which the Calvinistic Baptist theology of his youth moved, he was attracted in some respects to the patristic model that he finds, above all, in Augustine. But he is also aware that he is on *this side*

---

16. See, e.g., Charles Hodge, *Systematic Theology*, vol. 1 (New York: Scribner, 1872), 446, 490.

(1) of the Reformation, (2) of historical-critical research, and (3) of many modern philosophical proposals to understand God and time. In the tension of these swirling movements, he spies a theory that, to his mind, has the advantage of implicating *humanity* for its own shoddy theology and shoddy living.

Later, on a cassette recording from 1987, I fortunately found an instance of Willard renewing his theory of progressive apprehension and using the concept to again explain changes in theological thinking evident in the Scriptures. He gives examples such as the story of Achan and of corporate guilt, the Old Testament representation of women, and the response to intermarriage in Ezra 9–10. Interpreting these cases collectively, Willard says, "All through the Scriptures we see a progressive apprehension of God."[17]

When an audience member, confused about Willard's sense of the word *apprehension*, asks for clarification, Willard says, "I didn't use the word 'revelation' even. Apprehension. . . . The Bible is a record of that apprehension of God." Again, when an audience member asks him to explain his comment about not using the word *revelation*, he says, "Well, there have been a lot of theological wars which have been fought about it. . . . There are many people, for example, who are very ready to go to battle over progressive revelation. And I think, actually, there was not a progressive revelation. I think that those who drew near to God in his [*sic*] time understood his heart, but many of them did not. And so I distinguish the apprehension or comprehension from the revelation."[18] Willard's claim that *anyone at any time* who drew near to God could know his heart is certainly theologically interesting. But regardless of what he means by it, it is significant because it suggests that progressive apprehension has become for him *more* than a solution to theological divergence in the Scriptures.

Indeed, in his mature theology, a theory of progressive apprehension had become the historical, boots-on-the-ground counterpart of *his*

17. Dallas Willard, "Does God Talk to Girls?," *A Woman's Prerogative in Christ* (Valley Vista Christian Community, Sepulveda, CA, November 1987), MP3/cassette, 1:11:00.
18. Willard, 1:11:00.

teleology. It is the flip side of God setting up the world in such a way as to get a certain result. God, so Willard, is not standing by passively as humanity fights its way toward an adequate theology for life and for eternity. It is God's very aim in his "march through human history" that people are gradually led along so that they might *know*—above all, that they might know him but also that they might know themselves and the whole subject matter of theology. Scriptures with a unity yet a diversity in the ideas are a natural effect of the world being set up and stewarded in this way. For the flip side of an ancient people's progressive apprehension is purposeful providence.

So then, where does Christ come in?

The Kingdom and Its Christ

HOW EXACTLY WILLARD answered the Christ question in those early days when Augustine's vision of a heavenly fellowship was still in his mind is still unclear. But one thing is clear. He continues to think of the Christ event just as he said he wanted to read Acts: "in the context of the work of God throughout the ages."[19]

Now, the main function of any account of the history of redemption is to make sense of the place of Christ in history. Willard saw it no differently, for "the sweep of history [is] the field in which God is working to bring something about."[20] So what does Christ bring about within the sweep of history? Twentieth-century theologians have standard answers to this that have been taught in seminaries and churches. Willard, as a young person, heard and accepted one of these standard answers. But when he starts publishing his pentalogy, Willard's interpretation of what happened in the coming of the Son is *unique*, to say the least.

The Kingdom of God

TO BEGIN, HIS interpretation has a lot to do with the kingdom of God. Willard's starting point for interpreting the Christ event is not

---

19. Willard, "Kingdom Comes in Power," 2:30.
20. Willard, 2:30.

the incarnation, is not the cross and resurrection, but is Jesus's gospel, especially in the Synoptics. The kingdom of God, or kingdom of the heavens, *is at hand* (ἤγγικεν).[21] Willard argues persistently that Jesus's news in this announcement is not the kingdom of God per se but more precisely *the availability* of the kingdom of God. Willard cites I. Howard Marshall as saying, "It is universally agreed by New Testament scholars that the central theme of the teaching of Jesus was the Kingdom of God."[22] But Willard is keen to add that the modern scholarly consensus is not entirely accurate historically. *Availability* is what constitutes the *news* of Jesus's good news.

Where does he get this from? Frankly, not from any one particular school or scholar. In a 2002 interview, Willard confesses that he "didn't come to understand the kingdom through theologians."[23] It was, he says, his own experiences and study of the four Gospels that account for his view. And although this may be an overstatement, it is basically right that there are no theologians, exegetical or systematic, who are direct sources for Willard's mature views of God's kingdom and Jesus's gospel.

Toward the end of his life in 2010, he would look back to a book he read as a theology student in the 1950s, calling it "the best book on the biblical elements of the kingdom."[24] In 2011, he names the same book, John

---

21. Mark 1:15; Matt 4:17; Luke 10:9, 11. One reference he gives for understanding the Greek of these verses is the second chapter of C. H. Dodd's book *The Parables of the Kingdom* (New York: Scribner, 1958), which he also references in Willard, *Conspiracy*. See Dallas Willard, "Salvation, Life in the Kingdom of Heaven, the Gospel according to Jesus," *Jesus' Words of Eternal Life: What Were They?* (Bel Air Presbyterian Church, Los Angeles, CA, April 9, 1989), MP3/cassette, 32:15.

22. I. Howard Marshall, quoted in Willard, *Conspiracy*, 59.

23. Willard, "Kingdom Living," 18. The theologians in question are John Wimber and especially George Eldon Ladd, who was influential for Wimber and others with respect to the centrality of the kingdom of God for theology. From a biographical perspective, the basics of Willard's teaching on the kingdom of God, which only came into print in the late 1990s, stem from his years as a University of Wisconsin–Madison graduate student in the early '60s (Johnson, Matthews, and Willard, *Dallas Willard's Study Guide*, 1). The first documentation of what Willard was teaching about the kingdom, as far as I know, comes from a handout for a Sunday school class in 1972 (Willard, "Handout for 'Jesus' Good News'").

24. Dallas Willard, "The Gospel of the Kingdom and Spiritual Formation," in *The Kingdom Life*, ed. Alan Andrews (Colorado Springs: NavPress, 2010), 59.

Bright's *The Kingdom of God*, as one of five books personally meaningful to him.[25] But when compared in detail with Willard's theology, there are a few glaring dissimilarities.

The most significant similarity, however, is that Bright believes that the *idea* of the kingdom of God is more widespread in Israel's theology than the *term*, giving as a hermeneutical rule that "we must look for the idea where the term is not present."[26] Without being explicit about it, Bright shows in practice how one might approach the Scriptures with a largely discarded philosophy of mind, of ideas, and of language. Let us call this approach *realist hermeneutics*. As we will see, Willard agrees wholeheartedly with it and by means of it finds the idea of the kingdom of God in places even Bright does not.[27]

After Willard's graduate student days, other exegetical books came in and out of favor with him, such as George Eldon Ladd's books on the kingdom, which he read in the 1980s and then called "the best writings that I know on the kingdom."[28] But later when *Conspiracy* was in circulation, it is clear that he is critical. Ladd, he thought, failed to communicate a clear sense of the kingdom's ontology.[29] Second, Ladd's distinction between the "already" and the "not yet" of the kingdom had the practical

---

25. Dallas Willard, "My Personal Top 5," in *25 Books Every Christian Should Read*, ed. Julia L. Roller (New York: HarperOne, 2011), 155. About John Bright's *The Kingdom of God* (1953; repr., Nashville: Abingdon, 1981) and the other four books, Willard comments, "I cannot be very precise about the effect but in general these all worked toward giving me a vivid sense of the reality of God with me and the importance of holiness and obedience to Jesus as the foundation of life and ministry" (155).

26. Bright, *Kingdom of God*, 18.

27. Willard sets out the case against the alternative in his article "The Absurdity of Thinking in Language," *Southwestern Journal of Philosophy* 4, no. 1 (1973): 125–32.

28. Dallas Willard, "What Is the Kingdom of God?," *Guidelines for Life in the Kingdom of God* (Rolling Hills Covenant Church, Rolling Estates, CA, January 13, 1985), MP3/cassette, 22:30. He explicitly names George Eldon Ladd's *Crucial Questions about the Kingdom of God* (Grand Rapids, MI: Eerdmans, 1952); and *The Gospel of the Kingdom* (Grand Rapids, MI: Eerdmans, 1959).

29. Willard once said, "We read the Bible with a built-in ontology that does not allow for the reality of God over the world and the world as an expression of the spiritual kingdom of God" (Dallas Willard, "What Is 'Ministry'?," *Spirituality and Ministry* [Fuller Theological Seminary, Sierra Madre, CA, June 11, 2002], MP3, 39:00). Later in the same lecture, Willard says, "Ladd doesn't tell you what it [the kingdom] is" (41:30).

effect that most people put off life in the kingdom until the "not yet."[30] Lastly, and I think most penetratingly, he calls Ladd's interpretation a "more finely nuanced" version of the old dispensational view.[31]

A pattern emerges. Direct association of the kingdom with dispensations and/or eschatology is something that Willard has very little time for. And this is in a century that Christoph Schwöbel rightly labeled "the century of eschatology."[32] For Willard, the kingdom of God is rooted in theology proper, is eternal, and is "simply what God is actually doing."[33] This, of course, does not exclude eschatology, which is *also* something that God is and will be doing. But as Willard sees it in Scripture, the kingdom is bigger than eschatology, bigger than redemption, bigger than any epoch in human history.

These tendencies in Willard, well established by the time *Conspiracy* is published, explain why he takes very little interest in N. T. Wright's theories or any other late twentieth-century eschatological interpretation of the Christ event.[34] Wright's work burst onto the scene right about the same time as *Conspiracy* and found an audience among very similar—that is, biblically minded—people. We know Willard familiarized himself with Wright's work but, as far as I can tell, took over

---

30. Willard, "Finding the Kingdom of God Now, through Jesus and His Words," *For Such a Time as This* (Baylor University, Waco, TX, February 24, 2004), MP3, 49:30. Cf. Dallas Willard, "The Self/Spiritual Transformation and Discipline," *Leadership & Spirituality* (Regent College, Vancouver, BC, May 17, 2000), MP3, 18:45, where Willard says the distinction is "dangerous because it's false." Cf. also Willard, "Kingdom Living," 20.

31. Willard, *Conspiracy*, 402n19. For a statement that clearly shows that Ladd still thinks of redemptive history in dispensational terms, see *Gospel of the Kingdom*, 123.

32. Christoph Schwöbel, "Last Things First?," in *The Future as God's Gift: Explorations in Christian Eschatology*, ed. David Fergusson and Marcel Sarot (Edinburgh: T&T Clark, 2005), 217.

33. Willard, *Conspiracy*, 45.

34. One of Willard's first encounters with Wright was at an InterVarsity Christian Fellowship conference, "Following Christ / Shaping Our World" (Hilton, Chicago, IL, December 29, 1998–January 2, 1999), at which Willard gave the lecture "Shaping Our Inner World" and Wright presented the material that became N. T. Wright, *The Challenge of Jesus* (Downers Grove, IL: InterVarsity, 2000), heavily relying on his *Jesus and the Victory of God* (Minneapolis: Fortress, 1996).

nothing substantial or unique from Wright's exegesis.[35] Not so much his disinterest in Wright as his disinterest in eschatology altogether marked Willard, among New Testament scholars especially, as not quite exegetically "with it." Later in chapter 5, we will revisit this impasse and give Willard the opportunity to offer his criticism of the majority approach in historical, exegetical scholarship to the Christ event.[36]

So while Willard has some company when he begins to interpret the Christ event with Jesus's gospel rather than with his incarnation, cross, or resurrection, he finds himself all alone when he disagrees that the kingdom refers to some dispensation or some realized or unrealized eschatology. As central as it is to the Christ event, the kingdom itself is *not* the event.

The First Listeners and Jesus

MORE CENTRAL TO the Christ event *as an event* are, believe it or not, the people listening to Jesus. As Willard conceives it, the Christ event is only what it is because of when it comes in the course of history and especially because *of whom it comes to.* This move is not to be missed,

---

35. We will return to this in chapter 5, but briefly put, Wright's understanding of God's kingdom is that it, in an unexpected fulfillment of Israel's eschatological hopes, is announced and *established* in the life and work of Jesus.

36. It may be helpful to note how Willard, while speaking to a seminary faculty meeting in 2008, testified to the legitimacy and place of biblical criticism: "If you want to deal with [subjectivity and the theory of the mind] at that level . . . And someone has to, not everyone does. Just like not everyone has to study critically the texts of the Bible, but someone needs to. We should have a community of scholarship in which what some people have worked out can be communicated to others" (Dallas Willard, "Faculty Q & A," *Spiritual Renewal Conference* [Bethel Seminary San Diego, San Diego, CA, October 2008], MP3, 42:00). Later on, he makes an important qualification:

> That's where we need to think seriously about the existence of God. . . . When you read people who are worrying about the texts, what you often discern is they don't believe in God. I would recommend as a test for anyone who is going to do higher or lower criticism of texts that they believe the twenty-third psalm. . . . That would give you a basis for thinking about the texts. You could use the best of whatever devices there are for studying the texts because as Christians, we don't want to duck or dodge anything. But the truth of the matter is you have many people defining what religion is who don't believe in God. (1:19:00)

for some very high-placed theologians teach as if what happened in the life of Christ on earth is significant in isolation of any historical or social context. What matters, they say, is that it happens to God. Or to the cosmos. But for Willard, it essentially involves what was happening *to the people who were physically present* with Jesus. It derives its cosmic significance not merely from the person of Christ, as important as he is, but also from the effect he, being who he is, had on his immediate social world.

What Willard has spotted and is drawing out is how Christ's coming is tied to what God was doing in history *before* the advent of Jesus. Christ comes amid God's chosen people. Moreover, Willard in the same way sees how Christ's coming is tied to what God is doing *after* the advent of Jesus, for the event happens to people who form the nucleus of God's redemptive community until the eschaton. Christ's life would not be what it is for the cosmos in general if it had not happened to this particular people with this particular effect.

But, needless to say, the main-stage event of the whole Christ event is still unspoken. If the kingdom of God is not attached to some dispensation or realized or unrealized eschatology, what news could Jesus or anybody possibly have to announce about this (apparently) *eternal* kingdom? The answer, perhaps unsurprisingly, is Jesus himself. He, his reality, brings into the world new connections to the eternal kingdom that were previously not possible. Because of him, the kingdom of the heavens is now at hand. It is available.

What, for Willard, the appearance of Jesus means is, I submit, best understood through the eyes of the first listeners, the group of Jews who first heard and responded to Jesus's gospel. Yet this is not a simple task and is not made any easier by the fact that quite a number of Willard's doctrines—of God, the kingdom, sin, and so on—are not commonplace in today's churches or theological schools. But in sum, this book will look at precisely that: the gospel of Jesus, those new connections to the kingdom of God that were previously not available, through the eyes of those who encountered it first.

Christology sub specie aeternitatis

I SHOULD CONFESS that I have already taken a turn at a theological crossroads, for there are two canonically sanctioned and wholly orthodox ways of viewing the life of Jesus. And yet, one has become more standard in systematic theology and more familiar in today's church: to order what happened in the Christ event *according to the way that Christ looked to God.*

This means that one starts with him as "the only Son of God, begotten from the Father before all ages, God from God, Light from Light, true God from true God," as formulated in the Nicene Creed. One proceeds then to take a "God's eye view" of *Christ's person* in his coming—which is, namely, his incarnation as the second person of the Trinity, when, as the creed states, "he came down from heaven . . . and was made human"—and then to take a God's eye view of him in his earthly ministry, with or without a doctrine of kenosis, and in his cross and resurrection. When turning to *Christ's work* in redemption, this God's eye view brings to the forefront aspects of his coming that depend on his being *both* true God and true man. After all, that is what he is, and it would be bizarre if the salvation of our race and the whole cosmos did not have *something* to do with him being what he is. It is often taken to follow, though it does not follow, that anything that Christ did, for which a full God's eye view of his person is irrelevant, is superfluous to redemption.

But what this means, when that doctrine of salvation is turned around and formulated as a gospel that was and is to be preached, is that the God's eye view of Christ's person is made a prerequisite to understanding the good news; it is made a premise to the gospel's conclusion. In order for the one hearing the gospel for the first or thousandth time to make any sense of the salvific nature of the Christ event, he or she must take for granted a very high Christology. After all, Christ *is* true God and true man; why should the gospel not take this ontology into account?

Indeed, it should. But there is a problem if this is the only way that systematic theologians or churches view the life of Jesus. The first listeners did not have *any idea* of Jesus's true nature when they met him in Galilee, nor was their knowledge of him complete when he died on the cross, or even when he stood before them as a resurrected human being. It is historically debatable how long it took for those who were with him in Galilee to have something like the high Christology that we see in the New Testament and afterward. It is clear that it was a process.[37]

And yet all through the Gospels and through Acts, there is talk of a gospel and of a church that was gathered by this gospel. How was this possible, if a God's eye view of Christ and his life was not yet present? What was the gospel that the apostles and the embryonic church, not to mention Jesus, were preaching and responding to? How were they making sense of the Christ event without something approaching Nicene or Chalcedonian Christology?

Because these questions for the history of redemption are hard to answer if all one takes is a God's eye view of Christ, we can be glad that there is another canonically sanctioned and wholly orthodox way of viewing the event as a whole. It is one that orders the event *according to the way that Christ looked to his first listeners.* It is indisputable that these first listeners did not see Jesus for the first time, or even the second time, and think, "The only Son of God, begotten from the Father before all ages, God from God, Light from Light, true God from true God." And yet they did see him *somehow* and heard his gospel and watched his ministry—even joined his ministry and walked with him as he went to the cross and rose again and continued with them as they went out as his witnesses into the ancient world. Their self-understanding during all this time was that they had heard and responded to *the gospel.* They, in turn, understood themselves to be preaching and teaching *the gospel* to others. We know all of this because years later, some of them took it upon themselves to tell this story of the church's less-than-orthodox beginnings. By contrast, we know relatively little of how the followers of

---

37. As Willard puts it, "The disciples struggled with this endlessly. In the New Testament, you'll find really a kind of failing effort to grasp who this person was, who was Jesus" (Dallas Willard, "The Primacy of the Word," *In Search of Guidance* [Bedfordview Methodist Church, Bedfordview, South Africa, August 6, 1987], MP3/cassette, 39:30).

Jesus looked in the later part of the first century, when, as we see from the New Testament, a more mature Christology was more standard.[38]

In all the frenzy over the last two centuries about finally "uncovering" the historical Jesus ("who, after all, is *just* a man"), theologians disposed to trust the Scriptures have leaned on its testimony to Christ's fuller, divine-human ontology. A theology of the first listeners and their experience of Christ was confused with a skeptical search for the context that explains what really happened ("since he, after all, was *just* a man"). And one thing that was forgotten about the first listeners in this confusion is how the Bible tells their story sub specie aeternitatis, from the perspective of the eternal.

In the canonical history books of the New Testament, we are (presumably) given a God's eye view of *the first listeners* as they progress toward a more mature understanding of Christ and his gospel. This is one of Willard's major theological insights: "The story of the New Testament," he writes, "is the story of increasing understanding of who Jesus was."[39] No doubt a similar story is happening with respect to God and his ways in the Old Testament period. Some of this story is obvious to all readers of the Old Testament. With some specialized training and some (or much) speculation, Hebrew scholars have been able to see more of it. Yet in the New Testament, "the story of increasing understanding" is not something we must read between the lines for. It is recounted to us directly, sub specie aeternitatis.

Now, the New Testament is patently not an apologetics textbook. The more elementary christological claims are not introduced and made premises for more complex claims. Rather, the evangelists, though not always as explicitly as John, assume a very high Christology from the beginning yet tell the story of people who do not share this high view but are only moving toward it. Hence, we the readers are often told

---

38. N. T. Wright, *The New Testament and the People of God* (Minneapolis: Fortress, 1992), 341. He further states, "We know far less about the history of the church from AD 30–135 than we do about second-temple Judaism. . . . Even if we were to assign the highest historical value to Acts, the bright light it would shed on a few areas would only emphasize the total darkness elsewhere" (341).

39. Willard, *Guidance*, 132.

things and know things about Jesus that the first listeners were still gradually coming to terms with. Sub specie aeternitatis, we, even if we ourselves do not believe it, are allowed to observe the gradual apprehension of Jesus's followers. By this means, we ourselves are invited to make sense of the Christ event through how Christ looked *to them.*

This is precisely what Willard calls progressive apprehension. That it is so blatant in the Gospels and Acts might tip us off to its importance to the history of redemption as a whole. Is there, we might wonder, a deeper reason, a redemptive reason—one we miss in our efforts to guard orthodoxy—for why Christ did not come with his Nicene ontology on public display? Willard argues from the Scriptures that genuine understanding of the gospel and of Jesus and the kingdom of God began very early on, before the writing of the New Testament, before the explosion of the church in the Mediterranean, before the crucifixion and resurrection of Christ, and even before Peter's confession of Christ. It began in Galilee *with those who first listened to Jesus.* There, this small group of mostly Jewish nobodies began to see the new connection to the kingdom of God that Jesus himself brought into the world. And this, as Mark's Gospel indicates (Mark 1:1), is the beginning, though certainly not the end, of the Christ event.

Three Stages of Evangelical Knowledge

SO HOW ARE we to give this process—beginning, middle, and end—an order for teaching others but also for understanding it ourselves? Sadly, Willard is not going to give us much assistance. He will, at times, mention shifts and changes in the first listeners' understanding, but he does not appear to have an explicit mental architecture to understand the process.

For that reason, I suggest we turn to Paul, a disciple of Jesus but one with an explicitly high view of his teacher. In Colossians 1:16, he gives a distinct statement about his teacher's ontology:

> ὁτι ἐν αὐτῳ ἐκτισθη τα παντα ἐν τοις οὐρανοις και
> ἐπι της γης τα ὁρατα και τα ἀορατα εἰτε θρονοι εἰτε
> κυριοτητες εἰτε ἀρχαι εἰτε ἐξουσιαι τα παντα δι᾽αὐτου
> και εἰς αὐτον ἐκτισται.

> *For by him (ἐν αὐτῷ) all things were created—in the heavens and on earth, things visible and invisible, all thrones, dominions, rulers and authorities—all things were created through him (δι' αὐτου) and for him (εἰς αὐτον).*[40]

Paul in this passage describes Christ in terms of three ontological relations that he expresses through three prepositions. The first relation (ἐν αὐτῷ) is one of direct cause, which inverted could be expressed as "Christ created all things." The form of the last expression (εἰς αὐτον) suggests that it is a relation of benefit, in which something exists or is done for someone for their benefit. This might be reformulated as "All things were created for Christ." The middle relation (δι' αὐτου) is best understood as a relation of instrumentality. In other words, "All things were created by means of Christ." One might be tempted to think that this is merely rhetorical flourish for Paul, but since the same three relations are echoed in Romans 11:36, they are likely a significant piece of his Christology.

Now prepositions are, as Willard has said, "the most unruly members of the grammatical family."[41] So carefully, I submit that these three ontological relations, foundational to a mature understanding of Christ, are also three stages through which Jesus's first listeners passed as they approached this mature view. Second, I submit that, if gently applied, these three stages can serve as interior architecture—movable walls, so to speak—to understand Willard's own account of that learning process. To see how this works, and that it is not foreign to Willard's thought, I will briefly summarize how I read Colossians 1:16 in light of Willard's biblical ontology of the kingdom—that is, in light of Willard's view of "what the Bible teaches about the kingdom of God as a whole."[42]

---

40. My translation.

41. Dallas Willard, "Holiness, Divine Presence, and Divine Power: Reflections on John 14," *Malcolm R. Robertson Lectureship on Holy Living* (Azusa Pacific University, Azusa, CA, September 28, 2010), MP3, 33:00.

42. This phrase of Willard's will be discussed at greater length in chapter 5. Dallas Willard, "Q & A: Prayer," *The Divine Conspiracy* (e4, Hollywood, CA, July 8, 2004), MP3/video, 43:30.

First of all, kingdom of God, as Willard sees it in the Scriptures, is rooted in theology proper and is ontologically prior to creation. What's more, the acts of creation and providence (as named in this passage) as well as the acts of redemption are all acts of the kingdom of God. They are all, as Willard occasionally defined the kingdom, "God in action." The kingdom is *before* creation. It is primarily, as systematic theologians say, an immanent not an economic reality. Since God expresses his kingdom in creation without exhausting it, talk about creation in the Bible is eo ipso talk about the kingdom of God. Therefore, Colossians 1:16 is a kingdom of God verse expressed in terms of the economic action and ontology of the second person of the Trinity, "the firstborn of all creation."

Second, if this is also how Paul thinks of the kingdom and creation—and Willard knows that contemporary scholars strongly disagree—then the verse invites the wider interpretation that these three relations between Christ and the kingdom of God in creation (by, through, and for) are also present in between Christ and the kingdom *in redemption*.[43] If Paul is as kingdom-preoccupied in his theology as Jesus—and here contemporary scholars agree—then why would Paul not be giving expression to how he thinks of Christ's ontological relations to the kingdom in *all* its actions with respect to the economy?[44] Paul's ontology is that Christ, "the image of the invisible God," in the economy at least, relates to the kingdom of God in a threefold way—as its direct agent (by Christ), its instrumental agent (through Christ), and its beneficiary (for Christ).

But Paul was not one of Jesus's first listeners, and he was in a different place than they when he wrote these words. If any of Paul's three relations came to the first listeners' minds when they first met Jesus and heard him talk of the kingdom, it would have been that Jesus had a

43. Especially if one considers Matt 28:18.

44. There is a deeper reason for this as well. Willard's view of redemption could be described as what happens as the first listeners gradually understand Christ's position in creation. Christ does not need to assume a new posture as humanity's redeemer. His creational ontology is sufficient. The economy, by the way, is a concept systematic theologians use for the sum total of *all* that was not with God from the beginning.

relationship to the kingdom that was beneficial *for him*. Let us call this stage 1 of their formation. Soon some understood Jesus to be announcing that that same beneficial relationship was possible for them as well and that he offered to be its facilitator, insisting it would come increasingly into their lives *by means of* him. This is stage 2 of their formation.

And after many twists and turns, some further understood Jesus to be announcing that their ongoing relationship to the kingdom was actually a form of their ongoing relationship to Jesus, for the kingdom was his kingdom. Creation, redemption, and their ongoing, everlasting life in God's world were enacted, were to be ruled, *by him*. This is stage 3 of their formation and, significantly, where Jesus's disciple Paul finds himself, which means he is ready to see Jesus's *whole* gospel. I submit that these three stages are a sufficient mental architecture by which one can understand the progress of the first listeners. They are also, if one glances at its table of contents, the arc of this book and an order I am recommending for teaching Jesus and his gospel to others.

Is this how Willard sees the progressive apprehension of the first listeners? Well, not exactly. I fully admit that the three stages are my and, it seems, Paul's way of cutting the cake. But I also admit that I found the building blocks for it all in Willard's thought. He spoke often of stages of faith, of horizons of knowledge, of progressions of life.[45] All that was missing was this interpretation of Colossians 1:16.

I will say this much about my theology: I agree with Willard that the kingdom of God is an immanent reality in existence before creation and expressed in creation and redemption. This seems to me to be the best way of understanding what the Bible as a whole teaches about God and his kingdom. When I read Paul and the Gospels, I read authors who are coming to terms with the fact that the eschatological dreams for the kingdom that first-century Judaism taught them were mostly wrong, for they were incompatible with the Old Testament Scriptures, with Jesus's

---

45. Willard urges that "the spiritual life is a flow of the relationship. You cannot cut it up and ultimately make sense of it and if you do, people will die on it" (Dallas Willard, "Atonement in the Spiritual Life," *Elective Seminar* [National Pastors Convention / Youth Specialties, San Diego, CA, March 10, 2004], MP3, 1:06:00).

own teaching, and above all, with Jesus's transcendent life in which they shared.

Though the three stages of this book are mine, this is a systematic *interpretive* work aimed at giving you, the reader, a greater understanding of how Dallas Willard conceives of the Christ event as a whole. Even if you are inclined to agree with me, remember that I have set up the book's interior architecture as movable walls. They do not sit perfectly in history, nor do they sit perfectly in Willard's theology. But if one is not too rigid about them, they do sit passably well, I believe. And as I began using them to retell, through Willard's eyes, the story of Jesus's gospel in the ancient world, it became clear to me how helpful they were for organizing Willard's thought, if not also the biblical material.

Now, before we get to the details of these ontological relations and their corresponding stages, there is a need, especially for theologians, to understand something of Willard's biblical hermeneutics. Willard does not read the Bible as we, who went through theological education in the twentieth century, were taught to. This was not because he was still some Missouri hill country revivalist with a hayseed in his mouth. He over the years built up a quite sophisticated theory of what the Bible is and how it should be read today, and he called upon scholars to work out an "epistemology of the Bible."[46] A whole book is required to lay out Willard's theory, but in the next chapter, some general guidelines will be addressed.

---

46. Dallas Willard, "Christian Teaching Banished from Knowledge," *Spiritual Formation in the Academy: 2008 Midwest Faculty Conference* (InterVarsity, Cedarville, MI, June 2008), MP3, 54:00.

3

THE ONTOLOGICAL APPROACH TO THE BIBLE

> Christian faith today must come from an ontology. Ontology is the basic questions about reality. Secularism is not a conspiracy. It is a theory of reality authorized by [the] Western intellectual world.
>
> —Dallas Willard, Fuller Theological Seminary, June 10, 2002

IN A REVEALING moment from a 2004 lecture, Willard named why he read the Bible in the peculiar way that he did, advising everyone to do the same. He says, after some remarks on modern attempts to understand the kingdom of God and, particularly, the perennial difficulty among modern exegetes to imagine a kingdom that is *not* sociopolitical,

> *Here's what I'm saying to you, and it's extremely important to get this, because you have to be in a certain manner an ontologist if you're going to understand the Scripture.*
>
> *An ontologist is one who understands being, what it is for things to be and what kinds of things there are. We talked about the Trinitarian nature of God, the spiritual nature of God and so on. What we have to understand is that the kingdom of God is simply God's ruling. . . . the basic reality of the kingdom of God is simply the person of God and the instrumentalities by which he rules.*[1]

1. Dallas Willard, "The Kingdom Gospel," *The Divine Conspiracy* (e4, Hollywood, CA, July 5, 2004), MP3/video, 4:00.

The latter sentences provide a glimpse of the kingdom ontology that emerged when Willard read the Bible as "one who understands being." But his hermeneutical imperative is what interests us the most in this chapter: *only ontologists can understand Scripture*. It explains much about how Willard sees what he does in the Bible.[2]

Reading the Bible as an Ontologist

AN ONTOLOGIST, FOR Willard, is a person who is working on their own intellectually responsible theory of being. An ontologist asks both what it means to be and what in fact *is*, especially what most fundamentally is.[3] In terms of Willard's famous "Four Great Questions," ontology is the domain of the first: What is reality? Answering this is not, according to Willard, elite philosophical work but the basic work of all who propose to lead and teach humanity. Even those who are not in a teaching role must come to terms with what reality is because humans have no choice but to act on their beliefs about it.

Yet that ontology is basic, even unconscious work does not imply that it is done in an intellectually responsible manner adequate to human life. Willard, whom one might call a "professional ontologist," did not tire of helping people do their ontology better. Consider, for example, his many attempts to explain the nature and fundamentality of *spirit* to lay audiences who, consciously or not, already had a working concept of it.

So what does reading the Bible as an ontologist mean for Willard? First of all, it means that *the biblical exegete must be an intellectually responsible ontologist*. Second, it means that *the biblical exegete must consider the Bible's own answer to the ontology question*. With an eye to her own developing theory, the responsible exegete reads the Bible with an

---

2. Other than his publications and public lectures in ontology, he regularly taught courses at USC on ontology and metaphysics, and some of his syllabi, lecture notes, and class recordings have been preserved.

3. This follows Willard's own two-part division of ontology: "I take Ontology to be a field of research that aspires to a plausible theory of being. It has two main parts: a clarification of what it is to be or exist, and a determination of what ultimate sorts of things there are" (Dallas Willard, "Phenomenology and Metaphysics" [paper presented at the American Philosophical Association Pacific Division Meeting, San Francisco, CA, March 30, 1995], Dallas Willard Collection).

eye to its explicit and implicit description of reality.[4] Though the first task and second are pursued simultaneously, Willard believes the exegete should not give a priori authority to one over the other. All arguments relevant to answering the question of the nature of reality are to be taken into account.[5]

This is shocking to some who are used to separating the work of faith and philosophy. However, Willard held them together, as have many in the past. When asked which authors he would recommend to younger persons looking to explore the relationship between faith and philosophy, Willard said without hesitation, "St. Augustine, who turns out to be remarkably contemporary." But he sensed he would surprise people by also naming John Wesley. He explains, "[Wesley] was trained philosophically. But then Calvin and Luther also were. We don't know this now because philosophy has really come to stand for something different in the contemporary period—which is a kind of alienated academic position."[6] It should not be surprising that Willard's way of doing philosophy was different from that of his professional colleagues and more in line with what Augustine and Wesley thought it should be. He was, I would like to think, the type of modern philosopher Augustine, Luther, Calvin, and Wesley would have liked to meet, for they too, in Willard's sense, were ontologists and knew that an intellectually responsible exegete must read the Bible ontologically.

This, however, is not what mainstream exegetical scholarship believes. It is a main reason why Willard, even though he read and

---

4. Seeking the Bible's internal answer to the reality question does not mean to Willard that we will necessarily find a unified biblical ontology common to every biblical author. Willard recognizes development in the covenant people who wrote the Scriptures and in one important area fully admitted, after his own careful study, that *no* authoritative and consistent ontology was to be found. See chapter 6 note 20 on Christian psychology.

5. Commonsense philosophy applies here as well. If we are reading the Bible, ontological interpretation is not something we can avoid. All readers read with a tacit strategy for determining what the things mentioned in the Bible *are* (even if they decide in the end that they are no more than figments of the author's imagination) and tacitly integrate those findings with their general search for what is real.

6. Dallas Willard, "On Philosophy and Christianity," *Slipstream: Leaders in Formation* (Evangelical Alliance [UK], Sierra Madre, CA, June 2010), MP3, 1:45.

trusted his Bible with a voraciousness unheard of among philosophers and even theologians, spent little time studying the commentaries and monographs produced by contemporary Old and New Testament scholars. This was not because he was retro-confessional or, worse, lazy. Nor because he was an "alienated academic" who only left his professional guild to give inspirational Bible studies based on his "morning quiet times." He fundamentally disagreed with the whole approach to the Bible of mainstream exegetical scholarship, and though he rarely went public with it, he had a well-refined critique of its ethos, both conservative and progressive.

Mind you, his critique is not of the prudish type that fears higher (or lower) criticism. The Bible can be subjected to criticism, he believes, but he says, "What would be nice [is] if we did not have vacuous theories cycling around about it, if people would indeed be scientific. But they're not. Higher criticism has always been dominated by ungrounded philosophical assumptions, the foremost of which is, 'The miraculous is illusion.'"[7] Now, an adequate treatment of Willard's critique requires more than I can do in this book. It is the job of a full-length study, systematically addressing all pertinent issues. Nevertheless, Willard's views on the kingdom, Jesus, and the gospel will make little sense to us unless we are aware of a few important philosophical and theological *guidelines* that governed Willard's own approach to the Bible and to biblical ontology. The four I will cover here are (1) the existence and nature of God, (2) the presence of "Greek thought" in the Bible, (3) metaphysical and epistemological realism, and (4) the role of the word of God and faith in religious epistemology.

Guideline #1: The Existence and Nature of God

THE FIRST GUIDELINE concerns what Willard knew, or presumed to know, in theology proper. According to him, it is an imperative of rational inquiry *of any kind* to determine the existence and, as far as possible, the

---

7. Dallas Willard, "Study," *Spirituality and Ministry* (Fuller Theological Seminary, Sierra Madre, CA, June 18, 2002), MP3, 1:23:45.

nature of God and to determine their relevance to the subject matter.[8] This applies just as much to rational inquiries in chemistry as it does to inquiries in Old and New Testament studies.

Willard was aware of his finite existence and readily confessed, "I don't know the ultimate nature of God."[9] But this fact did not entail for him any confinement to negative theology. For similar reasons, he was opposed to vacuous meditation, as he called it. On these two postures, he says, "I would challenge anyone to find that [i.e., vacuous meditation] taught in any of the great Christian teachers except Eckhart. And Eckhart is a person—and Jakob Boehme who influenced [William] Law—they are people who are working a view called negative theology. [It] comes out of Pseudo-Dionysius the Areopagite. The idea that you can't know anything about God except he's not this, he's not this, he's not this, he's not this. And that contradicts the revelational teaching of the Bible that you can know."[10] Statements like this are parallel to Willard's general disinterest in mysticism as a means of theological knowledge. "For every property, there is a corresponding concept," he says in a lecture on intentionality. But mystics are those who believe that there are some things, like God, that can be experienced but for which we lack corresponding concepts.[11]

For epistemological reasons different from those that inspired the tradition of negative theology, the Western university culture in which Willard worked had also given up rational inquiry into the nature of God or theology as a field of knowledge.[12] In order to reestablish theology's place in the university and the Western mind, which Willard thought

---

8. See Willard's characterization of theology quote in chapter 1.

9. Dallas Willard, "Tough Questions 1," *Menlo Park Sermons* (Menlo Park Presbyterian Church, Menlo Park, CA, December 2009), MP3, 44:45.

10. Dallas Willard, "Confession, Meditation, Rules of Life," *Spirituality and Ministry* (Fuller Theological Seminary, Sierra Madre, CA, June 19, 2002), MP3, 40:30. Willard was aware, as far as I can tell, that Meister Eckhart was a Dominican and, despite his interest in negative theology, was likewise interested in positive, revelational theology.

11. Dallas Willard, "Intentionality," *Colloquium* (Biola University, La Mirada, CA, November 22, 1994), MP3/cassette, 54:00.

12. Cf., e.g., the section "The Discrediting of Religion as a Source of Knowledge of Reality, and, Specifically, of Moral Reality," in Willard, *Disappearance* (New York: Routledge, 2018), 8–9.

was necessary, he did not simply turn to the Bible. He thought rather that there were "three stages" for affirming the existence of God and knowing something of his nature. These stages were standard parts of his philosophy of religion and metaphysics courses at the University of Southern California (USC) and, in print, were worked through in his 1990 article "Language, Being, God and the Three Stages of Theistic Evidence" and more accessibly in *Knowing Christ*, chapters 4 through 6.[13] In brief, the first stage is built on the cosmological argument for God's existence and results in "demonstrated extra-naturalism." The second, built on the argument for design, comes out to "a quite plausible cosmic intellectualism." The third stage deals with human experience—with miracles in human history and direct interactions with God.[14]

Regarding this third stage and Willard's view of the role of experience in theology, valuable insight can be found in a 1973 seminar Willard held on the "Justification of Faith by Experience," of which, sadly, only the handout survives.[15] In these four sessions, Willard works through his argument for "rationally justified religion." The word *faith* in the title and notes is, I claim, one of Willard's attempts to be clever with words (he is playing with the familiar phrase in philosophy "justified true belief"), and it does not express his mature view on faith, which we will consider at the end of this and in the next chapter. What Willard has in mind here with *faith* is what theologians call doctrines—that is, theological propositions or thoughts. And his argument is that these doctrines do not hang in the air or solely on the potent revelation of God. Doctrines are shown to be justified *in the experience* of the biblical characters, of Jesus, and of one's own life.

13. Dallas Willard, "Language, Being, God, and the Three Stages of Theistic Evidence," in *Does God Exist?*, ed. J. P. Moreland and Kai Nielsen (Nashville: Thomas Nelson, 1990). There is also a handout for his philosophy of religion class that lists a moral and an ontological argument. Willard thinks that the other three listed, the cosmological, "teleological," and experiential arguments, are the most successful. Dallas Willard, "Handout for Willard's USC Course on Philosophy of Religion, Phil 361," n.d., Dallas Willard Collection.

14. Willard, "Language, Being, God," 213.

15. Dallas Willard, "Handout for 'Justification of Faith by Experience,'" 1973, Dallas Willard Collection.

There is much more that could be said about Willard's groundwork in theology and the knowledge he considers essential to doing good work in *any* rational inquiry, both in and out of the university setting. For our purposes, let us consider one conclusion about God, touched upon in Willard's first stage, which played a significant role in his approach to biblical ontology—namely, the self-sufficiency of God.

The Self-Sufficiency of God

TWO LECTURES FROM 1989 on "God in Himself" draw this conclusion with rhetorical force. They include the following statement in which the theological issues are brought together with the pastoral issues:

> *Every time that we look at a piece of matter, what we see is stuff that is not self-sufficient. It is not self-sufficient. What we know about every piece of matter that you can put your hand on or you can even think of is that it came from something else, and it is going to go to something else. That's matter. That's why Paul says when you look at the things that are created, you go directly to God because everything you see that is created is perishing, is de-pend-ent.*
>
> *And it points, by means of an argument which you will probably be thankful I'm not going drag you through . . . to a being that is totally self-sufficient, that is so grand that it is easier for him to exist than not to exist, who out of his mere nature pours forth being in infinite quantities that are incomprehensible and everlasting and will never cease and will never be exhausted! That's God.*[16]

It is impossible to overstate the importance of this conclusion for Willard's theology. Though his earlier thought is still too inaccessible to

16. Dallas Willard, "God in Himself—Part 1," *Life without Lack* (Valley Vista Christian Community, Sepulveda, CA, February 5, 1989), MP3/cassette, 40:00. See also Dallas Willard, "The Sufficiency of God to Your Soul," *The Soul* (Valley Vista Christian Community, Sepulveda, CA, August 12, 1990), MP3/cassette, 33:30.

justly analyze, his mature thought (from about 1990 onward) is saturated with a doctrine of God's self-sufficient nature. For him, this was the sort of deduction that followed from very simple premises (all matter is dependent) but concerned matters of ultimate reality and, therefore, should be counted as *rudimentary knowledge* in theology, philosophy of religion, and in the end, all academic disciplines.

One important thing that the deduction *does not* presuppose for Willard (who freely laid out such arguments in his USC courses) is the authority or even the authenticity of the Old or New Testaments texts. On the contrary, it is the sort of rudimentary knowledge that ought to be granted in any open-minded study of such texts. Because it is rudimentary knowledge, it is basic to an intellectually responsible approach to the Scriptures and to the biblical ontology of those Scriptures. It is basic to any intellectually responsible form of research.

That said, Willard also noticed the self-sufficiency of God *in* the testimony of the Scriptures. The self-sufficiency of God was not something, like geometrical properties or the geography of Egypt, about which the Scriptures had nothing to say but could or ought to be externally woven into the cosmic vision that comes from them. The self-sufficiency of God is, though admittedly with some different language, the explicit teaching of the Bible.

In the "God in Himself" lectures, Willard works through multiple texts in which testimony to the self-sufficiency of God can be heard. We see that, to his mind, self-sufficiency was not only a general scientific point but also a result of God's self-revelation of himself to the people of God. The Hebrews did not have to wait for "the philosophers" to come around in order to know it. It was a part of the "Jewish experience" of God. In print, Willard addresses a few of these passages in *Conspiracy*'s third chapter. For example, Willard writes, "And as for God, the highest biblical revelation of God's metaphysical nature is Exod. 3:14." From this and other texts, we learn that "nothing other than God has this character of *totally* self-sufficient being, or self-determination."[17]

---

17. Willard, *Conspiracy*, 81. Another location is *Renovation*'s talk of "circles of sufficiency" (Dallas Willard, *Renovation of the Heart* [Colorado Springs, CO: NavPress, 2002], 179–80).

The Substantiality of the Spiritual

GOING FURTHER, THE arguments and exegeses leading to our knowledge of God's self-sufficiency are the same arguments and exegeses that point to the nonmateriality, or the *spiritual nature*, of God. This is, in a word, Willard's version of *dualism*.[18] From all we know about matter, it owes its existence to something else and eventually passes out of existence. But God is some *thing* that is uncreated, self-subsisting, imperishable, and radically different from all that is physical. Put positively, God is spirit; he is that which has life in himself.[19] Quite often, Willard links the spiritual nature of God with the second commandment, the prohibition of graven images. The inverse teaching of the second commandment, he says, is the transcendence of God to created being and especially to matter.[20] This point is important for Willard in consideration of the gradual apprehension of Jesus's divinity after his ascension, which I will address in chapters 10 and 11.

Following immediately after *Conspiracy*'s statement on God's self-sufficiency is the section entitled "The *Substantiality* of the Spiritual."[21] According to Willard, spirit is *substance*. It is, moreover, primary substance. In one lecture, Willard refers, by contrast, to "the insubstantiality of material substance."[22] Matter is dependent on spirit—that is, on a

---

18. When asked, Willard confessed, "I'm a stark raving dualist. And the first dualism is between God and the physical creation. . . . It is God who establishes spiritual reality. Now I also believe that the mind is not identical with the brain." Dallas Willard, "Spiritual Formation as a Natural Part of Salvation," *Wheaton College Theology Conference* (Wheaton College, Wheaton, IL, April 17, 2009), MP3, 1:13:00. See also Dallas Willard, "Session 1—Part 2," *The Contemporary Belief System as Prison, and Jesus as Savior* (National Pastors Convention / Youth Specialties, San Diego, CA, February 2003), MP3, 50:15.

19. John 5:26.

20. Since dualism has been mentioned and other references will be made to Platonism in this book, the false assumption may arise that Willard is an antimaterial dualist, as Plato and his followers were. This is not true, as readers who are familiar with the pro-body argument of *Disciplines* and the pro–"ordinary life" and pro-earth arguments of *Conspiracy* will know.

21. Willard, *Conspiracy*, 81–82.

22. Dallas Willard, "The Material World and the Rule of God: Matter or Physical Substance as Understood Today," *Prospects for an Evangelical Apologetics in the 1980s* (Bethel College, North Newton, KS, September 20, 1982), MP3/cassette, 36:00.

more primary substance. Though much contested today, the philosophy of substance remained an important aspect of Willard's theology as a whole and especially his theology proper.

In a valuable 1990 lecture titled "The Biblical Understanding of the Reality of God," Willard ascribes four biblical properties to God: (1) self-subsistence, (2) spirit, (3) substance, and (4) moral personality. Under the "Substance" heading, Willard makes the fairly traditional claim that "God is a being of specific properties and powers united into one person," and he describes substance generally as "a unity underlying things."[23]

Later in 1993, Willard makes a comment on the doctrine of God that gives an indication of how he interprets the history of theology regarding fairly traditional claims about the *substantiality* of the spiritual. Speaking disparagingly of a school of modern theological books, he says,

> *Even in most of the theology books that I see coming across my desk, books on theology, you will find theology is rarely ever described as, shall we say, the science of God. It will more likely be described in terms of the human quest for meaning, for example. Or spirit will be defined in terms of the interior reality, of interiority. Then God will be identified somehow with this interior, and the unity of man with God will be described in terms of that. A lot of that is nothing but an elaborate way of backpedaling off from a very robust, straightforward statement that a personal being that is spiritual, in the sense of being unbodily, is the fundamental reality and that this being is God.*

23. Dallas Willard, "The Biblical Understanding of the Reality of God," *Reality and Spiritual Life* (North Park Theological Seminary, Chicago, IL, April 24, 1990), MP3/cassette, 23:30. With respect to calling the soul a substance, he describes substance as "an individual entity that has properties and dispositions natural to it, endures through time and change, and receives and exercises causal influence on other things" (Dallas Willard, "Spiritual Disciplines, Spiritual Formation, and the Restoration of the Soul," *Journal of Psychology & Theology* 26, no. 1 [Spring 1998]: 101–2).

> *God as a substance and the human soul as a substance has [*sic*] a very hard time in the face of a world tendency to get rid of anything like that and replace it with some elaborately interpreted project of physical humanity. It goes back very deep into the origins of modern theological thought. . . . If you've ever read a book by Feuerbach called* The Essence of Christianity, *for example, or similar books where the spiritual is treated as some kind of spin-off of the physical . . . many times, the effects of people's views are nothing they intend. But the attempt to defend God against the scientific worldview that we find in [Karl] Barth historically eventuated in giving up God as a serious cognitive reality. And it goes through several stages such as you will find in a person I greatly admire, Paul Tillich. But if you look at what he has to say about God and about religion, it's a very easy step from there to "death of God theology." And liberation theology and various other forms of reinterpretation of God in terms of the human project then come on top of that.*[24]

Following this comment, he gives an impromptu, fairly traditional "definition" of God, aligning with what he says in the 1990 lecture. God is "a self-subsistent being of a spiritual nature, uncreated and undying, [and] at least of unlimited extent in all of his properties—his power, his goodness, his knowledge, and all of those things."[25] What should especially be noticed in the previous comment is the loss, in not exactly unorthodox traditions of modern theology, of God and the soul *as substance*.

---

24. Dallas Willard, "The Spiritual Disciplines," *Regional Minister's Conference* (American Baptist Churches of the Pacific Southwest, Crestline, CA, September 1993), MP3/cassette, 4:00. Cf. also Dallas Willard, "Temptation, the Cross, the Trinity, Knowledge and the University" for a comment on Barth's positive, if now limited, influence on the university (*Spirituality and Ministry* [Fuller Theological Seminary, Sierra Madre, CA, June 17, 2002], MP3, 1:12:00).

25. Dallas Willard, "Spiritual Disciplines," 7:00.

Though a standard part of Willard's teaching at USC, his extant writings only give glimpses of his philosophy of substance.[26] One glimpse is found on a handout created for his USC students where he lists four issues dealt with through talk of "substance": (1) individuation, (2) the unity of many qualities in one thing, (3) the unity of different properties in the same thing over time, and (4) the stratification of properties into those more or less explanatory of the whole.[27] And yet, though underrepresented in his publications and public lectures, these theological and philosophical points are crucial to understanding Willard's mature thought. Every reference he makes to "spirit," "spiritual," "spirituality," and certainly to "God" has some connection to this very finely hewn intellectual and theological conclusion of *the substantiality of the spiritual.*

But the spiritual is not just substantial; it is personal. The key biblical texts concerning the nature of God all testify (largely in contrast to the Hellenistic view) to the *personality* of God. As far as the argument from the physical universe goes, Willard affirms the modest conclusion that "the nonphysical source of the physical universe" has some capacity to both will and think—ergo, it is personal. As will be discussed in chapter 5, it is from the commonsense familiarity with *our own* personality that the categories necessary to recognize God's personality are formed. This too is not only a general scientific point. As Willard says on one occasion, "Many people say that the great genius of the Jewish religion is monotheism. No, it's not. The great genius of the Jewish religion is its revelation of a personal God."[28]

When it comes to reading the Bible's talk of the kingdom of God *as an ontologist*, Willard lets his notions of God's self-sufficiency and God's

---

26. Most of the best sources for his philosophy of substance—that is, his notes for his USC metaphysics course—I was not able to access for my research.

27. Dallas Willard, "The Issues Traditionally Involved in Discussions of 'Substance,'" n.d., Dallas Willard Collection, to which could be added his handout "Nominalism and the Theory of Substance," 1982, Dallas Willard Collection. A stable and robust interpretation of what Willard meant by his comments about the substantiality of the spiritual and especially of God is an important but outstanding research task.

28. Dallas Willard, "The Fundamental Issues," *Manifesting the Kingdom* (Valley Vista Christian Community, Sepulveda, CA, 1988), MP3/cassette, 32:45.

dualist relation to the physical universe play commanding roles. Indeed, *even if* Jesus and others had never used the phrase "the kingdom of God," a good portion of what Willard taught about the kingdom could be gathered from the Scriptures' teaching about God. This is so because undergirding Willard's study of that specific phrase is what he took to be an intellectually responsible ontology of God, one he had worked out over time with an ordered use of multiple theological sources—Scripture, tradition, experience, and reason.

Willard, furthermore, knew that an ontology entailing God's substantial spiritual nature and self-sufficiency was well represented in the Christian tradition. Theologians who challenged it (above all in the modern period) often did so not for biblical but for extrabiblical reasons—for example, in lieu of the supposedly defunct philosophy of substance. But here, Willard's wide-ranging competencies in intellectual history reassured him that nothing has been discovered (by a philosopher or theologian) to call this traditional ontology of God into question.[29]

Guideline #2: Greek Thought

BUT THERE IS one tradition of theological thought—more associated with history than with philosophy or theology—that also disdained the philosophically disciplined approach to biblical ontology that Willard pursued and, therefore, neglected if not explicitly rejected the knowledge of God just delineated.

I refer to a modern antimetaphysicalist school, most visible in the mid-twentieth-century biblical theology movement, that attempted to read the Bible "historically" while also disowning much of the ontological-exegetical reasoning characteristic of church history. Admittedly, this is a broad and internally diverse school of thought (I would trace it back to scholarly, continental Lutheran circles from the mid-nineteenth century) that extends up until the present day to encompass many confessional

29. As can be seen from his "Language, Being, God" essay, he was accustomed to walking through obscure tracts of intellectual history to remind inquirers that human accumulation of knowledge still substantiates this basic point.

traditions.[30] This school's prime objection is that ontological-exegetical reasoning in the study of the biblical texts imports "Hellenism" into culturally Hebrew texts and, by doing so, misrepresents the view of reality witnessed to therein.[31] Hearing Willard answer this prime objection will help us understand where he stands.

The assumption of the objection is that the metaphysical inquiries and insights Willard is making use of are fundamentally "Greek" and, ergo, absent as influences on the worldview of the non-"Greek" biblical authors and the possible meanings expressed in their texts. This is a familiar twentieth-century position. One can find it in one of Willard's favorite authors on the kingdom, George Eldon Ladd, who writes, "[C. H.] Dodd's work has the defect of understanding the Age to Come in terms of platonic thought rather than biblical eschatology." By contrast, Ladd prefers Oscar Cullmann, who "provides an excellent corrective for Dodd's platonic approach."[32]

In one of his many interviews with him before he died, Gary Moon asked Willard, "What do you think when you hear the statement that we need to separate Christian thought from Greek influences?" To this, his reply was,

> *I think that people generally don't know what they are talking about. In the first case, it is impossible; you can't separate it out. And, of course, the Greeks had some issues. Their view of the body was mistaken, and there were other problems with the Greeks. And certainly, the Hebrews had a different worldview*

---

30. For historical orientation, Martin Kähler's lectures on the history of German Protestant thought in the nineteenth century are excellent (*Geschichte der protestantischen Dogmatik im 19. Jahrhundert* [Munich: Chr. Kaiser Verlag, 1962]). Read multiple times in Halle before his death in 1912, the lectures are valuable because they precede the two world wars and the influence of dialectical theology and Karl Barth. Kähler manages to present nineteenth-century thought without an ax to grind, despite having a horse in the race.

31. The most prominent expositor of this tendency, sometimes called the Hellenization thesis, is Adolf von Harnack.

32. George Eldon Ladd, *A Theology of the New Testament* (1974; repr., Grand Rapids, MI: Eerdmans, 1993), 9.

than the Greeks. For the Hebrews, it was a highly personalistic worldview, and the uniqueness of the Jewish people and so on is tied into their view of God and time and the world and everything else.

So there are differences, but you can't imagine an early church emerging from just Hebrew influences. It is impossible. Usually when people bring this up, they are arguing a point, like the famous contrast between resurrection and immortality. Immortality as a disembodied view is not a Hebrew view—it is a bodily resurrection.[33]

Sadly, this is an improvised comment and not a sustained argument, for it touches on something vital in Willard's approach to biblical ontology: whether biblical exegesis can ever be successful if one excludes "Greek" philosophical thought.

Willard's negative response has two pillars. First of all, Willard's *historical* assessment is that Greek thought is simply intertwined in the biblical and early Christian sources. Separating it out would alter the biblical testimony's original integrity. So long as it wishes to remain true to its original sources, Christian thought is welded to Greek thought.

To understand Willard's *historical* appreciation for Hellenic ideas in the Scriptures, two mental layers must be considered. The first layer is conscious or explicit Hellenism. In light of the Jewish Diaspora and Alexander the Great's conquests, the Second Temple Jews were no longer isolated from historical Hellenism. Willard concurs with this well-established point. His historical judgment is that Jesus and Paul, through the sheer metropolitan nature of first-century Jerusalem and Palestine, were aware of the major ideas that circulated in the ancient world.[34]

33. Gary Moon was kind to share with me this transcribed quote from his interviews with Willard (email correspondence with the author concerning Charles Finney, June 22, 2014).

34. So Willard, "In Jesus' day Jerusalem was a glorious city, routinely flooded by hundreds of thousands of visitors, including multitudes of brilliant people from all over the 'known' world. It was a cosmopolitan environment, interacting with the entire Roman

For example, an idea that was no longer simply in the possession of the elites but had become an unconscious part of even "low" Mediterranean culture was the role of exercises (disciplines) in pedagogy and especially in moral or sapiential pedagogy. This set of ideas is so pervasive, says Willard, that Paul and the other New Testament writers feel no necessity to include in their epistles to Jewish and Greek audiences a section on the disciplines.[35] Observation of the lives of Jesus, Paul, and others shows that disciplines were practiced, but as teachers, they never give a formal account of them. The reason being, argues Willard, that their audiences did not *need* such theorizing because such theories had already been worked out and were already deeply enculturated. The sight of a particular individual, Jewish or Greek, engaging in disciplines to imitate a person of importance, especially a person of religious or moral importance, was a common first-century sight. Culture is what needs no explanation.

The second mental layer for Willard is unconscious or inexplicit Hellenism. The idea here is that the Greeks were, in fact, right in *some* of their convictions about reality. Take, for instance, formal logic. This is an area of knowledge in which the Greeks were gaining explicit mastery. If they were correct in their basic convictions about formal logic, it was because, in Willard's view, they were merely describing the nature of reality—that is, describing how things stand in logical reality. But this does not mean that the Hebrews—who were, as far as we know, not seeking explicit mastery of formal logic—knew nothing of logic. Logic, being an element of what is real, was not incomprehensible to them, though what they knew was not explicit, rigorous, or extensive.

Willard's argument continues that because logic is a real and everyday entity, it is an entity about which most humans have some knowledge. The same applies to knowledge of logic today. Children need not

---

world and more. What was known and discussed anywhere was known and discussed there" (Willard, *Conspiracy*, 135–36). In the notes (410n5), he cites Richard A. Batey, *Jesus and the Forgotten City* (Grand Rapids, MI: Baker, 1991).

35. Dallas Willard, "The Disciplines of Abstinence: Solitude, Silence, Fasting," *Spirituality and Mission* (African Enterprise, Pietermaritzburg, South Africa, May 1985), MP3/cassette, 41:15.

wait until their first class in formal logic in order to finally be able to know something about logic and how to use it. The vast majority know something about logic and use it effectively because it is a part of their world. But what they know is implicit, nonrigorous, and limited.

Willard's philosophical grounds for affirming this layer of inexplicit Hellenism lie in his appreciation for commonsense philosophy.[36] The idea is that persons, ancient or modern, *can* exemplify genuine knowledge of ontological matters that the Greeks rigorously studied and wrote on without having read the Greeks or disciplined themselves as the Greeks had because these ontological matters are *real matters*. What's more, they are everyday matters. Put differently, in as much as they are real and everyday matters, there is no reason why the Hebrews should not have tacit knowledge of them. For this reason, the exegete's own ontology as well as the covenant people's tacit ontology are things that need to be explicitly pursued in order to make sense of the text and its subject matter.

Guideline #3: Metaphysical-Realist Exegesis

AS FOR THE second pillar of his response to Moon's question, Willard saw no intellectual advantage for biblical exegesis in jettisoning Greek thought and genuine advantages in embracing the best of it. This seems to be the background of his remark that one cannot imagine an early church emerging from just Hebrew influences—with an emphasis, I think, on *church* and not on *early*. The implication is not another factual statement about the historical-cultural situation in the first centuries but a normative statement about the providential sources of the church's overall vitality in its earliest period.[37]

---

36. One of Willard's first exposures to that position in philosophy was in G. E. Moore's article "A Defence of Common Sense," in *Contemporary British Philosophy (2nd Series)*, ed. J. H. Muirhead (New York: Macmillan, 1925). But later in his life, he would recommend the books of Michael Polanyi (Willard, "Bible, the University," 30). In his last conversation with Willard, long-time friend Trevor Hudson recalls that Willard urged him to read Esther Lightcap Meek's *Longing to Know* (Grand Rapids, MI: Brazos, 2003) and *Loving to Know* (Eugene, OR: Cascade, 2011). Trevor Hudson, interview by the author, June 2, 2014, interview 1, telephone.

37. Willard consistently thought that the life of the ante-Nicene period was a high point in church history and that making conscious use of the best of Greek thought was

In contrast to the above antimetaphysicalist school of thought, Willard simply continues the ancient practice of metaphysical exegesis, which profoundly marked the traditions of patristic, scholastic, post-Reformation, and modern theology, what is often called systematic theology.[38] At one academic speaking event, Willard confessed, "Frankly, Plato and Aristotle have meant more to me than any other book besides the Bible. They got in on the ground floor, and so they could make a better start. People after them tend to have to deal with other people who are already on the ground. So then Aquinas and Augustine, they come in from an angle that's different. And when you combine those two, you really get a very fine treatment of the human self, of knowledge, and of human value."[39]

After speaking about the modern period's preoccupation with knowledge and its crippling acceptance of empiricism, physicalism, and naturalism, he says, "In the modern period, the one person who has been the most helpful to me is a man I mentioned named Edmund Husserl. He's absolutely impossible to read. . . . But he is one who sees how to deal with empiricism."[40] With this range from the classical to the modern, further research on Willard faces an immense task of reconstructing his general philosophical thought and its relevance to theology.[41] Only then will Willard's ontological approach to the Bible be on hand for future scholarship.

---

a key to that vitality. The only sense in which Willard can sympathize with the worry historically associated with Tertullian is in the details. Hence, he welcomes it when a point is being argued like the point about resurrection and immortality.

38. Cf. two historical works significant for their timely, if unheeded, critique of the growing antimetaphysicalism in theology: A. B. Bruce, "Theological Agnosticism," *American Journal of Theology* 1, no. 1 (1897): 1–15; and B. B. Warfield, *The Right of Systematic Theology* (Edinburgh: T&T Clark, 1987).

39. Dallas Willard, "Worship and Holiness," *National Faculty Leadership Conference 2002* (Christian Leadership Ministries, Chicago, IL, June 29, 2002), MP3, 39:00.

40. Willard, 40:30.

41. Throughout his life, Willard held a providential view of science or what for centuries was simply called philosophy. For example, he says, "One of the fields I worked on in my graduate studies years ago was the history of science. I took a minor in that for my Ph.D. at the University of Wisconsin—the field was just opening up. One of the most interesting things is how much progress is due to 'serendipity,' over and over and over.

Here again, I can only describe a few elements of the metaphysical-realist exegesis that Willard practiced, focusing on the guidance he received from the man "who saved him from Kant"—namely, Edmund Husserl.[42] For Willard's most consuming professional interest, the "absolutely impossible to read" philosophy of Husserl, was also providential in the formation of his own philosophical views.

Openness of Inquiry

OF THE MANY commonalities to speak of, one of the first and easiest to mention is *openness of inquiry.* "Voraussetzungslosigkeit" is Husserl's term, giving it initial description in *Logical Investigations* (1900/1901).[43] Willard often highlights the importance of intellectual openness when critiquing the closed-mindedness of what is today called "science," wittily contrasting on one occasion "Baconian science" with "Draconian science."[44] The former, Willard's obvious preference, does not so much claim an allegiance to Francis Bacon as indicate the openness of inquiry and openness to facts that characterized scientific research into the end of the nineteenth century.[45] In biblical exegesis, Willard refers

---

It just bowls you over when you get to know the history of science." Then, asked about whether it was not rather "ordained from before the foundations of the world," Willard responds, "Absolutely right. This is God at work in human history. This is a part of the story, and not just in science but in other areas. When you survey the overall scene you realize how little of what we call progress is due to human inventiveness." In Dallas Willard, "Spiritual Disciplines in a Postmodern World," *Radix*, no. 2 (2000): 6.

42. A great deal of primary source material can be found only in his unpublished class notes, which are located in the Dallas Willard Collection.

43. Edmund Husserl, *Logische Untersuchungen 2. Teil* (Halle, Germany: Niemeyer, 1901), 19–22. Willard relates "presuppositionlessness" to Husserl's famous bracket in his *Ideas* and connects them both with the informal fallacy of ignoratio elenchi. On understanding what Husserl means by the bracket, Willard recommends Forrest Williams's paper "Doubt and Phenomenological Reduction." See his lecture on February 7, 1994, in "Transcript of USC Course Seminar in Phenomenology: Phenomenology and Postmodernism, Phil 525," 1994, Dallas Willard Collection.

44. Dallas Willard, "Science and Knowledge of the Human Soul," *Wheaton Theology Conference* (Wheaton College, Wheaton, IL, April 9, 1999), MP3/cassette, 54:30.

45. On this point, Willard actually follows Galileo, who is similarly analyzed by Husserl in his *Crisis*. Cf. Dallas Willard, "Understanding the Opposition to Knowledge of Christ in Today's World," *The Knowledge of Christ in the Contemporary World* (Eidos Christian Center, Newport Beach, CA, June 27, 2003), MP3, 40:00. There he

to this principle when, in *Conspiracy*, he urges for a hermeneutics "not governed by obscure and faddish theories or by a mindless orthodoxy."[46] On the contrary, he urges an "intelligent, careful, intensive but straightforward" reading.[47]

But beyond openness of inquiry, two of Willard's most profound commonalities with Husserl can be seen in his two major works on Husserl: respectively, his PhD dissertation, "Meaning and Universals," and his major philosophical monograph *Logic and the Objectivity of Knowledge.*

Antinominalist Hermeneutics

WILLARD'S DISSERTATION IS especially illuminating because he explicitly deals with the ontology presumed by *metaphysical-realist* hermeneutics. The first chapter, adapted from one of Willard's first philosophical pieces to be celebrated by his peers, deals with the nature of meaning and is partly critical of Husserl.[48] In it, Willard makes the case that the act of meaning is something only attributable to minds, to spiritual beings.

According to Willard, there has been a perennial tendency in philosophy to treat *words*—that is, a physical thing or event—as entities that mean. But there has been no coherent account given of how a physical thing or event could possibly do such a thing—that is, to mean. Words don't mean; minds mean. Willard reprimands Husserl, despite his excellent analysis of mental acts and especially their *intentionality*, for at times treating words as if they had mind-like abilities.[49] In chapter 1,

---

begins, "We often think of science as observational. . . . That's the Baconian idea of science. . . . But that's an extremely limited view of science and the Galilean version is: you form hypotheses and you test them against observations but you don't allow your observations to provide your hypotheses."

46. Willard, *Conspiracy*, xvi.

47. Willard, *Conspiracy*, xvi. As stated above, Willard believed this principle guided two prominent theologians—namely, Augustine and Wesley—who were models for how philosophy and theology are to be integrated. Augustine in particular is commended for not privileging Athens or Jerusalem but simply "following the argument" (Willard, "On Philosophy and Christianity," 1:45).

48. Willard, *Meaning and Universals*, chap. 1; Moon, *Becoming Dallas Willard*, 99.

49. One can see in this argument the roots of Willard's account of words as spiritual or as personal. This account is then tied into his account of how the word of God functions and how the kingdom of God, as a personal kingdom, is a kingdom of words.

section 4, Willard gives a quick account (a phenomenology) of how words relate to acts of meaning and understanding.[50]

This basic ontology of meaning or of the act of meaning is supplemented in the subsequent chapters of his dissertation, in which Willard argues that Husserl was not a nominalist but a realist with respect to universals. Though Husserl is not the person from whom Willard first learned this so-called Platonic realism (his graduate school was led by the realist W. H. Hay), he laments nothing in Husserl's account of universals except an obscure mode of expression. The fact that Willard was a self-aware and highly trained "Platonist" realist from his earliest days is *vital* for making sense of his approach to the Bible and to biblical ontology in our day, in which some form of nominalism is assumed (often without any corresponding awareness or proper training in the subject matter) by most theologians and philosophers.

Undoubtedly, one of the most profound things that Willard did learn from Husserl was an appreciation for the philosophy of mind known as *intentionality*. This theory, which was lacking in the classical realist tradition, holds that thoughts in the human mind have the unique character of pointing at things distinct from them. Every thought is a thought *about* something. The challenge the theory puts to the skeptic is to produce and describe a thought that lacks this property of *being about*. Whether about Hannibal of Carthage, about one's knee, about the number 6, about courage, about a unicorn, about the word *walnut*, about a mirage, or about another mental act, every thought has a direction, a pointedness. The object at which it is pointing may be real (one's knee), not real (unicorns), imagined (Middle-earth), or real but purely mental (the thought one is now having). What remains common to all variety of thoughts is they are about something. This aboutness is an inseparable property of thought.

Furthermore, the most illuminating section of the dissertation regarding Willard's approach to the Bible is found in the conclusion,

50. Willard, *Meaning and Universals*, 54–88. This section is extremely valuable for understanding the linguistic and mental ontology fundamental to his approach to biblical ontology in the Scriptures, and I refer the reader to it for more detail.

where he gives his rationale "for combining in one paper investigations into the nature of meaning and investigations into the question of the reality of universals."[51] He writes, "Just as act-characters, in their function of reaching out beyond the mind, make it possible for many people to have presented to them and think about the same thing—which therefore is objective—, so the reality of universals makes it possible for many persons to have thoughts which are *identical* in important respects with those of other persons. The same mental determinations, given the reality of universals, is instanced, or can be instanced, in many minds; and insofar, one's very thoughts are objective, just like what is thought of."[52] His theory of intentionality is what one hears when he writes of "reaching out beyond the mind" and "thinking about the same thing." What he is saying about universals is that, in thinking about Hannibal, my thought of Hannibal and your thought of Hannibal have an identical property. Both thoughts have the property of *being about Hannibal*. This is explained by their instancing of a universal—namely, *of Hannibalness*. Furthermore, only mental acts among all real entities (including words) have these properties that reach out asymmetrically beyond their bearer—that is, beyond the mental act as a particular entity.

"But there is more to it," Willard says. He continues, "Qualities [i.e., properties] not only are identical in many things or minds, they also have necessary connections between each other. One does not have to examine every dog to see if they are all sure enough going to be animals. . . . He has found a necessary and universal connection between certain complex properties, which allow him to know that whatever instances the one also and of necessity instances the other."[53] What Willard calls "necessary connections" are, one might say, the ontological building blocks of logic—that is, the real relations that exist between things such as between the numbers 2 and 4. Like universals, these building

51. Willard, 240.
52. Willard, 237–38.
53. Willard, 238.

blocks are, indeed, also universal, a point that Husserl belabored in his day against what was then called psychologism.[54]

Putting it all together, Willard says,

> *Now, put very crudely, all of this means that not only do other people have "my thoughts," i.e. intentional qualities [i.e., properties] which are instanced in my mind, but in their minds intentional qualities, simply or very complex, have the very same predicates and relationships to other qualities which I by reflection upon my own thoughts and perceptions have seen them to have. . . .*
>
> *And so, finally, a judgment which is true will be true regardless of the mind in which it is instanced, and a line of reasoning which is valid will be valid regardless of who executes it. In this way, the genuine objectivity of the truth is seen to rest upon its* überempirischen Idealität *[sic].*[55]

Though Willard will refine it over the years, these are the basic realist elements of an ontology of meaning and understanding that he regards as essential to hermeneutics and to biblical ontology. The existence of universals is what lies behind the possibility that a biblical author and a biblical reader can communicate and have identical thoughts, for their thoughts may instance the same universal, the same "aboutness," even if that object does not exist. The existence of "necessary connections" allows for the fact that these thoughts stand in the same logical order for both author and reader.

Willard does believe that universals are instanced in nonmental entities, in sunsets and guitar chords. So in claiming that identities hold between mental acts, he is not merely advocating for what is called conceptualism. Conceptualists have the difficulty of explaining how the precise concepts of one mind end up in another mind, and some Christian

54. See Edmund Husserl's "Prolegomena zur reinen Logik," in *Logische Untersuchungen 1. Teil* (Halle, Germany: Niemeyer, 1900), §§1–72.

55. Willard, *Meaning and Universals*, 239.

philosophers have sometimes resorted to invoking God to account for the transfer. This move is what Willard called, in a short response paper, "hermeneutical occasionalism."[56]

Conceptualist and nominalist metaphysics have a much more difficult time explaining the ontology of meaning and understanding. Denying the existence of universals, a nominalist claims that each act of meaning and each intentional mental act is a unique particular. For the nominalist, an act of meaning and an act of understanding cannot be, as Willard says, "*identical* in important respects." That would imply that two thoughts of two minds share an identical property (e.g., being *about* Jesus of Nazareth) whose existence could only be made possible by recourse to the existence of a universal (e.g., Jesus-of-Nazareth-aboutness). The best a nominalist exegete can hope for is a thought *in the same class* as a biblical author's thought.

What's more, for the nominalist, the necessary connections that follow from a person's intentional acts are unique to that person *alone*. There are no real relations that exist and apply universally to one person's mental acts *and* to any identical mental acts. Hence, it is impossible to deduce another person's *ideal* train of thought or assume that it *should* be the same as one's own ideal train of thought. A nominalist exegete can only search for a biblical author's *next* thought and, perhaps, try to find some causal reason for it outside of their rational intelligence (i.e., in their psychology or cultural history or in their physical environment).

To Willard's mind, the theory of intentionality, combined with the theory of universals, better explains how books written over many centuries *could*, despite the variety in linguistic expression, have an underlying ontological unity in their accounts "of God and of his relations to creation." What's more, this ontological unity can be subjected to systematic or logical analysis. Willard was adamant to say that the Bible, as a record of the people of God's progressive apprehension, is

---

56. Dallas Willard, "Hermeneutical Occasionalism," in *Disciplining Hermeneutics: Interpretation in Christian Perspective*, ed. Roger Lundin (Grand Rapids, MI: Eerdmans, 1997), 167–72.

not a systematic theology textbook or even a catechism.[57] Indeed, this blatant fact complicates the ontological task of the exegete (and in God's wisdom, keeps the Bible from being a book that we can dissect and control) but does not hamper the approach to biblical ontology in the way that the theories of representationalism and nominalism do.

Conceptual Analysis

ANOTHER ELEMENT OF Willard's appreciation of Husserl that is relevant to his metaphysical-realist approach to the Bible is Husserl's strategy of *conceptual analysis*, which Willard describes in *Logic* and elsewhere.

In the world of Husserl interpretation, Willard was keen to point out that Husserl was an ontologist. Husserl began his scholarly career in the 1880s with an inquiry into the foundations of arithmetic and began that inquiry with the hypothesis that arithmetic is based on the ontology of number. So he set out to determine what number *is*. But in the process of investigating number, he discovered that arithmetic is not dependent on it, and he abandoned his project. Nevertheless, his ontology of number and especially his *means* for determining what number is remained with him, so Willard, throughout his life. It is incorporated into Husserl's analysis of the ontology of knowledge and logic in his landmark book *Logical Investigations* (1900/1901).[58]

This method is what is referred to as conceptual analysis. It may also be fairly called "essence analysis," writes Willard, because it seeks, by means of an analysis of the concept, to determine the essence of that to which the concept applies—for example, of number.[59] "Conceptual analysis," Willard tells us, "is simultaneously an analysis of the essence of an object *insofar as* it is an object of the concept in question."[60]

---

57. Dallas Willard, *Jesus's Gospel and Ours* (Regent University, Virginia Beach, VA, 1992), 6:00.
58. Husserl, *Logische Untersuchungen 1. Teil*; *Logische Untersuchungen 2. Teil* (Halle, Germany: Niemeyer, 1901).
59. Dallas Willard, "Concerning Husserl's View of Number," *Southwestern Journal of Philosophy* 5, no. 3 (1974): 97–109, esp. 98. The best description of Willard's work on Husserl's early philosophy is in Burt Hopkins, "Dallas Willard's Contribution to Phenomenology," *Husserl Studies* 35, no. 2 (2019): 117–30.
60. Willard, *Logic*, 26.

Here is Willard's summary of how this works for Husserl with respect to number: "The general assumption in Husserl's early studies of number is, then, that in order to analyze *number* we must analyze the concept of number, and in order to analyze *the concept of number* we must psychologically analyze *experiences* of number—in which, of course, the concept of number is somehow resident."[61] For the moment, the mention of *experience* should be highlighted. There are many versions of conceptual analysis in contemporary philosophy, but Husserl's version elicited assistance from *psychology*, leading him to include *psychologisch* in the title of his first two publications. The reason for this is that concepts, if they are valuable to us at all, are so as constituents of knowledge. And knowledge and its concepts are found, if anywhere in reality, in the experiences of those who know. Psychology studies human experience and, therefore, is helpful for coming to terms with concepts.

Willard has much to say about Husserl's method of conceptual analysis when treating Husserl directly but never introduces it by this name or any other when teaching on theological topics.[62] Yet without the name, something virtually identical is nevertheless present. While lecturing, especially when he lacks the time to go into a topic, Willard will at times tell his audience to take a word/concept (angels, for instance) and trace it through the whole of the Scriptures with an eye to what the various texts say about what it is. Basically, he is recommending the traditional Bible study method of a "word study," something Willard himself did with biblical concepts on many, many occasions.[63]

Importantly, a whole theory of Scripture lies behind this practice. Suffice it to say, Willard holds that the Scriptures meaningfully express the authors' epistemic experience with an object—say, angels.

---

61. Willard, 26.

62. Cf. another reference to concept analysis in Dallas Willard, "Translator's Introduction," in *Philosophy of Arithmetic: Psychological and Logical Investigations—with Supplementary Texts from 1887–1901*, ed. Edmund Husserl (Dordrecht, Netherlands: Kluwer Academic, 2003), xv.

63. Because of reigning misconceptions, he often recommends doing this with the word *grace*. See Dallas Willard, "My Grace Is Sufficient," *Renovaré Regional Conference* (Renovaré / C. S. Lewis Institute, Fairfax, VA, May 2, 2003), MP3, 22:30.

The authors *mean*, through the words of the text, their epistemic experiences. That is to say, they reproduce in words for the sake of their readers the mental act that gave *them* initial knowledge of angels. Hence, by analyzing the object-oriented mental experiences of the authors as expressed through the word *angel*, we the readers may come to clarity about the concept (angel-directedness) employed (a) in their knowledge of the object—that is, of angels—and (b) in their expression of it to us.

This approach is especially expedient if a cognitive experience of the object can be reproduced in us, and in certain cases, this is not difficult. Water, donkeys, and even Jerusalem can be reexperienced by the reader. In other cases, such as with angels, joy, or Ezekiel's wheels, this may be more difficult or even impossible. But that does not mean that conceptual analysis is useless. Even if we have never experienced angels ourselves, through disciplined conceptual analysis, some degree of conceptual clarity concerning angels can be attained. This would prepare us for a fulfilled (or frustrated) experience with an angel—should we be so privileged.

A 1999 philosophical paper, "How Concepts Relate the Mind to Its Objects," clarifies that what Willard has in mind with the word *concepts* are the intentional act characters we previously encountered in his dissertation.[64] A concept is a particular directedness of the mind. More specifically, concepts are *properties* of mental acts—of beliefs, judgments, wishes, assertions, presentations—and instances of universals. In other words, the many things that exegetes attempt to make sense of through the texts and that systematicians order and relate are, philosophically stated, *concepts*—which, in Willard's theory of intentionality, means they are the properties of aboutness that thoughts (e.g., about angels) have.

---

64. Dallas Willard, "How Concepts Relate the Mind to Its Objects: The 'God's Eye View' Vindicated?," *Philosophia Christi* 1, no. 2 (1999): 5–20. Willard's account of how such intentional properties relate the mind and the world is complex and would take us too far afield. Other than "How Concepts Relate," his paper "Perceptual Realism," *Southwestern Journal of Philosophy* 1, no. 3 (1970): 75–84, is an excellent place to start. Likewise, one should consult the first five recordings for the 1997 class "Ontology of Knowledge," *Ontology of Knowledge* (Biola University, La Mirada, CA, May 27–June 13, 1997), MP3/cassette.

Altogether, these formed a biblical ontology that Willard sought to elicit from the presentation of the Bible as a whole. In the following chapters, many of the biblical concepts that Willard found to be important will be dealt with. But of these, there is one concept that deserves special attention before we leave Husserl and Willard's third guideline: the kingdom of God.

The Kingdom of God in Regional (and Systematic) Ontology

THOUGH CONCEPTUAL ANALYSIS is important for understanding the Scriptures as a whole, it has a particular responsibility, thought Willard, to their testimony to the concept of *the kingdom of God.* Willard thought this for two reasons. First, he had identified the kingdom of God as one of those "larger pieces" of biblical conceptualization that would unlock the smaller pieces and unify the whole.[65] An exegete must understand, in accordance with what it means *to be*, what the kingdom of God *is.* Though all readers will get the job done somehow, Willard's philosophical refinement meant, for one, that he made disciplined and conscious use of conceptual analysis.[66]

That meant, of course, something similar to Husserl's strategy as quoted previously. Allow me to adapt it as follows: "In order to analyze *the kingdom of God*, we must analyze the concept of the kingdom of God, and in order to analyze *the concept of the kingdom of God*, we must psychologically analyze *experiences* of the kingdom of God—in which, of course, the concept of the kingdom of God is somehow resident."[67] Note again the role that *experience* plays in this approach. If one wants to know what the kingdom of God is, one must be ready, so Willard, to

---

65. Willard, "Q & A: Prayer," 43:30. See chapter 5 for more on this.

66. It is significant for Willard's life history, I believe, that he was working on his translation of Adolf Reinach's *Über Phenomenologie* during the 1960s, when, as we know, he first started preaching and teaching on the kingdom of God in ecclesial circles, first in InterVarsity groups on the University of Wisconsin–Madison, then in the Congregationalist churches Willard pastored in 1964–65. Reinach's famous phrase "zu den Sachen selbst" (to the things themselves) and numerous other references to essence analysis occur in this lecture. Dallas Willard, "Concerning Phenomenology, Trans. of Adolf Reinach's *Über Phaenomenologie*," *Personalist* 50, no. 2 (1969), 194–221.

67. Adapted from Willard, *Logic*, 26.

exegete with experience. And the most important experiences to be psychologically analyzed are the experiences *of Jesus and his followers* as recorded in the Scriptures. But a thorough analysis of experience would, second, require, as it did for Husserl in the analysis of number, analyzing *one's own* experiences. The results of this second analysis may have positive or negative implications for one's trust in the New Testament.[68] But the strategy is not complete until, third, one has analyzed the experiences *of Hebrew biblical authors* and *of extrabiblical Christian authors up until the present day*.[69]

Beyond being commonsensical, these three steps recommend themselves because they mirror Willard's threefold account of sources in theology: *Scripture*, *tradition*, and *personal experience*.[70] This account would not be complete without adding *reason*, not so much as a fourth source, but as the mental activity that sifts and integrates these three, also discovering new truths by following the necessary connections.[71] It is by means of these sources that one is given the opportunity to know, this side of eternity, the kingdom of God.

We can roughly sketch how this epistemic process worked for Willard in practice, though he would be the first to say that we should do our own research—to not be "Willardian" but look for ourselves. Recalling his journey, Willard says, as quoted in the previous chapter, that it

---

68. Willard's humorous remark about his dispensationalist upbringing is relevant here: "I was raised under a system known as dispensationalism, and it was a very comfortable system. I learned later why. Because basically what it did is go through the New Testament, and anything that we didn't have, we said that's for another age. I came to call that 'selective dispensationalism'" (Willard, "Science and Knowledge," 40:45).

69. Sociologically, knowing by authority or knowing by a source is massive in human knowledge. But sociological quantity does not dictate epistemic ontology or, as Willard's 1982 study calls it, "the objectivity of knowledge" (Dallas Willard, "Wholes, Parts and the Objectivity of Knowledge," in *Parts and Moments: Studies in Logic and Formal Ontology*, ed. Barry Smith [Munich: Philosophia Verlag, 1982]).

70. They also map on to the three sources Willard mentioned in his 2004 email to me, quoted in the first chapter.

71. See Willard's book *Knowing Christ Today*, 58–61, for one place where Willard makes a pass at naming theological sources. Husserl is one who did not contrast ideal laws—that is, pure logic—with the phenomenological imperative, as the foregoing appeal to experience has been called (see Husserl, *Logische Untersuchungen 1. Teil*). See Willard's judgment to this effect in his *Logic*, 73.

was not "theologians" through whom he came to understand the kingdom. Starting the late 1950s, likely after he had left Baylor and while he was living in Georgia (1958–59), Willard's word studies of the phrase *kingdom of God* (conceptual analysis) inevitably led him to employ the same hermeneutical principle that John Bright (whom he had already read) did: separating the idea (the concept) from the term (the physical word). That is, the study of a word led him to a mental property, a concept, which may have many words associated with it throughout human history. It seems that by this means, Willard, while in his twenties and not without help from Bright, discovered that the concept of the kingdom of God permeated the Scriptures. I believe Willard's emphasis in hindsight on the biblical priority of his discoveries is not so much an outworking of his commitment to *sola scriptura* as it is a mere biographical description. He sincerely felt he had first discovered something "on his own" about the kingdom of God, albeit with God's help, merely through his reading of the Scriptures.

Only then did he begin looking for that same discovery in church history and discovered that the realist hermeneutical principle that served him well in the Scriptures served him as he read "the theologians" and spiritual classics. This, based on Willard's rare recollections of his mental history, began during the 1960s and his graduate school days in Wisconsin and probably was not finished until the '80s. Willard came to believe that though *kingdom of God* was not always an explicitly central theological term in the history of Christian thought, the concept was present throughout and was indeed central.

In graduate school, Willard's go-to authors were Thomas à Kempis, John Wesley, and Charles Finney. But his lifelong historical investigation advanced to the point where he could confidently say of the first books of his pentalogy, "In these three books there is very little that is new, though much that is forgotten," and then refer his readers to the writings of Athanasius, Augustine, Anselm, Thomas, Luther, and Calvin.[72] This should not be mistaken as a quickly conceived bit of "window

72. Willard, *Conspiracy*, xvii–xviii.

dressing" for a potentially provocative book about the kingdom of God. Willard had by that time, in fact, *looked* at all of these people and more and had found the *concept* of the kingdom of God, as he came to know it. He remarked once that "many times in the history of the church, you've had the reality without the language."[73]

Finally, and perhaps above all, Willard sought to understand the kingdom of God via his own life experience. Just as one might hear that one's car had been stolen and walk out to the original parking spot to confirm it, Willard did the same with what he had learned from the Scriptures and the great voices of the church, making attempts to confirm these witnesses through his own experience, or what he called in 1973 "the justification of faith by experience." This led him to draw on life experiences before he began formally studying the kingdom of God. Examples can be found in the current biography of Willard, *Becoming Dallas Willard*.[74] But it was not only witnesses to the kingdom with which he did this sort of thing. Before Willard was interested in the kingdom, he attempted to imitate great revivalists in prayer and extemporaneous speaking in order to see revival as they saw it.

All this is to say that as he draws from these three sources, a quite consistent ontology of the kingdom emerges in Willard's mind, especially in the late 1980s, one that stays with him through decades of further teaching and research. But with this concept of the kingdom forming in his mind, the kingdom's essential connection to metaphysics or systematic ontology becomes clearer for him. This is the second level of ontological research—namely, the level of determining whether something is a *fundamental* reality. The exegete must determine both whether a reality is fundamental for the biblical authors, and especially for Jesus and his followers, as well as whether it is for the exegete as an ontologist and human being. For Willard, the answer is affirmative on both counts. He puts it this way in one of his essays: "The biblical tradition teaches that reality consists of *a personal God and his kingdom* (all he arranges for), and that every subject matter of human

73. Willard, "Kingdom Gospel," 10:00.
74. Moon, *Becoming Dallas Willard*.

thought, along with human thought itself, exists within that overarching reality."[75] Though many biblical realities are in need of ontological analysis (peace, heart, world, Israel, anointing, heaven, etc.), it is the metaphysical *fundamentality* of the kingdom of God in the biblical tradition's conception of reality that sets it apart for *special* ontological treatment. It is this metaphysical fundamentality that recommends it, above all, to our own quest for a plausible theory of being.

Guideline #4: Faith That Comes by the Word of God

THE ABOVE GUIDELINES represent how Willard would respond to those who would exclude "Greek" ontological exegesis on *historical* (guideline #2) and/or *philosophical* grounds (guideline #3). There is one more guideline to Willard's approach to the Bible that we should have before our minds before we discuss Willard's view of the gospel.

Having studied philosophy in the 1950s, during which many questioned philosophy's and even reason's applicability to the work of God and the church, the objection Willard was most likely to hear to his approach to the Bible was a theological one.[76] Having arisen historically in some branches of Lutheran and Reformed thought, this quite forceful objection eventually filtered into young Willard's Calvinistic Baptist tradition. These theological objectors worried that a disciplined use of philosophical insights in doctrinal reasoning or hermeneutics or ministry compromised the important biblical teaching that faith is a gift of God that comes by the word of God. A disciplined use of philosophy presupposed a "too summery" view of the human condition and a "too wintery" view of divine grace and the disposition of faith.

Because of its crucial role in his soteriology, Willard's view of faith will be a major recurring theme of *The Kingdom among Us*. At this juncture, allow me to say that Willard gave lifelong, careful consideration to

---

75. Willard, "Bible, the University," 21 (emphasis mine). "God and his kingdom" is Willard's standard response to the question, What is real? Cf. Willard, *Knowing*, 50.

76. Dallas Willard gives a list of objections in "The Gospel Ministry of Apologetics: A Neglected Field of Christian Service," *Prospects for an Evangelical Apologetics in the 1980s* (Bethel College, North Newton, KS, September 20, 1982), MP3/cassette, 22:00.

the workings of grace and faith in the human soul and to the corruption that had fallen on the will and mind. To make a long story short, he did not conclude that God was made uneasy by rational inquiry into the most fundamental issues. What's more, Willard remained profoundly indebted to the teaching that the word of God is the divine and gracious agent that produces faith as a gift (Eph 2:8).

One of the best places to see his view is in his occasional paper "Faith, Hope and Love as Indispensable Foundations of Moral Realization." There, in defending the ideals of Christian ethical theory against the criticism that it is simply *too* ideal, Willard writes,

> *When told that they must forgive a brother seven times in a day the apostles cried out: "Lord, increase our faith!" (Luke 17:5). They were exactly right in doing so. Faith, love and hope must be given. That, by the way, is why they are, fundamentally, not virtues, which are, as Aristotle correctly saw, acquisitions or attainments. I do not suggest that faith, hope and love enter those who do nothing to receive them. The merest gift must, after all, be accepted, received, in some way. But the New Testament teaching clearly places them all much more on the side of gifts or graces than on the side of attainments, even attainments divinely assisted. Thus, faith is created in our hearts, we are told, as we listen to the word of God in the Gospel of The Kingdom (Romans 10:8–17, & cf. 1:16–17).*[77]

Two of Willard's standard moves are present here. First, we see that biblical faith is not something that human effort produces. The initiative and the growth are entirely God's. Second, we see that the word of God and especially the gospel of the kingdom are the means by which

77. Dallas Willard, "Faith, Hope and Love as Indispensable Foundations of Moral Realization" (Society of Christian Philosophers, Loyola Marymount University, Los Angeles, CA, March 25, 1987), printed lecture, Dallas Willard Collection, section 7.

faith grows. Let us look at these two moves in turn to fill out the content of the fourth guideline to Willard's approach.

The Gift of Faith

FIRST, CONSIDER WILLARD's exegeses of Ephesians 2:1–10. In a lecture from 2002, he works through the whole passage, saying this about 2:5:

> *Grace comes in also at the point when you can do absolutely nothing about it. The grace of God that comes to us in Jesus Christ comes to us, first of all, at that level. This totally upsets the human applecart. Because the whole message of the Bible, in dealing with the Jews and later, is [this]:* it is the initiative of God that is the foundation of all the good that comes into our lives. *You're dead. You can't do anything. God sends his word and he sends his Spirit into us and things begin to move. . . . The first move in salvation is life.*[78]

A month later, Willard would say of himself in an interview, "If you were to get to the bottom of my theology, you would find me pretty Calvinistic."[79] The exegesis of Ephesians 2 is one of the most glaring examples of how Calvinistic he was. In focus is the divinely initiated gift of *grace*—for Willard, a catchall term for all of God's activities toward humanity, especially his life-giving and salvific activities.

Faith, then, is a part of grace, and Willard brings it into the picture while working on Ephesians 2:8:

> *Faith is confidence. Now note the relationship here: faith is the instrumentality. "By grace you have been saved through faith." Faith is how grace works to save you. Now, this is pretty*

---

78. Dallas Willard, "Kingdom Living 3," *Kingdom Living: Walking in the Character and Power of God* (Southside Vineyard, Grand Rapids, MI, April 12, 2002), MP3, 12:00; cf. Dallas Willard, "The Specific Disciplines: Study and Prayer," *The Spirit of the Disciplines* (Canoga Park Presbyterian Church, Canoga Park, CA, March 3, 1993), MP3/cassette, 20:15.

79. Willard, "Kingdom Living," 18.

> *important for the issues that we're dealing with because a common way of presenting it is, "You have faith and then you get grace"—in fact, "You get grace* because *you have faith." In fact, in many places, faith is turned into a work by which you get grace. You get grace because you have your faith right.*
>
> *Notice the order here is very different: you're saved by grace through faith. Faith itself is, notice here, "a gift of God." "Through faith" is an expression of grace. It's not something that leads to grace. Grace leads to it. See now, it is a pretty common understanding that faith is a miracle. . . . If we have faith, it is because God has given it to us through his grace.*[80]

Willard's criticism is directed at certain "Arminians" who make faith a precondition of receiving grace.[81] Faith's value is found in its occasionalist effect upon God, who, upon recognizing this attractive or meritorious feature in a person, confers on them "grace," be it forgiveness of sins or protection against evil or vindication at the last judgment.[82] On the contrary, says Willard, faith is a manifestation of divine grace having already entered a person's life. The same dynamic is also attributed to love and hope in the "Faith, Hope and Love" paper.

In terms of pastoral guidance, this view leads Willard to say things like "Faith is not something we work up and produce. One of the worst things that happens to folks is they try to believe. Do not try to believe! . . . Belief is not something you do by trying. Belief is something you grow in by experience of the word and grace of God as you live in this world."[83] Faith grows or emerges because the word of God comes into a person's life as a gift and produces faith as an effect. This does not

---

80. Willard, "Kingdom Living 3," 22:45.

81. This is connected to Willard's criticism of "bar-code faith" (Willard, *Conspiracy*, 36–37) and an occasionalist view of faith.

82. He associates the development of this view with the fundamentalist-modernist controversy, wherein both Calvinists and non-Calvinists taking the fundamentalist side rose up to defend basic Christian doctrines against the modernists who had called them into question.

83. Dallas Willard, "The Human Disaster of Unbelief," *Learning to Live an Eternal Life Now* (Ojai Valley Community Church, Ojai, CA, May 1, 1994), MP3/cassette, 35:30.

mean that the person is entirely passive in the process; rather, "the merest gift must, after all, be accepted, received, in some way."[84]

The Creation of Faith

FOR WILLARD, THE primary way in which God creates faith in himself and his invisible kingdom is through speaking—that is, through the word of God. This is the second move mentioned previously, that faith comes by hearing the word of God. In other words, the grace that occasions faith (Eph 2:8) comes primarily in the form of the word of God and involves a revelation of the unseen world and especially the unseen God.

In one important respect, believes Willard, the unseen God has already been revealed in the person of Jesus. And yet, though this "unmerited favor" is given and the unseen has become seeable, it remains unseen by many.[85] *Jesus* is the word of God. In his incarnate advent, God has spoken. But many who have eyes do not see, and many who have ears do not hear. God has publicly revealed himself—but in a way that is *gentle* and that can be pushed aside if that is what is most wanted. So even though faith comes by the word of God, faith is not produced simply by the operation of the word of God alone. How this works will be clearer if we consider Willard's theology of preaching.

His reputation as a spiritual-disciplines guru may obscure the fact that Willard was a firm believer in the power and primacy of preaching.[86] His high view of preaching did not limit it to an ordained minister's word from the pulpit during a sacred service; rather, it applied to all events in which the word of God is spoken through one human being to others. This would paradigmatically include the writing and reading of the Scriptures.

Preaching for him was much more than conveying information and explanations—as one would do in a lecture on the anatomy of the

---

84. Willard, "Faith, Hope and Love," section 7.

85. This is the paradoxical part of the divine conspiracy, which Willard thought characterized the history of redemption (Willard, *Conspiracy*, 11).

86. I make a case for an improved view of Willard's philosophy of ministry in my "Dallas Willard, Philosopher of Ministry, Teacher of Christlikeness," *Theology Today* (forthcoming).

foot—but an occasion in which God *may* speak to us as others speak to us. Often Willard would, illuminatingly, phrase this in terms of "the Spirit working with the Word."[87] In the 1970s, when the theology of the word of God was much more prominent in his mind, he said,

> *Pray that your ministry [i.e., the pastors and priests] will speak to you in such a way as to create faith in that fact [that where you are is God's holy place]. The function of the ministry is to speak the word of God in such a way that people believe. Pray that you will be given such a ministry from your midst or whoever comes by or on the radio or wherever it may be. That God will speak the word and you will see as Moses saw that burning bush and heard that voice and you will know—pray that you will know—that where you are is God's holy place.*[88]

The theology of preaching and hearing the word of God represented here was something that became an undercurrent in Willard's later teaching career. He discovered that other things, such as spiritual disciplines, needed more explicit emphasis in his ministerial context.[89] But this theology still cropped up in a few places, most visibly in the chapter on "Redemption by the Word of God" in *Guidance* and in the apex of his "Golden Triangle." In his final years, Willard, still in accord with his high view of preaching, would emphasize the sheer power of "the word

---

87. Willard thought that Finney was a model preacher in knowing how the word and Spirit worked together.

88. Dallas Willard, "Confidence," *Faith Evangelical Sermons* (Faith Evangelical Church, Chatsworth, CA, March 5, 1978), MP3/cassette, 31:15. Later in 1990, he said, "How you come to believe is another one of those matters we need to speak of. See the primary responsibility for the regeneration and growth of the people in the kingdom of God lies upon the ministers of the Word of God, people who do things like I do, standing around here *talking* to you. Now I as a talker must never believe that the force of my intelligence is going to bring you to spiritual life. As a minister of the Word I am practicing being in the kingdom. . . . But I know . . . it is the ministry of the Word that creates faith" (Dallas Willard, "The Rule of Heaven in the Old Testament, In Israel," *A Series on What Jesus Believed and Taught—and Lived* [First Hollywood Presbyterian Church, Hollywood, CA, February 18, 1990], MP3/cassette, 18:45).

89. Another instance of his "shoot where the enemy is" approach.

of the kingdom," citing Mark 4:26–29 as the passage that taught him this.[90] The word that the kingdom is available has the power to come into the will and mind to create faith, especially the initial faith that is the fruit of regeneration.[91]

Now the point about the Spirit and the word working together in preaching is developed in his thought in the following way: The human preacher takes the word—that is, adequate representations of God, man, and Christ—and communicates it. In instance A, there is among the hearers no corresponding conviction of or faith in the truth presented. In instance B, there is a corresponding conviction of and faith in the truth presented. One cause for the difference between A and B is the operation of the Spirit *with* the word. Though a human can preach the word faithfully, this Spirit's action is not something the preacher is ever in control of. However, some preachers are more sensitive to and prepared for working with it than others.[92] Viewed from the other side, the Spirit does not accomplish this work in creating faith without the human preaching of the word. Divine oracles and images are a fundamental part of how Willard believes the grace of God goes forward and creates faith in the human soul.[93] And if humans effectively restrict the dissemination of the word, either actively or passively, then God the Spirit does not circumvent the word and create faith without the preaching of it.

Returning to Jesus as the word of God, even though God *has* revealed himself in Jesus in a way that he had not revealed himself to

---

90. He often did this to explain the weakness of the churches who thought they stood with him in some perceived "spiritual formation movement." Though these churches longed for spiritual formation among their congregants, they did not preach the kingdom of God but some other gospel. Therefore, they did not see the fruit of Jesus and the apostles' ministry. For a detailed exegesis of Mark 4:26–29, see Dallas Willard, "The Secret Manner of the Kingdom's Working: The Leaven and the Seed," Parable Teaching (Harbor Church, Lomita, CA, March 20, 1983), MP3/cassette.

91. Many of these issues in Willard deserve their own systematic interpretation.

92. Here is another place where Finney's theologies of preaching and of the Spirit are a direct influence on Willard. But looming large is Calvin's theology as well, though probably only indirectly.

93. See the role of both of these in Willard, *Renovation*, chap. 6.

previous generations and even though this word of God *has been* spoken and lies, as Willard writes, on "the pages of human history," many do not have ears to hear or eyes to see it.[94] This publicly revealed word may be taken in the hands of human preachers—with diverse levels of understanding and belief—and increase and multiply (Acts 12:24). This all may take place without the operation of the Spirit. But only when it is accompanied by the Spirit does the word of God have the effect of *faith*.

Now as described here, this fourth theological guideline about the workings of grace and faith in religious epistemology assumes one knows what faith *is*. To this discussion, we turn in the next chapter.

94. Dallas Willard, "The Craftiness of Christ: Wisdom of the Hidden God," in *Mel Gibson's "Passion" and Philosophy: The Cross, the Questions, the Controversy*, ed. Jorge J. E. Gracia (Chicago: Open Court, 2004), 173.

4

THEOLOGY AND THE OBJECTIVITY OF FAITH

> Faith is a reality that has its causes and its effects. . . . Faith is a confidence that leads you to interact with reality in such a way that a result comes.
>
> —Dallas Willard, Azusa Pacific University, October 26, 1992

WHEN TRACING THE history of theology, one can watch as many leading theologians of the nineteenth and twentieth centuries take an increasing interest in faith as an epistemological act or method. This includes famous names such as Kierkegaard and Barth but also lesser-known figures like Franz H. R. von Frank and Martin Kähler. Some attempted to defend this as the orthodox view of the church and treated opponents as deviations from the Christ and his apostles. Thomas Aquinas was a commonly cited example of the deviant view. Aquinas had seen "philosophy"—meaning thereby all general human attempts to understand reality, including what we today would call history and natural science—as irreplaceably supportive of theology. In the centuries after Aquinas worked, there were many minor shifts in the knowledge base of "philosophy," understood again as all fields of knowledge outside theology, but in the eighteenth and nineteenth centuries, this knowledge base began to shift drastically to the point that it no longer served as a stable foundation for many traditional and orthodox theological positions.

Dallas Willard accused empiricism of being the theory that "wrecked" the Western philosophical train.[1] And since most theologians could never accept the full empiricist package of, for example, Locke or Hume, it was rather the various attempts to avoid or improve upon the empiricist theory, thinkers such as Immanuel Kant or Thomas Reid, that dominated the theological discussion. In this altered and potentially precarious philosophical landscape of recent centuries, a few viable options presented themselves to theologians.

The first was the abandonment of theology and a capitulation to modern philosophy or to naturalist historical criticism as the highest, most comprehensive pursuit of knowledge. The second was a mediating position in which theologians embraced a lot of modern philosophy and historical criticism (empiricist or postempiricist) but still found a niche for theology from which they could negotiate creative compromises for traditional theological views. However, there were, third, those who refused to negotiate with modern philosophy and compromise on traditional theological positions. And this is the group that in the nineteenth and twentieth centuries saw an advantage in promoting *faith* as an organ of knowledge.

Faith as Supplanting Knowledge

ONE SUCH THEOLOGIAN was Herman Bavinck. In his prolegomena to his *Reformed Dogmatics*, he makes a sustained argument for *faith* as the human act that underlies all attempts to know the external world.[2] No thinker, he says, is free in their pursuit of knowledge from the functioning of faith *in the form of presuppositions*. The same is eminently true of theology, and the best of the church's theologians, he says, have accepted this. When the church's best theologians make their faith—that is, presuppositions—the scientific starting point for studying God and his revelation, they are accepting the only viable option for scientific

1. Willard, "Worship and Holiness," 39:00.

2. Herman Bavinck, *Reformed Dogmatics* (Grand Rapids, MI: Baker Academic, 2003), 50–58, 71–76, 86–93, 563–68.

knowledge of anything.[3] Vice versa, people who are not prepared to let their faith launch their study of God and his revelation are not able to know this subject matter at all.[4] There is no other way to scale the mountain of theology or any science. Knowledge without faith is dead.

The crucial step I wish to draw out in Bavinck—because it is characteristic of other theologians in the modern period—is how he uses the act(s) of faith to jump over the "philosophical work" that older theologians thought was an adequate entry point to viable theological work.[5] Thereby, he is able to and justified in avoiding direct engagement with "philosophers" and specific theories that might make his theology tenuous or unjustified. There is simply no common ground on which Christian theologians and their "philosophical" detractors can stand. The theologians have their faith and the detractors theirs. Never the twain shall meet. Bavinck, in the prolegomena of *Reformed Dogmatics*, is at great pains to insist that he is not, in describing this, promoting anything that the Reformers, Augustine, and the early church would not recognize as superb theological method. And many today agree with him.

It should be no surprise at this point to hear that Dallas Willard does not agree with Bavinck. In fact, his reading of the history of theology informed him that Bavinck's position was not the traditional one but only a late nineteenth-century compromise. He was prepared to argue that Augustine and the Reformers were as philosophically attuned and serious as the medieval and Protestant scholastics. Being open to any well-established "philosophical" finding—metaphysical, historical, natural, psychological, and so on—theologians before the mid-nineteenth century largely thought of theology as a matter of *knowledge*.[6] Faith, of course, was important for salvation and for life, having its own role to play, but was not an alternative or rival to knowledge.

This balance between faith and knowledge served theologians passably well until the modern era, thinks Willard, when it ran aground

3. Bavinck, 564.
4. Bavinck, 501–600.
5. Bavinck, 55–56, 503–4, 507–17.
6. Willard, "On Philosophy and Christianity," 1:45.

due to the inherent weaknesses of its inherited ontology of knowledge. These were, generally speaking, *lacuna* and *blurs* in the classicist ontology of knowledge—that is, places where classical, medieval, and early modern philosophers had not been thorough enough in describing what knowledge is and how it works. When empiricism and philosophers like Locke and Kant challenged the classicist model, the latter did not have sufficient muscle to stand its ground. There were too many blurs, too many loose ends in its account. Similarly, accounts such as Thomas Reid's, which extended the classicist model, also eventually lost position in intellectual circles for the same reason.

In terms of the philosophical trajectory, much of this history is documented in Willard's philosophical oeuvre, such as in recordings of his University of Southern California (USC) classes.[7] As I mentioned in the previous chapter, Edmund Husserl helped Willard develop an epistemology, an ontology of knowledge, in which he attempted to dispel all blurs and come to a clear account of what knowledge is and how it is possible.[8] Even if they have not read his philosophy, most of Willard's readers should be cursorily aware of his work there, for he often salted his theological writings with this theory of knowledge.

For at least a decade, Willard had been talking about these issues with seminary presidents, Christian faculty, and active ministers before he attempted in *Knowing Christ Today* (2009) to give a more popular account of how knowledge works *in theology and spiritual life*. It is a book that, from the perspective of theologians and well-read ministers, leaves a lot to be desired. The painstaking distinctions that characterize Willard's philosophical work are replaced by the broad strokes of a semipopular genre.[9]

---

7. See, e.g., in Dallas Willard, "Transcript of USC Course British Empiricism, Phil 320," 1993, Dallas Willard Collection.

8. Dallas Willard, "Ontology of Knowledge: Willard 1," *Ontology of Knowledge* (Biola University, La Mirada, CA, May 27, 1997).

9. Readers of Bavinck might wonder why Willard shows so little interest in *certainty*. Readers of nonfoundationalist theology (e.g., Stanley Grenz or Nancey Murphy) may wonder why Willard seemed *so certain* in his knowledge. For his part, Willard will say, "I don't do certainty." Dallas Willard, "Faith without Knowledge: Why Christians Court Disaster When Belief Is Not Intelligent," *Lecture* (MacLaurin Institute, St. Paul, MN,

In short, Willard advanced his own account of knowledge and faith—an account that does not lean on any well-known or leading *theologian* in contemporary thought. *Knowing Christ* may have been a poor medium for communicating that account to other scholars, but that does not mean that a scholarly understanding of Willard's writings will be possible without an understanding of his more sophisticated theory. Giving some assistance to that task with respect to the phenomenon of *faith* is the burden of this chapter.

Believing Christ Today

FOR REASONS OF space and because of its easy accessibility in his philosophical publications, I must assume that readers are, or at least can be, familiar with Willard's account of *knowledge*.[10] Here is his oft-repeated characterization (not definition) of knowledge: knowledge, according to Willard, is "the capacity to represent a respective subject matter as it is, on an appropriate basis of thought and/or experience."[11]

Willard's account of *faith*, by contrast, is much more obscure. This is regrettable because his view was not, shall we say, current, and yet it was integral to his whole theological system. One of the things that have led to some popular misunderstandings of Willard is that he never made his view of faith sufficiently public. There are a few short paragraphs in

October 23, 2008), MP3, 1:23:30. His sound-bite phenomenology of certainty is that "You can be certain and wrong and uncertain and right," often adding, "We all have experience with that." Dallas Willard, "Knowing Christ Today," *Open Word* (Bel Air Presbyterian Church, Los Angeles, CA, September 20, 2009), MP3, 44:45.

10. Recently Walter Hopp, one of Willard's PhD students, published *Phenomenology: A Contemporary Introduction* (New York: Routledge, 2020), and this book, while not about Willard, is unmistakably inspired by Willard. For most people, it would serve as a better introduction to the topics of consciousness, mental acts, and knowledge than any of Willard's writings.

11. Dallas Willard, "Knowledge and Naturalism," in *Naturalism: A Critical Analysis*, ed. William Lane Craig and J. P. Moreland (New York: Routledge, 2000), 31. This statement is fleshed out in many prominent places throughout Willard's oeuvre. See Willard, *Knowing*, chap. 1; and Willard, *Logic*, chap. 5. See also Dallas Willard, "How Naturalism Makes Knowledge of Knowledge Impossible and Thereby Destroys the Possibility of a Rational Moral Existence for Humanity" (paper presented at California Phenomenology Circle, San Luis Obispo, CA, April 4, 2008). See also Willard, "Handout for 'Justification.'"

his books that one can refer to but no cohesive argument of any length that one can expound and analyze. If we are to tackle questions of the gospel and salvation, this obscurity must be eradicated.

The most illuminating way, I submit, to pull together the different stands of Willard's account of faith is to see what he takes and leaves from the authors he read and interacted with on the topic. In later chapters—to Willard's doctrines of salvation, of Christ, and of the gospel—the details in this chapter will become increasingly relevant.

To make for a smoother ride through these comparisons, I propose to neatly, though artificially, divide the various authors into (1) those who primarily characterize faith according to its object or content—that is, what one has faith in, and (2) those who primarily characterize faith according to its function—that is, what a person with faith does or is. Among those important for Willard who order faith according to its content are John Calvin, John Wesley, John Baillie, A. W. Tozer, and looming behind them, Francis of Assisi and the early Franciscans. Among those who order faith according to its function, Willard found valuable insights in Edmund Husserl, William James, Charles Finney, and Martin Luther. Looking ahead to later chapters on salvation, the functional side of faith will be important for understanding salvation on the second stage (chapter 9), and the object-determined side of faith will be important for understanding salvation on the third stage (chapter 12).

Depending on the point Willard is trying to make with his audience, these two modes of characterization inform two often distinct presentations of faith in Willard's corpus. A content-based characterization informs the compact but revealing lecture "The Role of Faith in Prayer" as well as *Conspiracy*'s third chapter, "What Jesus Knew."[12] A functional characterization informs the discussion of faith in "Trust in God: Key to Life" (1989) and finds its way into Willard's book

12. This chapter contains remnants of Willard's original idea for the whole book as a discussion of Jesus's beliefs, the faith of Christ—for example, "Most hindrances to *the faith of Christ* actually lie, I believe, in this part of our minds and souls" (Willard, *Conspiracy*, 62; emphasis mine) and ". . . the faith and life [Jesus] came to bring" (66).

Knowing Christ, especially chapter 1, where he distinguishes faith from knowledge.[13]

One place where his ontology of faith comes closest to being put together in its entirety is a 1994 lecture, "The Human Disaster of Unbelief."[14] In this very important discourse, Willard strings together exegeses of many familiar biblical texts concerning faith and thus addresses both functional and content-based characterizations of faith. More typically, Willard's lectures and writings tend to emphasize one aspect or another, depending on the occasion. Though these named lectures and chapters can serve as anchors for his view, the roots of both perspectives actually extend far back in Willard's life. In all likelihood, Willard had been tweaking his account of faith since graduate school.

Faith as an Inescapable Function in Human Life

LET US LOOK, to begin with, at Willard's view of faith in terms of its function and then compare it to his more familiar view of knowledge. After this, we will consider faith in terms of its content.

William James: Commitment

WILLIAM JAMES WAS a prominent late nineteenth-century philosopher known for his work on pragmatism, and Willard required that both his theology and philosophy students read portions of James's work. In one lecture, Willard explains that "the essence of James's view here is that you do not have ideas that do not have impulses associated with them. . . . This is the basis of American pragmatism: it's the interpretation of ideas. It doesn't imply pragmatism, but it is one of the things that it is based upon."[15]

---

13. The presence of two perspectives does not represent, so I hold, a development in his concept of faith, though it cannot be doubted that Willard constantly tweaked his view.

14. Willard, "Human Disaster of Unbelief." Because this lecture was being video produced for distribution, it was given and recorded twice with minor differences in content.

15. Dallas Willard, "The Place of 'Disciplines' in Christian Discipleship and Spiritual Formation 2," *Spiritual Formation and Soul Care* (Denver Seminary, Monument, CO, January 7, 2010), DVD, 59:00.

Regarding James's view of faith, his famous essay "The Will to Believe" is relevant and a piece Willard required students to read.[16] In his own book on faith, John Hick describes James as a "modern voluntarist view."[17] It is true that James locates the disposition of faith primarily in the will, as Hick describes, but this should not suggest, as James's deferral to Pascal in the essay itself shows, that the intellect for James is uninvolved in instances of faith. Faith is more than an act of the will.

Generally, Willard took James and other philosophical pragmatists like him to be allies in two basic insights about human life. First, he agreed with James that action is an inescapable part of human life. We are the kind of beings who must act.[18] Second, he agreed with James that certainty or complete knowledge about the "rightness" of our action cannot be had in every instance where action is required. In light of these two insights, James argues for a disposition he calls "faith" and for our basic right to have it. Specifically, faith for James is a person's intent to act upon a hypothesis, whether stated or not. It applies to a person's intentions and dispositions to act in light of a thought that cannot be embraced with complete knowledge *or* with any knowledge at all. Here too, as on the two basic insights, one finds a correlation with Willard.[19]

---

16. William James, "The Will to Believe," in *The Will to Believe, and Other Essays in Popular Philosophy* (New York: Longmans, Green, 1897), 1–31. See, e.g., Dallas Willard, "Truth," *Feeding the Homeless Mind* (UCLA, Los Angeles, CA, February 21, 1992), MP3/cassette, 14:45.

17. John Hick, *Faith and Knowledge* (Basingstoke, UK: Macmillan, 1988), 33–44. See Willard, *Knowing*, 216n1.

18. Willard, "Bible, the University," 17.

19. On the final page of *Logic*, Willard sums up his criticism of Husserl (and many other great philosophers) by faulting his quest for and the pretensions of "*systematic* certainty, or certainty and rigor *throughout* the range of topics traditionally dealt with by philosophers" (Willard, *Logic*, 270). In lieu of this certainty applied across the board, some (many) topics *must* be handled on another basis. The book's parting word is that "*Wisdom*, which must in the nature of the case face up to life as a whole, has never been *knowledge*, nor will it ever be; and neither is diminished by that fact" (270). In life, phronesis must be called in to do duty because, though systematic certainty is without warrant, humans must "face up to life *as a whole*" (270; emphasis mine). A comprehensive philosophy (or theology) with equal amounts of certainty across the corpus is not an option.

These agreements can be seen most clearly in the introductory paragraph of Willard's article "The Bible, the University and the God Who Hides."[20] Willard claims, first, that action and willing are not options for a human being and, second, that mental content, in whatever form it is found in the mind, will guide a human being's intentions. Not only must we act, but we must act according to what fills our mind, which includes our feelings and emotions.[21]

However, James's defense of faith is not merely for the right to have an intention or a disposition to act in light of what cannot be known. It is for the right to have *voluntarily adopted* intentions to act. This is the so-called voluntarist element of James's account and the place at which the similarity with Willard's view ends. Though Willard does acknowledge our basic right to hold voluntarily adopted intentions to act, he includes these not under the genus of *faith* but under the genus of *commitment*.[22]

For James, "the right" to believe concerns the moral legitimacy of using one's will to select in one's mind the concepts and propositions on which one acts. This act of voluntarily prioritizing certain content in one's mind for action is what he calls "faith." But as Willard conceives it, this act has little to do with faith. On Willard's view, the will is important. Faith is not merely an act of mind, of a person's thinking and feeling. Faith's function essentially involves a person's will. Because of this, what a person wills may indicate where that person's faith lies. But not exclusively. On Willard's account, faith is not the only disposition indicated by a person's acts of will. *Mere* commitment is also expressed in what the person wills. It is this distinction between faith and commitment that James's analysis of human experience misses.

For Willard, commitment is a willing of something and a perseverance in that willing that *can* be detached from both knowledge and faith. Of course, one can (but must not) be committed to what one

---

20. Willard, "Bible, the University," 17.
21. The latter point is basic to Willard's theological anthropology and an entailment of the evangelized psychology to be spoken of in chapter 8.
22. Willard, *Knowing*, 16–17.

knows and believes. But it is psychologically possible, so Willard, to "commit yourself to something you don't even believe."[23] Willard goes on to defend "the right," the moral legitimacy of such a disposition in certain occasions, writing, "Sometimes we have to act . . . when we have no belief concerning what would be best."[24] James mislabels these commitments, even if they lack knowledge or belief, "faith" and then celebrates one's use of one's will to supply one's mental content. This celebration extends to one's willful commitments to what one does not even assert to be true, at least not yet. This turns into James's famous plug for "truths dependent on our personal action."[25]

This pragmatic voluntarism is far from Willard's intent. As we saw, Willard holds that "no one has ever yet made a belief true by believing it."[26] Positively put, Willard says belief is "a matter of tendencies to act." It is "a readiness to act, in appropriate circumstances, *as if* what is believed were so."[27] James's analysis omits the final phrase involving the assertion of truth or alters it to read, "As if what is believed *could be* so." For James, the assertion of truth in faith is optional.

Edmund Husserl: The Matter of Faith

THERE IS NO doubt that Willard had a working concept of faith before 1960. But it is only after 1960 that he encounters the work of Edmund Husserl and learns from him a new philosophy of mind (intentionality) and the so-called phenomenological way of thinking. What's more, Husserl helps Willard find a viable ontology of knowledge. Willard's phrase "the objectivity of knowledge" in the title of his major book on Husserl expresses his and Husserl's claim that knowledge is not a nebulous sort of thing. According to them, knowledge is an ontologically determinate

23. Willard, 16.
24. Willard, 16.
25. James, "Will to Believe," 25.
26. Dallas Willard, "Truth: Can We Do without It?," *Christian Ethics Today* 5, no. 2 (1999): 12.
27. Willard, *Knowing*, 16.

whole that can be analyzed and represented in thought and experience.[28] One task of philosophy is to give humanity an adequate account of "the constituents (parts, their properties and interrelations and relations to other things) of knowledge as an act and as a disposition."[29] Or in other words, an ontology of knowledge. The phenomenological way of thinking learned from Husserl shows how an adequate ontology of knowledge must make use of careful reflection upon experience.

In his account of faith, Willard is saying many of the same things as he and Husserl say about knowledge. Faith is not a foggy thing. It is an ontologically determinate whole that can be analyzed and represented in thought and experience. What's more, it is not particularly religious or spiritual. Faith, whether it concerns "religious" objects or not, has in all of its instances the same structure. Willard does not draw these points directly from Husserl, but Willard does subject faith to the same sort of careful reflection in experience to which Husserl subjects knowledge. Such reflection need not proceed under the banner of phenomenology or be explicitly attached to the legacy of Husserl. Without the language and the fastidiousness, all of the figures we will look at in this chapter derive much of their accounts of faith from careful reflection on experience. That is another way of saying that Husserl did not *invent* the type of inquiry he called phenomenology.[30]

According to Husserl, faith or believing is *a mental act*, a class containing other acts such as surmising, wishing, asserting, presenting, and doubting. Faith, in all of its instances, has the same functional structure.

---

28. Dallas Willard, "Ontology of Knowledge: Willard 2," *Ontology of Knowledge* (Biola University, La Mirada, CA, May 28, 1997), MP3/cassette, 17:00.

29. Willard, "Ontology of Knowledge: Willard 1," 18:30.

30. It will be noted that Husserl, especially in his Fifth Investigation, makes many references to qualities of mind called *Glaube* and *Unglaube*, or "belief" and "unbelief," respectively. But here is a place where the terminology is misleading. What Husserl has in mind is what would less misleadingly be called *assent.* Husserl means an act in which the truth of a presentation is accepted or posited. Husserl in no way is trying to defend a religious epistemology or a biblically informed theology of faith. He introduces *Glaube* mainly to differentiate such a mental act from an act of mere comprehension (mere presentation) without assent or dissent. For example, one can comprehend and hold the presentation *God is good* without (yet) assenting to or dissenting from it.

Apart from the insignificance differences of time, place, and the believing subject, instances of faith can differ from one another in two ways:

1. They can be performed with respect to two different external objects—for example, a chair versus a child.
2. They—that is, two differing instances of faith—can be performed with respect to the same external object (the very same chair) but in respectively different manners.

Husserl describes how a mental act, such as faith, is composed of (i.e., has as its *content*) two things: quality and matter. The *quality* of the act is what makes the mental act one of wishing versus one of judging, an act of presenting versus an act of doubting. In the case of faith or believing, the act's quality is believing.[31]

The *matter* of an act is the directedness of the act, its aboutness. The *matter* of a mental act is not the same as the external object *at which* the act is directed—for example, a chair. For instance, I have a believing

---

31. Another way Willard describes quality is by using Bertrand Russell's term "propositional attitude." However, Willard finds this term misleading because it suggests the object of the attitude is *the proposition itself* and not the same transcendent object of the proposition. In this, Willard is simply following Husserl in his Fifth Investigation. Willard writes,

> Propositions are not beliefs, though they combine with belief and the other propositional attitudes in the experiences of human beings. However, beliefs, etc. do not, on Husserl's view, have propositions as their *objects*. The objects of beliefs are precisely the same as what the propositions are about or of. The relationship between a propositions and a belief whenever they are concretely combined in an *act* of thought is co-instantiation. A proposition is a *quality* of the same act as is the belief. During one main segment of Husserl's career (especially in the Vth "Investigation") the proposition is called the "matter" of the act and the attitude is its "quality." But both are qualities in the usual sense: qualities of acts of thoughts. Propositions become objects of mental acts only in special acts of reflection (such as ordinary logical thinking) or in cases where one is, precisely, thinking about propositions—as one does in pure logical theory. (Dallas Willard, "A Realist Analysis of the Relationship between Logic and Experience," *Topoi: An International Review of Philosophy* 22, no. 1 [2003]: 74)

thought about a chair. My thought has a chair-aboutness. Moments later, I have a believing thought about my commanding officer. That later thought has an officer-aboutness. This aboutness or directedness is the act's matter. This is where intentionality as a philosophy of mind comes in. All thoughts or mental acts have a directedness; they are all about something.[32]

Importantly now, Husserl and Willard analyze the matter of a mental act further. Not only are mental acts about something; they are also about something *in some specific respect*. Thus, the matter is not only the act's directedness at this object (the chair) rather than that one (the officer). It is also the act's directedness at this object *as something*—the chair *as* wooden, *as* the officer's, *as* furniture. This directedness-at-something-*as* is part of an act's intentionality—that is, a part of the "properties, relations and categorical forms" under which the object is apprehended.[33]

This distinction is a fine point but a crucial one to understand before we enter the later chapters on Willard's Christology and soteriology. To illustrate, I may have faith in a substance *as* a medicine. Petroleum oil was trusted in the early 1800s as a treatment for tuberculosis and was administered by doctors and swallowed by patients in an expression of their mutual faith in petroleum as medicinal. However, I may also have faith in the same substance *as* fuel and correspondingly use it for lighting my lamps and heating my furnaces. In both cases of faith, the same external object, petroleum oil, is what my faith is directed at, and in this respect, the intentional object of the two instances of faith is the same.

For the sake of the argument, let us grant that petroleum oil has both salubrity and fuel value. What distinguishes an act of faith in petroleum that expresses itself in burning it from an act of faith in petroleum that expresses itself in swallowing it is the difference in what the

32. The term and many initial analyses stem from Franz Brentano, one of Husserl's teachers. There are many facets to the philosophy of intentionality, as can be seen in the differences between Brentano and Husserl.

33. Edmund Husserl, *Logical Investigations*, vol. 2, trans. J. N. Findlay (New York: Routledge, 2001), 121. Willard deals with this aspect of Husserl's thought in *Logic*, 218–25.

petroleum is grasped *as*. Though both acts have a petroleum-aboutness, the one is faith in the substance *as medicine* and the other is faith in the substance *as fuel*. The manner of directedness has changed. The result is that we have not only different mental acts regarding the same object; we also have respectively different effects in life. How an object is intended by the mind—that is, how the mind is directed at the object—is a crucial aspect of every act of faith. And the same could be said of other mental acts such as asserting, wishing, and presenting.[34]

To repeat, the matter is not the object itself (which may not exist) but a *property* of the mental act. Without this property, there would be no act of faith. Furthermore, the matter of faith is not merely the mind's directedness at the object the believer is trusting. The matter also includes what the believer is believing the object as. The matter is the quo of the mind's pointing—its direction, Husserl would say.

Charles Finney: Conviction

BETWEEN THESE TWO modern philosophical accounts, one heavily focused on the mind or consciousness and the other on the will, we can plot the "hybrid" account of a slightly older mental philosopher: Charles Finney.[35] Finney's early and mature thought developed at a time when

---

34. To clarify what is meant in Husserl and Willard's language by the act's *matter*, we could change the example and speak of a person who is trusted in one act of faith *as* a loving father and in another act of faith *as* a competent car mechanic. The external object (the one person) is both father and mechanic, but the acts of faith, though directed toward the same person, differ in respect to the properties in the person they aim at. In order to clarify what is meant by the act's *quality*, we change the act quality and consider *wishing* petroleum were a cure for tuberculosis as opposed to *believing* it is a cure. Likewise, we consider *positing* it as medicine in contrast to wishing or believing it. Despite these differences in quality, the matter of the acts is identical.

35. Apart from the thoughts and the will, some psychologists and theologians locate belief in the mind as a *feeling*. In *Renovation*'s chapter on feelings, Willard discusses faith as a disposition that results in positive *feelings* (117–39, esp. 129–30). In contrast to Willard, most mean by this description that faith is a feeling of *certainty* or *assurance* about some judgment. For his part, Willard commonly dismissed the importance of the feeling of certainty in life because it has no essential tie to truth, being right or wrong. Truth, not a feeling of certainty or sincerity, is what we are really after in our believing because truth alone integrates its holder with reality. Many certain and sincere people have had unpleasant encounters with reality (see Dallas Willard, "Post-modern

mental philosophy (essentially what Husserl and James also became representatives of) was considered an essential part of Christian *theology*. His systematic theology lectures from his professorship at Oberlin are riddled with claims and arguments concerning the constitution of the human person with respect to the action of God and his ministers.

Willard, as a young man, we know, was quite familiar with Finney's theology and philosophy of ministry through personal study of his sermons, his autobiography, his letters and lectures on revival, and finally, his volumes of lectures on systematic theology.[36] Importantly, Finney's view of "evangelical faith" (there are other kinds of faith for Finney) exercised a direct influence on Willard's view. This can be seen concretely in two lectures from Finney's *Lectures on Systematic Theology*.

Holiness: What Does It Look Like?," *Malcolm R. Robertson Lectureship*, MP3, 1:07:00). See also Charles Finney, *Lectures on Systematic Theology* (London: Tegg, 1851), lecture xviii, for a discussion of faith that differentiates true faith from acts of the intellect and from feeling.

36. Charles Finney's autobiography, *The Memoirs of Charles G. Finney: The Complete Restored Text* (Grand Rapids, MI: Zondervan, 1989), was listed as one of the five books personally meaningful to Willard ("My Personal Top 5," 155). What's more, Willard's first listed book, James Gilchrist Lawson, *Deeper Experiences of Famous Christians* (Anderson, IN: Warner, 1911), includes very high praise for Finney. Reading Lawson's book in 1954, nineteen-year-old Dallas Willard encountered statements from this Englishman such as, "The writer is inclined to regard Charles G. Finney as the greatest evangelist and theologian since the days of the apostles." Lawson calls Finney's autobiography "the most remarkable account of the manifestations of the Holy Spirit's power since apostolic days." Finally, Lawson judges that "Finney's 'Systematic Theology' is probably the greatest work on theology outside the Scriptures" (Lawson, *Deeper Experiences*, 243–44).

In Gary Moon's interviews with Willard, he asked him, "Which authors have influenced your thinking most?" to which Willard responded, "Well, I would have to put close to the head of the list, Charles Finney. For many, many years I just soaked myself in his writing, and his theology, I think this one of the greatest works [*sic*]. Almost no one even knows it now." Willard reports that this "soaking" began in 1956 (Moon, email correspondence with the author concerning Charles Finney, June 22, 2014). Stanley Mattson, one of Willard's close friends at Wisconsin (1962–65), wrote his MA thesis on Finney and remembers constructive conversations with Willard about Finney (Stanley Mattson, interview by the author, November 25, 2015, interview 1, telephone). In 1989, Willard required that participants in the first instantiation of the course he taught at Fuller Seminary read Charles Finney's *Lectures on Revivals of Religion* (1835; repr., Cambridge, MA: Harvard University Press, 1960). Let it be noted that religion, for Finney, is basically obedience to Christ.

In one of his lectures on the nature of love, Finney writes, "Evangelical faith is by no means, as some have supposed, a phenomenon of the intelligence. . . . Conviction, or a strong perception of truth, such as banishes doubt, is, in common language called faith or belief, and this without any reference to the state of the will, whether it embraces or resists the truth perceived. But, certainly, this conviction cannot be evangelical faith. In this belief, there is no virtue; it is essentially but the faith of the devils."[37] By ordering evangelical faith under love as he does here, Finney is saying that evangelical faith is defined not only by its function but also in part by its content, which, for Finney, is "the truth." This definition leads him, as we will see, to exclude from his general class of faith cases of persons believing falsely about something—for example, believing falsely in petroleum oil as salubrious.

But he also makes an important distinction that has a direct parallel to Willard's own view. For Finney, the disposition of faith includes both a "state of the will" *and* another psychological act—namely, "perception of truth." It is commonly assumed that a person who posits something (i.e., assents to its reality) or even intuits something (i.e., sees its reality) *automatically* has belief in that something with a willingness to act correspondingly (even if, for some other reason, they do not act correspondingly). This unity, or at least natural connection, between positing/intuiting and believing is denied by both Finney and Willard. Devils are paradigmatic for sentient beings who have a perception of truth but lack belief and willingness to act. In other words, unbelief for Finney and Willard is something akin to the root sin.

With this in mind, observe how Willard describes these two components of faith in a 1989 lecture "Trust in God":

> *You can't escape faith. You cannot live without faith*
> *because you have a future, and the only way you can deal*
> *with that future is in faith of some kind. You cannot deal with*
> *it in any other way.* In the attitude of faith there are two

37. Finney, *Systematic Theology*, lecture 18, 193.

> main parts. One is vision. The other is desire . . . desire or will. *There is a choice in faith. . . .*
>
> *Some of you are familiar with talk of "being under conviction." That was a bit of language that used to be used much more and was perhaps more common in other times. People were said to "be under conviction." The first part of the word* conviction *is* convict. *They were in the grip of something, but they were resisting, you see. Now, what characterizes a person who is under conviction is they have the vision but not the desire or the will. They are willing something other than what they see. They are in denial of their vision.*[38]

There is much here that is revealing of Willard's view. There is, first, the psychological state of *being under conviction*, which, when set in contrast to faith, gives us insight into the latter. To best understand conviction, one must have in mind Finney's paradigmatic case: an evangelist presenting the true gospel to his audience in a way that some in the audience *see it.* Until the listeners join their will to what they see or they decide to refuse it, these "seers" are said to be in the state of conviction, a hiatus between the arrival at a new level of understanding and the imminent disposition of faith. Among *some* of those seers, however, another psychological state inevitably sets in. Finney calls this "unbelief," and Willard calls it "denial."

Reflecting on denial in *Renovation*, Willard comments on the anguish of conviction, writing, "The will or spirit cannot—psychologically cannot—sustain itself for any length of time in the face of what it clearly acknowledges to be the case."[39] This inability leads a will that wishes to continue in opposition to the truth to a place where "it must deny and evade and delude itself."[40]

---

38. Dallas Willard, "Trust in God: Key to Life," *Life without Lack* (Valley Vista Christian Community, Sepulveda, CA, March 5, 1989), MP3/cassette, 21:15 (emphasis mine).
39. The psychological condition of denial is essential to Willard's vision for the ministry of apologetics.
40. Willard, *Renovation*, 52; cf. Dallas Willard, "Who Needs Brentano? The Wasteland of Philosophy without Its Past," in *The Brentano Puzzle*, ed. Roberto Poli (Brookfield,

Likewise, Finney writes, "Since it is naturally impossible that the will should be in a state of indifference to any known error or truth that stands connected with its duty or its destiny, it follows that a rejection of any known truth implies an embracing of an opposing error."[41] Though something has genuinely been grasped as true, it is intentionally put out of the mind because the person does not want to will it and, psychologically, cannot long endure the strain of being under conviction. Hence, another notion must rise up to take the vision's place.

Willard himself writes this potential hiatus of conviction into his "general pattern of personal transformation," which memorably distinguishes between the step of "Vision" and the step of "Intention," which is followed by "Means" (altogether, VIM). This creative language, meant to fit an acronym, should be expounded by Willard's accounts of epistemic and psychological progression elsewhere. That "Vision" stands for knowledge, for perception or intuition or logical conclusions, should be fairly obvious. Close attention to the prose of Willard's section on "Intention" in *Renovation* reveals its connection with his concept of faith. Willard writes, "Knowing the 'right answers'—knowing which ones they are, being able to identify them—does not mean that we *believe* them. To believe them, like believing anything else, means that we are set to act as if they (the right answers) are true and that we will do so in appropriate circumstances."[42] The concept of intention can stand in for the concept of faith because "the form that *trust* in [Jesus] takes" is "intending to obey the precise example and teachings of Jesus." It is "a mental impossibility," Willard says, to "actually believe the truth about him without trusting him by intending to obey him."[43]

MA: Ashgate, 1998). Cf. also Dallas Willard, "Knowledge and Biblical Faith," *Knowledge for Life* (Anaheim Vineyard, Anaheim, CA, April 17, 2010), MP3, 1:01:00.

41. Finney, *Systematic Theology*, lecture 54, 541.

42. Willard, *Renovation*, 88.

43. Willard, 87. Randall D. Engle, in his review of *Conspiracy*, insightfully points out that Willard's argument in chapter 8 would have been better served if, concerning discipleship, Willard had spoken of intent rather than decision (Randall D. Engle, "The Divine Conspiracy," *Calvin Theological Journal* 36, no. 1 [2001]: 219). But his choice of decision rather than intent is likely rhetorical. Willard would sometimes explain in lectures that some "saints," such as Robert Murray M'Cheyne, look back and cannot see

Looking again at Finney's description of evangelical faith, we can now point to a possible difference between Willard and Finney regarding *the source* of faith. Willard maintains that "evangelical faith" comes by the word of God. Though faith's function in human life remains the same, a subclass of faith—"evangelical faith," as Finney calls it—is generated by the impact of the gospel of God's kingdom on the human person. Thus in *Renovation*, faith is listed in the chapter on feelings as one of many "*conditions* of the whole person that are accompanied by characteristic positive feelings." In a statement that incorporates the material and functional modes of characterization of faith, Willard writes, "Faith sees the reality of the unseen or invisible, and it includes a readiness to act as if the good anticipated in hope were already in hand because of the reality of God."[44] This characterization of evangelical faith is furthered in his paper on the theological virtues, "Faith, Hope and Love," where Willard presents faith (with, admittedly, some lack of clarity) as an attitude or "presence" that is presupposed and included in love. With this, he means to say that it is more than an *attained* character trait or *virtue* such as courage or honesty. Love, including faith and hope, "is *communicated* to us through a course of experience which we have a part in but cannot reduce to a formula."[45]

Faith in this paper comes closer to being the supernatural reality to which Willard believes Hebrews 11:1 points: faith as "*substance* and *evidence*."[46] Because of its superhuman ontology, Willard regularly warns, as we may recall, against *trying* to have faith. It is with the superhuman substantiality of faith in mind that he writes in *Disciplines*, "The faith of the New Testament is a distinctive life force that originates in the impact of God's word upon the soul, as we see in Romans 10:17, and then

a decision to follow Jesus, but the presence of their intent is obvious (Dallas Willard, "Q & A," *Manifesting the Kingdom*, MP3/cassette, 37:30).

44. Willard, *Renovation*, 129.

45. Willard, "Faith, Hope and Love," section 6.

46. See Dallas Willard, "The Role of Faith in Prayer"; and also "Session 3" (*Doing What Jesus Did Conference* [Vineyard Columbus, Columbus, OH, November 16, 2002], MP3, 20:15), where he explains why faith is described as the substance of things hoped for, the evidence of things unseen: "If you have faith, it is because things unseen have produced faith in you."

exercises a determinating influence upon all aspects of our existence."[47] All told, there is an inescapable passivity for Willard to beginning and growing in faith.[48]

Finney's account of faith as an attribute of love is similar to Willard's in that the possession of love is essential to having morally commendable faith. But Finney's account is far less explicit on the *gifted nature* of such commendable conditions as love and faith—that is, on their *source* in God. This aspect is, if there at all, well hidden in Finney's theology and tucked into his concept of *influence*. Aside from truth, *influence* is Finney's most comprehensive word for what the theological tradition calls the grace that comes upon the person in their conversion.[49] Though Finney is intensely opposed to any doctrine of natural inability (an intensity that dominates the scope and proportion of his systematic theology), he is open to some notion of *gracious* ability in conversion.[50] If it is plausible that Finney's concept of influence entails the gracious communication of the superhuman reality of faith, hope, and love, then there is a deep resonance between Finney and Willard. The only difference, then, is that Willard, by ordering commendable faith under love and by viewing love as a "substance" that comes to the human agent enabling him or her to have faith, more clearly *explains* how faith is a gift.[51]

---

47. Willard, *Disciplines*, 41.

48. Willard writes, "Thus we have the biblical representation of repentance, as well as of forgiveness, as something *given* to us by God" (Willard, 40). Cf. also John Wesley's sermon 17, "Circumcision of the Heart" (in *The Works of John Wesley: 1–33. Sermons I*, ed. Albert C. Outler [Nashville: Abingdon, 1959]).

49. Wesley is the clearest case of a thinker in the tradition of those who investigate conversion who had a direct influence on Willard.

50. Finney, *Systematic Theology*, lecture 51.

51. Willard, "Faith, Hope and Love," section 7, makes this clear. For Finney's part, it is unclear that he has tucked *that much* into his concept of influence. He clearly describes the ideals of love (disinterested benevolence) and ascribes it descriptively to God and prescriptively to humans. But love and faith on the human side appear to be creaturely generated responses evoked with respect to the evangelical vision of divine love. Their source appears to be in God's creational endowments upon his creatures—in natural ability, in the language of New Divinity theologians—and out of these resources *alone*, humans rise up to meet evangelical truth for an exchange. This makes Finney's view of faith, indeed, more akin to the classical virtues, which, as Willard notes in communion

Charles Finney: Faith's Virtue

MOVING ON, ANOTHER lecture in Finney's *Systematic Theology*, "Faith and Unbelief," is especially illuminating when compared to Willard's view of the function of faith. In 1975, Willard copied two quotes from this lecture for a Sunday school handout distributed at a local Lutheran church.[52] Along with these from Finney, he attached a string of quotes on faith from Luther's "Preface to Romans," obviously inviting positive comparison between the two theologians.

From Finney's lecture, Willard extracts the following:

> *Since the Bible uniformly represents saving or evangelical faith as a virtue, we know that it must be a phenomenon of will. It is an efficient state of mind, and therefore it must consist in the embracing of the truth by the heart or will. It is the will's closing in with the truths of the gospel. It is the soul's act of yielding itself up, or committing itself to the truths of the evangelical system. It is a trusting in Christ, a committing the soul and the whole being to him, in his various offices and relations to men. It is a confiding in him, and in what is revealed of him, in his word and providence, and by his Spirit.*[53]

Generally, what Finney is trying to explain in this lecture is why the Bible praises faith morally, while it morally condemns unbelief. This

---

with Aristotle, are attainments or acquisitions. Finney would retort that this view is the only option in a theology in which God *justly* prescribes love to his creatures. Before one accuses Finney of Pelagianism, one should study his long series of lectures on sanctification, which are quite far from Aristotelian virtue ethics or any classical Greek ethical thinking. In these, Finney is further away from Pelagius than Augustine himself!

52. Dallas Willard, "Handout for 'Studies in the Gospel of Jesus Christ,'" lesson 5.

53. Finney, *Systematic Theology*, lecture 54, 533. We must note here a minor parting of ways between Finney and Willard. Finney holds that the Bible speaks of faith "in an evangelical sense" but also in another sense. He brackets virtuous, evangelical faith off from another biblical presentation of faith that he calls intellectual faith, "an undoubting persuasion, a firm conviction, an unhesitating intellectual ascent" (lecture 54, 532).

can only be so, he reasons, if faith is "a virtue," by which he innocently means a morally praiseworthy condition. And since the condition is *morally* praiseworthy, faith must be a property or function of the will.[54] A purely intellectual state could be praiseworthy but not *morally* praiseworthy. So faith, Finney reasons, is morally praiseworthy because it is a willful, ready embrace of God's truth that one has perceived. First and foremost, it is a willful, ready embrace of the truth of God's gospel.[55]

Though Finney begins with the case of "evangelical faith"—that is, faith in the gospel—he ends his analysis by saying, "Faith implies the reception and the practice of *all* known or perceived truth." Because Finney believed (as did all his peers in American higher education) that "all truth is harmonious," he is able to conclude that "the heart that truly embraces one [truth], will, for the same reason embrace *all* truth known."[56]

What Finney has in mind is a character trait, inextricably linked to the fundamental act of faith in conversion, which can be characterized as a moral disposition to never deny perceived or reasoned facts.[57] Willard, for his part, has some appreciation for such a character trait.[58] In

---

54. Finney's sense of the virtue and the virtuousness of faith has little in common with the Aristotelian sense of virtues as developed abilities. By *virtuous*, he primarily means "morally commendable" and has in mind something that can be immediately possessed.
55. Because of its external object (the gospel), the morally praiseworthiness of evangelical faith would *not* be applicable to all people (see Dallas Willard, "How Reason Can Survive the Modern University: The Moral Foundations of Rationality," in *Faith, Scholarship, and Culture in the 21st Century*, ed. Alice Ramos and Marie I. George [Washington, DC: Catholic University of America Press, 2002], 181–91). Growth in faith among those who have it would be an increasing readiness to embrace *gospel* truth or the Word of God with one's will when one encounters it.
56. Finney, *Systematic Theology*, lecture 54, 537 (emphasis mine).
57. Ten years earlier, Finney gives a slightly different view of faith in a letter on regeneration ("Prof. Finney's Letters No. 38," *Oberlin Evangelist* 3, no. 20 [1841], 156–57). Though it is an exercise of faith when the mind is "yielded up to the influence of mathematical, philosophical, or historical truth," evangelical faith "is not a conviction that the Bible is the word of God . . . nor is it a perception of its meaning, with the assurance that it is true." Faith has a generic sense and an evangelical species. Evangelical faith "is the yielding up of the whole being to be influenced by His testimony concerning His Son and by His Son" (157). This letter does show that Finney's doctrine of regeneration, at least at that point in Finney's life, was different from Willard's.
58. See Willard, "Knowledge and Biblical Faith," 44:00, where Willard says, e.g., "If you have knowledge, faith becomes a virtue."

his 2000 talk "Can Reason Survive the Modern University?," he argues that standing up for rationality is not enough unless one is prepared to stand up for our *moral duty* to be rational.[59] There is something similar going on in Finney. But while Finney thinks of the moral disposition to never deny truth as inextricably linked to saving faith in the gospel, Willard suggests that it might also be a virtue of those who have not (yet) embraced "the evangelical system."

Despite this commonality in faith's operation in regard to the truth, Willard's concept of faith embraces a wider psychological phenomenon, something neither morally good nor evil. It embraces a condition of human existence in general. Human wills must be joined to *some* intellectual content. As he said in 1989, all people "have a future" and must utilize faith (a combination of thought and will) to negotiate it. This fact of human existence may constrain persons to put their faith in a false gospel or other false thoughts, but one way or another, they will be believers.[60]

One must observe here that Willard's mental philosophy is simply richer than Finney's and that Willard has made good use of additional insights from Husserl, James, Augustine, and others.[61] But viewed from afar, much of the difference between the two accounts may simply be a matter of labeling. What Finney, following the Bible, condemns as unbelief, Willard is more likely to keep within the broad genus of faith and sublabel "denial." Because we are beings with, as I will discuss in chapter 8, *an evangelized psychology*, the person who rejects reality

---

59. Willard, "How Reason Can Survive," 187.

60. Finney has some appreciation for this general application of faith as well. Cf. Finney, *Systematic Theology*, lecture 54, 534. As an evangelist and college professor, Finney was a constant student of his audiences' and opponents' subtleties of thought that kept them from accepting the gospel and other Christian teachings in faith.

61. Finney, given his exegetical orientation and a number of his doctrinal commitments, has a peculiar way of combining the functional elements of faith with the material elements. Finney's faith is morally praiseworthy in light of *what* the person willfully believes in—that is, the truth and especially the gospel itself. He would see no virtuousness in a proclivity to believe mirages, mistakes, and lies. Hence, the real virtue he has in mind is something more like submission or obedience (what he calls "the soul's act of yielding itself up") to truth, goodness, and beauty. Unbelief, however, is vicious (morally reprehensible) because it is the refusal to submit to the presented reality.

when they see it will not be "let off the hook" from being a believer in something else.

Later in the lecture "Faith and Unbelief," Finney returns to the most important commonality with Willard: the essential joining between the will and the mind in faith. Faith, as Finney writes, "implies an intellectual perception of the things, facts, and truths believed. No one can believe that which he does not understand. It is impossible to believe that which is not so revealed to the mind, that the mind understands it. It has been erroneously assumed, that faith did not need light. . . . This is a false assumption."[62] Because he has the paradigmatic case in mind of an evangelist preaching to his congregation, Finney makes a strong case for the *conscious* intellectual basis of faith.

Yet here is another fine point of difference worth exploring. Though Willard affirms the truth claim involved in every belief, he allows for deep or unconscious beliefs. This is most evident in a few sections of *Conspiracy*, beginning with "Changing People's *Real* Beliefs" and including "Study What the People We Speak to *Actually* Believe."[63] Willard's underlying assumption is that the beliefs that are *really* functioning in our lives may be not obvious to us or those who work with us.[64] Our beliefs may not be obvious to those who work with us because we may *profess* to believe—in religion but also in education and family life—what we do not really believe.[65] But even in situations where we intend to be completely honest, we will still act in a certain way, and the intellectual

62. Finney, *Systematic Theology*, lecture 54, 534.

63. Willard, *Conspiracy*, 305–9 (emphasis mine). Willard recommends sections of Finney's *Lectures on Revivals* in *Conspiracy*'s subsection "Study What the People We Speak to *Actually* Believe" (308–9). Willard credits Finney as having a "profound theoretical and practical understanding of how belief governs action and how truth can be brought to bear to change belief" (414–15n12).

64. There is some admission of this in Finney when, after insisting that "intellectual light" is a condition of belief and unbelief, he admits that for unbelief, "it is a very common case, that the unbeliever denies in words and endeavours to refute in theory, that which he nevertheless assumes as true, in all his practical judgments" (Finney, *Systematic Theology*, lecture 54, 542–43).

65. This is due, he claims, to a cultural illusion about faith that stems (in the West, at least) from the post-Reformation era, when profession of belief was connected with personal safety (Willard, *Renovation*, 96–97).

judgments that correspond to our actions may not—especially not in the moment—be conscious. They may not even be immediately retrievable if solicited. Deep reflection (even therapy) may be required to unearth the intended truth claim. But an intended truth claim must be there if the condition is to count as a belief and not as a mere impulse, habit, or other bodily tendency to act.[66]

One of Willard's best examples of unconscious belief comes in the course of explaining his concept of worldview, which he calls in one lecture "your orientation in life whether you know it or not."[67] *Worldview* is his term for our total set of beliefs, the system we are prepared to act on. It is what he in *Conspiracy* is urging ministers to carefully study in their parishioners. He goes on in the lecture to explain that "you don't have to know what answer you're operating on to be operating on it. Because it is built into your body. How many of you, coming here this evening, were worried about dinosaurs? Anyone? See, that's part of your worldview. Your worldview does not include dinosaurs. . . . See, what governs our action without our thinking about it is the most important part of what our belief system consists in."[68] The extinction of dinosaurs is a retrievable part of the modern belief system and, though subconscious most of the time, governs the modern's behavior because of how it is "built into [the modern's] body." Though the judgments governing these actions may be tacit, they are vital for distinguishing beliefs from impulses, bodily tics, instincts, sensations, and senseless habits.

What Willard has in mind with subconscious beliefs built into the body should not be confused with two other genuine psychological states called at times by others "faith." The first is knowledge that

66. In a handout titled "What Is Belief?" used in his philosophy of religion classes, Willard writes, "Sometimes our beliefs emerge into consciousness as a feelable attitude toward what is represented in an accompanying thought. But by no means always! Our bodies have many beliefs, and some beliefs seem to live in our social environment." Dallas Willard, "What Is Belief?," n.d., Dallas Willard Collection, pp. 25–29.

67. Dallas Willard, "How People Perish for Lack of Knowledge," *The Knowledge of Christ in the Contemporary World* (Eidos Christian Center, Newport Beach, CA, June 26, 2003), MP3, 38:15. The way Willard describes worldview is, in a few respects, different from the way he describes ideas.

68. Willard, 38:15.

is resident in the body. Willard agrees very strongly that the body is a repository of knowledge, including knowledge that has never been and will never, before death, be made explicit to the mind.[69] Bodily knowledge is *knowledge* because it is tested and justified in experience. The other, not-to-be-confused psychological state is what he calls *ideas*, which are resident in the mind or body but not always articulated. Ideas are, he says, "patterns of interpretation, historically developed and socially shared."[70] Ideas may or may not be transferred into beliefs, the deciding difference being that people may be under the sway of grand ideas upon which they have no readiness to act (i.e., do not believe). "We always live up to our beliefs—or down to them, as the case may be," Willard writes.[71] The same cannot, thankfully, be said for ideas. Many people are, in their habits and beliefs, much better than their ideas.

Martin Luther: The Natural Entailments of Faith

IN THE BIOGRAPHICAL piece "When God Moves In," Willard mentions how his reading as a young man began to include Luther.[72] The fruit of that reading can be found, I suggest, on that handout for Shepherd of the Valley Lutheran Church, which attempts to bring Luther and Finney into one theological stream. Willard extracts two quotes from Luther's "Preface to Romans" that are too long to provide in full.[73]

The first quote includes the following:

> *But the Spirit is not given, . . . except in, with and through faith in Jesus Christ. So likewise faith cometh not, except only*

---

69. See Dallas Willard, "Spirit and Spirituality: The Gospel of the Kingdom," *Leadership & Spirituality* (Regent College, Vancouver, BC, May 16, 2000), MP3, 1:24:45; cf. Michael Polanyi, *Personal Knowledge: Towards a Post-Critical Philosophy* (Chicago: University of Chicago Press, 1962), esp. 265–68.
70. Willard, *Renovation*, 96–97.
71. Willard, *Conspiracy*, 307.
72. Dallas Willard, "When God Moves In: My Experience with *Deeper Experiences of Famous Christians*," in *Indelible Ink: 22 Prominent Christian Leaders Discuss the Books That Shape Their Faith*, ed. Scott Larson (Colorado Springs: WaterBrook, 2003), 54.
73. For another comment on faith in Luther's "Preface," see also Willard, *Disciplines*, 38–39.

> *through the Word of God, the Gospel, which preaches Christ, teaching that He is the Son of God and Son of Man, slain and risen from the dead for our sakes. . . . Hence it is that faith alone makes righteous (justifies) and fulfills the law, for it brings the Spirit through the merits of Christ. But the Spirit makes the heart free and willing, as the law requires; and then good works proceed of themselves from faith. This . . . [is how] we establish the law through faith; that is we fulfill it through faith (Rom. 3:31).*[74]

What stands out in this quote is the coming of faith by the word of God and especially the gospel, as was discussed in the previous chapter.

As is also evident in the quote, Luther has a phenomenology of faith that includes fulfillment of the law and good works as natural parts ("proceed of themselves from"). This takes place in the soul because, as he makes clear, the Spirit has come with faith, bringing willingness and free love. This analysis sounds a lot like the gratuity that Willard sees in the theological "virtues"—that is, dispositions. Yet the necessity of the Spirit's action in order for good works to proceed from faith does not comport with Willard's notion that faith is a basic human function distinguishable within persons only by *what* is believed in. Luther is quite specific. His is a phenomenology of *faith in Christ*, in the gospel.

The second passage includes the following famous lines:

> *But faith is a divine work in us. . . . O, this faith is a living, busy, active, powerful thing! It is* impossible *that it should not be ceaselessly doing that which is good. It does not even ask whether good works should be done; but before the question can be asked, it has done them, and it is constantly engaged in doing them.*

74. Willard, "Handout for 'Studies in the Gospel of Jesus Christ,'" lesson 5; cf. Martin Luther, *Luthers Vorreden zur Bibel* (Göttingen, Germany: Vandenhoeck & Ruprecht, 1989), 180.

> Faith is a living, well-founded confidence in the grace of God, *so perfectly certain that it would die a thousand times rather than surrender its conviction. . . . It is thus impossible to separate works from faith, just as impossible as to separate burning and shining from fire.*[75]

Here we can see how Luther's analysis does parallel Finney's in a general way. Both have *evangelical* faith in mind, a faith that is "a living, well-founded confidence *in the grace of God.*" Neither has much room in their analysis of human life for faith that is not evangelical, which looks to a false gospel and creates bad works.

And yet, functionally, faith has the two components spoken of by Willard in the 1989 lecture "Trust in God": vision and will. The impossibility of having faith and *not acting* in correspondence with that faith is the point that Willard takes from Luther.[76] Likewise, he could take the impossibility, hardly considered in Luther's pre-Enlightenment days, of having faith and *not seeing* something—that is, not having one's mind directed to anything definite. Evangelical faith is a leap not in the dark but to something the mind has before it quite clearly.

Interlude: Trust and Knowledge

WITH THE PUBLICATION of *Knowing Christ*, Willard brought together his vision for the Christian life as a life of knowledge *and* faith.[77] The

75. Willard, "Handout for 'Studies in the Gospel of Jesus Christ,'" lesson 5; cf. Luther, *Luthers Vorreden zur Bibel*, 183. Notably, these are descriptions of faith from the early Luther. Willard is aware that the late Luther had a different view of faith, since "the late Luther had to decide who is in and who is out because he had to be responsible for the ones who are in" (Willard, "Atonement in the Spiritual Life," 1:09:00).

76. So Willard, "'Works' are simply a natural part of faith. James's statement is about the inherent *nature* of faith, about what makes it up. It concerns what believing something really amounts to" (Willard, *Disciplines*, 38).

77. Willard's four-part seminar on "Justification of Faith by Experience" from 1973 is his first documented attempt to teach systematically on the relationship between faith and knowledge. *Justification* in the title is a play on words, since he was speaking on justification in the epistemological sense—that is, "justified true belief." His 2003 lectures "The Knowledge of Christ in the Contemporary World," which later became his book *Knowing Christ*, are another attempt in the same vein.

subtitle should be noted: "Why We Can Trust Spiritual Knowledge." In this phrase, trust and knowledge are paired such that trust responds in the presence of knowledge. The two are complementary, serving different functions in human life.[78]

Comparing knowledge to Willard's account of belief, let us first note what he sees as a shortcoming of knowledge: "Belief involves the will in a way that knowledge does not."[79] That is to say, knowledge is not a disposition of the will. It does not involve tendencies to act. It does not directly influence action. As Willard writes, "We sometimes do not believe what we know."[80] An example is the already mentioned circumstance of being "under conviction." The convicted person knows where he or she stands in life but is still acting as if the opposite were true.[81]

Western methods of teaching, Willard laments, often instigate this dichotomy by leaving students in a situation where they know the "right answers" in order to put them on their exams but are unprepared to *believe* what they know.[82] In briefly describing this predicament, Willard writes, "The teacher must get the information *into* them. We then 'test' the patients to see if they 'got it' by checking whether they can *reproduce* it in language rather than watching how they live."[83] To the point, analyzing a person's knowledge does not necessarily reveal their will and thus their life and vice versa.

On the other side, belief too has its shortcomings, says Willard. In contrast to knowledge, "belief has no necessary tie to truth, good method, or evidence. We can believe what is false and often do."[84] Faith may, therefore, be present where knowledge is missing. This is not an entirely undesirable situation, because, as Willard admits, "knowledge is not always available to guide action when we need it."[85] Nonex-

78. Willard, *Knowing*, 18.
79. Willard, 16.
80. Willard, 18.
81. See Willard, "Knowing Christ Today," 53:00.
82. Willard, "Truth: Can We Do without It?," 12.
83. Willard, *Conspiracy*, 112–13.
84. Willard, *Knowing*, 16.
85. Willard, 18.

perts and active students are two representative groups of persons who believe—that is, are prepared to act as if certain things are true—but who do not (yet) know. Knowledge brings with it an authority that belief does not bring—a fact that does not diminish belief's vitality to humans. Though belief has a tie to the will, belief "cannot reliably govern life and action except in its proper connection with knowledge and with the truth and evidence knowledge involves."[86] In the illuminating footnote attached to this statement, Willard cites Hume and Kierkegaard as two who "have wildly misconstrued Christian faith to be something opposed to knowledge."[87] On the contrary, the most desirable situation for the human being, says Willard, is one in which knowledge and faith work together *to guide action*. Their responsibility for guiding action means that they have an ideal moral relation: "Rational and responsible people are those who strive to base their beliefs and actions upon their knowledge."[88]

Faith as Knowledge of the Unseen World

AS CONVINCED AS Willard was that faith is a common inescapable human function and not anything particularly religious, he was similarly convinced that faith is a gift of God that one should not *try* to have. How do these convictions connect?

Indeed, even though he spoke of it all as faith, he undoubtedly divided faith into different species. As it turns out, the faith that operates exclusively in unregenerate, or "dead," human life (e.g., faith in the chairs we sit on or the electrical outlets we use) does not require for its existence and increase "the word and grace of God." This faith is "of the flesh," which in Willard's understanding of the Pauline concept is to say that it belongs to our "*natural human abilities*, considered in themselves and on their own, unaided by Divine assistance and direction."[89] As

86. Willard, 3.

87. Willard, 215.

88. Willard, 19 (emphasis mine). For a discussion of the relationship between morality and rationality, see Willard's 2000 lecture "How Reason Can Survive."

89. Dallas Willard, "Spiritual Formation and the Warfare between the Flesh and the Human Spirit," *Journal of Spiritual Formation & Soul Care* 1, no. 1 (2008): 81.

such, this general human faith is not bad but part of God's good creation, and regenerate persons of good sense should make use of it as well. By contrast, the faith that comes by the word of God distinguishes itself from general human faith not only in terms of its emergence, supernatural versus natural, but also in terms of its *content*—that is, in terms of the types of objects at which this faith is directed.

Willard was fond of explaining that "faith is not opposed to knowledge; it is opposed to sight."[90] But as it turns out, there are many real things that are not sense perceptible, are "unseen," some of which even the empiricist or naturalist (perhaps inconsistently) admits to perceiving. Moving up the metaphysical ladder to something like Husserl's realist philosophy, we enter into a world populated by innumerable things that are not sense perceptible (such as universals and minds), and yet we do not require divine intervention to have faith in or to know these.

For Willard, the need for grace for our faith in *certain* unseen realities has to do with the fundamental nature of these realities. In the case of chairs or electricity, the unseen realities are not personal—that is, not spiritual. But personal realities have intentions. A personal reality, as Willard holds, must want to be seen in order to be seen.[91] This freedom to be seen or unseen applies to evil spirits as well as to the Triune God, who in his mercy on a world soaked in sin wants to be hidden. But he also wants, in accordance with the accomplishment of his intentions, to be seen. For this reason, revelation or grace is inescapably antecedent to faith in Trinitarian reality. In this next section, we will focus on the gratuity of this faith but also on the object or objects of this faith and on their peculiar nature.

---

90. Willard, *Guidance*, 209.

91. Dallas Willard, "Recovering the Gospel of Jesus for Our Time," *Jesus' Gospel and Ours* (Whitworth Institute of Ministry, Spokane, WA, July 23, 1992), MP3/cassette, 40:30.

John Baillie and the Schoolmen: Direct Experience of God

LET US BEGIN with John Baillie, a Scottish theologian during the early twentieth century. In terms of importance to Willard, he is not the highest, but his books are so clear on the relevant issues that he can set the stage for other theologians who are.

Willard was, we know, aware of Baillie during the years when his basic doctrines were being formed. In 1984, when Willard first published *Guidance*, he quotes from Baillie's *Our Knowledge of God* (1959).[92] In 2008, he mentions the late nineteenth- and early twentieth-century scholarly interest in an account of divine revelation and claims that outstanding contributions were made by John and his brother, D. M. Baillie.[93] More than likely, Willard values these brothers because, though they were conversant on the leading issues of their time, they continued in their appreciation of both natural theology and spirituality (or what they might have called "mysticism" or "religion") in days when these pursuits had become suspect to some (e.g., Barth and Bonhoeffer). Their theology, I suggest, exhibited to Willard a balance he found lacking in their contemporaries.

Baillie's argument for revelation in *Our Knowledge of God* has a strong resemblance to Willard's position *if* one is able to set aside Baillie's polemic against what he calls inferential knowledge of God.[94] What Baillie has in mind are traditional arguments for the existence of God that began from observations of things that are not God and infer God's existence and nature from them. Baillie's criticism of this reasoning is, rhetorically, a springboard for his argument for a *direct knowledge* of God. But for Willard, this is a false alternative. In embracing direct

---

92. John Baillie, *Our Knowledge of God* (New York: Scribner, 1959), quoted in Dallas Willard, *In Search of Guidance*, 1st ed. (Ventura, CA: Regal, 1984), 28.

93. Willard, "Christian Teaching Banished," 55:00. Here he mentions John Baillie's *The Idea of Revelation in Recent Thought* (New York: Columbia University Press, 1964). In Willard, *Knowing*, 216, he mentions positively D. M. Baillie's book *Faith in God* (London: Faber & Faber, 1964).

94. Baillie, *Our Knowledge of God*, chap. 3.

knowledge of something (i.e., through experience), one must not reject the inferential knowledge one has of it (i.e., through reason).

As already discussed, Willard accepts in "Language, Being and God" the modest conclusions of two traditional arguments (one cosmological and one "teleological") and incorporates them into his doctrine of God. Avoiding Baillie's alternative, he finds himself free to also seek direct knowledge of God—much along the lines that Baillie recommends—but with the refined tool kit he learned from his disciplined study of Husserl and other philosophers. Willard's freedom to embrace both/and is seen not only in this article but also in *Knowing Christ,* in which the two traditional arguments are presented as the first and second epistemic stages that anticipate the more robust third stage, or source of knowledge of God—namely, of *direct* experience.[95] Though in the course of any given person's epistemic progression this strict ordering is rarely followed, for the purpose of a patient, systematic, and scholarly exposition of the existence and nature of God, this is Willard's recommended path to knowledge. Baillie's positive method for knowledge of God falls soundly into the third stage of Willard's recommended path.[96]

That said, the poignant alternative that Baillie's book lays out is whether direct knowledge of God is available *in this life* or whether it is only available after death, with the consequence that whatever we know of God *now* is mediated and inferential. It is, of course, Thomas Aquinas who stands for the latter option in stark contrast to his theological forebears and thirteenth-century contemporaries. Baillie writes, "We have, according to St. Thomas, no *direct* knowledge of any existence save the world of nature as perceived by the five senses. Our knowledge of all non-sensible realities is discursive in character, being reached by inference from the things we can see and touch."[97] Though this is an overstatement that makes Aquinas seem more in tune with modern

95. Willard, *Knowing*, chap. 6, represents the third stage.

96. In fact, the two overlap here in such harmony that one might even say that Willard announces the third stage of theistic evidence in order to do justice to Baillie's argument.

97. Baillie, *Our Knowledge of God*, 109.

empiricism than he in fact was, Aquinas, in clear preference for an Aristotelian view of knowledge, puts sense perception in the driver's seat of human knowing *in this life*. This restriction to sense perception is, however, lifted when souls come to enjoy, *after* their bodies die, the beatific vision of God. At that point, knowledge of God, says Aquinas, may be direct. But before then, all knowledge of God is uniformly mediated.

Baillie notices that Aquinas's forebears and contemporaries—Bonaventure, Bernard, the Victorines, and before them, Francis of Assisi and Anselm of Canterbury—disagree with Aquinas on this point. These persons represent a medieval, non-Aristotelean tradition that "teaches that some vision of God may be enjoyed even in this life, at the summit of the mystical assent, and without miracle."[98] Believing the truth is found more on the side of this pre-Thomist tradition, Baillie modifies and modernizes it in various ways to defend a view of "mediated immediacy" in our knowledge of God. Though this view is fascinating in its own right, it is rather his brief intellectual history and its theological topology that help us situate and make sense of Willard's concept of faith.

If the history of theology may be crudely divided into "Platonist" and "Aristotelean" parties, Willard is clearly aligned with the Platonists over and against the Aristotelean doctor of the church, Aquinas. This is even clearer if one takes into account the later, more refined Platonism of the early modern period and the arise of talk of *intuition*, which Willard explains as "a faculty for perceiving non-sense-perceptible qualities."[99] The "Platonist" party consists of those who believe that non-sense-perceptible realities can be perceived in this life and that in this category of objects lie not only mathematics, beauty, and ethics but also God and the kingdom of God.[100]

98. Baillie, 170.

99. Dallas Willard, "The Failure of Ethical Understanding in the 20th Century," *Staley Lecture Series* (Wheaton College, Wheaton, IL, November 1, 2001), MP3/VHS, 7:30.

100. Of course, a "Platonist" account of intuition with respect to God must exercise some restraint in order to match human experience. And Aquinas, if thought of as an impure Platonist, clearly agrees that non-sense-perceptible realities *can* be seen; he, however, limits the intuition of God and his kingdom to the afterlife.

Aquinas's position, mediated through Baillie, can further help bring Willard's concept of faith into relief by considering Aquinas's own concept of faith. As Baillie puts it, "It is plain that St. Thomas regards Scripture primarily as a body of communicated information, and faith as the acceptance of such information upon authority."[101] Faith is mainly associated with *authority-mediated* knowledge, most especially with the mediation of Scripture. Aquinas is not far from Augustine here, whose concept of faith builds strongly on trust in authority.[102]

One should not miss how Willard's notion of faith as *ideally* resting upon knowledge is, indeed, compatible with this. For Aquinas, reason and sense perception step in to *know* the value of an authority, and this *knowledge* may be, as Willard would say, "*a basis for belief.*"[103] To Baillie's mind, this stacking of faith on knowledge diminishes the value of faith even more because he thinks of faith in such instances as a superfluous addendum to knowledge. To Willard, however, combining faith with one's *knowledge* of an authority (or of anything) adds the morally praiseworthy element of a readiness to act, which knowledge on its own would not contain.

But what really dominates Aquinas's whole system is the conviction that a direct vision of God is not given *in this life* (though obviously, faith is) and his defense of this through an Aristotelean epistemology devoid of intuition. In his theological method, faith is only indirectly paired with those future visions, being, however, directly tied to the entities of mediation—that is, to created authorities. That is to say, the fulfillment of faith—no longer seeing in a mirror dimly but seeing face-to-face (1 Cor 13:12)—is not the direct vision of God and

101. Baillie, *Our Knowledge of God*, 112.

102. See especially Augustine, *On Seeing God (Letter 147)*, in Mary T. Clark, trans., *Augustine of Hippo: Selected Writings* (Ramsey, NJ: Paulist, 1984), 365–402.

103. Willard, *Knowing*, 19 (Willard's emphasis). In Willard's childhood and in Protestantism generally, the Thomist position has been represented by those who upheld faith in the authority of the Bible (its inerrancy, infallibility, etc.) as the epitome of faith for the Christian. The argument is that there is no knowledge of God apart from the testimony of the Scriptures. But faith in the authority of Bible is phenomenologically different from faith in the God represented in the Bible.

his kingdom but the direct vision of "the authority" of the believer's authorities.

The situation is different when one turns to Aquinas's forebears and contemporaries, Bonaventure and the like. In them, Christian faith corresponds *directly* to the visions of God, man, and Christ, which they hoped (even expected) to attain in this life and certainly in the next. This faith does not lead them to reject faith in their authorities and by means of their authorities. This would be to accept another false alternative. But their non-Aristotelean and certainly nonempiricist epistemology afforded them the freedom to expect and receive fulfillments of their faith in non-sense-perceptible realities by the appearance of those very non-sense-perceptible realities to their minds. This makes it much easier to acknowledge that the external object of their faith was God, man, and Christ.

John Wesley: Regeneration

SIGNIFICANT THINGS WERE happening in intellectual history between the medieval scholastics and the modern period. Plato had been "rediscovered," leading seventeenth-century intellectuals such as Henry Scougal to write things like "Faith hath the same place in the Divine life, which sense hath in the natural, being indeed nothing else but a kind of sense, or feeling persuasion of spiritual things; it extends itself unto all Divine truths; but in our lapsed estate, it hath a peculiar relation to the declarations of God's mercy and reconcilableness to sinners through a mediator; and therefore receiving its denomination from that principle object, is ordinarily termed 'faith in Jesus Christ.'"[104] What Scougal is alluding to is the early modern, Plato-inspired concept of intuition, the act of perception of the non-sense-perceptible, and something very similar can be found in early evangelicals like John Wesley, for whom Scougal was an important intellectual guide. In 2010, Willard has this to say about Wesley's concept of faith: "Faith comes in now as perception of the visible world. Faith is a kind of perception; it's the ability to make

104. Henry Scougal, *The Life of God in the Soul of Man* (Fearn, UK: Christian Focus, 2009), 54–55.

the spiritual world present to yourself in a perceptual manner. . . . If you read the great theologians of the past, you'll come to something like this. One of the most helpful things, I think, that Wesley did was to bring a new understanding of faith where it is a kind of perception of reality."[105]

Growing up with Methodist grandparents, Willard discovered John Wesley very early in life and began taking him seriously in graduate school. In the early 1970s, he held a series of lectures for a Wesleyan church in which Wesley's doctrines featured prominently.[106] Later in 1992, Willard gave a thought-provoking talk on "The Role of Faith in Prayer," in which he cites three of Wesley's sermons on faith. In addition to the 2010 quote, these sermons give us the best clues as to what Willard took from Wesley on the concept of faith.[107]

When mentioning Wesley's sermons, Willard drops the first major clue. He mentions that Wesley begins one sermon ("On the Discoveries of Faith") with the late medieval scholastic principle: "Nihil est in intellectu quod non fuit prius in sensu" (Nothing is in the intellect that was not first in the senses).[108] Wesley, in this sermon, goes on to dismiss this principle, arguing with Hebrews 11 that faith is precisely that which involves the mind with non-sense-perceptible realities. Later in 2008, Willard makes the following comment about Wesley: "This is where we have to go back and sort out what really have we learned since Wesley? One of the good things about Wesley was Hume had already happened. And he knew it. He knew Hume, he knew Locke, he knew all these people. Wesley is a remarkably modern person when you start thinking

---

105. Dallas Willard, "Salvation in Christ Is a Life: Eternal Living Now," *Spiritual Formation and Soul Care* (Denver Seminary, Monument, CO, January 5, 2010), DVD, 9:00.

106. Willard, "Handout for 'Justification,'" 1973.

107. Willard, "The Role of Faith in Prayer," *Living Prayer* (Renovaré, Azusa, CA, October 26, 1992), MP3/cassette, 11:15. Willard says he has in mind sermons 56, 60, and 72 of the "1872 edition" of Wesley's sermons. He means sermons 106, 117, and 132 in vols. 3 and 4 of John Wesley, *The Works of John Wesley*, ed. Albert C. Outler (Nashville: Abingdon, 1986–87).

108. John Wesley, "Sermon 117: On the Discoveries of Faith," in *The Works of John Wesley: 115–151. Sermons IV*, ed. Albert C. Outler (Nashville: Abingdon, 1987).

about it."[109] In other words, Wesley develops his theology in full view of the bold theory of empiricism.

One can at once see how Wesley begins to line up on the "Platonist" side of Baillie's topography. A vision of non-sense-perceptible realities, such as God and his kingdom, is enjoyed by some *in this life*. The only difference is that Wesley uses the term *faith* instead of *knowledge* to describe this vision. This is doubtless due to Wesley's intent, taking Hebrews 11:1 as his leading text, to let his concept be biblically informed. What's more, in Wesley's context, being himself a child of the Reformation, the concept of faith had taken on more theological centrality. But Wesley combines this with the early evangelical reinterest in regeneration to show that faith and a "birth" into new sensibilities stand quite close together. The result is an account of faith's core content that overlaps significantly with the "unseen" realities that Aquinas's rivals claimed to *know*—only in part, yes, but now in this life.

Seeing faith as marked out by a certain domain of objects that the mind grasps is the most dominant feature of Wesley's concept. For him, faith qua faith is directed toward the objects in the unseen world. However, this must be qualified if we are to understand Wesley accurately. He does have some appreciation for the functional, or existential, aspect of faith. He speaks in the sermon "On Faith" of a hierarchy of faith, and he reluctantly attempts to include the materialist's faith at the bottom level, adding, "If it be faith at all."[110] The third-highest level of faith, Protestant faith, has as its object the authority of the Scriptures, a level remarkably close to the Augustinian-Thomist position, which Baillie criticizes. This level stands in contrast to Wesley's second-highest level, which has "God and the things of God" as its object and, finally, the highest level, which has one's forgiveness and union with Christ as its object. Only the last two are what Wesley allows as *real* faith, or as the faith honored by the New Testament. He, however, concedes the point in mental philosophy

109. Willard, "Faculty Q & A," 40:45. What we have learned since Wesley, Willard goes on to suggest, is the philosophy of mind known as intentionality.

110. John Wesley, "Sermon 106: On Faith," in *The Works of John Wesley: 71–114. Sermons III*, ed. Albert C. Outler (Nashville: Abingdon, 1986).

that human faith, as understood functionally, may have other worthy objects and, therefore, have other species than the New Testament kind.

Nevertheless, his skittishness with the concept of "materialist faith" and his rejection of the Aristotelean-scholastic principle indicate that Wesley, prompted by Hebrews 11, is making an important qualification to the genus of faith. Faith, properly conceived, looks to non-sense-perceptible things. For example, a pure materialist believer would have no faith because they would have no grasp of unseen realities.[111]

This perspective on faith is strengthened in Wesley by the close identification of his second-highest sort of faith with *regeneration*. This state of affairs for Wesley entails, among other things, a new sensibility for God and the things of God. The regenerate person sees what they previously could not see, but not everything that they could see. The effect of this move is understood in the reverse admission that the unregenerate exist in a state of practical naturalism. The unseen heavens are closed to them no matter what they profess or how they define their worldview. Regeneration for Wesley (and Willard, as we will see) is not something that one can engineer by readjusting one's theories. Either the unseen world shows itself to you . . . or it does not. The connection between regeneration and faith is significant because Wesley—by employing the Reformers' insight that faith should characterize every true Christian—makes the vision of God, man, and Christ, which for medieval theologians stood at *the summit* of the contemplative's ascent, *the very starting point* of every truly regenerate person's journey.[112]

Something very similar can be found in John Calvin's attack on *implicit faith*, asserting that true believers believe directly in Christ. The difference between Wesley and Calvin, who we will turn to shortly, is probably not that Wesley is more of a supernaturalist or a mystic than Calvin but that Wesley, after Locke and Hume, needed to put more

111. This example is not perfect in light of what I have called the functional aspect of faith. Even a naturalist operates with faith in the unseen. They do not have sense perception of much of the matter, in terms of which they profess to live, *while* they act, and there is much to matter that they could never have sense perception of.

112. We will see in chapter 6 how Willard handles this doctrine.

emphasis on *the non-sense-perceptibility* of the objects of biblical faith—a position Calvin and his contemporaries simply assume. But in general, Wesley is fighting the same battle that Calvin was fighting in his day.

Though Willard takes the functional, or existentialist, aspect of faith much further than Wesley, the inclination to think of the spiritual domain as the primary object of faith is clearly present in Willard's thought. The reason for this Wesleyan inclination in Willard, I believe, is that the spiritual world, though not the only domain that is non-sense-perceptible, is the epitome of what is unseen. Feelings, universals, thoughts, numbers, logical relations, even the senses themselves—all of these are non-sense-perceptible realities about which we have, according to Willard, knowledge. But the epitome of the unseen is God. This helps us make sense of the fact that, though Willard will say faith is "not opposed to knowledge" and that it is "opposed to sight," he also will say "faith is knowledge."[113] For example, he said once that faith is "a kind of knowledge, a knowledge of the spiritual and invisible world."[114]

On another occasion, Willard says, "Faith is really knowledge of the unseen world."[115] That faith represents a category or source of knowledge may be inconsistent with Willard's view, discussed previously, that faith and knowledge are distinct and interactive dispositions in the person. Though there may be some shifts in his view, such a remark is best read, I think, as rhetorical, an attempt to get his audience to think about faith more along the lines of Baillie and the medieval theologians—that is, as potentially based on knowledge or, better, intuition of the spiritual world. In the same lecture, he says of Moses, who "endured as seeing him who is invisible" (Heb 11:27), "That's why he had faith, was because he saw him. He didn't see him because he had faith. You have to have the

113. Willard, "Human Disaster of Unbelief," MP3/cassette.

114. Unfortunately, I have not been able to re-locate this exact quote. One reference to faith as a "kind of knowledge" is in Dallas Willard, "Paul's Good News about God as Seen in Romans," *Studies in the Book of Apostolic Acts: Journey in the Spiritual Unknown* (Woodlake Avenue Friends Church, Canoga Park, CA, January 23, 1972), MP3/cassette, 48:30.

115. Willard, "Session 3," 23:30. Earlier, he says, "Faith is a vision of reality" (19:00).

order of causation right there."[116] With that order of causation in mind, we can best understand what he says next: "Faith is really knowledge of the unseen world. Faith is not opposed to knowledge. It is knowledge. Faith is opposed to sight."[117] Here one must be careful, I believe, to understand sight as sense perception, which is not as such capable of consciousness of the unseen world and him who is invisible.

In this vein, we recall again the subtitle for *Knowing Christ*, "Why We Can Trust *Spiritual* Knowledge." This distinction reintroduces the potential hiatus, discussed in connection with conviction, between the new spiritual knowledge that comes with regeneration (or perhaps in the prevenient grace that precedes it) and the faith one puts in what one knows by regeneration. We notice that in emphasizing the spiritual world as the primary object of faith, Willard is simply reiterating Wesley's view. Wesley's most biblical, most real levels of faith involve vision and knowledge of the Christian God and the unseen world.

Francis of Assisi and Bonaventure: The Active Life

ASSESSING THE CONNECTION between the early Franciscans and Willard is more difficult because there is, to my knowledge, no one text but many (modern and ancient) that transmitted the movement's emphases to him. It is mainly the aura and general direction of Franciscan teaching and spirituality that attracted Willard, and this should be understandable after having discussed Baillie and Wesley. Francis's groundbreaking emphasis on following Jesus *in his earthly ministry and ways of life* was always very important to Willard. The biographical stories of Willard's visits to Florence and Assisi suggest that these were partly undertaken in the mode of pilgrimage.[118]

But with respect to faith and knowledge, Francis and his early followers stand in the older "Platonist" tradition, with the expectation that the hidden world of God would be revealed in its time and in this

---

116. Willard, 23:15.

117. Willard, 23:30.

118. Dallas Willard, "Living in the Vision of God," in Willard, *Great Omission*, 91; and Richard Foster, *Longing for God* (Downers Grove, IL: InterVarsity, 2009), 128–29.

life. Perhaps the clearest example of this view is Bonaventure's *Journey of the Soul into God*, which Willard, along with *The Life of St. Francis*, required in his course at Fuller Theological Seminary.[119] But in line with the medieval mendicant movement and in contradistinction to the more contemplative Benedictine orders, Francis taught (mainly by means of his life) that the active life of love and service was not in conflict with the human pursuit of the vision of God; it was essential to it. And with this teaching, Willard heartily concurs.

In the early 2000s, Willard was asked by a group of leaders to comment on why churches and ministries tend to lose their founding visions and degenerate into institutions much unlike their founders. His reflection on this issue resulted in the essay "Living in the Vision of God," in which he begins with Francis and the history of the Franciscan movement. The essay's title encapsulates Willard's alignment with the early Franciscan ideal. Not waiting for death and the beatific vision, Francis lived, at least intermittently, in the vision of God. He *lived.* His divine vision was not the result of a life of solitary repose. This disposition of living in pursuit of and in the wake of a real revelation of the unseen, spiritual world is what Willard calls faith. And though the theological language of Francis's day did not call it faith, Willard, in his reading of Francis, recognizes the reality.

John Calvin and Horatius Bonar: The Gospel

MANY TIMES, WILLARD confessed to being a particular admirer of John Calvin's *Institutes*'s third book. One reason is that Calvin helped solidify Willard's skepticism toward the theology of faith popular in the fundamentalist churches of his upbringing and in the evangelical church at large.[120]

By the time Willard read Calvin as a young man, he was already skeptical of this aspect of his upbringing. Having been mentored by older evangelical writers, such as Wesley and Finney, he knew faith had

119. Dallas Willard, "Syllabus for 'Spirituality and Ministry' GM720," 1993–2012, Dallas Willard Collection.
120. Willard, *Conspiracy*, 36–37.

been shrunken into something impotent and susceptible to nominal Christianity. His exact reasons for turning to Luther and Calvin are unclear, but in reading them, he found them to be saying something different about faith and Christian life than his living teachers.[121] This gleaning echoes in one of his endnotes from *Disciplines*. Writing about how the first natural expression of regeneration, "the impartation of new life," is "turning from old ways with faith and hope in Christ," he attaches the following note, "I believe that this was the understanding of 'faith' accepted by the leaders of the Protestant Reformation," and points readers to Horatius Bonar's *God's Way of Holiness*.[122]

Who Willard has most in mind with this gesture to the Reformation is Calvin. The first thing that Calvin polemicizes in his teaching on faith is the notion of *implicit faith*. This medieval concept had come to describe, for Calvin, the many persons in Christendom who were instructed to trust the church and its teachings *as* their proper Christian faith. While Calvin has some respect for the reality of implicit faith as a precursor to true saving faith, he insists that the proper object of faith is not the church but Christ, "for faith consists in the knowledge of God and Christ."[123] Calvin's constant eliding of faith and knowledge here and elsewhere is important to note, especially because of its resonance with Baillie and Wesley. In fact, Calvin's statement "Faith rests not on ignorance, but on knowledge" is extremely reminiscent of Willard.[124]

Given Calvin's rejection of implicit faith, to what degree does he stand with the "Platonist" party in this matter? Are the realities of the spiritual, heavenly world *visible*, at least in part and in this life? What stands out immediately is how, for Calvin, the biblical faith he seeks to describe is so clearly defined by its proper object that the general

121. Willard, "When God Moves In," 54.

122. Willard, *Disciplines*, 38, 43; Horatius Bonar, *God's Way of Holiness* (Fearn, UK: Christian Focus, 2021). Bonar's point, which he tries to elicit from all the Reformers, is a censure against conceiving faith to be a meritorious deed. However, the historical consensus he presents on faith is far from convincing. Each Reformer seems to be defining faith in his own way in order to somehow align himself with the seminal insight of the day—namely, justification by faith.

123. John Calvin, *Institutes* 3.2, 3.

124. Calvin, 3.2, 2.

ontological and epistemological questions about faith are irrelevant to him. The most vital type of biblical faith does not have something so broad as "God and the things of God" as its object. Calvin even has some criticism for those who claim God as the object of faith, because this could suggest that sinful, fleshly humanity could have adequate knowledge of God *without* Christ's making him known.[125] Nevertheless, Calvin is comfortable with saying that the faith to which we are called is faith (1) in God and (2) in the divine will. This faith intends *Christ* because in Christ's person, God and especially the divine will are made known.

Calvin, to give him credit, recognizes many scriptural uses of faith. But his specific aim is to explicate *the faith* that distinguishes "the children of God from the unbelievers."[126] And not every aspect of the unseen world is intended by *this* faith. Properly, this faith intends Christ "clothed with his gospel."[127] This is an illuminating qualification to see him make because Calvin notes a few examples of faith *in Jesus* that were not proper, evangelical faith. In one example, the subjects believe that Jesus is the Messiah but have not received him in his gospel. This leads Calvin to focus even more on how Jesus in his person brings "a knowledge of God's will toward us."[128] He finally settles on Christ's revelation of God's *benevolence* or mercy. He defines faith as "a firm and certain *knowledge* of God's benevolence toward us, founded upon the truth of the freely given promise in Christ, both revealed to our minds and sealed upon our hearts through the Holy Spirit."[129]

Though Calvin probably only benefits from the aura of the non-Aristotelian tradition, it is nevertheless impossible to comprehend his teaching on faith outside of that tradition. While his emphasis is not on the non-sense-perceptibility of faith's object, he does not believe that faith's primary object is sense perceptible or something distinct from

125. Indeed, his insistence on the depravity of flesh does suggest a Platonist hue and one that Willard takes issue with.

126. Calvin, *Institutes* 3.2, 13.

127. Calvin 3.2, 6.

128. Calvin 3.2, 6.

129. Calvin 3.2, 7 (emphasis mine).

spiritual reality. This is clear in 3.2, 14, where he tries to justify his use of the word *knowledge* to define faith. He insists that faith is a comprehension *above* normal sense-perceptual comprehension.[130] His general point is that even the fulfillment of faith's comprehension is unlike sense-perceptual fulfillment because it does not grasp (*non capit*) its object and because a *certainty* is involved that does not accompany standard human epistemic acts. This certainty is the work of Spirit *added* to the bare understanding; it is a gift/grace that Calvin thinks the medieval scholastics have completely overlooked.[131]

The "Platonist" correlation between Calvin and Willard is the clearest, I think, in their mutual disregard for implicit faith, whether ecclesial or (and this is significant for modern accounts like Herman Bavinck's) scriptural. Reading Calvin as if his faith in the benevolence of God in Christ is fundamentally identical with a faith in the Scriptures invites Calvin's own censure against implicit faith. Calvin stands enough in the mystical traditions of the patristic and medieval eras to reject a secondhand knowledge of Christ. The Scriptures are a means to the more direct encounter that, for Calvin, the Spirit superintends. Granted, he is highly concerned with the manner in which sinfulness and fleshliness veil our perception of God (incidentally, another similarity with the mystical tradition). But his solution to this dilemma is not some version of implicit faith—ecclesial or scriptural—but a direct knowledge and faith *in Christ*, who broke and still breaks through the veil.[132]

---

130. His further distinctions are difficult to follow, especially his phrase *Neque etiam ubi pertigit quod sentit assequitur*.

131. Calvin, *Institutes* 3.2, 8.

132. Willard felt that a gospel of churchmanship was circulating in his lifetime, and even though he felt that believers in High Church traditions were most affected, he was inclined to see many in his own Baptist tradition in a very similar light. He characterized the churchmanship message as "You take care of your church, and your church will take care of you." For a brief introduction, see Dallas Willard, "The Failure of Evangelical Political Involvement in the Area of Moral Transformation," in *God and Governing: Reflections on Ethics, Virtue, and Statesmanship*, ed. Roger N. Overton (Eugene, OR: Pickwick, 2009), 77–78. The Protestant version of the churchmanship gospel, Willard thought, was centered on taking care of the church by believing the true teachings, which "happen to be" what that respective Protestant church teaches. In many churches,

A. W. Tozer: Evangelical Mysticism

THE PERHAPS CLOSEST, but unfortunately most pithy and most poetic, companion of all to Willard's concept of faith may be the evangelical mystic A. W. Tozer, for whom Willard had an appreciation ever since, at least, his days in graduate school. Tozer writes in his classic *The Pursuit of God*, "Faith creates nothing, it simply reckons upon that which is already there. God and the spiritual world are real. We can reckon upon them with as much assurance as we reckon upon the familiar world around us."[133] Later Tozer says, "At the root of the Christian life lies belief in the invisible. The object of the Christian's faith is unseen reality."[134] And in his previous book, *God's Pursuit of Man*, Tozer tells us that "wherever faith has been original, wherever it has proved itself to be real, it has invariably had upon it a sense of the *present God*. The holy Scriptures possess in marked degree this feeling of actual encounter with a real Person."[135] More quotes could be multiplied from Tozer's *The Root of the Righteous* and *Keys to the Deeper Life*, but unfortunately, Tozer is not given to analysis in his writings, so there is little more to do than note the similarity. Willard, when once asked about Tozer's influence on his thought, said the similarity stems from the fact that he and Tozer "were drinking at the same fountain."[136]

The Ontology of Faith

CLEARLY A DIFFERENT account of knowledge and faith is afoot in Willard than can be found in any well-known or leading *theologian* in contemporary thought. But to conclude this tour of Willard's faith companions, let us rehearse quickly the basic insights Willard is taking from this diverse

---

he observed that a prominent preacher taught from the Scriptures in a way that was reminiscent of the Roman magisterium. In all of this, *implicit faith* is the culturally dominant form of faith.

133. A. W. Tozer, *The Pursuit of God* (1948; repr., Camp Hill, PA: WingSpread, 1982), 53.

134. Tozer, 54.

135. A. W. Tozer, *God's Pursuit of Man* (Camp Hill, PA: WingSpread, 2007), 7.

136. Willard, "The Spirit of the Disciplines and the Academic Setting," *Faculty Luncheon* (Biola University, La Mirada, CA, April 10, 1989), MP3/cassette, 30:00.

group. With William James, Willard recognizes that belief has a tie to the will and to a readiness to act. Beliefs are necessary for humans who are not omniscient and, nevertheless, must act in life. From Edmund Husserl, Willard takes an elaborate and sophisticated toolbox for analyzing consciousness and mental acts such as the type involved in believing. He agrees with Husserl that acts of belief can be distinguished by their directedness on different aspects of the same object. One instance of faith in an object (e.g., Jesus of Nazareth) may be different from another instance of faith even though the object is the same.

Charles Finney, one of Willard's first companions, makes a distinction between "perception of truth" and believing, a distinction that allows for a psychological state called *conviction*, which may lead to a state of *denial* of "the truth." Willard, however, has a more elaborate description of the Spirit's role in moving people to faith. Yet both have an account of how faith is a praiseworthy disposition, ordering it with other virtues. Finney does not seem to have a category for faith in what is false, and neither, for that matter, does Martin Luther. Willard believes Luther agrees in a general way with Finney that genuine faith, whose source is in the Spirit and word of God, leads automatically to actions—good works and fulfillment of the law.

John Wesley was another one of Willard's first companions, and his timely theology, worked out after Locke's and Hume's empiricist projects had taken off, meant that he stands out for his emphasis on the non-sense-perceptibility of the objects of faith. This puts him in the company of theologians who thought that perception of eternal realities was possible in this life and who incorporated these revelations into their theologies. John Baillie polemicizes Aquinas, the poster child for those who restrict the first sources of theology to the sense perceptible, and aligns himself, as does Willard, with a "Platonist" tradition that passes in the medieval era through Francis of Assisi and Bonaventure. The Franciscan tradition stands out to Willard because its followers did not oppose perception of eternal realities with an active life. This tendency can also be seen in Wesley, who brings this perception or knowledge of the unseen into connection with the evangelical doctrine and common experience of regeneration. An earlier version of this can be found in

Calvin, who Willard thinks is particularly close to his view of faith. Calvin is helpful for his many distinctions about the precise object of the sort of faith that brings about regeneration and ultimately salvation. It, he says, is not just Christ but a particular aspect of Christ, which he calls "Christ clothed with his gospel."[137]

Willard's ontology of faith, as we find it in his oeuvre, is never found in a systematic whole such as we find his ontology of knowledge. There is some doubt, in my mind at least, as to whether the concept of faith can be stretched to cover *both* a basic human function in life that is distinct from knowledge *and* the specific "saving" disposition that, on Willard's account, is "a kind of knowledge." Whether this can be reconciled in Willard's thought or not, some grasp of Willard's concept of faith as a systematic whole is necessary to make sense of his doctrine of salvation and of faith in Jesus and his gospel.

As we go on to discuss Willard's view of "Christ clothed with his gospel" divided into three stages *of knowledge*, Willard's ontology of faith will be especially relevant at the end of each of these stages, where we ask what role faith plays in salvation through the gospel. In the first stage, to give readers a small preview, we will return again to the doctrine of regeneration much like we encountered in Wesley's view of faith.

But before we speak of the first listeners' faith and regeneration, we must speak of their knowledge of the gospel. And before we speak of their knowledge of the gospel, we must speak, in the next chapter, of a few other matters of knowledge that Willard believes were prerequisites to Jesus's preaching and the first listeners' adequate hearing of the gospel. We must speak of what the Jews knew.

137. Calvin, *Institutes* 3.2, 6.

Part II

THE FIRST STAGE

We have noted how he entered human history through the life of an ordinary family. But then, as God's flash point in reigniting eternal life among us, he inducts us into the eternal kind of life that flows through himself. He does this first by bringing that life to bear upon our *needs*.

—Dallas Willard, *The Divine Conspiracy*

5

WHAT THE JEWS KNEW

> Jesus' approach to these matters was, I believe, expressed in His statement: "Ye believe in God, believe also in me" (John 14:1 KJV). That's the right order. The religious ideas, history and context back of His life as an Israelite, *together with* his own teaching and action and character, provided for those who absorbed themselves in them something close to a *logical* demonstration, *not* of the existence of Jehovah, which was never in question for them, but of His specific nature.
>
> —Dallas Willard, "Language, Being, God, and the Three Stages of Theistic Evidence"

THE KINGDOM OF God, according to Willard, is biblical ontology. It is not eschatology or soteriology or a subdivision thereof. Though it has important expressions in those "mighty acts of God," it does not derive its nature from them.

This type of biblical philosophizing is not untypical in Christian history, but Willard has a historical claim to make as well. He is prepared to argue that the Jews of Jesus's day, without the sophistication of having ontological theories, knew that God and his kingdom are real and fundamental to reality. When Jesus comes, he speaks of neither in an ontological vacuum, in some barren philosophical world where metaphysical reflection remains fettered to Greek peninsulas. Jesus rather begins his ministry in an ethnic group that, as a result of its divinely supervised history and practices, knew of God's ontological kingdom. And he comes to them *not* with information about the kingdom's fundamental existence—of which they already knew—but with new information about its nature and latest movements.

Eschatological Hermeneutics

BY AND LARGE, mainstream historical, exegetical scholarship disagrees. In print, Willard largely sidesteps this large body of disagreement, seeming to act as if he were not aware that entire professional societies are convinced that he is wrong. Indeed, since Willard rarely interacts with other exegetes or theologians in print, his choice of Charles Ryrie as one of his few named opponents in *Conspiracy* may be read in a few less-than-flattering ways. It may be read mildly as a concession to a semi-academic genre of writing. It may also be read more sinisterly as an opportunity for self-aggrandizement by ignoring stronger contenders.[1] There is, I believe, something deeper going on, which I would like to explore before turning to Willard's positive historical claims.

Let it be noted that the late Charles Ryrie worked within a school of theology known as dispensationalism. In accordance with traditional dispensationalist hermeneutics, when Ryrie comes to Jesus's gospel of the kingdom in Matthew, he reads it as having "to do with the coming of the Messiah to rule the earth in the Millennium."[2] When Willard starkly criticizes this, he is criticizing a modern version of what *he* was taught about the kingdom as a young man.

Dispensationalism may not be our theological heritage, but there is an underlying connection between Ryrie and more academically fashionable traditions of exegetical theology: the use of eschatology as the lens to understand the kingdom of God and Jesus's gospel. And Willard is not blind to this connection.[3] One such tradition began at the turn of the twentieth century with Johannes Weiß and Albert Schweitzer. In their hands, the hitherto ignored *apocalyptic philosophy*, present socially

1. Charles Ryrie's view can be found in *So Great Salvation: What It Means to Believe in Jesus Christ* (Wheaton, IL: Victor, 1989).
2. Willard, *Conspiracy*, 45.
3. In *Conspiracy* (402n19), Willard recommends Wendell Willis, ed., *The Kingdom of God in 20th Century Interpretation* (Peabody, MA: Hendrickson, 1987). The book does not treat dispensationalism or other millennial interpretations.

in Second Temple Judaism, began to be drawn out exegetically in Jesus's teaching on the kingdom.[4] In a statement fitting for both Schweitzer and Weiß, Willard writes in *Conspiracy* about "Modernists" (albeit without naming any) who thought of Jesus as a great teacher but "present him as fundamentally mistaken about major elements of his own message, such as when his kingdom would come."[5] This inevitable consequence of Weiß's and Schweitzer's exegeses of the kingdom—that is, an ignorant Jesus—was, however, dissatisfactory to other exegetes. Thus there arose attempts to continue in the same eschatological tradition and yet to salvage Jesus's intellect by giving his apocalyptic message a factual referent either in this life or in the next. John Bright, Willard's favorite kingdom exegete, represents one such person.[6]

It was only after Willard's own views of the kingdom had been largely solidified and written up in *Conspiracy*—forty-five years after reading Bright and leaving dispensationalism—that he familiarized himself with a more modern attempt to rescue the apocalyptic Jesus from himself—that is, with the work of N. T. Wright.[7] Arising to popularity while Willard was at the height of his publishing career, Wright represents a new generation in twentieth-century exegetical theology whose work is unique in how it continues the "Modernist" eschatological tradition in a preterist and even historicist mode.

Making an important historical distinction, Wright criticizes Schweitzer for thinking that the Second Temple Jews expected an other-worldly kingdom, and he reports on the basis of vast, disciplined

---

4. Johannes Weiß, *Die Predigt Jesu vom Reiche Gottes* (Göttingen, Germany: Vandenhoeck & Ruprecht, 1892); Albert Schweitzer, *Von Reimarus zu Wrede: Geschichte der Leben-Jesu-Forschung* (Tübingen, Germany: Mohr, 1906).

5. Willard, *Conspiracy*, 56.

6. See chapter 2.

7. As noted in chapter 1 footnote 34, Willard encountered Wright at a 1999 intervarsity conference for university faculty, where Wright was presenting a popularized version of his *Jesus and the Victory of God*. Later, Willard wrote blurbs for a few of Wright's popular books and recommended *Jesus and the Victory of God* for further reading in his article "Jesus," in *Dictionary of Christian Spirituality*, ed. Glen Scorgie (Grand Rapids, MI: Zondervan, 2011), 63.

historical research that the first-century Jews sought a *this-worldly* "age to come."[8] According to Wright, this apocalyptic Second Temple worldview, now much more precisely defined than in Schweitzer's day, is what Jesus takes hold of in his kingdom gospel and reinterprets.[9] Jesus's intellect is salvaged by his being cast as a master reinterpreter who, as it were, commandeers the concepts and terms of his apocalyptic day by infusing them with unprecedented meanings. Always taking the New Testament seriously, Wright's view, in short, is that the kingdom of God, in a rather complex way, is announced and *established* in the life and work of Jesus.[10] And Willard disagrees.

Normally, such disagreement would not be a point worth mentioning in a book of this sort, which aims to shed light on Willard's views and on the sources, norms, and methods that led him to them. Willard disagrees with the whole herd of professional exegetes on the nature of the kingdom, and N. T. Wright is not unique in this respect. But in Wright's case, Willard gives a glimpse of *why* he disagrees. What it comes down to is two divergent approaches to the Bible, two divergent biblical hermeneutics. Because Wright in some ways represents the majority approach in historical, exegetical scholarship, we have in Willard's response to him a rare glimpse of his mature perspective on the whole herd. Willard was not in the habit of criticizing living theologians, so this is indeed a *rare* glimpse.[11]

The setting for this glimpse is a Q and A in which Willard fields a question about Wright's reconstruction of the first-century Jewish worldview and Jesus's ministry within it. After affirming that he was "a great admirer" of Wright, Willard gives an answer that reveals not only his take on Wright's approach but also how he thought the Scriptures and the ontology therein *should be* approached. Here is Willard's answer in full:

---

8. N. T. Wright, *The New Testament and the People of God* (Minneapolis: Fortress, 1992), 284–85.

9. Wright, *Jesus and the Victory of God*, 224, 226–29.

10. Wright, *Jesus*, 220–29, 364, 467–72.

11. Living philosophers were apparently another matter.

I don't believe you need to know all of that [about first-century Judaism, etc.] in order to understand what the Scriptures are saying. I think what you have to do is take a commonsense approach to reading it, and especially, that means reading not just verses but put[ting] the passages in context. As much as you can, of course, locate the larger pieces and contexts.

I don't think God set the Bible up in such a way that you have to know these details in order to understand what it's all about. I do believe that if you understand these things, they will often help you understand what it's about. So what comes out at the end is not just a function of that historical understanding. It's a function of the overall teaching of the Bible.

The reason why I came to this interpretation [i.e., of the message and teachings of Jesus] was because I believe the overall teaching of the Bible. Not just that passage or what first-century Jews thought about it. But rather the presentation of the kingdom of God in the Bible as a whole, which stretches over a long period of time, involves a lot of history. If you go back in the Old Testament and start reading about the kingdom of God and come up to the Gospel of Matthew and the New Testament, then I think you will get a version that is understandable, that is applicable, that gives practical guidance [on] what you're to do. That's basically how my reading proceeds.

Now, what N. T. [Wright] says about particular things [is] often very helpful. But you can't take the principle of first-century Judaism as the *key to it. It can help. But for one thing, the principle of first-century Judaism will give you an entirely different picture of what the kingdom is than the Bible as a whole does. In first-century Judaism, it was clear that the kingdom of God was supposed to be something political that appeared and led the Jews to triumph. You know how, if you look into the history of the interbiblical period [and] you see what they were struggling with, you can see why that would be an obsessive picture. But the picture that Jesus is presenting is* contrary *to that vision.*

So, you want to look at the history, learn as much as you can. You never in any *circumstances want to deny a fact. Never. That's true of biblical criticism in general. But you also have to take* all *of the facts into consideration. The truth is, from the very beginning of the history of Israel, there is a tension between the kingdom of God and political leadership. You see it beginning, for example, in Samuel and the book of Judges, even. You see that tension emerging. And when it goes in the political, it always goes wrong. When you have the building of the temple, the establishing of the nation, the kingdom in the political sense is established, God explicitly says to Samuel, "This is not my will, but I'm going to let it happen." He says, "They've not rejected you; they rejected me."*

So you have to look at the Bible as a whole to understand the central message. The central message is really, I think, best put in terms of God with us, God being with us. *So I use what I in other contexts call the* Immanuel Principle, *and you run that from Genesis to Revelation.*[12] *Then the kingdom of God emerges within that context as God's action in history. That's not a political system. That is something that is available to the lowliest of people who have nothing to do with the political system. In fact, it becomes opposed to the political system constantly, and the primary opposition in the day of Jesus was between the law and the prophets and the kingdom of God.*

So that's a long-winded way of saying, you just have to look at the whole picture. You have to be very serious and thoughtful about that. Then, if you can learn something from historical criticism, higher criticism, lower criticism, whatever—by all means, learn it. But the primary task

---

12. The Immanuel Principle is a key part of Willard's soteriology proper. For more, see chapter 11.

> *that Jesus had was correcting the view that people of his day imposed on the kingdom of God. Now, you can't get that from that view itself. Then you can go back and appreciate whatever truth there was in it.*[13]

Many things could be said about this answer that would be valuable for a full-dress treatment of Willard's hermeneutics. In passing, one might note some common ground between Wright and Willard: one must know *something* of the historical context to understand what the Bible is saying. Where they differ is in how much and how to weigh it.[14]

A more pertinent difference is with respect to what I called in the last chapter *realist hermeneutics*—that is, that one might and even must look for the idea where the term is not present. This is a rule that Wright is hesitant to use with respect to the term *kingdom*, and his hesitance restricts his ability to see patterns in Jesus's gospel *to linguistic expression and its use in a finite social group* and, ultimately, to one phase of biblical history—namely, Second Temple Judaism. The farthest he can go back in biblical history is the exile because this is when the mere terms were coined. Noting that social elites of first-century Judaism were more concerned with eschatology than with, say, atonement, Wright makes their prevailing apocalypticism the controlling factor (as Willard says, "the key") in his exegesis of the gospel.

Willard's alternative approach begins *positively*—with a comprehensive exegesis of the Old Testament and the history of Israel. Though he does not believe one needs an exhaustive or even scholarly understanding of the historical details to understand the texts, he does make use of such knowledge, saying later in the Q and A, "My assumption is

---

13. Willard, "Q & A: Prayer," 43:30.

14. When Willard was a teenager, an event took place that symbolizes his respect for history in reading the Bible. After seeing an advertisement for a copy of the works of Josephus, Willard exclaimed in his father's presence that he would like to have "that book." His father said, "If you'll read it, I'll buy it for you." Willard comments, "I still have that book and I read it" ("Confidence with Children," *Confidence in God: Men's Retreat* [Valley Vista Christian Community, Sepulveda, CA, June 1987], MP3/cassette, 1:11:30).

what the Bible teaches about the kingdom of God as a whole, and you have to know something about the historical realities to get that. But I don't think it is to be drawn from one particular phase of that history."[15] As he attempts to make sense of the "overall teaching of the Bible," Willard recognizes that the Old Testament's vision is dissonant with the various first-century Judaist visions but also—and this helps confirm it for him—*consonant* with the New Testament's vision emerging from the texts and from Jesus himself. This consonance is what he means by "the presentation of the kingdom of God in the Bible as a whole."

So let it not be forgotten that Willard consistently grounds his own view of the kingdom *in biblical exegesis* and expects his view to be taken seriously *as exegesis*. Though he was neither an Old nor a New Testament specialist, he is claiming that his kingdom exegesis is superior to other modern and ancient ways of reading the Bible.[16] And according to Willard's exegesis, the kingdom of God is biblical ontology, and Jesus is one of its ontologists.

Jesus as Ontologist of the Ancient (First-Stage) Ontology

GIVEN TODAY'S OVERRIDING assumptions, it may be difficult for some to think of Jesus as someone with anything profound to say about ontology or of his basic message and general teaching theme as dealing with statements about reality at its very core. Yet this is Willard's exegetical-historical claim. Consider that while Willard in chapters 4–9 of *Conspiracy* addresses Jesus's answers to the latter three of the "Four Great

15. Willard, "Q & A: Prayer," 54:00.

16. This may seem to be a bold claim, but Willard firmly believed that theologically crucial biblical interpretation should not be left to the specialists and did not leave it to them. See Willard, *Conspiracy*, xvi–xvii. Willard gives an indication of his scholarly habits when he shares his traditional lament in a 1990 sermon: "Jesus' gospel was *not* the kingdom of heaven. I have to spend a lot of time mucking around in scholarly stuff, and it's just so discouraging sometimes to just keep reading all these things. It's as if Jesus came and said, 'The kingdom of heaven!' He didn't come and say, 'The kingdom of heaven.' He came and said the kingdom of heaven is now available. That was the gospel. The kingdom of heaven has been around ever since any 'since' there was" (Dallas Willard, "Prayer: A Working Relationship with God," *The Soul* [Valley Vista Christian Community, Sepulveda, CA, August 19, 1990], MP3/cassette, 29:00).

Questions," Willard in chapters 1–3 addresses Jesus's answer to the "First Great Question": What is reality? In these fundamental chapters, Willard, by contrasting Jesus's gospel and basic teachings with what is generally taught in churches, is reconstructing the ontology Jesus preached and himself believed in.[17]

To be certain, there is a great difference between *Conspiracy*'s first chapters and what Willard regularly taught in his University of Southern California (USC) courses on metaphysics.[18] In part, this is due to the hesitance among those universities aspiring to "secularity" to introduce the teachings of Jesus (a "religious" leader) as possible statements of knowledge. However, it is also due to Jesus's hesitance to give lessons in *general ontology*, the main subject of Willard's USC course. That is, Jesus did not systematically address the questions of universals, mind, substance, and so on. Given his place in "God's march through human history," Jesus had, according to Willard, more significant topics in ontology to address—more significant than even explaining ontology as a discipline or using the word![19]

Biographically speaking, Willard came to his views about Jesus's ontology gradually as his philosophical acumen and the depth of his exegesis grew together and then blossomed in the late 1980s and early '90s. At an early point in his life, he was interested in what he called "the faith of Jesus," or what Jesus himself believed in and taught. And of course, the main statement of Jesus's faith that Willard had to make sense of is

17. The original vision for *Conspiracy* was a book on Jesus's beliefs. *Disciplines*, by contrast, was a book on Jesus's practices.

18. See many of the syllabi, transcripts, and handouts for Willard's USC course "Metaphysics, Phil 460."

19. On one occasion, Willard says, "Christian faith today must come from an ontology. Ontology is the basic questions about reality. Secularism is not a conspiracy. It is a theory of reality authorized by [the] Western intellectual world" (Dallas Willard, "Reality, Spirituality and the Gospel," *Spirituality and Ministry* [Fuller Theological Seminary, Sierra Madre, CA, June 10, 2002], MP3, 6:00). But outside of formal philosophical settings, Willard tended to use the word *reality* and talk about "what is real." This is doubtless because Willard knew that the word *ontology* scares even well-educated persons. Because of the flexibility, generality, and historical pedigree of the concept of ontology, this is a fear that I will not take into account in this book.

Jesus's gospel: the kingdom of God "is at hand."[20] In his mature years, Willard, putting it as simply as he could, would claim that Jesus's new information about God's kingdom was *that it is available.*

But a lot of "the faith of Jesus" was not this gospel; it was simply biblical ontology. And this biblical ontology was not esoteric, at least not for Jesus's first listeners. Jesus may have stood out because he believed it, but any mildly educated Jew would have known about it. This will be important for us because Willard's interpretation of Jesus's ministry depends on the fact that *there is a basic biblical ontology* that a first-century Jew could have grasped and that they *must have* grasped—at least apperceptively (i.e., on the margins of consciousness)—before any proper understanding of Jesus's message was possible. This basic biblical ontology was probably not the "sophisticated" view in the first century, but this fact is, for Willard, largely irrelevant to Jesus's evangelistic work and overall mission. So before we look in the next chapter at the first and simplest meaning of Jesus's *gospel* of the kingdom, we must have before us this basic biblical ontology—what the Jews knew.

But note: this basic view is not primarily a sociological fact—that is, something present in the operative worldview of first-century Jews and discernable through ethnographic study. It is primarily *biblical.* According to Willard, there is a basic view of God and all things related to God *latent in the Hebrew Scriptures*, a basic view that Jesus's Galilean presence calls to mind and his gospel aims to say something new about.[21] The people who are capable of calling this biblical view to mind (the Jews) are precisely the people to whom Jesus comes and addresses his gospel. Hence, to say that the kingdom of God is biblical ontology is to say it is the ontology that one might find in the Hebrew Scriptures.

One *might* find it. Willard's crucial historical claim in New Testament exegesis is that mildly educated Jews of Jesus's day could find it and did find it. They were aware of the kingdom of God as biblical ontology.

20. Greek: ἤγγικεν, perfect, third-person singular of εγγιζω. Matt 3:2; 4:17; 10:7; Mark 1:15; Luke 10:9, 11.

21. The intertestamental literature is partly in conflict with this basic view, and this is one reason why Willard largely disregards it as Scripture.

First-century Jews were not so tainted by their own social setting and their elite members' interpretation of the Scriptures that they could not recall another, more pervasive ontology in their Scriptures. They could find it and did find it, as Willard will claim, *because* Jesus's life and ministry helped them find it. His Galilean ministry is the redemptive event that triggers their memory. Because of who he was and what he said to them, Jesus, through his spoken words, could invoke basic but likely forgotten teachings of the Scriptures and expect that *some* of his listeners would understand. Working with a particular philosophy of mind, Willard does not view the first listeners as "Kantians," critical realists, postmodernists, and so on who cannot get beyond their own or their culture's representations.

The Biblical Ontology of Ancient Israel

ACCORDING TO WILLARD, what is this biblical ontology accessible to mildly educated Jews and assumed in Jesus's gospel? There are four elements of it that need to be accounted for in this chapter: (1) God and his kingdom, (2) heaven, and (3) the prophets. Because of the fourth element's importance to the ministry of Jesus, this chapter will finish with (4) "the baptism of Moses." It must be separated from the others because Willard makes no attempt to say that a theory of this "baptism" lay at hand for Jesus's first listeners. In any case, it is something that is more caught than taught, as we will see.

As I expound on these, the question may arise: Where does Willard get this from? In short, he gets this from *his own study of the Old Testament*—a philosophical but no less exegetical-historical study assisted by others, *including* Jesus and the New Testament authors. In contrast to Wright, Willard is not claiming that the majority worldview of Second Temple Judaism should be assumed for the mildly educated individuals in that society and used a lens for studying the Scriptures. Rather, he is claiming that the Old Testament *clearly* communicates a surface-level ontology of (1) God and his kingdom, (2) heaven, and (3) the prophets and also that the Second Temple Jews, given their basic familiarity with the thirty-nine books' contents, could be brought to recall this Old Testament ontology without much fanfare.

In the Emmaus road periscope (Luke 24:13–35), Jesus appeals to "doctrines" latently present in the Scriptures to interpret contemporary events to Jews who had memorized or at least could recall the text and its stories. Just as Westerners, given their basic familiarity with the Star Wars saga or the Harry Potter series could, upon encountering them one afternoon, identify *real* persons or events that replicated the ontology of those worlds, so the Jews could do the same given their basic familiarity with the persons and events of their Scriptures. It matters little how firmly the Westerners believed in or lived according to the ontology of those literary worlds *before* they met the persons or events. It matters that they were *familiar enough* with the sources of that ontology that they could recognize Han Solo's spaceship or Harry Potter's owl if it appeared outside their window. This familiarity is what I am referring to when I speak of Jews being "mildly educated." It basically means that first-century Jews read their Bible.[22]

God and His Kingdom

THE FOUNDATION AND center of the Jews' biblical ontology was God. In this first section, we must explore how, for Willard, the doctrine of *the kingdom* of God was intertwined with the Jews' doctrine of God. For Willard, the inclusion of the kingdom of God into the Jews' central ontology follows from the Jewish experience of YHWH and YHWH's own self-revelation *as a person*. As explained in the previous chapter, Willard believes the Scriptures testify to and philosophy points to a God who is a self-sufficient, spiritual substance.[23] Personal, we will now see, is a large part of how Willard views spiritual. And "having a kingdom" is a large part of how he views personal.

---

22. Willard's 1974 characterization of "the Jews," as the term is used in Paul's Romans, is relevant here because it more or less expresses Willard's view until his passing in 2013: "You could think of [the Jews] simply as people who have a knowledge of the Bible, who have some indication that they have a vocation, a calling under God." Dallas Willard, "The Condition of Sin," *The Psychology of Redemption* (Woodlake Avenue Friends Church, Canoga Park, CA, April 21, 1974), MP3/cassette, 5:00.

23. More could be done in writing to show how substance is, for Willard, a biblical concept—not just a philosophical one. This would revolve around his exegesis of the word of God.

There Is No Knowledge of God's Kingdom without Knowledge of Self

MOVING IN REVERSE order, what is a kingdom? Politico-economic monarchies were everyday realities for first-century peoples. To alleviate the concept's foreignness for modern democratic peoples, Willard will occasionally translate the Greek βασιλεία as "the *government* of God." But more typically and effectively, he resorts to giving a description of kingdom rooted in experience. He is apt to say, as he does in *Conspiracy*, that a person's kingdom is the range of the person's effective will and that what a person genuinely has say over is in *their* kingdom.[24]

What Willard is doing with this description is approaching the reality of kingdom *phenomenologically*, which he understands as methodically, seeking to gain comprehension of some reality *by reflectively going into one's own experience*. Indeed, kingdom is the sort of reality, unlike atoms or dogs or star formations, that cannot be known without direct reflection on one's own experience.[25] For some, this may challenge the assumption that a kingdom is fundamentally what Charles Taylor calls a "social imaginary"—hence, a reality that can only be approached sociologically.[26] But Willard, a student of Husserl, holds that we may have reliable knowledge of *some* things through the careful methods of phenomenology. Through phenomenology, he finds knowledge of the human self, and from within that self-knowledge, he finds a reliable angle on kingdom as a universal reality. In short, he discovers that *he* has a kingdom and, as is typical of phenomenological claims to know, asks others to look into their own experience to discover and confirm that they too have a kingdom.

What we will discover, he claims, is that kingdoms are personal and, in their most basic construction, individual. I know what kingdoms are when I encounter them "in the real world" because I, as an

---

24. Willard, *Conspiracy*, 21.
25. Cf. Dallas Willard, "God in Himself—Part 2," *Life without Lack* (Valley Vista Christian Community, Sepulveda, CA, 1989), MP3/cassette, 13:45.
26. Charles Taylor, *Modern Social Imaginaries* (Durham, NC: Duke University Press, 2004), 23.

individual person, have a kingdom. For example, in dealing with a politico-economic monarchy, we all know what it means for the crown prince to have the kingdom he does by looking into our own experience of our own effective will. Such reflected, or even unreflected, experience allows us to appropriately approach the political monarchy with adequate knowledge of what it is.

The individual, personal nature of kingdoms ascertained through phenomenology explains why Willard treats his view of kingdom as *commonsense* knowledge. Willard assumes on this phenomenological basis that the first-century Jews, though they may have lacked a formal definition of kingdom, *knew* kingdoms as he describes them. It is the same basis on which he assumes that little children *know* kingdoms. A child's kingdom is an everyday reality for a child that she encounters as she learns to have say over more and more in her world or as she encounters areas over which she does not have say. Though a child has no word for the reality yet, a child knows what it is to have (and to not have) say over something. It is individual, personal experience of our own kingdom that gives us the knowledge to live adequately with respect to other persons—that is, other kingdoms, whether individual or corporate. We may lack a unified word for the general reality, but our experience, reflected or unreflected, helps us navigate the reality.

Just as the first-century individual's commonsense knowledge of their own effective will gives them the conceptual intensions necessary to recognize and understand the Roman emperor's effective will and to act accordingly, so too the same knowledge gives them the intensions to understand God's effective will. The progression does not work in the other direction. Humans are not given to understand the workings of God's kingdom or any others' before they understand their own. In 1993, Willard says,

> *Our closest approach to the understanding of the nature of God is through our knowledge of ourselves, on the one hand, and our knowledge of the created world and its source, on the other. I'm not telling you anything new. If you read Calvin's* Institutes, *you'll see he just lays it out. . . . Now, our*

> *Scriptures tell us in Romans 1 that everything that needs to be known about God can be known from observing the natural worlds. . . . We cannot by knowing ourselves know everything that we need to know about God. We will not know how great he is; we will not know how good he is. But we will be able to understand the fundamental spiritual nature of God by reflecting on ourselves. . . . But you, by reflecting on your experience, understand what spirit is. God is spirit, God is a person; he is personal.*[27]

Thus in *Conspiracy*'s chapter 1, Willard takes his readers through an analysis of *their* kingdom, both phenomenological and biblical, before describing *God's* kingdom. God's kingdom is described with the intensions hewn from his general analysis of human kingdoms.[28]

What is God's kingdom? It is "the range of his effective will, where what he wants done is done."[29] God's kingdom, as Willard says pithily, is *God in action*.[30] This may not be a definition that any first-century Jew would have uttered on the spot, but that is irrelevant to Willard. A mildly educated Jew knew that their God was a person with a kingdom, and that was the range of his effective will. Only after applying his phenomenologically hewn definition to God in *Conspiracy* does Willard show the biblical antiquity of Jesus's concept, especially in Psalms 145–50 and in Ezra, Nehemiah, and Daniel. In citing these biblical references, he expects them to be interpreted precisely as the Jews (when

---

27. Dallas Willard, "The Eternal Kind of Life Available in Christ," *Church Renewal Institute* (Bethel Theological Seminary West, San Diego, CA, February 22, 1993), MP3/cassette, 31:15. Regarding Calvin, Willard is referring to the first sections of the *Institutes*. Dallas Willard, "Spirituality and the Spirit," *Spirituality and Ministry* (Fuller Theological Seminary, Sierra Madre, CA, June 2012), DVD, 50:45. Willard also recognizes that human beings can only know what they are if they know what God is, especially his nonbodily nature. Only then can they know that they too are spirit (cf. Dallas Willard, "Trust & Obey: The Teachings of Jesus," *Learning to Live an Eternal Life Now* [Ojai Valley Community Church, Ojai, CA, May 3, 1994], MP3/cassette, 3:00).

28. *Intension* is a term that stems from Edmund Husserl.

29. Willard, *Conspiracy*, 25.

30. See, for example, Willard, "What Is 'Ministry'?," 39:45.

not under the influence of "sophisticated" theories) understood any reference to reigning—that is, through a commonsense phenomenology of which any child is capable.

Kingdoms and Persons

A more familiar theological way of putting Willard's point about God having a kingdom is to say that the Jews believed in a *personal God*.[31] This, in fact, is what Willard is teaching. But he is teaching it in a way that pulls in the biblical language of *kingdom* and *reign* and *dominion*.

"The great genius of the Jewish religion," Willard says, "is its revelation of a personal God."[32] When addressing Jesus's answers to the first of the "Four Great Questions," Willard writes, "In the language of technical philosophy, Jesus was a 'Personalist.'"[33] In this, Jesus was no different from the Jews before him. Over many years of struggle, the Jews were learning to not associate YHWH with the gods of their neighbors. The latter, characterized as mere idols, are not personal and, insofar as they have any power at all, represent a power that one may use. By contrast, YHWH is characterized by personal power—that is, "a power that consists of thoughts and feelings and choices and acts by means of them. That means our relationship to this power is one where we have to respect their personality."[34] Although *personality* is more familiar theological language, useful in comparison with the impersonalistic philosophies of Spinoza and Hegel, it is actually less familiar biblical language than *kingdom*.

---

31. The personality of God is a central piece of Willard's doctrine of God, as it has traditionally been in history. If we were treating it fully, then space should be given to his evidential argument for God in which he explains why we must attribute will and mind (attributes of persons) to the yet unidentified causal source of the universe (see Willard, *Knowing*, 110–11).

32. Willard, "Fundamental Issues," 32:45.

33. Willard, *Knowing*, 50. Willard, if it is not clear, has in mind Personalism as a philosophical movement in the nineteenth and early twentieth century, associated with names like Hermann Lotze, Josiah Royce, Edgar Brightman, and Borden Parker Bowne, all of whom, along with many others, were studied carefully by Willard.

34. Dallas Willard, "The Centrality and Vitality of the Pastor," *Ministering the Kingdom of God with Christ Today* (Association of Vineyard Churches, Cape Town, South Africa, August 2, 2000), MP3/cassette, 22:00.

What's more, Willard aims in his analysis to say something about the personality of God that may be overlooked by contemporary theologians. Our contemporary notions of personality involve thought (i.e., some form of interiority) and communication (i.e., the ability to relate to other persons).[35] It may even include a vague notion of will, or the ability to make decisions. But Willard calls to attention *rule* in personality. A *person* has a faculty not only of assent but also of *effective* will. A *person* has an arena where their will is done and done immediately.[36] Willard puts it this way in *Conspiracy*: "Any being that has say over nothing at all is no person."[37] No person! Notice that this statement applies to human beings as well as to God. God is being described as a person not in virtue of the three "persons" of the Trinity but in virtue of being a being, united in the Godhead, who has a kingdom.

On the human level, having a kingdom (or dominion) is what it means for humans to be created, says Willard again and again, *in the image of God.* Willard routinely turns to Genesis 1:26–28 to teach that humans were made like God by being given dominion or, as he will sometimes translate it, "responsibility." There is a back-and-forth in his interpretation of kingdom in Genesis and throughout the Bible. Our own experiences of our kingdom (phenomenology) help us understand the ancient revelation that God has a kingdom. In turn, the ancient revelation of God having a kingdom—and a quite fundamental and powerful one, as we will see—helps us understand what it means for *us*

35. One thinks here particularly of the dialectical Personalism of Martin Buber. But philosophically, Willard sees much more Judeo-Christian Personalism in Immanuel Kant, and he even footnotes Kant in *Renovation*'s chapter on the will. For more on Kant and his "realm of ends," see also Dallas Willard, "The Spiritual Kingdom of God," *Spirituality and Ministry* (Fuller Theological Seminary, Sierra Madre, CA, June 10, 2002), MP3, 24:30.

36. However, distinguishing himself from some "Arminian" and humanist conceptions, Willard makes an important distinction between the divine and the human wills, saying, "God is absolutely free. We are not absolutely free. But still we do choose" (Dallas Willard, "The Things That Are Above: The Present Presence of the Kingdom of God," *Hearing the Voice of God* [African Enterprise, Pietermaritzburg, South Africa, August 16, 1993], MP3/cassette, 42:15).

37. Willard, *Conspiracy*, 22.

to be beings with dominion whose small kingdoms are derived in our creation from his grand kingdom.[38]

In order to see the point more clearly, one might consider the case of angels. In 1988, Willard made this comment: "An angel is not made in the image of God. Did you know that? . . . And the reason they're not made in the image of God is they don't have a body. . . . You see, the reason that man is in the image of God is because God gave him a body, and that gave him a measure of independent power with which to act. Satan and none of the angels have independent power with which to act. They act in the power that God gives to them. They have a constant dependence upon God, which we don't have."[39] The body is the central part of any human being's dominion. It is the place where a person may act immediately.[40] The gist of the quote

---

38. Willard's reading of the Bible's metaphysics of kingdom and words has much in common with Husserl's philosophy of consciousness and ego—that is, of persons. The clearest example of this is found in Husserl's *The Crisis of European Sciences* §28, where he speaks of *Walten* with respect to the ego's relation to a—indeed, *his*—body. Husserl points out that "the living body is constantly in the perceptual field quite immediately, that through which I exist in a completely unique way and quite immediately as the ego of affection and actions, in which I hold sway [*walte*] quite immediately" (Edmund Husserl, *The Crisis of European Sciences and Transcendental Phenomenology* [Evanston, IL: Northwestern University Press, 1970], 107). Husserl's anthropological insight is identical with what Willard holds to be the primary realm of the human kingdom: the body. "There is one domain," Willard writes, "where the human mind but 'speaks' and it is done. That realm is in the voluntary motions of the body—of the hands, the feet, the face—and over wide ranges of our inward thoughts themselves" (Willard, *Guidance*, 129). There is no Malebranchean occasionalism here. A person's body—in more limited senses for the physically handicapped and the wicked and in more free senses for great athletes, painters, and indeed, saints—is where a person may speak and cause immediate results.

39. Dallas Willard, "The Kingdom of Evil on Earth," *Soul's Eternal Anchor*, MP3/ cassette, 13:00.

40. Willard, *Guidance*, 129. Willard will actually restrict this even more, saying that the very first place of a human being's dominion is in their thoughts—choosing to think about this rather than that. This Willard calls our first freedom. It is an insight that Willard shares with Husserl (Willard, *Renovation*, 95). It should be clarified that speaking in these cases of kingdom does not entail the use of language. In Willard's philosophy of mind, not even thinking requires the use of language (see Willard, "Absurdity of Thinking in Language"). Language could, however, if rich enough, express the command given to the body or mind.

is that angels would be persons if they had this one property that God and human beings do have—namely, the possession of a place where what they want done is *immediately* done. By contrast, angels live in "a constant dependence upon God." They may have a vague sense of will in an ability to assent or not assent to God's directives, but they have been given no power to act independently of God.

In summary, the exegetical-historical argument that Willard is making is that the Jews were long aware that they were dealing with a being who acted independently, and this state of affairs constituted what they came to describe as YHWH's reign and what modern theologians describe as the "personality" of Israel's God. Ancient Jews apprehended this much in the same way that we, so Willard, must apprehend it—namely, phenomenologically. Regardless of whether YHWH (1) verbally announces his personality to Israel or (2) merely acts as a person, the Israelites were required to make use of their own experience as persons to arrive at the intensions of the concept *person*. These intensions—that is, "the properties a thing must have in order to fall under [the concept]"—are (a) what YHWH may presume upon when introducing himself as an extension of the concept *person* or (b) what help the Israelites recognize by their observation of YHWH in his self-revelation that he too is a person like they.[41]

What Is the Length and the Breadth . . .

from this homely, phenomenological starting point, the grandeur of YHWH's personality, or his *sovereignty*, can be gradually apprehended by the Jews and by us. What is the extent of God's kingdom, its length and breadth? This is a place where Willard's soft Calvinism shines through. As early as 1978, he says, "I wish to stress this fact that God has a kingdom, that he is king over all of this earth, that there is not one bit of it that is not beyond his direction in some measure and ultimately."[42]

41. Willard, "How Concepts Relate the Mind to Its Objects," 9.

42. Dallas Willard, "Presence of the Kingdom of God," *The Kingdom of God* (Faith Evangelical Church, Chatsworth, CA, April 2, 1978), MP3/cassette, 13:30; cf. Willard, *Conspiracy*, 25–26.

This, he believes, is what the Old Testament (as a whole) teaches about God's reign. Because of this, the Jewish people needed no repetition of it from Jesus. Willard would work through passages like Isaiah 52 or Psalm 145 in his lectures to make his point. Above all, he recommended that his listeners study the Psalms should they be in doubt about whether the Jews knew about the kingdom's existence or thought of it in highly restricted terms.[43]

The sovereignty of God's kingdom "over all of this earth" is not reason, explains Willard, to assume that all that is done on earth proceeds from God's effective will. As we will see in the next section, it took the exile for the Jews to learn existentially that God and his kingdom were self-sufficient *apart from* them and their political rule, perfectly capable of existing without them. "They did not know the kingdom of God," says Willard, "until they had been ground to pieces in their efforts to be a political unity and nation had been crushed by the Babylonians and spit out on the banks of the Euphrates."[44]

But for Willard, the opposite is also true. The Jewish monarchy was a human project that God permitted to function independently of himself, if the king and those responsible so chose. For those who use the evil of these all-too-human circumstances to insist that God is not ruling on earth, Willard points, as he does in *Conspiracy*, to "the fact that *other* 'kingdoms' are still present on earth."[45] Other kingdoms do not compromise the sovereignty of God, he believes, saying on one occasion, "We pray 'Thy kingdom come, thy will be done on earth as it is in heaven.' That acknowledges that there is some place where God's will is not done. That acknowledges that there is something outside of the will of God. Now, if you're worried immediately about the sovereignty of God, just understand that it is God's sovereignty that allows that. God has permitted certain beings to be outside of his effective will. He gives

43. See, e.g., Dallas Willard, "The Saving Message: Life in the Kingdom of God Now through Confidence in Jesus," *Bringing Christ to the World of the 21st Century* (Northfield Methodist Church, Benoni, South Africa, July 25, 2000), MP3/cassette, 19:00.
44. Dallas Willard, "Life in the Kingdom 1," *Atlanta Cohort—Session One* (Renovaré Institute, Atlanta, GA, October 12, 2011), MP3, 2:30.
45. Willard, *Conspiracy*, 29.

them the choice of being within his effective will."[46] The personhood of human beings—that is, their being made in the image of God to have dominion—is an indispensable part of God's perfect plan for his creation, and he *in his sovereignty* has made a provision for that.

The grandeur of God's kingdom, Willard will argue, is not only one of extensive range. It is also one of enduring existence. As already noted, Willard had very little time for New Testament theologies that contemplated how God or Jesus went about establishing the kingdom of God through Jesus's earthly lifetime. In 2000 in South Africa, he said, "There is so much scholarly ignorance about all of this that it is shocking. You find very distinguished scholars suggesting that Jesus actually brought the kingdom of God into existence. He didn't even think of doing such a thing. The kingdom of God has actually existed from everlasting to everlasting. Because the kingdom of God is nothing but the reign of God. And God has always been reigning. And he always will."[47] Though Willard never took any particular scholar to task for disagreeing with him, Willard repeated this point often in his speaking.[48] On one other occasion, he said, "The kingdom of heaven has been around as long as God has been around. It's not going anywhere."[49]

How, then, does Willard argue for the enduring existence of the kingdom? There are three crucial points to mention. First of all, he argues that within the created order, especially within the history of Israel, the

---

46. Unfortunately, I have lost the reference for this quote from one of more than 1,200 audio recordings.

47. Willard, "Saving Message," 18:00.

48. Cf. Willard, *Conspiracy*, 26, 31. In 2002, Willard glossed Jesus's gospel, "'Repent, for the kingdom of heaven is at hand.' He doesn't bring it into existence. The kingdom of God, the kingdom of heaven, has always existed because it is God's kingdom. It will never not exist. It has never been in trouble. But it has not always been available to human beings. It especially had not been available to human beings generally in the way that it became available through the person of Christ" (Willard, "Reality, Spirituality and the Gospel," 43:30). In the same year, he said, "The kingdom is from everlasting to everlasting, never came into existence and will never end." Dallas Willard, "Ultimate Reality and the Kingdom of God," *The Realism of the Kingdom of God for Life Today* (Living Waters, London, UK, May 24, 2002), MP3, 23:00.

49. Dallas Willard, "Your Kingdom and God's Kingdom," *Living the Eternal Life Now* (Church of the Apostles, Fairfax, VA, February 19, 2010), MP3, 11:30.

kingdom of God has long been an active reality. To get this from the Scriptures, Willard (or a first-century Jew) must distinguish the term from the reality, leaving out explicit passages like Isaiah 52 and Psalm 145 and finding testimony to the kingdom in expressions of its essential properties—above all, in God's action with people. Willard calls this the Immanuel Principle and connects it especially to the common Old Testament refrain "God was with X."[50] This is a statement not of God's omnipresence but of his readiness to act on behalf of the person or group in question. More will be said about the Immanuel Principle later (chapter 11), for it is a key part of Willard's thesis—however, much of it conflicts with the "sophisticated" first-century view—that the kingdom of God was an important part of the Jewish experience long before the term was coined.

The second crucial point is the long-standing connection between God's rule and his creation and providence. Willard's exegesis of this point is perhaps less within the immediate grasp of the first-century Jews, so we will turn to it later in chapter 11. Suffice it to say, the exegesis works with a metaphysics of the word of God and with the revelation that YHWH creates and sustains his creation *by his word*. Once Willard discovers a connection between the kingdom of God and the word of God, he is again off to the exegetical races, seeking kingdom reality apart from kingdom terms.

However, some of this long-standing connection between kingdom and creation is derived, for Willard, from commonsense philosophy. The Jewish experience of YHWH as a personal God (understood on the basis of commonsense phenomenology of kingdom and personhood) naturally raises the question of his rule over the material universe and of his role in that universe's origin. The Jews witnessed their God's power over natural events (be it miracles or natural events; e.g., Ps 147), and

50. See Richard J. Foster et al., eds., *The Renovaré Spiritual Formation Bible* (San Francisco: HarperSanFrancisco, 2005), xxvii. This introduction was a group effort, though Willard was responsible for drafting this section on "Catching the Vision," and the theology is thoroughly his. Later editions of this *Bible* are more commonly known as *The Life with God Bible*, as I will refer to it in the text. For historical purposes, I provide references to the first edition published in 2005.

their experience of YHWH's microrule in nature was the most tangible evidence they (or anyone) had for a theory of YHWH's macrorule—that is, that God's kingdom included *all* of the material universe. This line of armchair philosophical reflection does not detract from any divine revelation to the effect that YHWH is the creator and sustainer of the whole world. But the evidence that the Jews had that their God was a person like them and acted immediately in the realm of material objects was genuine intellectual fodder for the Jewish doctrine of creation and providence—that is, that YHWH's personhood included general rule over the material realm. More of Willard's philosophical-exegetical reflection on this point can be found in *Guidance*, chapter 6.[51]

Willard's association of the kingdom of God with heaven—that is, the unseen spiritual realm and the topic we will turn to next—could actually be confusing for listeners trying to understand his comprehensive view. One audience member asked if Willard equated the spiritual world with the kingdom of God, to which Willard responded, "There is a lot of God's kingdom that is created, so you have to distinguish the parts that are created from the parts that are not. Actually, nature is a part of God's kingdom."[52] In emphasizing nature, Willard seems to be forgetting the possibility of created members of the spiritual world such as angels. We will presently see that they are not forgotten.

The third point of Willard's argument was in all likelihood *not* readily at hand in the first-century knowledge of the Scriptures. However, it is unavoidable for those reading the Bible as ontologists and thus important for Willard's own view and worth mentioning here. It concerns the nature of the kingdom *before* creation. In *Conspiracy*, Willard writes, "God's kingdom has existed from the moment of creation and will never end (Ps. 145:13; Dan. 7:14)."[53] This could be read as if the kingdom began with creation, and this would fit with Willard's statement that being a person is about having a place where one's will

51. Willard, *Guidance*, 124–31.

52. Willard, "Salvation in Christ Is a Life," 10:15; cf. Dallas Willard, "Q & A: Knowledge & Will," *Divine Conspiracy*, MP3/video, 21:00.

53. Willard, *Conspiracy*, 25.

is immediately done. For humans, this, says Willard, is their body. For YHWH, is it not his creation? As one senior theologian put it to me once, "*Reigning* seems to be a transitive verb. How can one speak of God reigning without naming a realm (e.g., the created universe) over which he reigns?"

Willard resists this plausible line of reasoning and opts for another, indicated later in *Conspiracy*, when he writes, "But time is within eternity, not outside it. The created universe is within the kingdom of God, not outside it."[54] What Willard is referring to here is his view that "the kingdom of God is from everlasting to everlasting. . . . There was a kingdom of God before the world was created."[55] Exegetically, the point is simple. Apart from God himself, only the kingdom of God is described in the Scriptures with such sweeping properties of enduring existence.

Philosophically, the point is more subtly developed. Once anyone, ancient or modern, has accepted the previous biblical point that creation, visible and invisible, is an act of the kingdom of God or of "the word of God," to use Scriptural language (Heb 11:3), that person must develop an ontology of the kingdom that gives it chronological and logical priority over creation, or what theologians call the economy. For Willard, this ontology is easily derived from the personalist ontology of the Scriptures and refined through reflected or unreflected phenomenology. God *is* the sort of being that has a kingdom and always has been.[56]

Now, Willard was thorough enough as a metaphysician to have a theory on the nature of the kingdom with respect to God *in se*. But he was rarely teaching in situations where audiences were asking such questions.[57] On one occasion, Willard said, "God's kingdom is his effective

54. Willard, 392.

55. Willard, "Q & A: Knowledge & Will," 21:45.

56. There is loophole in this reasoning if one goes the route of antisubstantialist philosophy, such as in process theology, as well as weaker forms, such as in the biblical theology school and the theology of Karl Barth and many who have followed (cf. chapter 3). Willard, however, affirms substance theory.

57. The doctrine of God *in se* is fairly standard to Christian thought before the rise of modern theology, especially in German-speaking Europe.

care *over his own person* and over his creation."[58] Lest this be misunderstood, Willard said in a lecture already cited, "And of course, God is a part of God's kingdom only in a kind of extended sense. He's the one that has the kingdom. . . . Obviously, God is a part of his own kingdom, but he's the ruling part and not the ruled part."[59]

Knowing that more evidence may one day be found, I am cautious about engaging in too much speculation on this point. I submit the following, therefore, as my working hypothesis: Willard's ontological theory regarding the scriptural testimony to God and his kingdom seems to identify God's kingdom with God's eternal attributes of power, especially his *free* and *immediate* power. (We will see immediacy come up again later in chapter 11 in a section on "The Faith of God.") This fits with Willard's account of divine omnipotence, which, as Willard will say, is a doctrine that says not that God is doing everything but that he can do everything.[60] In other words, biblical talk of the kingdom of God before the foundation of the world refers to the infinite potentiality of God or to his eternal sovereignty. The kingdom, ultimately, is not an event in the infinite life of God but how he eternally is.[61]

Regardless of how those hairs are split, the kingdom of God, in terms of placement in a systematic theology arranged on the order of being, comes first for Willard. The creation of the heavens and the earth, all things visible and invisible, comes after, for it was the independent act of a being whose will was effectively done. If YHWH were no king and

---

58. Dallas Willard, "Bringing the Kingdom into Our Life," *Training for Reigning* (Benoni Central Methodist Church, Benoni, South Africa, August 12, 1993), MP3/cassette, 48:00 (emphasis mine).

59. Willard, "Salvation in Christ Is a Life," 10:15.

60. See, e.g., Dallas Willard, "'Routine' Hearing of God: How It Works as Part of Life," *Atlanta Cohort—Session Two* (Renovaré Institute, Atlanta, GA, March 2012), MP3.

61. If I am correct, it would be biographically helpful to learn when and how Willard combined this traditional doctrine of God with the New Testament witness to the kingdom of God. The only person I have discovered who comes close to having the same hermeneutic is E. Stanley Jones, though, it seems, without the elements of scholastic and patristic theology evident in Willard's view (e.g., E. Stanley Jones, *Victorious Living* [Nashville: Abingdon, 1938]; and Jones, *Kingdom of God*). Given what Jones says about the doctrine of God and the kingdom of God, I doubt, however, that Jones was the starting point for Willard's view.

had no kingdom, he would not only be no person; he would not have created the universe as the Jews understood it to be created. Namely, he would not have created it out of his own rational and good will.

In summary, the Jewish conception of the grandeur of God's kingdom, its extensive range and enduring existence, grew up with the ancient Jewish conception of their God. This may or may not have been part of the "sophisticated" view of the kingdom in the first century. But this is not relevant to Willard's exegetical argument. He relies on its being a part of the scriptural testimony "as a whole" and thus being readily accessible to persons with basic familiarity with that testimony. What should be clear at the end of this subsection on "God and His Kingdom" is that, in Willard's view, the mildly educated Jews, upon hearing about the kingdom of God, had the mental resources to think of God, *their God*, as an eternal person (i.e., one having independent rule) and as one who created and ruled over *all things*.[62] "The kingdom of God was very old news by the time Jesus got there," says Willard. "It had been worked out in the bloody history of the Jews."[63]

Willard's historical claims aside, his own view is that the kingdom of God is an extremely basic part of reality, referring ultimately to something about God himself, who is personal, sovereign, and eternal. "The kingdom of God" is not language for something God does or is only within the economy subsequent to the act of creation. The kingdom of God is ultimately, but not exclusively, theology proper. This point must be remembered when encountering some of Willard's descriptions of God's kingdom, for in his eagerness to present the gospel of *the availability* of the kingdom with rhetorical effect, he sometimes uses language that can be read otherwise. This must also be remembered because most if not all of the most enthusiastic spokespersons and

62. If this sounds historically implausible to us, it may only be a sign of how we have allowed theology to be absorbed into Christology and then "an absorption of Christology into soteriology" (Willard, *Conspiracy*, 403n8). This is a progression that would have been less likely for first-century Jews (despite their preoccupation with eschatology).

63. Willard, "Life in the Kingdom 1," 2:30.

scholars on the kingdom of God in the last two centuries do not share this philosophical-exegetical point with Willard.

Heaven

ALONG WITH THE first listeners' personal, regnal view of God, something else in the biblical ontology of ancient Israel prepared the way for their understanding of Jesus's gospel. Willard returns again and again in his teaching to a particular part of the historically formed Jewish cosmology—namely, *heaven*. The concept is ancient in the Jewish history and becomes shorthand, in Willard's mind, for the gospel to Abraham's children, to those who participated in "the Jewish experience."[64]

THE LESSON OF METAPHYSICS

HERE WE MUST be careful. To keep from muddying the waters, we must begin with some metaphysical distinctions before building up to the basic view of heaven that mildly educated Jews were well equipped to glean from their Scriptures.

The Old Testament testifies, in Willard's view, that the center of all reality is a self-sufficient person, spiritual in substance, who created all things in heaven and on earth. The Old Testament also testifies to a God who inhabits and acts "from surrounding space, the atmosphere—that is, from the 'first heaven.'"[65] As readers, we will not get far with Willard if we do not carefully distinguish between (1) an *immanent*, or eternal,

---

64. In terms of sources, the tip of the iceberg is a few pages on heaven in the third chapter of Willard, *Conspiracy*, 66–74. But the real bulk is found in older audio recordings from Willard's lectures. Two are of particular note: (1) A weighty eight-part series entitled *The Soul's Eternal Anchor* from 1988 introduces his doctrine of heaven in the early sessions in a way that frames and informs the whole curriculum. (2) Another eight-part series from 1990 at Hollywood Presbyterian begins much in the same way before turning to an exposition of the Sermon on the Mount and a few other topics. In the latter, Willard says, "Indeed one of the things that you can gain the most from so far as this series is concerned is to think very deeply and to study carefully what the Bible says about heaven" (Dallas Willard, "The Meaning of the Rule of Heaven," *A Series on What Jesus Believed and Taught—and Lived* [First Hollywood Presbyterian Church, Hollywood, CA, February 11, 1990], MP3/cassette, 25:15).

65. Willard, *Conspiracy*, 48.

kingdom of God and (2) an *economic* kingdom, which is the expression of the former.

The immanent kingdom in Willard's thought is the kingdom of God *as basic to God in himself*—to God as an eternal, self-sufficient, spiritual substance, a *person* of effective will, who before creation was, as Willard would wryly say, "enjoying themselves."[66] The economic kingdom is the kingdom, the endless energy of God, *as it is effective in cosmic space and history.* The economic kingdom, one could say, is the sum of God's action with respect to the creation of heaven and earth and its redemption in history and everything beyond that.[67] On the most ultimate level, it is uniquely sovereign over the economy: "There is not one bit of it that is not beyond his direction in some measure and ultimately."[68] Together, the immanent and economic sides of God's kingdom constitute the Old Testament's *metaphysical* doctrine of God's kingdom. And without a doubt, this metaphysics of the kingdom is only adequately understood with the help of divine revelation and logical reasoning. Experience alone, Jewish or not, is insufficient.

But Willard believes the Old Testament also testifies to the manifest kingdom. The doctrine of God's manifest kingdom refers to the phenomenal, though not necessarily sense perceptible, expression of the kingdom. It is the kingdom of God as it interacts with individuals and groups directly, allowing for their knowledge of it *by acquaintance.*

This metaphysical/manifest distinction in Willard can be illustrated by means of his view of the presence of God. In the message "How God Is with Us," Willard says,

> *There are two ways that God might be with us. One we might call the metaphysical way, omnipresence.* Of course *God is*

66. Dallas Willard, "Beyond Personality: A Celebration of Mere Christianity, Part IV," *C. S. Lewis Summer Conference: A Celebration of Mere Christianity* (University of San Diego, San Diego, CA, June 21, 2003), MP3, 40:45.
67. Cf. Willard, *Conspiracy* 32–33, where Willard plays with the Greek word for "house" (οἶκος) and the English cognates, of which *economic* is one.
68. Willard, "Presence of the Kingdom," 13:30.

> *with us. "In him we live and move and have our being," as Paul says. So what's the fuss about?*
>
> *The problem is, you might not know it. He's with you, but he's not actively engaged with you. So we need to recognize the other form of being with us, which is manifest personal presence. It isn't just an arrangement. It isn't just a metaphysical fact. God's being with us is an ongoing interactive relationship.*[69]

For participants in the Jewish experience, the kingdom of God was not merely a metaphysical reality that they had knowledge of on the basis of God's authoritative revelation and their logical, even phenomenological reasoning. A great deal of their historically formed knowledge of the kingdom was based on its manifest reality. And the cosmographic location of the kingdom of God's manifestation to them was *heaven*.

The Lesson of Experience

IN *CONSPIRACY*, WILLARD makes heavy theological use of the fact that in Matthew, "the kingdom *of the heavens*" (e.g., 3:2) can be substituted for "the kingdom of God." Matthew's choice of words is not only first-century Jewish literary taste, he says, but points to the cosmology with which the whole Jewish nation had become accustomed. The heavens are not included in the phrase as the agent of the kingdom. The kingdom is God's kingdom. Nor are they included as the realm of the kingdom, though they are that as well. The heavens are a chiastic substitute for God because they are, in light of the Jewish experience of God,

---

69. Dallas Willard, "How Is God with Us? How Can We Know It?," *Faith-Learning Seminar* (Westmont College, Santa Barbara, CA, May 26, 2011), MP3, 12:30. See also Dallas Willard, "No Longer Alone with God as Jesus in the Eternal Kingdom—Now: The With-God Life under the New Covenant," *The With-God Life: The Dynamics of Scripture for Christian Spiritual TransFormation* (Renovaré International Conference / Spiritual Formation Forum, Denver, CO, June 20, 2005), MP3, 4:30; and Dallas Willard, "Coming to Terms with Christians Who Are Not Disciples," *The Magnificence of Ministry—Your Ministry!* (Baylor University / George W. Truett Theological Seminary, Waco, TX, January 30, 2009), MP3, 42:30. This is the exact same distinction and language Tozer uses in *Pursuit of God*, 32–33.

the seat of God's *manifest* presence and actions. Just as Moscow or London may be rhetorically substituted for the persons in government who reside and govern there, Willard notes that the heavens were recognized by the covenant people as the phenomenal residence of the government of God.[70] He says, "The very fact that *heaven* could be used loosely to refer to God at all is deeply instructive of how God relates to us, once you realize what 'the heavens' are."[71]

In many places, Willard explains why he prefers a literal plural English translation of οὐρανοι.[72] He uses it as an occasion to teach about the ancient Hebrew view that multiple realms of the created universe were labeled "heaven," and he recounts the three-part division as follows: The first heaven (*coelum nubiferum*) is the heaven of the air, the birds, and the clouds. The second heaven (*coelum astriferum*) is the realm of the stars and the planets. The third heaven (*coelum angeliferum*) is the realm of the angels and God's "throne."[73] His main pastoral aim in airing out this ancient cosmography is to show his contemporaries that heaven for the Hebrews called to mind not a fuzzy, remote location "away off" and "beyond the moon" but something familiar and near. Numbering them may give the impression that, since the second heaven is farther out than the first, the third heaven of God and his angels is farther out than all the stars and planets. But this is contrary, at least, to what Willard himself holds and what, according to him, the

70. Dallas Willard, "An Easy Way into a Life of Constant Prayer 2," *Prayer* (Valley Vista Christian Community, Sepulveda, CA, May 18, 1986), MP3/cassette, 25:00. Willard further emphasizes that heaven suggests "immediate access" to the kingdom.
71. Willard, *Conspiracy*, 74.
72. Dallas Willard, "Beyond the Righteousness of the Scribes and Pharisees—Part 1," *A Series on What Jesus Believed and Taught—and Lived* (First Hollywood Presbyterian Church, Hollywood, CA, March 4, 1990), MP3/cassette, 6:45.
73. Dallas Willard, "Handout for 'The Soul's Eternal Anchor,'" (Rolling Hills Covenant Church, Rolling Hills, CA, 1988), Dallas Willard Collection, 2; cf. Willard, *Conspiracy*, 405n5, where he provides the reference to the encyclopedia (John McClintock and James Strong, eds., *Cyclopaedia of Biblical, Theological, and Ecclesiastical Literature* [New York: Harper & Brothers, 1894], 3:903–4) from which he most likely found the names and information about the threefold view of heaven.

Jews knew through experience.[74] What they knew through experience was that the first, the *closest* heaven was the place where they would meet the inhabitants of the third heaven, God and his angels, and experience their action.[75] The third heaven is not spatial in essence.[76]

What Willard is arguing for here is an ontology of heaven that is decidedly dualist and nonnaturalist. The "third heaven," whatever other properties it may have, is an invisible and non-sense-perceptible counterpart to the visible and sense-perceptible atmosphere surrounding the earth (the first heaven) and the solar system and beyond (the second heaven). Thus, there are two "orders" (Willard's word) to God's creation, one that is largely sense perceptible and one that is not.[77] The first is the order researched by natural scientists and comprising the "life-world" of all humans. The second is the order that may indefinitely hide itself from any human.[78] A veil, as Willard understands from Hebrews 6:19, normally separates this heaven, this order, from the consciousness of humans.[79] But in key moments of Jewish history or an

74. Dallas Willard, "Exploring the Basic Concepts," *Becoming Transmitters of God's Life and Power* (Kempton Park Methodist Church, Kempton Park, South Africa, August 7, 1987), MP3/cassette, 50:00.

75. Cf. Willard, "Recovering the Gospel," 35:15.

76. Dallas Willard, "The Kingdom of Heaven," *Kingdom Living Today* (Kempton Park Methodist Church / Bedfordview Methodist Church, Kempton Park, South Africa, August 17, 1987), MP3/cassette, 21:00.

77. Cf. Dallas Willard, "Pastoral Ministry and the Spiritual Disciplines," *Spiritual Resources for Pastoral Ministry* (Kempton Park Methodist Church, Kempton Park, South Africa, August 12, 1987), MP3/cassette, 34:30; and Willard, "Salvation in Christ Is a Life," 10:15.

78. It is difficult to know *where* he would put entities like universals or other things that Husserl called ideal being. Contra Plato, they are not the inhabitants of heaven because Willard does not hold that they hide themselves from human consciousness.

79. He calls these "landscapes" in Dallas Willard, "Living Eternally in the Moment," *Westmont Commencements* (Westmont College, Santa Barbara, CA, May 7, 2011), MP3/video, 7:00. It is a little difficult to place humans themselves in this division of Willard's. As he admits, humans (excluding their bodies) as well as many other familiar entities are not sense perceptible. These non-sense-perceptible entities are not "behind the veil" and are regularly researched by those for whom the veil has never parted. Willard here is making not a dualist (i.e., nonnaturalist) distinction but a finer distinction between heaven and the rest of creation. Given this distinction, it is possible to have a vivid nonnaturalist view of reality but still be ignorant of the biblical reality of heaven.

individual's history, the veil parted, the heavens opened, and humans were able to see what had been there all along.[80]

In Willard's typical manner of reviewing this point, he covers passages such as Jacob's dream (Gen 28:10–22) or Elisha's vision of horses and chariots of fire (2 Kgs 6:8–23) to show the breadth of this experience in the Scriptures and its fundamentality in the Jewish cosmology. "The idea that God is God of the 'heavens'—that is, of the surrounding atmosphere—is a primary part of the revelation of Jehovah to His select people, from Abraham on," he writes.[81] Angels are an important piece of this order because the manifest presence of angels confirms the invisible order's reality just as much as the manifest presence and action of God. In a manner of speaking, the angels *live there* in a way that God does not. What's more, Satan lives in or at least has access to heaven (cf. Job 1:6–12). He is the prince of the first heaven—that is, "the prince of the power of the air" (Eph 2:2).[82]

Over time, it was the invisible and non-sense-perceptible order of created reality that earned the right of way when the word *heaven* is uttered. The English language readily affords this right of way because of the prevalence of other words that cover the sense-perceptible order—*sky, atmosphere, outer space*. But this simplicity can restrict the English speaker in recognizing the "overlap" between the visible heaven and the invisible heaven that Willard thinks was routine for the ancient Hebrews.

That this "overlap" ought to continue to be routine for moderns is the burden of Willard's discussion of heaven in *Conspiracy*. He collects stories of Hagar, Abraham, Jacob, and Moses to show that the familiar, visible heaven or atmosphere of planet earth was the space-time location out of which the invisible heaven of the angels and God broke through and showed itself: "It is precisely from the space immediately

80. The concept of a veil is very important for Willard's understanding of revelation and human sin. See, e.g., Dallas Willard, "The People of God into Eternity," in Foster et al., *Renovaré Spiritual Formation Bible*, 2259.

81. Willard, "Gospel of the Kingdom," 34.

82. Dallas Willard, "Why Such Lack and Evil?," *Life without Lack* (Valley Vista Christian Community, Sepulveda, CA, February 26, 1989), MP3/cassette, 4:00.

around us that God watches and God acts."[83] The concept of heaven as a non-sense-perceptible but created order commandeers, as it were, the Hebrew word for "atmosphere" (שמים). And not without some justification, argues Willard. The atmosphere *is* where that other order is to be expected.

Now in Willard's writing and speaking, heaven often will serve as rhetorical shorthand for the kingdom of God, despite the two being fundamentally different entities.[84] Even if we restrict ourselves to the manifest kingdom of God, heaven is no more than *its tent*. Heaven is a finite reality that itself would not stay in existence if it were not for God's sovereign eternal kingdom. Nevertheless, as the tent, it may symbolize that which inhabits it and is much greater than it.

One can see how Willard's theology of heaven as the kingdom's tent was shaped by Hebrews. Though, to my knowledge, we have from Willard no comprehensive exegesis of Hebrews, he had a very high regard for its theology, saying, "The book of Hebrews is the most exalted presentation of the life of the believer drawn from the kingdom of heaven."[85] In detail, the book's notion of heaven as the more perfect institution of what the Jewish temple institution was while the latter still stood seems to be the biblical cosmology Willard is conveying to his audiences. Throughout all history, God manifests himself in heaven as he more familiarly manifested himself for a time in Israel's tabernacle and two temples. But the true temple or tent in the economy of God was always the invisible heaven behind the veil.[86] If this comparison is accurate, then, on Willard's reading of the Old Testament, the author of Hebrews is not publishing new revelations. His cosmology and gospel of the kingdom are very old. Again, "the idea that God is God of the

83. Willard, *Conspiracy*, 68.

84. There is an important theological reason for this that cannot be dealt with in this book. Suffice it to say, the obedience to God's rule, which occurs in heaven and in the "invisible" body of Christ (the church), means that these created realms come to represent the kingdom of God/heaven.

85. Dallas Willard, "God Created the Heavens," *Soul's Eternal Anchor*, MP3/cassette, 17:00.

86. Though short exegeses are scattered throughout his lectures, the series *The Soul's Eternal Anchor* (1988) has the lion's share of his interpretation of Hebrews.

'heavens'—that is, of the surrounding atmosphere—is a primary part of the revelation of Jehovah to His select people, from Abraham on."[87]

The Lesson of Exile

NEVERTHELESS, IT WAS a long struggle before the people of Israel could *fully* associate God and his kingdom with heaven.[88] Even beyond the temptation to idolatry, the human temptation always has been to associate God and his kingdom with *earthly* institutions and their human ministers. This temptation is also noticed by John Bright and applied by Willard to Jesus's heavenly ministry.[89] The very real, accumulating Jewish experience of God and his kingdom *in the heavens* did not immediately result in a habit of rejecting attempts to co-opt it into an earthly, human project.

Indeed, it was the dissolution of one grand, sustained attempt to co-opt the kingdom of God that forged the "kingdom of God" language that survived into Jesus's day. In the exile, Willard spots the first *widespread* recognition (individuals may have known it before) that YHWH was the God of all peoples, and therefore new language needed to be developed to identify him:

> *Jehovah now becomes identified as "the God of heaven" (II Chron. 36:23; Dan. 2:17–19,28; and throughout Ezra and Nehemiah)—of* heaven, *which, like the air surrounding us, the "first heaven" in biblical terms, is over all and directly and sufficiently available to all. This God of heaven now blesses his people through influencing non-Jews, including political figures, such as gentile kings, as well as nature. This new understanding of where God is in relation to us, hammered out in the cauldron of exile, develops into the language of "the kingdom of heaven" that is used by Jesus in Matthew's Gospel to proclaim salvation to all, beyond any "official" religious or*

87. Willard, "Gospel of the Kingdom," 34.
88. Willard, "People of God in Exile," 1172.
89. Bright, *Kingdom of God*, 136–53.

> *political arrangements. The experience of the exile and of how God was with his people in judgment proved essential to a new and more adequate understanding of how "our God reigns" (Isa. 52:7).*[90]

This statement says many things at once. Two things that it is not saying are (1) that the kingdom of God only comes into existence in exile and (2) that the Jews only learned of the kingdom of God in the exile. Even if all the references and allusions to the ruling and reigning of God are to be traced to this time period, Willard's position is that this is new language for an old phenomenon. The phenomenon is God acting out of heaven.

What is for the first time understood in the exile and sets in motion the development of new language is that the action of God *need not* be tied to Israel's political and religious institutions because in the exile, these were suspended—and yet, the action of God in heaven continued.[91] This was all the more clear because the action showed signs of coming upon the gentiles, for their own benefit as well as for the benefit of the Jews. What the coining of the new language marked was one of many times in which Israel remembered the transcendence *and* nearness of YHWH. They remembered that their cohesion as a social group depended not on political or cultic arrangements but on God. According to Willard, Judges also recounts a time when at least political arrangements were left aside and God's kingdom, though without that language, was the basis of Israel's social reality.[92]

But the loss of their land and cultic practices in the exile would drive the point further home: "The Jewish religion and culture formed within the context of the monarchy would, in exile, survive in its essential features *through God alone*, and without a political and geographic

---

90. Willard, "People of God in Exile," 1172.

91. Cf. Dallas Willard, "Servanthood: Isaiah in the Exile and the Jesus Way," *The Jesus Way: Recovering the Lost Content of Discipleship* (Renovaré, San Antonio, TX, June 22, 2009), MP3, 18:00.

92. Willard, *Disciplines*, 239–43.

basis, as Jews were dispersed 'from India to Ethiopia' (Esth. 8:9–13)."[93] On the other side and far more important in the long run than Israel's self-understanding, they would form a better theology, "an understanding that God was not bound to a special place (Jerusalem, see John 4:21) and that He was still present and in action where there were no visible manifestations in the surrounding heavens."[94] The "special place," if there was one, was heaven—conveniently also a place accessible to all Diaspora Jews and all gentiles. God's "tent" was transcendent, yet near.

The Prophet

THE BASIC VIEWS of God and his kingdom and of heaven just reiterated help explain what lay at hand for Jesus's first listeners when they heard Jesus's gospel. To repeat, when Jesus announces *the availability* of the kingdom of God, a sort of rudimentary view of the kingdom of God can be apperceptively (or marginally) held in the minds of those who observe him and hear his words. But other than these two concepts, Jesus was counting on another basic piece of Old Testament ontology to help the first listeners make sense of his gospel.

The first listeners, when Jesus spoke of availability, "had no general understanding of what was involved, but they knew Jesus meant he was acting with God and God with him, that God's rule was effectively present through him."[95] How did they know this? How did they know that Jesus was not a charlatan or a magician with a bag of illusions? Willard explains, "The familiar stories, traditions, and rituals of Israel enabled them to know the practical significance of this. They were stories and traditions of individual human beings whose lives were interlaced with God's action. Abraham, David, Elijah were well known to all. And the routinely practiced rituals of Israel were often occasions when God acted."[96] To see this for ourselves, we must see how Willard pulls together this doctrine of heaven with the narratives of the Old Testament

93. Willard, "People of God in Exile," 1172.
94. Willard, "Gospel of the Kingdom," 35.
95. Willard, *Conspiracy*, 19.
96. Willard, 19.

characters to form a concept of *prophets* that is older than Second Temple Judaism and yet still part of the mental furniture of mildly educated Jews. In the first-century mind, "prophet" had come to be known as a universal of which multiple particulars could be instances.

The plainest place to see this is in Willard's exegesis of Hebrews 11. Keeping in mind the book's view of God's kingdom as resident in heaven and as transcendent but near, we note that Willard understands all of the listed characters as persons whose lives were open to God's heavenly tent. His clearest example is the description of Moses, who "endured as seeing him who is invisible" (Heb 11:27). On the surface, this is an absurd comment, but what it alerts the reader to is a kind of sight that is different from sight *as sense perception*. This is sight "with the mind," as Willard spoke of it.[97] Thus, Moses falls in line with the prophet Elisha, who saw chariots of fire while his servant, looking with his eyes alone, did not.

Let us recall what was said in the previous chapter about Willard's view of faith as a kind of knowledge, and let us grant Willard's point that Moses sees *and knows* "him who is invisible." It follows that those who "received their commendation" by faith are those with a nonnaturalist ontology as well as a nonnaturalist epistemology. What's more, they are those whose lives have been transformed through their contact with the invisible yet visible order and are now something different from the ordinary cut of humans. This extraordinary knowledge and transformation constitute their sanctification or "otherness." Now, Willard does not speak of those who bear this "otherness" only as prophets. He believes the Scriptures have many words for the reality.[98] But for the sake of rhetorical simplicity, I will call the person bearing this quality *a prophet*.

There are two related but distinct acts of God that feed into Willard's concept of a prophet: (1) the opening of the heavens and (2) the

97. It is also on a more general level how Husserl claims to be able to see a universal or an essence. Thus, it is not exclusively "religious" sight.

98. In Willard, "Presence of the Kingdom" (26:00), he refers to judges and apostles in very similar terms.

presence of the Spirit. Often in connection with teaching on Jesus's baptism, Willard will highlight other biblical witnesses to the experience of the heavens having *been opened*. Ezekiel 1:1 has the precise language, but Willard turns to other familiar stories like Jacob's ladder or even instances of God's action like Abraham's servant's supernatural discovery of Isaac's wife. The heavens being opened is often an experience that represents a mental breakthrough for the person concerned. Hence, it is often an event that marks out a special person—namely, a prophet—called to live in unusual awareness and interaction with heaven.

In what amounts to a very important move for his theology, Willard sees a conceptual unity between these dramatic, prophet-making events and the more common Jewish experience of heaven as the tent of God and his manifest kingdom. A low-level awareness of God's presence in the tabernacle or with oneself (e.g., Ps 16:8) is in the same genus as Isaiah's lofty vision of God and his throne room (Isa 6). The difference between a prophet and an Israelite "circumcised in heart" is one not of kind but of degree.

In contrast to this generalization of prophetic vision, the presence of the spirit of God is more restrictive. The doctrine of the Spirit in the Old Testament (namely, the one Jesus's first listeners were most likely to have available to them) is, for Willard, largely subsumed under the doctrine of the prophets. Reading from Psalm 51, Willard tells an audience, "The Old Testament is a book of great familiarity with the Holy Spirit."[99] Mainly, he has in mind the book's great familiarity *with prophets* and the common connection between the Spirit and the *empowerment* of these persons to fulfill a particular function in the community. Though *baptism* in the Spirit, he says, is a New Testament phenomenon, special individuals were known to have been "filled" or "anointed" with the spirit of God.

Because of how Willard identifies a unity between the opening of the heavens and the average Israelite's awareness of God's manifest presence, *prophetic vision* (in contrast to *prophetic power*) is a quite fundamental

99. Dallas Willard, "Spirituality and Mission," *Spirituality and Mission*, 4:45.

and pervasive experience in life under "the law and the prophets." It is essentially the experience of *faith* (cf. chapter 4), albeit communicated with Old Testament conceptualization. And prophetic vision, being associated with faith, comes to be connected with elements of New Testament conceptualization such as "entering the kingdom of God" and "regeneration" or "new life."

Less fundamental to Old Testament spirituality, by contrast, is the work of the Spirit, which has mostly to do with power for service. In other words, in Willard's account of spiritual life, the experience of empowerment by the Spirit is less fundamental than the experience of faith. This split comes to a head in John the Baptist. In Willard's words,

> *John was still under "the law and the prophets." Now, the spirit of God was present under "the law and the prophets." But it was not the center of a personal community. The center of the personal community in "the law and the prophets" was precisely the rituals of a religion, and it was centered on a cultural, on a nationalistic basis. You had to be a Jew or a proselyte to really get in on it. Now, the prophets had the spirit of God, and they did marvelous things. I mean, you see old Elijah sitting up on that mountaintop. . . . That's power! There is a spirit of God in the Old Testament, but it is not the center of the community. It is not committed to individuals as the basis for the religion of the Jews.*[100]

The prophetic power was there and recognized in ancient Israel, but it was not as central or as pervasive to the community as the prophetic vision that, as we will see later, was communicated under "the law and the prophets" through "the rituals of a religion." The difference between these distinct acts of God in the life of the prophet helps explain Willard's depreciatory view of John the Baptist.

---

100. Dallas Willard, "The Best News You'll Ever Hear," *Essentials of Kingdom Living*, MP3/cassette, 37:15.

In the 1986 lecture "The Best News You'll Ever Hear," Willard makes a distinction between two kinds of religion present in the New Testament and in the contemporary church—the religion of John the Baptist and Apollos and the religion of Jesus and Paul. Working from Acts 18:24–19:10, Willard calls the religion of John and Apollos a religion of forgiveness of sins through Jesus. These men preached a gospel of forgiveness (through Jesus) and baptized their listeners in terms of that reality. But the religion of Jesus and Paul included something different, the Holy Spirit, and their ministry to others made reference to *another* baptism. The problem with the ministry of John and Apollos, Willard tells us, was that their gospel as a set of ideas *had nothing to do with*—that is, was not logically related to—the Holy Spirit and this other baptism. Their gospel, therefore, left their listeners in the dark about these realities. The ministry of Jesus and Paul, by contrast, was centered on a gospel of the availability of the kingdom, a set of ideas that was intimately related to the Holy Spirit and the other baptism *and* also included forgiveness of sins.

John did not understand this. He shared in the prophetic vision as many Israelites did. But John's life, as great as it was for those "born of women," was still a life lived "under 'the law and the prophets'" and without the power of God, which was associated with the Spirit. This is the reason why those who are least in the kingdom of the heavens are *greater* than John the Baptist. Willard explains, "When you look at John's ministry, it really is rather sad. John had to stand by and watch. . . . There are some very haunting words in the gospel about John. In John chapter 10, the remark is made, 'John did no miracle.' . . . When he was concerned to reassure himself that the kingdom of God was really present in Jesus Christ, he sent to Jesus, you'll remember, and he asked this question, 'Art thou he that will come or should we look for another?' Do you remember Jesus's answer to him? In general, his answer was in terms of miracles."[101]

---

101. For more on this, see Willard's series on the parables: *The Parabolic Teaching about Christ's Kingdom by Christ* (Harbor Church, Lomita, CA, March 6–May 29, 1983), MP3/cassette.

John's shortcoming began with a failure to understand the kingdom of God in terms of the Holy Spirit. Though he preached the same thing as Jesus, Willard says, "he really didn't understand what he was saying."[102] His message and baptism were mainly centered on forgiveness of sins and still within the spirituality or religion of "the law and the prophets." His shortcoming was then manifested in a life that did not evidence the power of God associated with the Spirit. *Prophetic vision* is evident in his life—that is, he saw the invisible hand of God—but *prophetic power* was lacking. By way of contrast, "under Jesus, anyone in the kingdom of God is initiated and led into the exercise of the power of the kingdom."[103]

Though the notion that Abraham, David, and Elijah were "prophets" in the covenant people's history should be simply comprehended, a more comprehensive idea of what Willard had in mind can be had by glancing at one of the books that made a strong impression on him as a young man and, by his own admission, launched his lifelong research into Christian history and literature: James Gilchrist Lawson's *Deeper Experiences of Famous Christians* (1911).[104]

Deeper Experiences is, according to Willard, a book without literary or scholarly merits.[105] It uses the anointing or baptism of the Spirit to evaluate and commend various individuals to its readers, beginning with Enoch and ending with nineteenth-century Americans. This slant, as Willard admits, makes the book overly selective and, at times, forceful in its reading of the individual life histories.[106] Nevertheless, God is presented as having a relationship with people in a way that causes their lives to be out of the norm in terms of power for God's work. "No great work has ever been accomplished except through the power of the Holy

---

102. Dallas Willard, "Spiritual Formation in Christlikeness 2," *Transformation into the Likeness of Christ* (Belfast Kilmakee Presbyterian Church, Belfast, North Ireland, May 31, 2004), MP3, 14:00.

103. Willard, "What Is 'Ministry'?," 26:00.

104. Willard, "When God Moves In," 53–54.

105. James Gilchrist Lawson, *Deeper Experiences*, 49.

106. In the original introduction, Lawson provides a wide-ranging, ecumenical list of famous Christians he could not include in his book.

Spirit, who is the great Executive of God, carrying out the will of God in all things," says the writer.[107]

In the chapter on the Old Testament, Lawson sifts through the narratives of the patriarchs, Moses, Joshua, the judges, the kings, and the prophets looking for evidence of God's extraordinary activity or of "deeper experiences." For example, he writes, "Not only Moses and Joshua, but all the other great judges of Israel, were also qualified by the Holy Spirit's power for the work to which God had called them."[108] Aside from the overreaching pneumatology, Willard agrees with Lawson that the Old Testament (unless one had reason to doubt its nonnaturalist ontology) could and *would* be read with an eye to its prophets. In this, he assumes the agreement of mildly educated first-century Jews, who were not staunch naturalists. For Willard, Lawson's simple book captures something that *is* simple in Old Testament theology: God's presence and action were with certain individuals, separating them out from the norm.

This has implications for the understanding of Jesus's gospel. In both Willard and Lawson, we notice an antidispensational tendency, one that does not restrict "deeper experiences" to the work of redemption *following* Jesus's coming. This continuity in the history of redemption becomes pivotal in Willard's conception of it because it does much to explain how Jesus's first listeners understood his gospel and recognized him: they had a working concept of a class of people specially connected to God.

The Baptism of Moses

THERE IS ONE final element of biblical ontology that we should discuss before we look at the first-stage understanding of Jesus's gospel, ministry, and person. But it is different from the other three because it does not seem to factor into Willard's account of the basic view of the kingdom, which Jesus's listeners do lay hold of when they understand his gospel. Nevertheless, it is real and active in their coming to understanding,

---

107. Lawson, *Deeper Experiences*, 15.
108. Lawson, 21.

as Willard sees it, and is best discussed here: the baptism of Moses (1 Cor 10:2).

Two 1987 sermons on baptisms are illuminating sources for this.[109] The plural *baptisms* comes from Hebrews 6:2, where, as Willard points out, βαπτισμων (genitive plural) are listed as one among many elementary doctrines. In the first sermon, "The Heavens Were Opened," Willard begins with the text that Jesus is one who will *baptize* with the Holy Spirit (Matt 3:11). He draws attention to how, during Jesus's water baptism, *the heavens were opened to him*, again pointing out that they are never spoken of as closing on him. Concerning the consequences of this event, he makes this general comment about Jesus's ministry: "The life before an open heaven is mediated by one on whom heaven has come to rest. And that is a general law which we must all understand."[110] Noting, first, how this "general law" applies also to Old Testament cases like Elisha and his servant, Willard goes on to insist that it *does not* apply to the case of John and Jesus. With this interpretation, he again applies his distinction between John's religion and Jesus's religion. Though John was regenerate in terms under "the law and the prophets" and was a prophet, "John did not have the spirit of God on him to give to others." Because of this, Willard continues, "God gave [the Spirit] directly to his Son *on the occasion* of his baptism at the hand of John. A heavenly life was breaking in in a way which it had never had before."[111] Jesus is the prototype of those on whom heaven has come to rest.

In what manner does *Jesus* then mediate the life before an open heaven to others? To answer this, we must in our minds set familiar baptisms aside—that is, John's baptism, Christian water baptism, and even Spirit baptism—and work for a while on a major biblical theme. With help from the second sermon ("Baptisms") and a few other sources, we must reflect on a "baptism," the baptism of Moses, which is not often

109. Dallas Willard, "The Heavens Were Opened"; and "Baptisms," *Baptism* (Valley Vista Christian Community, Sepulveda, CA, 1987), MP3/cassette. When listening to these sermons, it is important to recognize that they are not about regeneration in the Spirit (Titus 3:5), which is ideally in the past, but about baptism and ecclesiology.

110. Willard, "Heavens Were Opened," 30:30.

111. Willard, 30:45.

categorized as a baptism and, on the whole, is quite important for Willard's theology. To begin, recall Willard's suggestion that there is a conceptual unity between the dramatic, prophet-making events of a few Israelite lives and the more common Jewish experience of God and his manifest kingdom in heaven. Under "the law and the prophets," the average Jew had low-level access to the object of prophetic vision.

Now according to Willard, this access began primarily in the ministry *of Moses* during Israel's time in the wilderness. It was access made possible *by the public presence of God* among his people during that time and afterward. This accessible presence began individually with the person of Moses, whose own personality radiated the presence of God. But it began to be manifested beyond Moses in such things as the pillars of cloud and fire in the wilderness, the events at Sinai, and the eventual filling of the tabernacle. These manifestations of God and his kingdom *surrounded* the people of Israel. Though one could resist them, they were, so to say, the atmosphere of the nascent people.

This fairly undisputed claim about God's work with Israel is what Willard thinks Paul is referring to when he says "our fathers . . . were *baptized* into Moses" (1 Cor 10:2; emphasis added).[112] Baptism in its multiple New Testament forms is fundamentally, for Willard, an act of *surrounding* something. He often uses the word *engulfment.*[113] But Willard looks beyond the surrounding of persons with water and with the Spirit to a surrounding of the people *with God's manifest presence.* And what God through Moses was doing among the people whom God led out of Egypt was precisely this.

Whether called a "baptism" or not, this phenomenon is fundamental in Willard's account of the history of redemption—*more* fundamental than the giving of the law—because, for the people of God, *the publically available presence of God among the people* is the typical source for their faith or regeneration. There are atypical ways God

112. Willard, 31:45; Willard, "Baptisms," 14:30; and Dallas Willard, "Vision: The Cooperative Friends of Jesus 1," *The Church as a Community of the Kingdom of God* (Church of the Open Door, Maple Grove, MN, November 4, 2004), MP3, 2:45.
113. Willard, *Conspiracy*, 278.

reached individuals in the ancient world, but it was through his presence among his people that the low-level participation in the prophetic vision of God and his kingdom was made possible. Note, it was made possible, not inevitable. The baptism of Moses does not force faith or even awareness or knowledge of God's presence.

More familiarly to his readers, Willard argues that this is a type of baptism that continues in the church. In his later years, Willard regularly taught that Matthew 28:19 included a commissioning of ecclesial fellowships to perform *Trinitarian baptism*, a charge to "surround [disciples] in Trinitarian reality," not just to get them wet while saying "In the name of the Father . . ."[114] His exegeses of Acts and the epistles highlight their testimony to the presence of God with the assemblies, often under the ministry of certain individuals. For Willard, there is a real continuity here in the experience of the people of God in time.

He goes so far as to say that "the *primary* baptism is simply the engulfing of the people of God in the presence of God."[115] As primary for the other baptisms, Willard called it on one occasion "the assumption of baptism"—namely, "*the real presence of God and his kingdom* in the life of the community and in the life of the minister."[116] When he goes on to give his views of water baptism or baptism in the Spirit or baptism into Christ, he says that these baptisms draw their efficacy from the "real presence" in the community, a phrase whose theological significance Willard understands and intends. In the case of water baptism, then, the "active ingredient" is not the water or the ritual or the minister and

---

114. Willard, "Failure of Evangelical Political Involvement," 90; cf. Willard, *Renovation*, 245–47, 267n4. See also Willard, "Session 3," 1:04:00.

115. Willard, "Baptisms," 33:30 (emphasis mine). See also Willard, "Heavens Were Opened," 35:30: "That manifestation as smoke or cloud is a common manifestation of the presence of God's Spirit in the Old Testament. When you come to the New Testament, you see the same kind of manifestation on the Mount of Transfiguration."

116. Willard, "Baptisms," 11:30 (emphasis mine). Willard also speaks of "people who are dominated by the real presence of Christ in them" ("The Desire of All Nations," *Spirituality and Mission*, 27:00). He adds, "I use that word purposely, and you'll know that that ties in with a lot of discussions about the nature of the Eucharist, the real presence of Christ."

the congregation assembled or the faith of the person being baptized but the manifest presence of God and his kingdom.

Jesus the Baptist

In what manner, then, does Jesus mediate the life before an open heaven to others? First of all, Jesus, physically present in Galilee, personally continues the more general Mosaic baptism into the presence of God.[117] The divine manifestation in Jesus is of a similar kind to what it was in the cloud and sea in the desert and afterward in the temple. Commenting on the phrase "the Rock was Christ" (1 Cor 10:4), Willard says, "The complete provision for the people of God in the presence of Christ, whether in rocks or in clouds or in fire or whatever may be required—that is the condition in which baptism [in the Spirit] occurs."[118] As one full of the Spirit, Jesus brings the "manifest kingdom" of God to others simply by being around them, regardless of whether they are open to it. In this vein, Willard says, "The important thing was that, when Jesus came on earth and people listened to him and they watched him, they realized that God was present. He was present in Jesus Christ."[119]

The same ministry of Mosaic baptism is passed on to Jesus's apostles, which is why Willard continues in the same message, "And when Jesus sent his own disciples out . . . the kingdom of God was present *in them*. And they preached exactly the same message."[120] Hence, when they are rejected, they are to say, "Nevertheless know this, that the kingdom of God has come near" (Luke 10:11). Commenting on this verse, Willard says, "They brought the kingdom of heaven in their own personalities."[121]

117. From a Christian perspective, this may be thought of in terms of Trinitarian presence.

118. Willard, "Baptisms," 32:45.

119. Willard, "Bringing the Kingdom," 1:13:00. See also Dallas Willard, "Parable of the Sower," *Parable Teaching*, MP3/cassette, 8:30: "In him the kingdom of God drew nigh. It was in him and in his presence that the kingdom of God had come to earth in a manner in which it had never been here before. . . . He took the kingdom of God with him. Wherever he was the kingdom of God was."

120. Willard, "Bringing the Kingdom," 1:13:00.

121. Willard, 1:14:30. See also Willard, *Conspiracy*, 29.

Or, as he comments elsewhere, the kingdom "came in the person of the people who were bearing it with them to do the works and to preach the kingdom of heaven. The kingdom of God came right by them."[122]

In terms of theological traditions, Willard's views here are in line with a broad stream of American and British revivalist theology. More than any other theological tradition, it was the revivalists of the eighteenth and nineteenth centuries who carefully analyzed what happened when human ministry was particularly spectacular—when there were profound experiences of God, occasions of physical healings, large groups or whole areas returning to God, and spiritual power in preaching, teaching, and counseling and when there was a prevailing spirit of prayer and a strong pull to lead holier lives. Prominent revival theorists such as Jonathan Edwards and Charles Finney described what they thought were the contributing factors to these remarkable works of God. Finney thought they were so clear and so accessible that ministers could be trained to instigate revival with God's help. In other words, God wants revival, but he is waiting for his church to be ready to work with him in it.

As already noted, at a young age, Willard had become quite familiar with Finney's philosophical theology. One of the aspects of Finney's philosophy of ministry that Willard held to long after he stopped actively studying Finney's books was the idea that a minister could become so full of the vision and power of God that he would almost automatically bring the presence of God into the spaces where he ministered.[123] This idea is a familiar part of the later theology of revival and is taken up by other authors Willard respected such as Jonathan Goforth and A. W. Tozer.

What we have here is a contemporary form of what Willard thinks is happening in the biblical record. Working from Acts 19:20, Willard talks about being those in whose presence the word of God acts as a force in its own right: "Let me use the old-fashioned word 'revival.' . . . If you read from the Old Testament on, a revival is a case where the presence of

122. Willard, "Pastoral Ministry and the Spiritual Disciplines," 30:15.

123. See Finney, *Lectures on Revivals*, lecture 1, 18–19.

God becomes tangible in a community. Not just in a church house, but all through the community. It's a situation where a people are smitten with the presence of God whether they are doing something religious or not."[124] Not only did Willard recognize revivals in church history and in his own life history, but as one notices here, he thinks they are something to be found as far back as the Old Testament records. And this is crucial for his exegesis of the Gospels and the New Testament. Though the people of Jesus's day may have had no idea of how "the baptism of Moses" worked, it was working. By just watching and listening to Jesus, "they realized that God was present."

Now as real as Willard thinks it is in the gospel narratives, "the baptism of Moses" should be distinguished from the other aspects of biblical ontology discussed in this chapter. There is little indication that Willard treats this biblical phenomenon as part of the basic view of the kingdom of God that was essential to the first listeners' understanding of Jesus's message about the kingdom of God. Of foremost importance is that listeners understand (1) that God is a king and has a kingdom, (2) that heaven is the location for manifestations of his kingdom, and (3) that prophets can see and work with his kingdom in unique ways. They do not need to know that they have access or may have access to the prophetic vision because of the presence of God with his people. And yet, even though they may not know about it, it happens. In Jesus, God makes it happen just as he made it happen in Moses and in the prophets before Jesus. In the presence of Jesus, unsuspecting listeners were baptized with the presence of God.

124. I have unfortunately misplaced the reference for this quote from one of Willard's many audio recordings.

6

JESUS'S POPULARITY, EXPLAINED

> Jesus expresses his kingdom, partly, through the healing work that he did for people. And so in verse 23 [of Matt 4], "Jesus went about all Galilee, teaching . . . , preaching . . . , healing . . ." and you have a mass of people that were drawn to him. Now, it's important to understand, you see, that these people came to Jesus just to have their needs met. Are we clear about that? See now, that's all right. There's nothing wrong with that. Nothing wrong. But we have to understand that Jesus will lead us beyond that. . . .
>
> It's all right for us to come to receive the ministry of Jesus. Most of us come that way initially. Some of us come because of the burden of our sin. We feel them so heavily. We know we are not right with God, and we come to Jesus and accept him as our Lord and Savior and our sins are forgiven. . . . Some of us come because he's answered our prayers. He's healed us. He's saved our children from something. Something of that sort. So there are many reasons why they come.
>
> —Dallas Willard, Kempton Park Methodist Church, August 17, 1987

JESUS'S LISTENERS HAD an *initial* understanding of his gospel that the kingdom of God is at hand. Willard says that this first understanding of Jesus's gospel is that the kingdom of God was *available for Jesus*. The verb ἤγγικεν (is at hand) meant on the basic level that God was with Jesus and that that enabled him to do the extraordinary things he did as a newly arisen *righteous man* or *prophet*.

Though this may sound like a deviation from the best church teaching to orthodox ears, according to Willard, this rudimentary interpretation of Jesus's message was not a mistake on the part of the listeners; it was no less than Jesus's authorial intent. Willard writes, "When [Jesus] announced that the 'governance' or rule of God had become available to human beings, he was primarily referring to what *he* could do for people, God acting with him."[1] Given how Willard thinks of the first listeners—what they knew of God and his redemptive plans as revealed in their Scriptures—it will come as no surprise that he thinks that, when they first heard Jesus's news of the kingdom, they did not learn anything new about God. Rather, Jesus's gospel *confirms* what mildly educated Jews knew or could have known. This is a very important point: Jesus's gospel falls on *a few ears* ready to receive it, ears that had already heard it, in a way.

In this chapter, I will break down and analyze this true but incomplete gospel understanding, the first stage of the first listeners' response to Jesus's ministry. To begin, I want to provide a working topography of reality as understood by the first listeners and as intended by Jesus. Entailed in this topography is an understanding of Jesus (a Christology) and of the good Jesus brings to the listeners' lives (a soteriology). But Jesus's gospel calls for more than mere knowledge; it calls for faith. So finally, I will provide an analysis of the faith that this rudimentary, first-stage understanding of the gospel calls for.

Jesus's Gospel as Responsible for His Following: First-Stage Topography

LET US BEGIN with this: Jesus was terribly popular for a reason. Around him, the people said, "A great prophet has arisen among us!" (Luke 7:16). What did that mean in light of Jesus's gospel?

The most basic meaning of Jesus's gospel of at-hand-ness, Willard writes, was the special openness of God in his kingdom *for Jesus*. Only intermediately would there be any benefit for others. The gospel, so

1. Willard, *Conspiracy*, 19–20.

understood by the first listeners, was not new theology. It was not a joy-inspiring but basically a puzzling new vision of God and his ways. They could and did understand it in light of what they *already* thought of God, his "throne" in heaven, and how he worked with the forerunners of their religion, the rare but celebrated prophets of old.[2] Hence, the *news* of the good news is simply journalistic. As good as great prophets are, their presence among the people of God is rather inconsistent. The news is that Jesus has now announced his prophetic status and, more to the point, has manifested it with bona fide miracles.

When Jesus's first listeners initially understand this, they position him, the kingdom of God, and his gospel by means of a certain familiar type of topography. In their minds, the kingdom of God is, crudely put, *above* Jesus, them, and the whole cosmos. It is the sovereign kingdom of God. In Willard's words, it "is over all, from everlasting to everlasting. There is no boundary to it. Everything that God made and that includes everything falls in that kingdom."[3] But according to Jesus's "word of the kingdom" and its manifestation in miracles, he stands in *direct relationship* to this above kingdom of God. Apparently, the sovereign kingdom is *available for Jesus*. God is *with him*.

There is, however, an important caveat to this topography of availability. The first listeners assumed that the average participant in God's covenant people *did not* stand in direct relationship to God's kingdom. The average participant thought they were only invited to interact with God and his kingdom via *intermediaries*. These intermediaries were perhaps dead, in the case of Moses and Samuel, or they were perhaps living, in the case of their priests and rabbis. They were perhaps socially organized, in the case of the Jewish rituals and institutions. Generally

---

2. A similar conclusion, based on the impressions of the first listeners, is arrived at by N. T. Wright, who writes, "How then was Jesus perceived by the villagers who saw and heard him? All the evidence so far displayed suggests that he was perceived as a *prophet*" (*Jesus and the Victory of God*, 196). However, Wright argues for a different view of prophets in the minds of the Jews than does Willard.

3. Dallas Willard, "Kingdom Righteousness in God's Service," *The Kingdom of God* (Faith Evangelical Church, Chatsworth, CA, April 30, 1978), MP3/cassette, 16:30.

speaking, the average Jew thought that human intermediaries were their main connection to God and his kingdom.

Because of this assumption, Jesus was received among his first listeners as one of these intermediaries. That is, *Jesus* stands in direct relation to God and his kingdom, and listeners may (or may not) stand in direct relation to Jesus and *his* kingdom. The availability ordering is linear and hierarchical. As their understanding increases, this topography will become more complex and other ontological relations will be added, but this is how the arrangement looks for listeners on the first stage.

"A Prophet Mighty in Deed and Word": First-Stage Christology

NOTICE THAT THIS topography includes Jesus. When interpreting Willard, it is very important to note that Jesus's gospel is a gospel about him all the way through. It entails *a Christology* and calls for a type of faith in Jesus by means of which the benefits of the gospel (soteriology) are had. To use traditional language, the person of Christ is the hinge upon which Willard's account of the work of Christ swings.[4] As he writes in *The Divine Conspiracy*, "But they were only responding to *the striking availability of God to meet present human need through the actions of Jesus.* He simply was the good news about the kingdom. He still is."[5] In Willard's view, the work of Christ moves forward in his listeners *as* the person of Christ is more and more fully understood or, to speak biblically, as Jesus is more and more "glorified" to the minds of his listeners. One may notice that Willard follows the Johannine description of salvation, which is evident in one of his favorite verses to exegete, John 17:3: "And this is eternal life, that they know you, the only true God, and Jesus Christ whom you have sent."[6]

---

4. The work of Christ, which is the narrow focus of this book, could be further distinguished from Willard's account of the work of the whole Trinity in salvation, or what I call *soteriology proper*, under which concepts like "the Immanuel Principle" fall. For more on this, see chapter 11.

5. Willard, *Conspiracy*, 17.

6. Charles Finney has a similar view, writing, "The newly converted soul knows Christ in but few relations. . . . The new convert embraces Christ so far as he knows him; but

So who is this man? Despite similarities, Jesus was not like the other *living* intermediaries that his first listeners knew—the rabbis, priests, and scribes. Let us try to get at Willard's view of who Jesus was to them by naming and describing Jesus's office (or his authority—ἐξουσια, as Willard would say) and then by describing his person or his character.

The Office of a Prophet

AS CAN BE anticipated by the previous chapter, the concept of "prophet" captures for Willard the first-stage listener's view of Jesus's office. Prophets are ministers to the people of God, but a special kind. They are both relatively rare and relatively authoritative and powerful. Willard writes, "The radical independence of the prophet from the 'establishment'—even from a Jewish establishment—is strongly imprinted upon the People of God during this period [of the exile], even though a prophet as 'outsider' had always been a major thread woven into the fabric of Israel. From Jeremiah and Ezekiel to John the Baptist, the *right* of the prophet to 'come out of nowhere' and speak for God is confirmed. The people welcome the prophets and expect them to fulfill their role."[7]

In contrast to priests or rabbis, it was not a common experience for a Jew to be in the presence of a David or a Jeremiah, to have direct access to them. This rarity, compounded with the out-of-the-ordinary power of a prophet, means that a genuine prophet of YHWH stood, from Willard's perspective, higher in the people's mind than the temple's priests or the synagogue's rabbis. This honor has to do with the prophets being "unhooked" from these important public institutions and, nevertheless, being "hooked" into YHWH and having their extraordinary power from him directly. A genuine prophet of YHWH had the right and power to

---

at first he knows but little of his need of him, except in his governmental relations" (*Systematic Theology*, lecture 67, 679). See also Alfred Edersheim, an author Willard quotes in *Conspiracy*: "To the first disciples all doctrinal teaching sprang out of fellowship with Him. . . . they believed, and therefore learned the truths connected with Him and springing out of Him. So to speak, the seed of truth which fell on their hearts was carried thither from the flower of His Person and Life" (Alfred Edersheim, *The Life and Times of Jesus the Messiah* [London: Longmans, Green, 1883], 365).

7. Dallas Willard, "The People of God in Exile," in Foster et al., *Renovaré Spiritual Formation Bible*, 1172.

speak and act for YHWH without the accreditation afforded by the human, Jewish institutions, and this special "office" or authority is what the first-stage listeners took Jesus to have.

In using the concept of "prophet" to identify Jesus's person and work, questions are raised about how the first listeners saw themselves in relation to the prophets and therefore to Jesus. Did the average covenant partner think of the prominent persons of their history as outstanding examples of *all* covenant partners? Or, more restrictively, as outstanding examples of a distinct and privileged class of persons? Did the average Jew look up to the great men and women of Jewish history as better versions of themselves, persons whose lives would potentially make them feel guilty or inspired? Or did they look up to them as their hierarchical superiors, ontologically set on another plane for the purpose of serving the greater good of Israel? Willard is clear that the average Jew knew that they did not stand in *direct relationship* to God's kingdom. They did not resemble the prophets and relied on intermediaries. But how did they think about the dissemblance?

Willard does not answer this question about the first listeners, and perhaps it cannot be answered. Regarding a later church context, Willard does speak of the issue, relating it to the heresy of the Nicolaitans, which Willard describes as "the heresy which divides between those special people who minister and the laity. . . . The idea is that there is a very special kind of work, which calls above any other kind of work for holiness and power and all those wonderful things. . . . The work of the minister of the gospel does require some special preparation, but it requires no more of the holiness and power of God than it does to run a service station."[8] Here Willard connects all human work to provisions of the kingdom of God—namely, holiness and power. The view he opposes is that these provisions are directly available for *some persons* due to their special position in life but are not required by persons in other

8. Dallas Willard, "Your Work in Life," *Essentials of Kingdom Living*, MP3/cassette, 17:30; citing Rev 2:6, 15.

positions—that is, those who run a service station—and therefore may not even be available for them directly.[9]

In *Conspiracy*, he approaches the issue from a different angle. In the context of recommending apprenticeship to Jesus within *all* human vocations, he speaks of "the master" Jesus in the following general way: "What is it, exactly, that he, the incarnate Lord, does? What, if you wish, is he 'good at'? The answer is found in the Gospels: *he lives in the kingdom of God*, and he applies that kingdom for the good of others and even makes it possible for them to enter it for themselves. The deeper theological truths about his person and his work do not detract from this simple point."[10] This passage signals another way of stating the topography that the kingdom was available *for Jesus*—namely, that Jesus lives in the kingdom of God *and he is good at it.* He lives *well* in the kingdom of God.

In Willard's theology, "living in the kingdom of God" is conceived of in degrees.[11] In an ultimate sense, every creature, even a demonic power, lives or exists in the sovereign kingdom of God. But in a narrower sense, only human creatures are capable of living *from* the kingdom of God, and only some humans (namely, the regenerate) actually do. This smaller circle of humans who live in or from the kingdom was God's ideal for Israel and later for the church. Working from Exodus 19:3–6, Willard says, "In the natural order, there is a social order. There is a relationship of God to a group of people, and God called out the Jewish nation. The descendants of Abraham were called out precisely to show what kind of life this was to be when it was lived under that direct governance of God."[12] So in covenant terms, *every* faithful but insignificant Jew ought to be counted alongside Jesus as a person who

9. Willard is clearly opposed to such a view (hence, heresy) when it arises in a New Testament context. That does not mean he was opposed to the ministry as a profession, which is to say that it "does require some special preparation." For more on this, see the syllabus and notes for his USC course on "Professions and the Public Interest in American Life," 2007, Dallas Willard Collection.

10. Willard, *Conspiracy*, 282–83.

11. Or "kingdom living," as Willard would often title a series of talks.

12. Willard, "Presence of the Kingdom," 24:45.

lives in the kingdom.[13] In an exegesis of the parable of the wheat and the tares, Willard makes an even further distinction between those *in* the kingdom but ultimately *of* the world and those *in* the kingdom and also *of* the kingdom.[14] Finally and crucially, the case of prophets or the cloud of witnesses (Heb 11) is a case of persons who best approximate the covenant ideal of living *fully* in the kingdom of God. Jesus falls soundly in this faith-full category. Living fully in the kingdom of God is what Jesus is good at.[15]

With these degrees of living in the kingdom laid out, and given Willard's Old Testament theology, it seems clear that the covenant partners *should have* felt guilty and inspired by the prophets.[16] But given their immediate first-century background, did the first listeners receive the prophet before them as someone who exemplified their ideal life? Or was Jesus simply living on another plane than they were? Though unclear, Willard's historical judgment appears to be the latter. The implied shock of Jesus's listeners that Willard identifies in Jesus's statement from Matthew 5:20 suggests that the covenant people had been systematically indoctrinated to think that the honorable, well-supplied life of the prophet was not for them. If they were to claim the bold blessings of the Beatitudes and the status of salt and light in the world for themselves, "the law and the prophets" would be overturned.[17] This *inadequate* assumption will be pursued further in the following chapters.

Suffice it to say, the first listeners assumed that the kingdom of God was directly available for some (mostly dead) individuals and perhaps for the covenant people *as a whole* under "the law and the prophets." But most covenant people would access it indirectly from someone or something else. They believed that they were, by and large, secondhand

13. Willard, *Conspiracy*, 333. Covenant will be looked at more closely in the next section.

14. Dallas Willard, "Growing Together until the Harvest: The Tares in the Wheat and the Net," *The Parabolic Teaching about Christ's Kingdom by Christ* (Harbor Church, Lomita, CA, April 3, 1983), MP3/cassette.

15. Willard, *Guidance*, 156.

16. Willard, "Presence of the Kingdom," 26:45. This will be further addressed when we discuss the Levitical priesthood.

17. Willard, *Conspiracy*, 125–26.

recipients of God's action. If they indeed lived in the kingdom of God, it was at the mercy of some other beacon of God. *They* were not the light of the world. Moses was. Perhaps some people in Jerusalem were. And, in God's mercy, Jesus was. That was the news of Jesus's good news. Standing before them was a person who, of all the people they knew personally, lived richly in the kingdom of God. Apart from his shocking statements to the contrary, they conceive of him and, hence, trust him as if he exists on a different plane than their own.

The Person of a Prophet

HOW IS THIS office cashed out, second, in terms of Jesus's person? To answer this, we must work from a wider view of the topic.

First, Willard's assessment of theology in the twentieth century was that conservative theologians and ministers had underemphasized to the point of forgetting, yes, *the humanity of Jesus*. The root of this practical Docetism concerning Jesus was located, he thought, in the mythology surrounding other leading biblical figures such as David and Jeremiah. If not as entirely fictional, they are perceived as somehow superhuman, not sharing in *our* humanity. To counteract this, Willard would often draw attention to Acts 14:15 and James 5:17, which teach that the life experiences of the prophets should be understood in light of our own experiences of being human. He writes, "[Elijah] was, after all, 'a man subject to like passions as we are' (Jas. 5:17), regardless of his fantastic feats in the power of God."[18] So for Willard, the first step in rehabilitating an orthodox doctrine of Jesus's humanity is to have an orthodox doctrine of the humanity of "the lives of the saints and heroes of the faith throughout the ages."[19] This is the category into which Jesus's humanity in the first instance falls.

Second, with an inquiry into the character of Jesus's person, we broach a topic too vast for a short treatment: the doctrine of the human

---

18. Willard, 25.
19. Willard, *Guidance*, 25.

person, or what Willard called "Christian psychology."[20] Toward the end of his life, Willard prescribed that future research in theology and specifically the psychology of redemption needed to focus on developing a comprehensive psychology of the human person from a biblically informed perspective. This "Christian psychology" should rival contemporary "secular" and "quasi-secular" psychologies. Two thousand years of Christian reflection have not yet produced, to his liking, an adequate theory from which theologians and ministers can responsibly work.[21]

---

20. Willard worked steadily on this topic throughout his life. As evidence, consider his interest since his graduate school days in the philosophy of mind (Willard, "Discovering the Difference"). Biographically speaking, the culmination of this lifelong interest is the publication of *Renovation*, which, though not magisterial, includes an overview of his doctrine of man, including man's fall into sin and restoration through Christ. In 2010, Willard said of his diagram of the person (*Renovation*, 38), "In all of this what lies back of this is working on the issue of the person from Aristotle and Plato up to the present. . . . One of our problems today is that psychology no longer deals with this" (Dallas Willard, "Considering the Whole Person: Heart, Soul, Mind, Strength and Neighbor," *Spiritual Formation and Soul Care* [Denver Seminary, Monument, CO, January 4, 2010], DVD, 1:27:00). He did not think that the Bible, taken on its own, would be much help, saying in 1993, as he did often, "Though I believe there is not anything you could defend as a coherent, complete, and consistent biblical psychology, I think we would do best if we would identify the spirit with the will primarily and in biblical terms with the heart" (Willard, "Spiritual Disciplines," 1:00). See also Dallas Willard, "Spring Arbor: Residency Part 2," *Spiritual Formation & Leadership* (Spring Arbor University, Spring Arbor, MI, January 2008), MP3, 22:00. In 1999, Willard calls a Christian psychology "a deep and penetrating theory of the human soul that is advanced by the development and application of the teachings of Jesus Christ" (Dallas Willard, "Jesus: The Smartest Man Who Ever Lived," *Jesus: The Smartest Man Who Ever Lived* [Biola University, La Mirada, CA, 1999], MP3/cassette, 12:45).

21. Regarding what he was looking for, Willard wrote in 2000,

> The processes of spiritual formation thus understood require precise, testable, thorough knowledge of the human self. Psychological and theological understanding of the spiritual life must go hand in hand. Neither of them is complete without the other. A psychology that is Christian, in the sense of a comprehensive understanding of the facts of spiritual life and growth, should be a top priority for disciples of Jesus, particularly those who work in the various fields of psychology and who consider it an intellectual and practical discipline. No understanding of the human self can be theoretically or practically adequate if it does not deal with the spiritual life. (Dallas Willard, "Spiritual Formation in Christ: A Perspective on What It Is and How It Might Be Done," *Journal of Psychology & Theology* 28, no. 4 [2000]: 256)

Lacking, from Willard's perspective, a biblically informed psychology, it is difficult to say *with precision* what it means for us and the prophets to be "men of like passions." This then makes it difficult to say with precision in Christology what it means for Jesus to be *vere homo*. But in this respect, we are no more disadvantaged than Jesus's first listeners, who, lacking a scientific or even reflective view of their humanity, nevertheless needed to have an answer to the question, *What is* Jesus? Who is *this man*? For the biblical appeal to self-comparison ("men of like passions") is an appeal not to a precise, phenomenologically hewn, scholarly theory of personhood but to an implicit, nonrigorous, and limited knowledge of what it means for us to be alive. This knowledge was in the first listeners' possession and could be called upon to help them make a judgment about Jesus.

This is a good example of how Willard takes a body of knowledge that was getting explicit refinement in the Greek world and, by means of a theory of implicit or tacit knowledge, recognizes it as operative in the lives of the covenant people.[22] Aristotle's *De Anima* is the most enduring example of what the Greeks were discussing centuries before Jesus's coming.[23] But regardless of whether educated Jews were reading this treatise or peripherally aware of its contents, they were not without knowledge of the human person, its principle parts and their relations. In some cases, Willard suggests that the implicit Judeo-Christian psychology *surpassed* that of the Greek world because the Jews and early Christians, though lacking the narrow treatises, were more capable of solving the problems of the human condition, man's fall into sin.[24] They were not codifying their knowledge as the Greeks were, but their successes, both then and now, prove their competence.[25]

---

22. Willard, "Residency Part 2," 22:30. He adds that first-century Palestine was an incredibly sophisticated place that discussed ideas discussed anywhere.

23. Willard notes this work and others in Willard, "Spiritual Disciplines," 102n3.

24. Willard says the problem of Greek thought and civilization is "thinking that the problem is an intellectual one" ("Understanding the Battle between the Flesh and the Spirit [Gal. 5:16–18]—and the Way Out," *Calvin Institute of Christian Worship* [Calvin College, Grand Rapids, MI, January 2008], MP3, 13:30).

25. This is an essential point to discuss in a treatment of Willard's *soteriology proper*. See chapter 11.

So although for Willard, the question of Jesus's personhood *could* theoretically be answered with help from a rigorous metaphysical psychology deeply informed by Christian sources, it is not the rigorous metaphysical answers that concern Willard at this juncture in the history of redemption. If the first listeners of Jesus were supposed to hear his self-referential gospel and trust him, *what was it that they thought they were trusting*? Since trust, according to Willard, is not a leap from ignorance, what was their metaphysical Christology at this level of their understanding?[26]

The first thing to mention is what Willard calls *incarnational spirituality*.[27] The reference comes from his article "Jesus," his contribution to the *Dictionary of Christian Spirituality*. In it, he speaks of the life story of Jesus, "his spirituality," as a constant model for the tradition of Christian spirituality, just as other figures are the model for other traditions of spirituality. He describes Jesus's spiritual life as "incarnational" and unpacks it in the following way: "To use that word, however, is not to refer only to the metaphysical nature of Christ, as is usually done. Rather, it is an indication of two different realms coming together to form a unique kind of life, in which human life *in* the world is an expression of divine life surpassing the world."[28] This combination of the experience of two realms in one life is precisely how Willard describes *the spiritual life of Israel's prophets and great persons of faith*. Incarnationalism, so to speak, is not new with Jesus; however, Jesus does (mainly because of his perfection of it and how he introduced others to it) become the poster child for it.

---

26. Having already made the point that Jesus falls initially into the traditional "office" of a prophet, what I will say here in terms of psychology should apply equally well to other persons having that level of authority. I remind readers that the use of *prophet* is an oversimplification of Willard's Old Testament theology, which encompasses patriarchs, judges, kings, priests, and prophets into one class. For an instance of him bundling these "offices," cf. Willard, "Presence of the Kingdom," 26:00.

27. This is bound to be confusing when referring to Jesus because in traditional theological language, *incarnation* is the proper name for the doctrine of the coming together of Christ's two natures. But Willard does not have this reality in view when he thinks of Jesus as a participant in incarnational spirituality.

28. Willard, "Jesus," in Scorgie, *Dictionary of Christian Spirituality*, 59.

Later in the article, Willard calls this "the two-fold life," a life immersed in the ordinary events of birth, death, family, solitude, work, rest, and play and a life immersed in knowing God by interactive relationship. This was central to the Christology of the first-stage listeners. They encountered a man with responsibilities and relationships who was just as embedded in human history as they were, but a man who, like the saints of old, interacted *on another plane* with the God of the universe. He was as embodied, incarnate, as they. Incarnation, as Willard is using the term here, was not a secret to the first listeners. The secret about Jesus was that he was spiritual—that is, he interacted directly with their spiritual God.[29] As Willard said on one occasion, "As the Son of God, [Jesus] is the preeminently spiritual man."[30]

Other than incarnationalism, an advantageous way to arrange what remains to be said about *who Jesus was* to the first-stage listeners is to use Willard's own theological anthropology and his six dimensions of the human person.[31] For our purposes, the Christology of the first-stage listeners will be satisfied by only looking at three of these dimensions: (1) Jesus's mind with respect to his thoughts, (2) his heart, and (3) his body.[32]

The Mind of a Prophet

ACCORDING TO WILLARD, Jesus's or any prophet's mind distinguishes itself from others' minds in its high quantity and quality of *firsthand*

---

29. These themes of incarnational spirituality are embodied in the sixth stream, the sacramental stream, of Richard Foster's organization Renovaré. Having begun with only five streams, Willard was the primary instigator for including the incarnational or sacramental as the sixth.

30. Dallas Willard, "Leaders, Christ and Power," *Together*, January–March 1992, 11.

31. One will recognize here the tradition of faculty psychology, which had its most prominent modern defense in Thomas Reid, *Essays on the Intellectual Powers of Man* (1785). Charles Finney, addressed in chapter 4, made heavy use of this tradition in his systematic theology. Willard, however, once said of the dimensions, "These aren't separable parts. . . . The unit of analysis is the person. The dimensions of the person are not like the spare tire and the door on a car. . . . That is what used to be called the old 'faculties psychology,' which tried to treat these as if they were distinct. So now you need another metaphysical truth: 'Not everything that is distinct is separable'" (Willard, "Considering the Whole Person," DVD, 1:34:00).

32. These are covered respectively in *Renovation*, chaps. 6, 8, and 9.

knowledge of God and his kingdom. Prophets were considered experts, not of the law per se, but of God, his heavenly hosts, and their workings. The heavens were opened *wider* to the prophet, allowing them to see the kingdom of God better—that is, God in action. Willard explains, "The prophet is fundamentally one who has deep insight into the nature of life, the nature of God, the nature of human society—and on the basis of that insight, they often say things about the future."[33] An exhaustive description of prophetic expertise is unnecessary. The point is that a prophet saw and heard what the average covenant Jew did not see or hear. Willard remarks, "In the Old Testament, you'll remember, the prophets early on were called 'seers.' Do you remember that? What they saw was the kingdom of God."[34] Being a seer (or perceiver) for Willard is an important component of knowledge. Prophets *knew* what God was doing and how he did it. They *knew* what else or who else was at work in the invisible order.[35]

Concerning Jesus, Willard has this to say about *his* possession of the prophetic and, indeed, the Jewish mind: "It was the manifest presence of the kingdom that the Jews learned, and it came down so that when Jesus was baptized, in all four gospels, it indicates that the heavens opened. It never says that they closed again on him. It was the presence of the heavens to him."[36] Though based on an argument from silence, Willard's claim is that Jesus stands out, even among the prophets, in that his mind was *always* able to perceive the realities of the heavens. As we have seen in the chapter on faith, Bonaventure and other older divines would wholeheartedly agree.

---

33. Willard, "Desire of All Nations," 1:00.

34. Dallas Willard, "Core Value No. 1," *Navigators International Council 2003*, MP3, 10:00. Willard says, "Once in a while, we get a little eye-opener. We need it all the time. You see, the great people of faith, they saw this all the time: 'Moses endured as seeing him who was invisible.' They looked right into this. Jesus lived in the full light of eternity all the time. That's what his faith was. His faith was just vision that this was so" ("Many Mansions," *Things That Accompany Salvation* [Rolling Hills Covenant Church, Rolling Estates, CA, October 25, 1986], MP3/cassette, 23:15).

35. For a similar treatment of prophets in contrast to scribes, see Tozer, *Pursuit of God*, 40.

36. Willard, "No Longer Alone with God," 3:00.

But because the slightest vision of God or the slightest opening of the heavens is so elemental to *any* sort of genuine faith in God, it would be inaccurate to say on Willard's account that *only* the prophets had the heavens opened to them. The prophetic "office" implies not exclusion but expertise. Though a nonmusician hears something when a piece of music is played, a musician hears what a nonmusician does not. In the sense of the expertise of seeing the invisible, all were clearly not prophets. But in the basic sense of seeing *something* of the invisible, all true Israelites were prophets. But probably they did not know this about themselves—hence, their shock at being called "the light of the world" (Matt 5:14).[37]

Much of what Willard has to say about Jesus's prophetic mind is said in the context of discipleship and the imitation of Christ, which we will look at in the next stage. Thus, in describing Jesus's mind, he very easily slides into describing the regenerate and sanctified mind of all humans, the "mind of Christ" (1 Cor 2:16). For example, in chapter 6 of *Renovation*, he describes a mind filled with the thought of God as the grandest, most intrinsically valuable being that exists. Yet the main distinguishing feature of the prophetic mind over the regenerate mind is its *wealth* of firsthand knowledge. A prophet has, in accordance with God's revelation to them, great *intuition* of God and his kingdom in the heavenly places. This would naturally extend to hearing the phenomenal voice of God as well as hearing him with the mind.[38]

Emphasis on *firsthand* knowledge of God should not detract from the first listeners' expectation that Jesus also knew what they knew—that is, that Jesus knew "the basics" of Jewish knowledge. He knew what every mildly educated Jew knew and more. In the dictionary article "Jesus," Willard explains, "[Jesus] was thoroughly immersed from his youth in the teachings, traditions and official practices of the Jewish religion of his day. He lived and died within the outward forms of that religion,

37. Willard, *Conspiracy*, 126–27.
38. Willard, *Guidance*, 101–5.

even while, as a true son of Israel, he drew from the Law and the Prophets a vision of the whole world under God's rule (Ps. 46:10; Isa. 49:6)."[39]

In addition to the four topics addressed in the previous chapter, Willard lays out more of the common understanding among the Jews in *Conspiracy*'s third chapter, entitled "What Jesus Knew." At one point, he calls this a chapter on "Jesus' worldview."[40] It is an assemblage of loci in Jesus's knowledge and of what Willard will call "the faith of Christ."[41] That is to say, Jesus did not just know it; he believed it. From a different perspective, the chapter is an account of the loci that the long-standing historical Jewish experience in the world *should have* bequeathed to later generations and *did* bequeath to Jesus. In a sermon entitled "Jesus' Family of Origin," Willard says, "In these [his early] years, Jesus was learning all the things he later taught."[42] Our earlier discussion of what it meant for the Jews to be *mildly educated* should be recalled here.

The Heart of a Prophet

WILLARD THOUGHT THAT spirit, will, and heart more or less approximate one another in the biblical testimony. *Will* became the preferred philosophical term. *Spirit* is significant because it recalls the human likeness to God, personality, and nonnaturalism. But *heart* is a useful term for naming the Christology of the first listeners because of its Old Testament prominence.[43]

Jesus, says Willard, uses the Old Testament talk of heart to criticize the focus on externals that was prevalent in moral reflection in his

39. Willard, "Jesus," 58.
40. Johnson, Matthews, and Willard, *Dallas Willard's Study Guide*, 2.
41. Willard, "Discipline for Spiritual (Eternal) Living," 1:06:00. Speaking of *Conspiracy*, he says, "The third chapter is where I talk about Jesus's faith. You know, he had one, and I think it's approachable in that way."
42. Dallas Willard, "Jesus' Family of Origin," *Life of Jesus* (Agoura Bible Church, Agoura Hills, CA, December 31, 2006), MP3, 14:45.
43. See Willard, "Spiritual Disciplines," 1:00. In another lecture (Dallas Willard, "Why Am I Here? The Four Great Questions in Life," *Denver Cohort—Session One* [Renovaré Institute, Colorado Springs, CO, October 12, 2010], DVD, 38:45), he compares the difference to the one between morning star and evening star, which mean different things though they point to the same thing. This is a favorite example in explaining Husserl's philosophy of intentionality. See the discussion of Husserl in chapter 4.

day. Thus, it is quite possible that despite the concept's antiquity and familiarity, very few of Jesus's first listeners thought of themselves and of others explicitly in terms of heart. This accounts for why it is a point that Jesus must stress in his teaching.[44] Nevertheless, heart or will is an everyday reality of personal and social interaction, so a few general things can be said about what the first listeners thought about Jesus's own heart.

At the most general level, the great individuals of Israel's history had hearts that were characterized by righteousness. Of what this righteousness consists is, nevertheless, a matter Jesus feels obliged to clarify because of the deformation under which the concept had fallen. But broadly speaking, the Christology of the first-stage listener was that Jesus had a *righteous* heart, as did the prophets before him. This does not mean that the first-stage listener thought of him in terms of sinless perfection. The prophets before him were not thought of as perfect, though they were thought of as righteous, which is clearly a relative concept for the Hebrews.

On one hand, the rightness of Jesus's heart was a matter of logical reasoning. His status as a prophet depended on it. In the Johannine case of the man born blind, the Pharisees debate one another on the premise that a prophet is not a sinner. If Jesus is not righteous, he is not a prophet and not in direct contact with God so as to heal the blind. But if Jesus is genuinely healing the blind, then he is "a worshiper of God and does his will"—that is, he is righteous (John 9:31).

On the other hand, Willard calls attention to another bit of evidence for the first-stage view of Jesus's heart. In *Conspiracy*, he retells the story of the harlot at Simon's house (Luke 7)—a harlot whose heart a prophet, if Jesus were one, could have scrutinized. But about the scrutiny in the reverse direction, Willard comments, "The woman *saw* Jesus and recognized who he was and who dwelt in him. That vision was her faith. She knew he was forgiving and accepting her before he ever

44. Willard, *Conspiracy*, 139–44. See, for instance, Mal 4:6, a verse that Willard believes speaks to the failure of the initial or old covenant ministry with respect to the heart (Dallas Willard, "The Better New Testament Good News about God's Kingdom," *Soul's Eternal Anchor*, MP3/cassette, 0:30).

said, 'Your sins are forgiven.' She knew because she had seen a goodness in him that could only be God and it broke her heart with gratitude and love."[45] According to Willard, Jesus's heart shined forth through his body and his previously performed acts of goodness. That he was powerful and thus performed signs and miracles was one matter, but *the character* of his miracles showed, above all to those who benefited from them, that Jesus was a *good* man.[46] "He went about doing good," says Peter in Acts 10:38, allowing observers to infer that he was, in fact, good in his heart. In the case of the harlot, Willard holds that Jesus's goodness is seen in his previous acts of forgiveness, of not holding peoples' unrighteous actions up as cause for breaking his relationship with them. The woman in Luke 7 must have seen this noncondemnatory righteousness in Jesus before she attempted to gain access to him. As a sinner, she would not have attempted it unless she had. This is the case with all of the healings as well. As acts of benevolence, they reveal his benevolent and righteous heart underneath.

A second thing to mention not necessarily subsumed under the foregoing is how the first-stage listeners perceived Jesus's heart with respect to God. Willard uses many concepts to describe the ideal heart disposition of an Israelite before God according to the Old Testament, but there is only one he uses to describe the first listeners' view of Jesus's heart. Willard speaks of the first listeners' perception of Jesus's *faith*.[47]

In *Guidance*, Willard writes, "The faith by which Jesus Christ lived, his faith in God and his Kingdom, is expressed in the gospel he himself preached. That gospel is the good news that the Kingdom rule of God is available to mankind here and now. His followers did not have this faith within themselves, and they long regarded it only as *his* faith. Even after they came to have faith *in him*, they did not share his faith."[48] Willard continues by retelling the story of the storm

45. Willard, *Conspiracy*, 19.
46. Jesus's works were "primarily acts of love done to help those in need" (Willard, 289).
47. What is said here will assume the phenomenological discussions in later chapters, which can be turned to for clarification if necessary.
48. Willard, *Guidance*, 165–66.

on the Sea of Galilee. In waking Jesus up, his listeners show that "they had great faith in him, but they did not have *his great faith in God*."[49] We will return to this passage later, but what is of interest to us for the moment is the disciples' recognition that Jesus was a person of faith. Jesus believed in the God whose name he evoked in his own gospel. And as we will see, though faith has a mental component for Willard, faith is also an attribute of someone's heart or will.

Though Willard does not speak of the first listeners' recognition of it, the faith of a true Israelite was expressed in *obedience*. Obedience gets to the core of what Willard (if not the first listeners) thought Jesus's heart was like and what it meant for Jesus to believe his own gospel.[50] In the aforementioned dictionary article on Jesus's spirituality, we read, "Unlimited abandonment to God is essential to the spirituality Jesus lived and taught."[51]

In Willard's role as a pastor and spiritual director, we hear much from him about the necessity of obedience and abandonment of the will to God's will.[52] His pastoral theology does not interest us aside from the fact that it is in the imitation *of Christ* that Willard urges the dispositions of surrender, obedience, submission, abandonment, self-denial, humility, and total reliance—which is to say, Christ instanced them.

---

49. Willard, 166. On various occasions, Willard makes much of Paul's phrase "πιστις Ἰησου Χριστου," translating it with theological conviction as a subjective genitive, "the faith *of* Christ." For more on this, see chapter 9.

50. For more on this type of Christology from a person Willard respected, cf. Andrew Murray, *Humility* (1895; repr., Minneapolis: Bethany House, 2001), 25–34. Humility, to Murray's mind, is the root virtue. It is exemplified in God, who became man, and in Jesus, who went to the cross. What's more, Christ redeems by humility. He reveals humility (living from God), and he imparts humility (he lives in us).

51. Willard, "Jesus," 62.

52. Three important talks in this regard are Willard, "Trust in God: Key to Life," MP3/cassette; Dallas Willard, "Trust and Death to Self," *Life without Lack* (Valley Vista Christian Community, Sepulveda, CA, March 19, 1989), MP3/cassette; and Willard, "Sufficiency Completed in Agape," *Life without Lack* (Valley Vista Christian Community, Sepulveda, CA, March 26, 1989), MP3/cassette. He addresses, in turn, faith, self-denial, and love.

The Body of a Prophet

FINALLY, THE CLASS of prophets differed from their covenant brothers and sisters in the character of their bodies. As an Olympic athlete has a body with different resources than the average person, so Israel's heroes and saints could do things with their bodies that the average Jew rightly knew they could not.

Likewise, the first listeners recognize this exceptional divine empowerment of Jesus's body. Willard speaks about it often in terms of the gospel's accompanying manifestation—for example, "the *manifestation* of God's rule from the heavens."[53] He means by this that Jesus's body was capable, with divine help, to put its hands on a leper and heal him. Or his hands could lift up Simon's mother-in-law and cure her fever. Along with Jesus's firsthand knowledge, this bodily ability (ἰσχυς; e.g., Mark 12:30) is a primary aspect of what the first listeners think Jesus means by availability. It is what leads the hemorrhaging woman to think that she merely needed to *touch* Jesus for her own healing. It was not only a matter of "praying" to him that he pray to God. A prophet channels the kingdom through *their body*.

In *Disciplines* and elsewhere, Willard teaches on the New Testament talk of "laying-on of hands."[54] His view is not that God recognizes touching as his cue to intervene, a kind of medical occasionalism. Rather, power from God is resident *in the body* of the ordinary disciple, which, certainly not without God's additional help in the moment, accounts for the extraordinary results.[55]

---

53. Willard, *Conspiracy*, 288–89.

54. Willard, *Disciplines*, 121–23; Willard, "Handout for 'Studies in the Book of Apostolic Acts,'" 10–11; Willard, "Best News," 49:00; cf. Lawson, *Deeper Experiences*, xi–xii.

55. It will be remembered that the combination of abandonment and increased power for service was a characteristic of Keswick and holiness theology of the nineteenth century. Willard had some sustained contact with this in his youth (Dallas Willard, foreword to *How I Changed My Mind about Women in Leadership*, ed. Alan F. Johnson [Grand Rapids, MI: Zondervan, 2010], 9) and continued to read prominent authors such as Andrew Murray, Hannah Whitehall Smith, and Frederik B. Meyer (cf., respectively, Willard, *Renovation*, 150; Dallas Willard, "Knowledge in the Context of Spiritual Formation," *EPS Apologetics Conference—To Everyone an Answer* [Evangelical Philosophical

Though there would be more to say concerning power in a full-dress orthodox Christology, Willard thinks that this augmented physicality applies to Jesus as *vere homo* just as it applied to the prophets.[56] We will return to this later in the chapter when speaking of Jesus's transfiguration as a revelation of true humanity and of matter.

The Point of Miracles: First-Stage Soteriology

AS MENTIONED, THE *news* of the good news at the first level has a journalistic quality. Jesus has announced his prophetic status and, more to the point, is manifesting it with bona fide miracles. These miracles alone demand a statement from Jesus about what is going on. Vice versa, the miracles that accompany Jesus are how the first listeners know that his evangelistic statements are more than hot air. The miracles show God's action, his eternal kingdom, is *with* the actions of his servant Jesus. Luke's Peter assumes it has been common knowledge in Palestine that "he went about doing good and healing all who were oppressed by the devil, *for God was with him*" (Acts 10:38; emphasis mine).

Society, Berkeley, CA, November 17, 2011], MP3, 25:00; and Dallas Willard, foreword to *The Secret of Guidance*, ed. F. B. Meyer [Chicago: Moody, 2010], 7–13).

56. Looked at in summary, this nonrigorous, metaphysical Christology may appear strange to some theologians. But this aura of foreignness may be reduced by remembering that Aquinas developed, albeit with a great deal of originality in his day, a very similar notion of Christ, found in his *Summa Theologiae* 3a. 7 on *de gratia Christi secundum quod est singularis homo*. Therein the reader is asked to ponder the presence of "habitual grace" in Christ. Grace for Aquinas is a compatible, though not identical, concept to Willard's kingdom of God: "It is through habitual grace that the Spirit is said to dwell in man" (3a. 7, 1). For Aquinas, grace is that which a human requires to be fully that which God created him to be, to share in "divinity." For Willard and Aquinas, Christ's humanity was not from its own creaturely resources "divine" in the 2 Pet 1:4 sense. But by reception of habitual grace, it is accidentally "divine." "Grace exists as a kind of accidental modification of the soul," says Aquinas (3a. 6, 6). Moreover, the "grace of union," as Aquinas terms the incarnation, does not make "habitual grace" superfluous. On this, Willard, it seems, concurs.

Other than Aquinas, see also A. B. Bruce's *The Humiliation of Christ* (Grand Rapids, MI: Eerdmans, 1955), 77–79, for a discussion of Aquinas. Bruce, familiar with modern views of Jesus, was someone for whom Willard had lifelong respect as a theologian and philosopher. More study should be made comparing their respective views of Christ and the New Testament.

In Willard's view, Jesus's miracles are an inextricable part of his sojourn on earth. They give, on one hand, the evangelist's *evangel* a certain meaning. In light of the miracles, Jesus's first listeners can initially understand the gospel in light of Israel's men and women of lore and their unique experience of God's hand in their affairs. Without the miracles, it is hard to imagine Jesus's kingdom message not collapsing into a human-powered project for temporal well-being.

The miracles give, on the other hand, the evangel's *evangelist* an introduction that goes beyond his work as an evangelist or mere messenger. His gospel is *about him*. Its meaning is he. John the Baptist, as famous as his ministry was, performed "no sign" (John 10:41). John had the same message as Jesus, but the message in turn said nothing about John.[57] But Jesus, with the miracles in tow, delivers the message, and it reciprocates to himself. His miraculous works were, so Willard, "signs (*semeion*), or 'indications,' of God's reigning. They showed God acting with the servants of the kingdom, soon to be known simply as 'saints' or 'holy ones' (Acts 9:32)."[58]

Though we will look at the Beatitudes briefly in the next chapters, the same interpretive principle Willard uses there applies here—namely, exegetes tend to "bypass contact with Jesus in his own Beatitudes." "Indeed," he writes, "most interpretations of his words manage to forget that he is even on the scene."[59] Such hermeneutics would be far less possible if interpreters had Jesus and his miraculous works before them as, according to the gospel writers, the first interpreters did. If they are a fact, then the gospel and the Beatitudes are in some way attempts to explain who *he* is, what *he* is doing, and how *he* is doing it. His statements *must* be somehow time-stamped and self-referential. The "Jewish experience" of their God filled in the blanks of the first listeners' understanding. God is *with Jesus*.

But the miracles had a more basic nature than that of signs. Willard writes, "Such works were, of course, *primarily* acts of love done to

57. We will discuss this difference further in chapter 7.
58. Willard, *Conspiracy*, 289.
59. Willard, 103.

help those in need."[60] This deeper nature is quite obvious to the first listeners because *they* were the ones in need. They celebrated his coming because he is one who helps *them*, and thus they put their faith in him as their helper. These pericopes cannot be discounted theologically. Jesus's ad hoc help of individuals in need is biblical *salvation*. Any theological attempt to spell out the doctrine of how Jesus saves that passes over these straightforward acts of love is, in Willard's view, deficient.

Willard seems to think this had been happening among divines and laypeople in his day. He emphasizes, in a way that suggests it would be news to his readers, that salvation in the Bible as a whole is primarily deliverance. In 1999, he wrote, "When 'salvation' is spoken of today, what is almost always meant is entry into heaven when one dies. One is 'saved' if they are now counted by God among those who will be admitted into his presence at death or some point thereafter. This usage of 'salvation' and 'saved' deprives the terminology of the general sense of *deliverance* which it bears in the Bible as a whole."[61] With reference to the debated statement in Acts 4:12 and salvation by the one name of Jesus Christ of Nazareth, Willard points out that "the 'salvation' spoken of here is 'deliverance,' which is the generic sense of 'salvation' in biblical usage (cf. Exod. 14:13, 1 Sam. 14:45). The specific case of 'salvation' and being saved in question here is the deliverance of the lame man from his lifelong affliction."[62] This brings the concept of salvation down to a grittier, more temporal level than is usual. But that is where it was for the first listeners because that *is* how Jesus saved them. If asking a first-stage listener about how Jesus is a savior in Israel, the response would be that he helps persons in their time of need.[63]

One place to see where this root element of soteriology finds further resonance in Willard's thought is in his lifelong appreciation of

60. Willard, 289 (emphasis mine).

61. Dallas Willard, "Idaho Springs Inquires concerning Spiritual Formation," in Willard, *Great Omission*, 110.

62. Willard, *Knowing*, 186–87.

63. Here is further evidence that the first-stage gospel is not new theology. Cf. Willard, "Handout for 'Jesus' Good News,'" lesson 5, where Willard makes mention of "the Jewish religion which is almost completely 'this-worldly' in its view of salvation."

John R. Rice's book *Prayer: Asking and Receiving.*[64] The book excels in making prayer a matter of ad hoc asking for God's assistance in everyday matters of provision, physical healing, and success in our work/ministry.[65] Rice's view of God as one who responds ad hoc to material and existential needs is the operant theology in Willard's account of the first listeners. Jesus is an intermediary, an intercessor, for YHWH. As such, he is Israel's savior, their deliverer.

Regarding this grittier, more temporal understanding, Willard asks us to consider salvation in Abraham's story as paradigmatic. In *Conspiracy*, Willard asks, "What did Abraham believe that led God to declare or 'reckon' him righteous?" and provocatively inserts, "Was it that God had arranged payment for his sins?" Abraham's faith, he answers, is faith that God would interact with him now. In the famous story, Abraham is counted righteous because he trusted that God would give him *a male baby* in his earthly lifetime: "He trusted God, of course, but it was for things involved in his current existence. He believed that *God would interact with him now*—just as those who later gathered around Jesus did."[66] Abraham's faith was in the availability of God's activity for matters of his own, this-worldly life. This temporal divine activity constituted salvation for Abraham.

For the first-stage listener, Jesus's gospel is "a claim," as Willard says about Acts 4:12 in *Knowing Christ*, "about the availability of the power of God to meet human need." This rudimentary proclamation of good news does not cease to be true when other levels of understanding are reached, for "this 'availability' was," as he continues in *Knowing Christ*, "a part of the 'good news' about the kingdom of God as that good news was lived and preached by the earliest disciples of Jesus."[67] That the God

---

64. John R. Rice, *Prayer: Asking and Receiving* (1942; repr., Murfreesboro, TN: Sword of the Lord, 1980). Discovered most likely before or during his undergraduate days when he heard Rice speak in chapel, he recommended it forty-five years later as one of his favorite books on prayer (Willard, *Conspiracy*, 412n9).

65. Dallas Willard, "How Prayer Works," *Essentials of Kingdom Living*, MP3/cassette, 18:30.

66. Willard, *Conspiracy*, 47.

67. Willard, *Knowing*, 187.

of Israel was like this was known from the Scriptures. That God used prophets or intermediaries to pass it on to the covenant people was known from the Scriptures. That such a prophet could be found in Jesus was the first *news* of the good news.

Alive to God: First-Stage Faith

UNTIL NOW, WE have considered various aspects in the first-stage listener's *knowledge* of the gospel Jesus preached. We have considered the "available for Jesus" topography that Jesus's gospel announces, and we have considered the person and work of Jesus in relation to this new topography: Jesus as a prophet and deliverer who lives life before an open heaven.

But knowledge is not the same as faith. What has been discussed previously falls in the category of the knowledge that the listener has about Jesus, the kingdom of God, and the gospel. They rightly understand reality to be a certain way, and they truly comprehend a basic gospel of availability. But now they face a decision, one that may be answered in a moment or over time. Will I *trust* what I have heard and what I know? Or will I not and thus find some way to *deny* it—that is, put it out of my mind? Will I *trust* Jesus? Or will I *deny* him?

In addition to chapter 4, I will say more in later chapters about Willard's views of knowledge and faith in the process of repentance (metanoia) and belief in the gospel (Mark 1:15). Here I have the more modest intent of explaining why, of all possible human responses to Jesus and the gospel, *faith* obtains salvation. That is, what is the relation between faith and salvation according to Willard?

Saved by Grace through Faith

AS ALREADY INTIMATED in the section on Jesus's heart, Willard uses the story of the disciples waking Jesus during the storm to distinguish between a faith in Christ and a faith in God: "[The disciples] had great faith in him, but they did not have *his great faith in God*."[68] But many

---

68. Willard, *Guidance*, 166.

in Jesus's day did not even have that. They had *an understanding* of all I have hitherto presented about Jesus, the kingdom, and the gospel but did not have any *faith* in him. They would not have woken Jesus in the boat or even have entered it with him. Many had heard and understood the gospel about Jesus the prophet but were still mulling over whether they should trust him.

The woman of John 4 says to her Samaritan village, "Come, see a man who told me all that I ever did. Can this be the Christ?" (John 4:29). Philip says to Nathanael, "We have found him of whom Moses in the Law and also the prophets wrote, Jesus of Nazareth, the son of Joseph" (John 1:45). Both the Samaritan village and Nathanael have the requisite information. They have the gospel about Jesus present to their minds and are given the previously impossible option of putting their faith *in* Jesus. But for an unspecified period of time, they lack "faith *in* Christ" (Gal 2:16; emphasis mine).[69] Jesus's hometown is famous for ultimately lacking faith *in him*, "the carpenter, the son of Mary," though they had the requisite information for making that step (Mark 6:3).

Taking a positive example, let us return to Willard's reading of Luke 7 and the harlot who saw and knew Jesus's love and acceptance. "That vision was her faith," he says about her. To understand how Willard is reading this passage, one must recognize how he connects faith with action. That that vision was her faith is revealed in *her action* of entering into Simon's house to embrace Jesus. In *Conspiracy*, Willard writes, "We always live up to our beliefs—or down to them, as the case may be. Nothing else is possible. It is the nature of belief."[70] The harlot lives up to her belief (faith) in Jesus as forgiving. Her action—the impingement upon Jesus and Simon and the weeping, kissing, and anointing—expresses this "faith *in* Christ." Her vision or knowledge of "who he was and who dwelt in him" is the fundamental *content* of her faith in Jesus.[71]

69. Willard, 166.

70. Willard, *Conspiracy*, 307.

71. Willard, 19. In chapter 4, there is a more exhaustive discussion of content.

The point is that the first-stage vision of Jesus is not necessarily the first-stage faith in Jesus. Merely having the correct vision of Jesus and his message but lacking the faith would result, so Willard, in a psychological condition of being *under conviction*. More importantly, merely having the vision does not result in the person's salvation. Faith is essential.

Faith, compared with knowledge, makes a real difference in the orientation and quality of human life as a whole. In *Knowing Christ*, Willard writes, "Belief involves the will in a way that knowledge does not."[72] Its tie to the will is the reason for God's special interest in the disposition of faith and why faith, in contrast to knowledge, *obtains* salvation. Faith by nature disposes a person to seek to live in accordance with the vision of reality intrinsic to it—even if that vision is false. Knowledge does not work that way. For example, the knowledge that eating vegetables is good for one's body is not a sufficient internal disposition to seek the good of eating vegetables. But if one *believes* that eating vegetables is good, then one *will* order one's will and life in terms of that good and obtain it when appropriate and when circumstances allow. It is the nature of belief to function in this way. "Belief puts us into action and makes contact with reality," writes Willard.[73] Again, "faith is important because it integrates our life with reality."[74]

Returning to the story of Abraham, Abraham's faith obtains the salvation (the male baby) he was promised and was seeking because it put him into action (a combination of having sexual intercourse and waiting) and in right relation with the gracious reality (God) that had promised and was able and faithful to provide this "salvation." The same dynamic is at work in the life of Jesus. Faith *in Christ* brought persons into contact with *the gracious reality* of Christ. Their faith obtains salvation at the hand of Jesus not because God has arbitrarily linked salvation to the disposition of faith in Jesus but because Jesus *is* savior. He is a

---

72. Willard, *Knowing*, 16.

73. Dallas Willard, foreword to *Apprenticeship with Jesus*, ed. Gary W. Moon (Grand Rapids, MI: Baker, 2009), 14.

74. Willard, "Human Disaster of Unbelief," 55:00.

person for whom the kingdom of God is available and through whom deliverance may flow.

Ignorant of later theological controversies about who could and could not be justified before God, this was the commonsense understanding of the first listeners. It is what Willard means when he says, "Everyone knew that whoever trustingly put themselves in *his* [Jesus's] hands, as this poor scandalous woman did, were in fact in the hands of God."[75] Their faith *in* Jesus the person obtained the accurately perceived benefits of his reality: that he *was* one who could and would deliver another in the power of God.

Such a theological analysis of the reason for God's interest in faith and why it obtains salvation is contrasted by Willard with what he calls in *Conspiracy* "bar-code faith." Years before appearing in print, he spoke of an erroneous teaching on faith that understands its primary value to be in the effect that it has on God. The upshot of this teaching is that "God will like us if we believe," and on that basis, we will be saved—that is, justified.[76] This theology ironically turns faith, so Willard, into a "meritorious deed" or a "saving work."[77]

In Willard's antimodernist Baptist context of the 1940s and '50s (in which heavy emphasis was put on coming forward and professing Christ publicly), it is not difficult to imagine how this view of faith was implicitly if not explicitly taught. But Willard found it to still be present in many contemporary circles. It went hand in hand with making the object of "saving faith" not Jesus but *a theory* about the atoning work of Jesus on the cross and other "correct" doctrines and with making no clear distinction between faith and the mere profession of a "correct" doctrine. In this view, faith obtains salvation because God has a faith

75. Willard, *Conspiracy*, 19.
76. Willard, "Human Disaster of Unbelief," 50:45.
77. Dallas Willard, "Getting the Good News Right," *Beyond Belief* (Grace Fellowship Church, Timonium, MD, May 2, 1998), MP3/cassette, 59:15. See also Willard, "Role of Faith," 30:00: "We take faith as a work of righteousness and faith is not a work of righteousness. Faith is a reality which has its causes and its effects. . . . Faith is a confidence leads that you to interact with reality in such a way that a result comes." See also Willard, *Disciplines*, 41.

fetish and lavishes gifts on those who manage to instance it.[78] But as Willard sees it, faith obtains salvation because faith—through its essential connection to the person's psychology, especially to their heart/will and not just to their mind—brings a person's intentions and eventually their whole psychology into contact with reality. In this case, with a gracious *God* who saves.

Regeneration

ABRAHAM'S STORY EXEMPLIFIES a feature that does not on the surface seem to be true of the harlot and other first-stage listeners. Abraham trusts *God*, whereas the first-stage listeners trust *Jesus*, the prophet among them. It seems that they do not trust God at all, only an intermediary. Are they really brought into contact with God through Jesus's service?

Willard makes an important distinction here. Not everyone who received the benefits of Jesus's deliverance believed Jesus's *gospel*, a gospel about Jesus but also about God. The Johannine version of the feeding of the five thousand tells of the crowd seeking Jesus on the other side of the lake. Jesus says to them, "You are seeking me, not because you saw signs, but because you ate your fill of the loaves" (John 6:26). Here is clearly a case of "people who believe in Jesus [who] do not actually believe in God," as Willard said.[79] They do not believe that *God's kingdom* is available for Jesus. They do not see "signs." They only see effects. That *God* sent and anointed Jesus to multiply the loaves, cast out the demons, and heal the sick—that Jesus's service is an act of the invisible God—is not in view. What is in view and what they trust is that "they may eat their fill." Thus, in seeking Jesus, they do not, as the harlot did, "put themselves . . . in the hands of God." In a sense, their faith and action obtain salvation, but in a more profound sense, it does not.

---

78. There is a type of Malebranchean occasionalism underway here, for faith is not understood as having its own causes and its own effects. See also the discussion of standing on proprieties in chapter 7.

79. Willard, *Conspiracy*, 91. This connects with Willard's criticism of vampire Christians who trust in Jesus's deliverance from hell but have no use for him, which will be discussed later. See more on believing Jesus but not believing what Jesus believes in *Conspiracy*, 318–19.

"Salvation Is a Life"

THE MORE PROFOUND sense involves an understanding of salvation that is more than deliverance from temporal ailments like hunger. This is salvation as *regeneration*. Regeneration is an extremely important doctrine in Willard's thought, and many of the building blocks of his view have already been discussed.[80]

Regeneration is an event that takes place in the person on account of the heavens being opened, even on account of the "small cracks" that were the more common Jewish experience.[81] At the basis of regeneration lies the prophetic vision or simply some vision of God, and whether they knew it or not, the difference between the vision of the prophets and that of the Israelite faithful was simply one of degree. A prophet is an expert and receives "commendation" for their exemplary faith (Heb 11:2), but all genuine covenant partners have seen *something*.[82] As discussed in chapter 4, the primary way that faith comes is by the word of God (Rom 10:17), whose coming in and of itself is a peculiar way of "seeing" the action of God—namely, his speaking.

Faith is the human response to this God-given vision, and it shows itself in human action or readiness to act. It shows itself in Abraham waiting for a son and in the harlot crashing Simon's party. Though faith is not explicit in the Old Testament texts, once the New Testament concept is psychologically understood, Willard would argue, it is not hard to detect faith's presence in the Old Testament accounts. And unless one wishes to exclude regeneration from salvation or exclude it from the salvation of the ancient Israelites (in the manner of dispensational or covenant theology), one must explain how it is a pervasive experience

---

80. As evidence of how important regeneration is for Willard, see *Conspiracy*, 42; and "Spiritual Formation as a Natural Part," 49.

81. Not, I submit, with the baptism or filling of the Spirit.

82. Again, see Willard, "Many Mansions," 23:15. In his doctrine of regeneration, Willard is leaning on John Wesley. Cf. John Wesley, "The Great Privilege of Those That Are Born of God," in Outler, *Works of John Wesley: 1–33. Sermons I.*

in the whole history of redemption. Regeneration must include in a real way Abraham's experience and those who followed him.[83]

That Abraham is included is Willard's argument in the following: "Abraham's confidence was that God would give him a male heir. That's the faith that God looked at and accepted as righteousness. That's the life of faith. That's counting on God for life. That's the kind of faith—Abraham's kind—that Paul spoke of in Romans 4. This awakening of faith—which, by the way, need not be just a moment but can also be a process—is, in fact, regeneration."[84] Though often worked out in experiences of deliverance (e.g., male heirs), regeneration is the more profound aspect of salvation in the Old Testament period.[85] More people in God's work in human history were regenerated than knew something of *the doctrine* of regeneration.

Before returning to Jesus's first audiences, let us rehearse another element of Willard's view of regeneration. Regeneration, according to Willard's reading of the New Testament, is a matter of *new life*, particularly life from above (John 3). At the 2009 Wheaton Theology conference, he spoke of it as "the event of *a new type of life* entering into the individual human being."[86] This may seem irreconcilable with his view of regeneration as faith and faith as a human *response* to the vision of God, but this is an instance where Willard's "Calvinism" rears its head. In the section on "Faith That Comes by the Word of God" in chapter 4, we looked at Willard's view of the *gratuity* of faith.

An important parallel to this teaching is found in *Disciplines*'s chapter "Salvation Is a Life," where *faith* is said to "display itself on the pages of the New Testament in three major dimensions."[87] These

---

83. See Dallas Willard, "Entering the Kingdom Today," *Soul's Eternal Anchor*, MP3/cassette, 4:30.

84. Willard, "Gospel of the Kingdom," 54.

85. Willard teaches that people enter the kingdom in all sorts of ways (Willard, "Entering the Kingdom Today," 15:15).

86. Willard, "Spiritual Formation as a Natural Part," 49.

87. In his lectures from that period, he usually says they are three dimensions of salvation (Willard, "You Can't Have One without the Other," *Discipleship and the Kingdom of God* [Western District Conference, Ventura Missionary Church, Ventura, CA, May 14, 1984], MP3/cassette, 22:45; and Dallas Willard, "The Biblical View of the Imago Dei,"

are (1) "the presence of a new power *within* the individual, erupting in a break with the past through turning in repentance and the release of forgiveness"; (2) the transformation of character; and (3) the power over evil.[88] With the latter two following from it, the first dimension is undoubtedly Willard's doctrine of regeneration, which includes, by its very nature, repentance and forgiveness. Much as Willard emphasized the gratuity of the theological virtues in "Faith, Hope and Love," emphasis is placed in *Disciplines* on all of this being *given*. "Faith is created in our hearts," he says in the 1987 essay, "as we listen to the word of God in the Gospel of The Kingdom."[89]

So the human response (which Willard will also describe as a surrender) is an effect of God's activity in the person both in the form of new mental horizons (the word of God as truth, the manifest presence of God) and in the form of an infusion of life (the word of God as substance, grace, or the action of God to accomplish what the person cannot accomplish on their own), which makes it possible for the person to believe what he or she sees.

Another typical move in the doctrine of regeneration for Willard is to recognize an overlap in the concepts associated with regeneration in the Bible's kingdom language. "Entering the kingdom" is familiar language in the Synoptics and John. But speaking about regeneration in the Wheaton Theology conference, he says, "'Life' is associated with seeing and entering the kingdom of God."[90] And "to enter the kingdom is to have the life 'from above.' *That life is the principle of kingdom inclusion.*"[91]

Deliverance from the Law of Sin and Death [Eastern Mennonite College, Harrisonburg, VA, January 15, 1985], MP3/cassette, 40:45). This is later expanded in Willard, *Conspiracy*, 366–69, to five dimensions.

88. Willard, *Disciplines*, 39–40.

89. Willard, "Faith, Hope and Love." See also Dallas Willard, "The Specific Disciplines: Solitude, Silence and Fasting," *The Spirit of the Disciplines* (Canoga Park Presbyterian Church, Canoga Park, CA, February 24, 1993), MP3/cassette, 8:30.

90. Willard, "Spiritual Formation as a Natural Part," 49.

91. Willard, 49.

In other words, "entering the kingdom" is the language Jesus gave to his first listeners to contemplate regeneration.[92] This key doctrinal conclusion is largely the result of his exegesis of John 3 and Colossians 1. When treating John 3, Willard points out in *Guidance* and elsewhere that Nicodemus comes to Jesus claiming to *see* the kingdom of God (faith). Jesus's response makes reference to a birth from above—that is, a birth from the above *kingdom*—without which the same kingdom is invisible. "Like all seeing," Willard explains, "spiritual seeing also requires the appropriate faculties and equipment."[93] Seeing God and his actions is a power of those who have been made alive by and alive to God and his actions.

From the human perspective, the step of regeneration is a catch-22, a situation that Willard believes Paul expresses when he speaks of being "dead in the trespasses and sins" (Eph 2:1). Coming alive to a new life principle is impossible from the standpoint of those currently dead to it. Crucially, this step is accomplished *by the very life principle to which* humans are made alive. Cats are *dead* to poetry. To explain regeneration, Willard asks us to "imagine an otherwise 'normal' kitten that suddenly begins to appreciate and compose poetry."[94] Taking this metaphor one step further, in human regeneration, it is as if *poetry itself* were responsible for making a cat alive to poetry. In being addressed by a poem, the cat is made aware of the poem and of poetry in general. That is to say, the experience of regeneration itself is the first kingdom event, which a regenerate person is empowered to have. God and his kingdom both make the human spirit alive and are the very thing to which and in which the human spirit is alive.

In terms of appropriation in the Trinity, the infusion of life that makes it possible for the person to believe what he or she sees is the

---

92. For more on the concept of entering the kingdom and regeneration, see Willard, "Entering the Kingdom Today"; Dallas Willard, "Entering at the Straight Gate," *The Kingdom of God* (Faith Evangelical Church, Chatsworth, CA, May 28, 1978), MP3/cassette; and Dallas Willard, "Entering the Kingdom of Heaven," *Manifesting the Kingdom*, MP3/cassette.

93. Willard, *Guidance*, 157–58.

94. Willard, 157.

work of the Spirit. Being "born of the Spirit," in contrast to "entering the kingdom," is less familiar language in the gospels. But in constructing the doctrine, Willard follows Jesus's change in metaphors in John 3 and refers to the event of regeneration, by which we "participate in God's governance, his 'Kingdom,'" as "an additional birth *of Spirit*."[95] The Johannine pneumatology at this juncture is important for Willard. Though ostensibly, Jesus's listeners are not in conscious contact with the Spirit and are still in a time when "the Spirit had not been given" (John 7:39), in reality, *if they have entered the kingdom of God*, they have been born of the Spirit.[96] Willard works this out in more detail in *Guidance* and elsewhere.

Now, returning to the case of Jesus and his first-stage listeners, there are two ways that Jesus is responsible for regeneration—that is, for salvation in this more profound sense. Ostensibly, he is feeding, healing, and teaching people and casting out demons. But at a profounder level, he is giving his audience a new mental horizon by preaching the word of God. In doing this, Jesus the man is depending on the Spirit to infuse life into his listeners, to make his listeners alive to the realities in the new mental horizon he gives them.

As the human minister, Jesus does two things. First, his gospel calls attention to the availability of God's kingdom *for him*. Hearing the word of God, listeners are invited to know and believe that *God* has sent Jesus and that *God* is with Jesus. They are invited to *see* the kingdom, the action of God, in the vocation of Jesus. Given that the Spirit is working with the word, some see it. But many, perhaps, do not. Without the life or power given for regeneration, they nevertheless see *the effects* of God and his kingdom and may want to benefit from them, to "get their fill." If so, they benefit from the effects of the gospel without believing it.

Second, Jesus's bodily presence radiates the spiritual presence of God. Here is where, for Willard, the theme of God's manifest presence

95. Willard, 158 (emphasis mine).

96. In response to a woman's question during a Q and A, Willard said, "I actually think the point of regeneration was when [the first disciples] decided to be with him" (Dallas Willard, "Q & A: Formation," *Divine Conspiracy*, MP3/video, 15:45).

with the people of Israel ("the baptism of Moses," as discussed in the previous chapter) enters the story of Jesus. On the whole, this biblical theme helps undergird the doctrine of regeneration, the profounder sense of salvation, with which Willard wishes to interpret the soteriology of the whole Bible. The manifestations of God among Israel in the desert continued, albeit in less spectacular form, throughout Israel's history and provided a basis for faith and regeneration among the "non-prophets" of Israel.[97] And individuals, we remember, are also capable of immersing those in their proximity with the manifest presence of God.

Filled with the Spirit, Jesus continues the pattern of Mosaic baptism among the people of God. Behind this claim lies a whole account of what Jesus's reception of the Spirit meant. That is to say, it is not so much an exegetical point for Willard as it is a systematic or logical point. Willard notices the "baptizing" phenomenon in Scripture, throughout church history, and in his own experience *and concludes* that Jesus, as one preeminently filled with the Spirit, also "baptized" others in this way.

In 1993, he says, "The important thing was that, when Jesus came on earth and people listened to him and they watched him, they realized that God was present. He was present in Jesus Christ."[98] In truth, Willard's best exegetical evidence for this comes from his analysis of Luke 10:11, where the apostles are told to tell those who *reject* their gospel that *nevertheless*, the kingdom has come near.[99] In other words, the kingdom was present in the form of the Mosaic baptism, which the apostles' physical presence occasioned. What was true for the disciples must be eminently true of the master, Willard reasons.

---

97. On this matter, Willard thought well of Daniel Fuller's *Gospel and Law: Continuum or Contrast?* (Grand Rapids, MI: Eerdmans, 1980). See Willard, *Disciplines*, 42–43.

98. Willard, "Bringing the Kingdom," 1:13:00. See also Willard, "Parable of the Sower," 8:30: "In him the kingdom of God drew nigh. It was in him and in his presence that the kingdom of God had come to earth in a manner in which it had never been here before. . . . He took the kingdom of God with him. Wherever he was the kingdom of God was."

99. Willard, *Conspiracy*, 29.

Faith in Jesus the Prophet as Regeneration

To conclude here, I want to make the important argument that for Willard, genuine first-stage faith in Jesus is also regeneration. I'm arguing this despite the fact that, as Willard writes, "the first *clear* manifestation of heavenly life in the individual [i.e., regeneration] is recognition, hearty confidence, that Jesus really is the Anointed One, Christ, Lord."[100] If what this statement means is that *only* those who confess Jesus as the Messiah are regenerate, then Willard's statements about Abraham, even those in the same paper, are incomprehensible. The fact is that genuine faith in the first stage is *hard* to identify in persons because there are many who obtain something of the deliverance Jesus brings who do not *believe his gospel* about God. For this reason, there is a need, as Jesus communicates in his early parables, for patience and discernment.[101]

Regenerate persons who have faith in Jesus according to the first stage are, therefore, those who see the kingdom *of God* in Jesus. This is the most rudimentary meaning of Jesus's gospel: not that Jesus can do extraordinary things and help persons in need but that the kingdom of God is at hand *for him*. The four Gospels give many reports of persons who saw the gospel effects but tried to deny the gospel explanation—that is, that "the kingdom of God has come upon you" (Luke 11:20).

By contrast, Willard describes the harlot as one who recognized Jesus's position in the realm of God's action and entrusted herself to Jesus in the expectation that she was entrusting herself to God, was "in the hands of God." A little bit further, Willard repeats, "From the very beginning of [Jesus's] work, those who relied on him had, at his touch, entered the rule, or governance, of God and were receiving its gracious sufficiency."[102] This quote explains how, though often worked out in experiences of deliverance, regeneration is the underlying event.

---

100. Willard, "Spiritual Formation as a Natural Part," 52.

101. For more on this, see Willard's series on the parables: *Parable Teaching*, twelve MP3s/cassettes.

102. Willard, *Conspiracy*, 20.

Granted, there were some sheep of the flock of Israel such as Simeon and Anna (Luke 2:25–38) who were not lost. These persons did not need to hear Jesus's gospel *in order to* be regenerate. They already were. And there are some who receive the merciful deliverance that is in Jesus but who nevertheless do not *see* the kingdom of God, who do not trust that "God anointed Jesus of Nazareth with the Holy Spirit and with power" (Acts 10:38). But finally, though they are harder to identify at this stage, there are some (like the harlot) who "hear the word and accept it and bear fruit" (Mark 4:20).

The Resurrection of Jesus and the Continuation of First-Stage Faith in Him

WHEN CONSIDERED AGAINST the backdrop of the history of theology, Willard is making a fairly bold theological claim. He is saying that a basic faith in Jesus and his gospel *and* a basic form of salvation (ad hoc deliverance and especially regeneration) were a possibility *before* Jesus goes to his crucifixion, resurrection, ascension, and heavenly session. Christian salvation is, in an initial and important stage, not dependent on the cross, the resurrection, or any of these climactic events in Jesus's life. It is merely dependent on the existence and presence of Jesus on earth as one who lives richly in the kingdom of God.

Nevertheless, the climactic events add key elements to Jesus's basic gospel of availability. For these first-stage listeners, Jesus's crucifixion, taken by itself, is pure tragedy. But coupled with his resurrection, its "sting" is absent (1 Cor 15:55). Willard certainly understands the resurrection as Jesus's return to natural bodily life, albeit in a glorified state, after his bodily death.[103] But the resurrection is also understood as an event that, in hindsight, proves the authenticity and durability of a life in Jesus that was not reducible to his natural bodily life. This Willard calls Jesus's *transcendent life*.

One remarkable and revealing passage is found in *Disciplines*. Willard begins by commenting on the Christology of the early church,

103. Willard, *Knowing*, chap. 5.

pointing out, "It wasn't Christ's death that gave rise to this courageous early church—but his *life*!" He then continues, "As the pages of the Gospels amply show, *Christ's transcendent life in the present Kingdom of heaven* is what drew the disciples together around Jesus prior to his death. And then resurrection and post resurrection events proved that life to be indestructible. They verified that all of Jesus' teachings about life in the Kingdom were true."[104] Jesus's life, his companions perceived, was not life as usual. Jesus lived richly in the kingdom of God. As such, his life was an instantiation of true human life. In Willard's reading of the New Testament, the resurrection does not reveal this transcendent quality of Jesus's life for the first time. It was something obvious to some before his death and was, as Willard says, what drew persons to Jesus as his students. Hence, the central fact of Jesus's presence in Palestine was not his life's climax in his death and resurrection in Jerusalem but rather his personal reality and presence, what Willard calls "his transcendent life." This fact, Willard believes, is what inspired the church of the first centuries to persist and thrive through marginalization and persecution.[105]

Given this more primary fact about Jesus's person, how Willard interprets the resurrection event is instructive. The resurrection is not merely a miracle, the regifting of breath to Jesus. What matters in the resurrection is not that *someone* was raised but that *this one* was raised—this one whose life was ostensibly higher and richer than that of others.[106] So Willard, "The resurrection was a cosmic event *only* [emphasis mine] because it validated the reality and the indestructibility of what Jesus had preached and exemplified *before* his death—the enduring reality and openness of God's Kingdom."[107] With *exemplified*, Willard here refers, I believe, to who Jesus was, the kind of transcendent life he instantiated.

---

104. Willard, *Disciplines*, 35 (emphasis mine).
105. Willard, 35. Willard doesn't explain, but one may wonder how Christ's transcendent life compares to "the baptism of Moses" or the Trinitarian baptism spoken of earlier.
106. Dallas Willard and Todd Hunter, "Kingdom Living 2 Q & A," *Kingdom Living: Walking in the Character and Power of God* (Southside Vineyard, Grand Rapids, MI, April 12, 2002), MP3, 23:00.
107. Willard, *Disciplines*, 37.

The presence of this enduring reality with the human Jesus is what made the resurrection *gospel* for the first listeners and why this event alone could in the decades that followed serve as shorthand for preaching the gospel of the kingdom.[108]

Transfiguration

FOR THE MOST part, Jesus's transcendent life was revealed to his audiences in extremely small doses. But Willard thought that certain events exposed it more nakedly. In *Conspiracy*'s discussion of the *personal* nature of the cosmos, of the cosmos's fundamental determination by and openness to *personal* factors, Willard writes the following: "These factors are God and his kingdom among us. They have announced themselves definitively in human history in the person and word of Jesus, but especially in his transfiguration and his resurrection. On these occasions, high points in the history of redemption, ordinary human beings *saw* the kingdom of God (Luke 9:27–28). Accordingly they lie right at the heart of the *knowledge* tradition that provides the basis for the historical and institutional reality of Christianity (2 Pet. 1:16–18; 1 Cor. 15)."[109]

What we should notice here is the coupling of the transfiguration and the resurrection. This coupling shows that Willard does not take the resurrection to be a passage for Jesus into a *new* metaphysical existence. The metaphysical existence *revealed* in the resurrection is the same metaphysical existence that was *revealed* in the transfiguration.

Later in *Conspiracy*, he teaches on the metaphysics of the postresurrection Jesus: "He had a body: a focus of his personality in space and time that was publicly observable and interacted with physical realities. But it was radiant, and therefore it was called 'the body of his glory'

108. Cf. Willard and Hunter, "Kingdom Living 2," 17:30. Here Willard exegetes Paul's statement in 1 Cor 15:3 that the death and resurrection are "of first importance," saying, "Because the death and resurrection of Jesus is the final note in the proclamation of what the kingdom of God is. If you don't understand that you'll never understand the kingdom. See that's what the fellows didn't understand. That's why even in the first chapter of the book of Acts they're still saying, 'Lord, at this time will you restore the kingdom to Israel?'"
109. Willard, *Conspiracy*, 377.

(Phil. 3:21). And it was not *restrained* by space, time, and physical causality in the manner of physical bodies."[110] This being who Jesus was revealed to be in and after his resurrection provides evidence of what, according to Willard, Jesus was *before* his resurrection. His resurrection body was nothing more than the transfigured body of Jesus manifesting itself again.

Though this quite high Christology does exceed a Christology of Jesus as a mere prophet, it is still not necessarily orthodox Christology. Willard typically inserts these descriptions into arguments about what is possible for *created* human life—that is, the future existence of Jesus's *followers*. In terms of his argument, the point of describing the metaphysics of the transfiguration and resurrection appearances was to display the potential of matter in its highest form—that is, in the *glorified human* form. The transfiguration and the resurrection are the greatest revelations to date of what *humanity* is. They are moments of humanity's glorification.[111]

Thus we read, "Indeed, the 'transfiguration' of Jesus must be regarded as the highest revelation of the nature of matter recorded in human history."[112] This is the basis of the hope that "at the initiative and guidance of the spiritual word of God (John 6:63), a person's finite energies can be meshed with God's in such a way that progressively—and, eventually, totally—he or she can 'put on incorruption' (1 Cor. 15:54: cf. 1 Pet 1:4 and Phil. 3:11)."[113] We learn that transfiguration and resurrection were primarily lessons not in Christology but in anthropology.

110. Willard, 395.

111. The quote Willard takes from William Temple is directly relevant here: "We must not form a conception of Humanity and either ask if Christ is human or insist on reducing Him to the limits of our conception; we must ask, 'What is Humanity?' and look at Christ to find the answer. We only know what Matter is when Spirit dwells in it; we only know what Man is when God dwells in him" (William Temple, "The Divinity of Christ," in *Foundations: A Statement of Christian Belief in Terms of Modern Thought*, ed. B. H. Streeter [London: Macmillan, 1912], quoted in Willard, *Guidance*, xi).

112. Willard, *Conspiracy*, 254. See the whole section for more on the Christology of the transfiguration.

113. Willard, *Disciplines*, 88–89.

As Willard says, "Just like Jesus appeared glorious on the Mount of Transfiguration, that's how you will appear."[114]

Seated at the Right Hand of God

THOUGH NOT TO a new metaphysical existence, Jesus as "the firstborn among many brothers" (Rom 8:29) does transition to a more strategic role. What his resurrection announces is, among other things, *a continuation* of the good news that the first-stage listeners had already accepted and rejoiced in. The kingdom is still available on earth through its most capable intermediary who still lives among them. As Willard says, "[The resurrection] meant that the Kingdom, with the communal form his disciples had come to know and hope in, would go on."[115] In the days after his ascension, Jesus is somehow ubiquitously present with his listeners and manifests his presence primarily through speaking.

But where is his natural, sense-perceptible body after the ascension? Is it any*where*? Not a major point in his teaching, Willard has an answer to this question, which has troubled Lutheran and Reformed/Catholic relations. In what is an aside leading up to discussing Acts 1:6 and the disciples' inabilities to think of the kingdom as something other than a sociopolitical order, he says, "He is ascending back to the place where he has [*sic*], at the right hand of the Father even now. It's a real place, by the way, in the universe. We don't know where it is, wouldn't know what to do with it if we did. We'd just try a Babel-thing, probably. Except this time, it would be a spaceship; try to get a spaceship to go there. I wouldn't want to approach it, really. That's a real place, and Jesus is still there. But he's also still here. The continuing incarnation of Jesus is in his people."[116] Jesus as a sense-perceptible, biological being is located and localizable *within* this vast universe. He is not in another space-time dimension called "heaven." In Willard's cosmology, there is

---

114. Willard, "Session 3," 1:22:30.

115. Willard, *Disciplines*, 37. In other contexts, Willard refers to this enduring communal form as "the body of Christ" of Paul's epistles or as, in a phrase of his own, "the continuing incarnation." One should not miss the resemblance to the Roman Catholic doctrine of the mystical body.

116. Willard, "Kingdom Gospel," 2:00.

no discussion of such a place.[117] Jesus has, indeed, left the disciples, taking his "resurrection body" with him. But he has not left our space-time cosmos.

This is a unique solution to Jesus's continuing existence in matter, and I know of no other theologian who holds it. It makes sense of how Jesus is literally in heaven, as the Scriptures testify, but without doing violence to the Jewish notion of heaven. For the Jews, heaven is the heaven*s*, including the atmosphere (the first heaven), the realm of the planets and stars (the second heaven), and the realm of the angels and of God (the third heaven). The older Christian cosmologies, based on Aristotle and Ptolemy, conflated the second and third heavens, or at least thought of the third heaven as geographically "up." Consequently, they had no problem with the upness of the ascension.

Since the Copernican revolution, the tendency has been to think of Jesus's ascended location as *outside* the physical cosmos in another realm, perhaps a spiritual realm properly called "heaven," and this has posed a problem for Jesus's continued bodily existence. But by claiming that Jesus physically ascended to the realm of the planets and stars, where he currently remains, Willard seizes upon the ambiguity of the Jewish notion of heaven in a way that can account for Jesus's bodily presence in heaven and his geographical absence from his listeners on earth. It is also unique in the way that it can make sense of the upness of the ascension to the post-Copernican astronomical mindset. Jesus does not go up because "the door" to the otherworldly dimension (a.k.a. heaven) is "up there." Jesus goes up because that is where he is. Examples of ill-advised attempts to find Jesus (a tower of Babel, a spaceship) would similarly have to work upward.[118]

Notice too how this view of the ascension is the complement of Willard's eschatology, for he envisions the redeemed community's future

---

117. Willard, *Conspiracy*, 392. Willard continues, "Much of the difficulty in having a believable picture of heaven and hell today comes from the centuries-long tendency to 'locate' them in 'another reality' outside the created universe" (392).

118. There does seem to be some diversity in Willard's thought on this point. At times, Willard will utilize the upness of ascension to ground the manifest presence of the kingdom "out of" heaven as in the Pentecost event.

as taking place in *this* universe. The place that Jesus is preparing, according to John 14, refers to places (perhaps solar systems and galaxies) in our universe.[119] One can see how both of these doctrines work together with an important part of his doctrine of creation: "The gospel of the kingdom sees the world of nature, from the tiniest particle to the farthest system of galaxies, as a great and good thing. There is, at a minimum, no reason to think that the world of nature will cease to exist or be destroyed."[120]

Salvation in His *Name*

HAVING LITERALLY TRANSITIONED to a new location of ministry, the basic form of Jesus's kingdom-augmented deliverance of humanity continues. What continues is, first of all, *Jesus* and, second, his ability as one who stands in the kingdom of God to deliver those who come to him. The paradigmatic pericope for this is the healing of the beggar at the Beautiful Gate in Acts 3–4. And the paradigmatic act of first-stage faith *after the ascension* is acting or praying "in the name of Jesus." The reality behind these events is what is traditionally called *the intercessory work* of Jesus.

Praying or acting in the name of Jesus is a biblical phenomenon that received a fair amount of reflection from Willard. The Lukan pericope is often a launching point for him—not least because it was historically significant in the development of the nascent church's theology of prayer and of Jesus's continuing work. In its basic form, this healing event is not different from any of the pericopes of Jesus's preresurrected life. A person comes or is brought to Jesus, who, by virtue of *his standing* in God's kingdom, delivers the person. It is proof that Jesus's work of going "about doing good and healing all who were oppressed by the devil" (Acts 10:38) continues thanks to his resurrection and ascension. Asking in Jesus's name is an activity that expresses first-stage faith in the gospel and obtains a first-stage savior.

119. Willard, *Conspiracy*, 378.
120. Willard, 377–78.

In fact, this alone explains the exclusivity of the name that we find in Peter's statement about salvation in Acts 4:12 ("No other name under heaven given among mortals"). Willard's argument regarding this text appears to be equivalent to the argument of Hebrews 1–3. Jesus's name is more excellent than the angels (Heb 1:4) and has been counted worthy of more glory than Moses (Heb 3:3). Moses's name or that of any angel is not one by which people may be delivered. Not even the name of "the Cosmic Christ" or the Logos is appropriate, or so Willard insists in *Knowing Christ.*[121] It is *Jesus Christ of Nazareth* who by virtue of his robust life in the kingdom of God owns the ministry of intercession.

Exclusivity follows from this not because the Cosmic Christ or the Logos is a different person or is not able. It follows because the deliverance that comes exclusively by the name of Jesus Christ of Nazareth makes a connection to *the gospel* of Jesus—namely, that the kingdom of God is at hand *for him.* As Willard often points out, the phenomenon of praying or acting in the name of Jesus continues in Acts and *becomes* part of the basic gospel message, most explicitly in Acts 8:12. Such prayer inclines people to trust the gospel of Jesus the person, not merely the benefits. Its corresponding exclusivity is merely the inverse of recognizing the uniqueness of who the historical person Jesus of Nazareth *was, is,* and *will be* in the kingdom of God.

A Gospel for "the Poor in Spirit"

NEEDLESS TO SAY, the Christian concept of salvation embraces far more than ad hoc deliverance from a great prophet now ascended on high. But as Willard is apt to say, God meets us where we are. As I argued at the beginning of this chapter, God met the mildly educated Jew who had a biblically revivable knowledge of intermediaries, of prophets. The topography between Jesus and the kingdom he announced was one in which they stood in direct connection, while others stood only in direct connection to Jesus. We then entered the details of what, according to Willard, Jesus was taken to be by his first listeners. He was taken to be

121. Willard, *Knowing*, 187.

a prophet and knew what other humans did not, was inwardly righteous and physically powerful. The concept of salvation to come of this "Christology" is an old Jewish classic: deliverance. Though this "Christology" will become richer, perhaps the most theologically interesting aspect of Willard's thought at this stage is how he ties in faith. "Faith is a reality with its causes and its effects," he says.[122] And faith obtains salvation by leading its possessor into contact with reality. This contact may result in mere deliverance from a temporal ailment, but Willard believes that even on this rudimentary view of God sending an intermediary to deliver people, persons can experience regeneration. And then this prophet is crucified, is resurrected, and is taken up into heaven, where he is still accessible. His gospel of the kingdom as available to him is still a gospel.

This is the gospel on the first stage. And now we move on to the second stage. But to speak about this, a larger view of the arrangement before Jesus, the system under "the law and the prophets," must be taken.

---

122. Willard, "Role of Faith," 30:30.

Part III

THE SECOND STAGE

The whole point of Christ's coming into the world was, in scriptural terms, to destroy the works of the devil. It is to make good people. We don't understand the gospel until we understand that Jesus Christ stands in flat-footed competition as a teacher of the human race with all of those who have stood up to try to show us how to live.

Now we are desperately in need of recovering that in our time because we have lost the concept of Christ as teacher from our churches, our culture. We've lost it. . . . And that is one reason why discipleship has become really marginalized, and it's been marginalized for decades at least, and we have a whole category, a culture of churches that are filled with Christians who are not by any sense of the term disciples of Jesus Christ.

—Dallas Willard, Southern Baptist Theological Seminary, September 20, 1994

WHAT ELSE THE JEWS KNEW (OR COULD HAVE)

> Staying, himself, within the Jewish forms of his day, at many points he challenged those forms as practiced around him, but always from within the resources of the Law and the Prophets. . . . By critiquing them, Jesus continued the ancient prophetic tradition of Israel: that of the insider who is also an outsider, standing among the people in the presence and power of God. The spirituality of Jesus Christ was in that precise sense *incarnational.*
>
> —Dallas Willard, *Dictionary of Christian Spirituality*

ON THE WHOLE, Willard's vision of God's work with humanity in time or redemptive history emphasizes continuity. This conclusion is what a reading of his publications will initially yield. Yet as Willard conceives it, there is *a transition* in God's redemptive work that took place in Jesus's lifetime, a transition that was announced and even initiated in his preaching and teaching. It is this transition in the midst of the history of redemption's underlying continuity that we will try to discern in this chapter before returning again to Jesus's first listeners and the gospel as understood with a second-stage topography.

Exactly how does Willard conceive of this transition to something new? In order to fully understand passages that deal with the transition in Willard's writings, we must take a wider view and rehearse some aspects of the redemptive arrangements that he sees in Scripture.

Election and Covenant

THE FIRST ARE *election* and *covenant*, concepts that seem to describe the same reality for Willard. In his understanding of God's work with humanity, a person or group is elected *to* covenant. There is no remainder to a person's election outside of some particular covenant. So to say that God elected Israel is another way of saying that they are the ones with whom he had a unique covenant. This should be said eminently of Abraham's election and covenant with God.

Now Abraham is at the apex of covenantal life with God because, for Willard, Abraham's covenant is the dominant one of the Bible. In the 1988 lecture "Old Testament Good News about the Kingdom," Willard asserts that the gospel in the Old Testament "has primarily to do with Abraham. It does not have primarily to do with Moses, but that is a big part of the story."[1] "Gospel" here refers to the availability of God's kingdom to Abraham and to his family. Thus, the notes for this lecture include the following statements: "The *Old Testament Gospel* is the covenant with Abraham. . . . His family was to bless, supply the need of all the families of the earth (Gen 12:3)."[2] In the lecture, Willard says in detail that Abraham's covenant was

> *simply an agreement [i.e., covenant] with an individual man, an individual person: "I will enter into your life and allow you to work and live with me, to live in my power, to work with my power, to show forth the glory of God through you, an individual, and through your family. . . ." That's the gospel of the Old Testament.*
>
> *Notice right away, it is restricted to a particular group of people: Abraham and his descendants. But on the other hand it was not restricted because the whole point of God making a covenant with Abraham, an agreement with him, was that all*

1. Dallas Willard, "Old Testament Good News," *Soul's Eternal Anchor*, MP3/cassette, 9:45.
2. Willard, "Handout for 'The Soul's Eternal Anchor,'" 6.

> *of the people of the earth should be blessed. It was particular, but it was not exclusive. It was particular in its opportunities and responsibilities, but it was not exclusive of anyone.*[3]

Abraham's election and the Abrahamic covenant, one should notice, are directly tied to Abraham's individual salvation, to his own life in the kingdom of God. His election also had effects that went beyond Abraham, but the purpose of his election is not restricted to the utility it had to others. In contrast to understandings of election that became popular in the twentieth century through Pierre Maury and Karl Barth, the election of Abraham was a covenant with benefits *for* Abraham.

The Abrahamic covenant being the paradigmatic covenant, all other divinely initiated covenants with the children of Abraham are rooted in this one. Its structure becomes the basic structure of the others. Willard speaks of two aspects of it.[4] First, there is the soteriological and beatitudinal aspect already mentioned—that is, God interacting with Abraham now. Second, there is the ministerial aspect. The covenant includes Abraham's and Israel's *commissioning as ministers*, as agents for God's blessing of others. In Abraham's case, it is his role as a father and a master that primarily communicates God's blessing onward.[5] But for those not in Abraham's direct household, it is his example ("the imitation of Abraham") that makes him a blessing to others. As discussed in the first stage, Abraham's faith and his salvation are biblically paradigmatic by showing to the world how God desires to interact with individuals.

Concerning the soteriological aspect, what was said in the previous chapter about Abraham's paradigmatic salvation should be recalled. Abraham was given the opportunity to live in the kingdom of God, to have God interacting with him now. This is salvation.

---

3. Willard, "Old Testament Good News," 15:45.

4. Compare with Daniel Fuller, for whom the covenant is "God's commitment and oath to save" (*The Unity of the Bible* [Grand Rapids, MI: Zondervan, 1992], 389).

5. For more on fathers, see Dallas Willard, "Fathers and Sons," *Father-Son Banquet* (Panorama Full Gospel Foursquare Church, Panorama City, CA, June 17, 1990), MP3/cassette; and Willard, "Confidence with Children."

Now God's choice of Abraham and of Abraham's children was, furthermore, an instance of what Willard called the Great Inversion.[6] This is the biblical theme under which the Beatitudes should enter the discussion and, hence, why I speak of a beatitudinal aspect.[7] The Great Inversion, so Willard, is a general biblical teaching about how those who are first in the human system are not necessarily on top in God's system *because* the kingdom or action of God also comes upon those who are last in the human system. This lifts them up to primary positions in the more fundamental system of God. Circumstances and proprieties on earth do not matter *because* God's kingdom, the greatest thing in the world, mercifully comes upon all. This will result in many specific cases of the first being last and the last being first (Mark 10:31)—a key verse for the Great Inversion.

Willard first recognizes this theme in the patriarchs who were simply "drifters" in the ancient world but who, in spite of this, became—because God chose to be with them—wealthy and powerful. He notes how God lifted up the Israelites when they were the lowest segment of Egyptian society. Throughout the Old Testament, we learn, "The barren, the widow, the orphan, the eunuch, the alien, all models of human hopelessness, are fruitful and secure in God's care."[8] In fact, "this inversion becomes so well known as the biblical revelation of God progresses that it is treated as a formal literary device in teaching God's perspective and how he works," and Willard gives Ezekiel 17 as an example.[9]

---

6. This is described as "a general structure that permeates the message of the Bible as a whole and the reality portrayed therein" (Willard, *Conspiracy*, 89).
7. Though he knows his exegesis of them is far from traditional, the Beatitudes (interpreted in light of "the Great Inversion") are extremely prominent in Willard's thought. It was sometime between 1965 and 1972 when his particular view of them developed and came to be described as a "breakthrough" in understanding the kingdom of God for himself (see Johnson, Matthews, and Willard, *Dallas Willard's Study Guide*, 1; cf. Willard, *Conspiracy*, 408n3). At one point he refers to them as "the deepest layer in *The Divine Conspiracy*" ("Discipline for Spiritual [Eternal] Living," 1:08:15). Though not the source of his view, Willard found that Alfred Edersheim had a similar exegesis (cf. *Life and Times*).
8. Willard, *Conspiracy*, 89.
9. Willard, 89.

Thus, when Jesus composes his Beatitudes, he is not bringing new theology to the people but reminding them of something old in how God works. So Willard: "The Beatitudes are about who is well off and who is not well off. And what [Jesus] does in the Beatitudes is . . . he takes the scriptural principle of inversion between man's kingdom and God's kingdom and he applies it."[10] The human conditions of the first half are not qualifications that must be met before the blessings of the second half can be had.[11] The human conditions explicitly named are *a few examples*, taken from the crowds gathered around Jesus, *of the many, many types of people* who can be blessed by the availability of the kingdom of God in Jesus.

Concerning the ministerial aspect of the covenant, Willard's view is that, beginning with Abraham, God "establishes a *public* presence in human history through a covenant people in which he is tangibly manifest to everyone on earth who wants to find him."[12] This notion of a public presence in human history seems far more applicable to the nation of Israel than it does to Abraham and his immediate household. But this notion points out how God's agreement with Abraham was fundamentally different from his positive interactions with other isolated individuals throughout history. Abraham was a minister—to his family and to his neighbors. What's more, from the commissioning of Abraham *as a minister* flows the rights and responsibilities given to all Israel as an ordered, ministerial people with appointed ministry leaders (patriarchs/fathers, judges, priests, prophets, kings, scribes, and rabbis).[13]

Though certain individuals and groups stand out as ministerial leaders, the ancient covenant ministry was a commissioning of the entire people. Willard makes this particular point in an exegesis of

10. Dallas Willard, "The Beatitudes as Gospel," *A Series on What Jesus Believed and Taught—and Lived* (First Hollywood Presbyterian Church, Hollywood, CA, February 25, 1990), MP3/cassette, 47:15.

11. "Because being in the kingdom of God is, on the usual interpretation of the Beatitudes, obviously not a matter of grace but of attaining to special conditions, the present age cannot be the age of the kingdom. That is the thinking of many" (Willard, *Conspiracy*, 105).

12. Willard, 333.

13. Willard, "Meaning of the Rule," 51:45.

Exodus 19:5–6, wherein he says, "God called the people of Israel to be, notice the wording, 'a kingdom of priests.' Every one of them was to be a priest. . . . What is a priest? A priest is one who deals directly with God. A priest is one who has not a series of religious bureaucracies to get through before he gets to God. But he has direct access to God."[14] The similarity here to what was said before about the ontology of prophets should not be overlooked.

But Willard sees a degeneration of the peculiar ministry given to Israel in which political bureaucracies like the monarchy were introduced and intermediaries and mediators supplanted the ministry of average covenant partners. Speaking in 1978, Willard says, "God spoke to the people through the prophets because they were in general a rebellious people from the word 'go.' Consequently God had to grab in that set of people . . . prophets and leaders and judges through whom he would speak."[15] But in its purity, all of Israel was commissioned to this ministry. Willard writes, "The people of all the earth must come to know that Jehovah is God, and Israel has the role of bringing that to pass. The Israelites were from the outset assigned to be witnesses to all the nations."[16]

By way of contrast, Willard distinguishes this public, ministerial aspect of God's interaction with Abraham and Israel from the secret, intermittent, and undefined interactions God had with every individual human being.[17] Compared to the latter, God is doing a new thing with Abraham. Whereas the covenant with Abraham was public, inclusive, and long term, God's other activities with individuals were often private, exclusive, and simply ad hoc. Thus, "Abraham and the tradition of faith that comes down from him through the ages was to be *the publically*

---

14. Willard, "Presence of the Kingdom of God," 26:45.

15. Dallas Willard, "From Resurrection to Ascension," *What Happened in Acts* (Faith Evangelical Church, Chatsworth, CA, May 14, 1978), MP3/cassette, 13:45.

16. Willard, "People of God in Exile," 1173.

17. In a passage from *Conspiracy*, Willard cites John 1:9; Acts 10:30–31; 14:17; and Rom 1:14–15 as examples (333). In Willard, "Meaning of the Rule," 44:30, he cites Job as an example. A summative expression of Willard's view on this is found in one contribution to *The Renovaré Spiritual Formation Bible*, his section introduction to Gen 1–11: "The People of God in Individual Communion with God."

appointed place in history where the nature of God's Father heart was to be accessible to all."[18] The latter phrase should be thought of in terms of the *availability* of the kingdom of God.

Willard's language of Abraham and Israel as a *public* presence, however, should not suggest that the purpose of Israel's commissioning was entirely or even primarily *extra muros* outside its own walls, as is suggested in highly missional readings of the people of God. To Willard's mind, the covenant that elected Israel to be a public location to find God also entailed that *they too* could find God through Israel and that this was of primary importance. Though distinguished, Willard does not separate or contrast the soteriological and the ministerial aspects of Israel's election. When, to take a New Testament example, Jesus gives the keys of the kingdom to Peter, the purpose of the handover is for *Peter* to go in. So Willard: "Having the keys is not a matter of controlling access to the Kingdom, as is often thought. Keys do not mean the right to control access, but the enjoyment of access."[19] Hence, Israel's *first* ministry under the covenant was to those who were associated with Israel, to its own house. Eventually, the failure of Israel as a ministerial people was not in their failure to lead the other nations to God; it was in their failure to go *themselves* to God.[20] Being in some fashion a recognized member of the ministerial people of God did not necessarily entail that one had found God and his kingdom oneself—that is, that the soteriological aspect of the covenant had been individually realized.

With that clarified, we can consider Willard's statement that "God's intention with Israel *always* lay beyond Israel."[21] When Willard makes such statements, there are two things on his mind. First, he means that *in the ancient world*, the family/nation of Israel was, as he came to call it, "the 'street address' of the kingdom of God on earth."[22]

---

18. Willard, *Conspiracy*, 333 (Willard's emphasis).
19. Dallas Willard, "The Key to the Keys to the Kingdom," in Willard, *Great Omission*, 33.
20. Willard, "Meaning of the Rule," 51:45.
21. Willard, "Gospel of the Kingdom," 35.
22. Willard, 39.

Going on, he says, "God was always beyond Israel, of course, but they had a special calling, and anyone who wanted to find God could find Him through coming to Israel. God intended to bring the kingdom to earth through the people of Israel. And He did just that!"[23] God's name was to be made known in the ancient world through the covenant people, and anyone alive then who wanted to come to this great God *could*—by joining ethnic and institutional Israel. From the Christian perspective, this does not seem inclusive because the Christian mind is accustomed to fewer preconditions. But Willard reads this period of redemption history as an instance of God's merciful provision of a way back to him suitable to its time. And it was effective. Those who sought YHWH in the ancient world could have found him and lived with him.

Second, Willard means with this statement that God's purposes with Israel were beyond Israel *in time*. This is an important aspect of Willard's conception of the unity of the Bible and accounts for why the Christ event must be seen through the minds of those who experienced it firsthand, the covenant people to whom Jesus primarily came. A long, ineloquent quote will put this idea before us:

> *This idea of the direct availability of God now, not through a special avenue—the institutions of the Jewish nation—but directly. Because that way of making the kingdom of God available to people had now fulfilled its function. That's what he means when he says in Mark 1 that the time is fulfilled. That work had been done. There was now a group of people who had been prepared by the Jewish experience, as the experience of a covenant people, a people who had an agreement with God that when Jesus came on the scene, they would be able to look at him and recognize him. . . . Not many people were able to do it, but a few were. That's why when we find him asking his disciples, "Whom do people say I am?" And they go through one thing or another. Finally, this*

23. Willard, 39.

> *ex-fisherman—well, he wasn't quite ex- yet—he said, "You are the anointed one. You're the one who's come to really make it happen. You are the person that fulfills everything that was promised under the covenant relationship with the Jewish nation. You're the one." That was no small thing, and Jesus acknowledged it by saying, "Simon, Son of Jonas, flesh and blood," that is, "Your own smarts didn't deliver that to you. You had some help."*[24]

The teaching here is that the election of Israel as a people was, in part, for their service to those who would be gathered to God *through Jesus* centuries later. Jesus's first listeners were not accidental passersby but providential listeners because they, out of all the people in the ancient world, had the mental furniture ("prepared by the Jewish experience") to see who was before them.[25]

In print, Willard elaborates, "But they had also been prepared as a people, through a long and painful process of historical development, to *tangibly* receive the kingdom of God and to make it accessible to others, even to the whole of humanity."[26] In one other lecture, he ties this in with Galatians 3:24, "The law is a schoolmaster to bring us to Christ" (Willard's paraphrase), saying "If you study the law rightly, you'll be able to recognize Christ when you see him." The law came "to teach a nation so that at a certain point there would be people who could say, 'This is the Messiah.'"[27] Getting to this point in history was not a speedy process.[28]

---

24. Willard, "Rule of Heaven in the Old Testament," 2:45. Hear a similar statement in Willard, "Presence of the Kingdom," 27:45, and in multiple other places in Willard's lectures.
25. Willard, "From Resurrection to Ascension," 24:30.
26. Willard, *Knowing*, 140.
27. Dallas Willard, "The Current Captivity of the Church," *The Book of Acts* (Skyline Wesleyan Church, Lemon Grove, CA, July 26, 1974), MP3/cassette, 25:30.
28. The slowness of the process ties into Willard's teleology, which I do not have space to consider.

"The Law and the Prophets"

THIS NEXT ASPECT of the divine arrangements in the history of redemption is important for Willard, but it is especially difficult to give an account of. It appears in two key biblical texts that more than any other text signal for Willard the transition to something new in Jesus. These texts are Matthew 11:13 and Luke 16:16, and Willard comments on them very frequently.

In these texts, the phrase "the law and the prophets" stands out for him and becomes one of his own bywords in speaking and writing.[29] Along with these two instances, Willard is aware that the phrase occurs in Matthew 5:17; 7:12; 22:40 and probably in Luke 24:27, 44. Generally, one could say "the law and the prophets" is something of which Jesus could be mistakenly considered an abolisher, something that the Golden Rule sums up and something that witnesses to Jesus.

What is the intended external object of this phrase? At first but tangentially, one should note how the phrase infers the ink-and-paper concrete copies of the written Tanakh. This is clearly not what Willard thinks the phrase refers to. All of these copies could be destroyed and "the law and the prophets" would presumably still exist. Clearly, the intended object is something transcendent, something that the concrete, physical Tanakh teaches. Yet its books teach many things (history, geography, ethnic culture, philosophy, Hebrew grammar). Many of these minor subject matters could have been curtailed, and "the law and the prophets" would not have suffered a loss.

To make quick work of a complicated topic, it is my assessment that Willard believes this phrase means *important instruction on life and religion* centered in the covenant people's Scriptures. This meaning is captured perhaps as closely as any in the Christian theological word

29. Aside from all the references in *Conspiracy*, see Willard, "Jesus," 58–59; Willard, "People of God in Exile," 1173; and Dallas Willard, "The People of God with Immanuel," in Foster et al., *Renovaré Spiritual Formation Bible*, 1787.

doctrine.[30] What Willard has in mind is an ever-growing body of knowledge that concerned the most important topics in life.[31]

As is the case with any body of knowledge (astronomy, ethics, Finnish grammar), it developed over time. But in this case, it arose through the interaction between God and the covenant people, through what Willard routinely calls "the Jewish experience." In light of the covenant people's privilege, some persons became knowledgeable of "the existence and nature of God and of his relations to creation, with special reference to the purposes of human life and salvation," to use Willard's own description of theology's subject matter.[32] Some of this knowledge is undoubtedly a direct oracle or revelation from God; some of it is an intelligent but nonetheless inspired reflection by a human mind. But the unifying principle of this knowledge is not formal but material. The body of knowledge named by "the law and the prophets" does not include *every last thing* the ancient Jews as a people knew; it includes the matters most important to life and religion, or life with God. Above all, it included knowledge of God.[33] This is why the many other things that the Tanakh includes (geography, etc.) are not intended in the phrase "the law and the prophets." What is intended is *doctrine*, or what we know about God and everything else that is central to human life. This Christian concept, I think, best captures what Willard sees in the phrase.

But care must be taken to remember the primacy of the Scriptures in Willard's meaning. As Willard observes, scripturality (writtenness) becomes typical of the body of knowledge dear to the covenant people,

---

30. For Willard, it is obviously related to the word of God, a concept that was central to Willard's thought. But the word of God, because of its intimate connection to the kingdom of God proceeding from God's own being, is more dynamic and much broader in employment than "the law and the prophets."

31. The claim of knowledge may be difficult to grasp because of Enlightenment sensibilities that religion falls outside of knowledge. Willard observes that, historically, the so-called religions thought of their traditional teachings *as knowledge* and that around the world, societies unaffected by the modern university still think of their traditional teachings *as knowledge* (though they may more appropriately be merely beliefs). The ancient Jews were no exception, according to Willard. Hence, "the law and the prophets" calls to mind that socially recognized ideal body of knowledge.

32. Willard, "Handout for 'Spiritual Formation Track.'"

33. This will be an important theme when we come to consider Mal 4.

especially as they go in and out of exile. Other bodies of knowledge (mathematics, biology) are not necessarily tied to specific, original texts, but scripturality is something that Jews come to *know about* what they are privileged to know. Concerning the exile, Willard tells us, "A major part of the true blessing in and beyond judgment was the emergence of 'the law and the prophets' as the heart of the covenant relationship with God."[34] What he means is that the knowledge of Israel's leading lights, which is *essentially accessed through their writing*, becomes a known standard for Jewish life and religion in a way that it was not before. This happens in the exile before or coinciding with when the exilic Jews compiled these written texts. In the exile, the covenant people take it into their explicit knowledge of God that certain writings and their authors are in fact how God wants to bless them and make them a blessing.

Let us call this scriptural primacy Biblicism. And though related to it, Biblicism is not what is meant by the phrase "the law and the prophets." That is to say, "the law and the prophets" was a real entity before the principle of Biblicism emerged to make "the law and the prophets" the heart of the covenant relationship. Some of Willard's uses of the phrase suggest that he has a pure or ideal version of the Scripture's teaching in mind, something like scriptural doctrine in concentrate.[35] This is what I think is most plausible. It would fit with Willard's statements to the effect that "the law and the prophets" is "a different arrangement of access to the kingdom."[36] Though that is no doubt included for Willard,

34. Willard, "People of God in Exile," 1173.

35. Indeed, Willard, given his philosophical convictions, does believe in the existence of such ideal realities.

36. Dallas Willard, "Spiritual Formation in Christ: Discipleship and Disciplines," *Bringing Christ to the World of the 21st Century* (Northfield Methodist Church, Benoni, South Africa, July 26, 2000), MP3/cassette, 11:30. See also Dallas Willard, "The Kingdom of the Heavens and a Universe Suited for Prayer," *Pastors Conference* (Hawaiian Islands Ministries, Honolulu, HI, March 29, 2007), MP3, 1:02:00; Willard, "What Is 'Ministry'?," 25:00; and Dallas Willard, "Vision," *V.I.M.: Renovation of the Heart* (St. Ninians Church of Scotland, Prestwick, UK, May 17, 2002), MP3/cassette, 21:30. The one statement that Willard made about "the law and the prophets" that challenges my interpretation but also many of his other statements about "the law and the prophets" (as well as, it would seem, a few of the Bible's statements) can be found here: Dallas

there is more to "the law and the prophets" than a description of Israel's unique arrangement of access to the kingdom.

Most importantly, "the law and the prophets" is not a sociologically conceived worldview describing the collective mind of the people of God *at any given time* concerning the most important topics in life. It is something that any Jewish individual or group of individuals may have in varying degrees but that will not go out of existence if no living person instantiates it. This ideality is easy to overlook because of Willard's belief that the Hebrew Scriptures witness to a "progressive apprehension" of God by the people of God. And yet an ideal reality, something not subject to human acts of transmission and forgetfulness, is what Jesus's first-century phrase picks out.

So concerning the formation of Jesus, Willard writes, "He was brought up and lived for the most part in outlying areas of the Jewish homeland under Roman occupation; but he was thoroughly immersed from his youth in the teachings, traditions and official practices of the Jewish religion of his day. He lived and died within the outward forms of that religion, even while, as a true son of Israel, he drew from 'the law and the prophets' a vision of the whole world under God's rule (Isa. 49:6; Ps. 46:10)."[37] Likewise, in a paragraph later in the same piece, Willard explains that "the law and the prophets" are what Jesus appeals to in order to criticize the covenant people's worldview in the first century. Clearly here the Scriptures' *pure teaching* is coming in to inform a more deteriorated version that dominated the first-century mind.

As we will see, the principle of Biblicism leads to a historical, sociologically identifiable worldview in which its adherents aim to live *under* "the law and the prophets." But the real and ideal "law and the prophets" work to show that this historical worldview has a skewed view of "the law and the prophets."

This pure object of reference fits with the various uses in *Conspiracy*. With respect to Matthew 5:17 and the supposed abolishment of

---

Willard, "The Sermon on the Mount 2," *Spiritual Formation and Soul Care* (Denver Seminary, Monument, CO, January 8, 2010), DVD.

37. Willard, "Jesus," 58.

"the law and the prophets," Willard glosses the phrase with "the entire established order as far as his hearers were concerned."[38] Jesus's hearers thought they were under the real "law and the prophets," but in fact, it "had been twisted around to authorize an oppressive, though religious, social order that put glittering humans . . . in possession of God."[39] To free them of this situation, Jesus "will explain what the law *really* means"—that is, he will exegete the pure law as found in the Scriptures.[40]

Commenting on the summation of the Golden Rule in Matthew 7:12, Willard gives two glosses for the phrase: (1) "everything that is intended for us by God" and (2) "God's revealed will." He points in two related passages to the ideality of "the law and the prophets" by speaking of their *real* meaning. A pure object of reference also accounts for why, "so long as creation stands, not the least element of the law—not 'one jot or tittle' of what God intended with it—will be retracted (Matt. 5:18)." Willard comments, "This must be simply because the law is good. It is right. That, and not some sense of his offended dignity, is why God stands behind it."[41]

Law

IT MAY BE proposed at this juncture, and some of Willard's glosses of the phrase suggest it, that the theological category of *law* as understood primarily in the Lutheran tradition is the object of Willard's phrase "the law and the prophets." Law, according to this tradition, is the sum of the *moral laws* required by God of Israel or, indeed, of all humans. This, for a few in post-Reformational traditions, is thought to be that on which Israel presumed to stand—a presumption that the theological category *gospel* somehow challenges and overturns. But law in this sense is not a useful category for interpreting Willard's view of the transition Jesus initiates.[42]

38. Willard, *Conspiracy*, 126.
39. Willard, 127.
40. Willard, 127 (emphasis mine).
41. Willard, 142.
42. As might be expected, Willard is explicitly quite far from the antinomian position (see Dallas Willard, "The Virtuous Life: The Substance of Holiness," *Personal Spiritual Renewal* [Renovaré, Wichita, KS, November 1989], MP3/cassette). We find praise for

Law is certainly included in "the law and the prophets," but one must grasp how Willard understands law ontologically. One notices he does not distinguish between doctrine and law on the levels of knowledge and action. Given Willard's phenomenology of doctrine—for example, creation, Trinity, or the gospel—it is not improper to speak of *obedience*.[43] Obedience to the doctrine of the gospel would not be anything other than conformity with that doctrine in all of the aspects of one's being. It would be, in another turn of phrase, really believing the doctrine.[44] From Willard's perspective, having faith in and embodying a particular view of the gospel (a doctrine) in one's mind, will, or body would not be fundamentally different from having faith in and embodying a particular moral law (again, a doctrine) in one's mind, will, or body. In the psychology of redemption, the effect is the same, so the distinction falls apart on this level.[45]

---

the law typical of Calvinist theologians who embrace all three uses (see Calvin, *Institutes* 2.vii.6–12). In one introduction to the moral teachings of Jesus, Willard writes, "The law that God had truly given to Israel was, until the coming of Messiah, the most precious possession of human beings on earth." And then, "We must understand that Jesus, the faithful Son, does not deviate at all from this understanding of the law that is truly God's law. He could easily have written Psalm 119 himself" (Willard, *Conspiracy*, 141). The law or Jewish moral knowledge lies solidly in what is continuous between Israel and Jesus.

43. Recalling chapter 4's discussion of faith and especially of conviction, there is a place in Willard's phenomenology for knowledge of something that one did not believe and integrate into one's life.

44. This is a more commonly shared point than may be initially thought. Extremely few of the traditions that attempt to tease apart doctrine and ethics teach that one should merely *mentally assent* to the gospel and other central doctrines without them affecting the rest of one's being. That the Scholastics, especially the Lutheran Scholastics, were encouraging this was the criticism of Johann Arndt and the continental Pietists of the late seventeenth century. It is epitomized in Philipp Spener's famous question, *Wie bringen wir das Kopff ins Herz?* (How do we bring the head into the heart?) Whether the Pietists had appropriately understood the Protestant Scholastic movement is another question. But this historical example only points out that mere mental assent is of little value to almost everyone. One group, however, that found much value in mental assent is the American fundamentalist tradition of the early twentieth century. Willard observes that in their conflict with modernism, they came to emphasize the eternal value of mental assent to basic, antimodernist theological tenets.

45. What is indeed happening phenomenologically when gospel is contrasted with law is that one set of doctrinal and ethical statutes is being prioritized over another.

But at a deeper level, this is because the basic ontology of both is the same. Moral laws are not arbitrary willings of a God who must be reckoned with because he is "bigger" or "earlier" than everyone else (which is existentialism as an ethical theory).[46] Moral laws are *descriptions*—often revealed by God, who, of all rational beings, *knows* them—*of how reality is*, or, for example, how wills and souls best interact with one another (which is realism as an ethical theory).[47] Moral laws are doctrines or, to use Willard's phrase, moral knowledge.[48] They are realist teachings about moral reality, just as physical laws are realist teachings about physical reality. The law of gravity can be defied by trying to jump up thirty feet in the air, but it cannot be broken. "In the moral realm, the same thing is true," Willard says. "You can defy moral law and you can defy the laws of God, but you cannot break them."[49]

---

46. Willard discusses the history of ethical theory in "The Human Function of Ethical Theory and Christ's Teachings, Historically Considered," *Staley Lecture Series* (Wheaton College, Wheaton, IL, October 31, 2001), MP3/VHS. This is doubtless a quick summary of the ethical history course he regularly taught at USC.

47. Obviously, Willard's fullest, most explicit defense of moral cognitivism (in contrast to noncognitivism and existentialism/voluntarism) is in *Disappearance*. Elsewhere it is not difficult to identify his cognitivist streak. Compare, for example, "God's true law also possessed an inherent beauty in its own right, as an expression of the beautiful mind of God" (Willard, *Conspiracy*, 141). Willard's main reason for affirming the law is phenomenological and realist.

48. Various theological sources for Willard's nonexistentialist appreciation for the law can be named. One is the study by Fuller, *Gospel and Law*, which Willard recommends for its contributions to "a proper understanding of the relationship between faith and law from the viewpoint of recent evangelical theology" (*Disciplines*, 42–43n4). From the viewpoint of older evangelical theology in which Willard immersed himself, he found another "proper understanding" in New School Calvinism and especially the deeply entrenched cognitivist Charles Finney (see Finney, *Systematic Theology*, lecture 2, 11–13). Not only did Finney hold that God's will does not *make* law; he did not oppose the work of Jesus to personal, new covenantal fulfillment of law (see *Systematic Theology*, lecture 15, 156). After decades of reading about and teaching ethics in the university, Willard, who believed love to be the center of moral theory, calls Finney's many lectures on love "the finest exposition of the biblical and moral concept of love I know of" (Willard, *Renovation*, 264n3). Nevertheless, older accounts of the ongoing place of the Mosaic moral law in the Christian life—such as that of Augustine, Aquinas, and Bonaventure or Calvin and Wesley—are places where he would have looked for support.

49. Dallas Willard, "How His Gospel Calls Us to Be Spiritual Person," *Jesus Our Living Teacher* (Kempton Park Methodist Church, Kempton Park, South Africa, August 6, 1993), MP3/cassette, 7:00.

With this possible misunderstanding out of the way, it would be helpful, as we did with covenant and election, to turn to Willard's view of the origin and purpose of the law in the history of redemption and to his view of the Sinai event and its repercussions. But as far as I am at present aware, Willard is very reticent about the institution of the Mosaic law in his writings and lectures. Nevertheless, a few general things can be stated about his view.

First, there is his notion that realism best describes the God of Israel's relationship to the law. This means that the fact that *God* gave the law to Moses has no bearing on the law's validity. The moral teachings of the Mosaic law would be valid even if they had not historically come to humanity from the mind of God.[50] Willard often quips that Americans can be thankful that God did not give Moses the multiplication tables because then they could not teach them in their public schools.[51] The multiplication tables, most agree, are valid regardless of who the first to formulate them was. They are not the arrangement of a discrete group. The implication is that the Mosaic law has validity regardless of the fact that God or "religious" leaders like Moses were the ones who formulated it. It is not a contract or an agreement between God and Israel that may be dispensed with when the parties go their separate ways.[52] Its validity is grounded in its correspondence to moral reality.

---

50. Willard believes that many moral teachings roughly equivalent to Jewish law did arise in other distinct cultures. He does not, however, account for this in terms of natural law.

51. E.g., Dallas Willard, "Taking the Kingdom of God to the World of Government and Business Today," *Elective Seminar* (National Pastors Convention / Youth Specialties, San Diego, CA, February 2003), MP3, 1:16:00. Or Dallas Willard, "Session 2—Part 1," *The Contemporary Belief System as Prison, and Jesus as Savior* (National Pastors Convention / Youth Specialties, San Diego, CA, February 2003), MP3, 9:00.

52. In his ethics classes, Willard uses a piece on contractarianism to bring this view before students (Jane English, "What Do Grown Children Owe Their Parents?," in *Aging and Ethics: Contemporary Issues in Biomedicine, Ethics, and Society*, ed. N. S. Jecker [Totowa, NJ: Humana, 1992], 147–54). His opinion of it is negative (Dallas Willard, "The Last Enemy That Shall Be Destroyed," *Kingdom Living: Rediscovering Our Hidden Life in God* [Church of the Open Door, Maple Grove, MN, August 26, 2000], MP3, 32:00).

Consequently and secondly, the law is more enduring than the covenant with Abraham, than the people elect to covenant with God: "Law as God intended it remains forever essential to the kingdom, and Jesus made it clear to his hearers that his aim is to bring those who follow him into fulfillment of the true law."[53] The law existed before the historical covenant with Abraham and was known and honored in part by individuals and groups, including Abraham and his family, long before it was formally given to Moses and Israel.[54] Furthermore, the law will exist into eternity after the covenant with Abraham has run its course. It was only noncontingently involved with traditions of Israel established at Sinai or at other points in time. The Sinai event depends on a genuine giving of the law, but the law does not depend on the Sinai event.

Third, the law is given to the covenant people quite simply because it is good and because God is good. It is an effect of the soteriological aspect of the covenant: "The law that God had truly given to Israel was, until the coming of Messiah, the most precious possession of human beings on earth."[55] In other words, God is good, and he mercifully gives his covenant people, as he would anybody, what is good when they are ready for it. The goodness of the law is also the reason why obedience to it is life-giving: "Fulfillment of God's law is important because the law is good. It is right for human life. And the presence of the kingdom brings us all that is right for human life."[56]

Fourth, as may be expected, one must distinguish in the Mosaic law between its core and its traditional and occasional expansions. A question about which law in the law is the greatest is a legitimate question with a definite answer. From this center all other moral teachings may be measured according to their distance from the center. A good example of Willard doing this in a Christian context is in his 1973 piece "Marriage and Divorce," where the "law of love" governs the laws on

53. Willard, *Conspiracy*, 136.
54. Unique to one of his earliest recorded lectures is an affirmation of Karl Jaspers's theory of the Axial Age (Willard, "Paul's Good News about God as Seen in Romans").
55. Willard, *Conspiracy*, 141.
56. Willard, 136.

marriage and divorce.[57] However, Willard thought that the law, as it was understood by the popular mind in Jesus's day, was not properly distinguished into its core and its occasional applications. It had become monolithic, and for that reason, Jesus's divergence on minor laws of ritual and institutional practice set him up as a breaker and abolisher of the whole law.

In sum, even understood in Willard's realist sense, law does not sum up the phrase "the law and the prophets." Doctrine, understood in a sense inclusive of law, is more accurate. Of Willard's "Four Great Questions," law would only relate to knowledge in the third, Who is a good person? But "the law and the prophets" would seem to also contain the Jewish knowledge of the other three, including (1) knowledge of reality and the gospel, (2) knowledge of the good life, and (4) knowledge of becoming a good person.[58] When Jesus in Matthew 5:17 calms the suspicion that he is dismissing "the law and the prophets," it is the whole teaching of the Scriptures that is at stake, knowledge of God included.[59]

Rituals and Institutions

THE RITUALS AND institutions of Israel, as Willard calls them, play an important part in Willard's understanding of the transition. In one text, he gives us a short list of some things he has in mind: "male circumcision, Sabbath observance, food laws, and other rituals."[60] To this must be added the Levitical priesthood and the temple cult. What divinely conceived role did these play in the soteriological and ministerial covenant with Abraham?

---

57. Dallas Willard and Richard Foster, "Contemporary Issues: Marriage and Divorce," *Quaker Life* (1973).

58. Regarding Jesus's teaching on who is blessed, Willard will often polemically remark that the Beatitudes do not tell us to do anything. They are not laws. They are *examples* of people who are blessed who would, however, not be thought to be blessed. They describe a different aspect of reality than do descriptions of good and bad persons.

59. The reason the phrase slants toward the third question is because of the faith in propriety that dominated the first-century mind.

60. Willard, *Knowing*, 179.

The clearest example of his thinking concerns circumcision. In 1988, Willard calls circumcision "the mark of the Abrahamic covenant" and explains how it symbolizes (my word) an individual's ideal relationship to God, "a tender and sensitive heart before God."[61] In the notes for this lecture, he writes, "God extended the opportunity of a personal relationship with him to every descendent of Abraham, who were to form a 'peculiar treasure unto me above all people,' being 'unto me a kingdom of priests, and an holy nation' (Ex 19:5–6)." The most important thing is this inner reality, a heart sensitive toward God. The rite was added to the already present reality of Abraham's inner life as a means for remembering and teaching it to Abraham and to Abraham's children. The rite was an aid to the attainment of the far more important, real thing—namely, Abraham's kind of heart.

In the same lecture notes, Willard writes, "The Mosaic institutions/rituals were designed to maintain in every person among the people an awareness of the presence of God in their midst (Lev. 9:6 & 23–24, 10:3)."[62] One notices in this statement that the rituals and institutions were *instrumental means* to the kingdom of God and of the Abrahamic covenant. This statement seems to suggest that Willard thinks of the rituals and institutions as aids for remembering, teaching, and ministering something more important. In a lecture given in the same year, Willard says, "Now, in the Jewish nation he very carefully prepared arrangements where people could go in and out of the presence of God. . . . What was it all about? All these sacrifices and priesthoods and tents and tabernacles and temples and all that sort of thing? . . . See, that was a way of arranging so that there was a place in the midst of the people where God was present. But you could move out of that place, and you could go to that place. There would be a function of choice as to how you related to it."[63] From this passage, it is clear that the rituals and institutions were aids for making contact with the presence of God. They were instituted

61. Willard, "Old Testament Good News," 11:00.

62. Willard, "Handout for 'The Soul's Eternal Anchor,'" 6; cf. Tozer, *Pursuit of God*, 34–35.

63. Willard, "Fundamental Issues," 31:30.

to sustain the covenant people in their interaction with the real presence of God in their midst.

In the same lecture, Willard presents his standard exegesis of Exodus 19:5–6 and especially the phrase "kingdom of priests," which, he holds, is "a group of people, every one of which is in direct relationship to [God]."[64] In order to drive this point home, he gives his only description of the purpose of the Levitical priesthood that I have found: "The priesthood in the Old Testament was not designed to come between men and God. They were designed to keep operating a system within which each individual would be personally related to God. They were servants of the system."[65] This view of the priesthood's original purpose as servants to the "kingdom of priests" stands in marked contrast to what Willard holds was the first-century assumption. First-century Israel had developed the notion that the average participant in God's covenant people did *not* stand in direct relationship to God and his kingdom. Priests (and others) were necessary to come between God and the people as intermediaries. Priests were not servants of an arrangement that allowed for individual access but bureaucrats who controlled access. Their original purpose as instrumental means to the kingdom of God had undergone a historical degeneration. But in better times, the Levitical priesthood served a kingdom of priests. Other offices in the history of Israel (father/husband, prophets, rabbis, scribes) would fit into this category as well.

Another instrumental means to life in the kingdom of God was the Psalter, which is instructive for us to consider because Willard describes its misuse.[66] According to Willard, "Ideally, the Psalms were performed in suitable architectural and liturgical settings, beginning with the

64. Willard, 39:45.

65. Willard, 40:15.

66. Regarding worship and cultic activity, one could wish for more from Willard on the role of animal sacrifice. "Animal sacrifice is not God's will for his creation," he says in one Q and A session. He goes on to explain sacrifice's role in developing a clerical or leisure class in Israel, which resulted in growth of language, of the Bible, and of Jewish history. But one can only wish he had given much more detail (Willard, "Tough Questions 1," 37:00).

tabernacle in the wilderness and continuing up through the glorious Temple of Jesus' day."[67] But teleologically, "the Psalms are primary *instruments* for forming the inner life of the faithful, but much of their effectiveness derives from the fact that they are also *about* how such formation occurs."[68] As grand as the Psalter is as an instrument of the Abrahamic ministry, it has limitations that relativize its use: "Any activity can become *mere* performance. As we have seen with the law, the limitation of liturgical language and ritual is that it can remain external and not touch the heart."[69] Thus, even in the institution of some perfectly suited instrument for the ministry, there is a qualification that would recommend its disuse by the people of God so as to avoid its misuse. One can externally sing the content of the Psalter and internally avoid participation in its reality.

So with an eye to instrumental means wider than the Psalter, practices that remain external, writes Willard, "can also bind one's devotion to God to times and places ('church work'), and to legalism, or to culture (ethnicity). When this happens, our religion becomes a performance—or worse yet, turns us into being spectators of a performance. Worship of God can be replaced by worship of beauty or merely 'propriety' and even become simply entertainment."[70] Good means can be misused. This is a standard criticism of the prophets, Willard observes. But Jesus makes use of it as well, and Willard's mention here of "propriety" (to be discussed shortly) flags the form of criticism Willard identifies in Jesus. The scenario involves a person who rightly uses the Psalms to worship God but who assumes that God's blessing will follow the *rightness* of their use.

But later Willard tells us that "merely external worship leaves us incapable of devotion when the 'props' are taken away."[71] Misuse aside, good means need not be used. The classic historical example is the loss of the temple in the Jewish exile. In this context Willard tells us, "The

---

67. Willard, "The People of God in Prayer and Worship," in Foster et al., *Renovaré Spiritual Formation Bible*, 769.
68. Willard, 770.
69. Willard, 771.
70. Willard, "People of God in Prayer and Worship," 771.
71. Willard, 772.

Jewish people are stripped of all the externals that they had come to think of as the substance of their lives: their king, their temple and its city, and their land. They could no longer look to these externals, but were left with what they could carry with them and in them: mainly, their sacred writings and their memories and customs."[72] The nonuse of the temple in the exile was not due to there being anything fundamentally wrong with the temple as an instrument. However, inherent in the nature of an instrument is its subordination to an end. If the end can be accomplished without a particular instrument, then the instrument may or may not be used. But externalization muddies this distinction.

But having clarified Willard's view of what the Jews knew (or could have known) about rituals and institutions, about the law, about "the law and the prophets" (i.e., of doctrine), and about covenant, we are ready to discuss the "cataclysmic change," as Willard calls it, that comes in human history.

The Continuation and Transition of God's Covenant

TO THE AUDIENCE gathered at Hollywood Presbyterian Church, Willard says,

> *"The law and the prophets were until John"—when you look at this and other passages, you realize that there is this cataclysmic change that happens. It was marked in the first passage we read from Mark 1 by Jesus' saying, "The time is fulfilled," or Galatians 4:4, "in the fullness of time." There is an economy; you see, God is doing something in the world. World history means something. It is significant.*[73]

On the whole, Willard's vision of God's work with humanity in redemptive history emphasizes continuity. But there is *a transition*, as he sees it, in God's redemptive work. It takes place in Jesus's lifetime and was

---

72. Willard, "The People of God in Exile," in Foster et al., *Renovaré Spiritual Formation Bible*, 1172.
73. Willard, "Meaning of the Rule," 45:15.

announced and even initiated in his preaching and teaching. How does Willard conceive of this transition?

Other than the one above, a few quotations will serve to help introduce the topic. In 2010, Willard writes,

> *But when Jesus said in Matthew 4:17 and elsewhere, "Repent, for the kingdom of heaven is at hand" (NASB), He was announcing the availability of the kingdom of God* beyond all existing assumptions. *Paul called this worldwide availability a "mystery which has been hidden from the past ages" (Colossians 1:26, NASB). And this hiddenness was necessary because the kingdom of God had been committed, in a special way, to the people of Israel. Others did not share in it prior to Jesus' announcement.*[74]

One should notice that the kingdom of God was committed to Israel—that is, it was operant in the life of Israel. But this kingdom is going to become available "beyond all existing assumptions." These assumptions are, more precisely, the ideas typical of the Second Temple Jew on which Jesus in his call to "repent" is encouraging serious reflection.[75] What specific assumptions does Willard have in mind?

A subsection called "Proprieties Aside" in *Conspiracy* includes the central published text wherein Willard expresses his vision of the transition. Unfortunately, it is extremely terse. Yet because of its importance, it is given in whole:

> *Some time later, toward the midpoint of his years in public ministry, Jesus reflected on* a remarkable change *that had occurred when his cousin, the Baptizer, passed the torch of God's word on to him.*

74. Willard, "Gospel of the Kingdom," 34.
75. This is metanoia, a reexamination of one's "ideas," which will be discussed in the next chapter.

> *John was, Jesus remarked, as great as any human being who ever lived. Yet, he still functioned from within the limited framework where* God's action, rule, or governance was primarily channeled through the official practices of Jewish rituals and institutions*: through "the law and the prophets," as that phrase was then used.*
>
> *But since John, Jesus continued, we no longer* "stand on proprieties." *"The Kingdom of the Heavens is subjected to violence and violent people take it by force" (Matt. 11:12). That is, the rule of God, now present in the person of Jesus himself, submits to approaches that were previously not possible. Personal need and confidence in Jesus permit any person to blunder right into God's realm. And once in, they have an astonishing new status: "Those least in the Kingdom of the Heavens are greater than John."*
>
> *The parallel passage in Luke 16:16 records Jesus as saying, "The law and the prophets governed until John. But since then the kingdom of God is announced, and everybody is crowding into it."*[76]

For Willard, the most important biblical texts concerning the "remarkable change" are Luke 16:16–17 and Matthew 11:11–13. These describe the transition that Jesus's person and work occasion.

Consider, finally, a quotation from *Knowing Christ* where he briefly gives new expression to this topic:

> *In the times of Jesus, Peter and Paul being a "good Jew"—an acceptable Jew—essentially involved observance of ceremonial law, especially male circumcision, Sabbath observance, food laws, and other rituals. Can one be acceptable to God and not keep these laws distinctive of Jewish religion and culture?*[77]

76. Willard, *Conspiracy*, 17; emphasis mine.
77. Willard, *Knowing*, 179.

The existing assumption in the times of Jesus to this burning question was no. But Willard goes on to explain how Jesus announces that the kingdom of God is *now* primarily channeled through another means—namely, through *his own person.*

Standing on Proprieties

ABOVE I CHARACTERIZED "the law and the prophets" as important instruction on life and religion that exists ideally but was gradually known by the covenant people and their leading lights and is found in their Scriptures. If this reconstruction of Willard's concept of "the law and the prophets" is sound, we must still make sense of the phrase's instance in the long quote from *Conspiracy* above, for there it seems to be epexegetical for the rituals and institutions.[78]

It would be easiest to take this sentence as a rough-and-ready formulation, without the semantic precision with which Willard usually composed his writings. If taken, however, as a thoughtful, compact statement, we must be careful. Because it is tied to the verses Willard is explaining (Matt 11:13 and Luke 16:16), one's reading cannot stray too far from his general interpretation of those verses. Though it is tempting to equate the phrase with "the official practices of Jewish rituals and institutions," I think Willard has something more substantial in mind. He has in mind that from which not one iota or dot will pass, that ideal reality that, he believes, also remains for the people of God under Christ. Rituals and institutions are better seen *as a part* of what Jesus's listeners consider the pure "law and the prophets" to contain. They are part of what the covenant people know, quoting again Willard's description of theology, of "God and of his relations to creation."[79] They are accentuated because they are the part that Jesus seems to threaten. He seems, therefore, to be threatening *the whole thing*: "Do not think that I have come to abolish the Law or the Prophets" (Matt 5:17). "Obviously he

78. Willard, *Conspiracy*, 17.
79. Willard, "Handout for 'Spiritual Formation Track.'"

had to say this," Willard comments, "because that is precisely what his hearers *were* thinking! They could think nothing else!"[80]

The first significant aspect of the main quote from *Conspiracy* is the subject "God's action, rule, or governance." John was a minister in an arrangement under the law and the prophets whereby the never-needing-to-be-established *kingdom of God* was met through official rituals and institutions. Though they were not above human corruption, they were genuine means to the presence and action of God. This arrangement was understood as part of the pure "law and the prophets" both because of its scripturality and because no other arrangement had challenged it with much success.

This is a fairly unproblematic interpretation of the passage until Willard's next sentence signals a contrast: "We no longer 'stand on proprieties.'"[81] What are these proprieties on which Israel stood or presumed to stand? They would seem to be not just the official practices of Israel but *everything good* that the pure "law and the prophets" recommended—that is, the whole body of knowledge stemming from God and the Jewish experience and witnessed to in writing. Standing on proprieties seems then to refer to the Second Temple principle of Biblicism and the ideal of being a people who live *under* "the law and the prophets." Though "the law and the prophets *were* until John" (Luke 16:16), something about them is no more.

Propriety is a key concept in Willard's theology. In a 1989 lecture on faith, which we do not have space to consider in detail, Willard speaks of three stages of faith in Job, the first of which is called "the faith of propriety" and typifies "Pharisaical" faith. Propriety is a relation of fittingness. Propriety in Judeo-Christian religion is a sense that God's blessing (recalling Willard's second great question, Who is well-off?) is *fitting* with moral goodness (recalling Willard's third great question, Who is a good person?). Those with *the faith of propriety*, like the pretribulation Job, are those who believe that the sovereign God *always* (this being the key word) interacts with his creatures according to a principle of

80. Willard, 126.
81. Willard, 17.

propriety. So standing on proprieties is the disposition of awaiting God's blessing on account of one's obedience to him, one's moral goodness. As Willard thinks of it, having this sense of propriety is not un-Christian or wrong. It is not un-Christian or wrong because blessing *is* fitting with moral goodness. But a sense of propriety inevitably frustrates those whose *faith* in God is characterized by it because God does not *always* work according to it.

What does it mean to *stand on* proprieties? This is difficult because I think Willard has two meanings—one negative, one positive, and both set aside by Jesus. In the negative sense, standing on proprieties is the faith of propriety and is occasioned by thinking that God's blessing follows mechanically upon those who are good and do good and worthwhile things. Therefore, even something good that channels the kingdom of God, such as public worship, is not used because it truly channels the kingdom of God. It is used because God supposedly observes those who use good things and rewards them according to the principle of propriety.[82]

Ultimately, standing on proprieties is belief in a form of occasionalism, a theory of causation that Willard often uses to critique various religious thinking. We've already seen it in chapter 3 with regard to hermeneutics and faith, in chapter 5 with regard to persons ruling over their own bodies, and in chapter 6 with regard to healing. Here we find Willard using it with respect to the law and the prophets and the rituals and institutions of Israel. In effect, occasionalism is the view that God directly causes something (thing B) to change, having noted that something else (thing A) has changed. A nonoccasionalist view is one that *can* leave God out of it (but need not) because things (A and B) have their own causes and effects.

The occasionalism of standing on proprieties works by using the instrumentalities of the Jewish religion to trigger God. By way of analogy, faucets channel clean water for those who use them properly and are, as such, good things. But a person who stands on proprieties

82. See, for example, the section on "Legalism Is Superstition," in Willard, *Guidance*, 146–47. The legalist "departs from the natural connections of life."

does not turn on the faucet expecting to engage the faucet's own natural connection to good but turns it on to trigger God's supposed sympathies for faucet turning. They turn on the faucet believing that God will make a mental note that they are doing something he likes and will bless them on the basis of a principle of propriety. It may not matter to them if water comes out of the faucet or not. What matters is that God notes their rightness in turning on the faucet and blesses them.

What is ironic about this attitude is that the person may in fact *be* doing good and worthwhile things. Willard's clearest case of this is Job with his faith of propriety, though he also has many respectful things to say about the Pharisees' moral goodness. But in addition to doing good, such persons make the mistake of expecting God's blessing as a direct result. Taking a principle of propriety to be the divine arrangement leads inevitably to persons who are, in fact, *not good* because they become less concerned with actually being good than with *appearing good* and therefore with external actions that seem good *to others*.[83]

In the positive sense, standing on proprieties means simply being a "good Jew," which entailed being *knowledgeable* about God and his ways and *obedient* to this knowledge, including its moral knowledge and ceremonial law. Now, there is nothing wrong, according to Willard, with being a good Jew. In light of the alternatives in the ancient world, there was everything right with it. The prophets, in my general sense, were good Jews, and "among those born of women none is greater than John" (Luke 7:28).

There was never any need in God's economy to stand on proprieties in the negative sense. This is simply a misunderstanding of God. The story of Job and the biblical theme of the Great Inversion, which Jesus restates in his Beatitudes, teach that YHWH is not a god who always interacts with his creatures on the principle of propriety. But in light of Jesus's coming and his gospel, there is *also* no longer any need to stand on proprieties in the positive sense. This is the primary meaning

83. Willard says that different groups want to take one dimension of the self and "try to make them the whole thing." The scribes and the Pharisees, he says, "wanted to make the social the whole dimension" (Willard, "Residency Part 2," 27:15).

of the *Conspiracy* quote, and it refers especially to institutions and rituals. These genuine means to the kingdom of God are no longer essential because "the rule of God, now present in the person of Jesus himself, submits to approaches that were previously not possible."[84] This is why those in the kingdom of God are greater than John the Baptist (Luke 7:28):[85] "The 'greater' is not inherent, a matter of our own substance, but *relational*."[86]

This new possibility may offend (cf. Matt 11:6) *any* who have been standing on propriety, even those who have been rightly "looking for the kingdom of God" according to the best knowledge of the covenant people and through the appointed means (Mark 15:43). Jesus's gospel bruises everyone's sense of propriety.[87] The elder brother in Jesus's parable of the prodigal son is Willard's prime example. "Elder brothers" experience the new approaches to God's kingdom through Jesus's gospel as "violence," which is Willard's preferred way of reading "the kingdom of heaven has suffered *violence*, and the violent take it by force" (Matt 11:12). Violence is a description of the situation from the viewpoint of the prodigal son's elder brother, who watches harlots and tax collectors go into the kingdom (Matt 21:31–32).[88] But these genuinely good Jews might also put "Proprieties Aside," as the subsection's heading suggests. This would consist of considering and believing Jesus's gospel that "personal need and confidence in Jesus permit any person to blunder right into God's realm,"[89] in which case, one might still see the wisdom in being a good Jew but not regard this arrangement as *the only way* God will let his kingdom come (Matt 6:10).[90]

Thus, propriety is what could be called a *right use* of the Jewish body of knowledge, "the law and the prophets." But this right use must

84. Willard, *Conspiracy*, 17.
85. Willard, 20.
86. Willard, 20.
87. Willard, 149.
88. For more on this theme, see Dallas Willard's "Two Sons, Two Debtors and Another Two Sons," *The Parabolic Teaching about Christ's Kingdom by Christ* (Harbor Church, Lomita, CA, April 17, 1983), MP3/cassette.
89. Willard, *Conspiracy*, 17.
90. This is a topic that Willard treats in his many series on Acts.

be distinguished from *wrong uses.* As we observed in his approach to the Scriptures, Willard does not hold that first-century Judaism and its leaders should be set up as *the* authority on "the law and the prophets," the real but ideal set of teachings under which Israel lived. "The law and the prophets" is not a sociologically identifiable worldview but the body of knowledge apprehended through the centuries-old Jewish experience and put to expression in the written Scriptures.

On this basis, Willard resists the historicism implied by using the principle of first-century Judaism to gain access to the minds of Jesus and the other New Testament authors.[91] Given the transcendence (or ideality) of "the law and the prophets," the question may be reasonably and impartially raised as to whether first-century Judaism ought to be sorted into John the Baptist's or Jesus's conceptions of "the law and the prophets." This is Willard's view. There was a "cut-down and distorted version of the law that dominated their social setting," he says. He continues, "But this 'righteousness of the scribes and Pharisees,' as Jesus called it, was *not* the law of God."[92] That is to say, the dominant first-century concept of "the law and the prophets" was not consonant with the ideal expressed in the Scriptures.

The Transition

WE ARE READY now to speak about Willard's vision of the transition itself, the fulfillment of the time (Mark 1:15), which the Christ event occasions. Discussing Matthew 11:11–12, Willard says, "The translators struggle with this verse partly because it doesn't fit with their ideas about how things should be. But you have to see it in its context. It is announcing a new dispensation. There are dispensations. They're not often what they are cracked up to be in some quarters, but there are

---

91. This historicism often assumes that the sociology of knowledge is a sufficient theory of knowledge, which Willard does not. See Dallas Willard, "The Relativity of Belief and the Absoluteness of Truth," *Indiana University* (Veritas Forum, Bloomington, IN, December 31, 1994), MP3/cassette, 34:00.

92. Willard, *Conspiracy*, 141.

dispensations. And here's a dispensation."[93] How is it that redemptive history moves from the time until John when "the law and the prophets were" to the time when the kingdom of God "is preached"? Very simply, the movement out of the old phase of God's work corresponds to two uses of "the law and the prophets" and has two aspects for Willard. The first is the criticism and abandonment of the Jewish leaders and the *assumptions* they represented and supported. The second is the appearance of the superiority of Jesus's ministry of the kingdom.

Resisting the Wrong Use

GENERALLY SPEAKING, THE Jewish authorities, whom Willard, along with the four Gospels, labels as "the scribes and Pharisees," were corrupting the ministerial aspect of the covenant such that its good function was diminished to the point of being absent. Willard reads Jesus as agreeing with John the Baptist that they, as a social group, are a "brood of vipers" who do "not bear good fruit" (Matt 3:7–10). Poignantly, Willard reminds us of Jesus's criticism: "You shut the kingdom of heaven in people's faces. For you neither enter yourselves nor allow those who would enter to go in" (Matt 23:13). The underlying assumption of this Matthean critique is that the commissioned ministry entrusted to Israel made Israel a place where anyone could seek the kingdom of God and find it. Though this ministry was entrusted to the whole people, certain "professionals" (fathers, priests, judges, etc.) were called upon to teach, lead, and catalyze the people's ministry and sometimes to perform special functions in the name of the people.

In the time of Jesus, "the scribes and the Pharisees" were in the role of being some of the leading ministers of the covenant people. The leading ministers could not block the way to the kingdom of God (Matt 23:13) if there was no way or if the ministry was not meant to be a way. *They* could have gone into the kingdom. Willard says at one

93. Willard, "Entering the Kingdom Today," 11:45. Though it is not accurate to call Willard a dispensational theologian given what that commonly means, compared to a theologian who does not recognize a diversified history in God's work with humanity, Willard is a dispensationalist.

point, "'Repent, for the kingdom of the heavens is at hand' means that it is now accessible in a new way. Now, that has a definite reference to an old way that it was accessible. The old way that was accessible is called in the Bible 'the law and the prophets.' It was identified with the social organization of religion that existed in Jesus' time in the nation of Israel. God had made the kingdom of the heavens available through the people of Israel, through the Abrahamic covenant through the Mosaic law."[94] The Pharisee Nicodemus is scolded for not knowing better about the kingdom of God because he, with the privileges of a "professional," could have known better.[95] Though Jesus calls the Jewish leaders *blind* guides (Matt 23:16), they are still guides—guides to the kingdom of God and his righteousness.

As Willard understands it, the center of Jesus's critique of the scribes and Pharisees—that is, the crux of their ministry's corruption—is their concept of *righteousness*.[96] Willard's central verse to this effect is Matthew 5:20: "Unless your righteousness exceeds that of the scribes and Pharisees, you will never enter the kingdom of heaven."[97] Their concept

---

94. Willard, "Getting the Good News," 26:00. See also Willard, "Saving Message," 4:00.

95. Willard, *Conspiracy*, 68.

96. Willard provides a section in chap. 5 of *Conspiracy* on the convergence of the high Greek classical tradition (Plato and Aristotle) and the Hebrew tradition (with Amos, Micah, and Isaiah as high points) in the term δικαιοσυνη. The convergence is an agreement about what the terms δικαιοσυνη and ἀρετη refer to. Willard attempts two paraphrases of the terms: (1) "what that is about a person that makes him or her really right or good" and (2) "true inner goodness." With this convergence in mind, the scribal concept of righteousness stands in contrast not only to John and Jesus but also to formulations in the Jewish tradition as well as classical formulations: "Actions do not emerge from nothing. They faithfully reveal what is in the heart, and we can know what is in the heart that they depend upon" (Willard, *Conspiracy*, 144).

97. In almost every exegesis of the text, he explains that this calls for a different kind of righteousness (righteousness from the heart), not more of the same righteousness. E.g., in the handout for one of his earliest teaching series on Matthew (Willard, "Handout for 'Studies in the Gospel of Jesus Christ,'" lesson 5), he writes,

> The righteousness of the Sc. and Ph. is not to be despised, but to be exceeded. Seldom if ever is there a person who is able to enter into "the Kingdom of God and His righteousness" without previously being deeply concerned about the external righteousness of the Sc. and Ph. It seems as if conviction of the importance of right external behavior is a necessary

of righteousness, and their actual righteousness, was a righteousness of *externals*.[98] Their ethical theory came down to believing that righteousness is a matter of action and particularly of avoiding wrong action, or "not doing anything wrong."[99] Their "fundamental mistake" is that "they focus on actions that the law requires and make elaborate specifications of exactly what those actions are and of the manner in which they are to be done. They also generate immense social pressure to force conformity of action to the law as they interpret it. They are intensely self-conscious about doing the right thing and about being thought to have done the right thing."[100]

What Willard spies in the moral theory of Jewish leaders is the view that came to be known in ethics as *externalism*. In one instance, he describes this as emphasizing "the (presumed) moral worth of the right action as an abstract type, treating actions as having a moral quality separable from the moral praiseworthiness that involves the action's ground in the life of the agent."[101] Jesus's moral theory, by contrast, takes seriously the "ground in the life of the agent." For Willard, this finds expression in Jesus's word *heart*, as already discussed. The heart is the inside of the agent. Though other hidden dimensions of the person are at play in moral action, the heart or will is the most important for assessing the moral worth of a person.

This should be a fairly obvious point to Willard's readers. But his biblical exegesis can be brought into connection with his work as an ethical theorist.[102] The 2000 paper "Naturalism's Incapacity to Capture

---

condition for penetration of the law of God directly into and throughout the heart. Jesus did not scorn external rightness of action, but pointed out its insufficiency without a deeper righteousness. This is true of all the great Christian leaders, such as Paul, Augustine, Luther and Wesley.

98. Willard, *Renovation*, 23.

99. Willard, *Conspiracy*, 187.

100. Willard, 143.

101. Willard, "Faith, Hope and Love," section 3; cf. also his statement "Spirituality without ontology produces legalism" in "Kingdom Salvation," *The Divine Conspiracy* (e4, Hollywood, CA, July 6, 2004), MP3/video, 33:00.

102. A full-dress account of Willard's history of ethics and his ethical theory would be helpful at this juncture but lies outside of the bounds of this book.

the Good Will" is currently the best evidence for his own standpoint in the history of moral theorizing. Consider the following excerpt:

> *I mention Hume and Kant not to enter into exposition of them, but simply to locate a broad tradition of ethical theorizing that locates moral value not in action but in the sources of action, and not in the formal features of moral experience, but in the material aims of action and dispositions organized around them. This is a tradition that reached a sort of maturity in the work of late 19th century thinkers such as Sidgwick, Bradley and especially T. H. Green, and I want to identify with that tradition [i.e., the broad tradition, including Hume and Kant]. For the following one hundred years after these thinkers this tradition has been paralyzed if not killed off by the effects of Moore and his followers and critics. It was a tradition that focused upon the will and the role of the will in the organization of the "ideal self." The "ideal self" was, of course,* the good person, *which everyone finds themselves obliged to be.*[103]

It is illuminating that Willard sees Jesus as a part of this tradition and even as the *source* of this tradition. But even Jesus is not wholly original here. We have already met Willard's description of the Old Testament gospel as "a tender and sensitive heart before God." Tender and sensitive are not the same as morally good, but the focus on the sources of action, the inner person, is there.[104]

---

103. Dallas Willard, "Naturalism's Incapacity to Capture the Good Will," *Philosophia Christi* 4, no. 1 (2002): 21.

104. Willard does not say it in the context where he introduced the phrase, but "a tender and sensitive heart before God" sounds remarkably like faith (cf. Tozer, *Pursuit of God*, 63–65). But this introduces a tension in Willard's understanding of the time until John the Baptist. Up until the end of his life, Willard gave a consistent exegesis of Mal 4:6, explaining it taught the failure of what had been given since Moses (Dallas Willard, "Life in the Spirit: Session 1," *Life in the Spirit* [Grace Long Beach, Long Beach, CA, June 30, 2012], MP3, 1:06:45; cf. Willard, *Conspiracy*, 339). What Willard has in mind is the law of Moses *understood* as a set of axioms to govern behavior externally. This is

How then does one exceed the righteousness of the scribes and Pharisees (Matt 5:20)? First, one gives up on the moral theory of externalism, the misguided exclusive focus on external conformity to propositional laws. Second, one recognizes that the law the scribes and Pharisees aimed to externally conform to was not even the law of God: "It was a contemporary version of religious respectability, very hard and oppressive in application."[105] It was what Jesus in Mark 7:8 called "the tradition of men."

Third, one dismisses these leading ministers' faith in propriety that leads them to count on their righteousness (albeit external and mixed-up laws of men) to qualify one for blessing. The dominant thought of the day was that the blessed action of God (probably understood mainly in terms of the reinstitution of Israel's sociopolitical kingdom) would follow, by rule, the covenant people's instantiation of righteousness. This, it turns out, is false. Aside from the *general* unmerited blessings of life ("For he makes his sun rise on the evil and on the good" [Matt 5:45]), blessing within the Abrahamic covenant did not follow by rule on a person or the group's righteousness. It followed on their faith in God and, even then, not by rule but by grace. For Willard, this is not a teaching that Jesus introduces so much as clarifies in "the law and the prophets" and that Willard calls the Great Inversion. The God of Israel does not operate *exclusively* according to the principle of propriety.

What's more, this faith in propriety led many Jewish leaders to misinterpret the *point* of being a good person. They assumed that one of the reasons for the moral worth of a particular intention or action was that it had the effect of triggering God's sense of propriety, a certain

---

inadequate, as the verse points out, and requires someone additional to come to turn *hearts*. Other than being a historically unparalleled source of pure love, hope, and faith (i.e., grace) to the moral agent, what this someone (Jesus) mainly does is *explain* in his example and teachings how righteousness is a matter of the heart and how the law of Moses should be understood as exemplifying the moral life that flows from an internally good person. Such a person was missing in the time until John. But this is conflicting with Willard's view that the heart *was* a subject of moral discourse under "the law and the prophets." Jesus's teachings on the good heart are perhaps more pointed but not new for "the law and the prophets."

105. Willard, *Conspiracy*, 136.

law-like psychological mechanism in God.[106] It is interesting that Willard never mentions the afterlife as one of the blessings the Jewish leaders aimed to secure. The blessings Willard names are this-worldly blessings such as wealth, safety, and honor. Jesus counters the prevailing moral theory with its assumed ethical ends by preaching the Great Inversion, especially in his Beatitudes. God bestows blessing irrespective of one's life condition. Righteousness must have another end.

What's more, in statements even more scrutinizing, Willard recalls Jesus's criticism of religious and human *respectability* among the Jewish elite. The real end of being righteous according to the dominant Jewish social order was not really to gain *God's* attention. It was to gain *man's* attention. This is doubtless not a description of ethical aims that any historical Second Temple leader would have defended publicly. Willard himself pulls it not from extrabiblical rabbinical texts but from Jesus's criticisms in Matthew 23:5–7 and 6:1–18.[107]

If accurate of the social situation, not even God and his sense of propriety was in view as the end of righteousness so much as human and especially religious acceptability. This behavior among the elite had the effect that "the Law and the Prophets had been twisted around to authorize an oppressive, though religious, social order that put glittering humans . . . in possession of God," an order that would have been

---

106. It is curious on this point that Willard never, to my knowledge, discusses the traditional, Reformational view of Second Temple Judaism—the view that the Jews believed that the end of righteousness was to trigger God's sense of propriety or to invoke some promise of propriety he made long ago *in order to* gain their entrance into heaven or the blessed afterlife. One stream of contemporary research into Second Temple Judaism gives us the picture that, on the view of many leading Jews, righteousness or faithfulness to God's covenant was considered useful for installing the kingdom *of Israel*, a sociopolitical reality initiated by God, or at least indicative of who would be included once installed (cf. the seminal works of E. P. Sanders, *Paul and Palestinian Judaism* [Philadelphia: Fortress, 1977]; and E. P. Sanders, *Jesus and Judaism* [Philadelphia: Fortress, 1985]). This longing is likely encapsulated in the late question from Jesus's own disciples: "Lord, will you at this time restore the kingdom to Israel?" (Acts 1:6). I have no evidence of what Willard thought of *covenantal nomism* as a theory of the majority worldview in the first century. But on this point, see Willard, "Handout for 'Jesus' Good News,'" lesson 5.

107. Willard extracts this insight from Matt 6 as well. See Willard, "Kingdom Righteousness," 25:45.

opposed by the ancient prophets just as it was by John the Baptist and Jesus.[108] In an early lecture, Willard summarizes Jesus's evaluation of the religion and society of his day by saying, "Their religion was more than anything else a way of currying the favor of their fellows, of cultivating their in-group and getting those around them to look at them and say, 'Yes, you're alright.' They were developing what we sometimes call a mutual appreciation society."[109]

Jesus's positive alternative to the whole social-ethical order, so Willard, is centered in the Great Inversion and the ethics of love.[110] The good person is the loving person because the loving person seeks the good of the other. The material end that determines the moral value of a person and their intentions is *the intrinsic value of the objects* that those intentions promote or do not promote. The ends are chosen for their own sake. Thus, Jesus's central moral statement isolates God and one's neighbor as *the* objects of greatest intrinsic value. Willard, who bases his own ethical theory on Jesus's and on the tradition of Jesus, gives this formal definition: "The morally good person, I would say, is a person who is intent upon advancing the various goods of human life with which they are effectively in contact, in a manner that respects their relative degrees of importance and the extent to which the actions of the person in question can actually promote the existence and maintenance of those goods."[111]

Going beyond the Right Use

NOW, THIS CRITICAL, prophetic act of restoring Israel to her true faith is only a sideshow in Jesus's fulfillment of the time. The more sweeping fulfillment is found in his *surpassing* of Israel's genuine covenant ministry. How is it that redemptive history in Jesus moves from the time when "the law and the prophets *were*" to the time when the kingdom of God "is *preached*"? In the next chapter, we will consider what, according to

108. Willard, *Conspiracy*, 127.
109. Willard, "Kingdom Righteousness," 26:30.
110. Willard, *Conspiracy*, 182.
111. Willard, "Naturalism's Incapacity," 21.

Willard, Jesus is and does. Leading up to that, we ask, How should one characterize the transition?

In comparison to his tough resistance to the wrong understandings and uses of "the law and the prophets," Jesus's response to the right understanding and use is much gentler. Jesus simply offers what the covenant ministry of Israel offers without full recourse to that covenant ministry. The covenant ministry of Israel, growing in complexity over time, was instituted with the people with the ideal that it should bring the kingdom of God and heart-circumcised individuals together. As Willard writes, "The system that was present in the Jewish institutions were [*sic*] the officially appointed *doorway* into the kingdom of God. That is, what God has appointed in an orderly way to do upon earth was done through the Jewish system."[112] But Jesus comes and offers the exact same thing, a doorway into the kingdom of God. And he does so via means that, though perhaps conceivable in the past, were not "at hand" until he came.

How God brings about this cataclysmic change recalls an important strategy in God's plan for redemption in history: *gentleness*. According to Willard, God intends his major movements in history to be *gentle*. In one of the earliest recordings of Willard's teaching from 1971, he says the following about such changes: "God always follows a principle of connexity. He never makes abrupt changes. Now, this may be contrary to what you've been led to believe. But if you will watch, you will see that slowly, slowly, slowly he leads us along."[113] Forty years later, it remained a major theme for Willard that God slowly prepares individuals and groups for more advanced levels of interaction in his kingdom. For example, what was said about the nature of God, of heaven, and of the prophets in the first stage should be recalled. These are, by the time of Jesus, familiar elements of "the law and the prophets." They, among

---

112. Dallas Willard, "God and His Kingdom," *Divine Conspiracy* (e4, Hollywood, CA, July 5, 2004), MP3/video, 1:02:00.

113. Dallas Willard, "The New Community of God Reaches Out in Power to the Old Jewish Community," *Studies in the Book of Apostolic Acts: Journey in the Spiritual Unknown* (Woodlake Avenue Friends Church, Canoga Park, CA, December 5, 1971), MP3/cassette, 4:30.

other things, are what help some persons recognize Jesus and the new thing that God is doing in Jesus.

In a 1978 sermon on Acts 3, he gives an illuminating image for how he sees the gentleness of the transition playing out:

> *Here we find Peter and John . . . going up the hour of prayer, the ninth hour. One of the beautiful things, by the way, now, about the story in the book of Acts is simply this. They didn't have to tear the temple down. They didn't say, "Let's quit going through these dead rituals." They stayed in the place they were until the power which entered into them blew it apart.*
>
> *Now, that was what Jesus taught them. You see, Jesus taught them that you do not put new wine in old wineskins. We read that as saying, "Let's don't try to do anything new. We might ruin the wineskin." But you see, there's another side to that teaching which says, "If you've got new wine, it'll take care of the wineskins." You don't need to get an axe and chop the wineskin up. If you've got new wine, the wineskin has had it. Just give it time. The fermentation process will eat the thing up and blow it apart. They didn't need to tear the temple down.*
>
> *You see, the mark of the fleshly revolutionary is that they get the idea "We ought to go up and tear the building down. We ought to change everything around." No! Receive the word of God into the wineskin! Let it blow it apart! There is a time for conscious change, but it is to be taken in dependence on the word of God to accomplish the end.*[114]

---

114. Dallas Willard, "Preparation for Persecution," *What Happened in Acts* (Faith Evangelical Church, Chatsworth, CA, May 28, 1978), MP3/cassette, 39:45. Whether this is a careful interpretation of Matt 9:17 and Luke 5:37 is not at issue here. After the 1970s, I have never heard Willard use the wineskin metaphor. See also Dallas Willard, "The Great Inversion of the Kingdom of God: Righteousness," *The Kingdom of God* (Faith Evangelical Church, Chatsworth, CA, April 16, 1978), MP3/cassette, 21:45: "Jesus is not a revolutionary. He does not say, 'Go tear the institutions down.' Jesus stands beyond that level of change."

In comparison to other ways of characterizing the transition in redemptive history from some older phase, Willard's view stands out by the fact that it allows the covenant ministry of Israel to stand and remain what it is and was: "the officially appointed doorway to the kingdom of God."[115]

This is in contrast to those who characterize the transition as *evolutionary*. In this view, Jesus works *from within* the established system and fulfills it by changing it, completing its outstanding requirements, or absorbing its functions. For example, Jesus is seen as the fulfillment of the temple cult, which is understood either as a merely typological ostentation of the real and effectual sacrificial cult of Jesus or as an authentic cultic process in which Jesus's sacrifice stands as the final and enduring act.[116] The wineskin metaphor does have some resemblance to the evolutionary view because of the emphasis on the new being *inside* the old. But the result is not the preservation of the old in a new, mutated form but a breakaway from the old.

On the other hand, there are those who characterize the transition as *revolutionary*. Jesus overturns the former system, deposing it and asserting himself in its stead. This is not a matter of prophetic critique of false religion but a matter of deposing the divinely appointed rituals and institutions such as circumcision. Such formerly legitimate elements of Jewish religion are supplanted ("fulfilled" in the sense of being permanently discarded) by God to make room for Jesus's own "institutions and rituals."

Yet another way of characterizing the transition attempts to bring together both the continuity and discontinuity in redemptive history by an appeal to the arbitrary workings of a sovereign divine will. This is an *existentialist* view because the value of Jesus's new arrangement over the old is both voluntarist in substance and otherwise noncognitive. Apart from the fact that God willed it, the question of whether the initial or the subsequent arrangement is intrinsically better is irrelevant.

---

115. Willard, "God and His Kingdom," 1:02:00.

116. E.g., Charles Hodge, *Systematic Theology*, vol. 2 (New York: Scribner, 1872), 465; cf. also Augustine, *City of God* XVI, 2.

It is better only because God, in his voluntarist view of salvation, has decided to change the game. Because he is the sole sponsor of any and all "games," his decision stands. In the existentialist view, God is like a physical education teacher who calls an end to a game of basketball and announces a game of volleyball.[117]

In contrast to these views, Willard's view is what could be called a *competitive* view. When the new comes, it allows the old phase to stand and remain what it is—namely, "the officially appointed doorway to the kingdom of God."[118] But the new phase is *also* an officially appointed doorway to the kingdom of God. It is, moreover, a *better* doorway. Both arrangements have a common end in their ministration, their throughness. To Willard, both are a ministry *to having life from the kingdom of God now.*[119] Willard's view is akin to a service provider who enters a particular market, sets up shop beside another's shop, outperforms the other, and indirectly puts it out of business. The oddity of this scenario when considering the history of redemption is that both shops are God's.

So when Jesus offers to help people enter the kingdom of God, the old ministry to help people enter is still standing. In Jesus's lifetime, both arrangements are simultaneously viable and thus open to evaluation concerning their intrinsic value. God, too, from the perspective of eternity and of his purposes for his creation, evaluates both arrangements and, in his wisdom, institutes the more appropriate one when the time is right. He does not impose an arbitrary arrangement when he feels like it (existentialist). But when the time is right, he announces and institutes his wise plan. At the same time, he does not tear down the old (revolutionary) or try to attain the new from within the old (evolutionary). He just brings in the new.

117. This position is consistent with a doctrine of resistible grace—that is, of persons freely choosing to associate with the covenant they are presented with. The irresistibility is found in the matter of which covenant they are presented with.

118. Willard, "God and His Kingdom," 1:02:00.

119. "The words and acts of Jesus naturally suggest that this is indeed salvation, with discipleship, forgiveness, and heaven to come as natural parts. And in this he only continues the teachings of the Old Testament. The entire biblical tradition from beginning to end is one of the intimate involvement of God in human life—or else alienation from it" (Willard, *Conspiracy*, 47).

Now, in order to properly evaluate the old arrangement against the new, one must know what the old arrangement was for. One must understand its intrinsic value, its nature, and its ends. The telegraph and the cellular phone both present themselves as options in the field of telecommunications. Choosing one over the other is a matter of understanding what they *are* (telecommunication devices) and that they are *for* telecommunication. Then one can determine which is more adequate to that end. In the same way, the old arrangement under "the law and the prophets" and the new arrangement of Jesus both have the common property of being a ministry to human life in the kingdom of God. Standing on this equal footing and being for a time offered simultaneously, it is possible to submit them to comparison and to make the right decision that Jesus's option provides a *superior* ministry to the kingdom of God. On Willard's view, Jesus does not demarcate the transition as much as instigate it. He need not be antagonistic toward the alternative or take it over. He only needs to be what he is and offer what he offers. As such, he outperforms the alternative. In like manner, Jesus does not overthrow or absorb John's ministry. He begins by ministering *beside* it such that John's disciples have reason to say, "Look, he is baptizing, and all are going to him" (John 3:26).

We see that the wineskin metaphor does not quite capture the competition involved in Jesus's coming, though it does capture the indirect manner in which the old is done away with. The ministry "under the law and the prophets" and Jesus's ministry are comparable in a way that the new wine and the old wineskin of Jesus's metaphor are not. The new wine resembles the blessing (the kingdom of God, the word of God, the power of God), while the old wineskin resembles the means to the kingdom of God (the temple, the hours of prayer, etc.). By using the wineskin metaphor to describe the transition, Willard seems to suggest that God is suddenly offering the kingdom of God without *any* mediation. It is more consistent with his thought, however, that access to the kingdom of God (new wine) via a new means gradually makes Jesus and his earliest followers' usual participation in old means obsolete. They may be exiled from Palestine, have their temple destroyed, or refuse circumcision and not lose their means to the kingdom of God.

Having received a cellular phone, one may still communicate for a while with a telegraph. But long-term cotemporaneous use of both systems is unlikely *unless* one has simply missed the point of using a telecommunication device. According to Willard, there were many in Jesus's day who had missed the point.

In sum, Willard sees much continuity in the passing from the old to the new, almost to the point of Jesus's ministry being sheer repetition and renaissance. But Jesus does effect a "cataclysmic change" that is inconsistent with conceptions of evolution, including systems of reinterpretation or Hegelian *Aufhebung*.[120] And Jesus does not institute this cataclysmic change in the way of the "fleshly revolutionary" but gently lets his first listeners make up their own minds.

The Fate of Israel

IF THE FIRST phase of covenant ministry is not absorbed or dispossessed or dismissed but rather outplayed, what becomes of it historically in the advent of Jesus? Willard isolates a couple of Jesus's statements in answering this question, especially "Therefore I tell you, the kingdom of God will be taken away from you and given to a people producing its fruits" (Matt 21:43). Another is "I tell you, many will come from east and west and recline at table with Abraham, Isaac, and Jacob in the kingdom of heaven, while the sons of the kingdom will be thrown into the outer darkness" (Matt 8:11–12).[121]

When Jesus comes on the scene as a serious competitor to an ancient arrangement, his competition does not change or negate the reigning system *immediately*. It is sidelined but still functional during Jesus's earthly ministry and shortly after. Thus, Jesus does not say the kingdom of God has been taken from you but that it *will be* taken from you. He tells his first-century listeners, "The scribes and the Pharisees sit on Moses' seat, so do and observe whatever they tell you" (Matt 23:2–3). Likewise, he commands the leper, "See that you say nothing to anyone,

120. Willard, "Meaning of the Rule," 45:15.
121. Willard, 51:30.

but go, show yourself to the priest and offer the gift that Moses commanded, for a proof to them" (Matt 8:4).

This delay has meant to some interpreters that Jesus's death and resurrection are the direct cause of the ancient ministry's demise. However, Willard's reading is that verses like Matthew 21:43 and 8:11–12 are applicable to a historical period *after* the ascension and Pentecost.[122] Referring to Matthew 21:43, he says, as he often does, "The book of Acts is an account of how that happened."[123] This is a significant claim for the theology of Acts, and tracing out Willard's interpretation in detail would take us beyond the intent of this chapter.[124] In summary, he says, "The book of Acts is the story of how God's kingdom and grace manifested itself far beyond religious organization, because in that story, religious organization drops away."[125] The end result of the process that unfolds historically in Acts is ethnic Israel's *loss* of the kingdom of God—loss not in the sense that individual ethnic Jews could not enter but in the sense that "it was not in their peculiar possession to make it [the kingdom] available to the world."[126]

Commenting on Matthew 8:11–12 and the sons of the kingdom who are thrown out, Willard says, "If you're a child of the kingdom, aren't you in?! You see, he's referring to people who were in only in the sense that they were a part of the people of Israel who had previously to John been *given the responsibility and right of exercising the power of the kingdom of heaven*. They were under authority. But they had perverted

---

122. "Thus was fulfilled Jesus' statement to the Jewish nation—not, we emphasize, to individual Jews—that 'the kingdom of God shall be taken from you and will be given to a people producing its fruits' (Matt. 21:43). And those people were the people of the name 'Jesus'" (Willard, *Conspiracy*, 281).

123. Dallas Willard, "On Acts, Pt. 1," *2012 Renovaré Ministry Retreat* (Renovaré, Los Angeles, CA, June 2012), MP3, 36:30. See also Willard, "God and His Kingdom," 1:06:30: "That's what happened in the book of Acts. The book of Acts is the description of how Matthew 21:43 was carried out."

124. Needless to say, Willard is reading Acts as part of a larger literary world than the book itself admits—namely, as part of redemptive history or, in Willard's idiosyncratic language, "God's march through human history." See Willard, "Plain People Lifted," MP3.

125. Willard, "On Acts, Pt. 1," 23:00.

126. Willard, "God and His Kingdom," 1:06:30.

that. And because they lacked the faith that put them in touch with God's heart, the reality of God."[127] All ethnic Jews were sons in the kingdom in the sense that they were all commissioned as ministers of the kingdom—that is, "were under authority." Though formally *in*, not all of this group were *of* the kingdom and had the faith of Abraham, putting them in touch with God. In light of Jesus's coming, there were persons like Peter and John whose "responsibility and right" *as natural and ethnic Jews* were lost but who nevertheless retained that responsibility and right on another basis. This can be seen if we consider Willard's careful analysis of the Abrahamic covenant in light of the Christ event.

Given his understanding of the Abrahamic covenant in its inception, Willard notes a history in its application. In *Conspiracy* he says, "The people that later came to follow Jesus, a child of Abraham . . . understood themselves to be the continuation and fulfillment of the covenant with Abraham."[128] Jesus's followers continue in the Abrahamic covenant with its beatitudinal and ministerial aspects, but they do so with different instrumentalities. Talk of fulfillment should be understood in this context not as the termination of the Abrahamic covenant but as arrival at its *intended* culmination and extension. The people of the "new covenant" were what the ancient covenant people were, at least in part, aiming at.

Though it is unclear, I think Willard fundamentally believes there is only one covenant in biblical history—that is, the Abrahamic covenant. The biblical language of *new* covenant has to do with the changes noted above. The *conditions* for being covenant partners and being its commissioned ministers change such that some persons (e.g., Peter and John) continue to be partners of the same covenant but now on different conditions. Willard's phrasing later in the section bears

---

127. Willard, "Meaning of the Rule," 51:30 (emphasis mine). For a reference to how Willard understands God's righteousness, see his brief comment about Rom 1–8 (Willard, *Conspiracy*, 146) or his 1977 sermon series on Romans (*Romans* [Faith Evangelical Church, Chatsworth, CA, September 18–November 20, 1977], MP3/cassette). For more on this distinction, see Willard's lecture "Growing Together until the Harvest," MP3/cassette.

128. Willard, *Conspiracy*, 333.

witness to this mixed form speaking of "the transition and continuation of the covenant through Jesus."[129] Jesus changes the conditions of being a partner in the Abrahamic covenant. The question of responsibility and right ceases to be *Are you a member of Abraham's biological and ethnic family?* and becomes *Are you a believer in Jesus?* Thus, there is transition *and* continuation in the covenant with Abraham.[130]

The natural and ethnic descendants of those who left Egypt could still enter the kingdom and be its ministers. Because of the advent of Jesus and the superiority of his ministry, the kingdom had become, indeed, more expediently available *to them* than it was when they were its exclusive, commissioned ministers. But the purpose of their *exclusive* commissioning as ministers of the kingdom has been fulfilled.[131] Just as their political rule had expired, so their ministerial rule has also expired. Of course, Willard is not suggesting that Israel as an ethnic group among other ethnic groups has somehow run its course.[132] In fact, the transition that Jesus's advent instigates is what gives meaning to talk of Israel as an *ethnic* group and not as a chosen and "official" group. For the setting aside of Israel is the setting aside of Israel as a human organization, as an ordered ministry. But Israel as an ethnic people remains and remains important to God.

---

129. Willard, 333.
130. He is here on a similar track as John Bright. Bright writes of God's covenanting, "To be sure, the New Testament repeatedly contrasts the Old Covenant with the New (e.g., Gal. 3–4; Heb. 7–9) and declares the New to be the 'better' (Heb. 7:22; 8:6). . . . But we cannot state the relationship of the two Testaments in terms of contrasting theologies, or regard the New merely as the last and highest upward step in the understanding of God. Christ came, indeed, to announce the decisive redeeming act of God, and to perform it. But he did not come to inform Judaism of a new and unknown God" (Bright, *Kingdom of God*, 195–96).
131. On Willard's view, one need not accept the decommissioning of Israel on divine authority alone; rather, God's recognition may be shared by a realistic consideration of the matter itself (cf. Willard, *Knowing*, chap. 7). In particular, we should consider whether the grace of God—the treasure of Israel's ministry and the reason for its commissioning in the first place—manifests itself effectively *apart* from this structure.
132. In the 2004 series *The Church as a Community of the Kingdom of God* (Church of the Open Door, Maple Grove, MN, November 4–6, 2004), Willard attempts to say, though he cannot in the moment recall the word, that he is not a supersessionist.

Now, in this chapter, I have brought to light a crucial piece of Willard's history of redemption. Without this piece, Willard's understanding of Jesus's gospel would be incomprehensible. I have said a lot about how, according to Willard, the old ministry worked, or was intended to work, in Israel. I have spoken about the change that Jesus introduces and how the transition took place. But I have not shared how Dallas Willard thinks Jesus's own ministry works. This is intentional and will be discussed in the next chapter as we discuss the ontology of Jesus's gospel of availability as understood by listeners on a second stage.

8

THE (LOST) GOSPEL OF JESUS THE TEACHER

While I was teaching at a pastor's conference recently, one pastor asked me what was the human issue, irrespective of church life or religion, that Jesus came to answer. The answer is that Jesus came to respond to the universal human need to know how to live well. He came to show us how, through reliance on him, we can best live in the universe as it really is.

—Dallas Willard, *In Search of Guidance*

You would never be a Pelagian unless you refused to take sin seriously. Once you take sin seriously, then you're going to cry for help. But Pelagian thinking is essentially a kind of Greek thinking about human beings and how they can fix themselves up. Plato's view of spiritual formation . . . is a self-help project. That's what Pelagius is about. Once you look into the depths of sin and realize what you have done, you'll never be tempted to be a Pelagian. Because you'll always know, you did that. Actually, we have a lot of Pelagianism in our evangelical churches, practical Pelagianism.

—Dallas Willard, Regent College, May 16, 2000

CONSIDER WILLARD'S STATEMENT in *Renovation*:

Most professing Christians today have "prayed to receive Christ" because they felt a need and would like him to help them deal with it. Now one cannot lay a satisfactory

> *foundation for spiritual formation or growth in grace by approaching people in terms of "the trouble they are in." I do not say that "felt needs" are to be disregarded, but in human affairs the "presenting problem"—the thing that needs to be* fixed now—*is rarely the real problem. One should of course be sympathetic with people who are lonely, guilt-ridden, and incapable of dealing with life, and so on, but these are not their problem.*
>
> *Their problem is that they have rejected God, for whatever reason, and have chosen to live life on their own. They have not surrendered their will to him. They do not want to do what God says to do, but what* they *think is best. And they are lost because of that, in the sense explained in an earlier chapter. They do not know what their real needs are and do not think of themselves as rebels and outlaws who must radically change because they are not acceptable to God. They do not think they need the grace of God for radical transformation of who they are, but that they just need a little help. They are good people. Or so it seems to them.*[1]

Willard, on one hand, recognizes an initial understanding of salvation in which Jesus has come to help individuals in their need and recognizes that faith in Jesus as a savior *of this kind* was genuine faith, obtained genuine deliverance, and was the occasion for some people's regeneration.

But on the other hand, Willard confronts a needs-based practice of evangelization in the contemporary church that sidelines discipleship and spiritual formation because it does not concern itself with "the *real* problem," with their rejection of God. In another place he says, "In the one case, the person actually does experience repentance. And the other, they don't experience repentance any more than when they buy a new vacuum cleaner. They just find something that is better for their needs."[2]

---

1. Willard, *Renovation*, 243.
2. Dallas Willard, "Understanding Spiritual Transformation," *The Place of Spiritual Transformation* (Bethel Seminary & College, St. Paul, MN, May 20, 2003), MP3, 57:45.

One thing that the listeners on the first level did not take into full account was the condition of sin, their rebellion against God. One could say that the gospel as understood at the first stage is not even one of Willard's pejoratively dubbed "gospels of sin management" because sin is almost a nonissue. This is not necessarily a failure in thinking, for it fits with Willard's understanding of the Beatitudes and the Great Inversion. Sinners like Abraham and Sarah are, for him, examples of the many sinful people whose lives are undeservedly blessed by the at-hand-ness of the kingdom. Abraham's sin is mercifully *not* taken into account, and this fact is the Great Inversion.

But according to the statement above, a gospel that involves discipleship will bring conviction of sin. It will not simply manage it but save people from it. How, according to Willard, do the first listeners make sense of their sin and Jesus's gospel? This question ties in with a question left open from the last chapter: What does Jesus *do* as a minister of the kingdom of God? Put differently, How does Jesus's ministry of the kingdom work? Or how is the kingdom of God made available to his listeners *through him* as opposed to how it was made available through the ministry commissioned to Israel under "the law and the prophets"?

The answer to these questions is the basis of a new understanding of Jesus's gospel of the kingdom. This higher stage is spoken to by Willard in chapter 1 of *Conspiracy*: "When [Jesus] announced that the 'governance' or rule of God had become available to human beings, he was primarily referring to what *he* could do for people, God acting with him. But he was also offering to communicate this same 'rule of God' to others who would receive and learn it from him."[3] The "also" of the second sentence signals an aspect of the gospel invitation that is *in addition to* their first understanding of the invitation—that is, in addition to the offer to have one's needs met ad hoc by coming to one who has access to the kingdom of God. If the first stage draws from a relation in which Jesus is the recipient and vassal of the kingdom, this higher

3. Willard, *Conspiracy*, 20.

stage names a relation in which Jesus is the *minister* of the kingdom.[4] Not its intermediary but its mediator.

Though not always explicitly distinguished from other relations as I am doing here, this is a *very* common mode for Willard to think about Jesus and the kingdom.[5] Considering Willard's publications as a whole, it is fair to say that this is the aspect of Christology that he most wished to communicate in his day, the aspect he felt was most pertinent for contemporary theological reflection. Thus, when he expresses in the first sentence of *Conspiracy* that his "hope is to gain a fresh hearing for Jesus," it has mostly to do with Jesus's role as the kingdom's minister.

Before we turn to describing Jesus's ministry, his method of saving people from their sins, we must know something of how Willard makes sense of the ruin into which the human race fell. Though I cannot give a comprehensive summary of Willard's hamartiology and anthropology, I will focus on one key part that, once clarified, should set the stage for his view of Jesus's ministry and salvation through it.[6]

Sin and the Evangelized Psychology

ON WILLARD'S VIEW, sin in the person stems from inaccurate thinking and especially from inaccurate thinking about God. Because of the God-intended function of the mind in the human person, those who think inaccurately about God (and all things related to him) will find

4. The last stage works with a relation in which Jesus is the *master* or *author* of the kingdom.

5. Consider the fact that the prospectus for *Conspiracy* portrayed the unwritten book as a companion volume to *Disciplines*. Whereas *Disciplines* dealt with Jesus's practices, the new book would deal with Jesus's beliefs—on which his practices rested (Dallas Willard, "Prospectus for *The Kingdom Next Door* [*The Divine Conspiracy*]," 1991, Dallas Willard Collection).

6. There are various historical sources from which Willard could have derived this view of sin. But one of the oldest and most prominent sources for him was Finney. Finney's method of bringing the knowledge of sin to his listeners' minds is penetrating. He repeatedly raises examples of actions and intentions that seem to be good on the surface but fail to measure up to our highest vision of moral reality. In a word, that vision of moral reality is love—that is, disinterested benevolence.

themselves sinners.[7] This basic point is not sufficient to give a full account of Willard's ontology of sin, its origin in God's good creation, or its wrongness. But it is important in order to understand something of sin's cure—the focus of this chapter. There will be no final cure of sin that does not rectify the false thinking characteristic of the fallen mind.[8]

If one is intent on ruining a human being, then a crucial place on which to work is their thoughts. Consider the following excerpt:

> *Ideas and images are the primary focus of Satan's efforts to defeat God's purposes for humankind. They form the primary arena of the battle of spiritual formation. When we are subject to Satan's chosen ideas and images, he can take a holiday. When he undertook to draw Eve away from God, he did not hit her with a stick, but with an idea. It was with the idea that God could not be trusted and that she must act on her own to secure her own well-being.*
>
> *Here is the basic idea behind all temptation: God is presented to our minds as depriving us of what is good (or at least of what we want) by His commands, so we think we must take matters into our own hands. This image of God leads to our pushing Him out of our thoughts and putting ourselves on the throne of the universe. We can see that the single most important thing in our minds is our idea of God. The process of spiritual formation in Christ is one of progressively replacing our destructive images and ideas with the images and ideas that filled the mind of Jesus Himself. We thereby come increasingly to see "the light of the gospel of the glory of Christ, who is the image of God" (2 Corinthians 4:4, NRSV).*[9]

---

7. Willard bears a strong resemblance here to A. W. Tozer. See A. W. Tozer, *The Root of the Righteous* (1955; repr., Milton Keynes, UK: Authentic Media, 2011), 7–9.
8. For more on this anthropology, see Willard, "Study and Meditation," 12:00.
9. Willard, "Gospel of the Kingdom," 49–50.

The upshot of this excerpt is that human beings were created to be beings whose choices and course of life depend in great measure on the contents of their minds. This means that they, in their integral state and much more so in their fallen state, are vulnerable in their thoughts.[10]

Let us call this anthropology the human creature's *evangelized psychology*.[11] On this, I grant liberal use of the word *gospel*; Satan's word to Eve is a gospel. It is a message that concerns her well-being. But because it is a *false gospel*, it affects her well-being negatively. The immediate effect that falsity has upon Eve is to keep her from integrating her life with reality, which is the primary function of truth in the human soul. This is her ruin.[12] The reality about her is that she cannot secure her own well-being on her own. Trying to do so will only engage her in futile activities that will eventually exhaust her life. Reality itself is not the sort of thing that will bend in light of her notions of it. If Eve believes falsely about the reality of herself, reality will not change its stance in light of Eve's belief or her attitudes (sincerity, certainty, commitment, willingness to profess it, etc.). Likewise, believing that God is untrustworthy will not *make* God untrustworthy. "No one has ever

---

10. Willard describes ideas as "very general models of or assumptions about reality. They are patterns of interpretation, historically developed and socially shared. They sometimes are involved with beliefs, but are much more than belief and do not depend upon it. They are ways of thinking about and interpreting things. They are so pervasive and essential to how we think about and how we approach life that we often do not even know they are there or understand when and how they are at work" (Willard, *Renovation*, 96–97; cf. also Dallas Willard, review of *Welt, Geschichte, Mythos und Politik*, by Gerd Brand, in *Contemporary German Philosophy*, vol. 4 [University Park: Penn State University Press, 1984]). According to Willard, ideas should be distinguished from knowledge and beliefs and are mostly unconsciously held. For an example of how *ideas* function in human life, see Willard's discussion of why churches do not make disciples of Jesus despite their conscious awareness that they should (Willard, *Conspiracy*, xv).

11. A similar usage of the word *gospel* can be found in Paul Tournier, *A Place for You* (New York: Harper & Row, 1968). Writing about "the gospel of psychology," which he clearly does not hold is a true gospel, he says, "I am using the word gospel in a loose, secular meaning, as when one speaks of the communist gospel. . . . What I am talking about is the advice that might be given by a psychologist compared with that of a theologian—or the advice that people *think* the psychologist and the theologian are giving, apparently in contradiction of each other" (92).

12. Cf. Willard, *Conspiracy*, 308–9.

yet made a belief true by believing it," says Willard.[13] This is the reality about reality: Human consciousness does not construct it. Human perception does not shape it, holds Willard.

What's more, given what Eve is, a human creature, she may not excuse herself from evangelized existence, an existence in which messages *will* fill her mind and thus delimit her actions. She is the kind of being that is, to use one of Willard's pithy phrases, "at the mercy of her ideas."[14] Though this form of existence is God's good gift to humans in his creation of them, it does entail that false gospels may enter the mind and wreck the person.

Often in full view of the great destruction visited upon humanity in light of false gospels, a false solution to this potentially perilous situation is worked out: the rejection of our evangelized psychology. This may happen in a variety of forms, be it a form of pragmatism (James, Rorty), anti-intellectualism (Pol Pot), skepticism (Hume), existentialism (Kierkegaard) or "Eastern religion" and meditation (what Willard called "the nirvana story").[15] This solution is both false and disingenuous because in practice, these solutions unavoidably *also* come to the human person in the form of a message, a representation of reality, and have precisely the effect that one would expect for an evangelized psychology. These false gospels fill the mind and direct the person's actions toward blessedness, goodness, or at least self-will.[16]

Another entailment of our evangelized psychology is that the origins of the first gospels that shape us are often deep and almost unsearchable. For Willard, a child's mind is not a tabula rasa in the sense that it could *decide* not to receive an education (or a spiritual formation) or *decide* in advance which one it wants. But it is a tabula rasa in the sense that its circumstances and the teachings or gospels of the persons with whom it first shares life inevitably come to inhabit it to the point

13. Willard, "Truth: Can We Do without It?," 12.

14. Willard, *Guidance*, x.

15. Willard, *Knowing*, 62.

16. This is a place where my focus on the mind does not allow space to discuss Willard's view of the heinousness of sin as a willed phenomenon. In print, cf. the section "Evil Now a Non-category" (*Renovation*, 46–47) as well as *Renovation*'s chapter on the will.

that their presence can be assumed. This is the point of the past particle "evangeliz*ed*." The gospels are there; it is human nature to be nurtured. "Who teaches you?" asks Willard in this vein. "One thing is sure: You are somebody's disciple. You learned how to live from somebody else. There are no exceptions to this rule, for human beings are just the kind of creatures that have to learn and keep learning from others how to live."[17]

These early childhood evangelists and their gospels are, to a degree, deep and unsearchable because of the absence of the individual's conscious decision in the process. In a lecture on spiritual formation and in exposition of the parable of the sower (Luke 8:4–15), Willard carefully explains the psychology he has in mind:

> *When you receive the word into "an honest and good heart," that means you join your will to it. There are a lot of theological issues here, but let me tell you at the outset, because I certainly want to make sure that this is said: how this works is a mystery. No one can program their own heart. There's a circle there. Because if they programmed their own heart, then their own heart has to be programmed before they can program it. And it is impossible. No one can do that. That's why at this center of the being, it was never meant to run on its own. It was meant to run in union with God. The basic problem with human beings is they are trying to program their own hearts. They are trying to find someone to do it.*[18]

This, beyond being one of Willard's arguments against some forms of Arminianism and Pelagianism, reveals how Willard thinks of the human being as necessarily "programmed" by others. The attempt by many, especially modern and structuralist thinkers (Freud, Marx, etc.), to teach without being taught is what he calls the "bootstrapping process among

---

17. Willard, *Conspiracy*, 271.
18. Dallas Willard, "Changing the Depth of the Heart," *Spiritual Formation* (NavPress / Theological and Cultural Thinkers, Colorado Springs, CO, April 1997), MP3, 31:45.

human beings." This vicious circle points, he says, to "the absolute centrality of revelation in human life—the word of God comes to man."[19] But when this new "programming" comes, it comes upon a soul in which other "programming" is already present, the origins and even contours of which may be hidden from the individual. Humans come into the world with the need to be told about reality and their ideal place in it. Our social setting, without exception, fulfills this role for us.

To be clear, for Willard, thinking a false gospel is not in itself a sin. Sin is fundamentally a matter of the will. But evangelized personalities are led automatically into sin by the false gospels their minds entertain. It was not Eve's *thought* (God cannot be trusted and I must act on my own to secure my own well-being) that was her sin. It was her *readiness to act as if her thought was true* that was her sin. As we saw in chapter 4, the readiness to act as if *x* is true is what Willard calls belief. And belief involves the will and produces the act, which is sin.

That being so, it is the God-given necessity of the human person for *gospels*, even if they are false, that generates further sin and corruption in the world and in the person. It is a grim set of affairs that calls for salvation that comes in the form of an evangelist and a new message. Such a savior would not merely inform Eve's children *about* salvation. This evangelist would *save* Eve's children by preaching to them a true gospel that supplants the false gospels that are currently wrecking their lives. Given such a state of disrepair, the act of salvation *is* the act of evangelization.

Other than evangelization, Willard could also speak, with the Bible, of the acts of *preaching*, or of *teaching*, or of *revelation*. The latter is a uniquely helpful concept for naming Willard's view because it highlights the importance of the gospel that saves *to come from outside human history*. Eve and her children were not capable of "reasoning up to" or

19. He continues, "And it comes in such a way that one never even says, 'Hah! Here is a wonderful resource that I can use to straighten out my life.' No, no, you simply fall down. You surrender" (Willard, "Changing the Depth," 33:45).

"stumbling upon" the gospel. It is, as Willard titles one subsection, a "Word *from a Different Reality*."[20]

Jesus's Gospel as Responsible for Bewilderment: Second-Stage Topography

BUILDING UPON THEIR initial understanding of the gospel in which Jesus is a prophet, some of Jesus's first listeners begin to make sense of his gospel in another way, a way that could be quite perplexing to them at first. When Jesus says the kingdom of God is "at hand," these listeners begin to think that he means more than that the kingdom is "at hand" *just for himself.* Jesus's message and early teachings suggest to them that the kingdom of God is available *for them* in the same way as it is available *for Jesus.* These are precisely the listeners who think that Jesus is thereby abolishing the law and the prophets (Matt 5:17).[21] Willard is fond of using this verse to argue that Jesus's gospel was quite lofty for his average first listener. As good Jews, they were accustomed to the kingdom being available *only* through their participation in the rituals and institutions of Israel. The rare prophet might be an exception to the rule, but this was not thought to be a reliable path for the masses.

Though it was beyond the first listeners' purview, sub specie aeternitatis Willard explains that Jesus "was simply *announcing* God's new move forward in human history."[22] As a result of his coming, Jesus proclaims that the kingdom of God is not just available to him; it is "now available to every one."[23] The Beatitudes, as should be familiar from *Conspiracy*, are teachings on the reality of human blessedness in light of *this fact*—namely, that the kingdom of God is directly available to the diverse kinds of people who simply were within earshot of Jesus. The first Matthean and Lukan Beatitude both include a conceptually equivalent blessing, "*theirs* is the kingdom of heaven" (Matt 5:3; emphasis mine).

20. Willard, *Conspiracy*, 11 (emphasis mine).
21. Willard, 126.
22. Willard, 288.
23. Willard, 288.

The first listeners are now confronted with the idea that their condition might prove no hindrance to the kingdom's at-hand-ness *to them*.

Though it may not seem so to us, this is a rather hard pill for Jesus's first listeners to swallow, which is why, according to Willard, Jesus encourages the practice of metanoia.[24]

Metanoia

METANOIA IS THE social-psychological entryway for "God's new move forward in human history." In reading Jesus's use of the word, Willard follows the connotations of the Greek rather than the traditional Latin (*paeniteo*) or English (*repent*) translations. Metanoia, for him, is a familiar mental act in which a person reviews his routine course of thought in light of some new information. Willard paraphrases it as "Think about how you have been thinking," and it is not exclusively related to moral matters.[25] An arachnologist could review and reverse her thoughts about the classification of spiders in light of reading a recent peer-reviewed journal article. This would be an act of metanoia, even though there was nothing morally wrong with being a person who believed something inaccurate about spiders.

By way of contrast, some theologians have a system of God's purposes, human nature, and sin within which this metanoia is not necessary. For them, salvation is the removal of God's problem with sin (guilt) in a way that is cosmically imposed on the world and/or imposed on individuals. In a familiar Arminian scheme, though secured and imposed cosmically, salvation from guilt is not imposed on individuals. Instead, their repentance (by which is meant remorse for their sins) and faith (whose object is usually that God has sufficiently dealt with his problem with sin) are preconditions for receiving salvation individually. In a familiar version of this captured in the Westminster standards and in reaction to the Arminian scheme, a person's repentance and faith are thought of as entailments of God's antecedent imposition of salvation on the person.

24. Willard, 15–16.
25. E.g., Willard, "Gospel of the Kingdom," 36.

In such systems, that from which the person is primarily suffering is not the real-world consequences of their own rebellion—namely, their distance from God and the corruption of their whole selves. The person is suffering from a divine verdict of condemnation. This verdict may not have any effect on their lives now, but it nevertheless keeps them from entrance into the blessed afterlife. To rephrase a question Willard asks of the needs-based method of evangelization, If persons come to Jesus because they need entrance into the blessed afterlife, will this "bring the saving transaction into [their] life"? If all that is at stake is one's need for eternal security or release from the burden of guilt, there is no need for metanoia concerning one's life *as a whole*. Metanoia is reduced to the same level as choosing a new diet.[26] And otherwise, one is free to think, believe, and live as one wants.

If, as in the late medieval period, a false theology of how God's forgiveness and entrance into the blessed afterlife are secured (so-called works righteousness) has entered people's minds and dominated their culture, these people, in light of hearing the rightful preaching of the word, will have to "think about their thinking." Willard believes that it was the presence of false theology in the prevailing late medieval, early modern culture that accounts for the fact that for persons like Martin Luther or John Owen, a more biblical teaching on forgiveness and eternal security led to profound changes in their lives *as a whole*.

How Willard tells the intellectual history of the Reformation is interesting but beyond our purview. Suffice it to say, Willard differentiates between (A) the intellectual breakthroughs of the Reformation regarding forgiveness and so on, (B) the perennially human event of seeing one's rebellion against God and the false gospels by which one has lived, and (C) compunction for one's sins, or what Willard called "wanting to beat your head against the floor."[27] (A) is what was really happening in the Reformation and what gives this period of intellectual history lasting importance. But the Reformers followed the medieval era in mistakenly thinking that the Greek metanoia meant (C). Yet much

26. Willard, "Understanding Spiritual Transformation," 57:45.
27. Willard, "Servanthood," 16:45.

like the reclassification of spiders for the arachnologist, for theologians caught in the false theology of the late medieval period, (A) was a kind of metanoia in the true Greek and biblical sense. Finally, for some people, the experience of (A) was so personally meaningful that it was the occasion of (B), which is the true soteriological experience of metanoia. But in reality, (B) does not have to be connected with (A). And (B) may lead to (C), felt sorrow for one's sins, but is distinct from it.

When Reformational concepts and events enter the twentieth century four hundred years later, they no longer have the redemptive-psychological power they had in late medieval and early modern society *because* the false gospels that capture contemporary society have changed. Thus, theological systems that are constructed and preached today in the attempt to honor the Reformation, its hermeneutical patterns, and its psychology of redemption have an effect that their proponents probably do not intend. They *do not* lead, as they did for Luther and Owen, to profound changes in their adherents' lives as a whole.

The Achilles' heel that Willard spots in such systems is that they are prone to leave intact many of the false gospels that plague Eve's children and corrupt their lives. What's more, they leave Eve's children with no notion of where to turn for help or even that they need it. This is because belief (X) that God has arranged for forgiveness of our sins is logically independent of belief (Y) that we are evangelized personalities who have fallen into "whole life" ruin stemming from a corruption of our minds *and* belief (Z) that God has uniquely entered the world to help us be transformed by the renewal of our minds. In other words, one cannot assume that a person who only believes the former (X) will eventually come to believe the latter (Y, Z) because of their inherent logical relation. By contrast, when Luther, Owen, and others come to believe the former (X), they do so in an intellectual context in which the latter (Y, Z) are simply assumed. But this cannot be assumed of Christians or non-Christians today.

Now, only in the latter (Y, Z) does metanoia have a key role to play in the person's salvation. For Willard, though conscious choices may have led them into it, humans function in a state of rebellion against God—willing that which is not God's will—because they do not know

God and his world rightly. Willard speaks of how "this [false] image of God leads to our pushing Him out of our thoughts and putting ourselves on the throne of the universe."[28] Therefore, God must bring such persons to understand that they think wrongly about him and all things related to him, including their own well-being.

Thus, metanoia, according to Willard, is far broader than recognizing upon reflection that one has committed sins and is, therefore, a sinner. That recognition alone would do very little to solve a person's "whole life" problem. Evangelized personalities like Eve commit sins thinking and believing that God and his relation to their well-being is different from what it is in reality. Only changing their minds about these fundamental gospel issues treats the person in a way that has an effect on their *whole life* while respecting God's purposes in history.[29] It puts them in a position to *believe* the gospel and end their rebellion against God. Then, having reconciliation with God, further metanoia saves them from their sins.

Identification of and Trust in a Minister

JESUS PUTS INTO the minds of his first-century audience the idea, contrary to what they have been led to think, that the kingdom of God is theirs (Matt 5:3, 10; Luke 6:20). This is all the more perplexing because the best and clearest example of what Jesus means by this is *he himself*, the one who is standing in front of them speaking, teaching, healing, and caring for others in the extraordinary power and wisdom of the kingdom. Willard writes with emphasis, "*He was himself the evidence for the truth of his announcement about the availability of God's kingdom, or governance, to ordinary human existence.*"[30] Suddenly believing Jesus's message involves comparing oneself to Jesus, a comparison that led Peter to say, "Depart from me, for I am a sinful man, O Lord" (Luke 5:8).

---

28. Willard, "Gospel of the Kingdom," 50.
29. To hear Willard develop the idea of a "whole-life gospel," see "Kingdom Gospel," 9:30. There are many other issues to deal with here in Willard's soteriology.
30. Willard, *Conspiracy*, 20.

Now, the identification of Jesus's own life on earth with the end result of the kingdom's availability to human beings is an essential point in Willard's reconstruction and should not be overlooked. It must be understood that the kingdom of God was available for Jesus (stage 1) before any deeper meanings of Jesus's message are grasped. Only on the basis of Jesus's perceived greatness in the kingdom of God does the invitation to join him strike the listeners as it should. And only on the basis of Jesus's perceived greatness does the invitation's sense of solemnity, audacity, and sheer incredulity for those first listeners strike us as it should.

Jesus tells his first listeners that "among those born of women there has arisen no one greater than John the Baptist. Yet the one who is least in the kingdom of heaven is greater than [John the Baptist]" (Matt 11:11). As great as John was in the minds of Jesus's audience and in reality, Jesus audaciously announces that some of his listeners have already gone *beyond* the spirituality of John and have an even greater relationship to God and his heavenly kingdom than he.[31] As already discussed, Willard makes sense of this himself by arguing that John's spirituality was a spirituality without the prophetic power of the Spirit. Jesus's spirituality is a significant step up from John's.

But for the first listeners, being greater than John (when one is only a lowly worker in the kingdom) could only mean that Jesus is continuing his incredulous proclamation of the radical availability of the kingdom that he laid out in the Sermon on the Mount. It is an availability without regard to one's condition as one "born of women." This radical availability apparently comes packaged with a kind of greatness, one modeled on *Jesus's own* greatness and not on John's. This is not exactly good news to a Jewish audience. Jesus's greatness in the kingdom is untroubling to his listeners so long as he remains their intermediary

31. Willard, 20. See Dallas Willard, "Session 4," *Doing What Jesus Did*, MP3, 5:45: "Now, why would you be greater than John the Baptist? Because now there is a relationship to the kingdom of God that you have because of the work of the person of Jesus Christ that John the Baptist himself didn't have."

to supplicate and not their example to follow. Jesus's first listeners know enough about their God to know that he is not one to be trifled with.

So here is how Willard puts this together. While it is true that the kingdom is available for everyone as it is for Jesus, that is not the gospel. The gospel is that it is available for them *through Jesus* and not apart from him. Jesus's gospel and his statements such as Matthew 11:11, Luke 7:28, or the Beatitudes are not good news, or possibly even true, if Jesus is removed from the scene.[32] He is not proclaiming a radically individualistic spirituality such as is typical of Eastern religions or various instantiations of Western spirituality ranging from Hegelianism to witchcraft. Jesus's intended news is that the kingdom is now available for everyone *through himself*.

Willard's theology of Jesus's gospel is best understood if we recall a way Willard regularly expressed the gospel to his own audiences. The gospel, he says, is "trust Jesus."[33] What this means in light of the fact that the kingdom is radically available for everyone regardless of their circumstances is that the gospel is *Jesus's ministry*. Jesus presents himself as one who will *mediate* a relationship between the listener and this radically available kingdom. This is the heart of his gospel: that Jesus is

---

32. Willard, *Conspiracy*, 103.

33. See Willard, 48–49; Dallas Willard, "Gospel and Salvation," *Pursuing Truth in Love* (Desert Stream Spring Conference, Anaheim, CA, May 2003), MP3, 14:45; and Dallas Willard, "The Fine Textures of Life in the Kingdom of the Heavens," *Renovaré Regional Conference* (Renovaré, Folsom, CA, April 19, 2002), MP3, 8:00. Consider also these statements: "What Jesus was saying was the kingdom of God is now available to you in a new way by trusting me" (Dallas Willard, "The Background of Reality," *NavWorld Laying Foundations Conference* [Navigators, January 19, 2001], MP3/cassette, 20:30) and "Jesus came into the world so that we could trust him and follow him into his kingdom" (Dallas Willard, "Living in the Kingdom of God Is Walking in the Character and Power of God," *Kingdom Living: It's a Wonderful Life* [Valley Vineyard, Reseda, CA, February 9, 1999], MP3/VHS, 11:30) and "He's [Jesus is] simply saying, 'Look, trust me,' because the kingdom of heaven was at hand in him" (Willard, "Finding the Kingdom of God," 17:00) and "The whole gospel is contained in trust Jesus" (Dallas Willard, "Ordering the Spiritual Disciplines," *Where New Life Begins* [Renovaré, Wichita, KS, April 13, 1991], MP3/cassette); cf. also Dallas Willard, "On Acts, Pt. 2," *2012 Renovaré Ministry Retreat*, MP3, 4:45.

offering *himself* as a reality for trusting. Without trust in him as a minister, his ministry does not work.[34]

The Mechanics of Ministry: Presence and Preaching

SO WHAT IS Jesus's ministry? How does *his* ministry to the kingdom work? First of all, it works by a kind of baptism. Recall here the discussion from chapter 5 on the baptism of Moses. To Willard's mind, the Mosaic baptism is the equivalent of the waterless(!) Trinitarian baptism of Matthew 28:18–20. Second, it works by means of an invitation, available only through Jesus, to go *beyond* the religion of John and become greater than he. How this upward mobility would take place is largely unclear to the first invitees, but here are two fundamental aspects. First, they know that Jesus invites them to be with him and that somehow this togetherness will impart to them some kind of kingdom *greatness*.

Willard, for his part, highlights this element of people being *with Jesus* (e.g., Mark 3:14). The μαθηταὶ (or Jesus's apprentices) are exemplary of those who, *by being physically close to Jesus*, came into deeper contact with the spiritual kingdom of God—deeper, that is, than what their regeneration and ongoing participation in the Jewish institutions afforded them. "Christ's transcendent life in the present Kingdom of heaven," as I quoted in chapter 6, "is what drew the disciples together around Jesus prior to his death."[35] Having gathered them together around him, he did not keep his "transcendent life," or his spirituality, to himself. He communicated it.[36]

As also discussed in chapter 6, Jesus's spirituality is "incarnational" or embodied. On account of this, Willard had great respect for how

---

34. Before unpacking this, I wish to note in passing how Christ-centered Willard's notion of the gospel is. At the bottom of Jesus's gospel of the kingdom's availability is not some theistic metaphysical teaching. At the bottom is the reality of Jesus. This conforms to Willard's exposition and affirmation of the Johannine description of salvation (John 17:3). The work of Christ moves forward in his listeners as the person of Christ is more and more fully understood.

35. Willard, *Disciplines*, 35.

36. This is not to suggest that his life is something that is detachable from him like an electrical charge. At least this is not Willard's view, who eventually connects this with the indwelling Christ of Col 1:27.

spirituality is transferred from body to body. In an important lecture from 1985, he speaks of "the matrix of mission," saying, "[A matrix] is that source from which something arises, as from a womb. Matrix is the womb of mission. The womb of mission is the body of the believer. . . . When I say 'body,' I mean that thing sitting in the chair. . . . I am talking about that physical body. And it is that which is the repository from which the life of God (that is the inevitable mission) [flows]; it is from this body that mission flows."[37] The same, Willard believes, is eminently true of Jesus. His transcendent life is passed on to others through contiguity.[38] How this happens is a mystery (at least Willard seems to believe it mysterious), so it is not unusual for him that the first listeners have no comprehension of its operation. What is clear is that Willard does not think of contiguity in terms of automatic physical reactions like bodies that become hot near a fire. Since this is a *spiritual* process, the recipient's will is involved to the point that a person disinterested in or resisting the process *will not* be affected by it.[39]

But spiritual contiguity is not the nucleus of how Jesus proposes to make his listeners greater than John. Recall the verse that, for Willard, signals the transition in God's redemptive work: "The Law and the Prophets were until John; since then the good news of the kingdom of God *is preached*" (Luke 16:16; emphasis mine). In other words, Jesus's ministry to the kingdom will work—in marked contrast to what was done under "the law and the prophets"—through *preaching*. This is the second fundamental aspect of how Jesus's ministry works.

As I said in chapter 3, preaching is an often missed element in Willard's philosophy of ministry because his reputation for promoting spiritual disciplines tends to obscure it. Though his Calvinistic Baptist

---

37. Dallas Willard, "Matrix of Mission 1," *Spirituality and Mission*, 1:45.
38. Willard, *Knowing*, 159. Willard develops this theme in many places, but especially in "The Matrix of Mission 1."
39. This process is a remnant of Willard's revivalist theology, which he pursued intently as a young man (Dallas Willard, "The Good Life and the Good Person Made Real by Jesus: Rethinking the 'Sermon on the Mount,'" *Spiritual Renewal Conference* [Bethel Seminary San Diego, San Diego, CA, October 10, 2008], MP3, 6:30). Though he left revivalism as a complete tradition, this aspect of it remained with him throughout his life.

upbringing introduced him to the power of preaching, studying how "the word" functioned in Jesus's ministry and Acts breathed perpetual life into his tradition's "high view" of preaching.[40]

Now, as a preacher, Jesus announces or proclaims knowledge. In identifying Jesus as a trustworthy preacher, his listeners simply recognize him as someone who is speaking accurately about reality. In a sense, they are saying, "Here's a journalist one can trust." The deeper aspects of what God is doing in their souls through the preaching are largely unknown to them. This means that when initially thinking of Jesus as a preacher, the first listeners are not thinking of him very highly. Their appreciation of him does not exceed the appreciation of those who welcomed his extremely unexperienced apostles when Jesus sent them out to preach the same message.

To be more specific, Willard believes the initial ministry of Jesus is evangelism, or what he also calls proclamation. When Willard uses the word *evangelism*, he often strictly distinguishes it from soul-winning.[41] Soul-winning, put in the best light, is an activity of helping people make a decision about their relationship to what they know in the gospel. Evangelism, however, is simply putting some good, new information out there—regardless of the outcome. Willard compares it to putting up billboards. Evangelism takes the idea or fact and publishes it in brief, memorable expressions.[42] It is often confused with soul-winning because many do not understand that evangelism can be successfully

40. More of this will be discussed in the next stage because Jesus's second-stage listeners are not quite ready to think of Jesus in that way.

41. Dallas Willard, "Jesus as a Logician and Apologist," *Apologetics Track* (European Leadership Forum, Eger, Hungary, May 2006), MP3, 28:00, 30:30.

42. Willard's most sustained reflections on this act are in terms of the metaphor of a seed. His exegeses of the parables of the sower and of the seed treat them as analyses of how kingdom *proclamation* works. Willard works through the parables in multiple settings but extensively in "The Diverse Receptions of the Word of the Kingdom: The Sower," *The Parabolic Teaching about Christ's Kingdom by Christ* (Harbor Church, Lomita, CA, March 13, 1983), MP3/cassette; and "The Secret Manner of the Kingdom's Working: The Leaven and the Seed," *The Parabolic Teaching about Christ's Kingdom by Christ* (Harbor Church, Lomita, CA, March 20, 1983), MP3/cassette. Also in Dallas Willard, "Word of the Kingdom as a Life Force: How to Respond," *Kingdom Living: It's a Wonderful Life* (Valley Vineyard, Reseda, CA, March 16, 1999), MP3/VHS.

done without resulting in any conversions. Soul-winning, however, always involves additional measures—some Willard applauds, some he deplores—to lead people to a decision and/or to a conversion.

Even though evangelism was a part of how *first-stage* listeners heard the gospel and came to faith in Jesus, for listeners at that stage, his preaching was not in focus. It mattered little *how* a first-stage believer came to know what they knew about Jesus or about God. In the second stage, however, the listeners *must* negotiate the idea of Jesus as an evangelist, as a preacher. Jesus's statement that "yours is the kingdom of God" (Luke 6:20) is quite radical and calls for a decision as to whether Jesus knows what he is talking about. Deciding that he is speaking the truth in this instance, that he is a trustworthy preacher, does not indicate a very high Christology. Presumably, Judas Iscariot was also a preacher of the kingdom and sent out with the Twelve to repeat the exact same message Jesus preached in the Jewish towns and villages. But thinking of Jesus as a trustworthy preacher does situate the listener in a different *set of relations* with Jesus and the kingdom, a set of relations that will be very important for the development of higher views of Jesus.

The Topography of Jesus's Ministry

LET US LOOK for a moment at this set of relations. In order to be precise about Willard's theology here, it is necessary to go in for a little abstraction. What is the ontology presumed by the gospel in the *second* stage? In the first stage, it was held that the kingdom of God was *generally* made available to Israel and the world under "the law and the prophets" and especially through the rituals and institutions of the covenant people to whom "the law and the prophets" were entrusted. Jesus, however, was one of those unique persons, familiar from biblical history, to whom the kingdom was directly and abundantly available. In the first stage, trust in Jesus was a trust in a person with special standing in the kingdom of God (a prophet) who could and would on that basis act benevolently toward those who came to him. This trust in him as their deliverer put them in effective—that is, saving—contact with Jesus and his God. This was the meeting place of human trust and Jesus's work of making the kingdom available.

The ontology presumed by the gospel in the second stage is more complex. At the basis of Jesus's proposed ministry to the kingdom of God, at the basis of this new state of affairs in biblical history (the new "age"), there is a different set of ontological relations between the relevant parties. To begin with, the listener acknowledges that the kingdom of God is topographically nearer to himself than in the first stage. The previous stage had a kind of buffered nearness. The kingdom of God had first come near to Jesus, and then Jesus had come near to the people. Between the kingdom of God and the listener stood, almost as an obstruction, the man Jesus and his human "kingdom." All access to the kingdom of God was thought to go directly through his human personality, especially his will. "Lord, *if you will*, you can make me clean," is expressive of first-stage ontological relation.[43]

But the topography of this next level is the *direct proximity* of the kingdom of God to the listeners without any "stopover" in the man Jesus. If true, this implies that Jesus stands in a different relation to God and the kingdom of God. His role in God's plan of salvation is different from that of God's "charity worker." His role is less central and profoundly *instrumental* in establishing a more important relationship. If his listeners trust him as he preaches this radical gospel, the trust placed in him is the trust conferred on a human "instrument," a helper or a minister for those seeking the kingdom of God.

So one way of describing Willard's notion of Jesus's ontological position ministry that lies at the heart of the second-stage presentation of the gospel is to point to a real *distinction* between the kingdom and Jesus. If in the most mature stage Jesus's position as the kingdom's king leads one to see that the kingdom is indivisible from Jesus, this second stage recognizes Jesus's external position with respect to the kingdom. He is the kingdom's associate, its counterpart. He stands alongside it and refers to it, gives access to it by speaking of it, manifesting it, and baptizing others in it. If in Willard's first stage Jesus stands between the kingdom and his first-century listeners, such that the "secrets" of

43. Matt 8:2; also Mark 1:40; and Luke 5:12.

the kingdom are hidden from their view (Matt 13:11) and only Jesus's amplified actions are visible, this second stage has Jesus stepping aside, as it were, and exposing the kingdom to his listeners and vice versa. There is an identifiable distinction here. Jesus is not identical with the kingdom that he announces. And what this distinction amounts to is a relation between the kingdom of God and all human beings that is characterized by direct proximity. *Jesus* is not "in the way."

Another way of describing the availability of the kingdom that Willard has in mind is to say that the kingdom is *not prophetocentric*. A prophet in the minds of mildly educated Israelites is an intermediary who, among other things, has access to the kingdom of God. When Jesus the prophet makes his big gospel announcement, he is saying that the kingdom of God is available to people without their being dependent on him, the prophet. To them, this would certainly mean that they might themselves be or become prophets. Since the kingdom of God is available to them, they may interact with it *independently* as any of the prophets have—if they so wish and if they know how. Jesus's role is as this new situation's evangelist or preacher. He announces it, and *in an important respect*, his listeners may access it without him. He is their brother not their "charity worker." As it has been for him, the kingdom of God is *simply there* for them. Jesus's distinction from the kingdom leaves room for a more intimate, more direct relationship between the kingdom and other individuals.

In light of this ontology, a quite fitting concept for Jesus's work at this stage is that of *mediation*.[44] Willard uses the concept strategically, though not always consistently, to express Jesus's second-stage ministry. I have mostly

44. For example, "The life before an open heaven is *mediated* by one on whom heaven has come to rest" (Willard, "Heavens Were Opened," 30:30). One other valuable instance of the concept is in *The Life with God Bible*, where Willard describes the difference between God's direct interaction with individuals before Abraham and his interaction with individuals after Abraham as a difference in *mediation*. Missing in God's interactions before Abraham was mediation (Dallas Willard, "The People of God in Individual Communion with God," in Foster et al., *Renovaré Spiritual Formation Bible*, 4; see also Willard, "People of God into Eternity," 2261). This reference fits well with our descriptions of the covenant ministry from Abraham on through Jesus. See also Willard, "God and His Kingdom," 36:00, for another reference to mediation.

used the word *ministry* because this is most consistent with Willard's idiom. But ministry can be quite general as a concept concerning Jesus's work as well because it has a place in the soteriology of all three stages. Generally conceived, Jesus's ministry is about his doing *everything* possible to promote the good of those whom he is serving. As such, it is a synonym for salvation.

But mediation describes a unique position and function that Jesus maintains toward his listeners. The concept calls to mind a third-party facilitator. In Willard's thought, it expresses that two other parties, the kingdom of God and the individual person, are what need to be brought into relationship and alignment. As a third-party facilitator, Jesus is fundamentally auxiliary and ancillary to the formation of this primary relationship. His auxiliary position is essential to his ancillary work of mediation. Importantly, the goal in an act of mediation is not *more mediation* but perfection of the relationship between the two other parties—in this case, the person and the kingdom of God. The goal in Jesus's mediation is a person—ultimately like himself—who lives fully in the kingdom of God.

Solus Christus?

THE BIGGEST DISSENTERS from Willard's ontology here are the two perhaps greatest christological theologians of the early twentieth century: Karl Barth and Dietrich Bonhoeffer. What such theologians object to is that Willard's topography of Jesus's ministry with his first listeners admits a distinction between Jesus and the kingdom. They object to the notion that access to the kingdom was possible for the first listeners without knowledge of Jesus as the kingdom's direct agent or of his unique role in opening the kingdom to others.

Their position was a variation on a view popular in the Reformation era about whether and how *faith* saved individuals before the coming of Jesus. The Second Helvetic Confession is typical in confessing, "This Jesus Christ our Lord is the unique and eternal Savior of the human race, and thus of the whole world, in whom *by faith* are saved all who before the law, under the law, and under the Gospel were saved."[45]

45. Second Helvetic Confession 5.077 (emphasis mine).

In other words, the object of faith for Abraham or those after him is the ancient "gospel promises," which, though they do not name Jesus and his life history, allude to his peculiar function in the history of redemption. By means of this move, the Reformers and their followers were able to claim *solus Christus*. But it did entail for New Testament interpretation that Jesus's first listeners could not have had saving faith in him or his gospel so long as they did not yet understand his *divine* functions in the kingdom and in salvation.

The christological theologians worked on a similar account of Jesus's ministry under the banner of *solus Christus*. It is noteworthy that their theology was forged in a time when the liberal, often German theologians of the late nineteenth century regularly *and radically* distinguished Jesus from the kingdom of God and the gospel. Though his message of the kingdom would remain true for future generations, Jesus was regarded by liberal theologians as dispensable in his listeners' appropriation of the saving effect of his message. Jesus was a genius whose life history or whose continuing presence was irrelevant to future belief in his eternally relevant thoughts.

The alternative ontology that the christological theologians accepted was designed to strike at the heart of liberal ontology. The message of Jesus could not be made sense of, and salvation could not be obtained *apart from knowledge of Jesus in his divinity* because the kingdom could not be distinguished ontologically from Jesus. In their unique way of exegeting the Scriptures, the incarnation of the second person of the Trinity was brought into the ontology of the kingdom. That means the Triune God did not have a kingdom whose essence was or could be independent of the incarnation and of the man Jesus. That historical state of affairs was an inseparable part of the kingdom's reality. The planet Venus, the healing of the blind beggar, the writing of the book of Hebrews—all these historical acts of God were *in* his kingdom as separable parts, as noncontingent manifestations of its reality. Had they not come into existence, the essence of the kingdom of God would have remained the same. But the incarnation and the resulting divine-human person were different. When the Scriptures speak of the kingdom of God, they are speaking of Jesus's kingdom as a God-man whom the

Father sent and the Spirit glorifies. And that kingdom's *essence*, irrespective of how the individual theologians worked out the rest in their Trinitarian theology, was tied up with the second person's divine *and human* reality.

Now, Willard will fully admit that the second person of the Trinity is essential to the kingdom of God as its direct agent. But his incarnation is not. His incarnation is an essential part of God's plan of salvation in light of God's purposes for his creation. But the kingdom of God is not subsumed under this salvific plan; it is not a subdoctrine of soteriology or teleology. Though it has manifestations in the outworking of salvation, it is fundamentally a part of who God is in his immanence, whether he is creator and savior of the world or not.

For the christological theologians, this ontology of the kingdom—that is, its indistinguishability from Jesus as the divine incarnate king—meant, as it did in the Reformation era, that no preaching of the gospel of the kingdom could have saving effect on its listeners without their knowledge of Jesus's divine or divine-human functions. The ministry of evangelism either brought to light Jesus's divine-human reality or was not salvifically effective. To admit that Jesus's own ministry of evangelism was effective *without* the deeper aspects of his person being known would compromise their sense of *solus Christus*. Focused as they were on the latter events of Jesus's life, on his church, and on Jesus's functions in his church, generally the christological theologians ignored Jesus's ministry in Galilee. It did not fit well into their ontology and was, for that reason and others, theologically uninteresting.

Between the liberal theologians and the christological theologians, Willard took a third route. This is evident in one of his oldest maxims. Studying philosophy in the late 1950s and early '60s, when the christological theologians had won the day and American fundamentalists were beginning the neoevangelical movement, Willard encountered many Christians who were worried about his engagement with philosophy and the increasingly secular-minded university. Would his faith not be safer and more robust if he kept himself from exposure to views that did not explicitly trace their origin back to Jesus? In other words, is not Jesus the sole source of all important knowledge in this world? Are not those who do not exclusively immerse themselves in his word introducing themselves to sources of error? In this climate, Willard was inspired to formulate a maxim that he continued to give to his audiences until his death: "If you could find a better way, Jesus would be the first one to tell you to take it. And if you don't believe that about him, you don't have faith in him, because what you're really saying is that he would encourage you to believe something that is false."[46] In other words, Jesus as preacher and teacher does not assume the role of the sole source of knowledge. He may, when appropriate, assume the role of one pointing another to knowledge.

Of course, the latter is the role in which the liberal theologians had exclusively thought of Jesus. But for them, his message did not have a self-referential element. The gospel of the kingdom would have been true and good had he not existed. By means of a crucial compromise, they managed to continue the pedagogical realism with which Jesus's teachings had been taken since the apostolic era. But this compromise was the careful disregard of all self-referential elements of Jesus's teaching and ministry. As historians, they associated these with the apostolic distortion of Jesus and his message in the years following his death and not with Jesus's original intent.

By holding to the pedagogical realism of Jesus's teachings and yet resisting this compromise, Willard took his third route. Jesus spoke as a realist about God and the world, but he also spoke as a realist about himself. He could not be separated from his message as a whole because he was a part of his message as a whole. That did not mean for Willard that Jesus's message was *about* his being the incarnate Son of God. He *was* the incarnate Son of God, but that is not what his message was about.

Jesus's Bewildering Ontology

RETURNING AGAIN TO the Galilean situation, Jesus's gospel of trust in him as a preacher and its underlying topography put the first-century listener into quite a lofty epistemic situation. But we must recall that

46. Christine A. Scheller, "A Divine Conspirator," *Christianity Today* 50, no. 9 (2006): 46. See also Willard, "Handout for 'Justification,'" 1973.

listeners are not being asked to rethink their theology of how the kingdom of God might interact with any given individual. If they take Jesus at his word, they assume the kingdom will exist and operate much in the same way they believe it did for the prophets of old. They know what this means from their basic familiarity with their Scriptures.

The proposed difference is that this is all possible *for them* because of the kingdom's immediate presence *to them*. The rituals and institutions of their people and the intermediaries through which they had accessed the kingdom are seemingly sidelined.[47] Jesus, if they trust him, will now mediate the relationship. Again, this is a mind-boggling change and can only be accompanied by Jesus's call to metanoia. Believing that the kingdom is immediately present to a present-day prophet is, of course, news but is not a cause for wide-sweeping revision of one's thoughts. Believing it requires no restructuring of their scriptural theology of the kingdom nor of the genus of the person speaking to them. It is journalism—neither theology nor heresy. However, that the kingdom is present *to them* as it was to the prophets is groundbreaking theological information.

And yet, though mind-boggling, this, too, according to Willard, is not *new* Jewish theology. It is forgotten Jewish theology. As discussed in the previous chapter, God's original vision for his elect people was that they would all be a "kingdom of priests" (Exod 19:5–6), interacting with God directly. Though God used them, intermediaries were not God's original intent for Israel, and groups like the Levitical priesthood were meant to be servants in the priesthood of all "believers." So while it is not new theology—*if* the listeners could recall key portions of "the law and the prophets"—it was still hard to believe. That it countered the ideas that their religious leaders had communicated to them did not help.

But now I want to turn to how this bewildering ontology comes to influence the first listeners' view of Jesus, of the salvation he proposed to accomplish in them and finally the faith he called them to—all the same themes from the first stage, only a new chapter.

---

47. See Willard, "Presence of the Kingdom" (MP3/cassette) and his other attempts to exegete Exod 19:5–6; cf. Willard, *Guidance*, 39.

9

THE (ONLY) GOSPEL THAT MAKES DISCIPLES

> Jesus came among us to *show* and *teach* the life for which we were made.
>
> —Dallas Willard, *The Divine Conspiracy*

> When Jesus comes . . . he is the world's primary educator. . . . The force of Jesus in the world has been mainly through education.
>
> —Dallas Willard, Denver Seminary, January 4, 2010

> Knowledge is the basis of our salvation. It is our salvation more than anything else. It is knowledge. It is knowledge which saves. Put that to the test of reading the New Testament to see. Our feelings, our will are based upon our knowledge. That's why the work of the ministry is the teaching of truth. And when that is done effectively, feelings follow, wills follow. It's the teaching of truth.
>
> —Dallas Willard, "Skyline Wesleyan Church, July 26, 1974"

IN THE LAST twenty years of his life while he was traveling the globe to speak in churches and seminaries, Willard repeated a provocative theological position: only Jesus's gospel of the availability of the kingdom of God would lead naturally to discipleship among those who received it. With this he was pointing out—and he thought it was empirically verifiable—that the other gospels that were popular in the West did not result in much, if any, discipleship. He used this criterion to prophetically call the church to metanoia about its theological system and methods of ministry.

Granted, this is potentially disconcerting for theologians and ministers who perhaps have centered their theology or ministry or both on a certain concept of the gospel. In this chapter, as a continuation of the previous chapter, we will discuss the topics that led Willard to speak in this provocative way. Why only one gospel? Why this gospel? Why a natural progression?

In the previous chapter, we started with Willard's criticism of a needs-based method of evangelization—precisely the sort that relies on the first-stage view of Jesus. Willard called out this ministry method because it did not take into account human rebellion, the rejection of God, or sin. Though it is not exhaustive of his view, part of what sin means for the human race is that it is affected by inaccurate thinking about God and the kingdom of God. Having an evangelized psychology, or at least an evangelize-able psychology, humans are "tossed to and fro by the waves and carried about by every wind of doctrine" (Eph 4:14). Thus, the means of saving such creatures must address their "rational soul," as older theologians called it.

This is what Jesus does when he proclaims his gospel of the kingdom's availability to everyone, regardless of their life circumstances or moral character. To accept this message, Jesus's first-century listeners must rethink their thinking. Specifically, they must rethink their lives in light of the kingdom of God being theirs. But this is not easy to accept because Jesus's own transcendent life is the clearest case of what that would mean. At the same time, they must rethink how the kingdom of God will be mediated to them. No longer is it not exclusively through "the law and the prophets" as they have been taught. It is now through putting their trust in Jesus as their mediator. And Jesus's mediation to the kingdom works by means of his presence and his preaching. By these means, Jesus will make those who come to him greater than John the Baptist and able to live in the kingdom as he himself does.

"The Wisdom of the Just"

BUT BY AND large, Jesus's first listeners did not expect him as he came. The covenant people did not expect a preacher-savior. They did not know that their psychology and the nature of their sin were such that they needed a teacher to come to save them.

If there was any recognition that the *real problem* was that false gospels had caught the minds of the covenant people (and indeed the whole world), leading them into sin and necessitating their rescue by a preacher-savior, it was among the Jewish prophets up to and including John. But generally, this was not recognized. Even John, as already mentioned, was confused by the appearance of *this kind* of savior (Matt 11:2–3).[1] So it is not on the basis of any historically ascertainable worldview among the covenant people that Willard makes his argument for this understanding of Jesus and his gospel. One place he starts is with the book of Malachi.

Malachi 4:5–6, he says, is a promise but "looks back on the failure of the old testament."[2] Translating *testament* as a covenant agreement or will, it is not a discrete covenant that Willard has in mind so much as what he in another context calls "the Jewish *system*."[3] He goes on to say, "That old covenant failed for lack of the perfection which would come in through Jesus Christ."[4] This much has been rehearsed in previous chapters.

He then adds, "The curse of sin rests upon the unhealed relationships at the heart of our families, between fathers and sons, between brothers."[5] This curse is what "the old testament"—that is, the Jewish system—failed to lift:

1. Cf. Willard, "Jesus as a Logician."
2. Willard, "Fathers and Sons," 2:30.
3. Willard, "God and His Kingdom," 1:02:00. This use fits the author of Hebrews' use of covenant to stand for the Levitical priesthood's ministry.
4. Willard, "Fathers and Sons," 3:00. See also Dallas Willard, "An Introduction to Your Soul," *The Soul* (Valley Vista Christian Community, Sepulveda, CA, August 5, 1990), MP3/cassette, 38:45.
5. Willard, "Fathers and Sons," 4:00.

> *The Old Testament is a family book, and when it comes down to the end of it, for all the grace of God that is manifested in it, there is still the unhealed relationship at the center of human life. The fathers whose hearts are turned away from the sons and the sons whose hearts are turned away from the fathers.*
>
> *And now what this does, you see, [is] it robs us of the ability to enter into the great stream of life and the wisdom of God that comes down to us through past generations and is present in the Bible and should be present in the elders who lived in our family. See, we're meant to learn from our elders.*[6]

In God's original plan for human families, our elders were intended to introduce us to "the great stream of life and the wisdom of God." But this tradition, the most eudaemonious human tradition, has been broken because of sin. The tradition, as broken, is itself not sin but *the curse* of sin. And it was the curse that "the Jewish system," for all its focus on the family, was unable to lift.

In the same message, Willard goes on to address the Lukan version of the Malachi text that renders the last part of the couplet "turn . . . the disobedient to *the wisdom of the just*" (Luke 1:17; emphasis mine). Bringing his exegesis back full circle, he asks, "What is the wisdom of the just?" His answer is simple yet profound: "Primarily 'the wisdom of the just' has to do with the knowledge of God. It has to do with the knowledge of God's rule."[7] In other words, "the wisdom of the just" boils down to the gospel, the availability of the kingdom. But how is a family that is under a curse that affects their knowledge *to know* that they are under a curse? Willard's answer is that word must come from the outside—*word from a different reality.*

Thus, it was the factual coming of a preacher-savior that revealed the underlying hamartiology and soteriology that Willard espouses.

6. Willard, 6:30.
7. Willard, 18:00.

Only in the appearance of Jesus does the nature of the problem become clear as well as the form of salvation necessary.[8] What Jesus brings into the world and into an incomplete Jewish system is "the wisdom of the just." Or, in a word, knowledge. As should be familiar, Willard was accustomed to categorizing Jesus's gift of knowledge into four answers to "Four Great Questions." He claims that Jesus offers knowledge about these questions that is superior to other offerings, *including* what Moses and the prophets offered. The Sermon on the Mount is the archetype of this gift of knowledge, but Jesus's whole earthly ministry is devoted to it in various ways.

Now, sub specie aeternitatis, Willard will argue that the problem—belief in false gospels—is solved by the appearance of somebody who lives in the truth and preaches it. But for the first listeners, the progression is reversed. First appears to them a person who lives in the truth and preaches it. Second-stage listeners are those who see this and are invited to put their trust in him as their teacher. Only after this does their recognition of false gospels, "the futile ways inherited from your forefathers" (1 Pet 1:18), and a more complete understanding of their corruption follow.[9]

"A Great High Priest": Second-Stage Christology

SO FIRST WE have the appearance of somebody who lives in the truth and preaches it. Through a mind-boggling gospel, Jesus offers himself as a reality for trusting. In the very least, he offers himself as an evangelist who is to be trusted as giving a true testimony of the availability of the kingdom. But he is offering more than this. As I said in the previous chapter, Jesus's listeners have the opportunity, previously unavailable, to be *great* in the kingdom—to be, so it would seem, like Jesus. Even the least of them, Jesus says, is already greater than John. Though they

8. His approach here more closely resembles Karl Barth's approach in *Kirchliche Dogmatik IV, 1–3* (Zürich, Switzerland: Theologischer Verlag Zürich, 1953–58), in which the revelation of the savior reveals the nature of sin from which humanity needed to be saved.

9. Willard, "Study and Meditation," 26:30.

probably do not even believe the promise of greatness and though some of Jesus's closest followers profoundly misunderstand it, at least, as Willard writes, "they know that Jesus does believe this."[10]

Again, from the perspective of the first listeners, how this upward mobility would take place is largely unclear. They know, first, that Jesus invites them to be with him in physical proximity. And they know, second, that Jesus invites them to trust him as a mere preacher, as one who proclaims knowledge. These are the fundamental aspects of how Jesus's ministry works. But they also know, third, that Jesus the preacher has invited some of them to be with him for a time of what we might call *preparation for greatness* in the kingdom. Greatness will be given to them not by association or infusion but by their diligent action in response to his intelligent direction. This *preparation* of those who respond, so Willard, will be Jesus's primary precrucifixion ministry.[11] This is what the μαθηταὶ, or those who are with him, trust him for. So let us try to state who this man is that they are invited to trust. What, in other words, is Jesus?

The Office of a Mediator

THE CHRISTOLOGY OF the listeners up until now, given their rudimentary understanding of the gospel, was focused on Jesus's person, his *own life in* the kingdom of God. Known as a person for whom the kingdom was available, his service to others was a side effect, "the crumbs that fall from their masters' table" (Matt 15:27). But in the second stage, the

---

10. Willard, *Conspiracy*, 319.

11. In his many lectures on Acts, Willard speaks of Jesus's work as the preparation of a people for the coming of the Spirit. See Dallas Willard, "The Meaning of Pentecost," *The Book of Acts* (Skyline Wesleyan Church, Lemon Grove, CA, July 23, 1974), MP3/cassette. Willard thought highly of A. B. Bruce, *The Training of the Twelve* (Edinburgh: T&T Clark, 1871), recommending it to individuals and quoting from it occasionally (e.g., Willard, *Disciplines*, 125–26). The Pentecost event would not have happened to a people who had not had the kind of durative and formal proximity to Jesus and the previous experiences with the Spirit that the apostles and the others had. One example of their previous experience is discussed in Willard, *Conspiracy* (278). More about the event of Pentecost and Jesus's transition from his earthly to his heavenly ministry will be discussed in chapter 10 and the third stage of the first listener's knowledge of the gospel.

focus turns to Jesus's person *as a minister*. Let us frame this Christology again in terms of Jesus's office and his person or character.

As already intimated, *mediator* or *minister* both capture Jesus's office. In *Conspiracy* and elsewhere, Willard breaks down Jesus's Galilean ministry into three things: proclaiming, manifesting, and teaching.[12] Missing from this threefold "ministerial method" is the crucial phenomenon of *baptizing* audiences in the presence of God. Since we have already discussed proclaiming and baptizing, let us turn to *manifesting*.

Manifesting

MANIFESTING, FOR WILLARD, is a matter of showing the presence of God's rule in words and deeds whose effects lay beyond natural human powers. For those who are trying to understand the kingdom in terms of its direct availability to Jesus or to themselves, the manifestations of God's rule through Jesus's own body lead them to greater insights into what *abundant* life in the kingdom entails. Examples of this include the calming of the storm, the raising of Jairus's daughter, the cursing of the fig tree, the transfiguration, and the resurrection body of Jesus.

For example, Jesus's manifestation of his conversational relationship with God showed listeners the possibilities for their own life. Willard's words about this in *Guidance* also describe well the role of manifestation for Jesus's ministry more generally. He writes, "The model for divine guidance is therefore taken from what communication and guidance is at its best among human beings at *their* best. But 'their best' is interpreted in light of Jesus Christ and His followers. We should not judge the possibilities of humanity from a consideration of the dreary normalcy of human existence."[13] By his manifesting the "best" life in the

12. Willard, *Conspiracy*, 288–91.
13. Willard, *Guidance*, 7.

kingdom of God, Jesus shows his μαθηταὶ the high-water mark of being greater than John.[14]

Teaching

NOW, IF PROCLAIMING and manifesting are the opening steps of Jesus's mediation of the life before an open heaven, then the perfecting step is *teaching*. Teacher is really Willard's archetypal concept for Jesus's mediatory office. It is inclusive of both proclaiming and manifesting, which is why *Conspiracy*, in its "attempt to gain a fresh hearing for Jesus," is mainly concerned about "The Case of the Missing Teacher."[15] As he writes in that book, "Jesus came among us to *show* and *teach* the life for which we were made."[16] In other words, Jesus's ministry to the kingdom works by offering himself as a teacher to be trusted. This gospel is not lost on the first-century listeners, who know Jesus the preacher invites them to be with him for a time of *preparation for greatness* in the kingdom. They know, at least eventually, that greatness will be given to them not by infusion but by his intelligent direction of their diligent action. Indeed, preparation or training is how the μαθηταὶ, so Willard, would characterize what Jesus was doing with them "during all the time that the Lord Jesus went in and out among [them]" (Acts 1:21). By contrast, proclamation and manifestation, as simpler mediatory activities, are delegated to less experienced persons like John the Baptist and the apostles. But teaching is Jesus's magnum opus, his chief and most providential mediatory work while living in Palestine.

To the modern world looking back on the life of Jesus, Willard advances the priority of teaching as a sheer statement of historical fact. Considerations of God's cosmic purposes and Jesus's role in them aside, Jesus stands in world history as one who is prepared to teach and to

---

14. In a profound and mysterious way, Jesus's crucifixion also manifests the abundant life in the kingdom.

15. See, for example, the subsection titled "The Case of the Missing Teacher" (Willard, *Conspiracy*, 55). *Teacher* in this instance stands in for all of Jesus's ostensive ministry.

16. Willard, 27.

will the good of others by teaching.[17] In modern terms, he might be described as a pastor.[18]

The Person of a Mediator

WITH THE NOTION of an expert practitioner in mind, we can understand why, for Willard, one of the essential components of Jesus's teaching office is that Jesus *is* a prophet with the corresponding privileges and abilities spoken of in the previous chapter. He, as *vere homo*, truly does live richly in the kingdom of God. Jesus is not a mediator in the sense of a Harley-Davidson showroom salesman who can effectively bring together a potential buyer and a motorcycle but does not himself have the money, skill, or relevant driver's license. Jesus's second-stage office entails that he has the dispositions that he will encourage in others.

This means that all of the qualities of mind, will, and body that could be predicated of Jesus's soul in the previous stage are assumed and even intensified in the Christology at this stage. These remain the main things that characterize Jesus's mind, will, and body and distinguish him

17. The cosmic reasons why Jesus's ministry is centered on teaching are also an indispensable topic for reflection and essential to a treatment of Willard's teleology. But Willard's anthropology has an influence as well. Clearly, Willard is not a voluntarist. Once asked what he thought of John Piper's book *Desiring God* (Portland, OR: Multnomah, 1986), he traced its anthropology back through Daniel Fuller (one of Willard's personal acquaintances) to Jonathan Edwards and through Edwards to John Locke, "who just made a mistake." Explaining, he says, "It is a mistaken psychology to believe that we only act for the sake of pleasure. Probably not a person in this room has acted for pleasure today. . . . In the rise of modern thought, value disappeared, and it had to be revived. John Locke was a sensible man, and he revived it in terms of pleasure and pain because that would pass the criteria of feeling" (Dallas Willard, "Discipleship and Living Well," *How to Put Christ into Your Everyday Life* [West Valley Christian Church, West Hills, CA, March 6, 1993], MP3/cassette, 53:30). It is, however, not appropriate to assume that Willard had an intellectualist anthropology. Compared to clear intellectualists such as Aquinas, Willard's anthropology is highly nuanced and should be studied for itself.

18. Strange as it may seem, Willard rarely uses the rabbinic-synagogal educational system of Jesus's day to describe Jesus's own work. Though I have no word from Willard on this, I believe it has to do with the fact that the goal of teaching in rabbinic education was, in Willard's mind, different from Jesus's goal. The similarities, Willard would argue, derive from the fact that the rabbis, as did almost all ancient teachers, used the master-apprentice model of education. Cf. Dallas Willard, "Spiritual Formation Meets the Gospel," *Summer Lectures* (Regent College, Vancouver, BC, May 17, 2000), MP3.

from others. Nevertheless, there are some aspects of Christ's soul that are unique to this stage. In his gospel, Jesus offers himself to these people as a reality for trusting. So what did these people think they were trusting? Who, once again, is this man?

The Heart of a Mediator

THE MAIN DIFFERENCE between the second-stage Christology and the first-stage Christology, in which Jesus's righteous heart resembles Elijah's and Moses's heart, is the awareness of Jesus's *intent* to mediate, to teach. The listeners have this crucial knowledge concerning Jesus's will. They know he intends to accept them as students to imitate his expertise and character. This glimpse of Jesus's inner life is revealed in his public invitations to follow him.

Though this may seem a simple observation, it is possible for church history, so Willard, to produce persons who do not know this about Jesus. One of Willard's long-standing frustrations with the contemporary Western church is that Jesus's will to teach long ceased to be proclaimed from the pulpits. By contrast, in Jesus's formulation of the gospel and his early teaching, his intent to share his expertise and character was made public. Introducing *Conspiracy*, Willard writes, "The really good news for humanity is that Jesus is now taking students in the master class of life." This is not Jesus's only good news for humanity. But it is Willard's primary burden in *Conspiracy* as he aims to "present discipleship as the very heart of the gospel."[19]

The Body of a Mediator

DEPENDENT ON THEIR vision that Jesus was willing to teach, Jesus's listeners knew or at least assumed that their teacher would be *with them bodily*. This, too, seems to be a rather banal point. But if they are to learn *from him* how to live in the kingdom of God as *he* does, they trust that he will be with them and they with him in order for the learning process to work. Willard explained this assumption so: "But if I am to be

---

19. Willard, *Conspiracy*, xvii.

someone's apprentice, there is one absolutely essential condition. I must be *with* that person. This is true of the student-teacher relationship in all generality. And it is precisely what it means to *follow* Jesus when he was here in human form. To follow him meant, in the first place, to be with him."[20] Willard's insistence on the importance of bodily presence in his Christology should be commonsensical. That it would be questioned may have something to do with differing assumptions of modern and ancient audiences.

First, the ancients assumed that teaching took place via *personal demonstration*. Modern attempts to mass-produce education or to maintain professional or objective distance from students and even from the subject matter are at odds with ancient theory. When Jesus's first-century listeners see that he intends to teach, they as ancients conclude that he will be bodily present with them for purposes of personal demonstration—that is, for manifestation.[21] And indeed he *was* with them. He was accessible to them in ways that were bodily and quite obvious. This seems, as I said, like a banal point of Christology, but in Willard's account, it is not. In the office of teaching, Willard insists, "the 'being-with,' by watching and by hearing, is an absolute necessity."[22]

---

20. Willard, 276.

21. An expert in ancient philosophy and one of Willard's lifelong colleagues at USC, Kevin Robb, writes that the ancient Greeks' practice of *sunousia* "refers to the constant association of a younger generation with the older. . . . The young listened, they absorbed the accumulated wisdom and skills of elders, and they sought to imitate their virtues" (Kevin Robb, *Literacy and Paideia in Ancient Greece* [New York: Oxford University Press, 1994], 197). As he later observes, "It did not fade away or become a cultural anachronism until the knowledge on which the culture's major institutions depended had found its way into texts that could be read by those who must make daily use of the contents" (198). Cf. also Dallas Willard, "Concerning the 'Knowledge' of the Pre-Platonic Greeks," in *Language and Thought in Early Greek Philosophy*, ed. Kevin Robb (LaSalle, IL: Hegeler Institute, 1984).

22. Willard, *Conspiracy*, 276. The argument could be pursued in the opposite direction. In fact, Jesus *was* with people during his lifetime. So why was he with them? For the purpose of teaching them to live in the kingdom of God as he does. This argument has an important implication for the purpose of the incarnation in Willard's thought. Other reasons aside, one reason why God took on flesh was to make possible his redemptive purposes in discipleship. Merely speaking to disciples from heaven (such as discipleship

The second differing assumption is as follows. It does not occur to Jesus's very first listeners that he might teach *without* being bodily present. Though this possibility will become relevant as Jesus leaves his students, at present, it is a nonissue. To the first listeners, Jesus was emphatically a spatiotemporal, physical being. Learning from him meant being with him and being with *him* meant, unavoidably, being with his body or at least with the physical effects of his body, such as his temporal arrangements and words.

Thanks in part to his theology of the body, Willard conceives of Jesus's mediation as *purposefully* bodily. Though incarnation is not in the first listeners' minds, from Willard's perspective, sub specie aeternitatis, he claims that embodiment is not superfluous to the Son's mission from the Father. Willard speaks in *Disciplines* of a practical Docetism that haunts modern Christianity and cannot accept that Jesus had a body. This tendency, he believes, comes from the old Platonic dualist tendency "to think of the body and its functions as only a hindrance to our spiritual calling."[23]

But the first-century temptation, Willard believes, was the reverse. It was obvious that Jesus had a body. It was, as I observed in the first stage, his "spirituality" that was difficult to accept. But once it was accepted, or at least supposed, and once his intent to teach was made public, the first listeners had an immediate interest in the happenings of his body. They knew "he shared the human frame, and as for all human beings, his body was the focal point of his life."[24] In other words, they knew his life was the way that it was because of the history and circumstances of *his body* in the world.[25] This is the commonsense assumption of the master-apprentice form of education.

This bodily entailment of discipleship is somehow lost on the modern audience when considering Jesus. But not because the principle

---

worked for Moses) would not have been as effective. Human psychology is such as to need bodily presence and demonstration.

23. Willard, *Disciplines*, 30.

24. Willard, 29.

25. For more on how personal and cultural circumstances form our body and soul, see Willard, "History and Personality," MP3/cassette.

has ceased to be common sense. Willard observes that all without question know that a particular Olympic athlete, systems engineer, or Baptist preacher have become what they are because of the history and circumstances of their body. We know we can approximate the life of the Baptist preacher by a process of reproducing the relevant history and circumstances of his body in our own body. It is common sense that "the human body *is* the focal point of human existence."[26]

The snag for the modern audience is the logic that in the Son of God's assumption of flesh, *his body* became the focal point of his life. It is hard to believe that he was the way that he was *not in spite of* but *because of* his body's history and circumstances in the world. Again, this is not a snag for the first listeners, and therefore "the idea of *really* following him and becoming like him" was not, as Willard says it is for moderns, "a practical impossibility."[27]

Disciplines on one level is an attempt to revive for a modern audience what Willard thinks was common sense to Christology and discipleship in the first century. Consider the following from the book:

> *My central claim is that we can become like Christ by doing one thing—by following him in the overall style of life he chose for himself. If we have faith in Christ, we must believe that he knows how to live. We can, through faith and grace, become like Christ by practicing the types of activities he engaged in, by arranging our whole lives around the activities he himself practiced in order to remain constantly at home in the fellowship of his Father. What activities did Jesus practice? Such things as solitude and silence, prayer, simple and sacrificial living, intense study and meditation upon God's Word and God's ways, and service to others.*[28]

---

26. Willard, *Disciplines*, 29.

27. Willard, 30.

28. Willard, ix. On this basis, Willard would tell us that Jesus engaged in spiritual discipline for interaction with the kingdom of God in order to accomplish the work he had to do and the life he was determined to live before God. If this is perceived as odd from the orthodox view of the sinlessness of the Christ, it may lose this stigma if it is granted

The first listeners' Christology entails that certain things he does and did with his body are important for explaining who he is.[29] They expect that these things will be revealed to them, probably through personal demonstration, in the course of their study. For this reason, they expect that Jesus will be *with them* in body.

The Mind of a Mediator

THE FOREGOING IS, I think, the most that can be responsibly predicated of Willard's view of the Jewish first listeners' Christology on the second stage. But concerning Jesus's mind, there is a relevant aspect of *Willard's own* Christology that should be inserted here.

Jesus is a Jewish prophet, broadly conceived, and one who lives richly in the kingdom of God. This is his expertise. But does that automatically mean that he can pass on his expertise to others *well*? Because of the pervasiveness of the master-apprentice model in the ancient world, this question may never have been explicitly raised by the average person. But Willard holds that it was a primary question for all great thinkers. He calls this "the development question," pointing out that the Greeks had been working on it for centuries. In this context, we hear

---

that "the spiritual" (i.e., the kingdom of God) would have been necessary for human life in the body even if humans had never sinned. What "sin management gospels" miss, as Willard often says, is that "if we had not sinned, we would still have great need of God" and likewise great need of grace. Willard, "Curriculum for Christlikeness 2," *Transformation into the Likeness of Christ* (Belfast Kilmakee Presbyterian Church, Belfast, North Ireland, June 1, 2004), MP3, 3:00; Dallas Willard, "My Grace Is Sufficient for You," *Renovaré Regional Conference* (Renovaré, Menlo Park, CA, November 11, 2005), MP3, 8:00.

Working from the perspective of orthodox Christology, Willard observes, "Being the unique Son of God clearly did not relieve him of the necessity of a life of preparation that was mainly spent out of the public eye. . . . Out of such preparation, *Jesus was able* to lead a public life of service through teaching and healing. *He was able* to love his closest companions to the end. . . . And then *he was able* to die a death unsurpassed for its intrinsic beauty and historical effect" (Willard, *Disciplines*, 5; emphasis mine). In his refrain "he was able," Willard points to the unique power that he believes spiritual disciplines bring to the *embodied* person irrespective of being divine and sinless. Being creaturely and sinful only increases one's need.

29. Again, if this can be predicated on the first listeners, it is not a statement representing a precise, phenomenologically hewn theory of personhood but, as already intimated, an implicit, nonrigorous, and limited knowledge of what it means for us to be alive.

the words, "The first great treatise on education is actually a treatise on spiritual formation. It's Plato's *Republic.* Plato's *Republic* is precisely an account of the inner nature of the self and how you train it so that the right behavior comes out of it."[30]

In an ancient context, where this question had been explicitly worked on, it might be genuinely questioned whether Jesus was a person whose *mind* had sufficiently understood the dynamics of human development such that he could effectively produce persons like himself. If not, then there seems to be reason to withhold one's trust in him as one's teacher despite his benevolent will to teach.

On this question, let us begin with some of Willard's comments about Paul of Tarsus:

> *We customarily think of Paul as a great theologian, not as a master psychologist. But he clearly perceived and explained the fundamental structures and processes of the human self related to its well-being, its corruption, and its redemption. His Letter to the Romans can never be fully appreciated unless it is read as, among other things, a treatise on social and individual psychology. The fact that he viewed his doctrine of redemption as a doctrine of the transformation of the self required him to be a psychologist. In fact, our ability to imagine that a great theologian would not at the same time be a profound psychologist, a profound theorist of human life, shows how far off-course our thinking is today. Only the fatal separation of salvation from life in modern thinking makes it possible to separate theology from psychology.*[31]

---

30. Willard, "Spiritual Formation Meets the Gospel," 15:00. A day earlier, he calls Pelagian thinking "a kind of Greek thinking" that does not take sin seriously and holds that you can fix yourself up (Willard, "Spirit and Spirituality," 1:08:45). Previewing his evening lecture "Spiritual Formation Meets the Gospel," he goes on to say, "Plato's view of spiritual formation . . . is a self-help project. That's what Pelagius is about. Once you look into the depths of sin and realize what you have done, you'll never be tempted to be a Pelagian."

31. Willard, *Disciplines*, 112.

Willard's notion of psychology here is broad; it is inclusive of education and spiritual direction and certainly far from the modern scientific and professional notion of psychology. He is referring to the tradition, Christian or otherwise, of analyzing the nature of the human person for the purpose of healing, educating, and empowering it, and in numerous places he recounts the high points of this tradition.[32] Paul is not currently thought of as a psychologist in this broad sense. But Willard thinks he should be. In detail, Willard thinks, "Paul's fundamental psycho-theological insight has to do with the nature of the human body as a bearer of active tendencies to evil and to good. In other words, it had to do with *spirituality and habits*."[33]

The parallel with Jesus should be obvious. "[Jesus] is the master psychologist," says Willard, summing up his view at one point.[34] And in light of there currently being (to his satisfaction) no consistent *biblical* psychology, Willard consciously took his divisions of the person from *Jesus's* statement of the greatest commandment (Mark 12:29–31).[35] These divisions structure his book *Renovation*. Again, after *Conspiracy*'s many excurses into Jesus's deep understanding of reality, especially moral reality, we read in the section on "The Law and the Soul" that "it is precisely *Jesus' grasp of the structure in the human soul* that also leads him to deal primarily with the *sources* of wrongdoing and not to focus on actions themselves."[36] This is Willard's acquiescence to Jesus as a "master psychologist." Of course, we could also draw from these texts Willard's vision of Jesus as a master ethicist (the third great question). But master psychologist (the fourth great question) resides deeper in this Christology of Jesus as a mediator.[37]

---

32. Willard, "Spiritual Disciplines," 109n4; Willard, *Renovation*, 265–66n4; as also Willard, *Disciplines*, 112.
33. Willard, *Disciplines*, 113.
34. Dallas Willard, "Progress in the Blessed Life in Christ," *Valley Vineyard Sermons* (Valley Vineyard, Reseda, CA, 2009), MP3, 17:30.
35. Willard, "Spiritual Disciplines," 1:00; cf. Willard, *Renovation*, 31.
36. Willard, *Conspiracy*, 139.
37. Indeed, these competencies run together for him. One of the problems that moral reasoning ran into in the twentieth century was the stagnation and loss of knowledge of the human person.

For the first listeners, trust that the kingdom of God is available *through* Jesus entails an implicit Christology that Jesus is at least a tolerable psychologist. He knows not only the structure of the human soul but also how "to speak to, to heal and empower the individual human condition."[38]

Saved to Faith: Second-Stage Soteriology

HOW, THEN, DOES Jesus save his people from their sins (Matt 1:21)? What answer might those who understand his gospel on the second level give? Consider Titus 2:11, a verse Willard uses in his lectures: "For the grace of God has appeared, bringing salvation for all people." Typically, Willard stops here and asks his audience to see if they can complete the sentence.[39] The verse continues: "Training us to renounce ungodliness and worldly passions, and to live self-controlled, upright, and godly lives in the present age, waiting for our blessed hope, the appearing of the glory of our great God and Savior Jesus Christ, who gave himself for us to redeem us from all lawlessness and to purify for himself a people for his own possession who are zealous for good works" (Titus 2:12–14). What Willard sees in this verse is a summary of Jesus's earthly ministry (as well as his heavenly ministry). He sees the lessons of Jesus, which two of his favorite books on the spiritual life center on: Thomas à Kempis's *The Imitation of Christ* and Jeremy Taylor's *Holy Living*.[40]

"Training us," as the verse puts it, is also the answer that Willard thinks those in the second stage of understanding would give. In light of the gospel, they would answer that Jesus will save them because he,

38. Willard, *Conspiracy*, 13. Of course, Willard famously asserted that Jesus "was and is the most powerful thinker the world has ever known" (*Renovation*, 105). But he does not argue for this as a first or even second impression of Jesus amid his first listeners. Superlative as it is, it is more appropriately a reflected, mature judgment.

39. E.g., Dallas Willard, "Salvation Confusion," *The Divine Conspiracy* (e4, Hollywood, CA, July 6, 2004), MP3/video, 0:30.

40. Cf. Willard, *Knowing*, 227n12. Taylor's book is explicitly structured on Titus 2:12 (Jeremy Taylor, *Holy Living and Dying* [1650; repr., London: George Bell & Sons, 1883]). Without mentioning Titus, à Kempis in *The Imitation of Christ* (many editions) presents the imitation of Christ as an imitation of him specifically in the qualities named in Titus, qualities that Christ also exemplified.

having gone before them in his own experience, will teach them the truth concerning life's most pertinent aspects so that they might put it into practice in their own experience. If we put this answer in yet different language, it may enlighten for some the place of *Disciplines* (a book on Jesus's practices) and *Conspiracy* (a book on Jesus's beliefs) in light of Willard's whole systematic theological project.[41] For second-stage listeners, Jesus saves *by education*. Jesus is inviting a few Jews into the process of spiritual formation that will transpire under his pedagogical guidance. This is how Jesus's ministry works. This is how he will save his people from their sins.

Clearly, a unique concept of salvation is afoot in Willard's theology.

Reassessing the Target

WHEN ANALYZING THE various theories of salvation, including Willard's own, one can distinguish between the mode of salvation and the target of salvation. In *Conspiracy*, for example, Willard writes of how those in the "Lordship salvation" debate are in agreement about "the *target* of divine and human efforts for salvation." They agree that "getting into heaven after death" is "what being 'saved' amounts to." But Willard, as should be familiar, writes of how "a totally different picture of salvation, faith and forgiveness" comes into view if we regard *something else* as the target.[42]

Given what was said in this stage about the mode of Jesus's saving, it might be assumed that this target, according to Willard, is knowledge. If correct, Willard would be rehearsing a familiar soteriological theme in the history of theology. Thomas Aquinas is the theologian most associated with making knowledge central to the target of salvation.[43] In his *Summa*'s questions on teleology and happiness, he lands on *the beatific vision* as the ultimate prize that we might attain through

---

41. See Willard, "Book Prospectus."
42. Willard, *Conspiracy*, 46–47 (emphasis mine).
43. In the Reformational tradition, the Protestant Scholastic Francis Turretin could be mentioned. The target for him is worship, but largely on the basis of knowledge and contemplation.

God's redemptive involvement in our life. This is a kind of knowing in which the saints directly contemplate God, being united with him.

For Willard, this is not the target. Doubtless, knowledge is involved. But knowledge is only the entryway into a more comprehensive condition of salvation. In order to understand how knowledge functions in the mode of salvation, we must see it in light of Willard's reassessment of the target to which Jesus brings his people in salvation.

To begin, it should be recalled how in the last stage the dominant motif for salvation was deliverance—in fact, *temporal deliverance* from the troubles that plague humanity. Viewed from this perspective alone, Jesus's gospel is, as Willard says about Acts 4:12, "a claim about the availability of the power of God to meet human need."[44] This gospel is true, but if divorced from faith in Jesus the person, then this gospel quickly slips into the needs-based invitation to church ministry, which Willard criticized.

For, in fact, deliverance from temporal suffering is only part of what Jesus brings in salvation. And this is clear to those in the second stage. They know that the target of salvation is eternal life, or as Willard reformulates it, *the eternal kind of life*. Like Jesus himself, Willard uses many turns of phrase to name the same reality. Other favorites of his are *life in the kingdom of God*, or *life in the Spirit*, or simply *spiritual life*. With the emphasis on life, this target stands in marked contrast to the target accepted by those on the theological right—that is, getting into heaven after death. The eternal kind of life is, so Willard, a target that can be entered into now. It also, much like the beatific vision, entails a different quality of human existence.

This explains why so many of Willard's books *on the theology of salvation* could be classified as "spirituality" or "Christian life." His theory of salvation took seriously a target that, so Willard, was enjoyed (1) *now* and (2) *as a part of one's very psychology*. Therefore, writing on the theology of salvation was nearly impossible without writing on the experience of it. Not to mention that the genre of curricular theology in

44. Willard, *Knowing*, 187.

which he wrote, as opposed to the genre of theological treatises, entailed that there was no rhetorical reason to divorce his conclusions from his intent to edify.

Willard's oldest and most rudimentary formulation of the target, to my knowledge, is in the handout for a Sunday school lesson from 1972. There he writes of a view of salvation in which "your life is *taken over* in every aspect by the spirit 'of power, and of love, and of a sound mind.' (II Tim 1:7) The home, work, place, *all* is permeated by 'Love, Joy, Peace, Longsuffering, Gentleness, Goodness, Faithfulness, Meekness, Self-control'" (Gal 5:22–23). He adds that "[this] is Jesus' view of 'Salvation': Eternal life is (John 17:3) entered into now, here, with death being but a minor transition from God here to God beyond. In this regard, he is faithful to the Jewish religion which is almost completely 'this-worldly' in its view of salvation (Ps 27:13–14, 30:9,12, 142:45)."[45] Notice how even in this early source Willard cites John 17:3 as a central text.

After 1972, Willard continued to refine his theory, becoming accustomed to speak of three main parts to salvation in the New Testament.[46] His theory increasingly attempted to account for the biblical vision of salvation as *a natural* or *automatic principle* that carries "the saved" on to the culmination of their salvation. This is why the three parts of salvation are described in *Disciplines* as the three major dimensions of *faith*. Willard is at pains to describe this faith with the help of Luther as a "powerful life force."[47] In other words, the target of salvation, the eternal kind of life, is not an addendum to or a reward for the faith in Jesus that characterizes "the saved" in this life. Faith in Jesus is part of the gift of salvation that blossoms (Willard tends to use biological or mechanical metaphors) into salvation in its fullness.

45. Willard, "Handout for 'Jesus' Good News.'"
46. Willard, "Biblical View of the Imago Dei," 43:30; Willard, "You Can't Have One," 22:45; Dallas Willard, "What Christ Did to Save Mankind," *Faith Evangelical Sunday School* (Faith Evangelical Church, Chatsworth, CA, 1979), MP3/cassette, 10:00.
47. Willard, *Disciplines*, 39.

The first of these three dimensions of salvation Willard calls "the presence of a new power *within* the individual." Regeneration is the classical doctrine that, as Willard well knows, best captures this fundamental part of salvation he is expounding. His oldest formulations of salvation's three parts simply spoke of the first as "forgiveness of sins," but one can see how, in *Disciplines*, regeneration has taken the lead and forgiveness and repentance are its natural entailments.[48] Other than life, faith is actually the best concept to describe what this first dimension is about. Faith, as had become typical for Willard by the time of writing *Disciplines* in 1984–85, is not so much salvation's trigger as it is the first element of its unfolding essence, as a seed is the first element of a mature plant.

In his early days, it was the latter two dimensions of salvation—transformation of character and extrahuman power over evil and for good—that Willard wanted to introduce to his audiences who by and large only thought of salvation in terms of forgiveness. But as faith and/or life become central in *Disciplines* and after, these two begin to sound less like elements distinct from the first and more like natural developments of it.

Sometime in the early 1990s, Willard began inserting two more dimensions. He explains that "they don't necessarily come one after the other, but there is an important priority in them."[49] Now after faith, he inserts discipleship and obedience for a total of five. Thus, Willard's most mature formulation of the target of salvation is found in *Conspiracy* under the section "Five Dimensions or Stages of the Eternal Kind

48. Willard seems to change his mind many times throughout his life about how forgiveness relates to atonement. Here in *Disciplines*, forgiveness of the individual person seems to be disconnected from atonement and an entailment of regeneration. But in other statements, he seems to connect forgiveness with God's cosmic act of atonement (an act that he also changes his mind about) and speaks of universal forgiveness (but not of universal salvation).

49. Dallas Willard, "Taking the Sermon on the Mount Seriously," *Church Renewal Institute* (Bethel Theological Seminary West, San Diego, CA, February 23, 1993), MP3/cassette, 13:15.

of Life." Though he admits the oddity of obedience preceding inner transformation, he claims that is often how it works psychologically.[50]

As in *Disciplines*, his emphasis in *Conspiracy* is on the extrinsic origin of the five dimensions. His formulation in one instance is that they are five "movements [of] the eternal life that flows through us."[51] And though they are all gift or grace, only the first, "confidence in and reliance upon Jesus," could be said to be passively received. After the gratuitous birth from above that typifies the first dimension, "we must be intelligently active in stages or dimensions 2 through 5."[52]

Together these five dimensions are Willard's view of the target of salvation. They spell out what Willard calls *the eternal kind of life* or *life in the kingdom of God*. They are what will make those least in the kingdom of God greater than John the Baptist. And they are, as Willard said back in 1972, "entered into now, here, with death being but a minor transition from God here to God beyond."

Salvific Progression: Moving from Faith to Faith

BUT JESUS'S MODE of salvation is education; he preaches, he manifests, he teaches, and he "baptizes." A great deal of the argument in this stage has been to explain the whole scriptural context within which Willard asserts precisely that. That is, Jesus saves by being one who brings knowledge to his listeners. And yet, as important as this is for sinners with an evangelized psychology, knowledge, so Willard, is not the target of salvation. Life is. A certain kind of life. And this life is, not just in its first dimension, a life *of faith*.

Confusing as it may seem, faith is not only that by which this salvation is obtained. Here Willard follows in this classic Reformational teaching. Faith is also, in an important sense, the salvation obtained. Faith is the target. Here is how that works for Willard. The first stone to be laid in the listener's soul is a stone of faith in Jesus as a competent mediator of the kingdom life. But granted that listeners have this faith

50. Willard, 17:45.
51. Willard, "Specific Disciplines," 7:30.
52. Willard, *Conspiracy*, 369.

in Jesus, Jesus is able to save them by taking them on a journey . . . *to faith*.

This is where the progression of faith briefly mentioned in chapter 6 again becomes relevant. According to Willard, the Bible speaks explicitly of a fiduciary progression from faith *in* Christ to the faith *of* Christ. The faith of Christ is the faith that Christ himself had and that guided his life. In Christ, as it may be in his followers, faith was not in any way disconnected from knowledge, which explains why Willard will call faith's content "What Jesus Knew." It is the faith that those who were with Jesus knew he had *but knew they themselves did not have*. If anything, they only had a faith *in* Jesus.

In *Guidance*, Willard provides a summary of his exegesis of Galatians 2:16–20, which he thinks follows this progression. Using the KJV because of its closeness to the Greek, he italicizes the relevant prepositions:

> *Knowing that a man is not justified by the works of the law but by the faith* of *Jesus Christ, even we have believed* in *Jesus Christ that we might be justified by the faith* of *Jesus Christ, and not by the works of the law. (Gal 2:16)*
>
> *I am crucified with Christ: nevertheless I live; yet not I, but Christ liveth in me: and the life I live I live by the faith* of *the Son of God, who loved me, and gave himself for me. (Gal 2:20)*

By reading the three genitive clauses as subjective genitives—that is, "Christ's faith"—Willard gives us the following exegesis of the passage: "Paul here presents faith *in* Christ—such as the apostles certainly had on the occasion of the storm of the sea and at other times—as that that leads to having the faith *of* Christ. This faith in Christ leads to the believer actually having the *same* faith in God that Jesus himself had."[53] The faith *of* Jesus plays a strong role in Willard's theology of the New Testament. It

53. Willard, *Guidance*, 166. In the storm on the Sea of Galilee, according to Willard's reading, the disciples had (A) great faith in Jesus, but they did not share (B) his great

is one of the major bridges for him between the Gospels (where the faith of Jesus is manifested through his life) and the Epistles (where the faith of Jesus is theorized for the formation of doctrine). About this concept, the faith *of* Jesus, I will have more to say in the third stage.

So the journey from faith to faith begins with the recognition that Jesus is a person who himself has faith in something. In what does Jesus have faith? Willard writes, "The faith by which Jesus Christ lived, his faith in God and his Kingdom, *is expressed in the gospel he himself preached* . . . that the Kingdom rule of God is available to mankind here and now."[54] In other words, Jesus's own life, as a result of his knowledge of and faith in God and his kingdom, is a historical manifestation of the eternal kind of life. Jesus's own life is an example of the "saved" life of faith.

But in order for listeners to obtain this extraordinary faith of Christ, their faith in him must consist of more than faith in him as a prophet with extraordinary faith. It must include faith in him *as* a competent mediator, *as* one who can and will teach them how to believe as he believes and thus to live as he lives. Hence, these believers do not trust in their raw initiative to be like Christ. They trust in a specific work of Christ. Of course, one of the essential things that such believers are trusting Jesus to do is to teach them to know what he knows. But they are also dependent on his help to believe as he believes.

In *Conspiracy*'s latter chapters, Willard strives to make clear that this work of Christ aims not at knowledge alone but also at belief. A second-stage listener is learning not just to view the world as Jesus does but also to live in the world as Jesus does. And life requires faith. The answer that he gives in *Conspiracy* to *how* Jesus brings this faith about is *a course of training*. But unfortunately, a lot of what Willard has to say about this course of training regards only what church leaders might do for the members. This boils down to a focused program of teaching about God's loveliness and individualized guidance about disciplines to

faith in God (Matt 8:23–27). His faith, which was by God's grace evident to them, "they long regarded . . . only as *his* faith."

54. Willard, 165 (emphasis mine).

undo habits of sin. Of course, Jesus stands at the vanguard of this course of training—both historically and eternally. But the focus, at least in *Conspiracy*, seems to be on adopting new habits of mind and body—that is, on growing in knowledge.

In *Conspiracy*, the jump from knowledge to faith remains somewhat obscure. But elsewhere there are two things that Willard is accustomed to saying on this matter. The first, his broadly Reformational view, we have already rehearsed in chapter 3. To Willard, faith is not something that anyone should try to have. It is grace, a gift of God, and it comes, more often than not, through the word of God. In both preaching and the life of Christ, God's plan is that his Spirit acts with the proclaimed word to create faith in the listeners' hearts.[55]

The second piece of advice Willard has for faith's increase is the third of the five dimensions of the eternal kind of life: obedience. Basically, Willard holds that acting on the small faith the listeners have in Jesus by obeying his teaching leads to increased faith in Christ but also in the realities he believed in.[56] What's more, learning to obey is also part of the responsibility of obeying, which is where, for Willard, an appropriate use of the disciplines for the spiritual life comes in.

A Natural Part of the Gospel Proclaimed: Second-Stage Faith

AS MENTIONED ABOVE, the cornerstone of faith in the second-stage listener's soul is faith in Jesus as a competent mediator of the kingdom life. Here it may help to note that Willard uses a common contemporary Christian term to denote this crucial form of faith. This faith is

55. Without the emphasis on the word, Willard deals with the increase of faith *by infusion* in *Guidance* (167–68). By and large, the first listeners did not understand this, though Paul and John later did. Regarding Paul, Willard emphasizes how union with Christ (see the book's preceding subsection) confers on individuals *Christ's faith* and *Christ's love*, which actually do the work. In a way that is strongly reminiscent of the theology in his 1987 paper "Faith, Hope and Love," Willard goes on to emphasize in *Guidance* how Jesus works *from the inside* of his listeners to infuse them with his faith, his hope, and his love.

56. Dallas Willard, "Handout for 'Life without Lack'" (Valley Vista Community Church, Sepulveda, CA, February 5–April 9, 1989), Dallas Willard Collection.

the faith of a *disciple*; it creates in its possessors the status of *discipleship*. Discipleship, so Willard, was Jesus's gospel—at least an essential part. When the first listeners do not just know but believe Jesus's gospel of the kingdom as available through him, they become disciples, learners, students, apprentices of him.

But after this cornerstone is laid, a context is created for further stones of faith to be laid in a listener's soul. What this means is second-stage faith, the faith of a disciple, is directed toward the man Jesus but does not terminate on the man Jesus. The listeners trust Jesus as a teacher, but they trust him *for* their acquisition of something else—namely, the trust that he has in God and the kingdom of God. This unique second-stage dynamic is described by Willard in the following passage:

> *Toward the beginning of their course they do not, for example, really believe that the meek and the persecuted are blessed, and certainly not the poor. That is, they do not automatically act as if it were so. But they know that Jesus does believe this, and they believe that he is right about what they themselves do not yet, really, believe. Further, they want to believe it because, seeing his strength and beauty, they admire him so much and have such confidence in him. That is why they have become his students and have trusted him—or* intend *to trust him—for everything.*[57]

This is how second-stage faith obtains salvation. It obtains a preacher-savior who can competently lead people to faith. This faith is the eternal kind of life.

In light of our discussion of the second-stage understanding of Jesus, the kingdom of God and the gospel, one of Willard's most common and most provocative theological contentions, can be better understood. As mentioned at the beginning of this chapter, Willard held that *the gospel* should lead naturally to discipleship, and any *so-called gospel*

57. Willard, *Conspiracy*, 319.

that does not lead naturally to discipleship is not *the gospel*.[58] The natural tendency toward discipleship was one of the sharpest criteria with which Willard regularly evaluated and dismissed the reigning "gospels" of his day.[59] They were dismissed not necessarily as false doctrine but as something *other than* the message that initiates whole-life salvation. How, then, does the message of the availability of the kingdom lead naturally to discipleship or second-stage faith? And how do the other messages fail and, by Willard's observation, fail so obviously?

To put this together, we must recall Willard's phenomenology of faith and especially the difference between faith and knowledge. With chapter 4 in mind, there are, as I see it, three characteristics of Jesus's gospel of the kingdom of God that, so Willard, make discipleship its natural entailment.

First of all, the gospel of the kingdom is what Willard calls a "whole-life gospel." That is, Jesus's gospel concerns something that has a sweeping existential scope.[60] It is about the kingdom of God, which is a comprehensive reality covering *the whole life* of a human being. Other gospels, by contrast, tend to focus on one narrow aspect of God's involvement with the human race.

In what Willard calls the gospel of the theological right, the focus is on God's will to remove human guilt. Though this is a fair and accurate description of God's merciful will, guilt is not a reality that covers the whole life of a human being. A gospel that treats only guilt leaves much of human life untouched. Even human sin, though more profound

---

58. Willard, 47–49, 304, 367.

59. Another criterion was that other gospels are not the gospel that Jesus preached. Before he started school at the University of Wisconsin, Willard was deeply affected by the realization that he did not preach the gospel Jesus preached.

60. See here Willard, "Kingdom Gospel," MP3/video. A day later in "Salvation Confusion" (44:00) Willard says, "So now, that is how discipleship and the gospel of the kingdom comes together. Because if you don't preach some kind of whole-life gospel, you'll never make disciples. You have to preach a whole-life gospel. I've used the word *kingdom* and so on. But however that works—I talked last night about how we shouldn't make a legalism out of the language kingdom of God and kingdom of heaven. Some people do that. We don't need to do that; we need to get the point. And the point is living now within the range of God's effective will. Whole life."

and pervasive than guilt, is not comprehensive or fundamental enough to permeate *all* of human life, past, present, and future. It was this recognition—the narrowness of sin and guilt in the scope of human existence—that led Willard to brandish present-day gospels as "sin management gospels." They are gospels that assume, as Willard at times says, that "if it wasn't for sin, we'd have no need for God."[61] Willard brings the same criticism of being focused on "sin management" against the gospel of the theological left. Here the sole focus is God's interest in displacing structural evils—that is, managing social sin.

However, the kingdom of God, if recognized to include the creation of the world and all of God's economic works subsequent to that foundational work, pervades all of human life, leaving no element untouched. Thus, a gospel pertaining to the whole range of God's activities gives proper place to God's concern for guilt, sin, or structural evils. But it does not stop there. When Jesus comes into history, he comes as one who is a master of the kingdom of God in all its comprehensiveness. By offering himself as a reality for trusting, he mediates comprehensive contact with this reality. The combination of the kingdom's existential scope and Jesus's offer to teach it makes discipleship an inevitable outcome of his gospel.[62]

The second characteristic that makes discipleship proceed naturally from the gospel of the kingdom concerns the object of the person's faith. The true gospel says, "The kingdom of God is available to those who put their faith *in Jesus*." The object of faith is not, according to Willard, "something he said or something he did" but the person, the living reality.[63] This object of faith secures the idea that even if a person comes to trust in Jesus *without knowing that he is a teacher*, that person will not

61. Willard, "Curriculum for Christlikeness 2," 3:00; also in Willard, "My Grace Is Sufficient for You," 8:00. Only a literally *total* conception of total depravity could possibly make a gospel focused exclusively on sin relevant to all of life. Even then, there would be no gospel for the already redeemed parts of life, and postsin, "we'd have no need for God."

62. It is hard to imagine how in any version of Christian ontology one's guilt could bring one to be a student of someone else—as a cause, as a result, as a condition, and so on. The connection between the two is not to be found.

63. Willard, "Fine Textures of Life," 8:00.

be confronted with yet another decision upon learning of Jesus's identity and intent as a teacher. Their faith in him as a personal whole allows for new aspects of his personhood to be discovered and naturally integrated into their ongoing disposition of faith in him.

Willard does admit that some may trust Jesus and enter the kingdom of God (be regenerated) *without knowing* that Jesus makes any offer of discipleship. This may have been the case of the harlot of Luke 7 who "loved [him] much," whom we looked at in the first stage.[64] Willard says elsewhere, "We will not say that failure to become the apprentice or disciple of Jesus is a metaphysical impossibility for one who has confidence that he is Lord of the universe. A certain degree of understanding of 'what comes next' is presupposed, and in the midst of confused teaching and example, things might not proceed as they naturally would."[65] But a person who has trusted Jesus *the person*, without knowing all of what that entails, will find it a natural move to trust Jesus as teacher and lord and, therefore, to become his disciple.

In the case of other gospel presentations, Willard claims that something else is being presented as the object at which faith is to be directed. It may be *the church* of Jesus Christ, in the case of his so-called churchmanship gospel. It may be *a state of affairs* regarding redemption, in which Jesus prominently features. For example, this state of affairs may involve Jesus's passion or his exaltation. It may be Jesus's *stated positions* on personal and social issues. The problem is that the object of faith in all of these is something other than Jesus the living person. Willard asks, "What exactly is a 'faith' that does not naturally express itself in discipleship to Jesus? It would be that of a person who simply would *use* something Jesus did, but has no use for him."[66]

There is a key phenomenological observation to be made here. The mind trusting in Jesus the person simply has a different disposition than the mind trusting in a state of affairs involving Jesus. Therefore, moving a person with faith in a state of affairs involving Jesus to a faith in Jesus

64. Willard, *Conspiracy*, 19.
65. Willard, "Spiritual Formation as a Natural Part," 52.
66. Willard, 53.

as a competent "whole life" teacher is not impossible or unheard of. But it is not *natural.* One does not proceed from one to the other as a matter of course.

Willard's point may be understood if one compares the "gospel" that would get someone to walk across the world's first suspension bridge with the "gospel" that would get someone to learn the violin. The gospel and faith required in the former is not opposed to the gospel and faith of the latter. It is not unheard of that a person would go on to have respective faith in both. But it is not a *natural* progression from the one to the next. By contrast, Willard holds that Jesus's gospel with its emphasis on faith in Jesus the person will *naturally* come to include second-stage faith in Jesus—faith in him as a superlative teacher—because in such a shift the object of faith stays the same. It will not require an entirely new evangelistic or catechetical program and a corresponding mind-changing decision to comply. It does not buck the system because it is part of the system.

Third, the unnaturalness of other messages is accentuated when they, as is usually the case in presentations of *the* gospel, are taught as God's plan for salvation *as a whole* or, even more grandiosely, as the center or foundation of all Christian theology. This *theological totality* associated with the concept of the gospel means that listeners who accept a gospel will naturally regard certain aspects of the Bible and Christian tradition as tangential and optional. Second-stage faith succumbs to that fate if there is not a natural or logical connection to what was first presented as salvation as a whole. Therefore, it will be difficult for the minister to cast discipleship as truly central to saved life, since another doctrine of salvation looms large at the center of the listener's mind that is already quite comfortable and in essence unrelated. A renegotiation of the believer's entire vision of God and their life is necessary.

So not merely the gospel's existential scope and its particular object of faith but also the weight or proportion given the teaching within the Christian system ("This is not just *a* Christian teaching; this is *the gospel*") may keep discipleship from being a natural part of another gospel.[67]

---

67. Though Willard's social criticism of contemporary North American Christian culture is not being treated in this book, Willard laments that a religion of disconnected

The Resurrection of Jesus and the Continuation of Second-Stage Faith in Him

AS WE SAW in the previous stage, genuine knowledge of the gospel and the salvation it concerns were mental possibilities before Jesus went to his death and was seated at the right hand of God. The same is true, according to Willard, for the knowledge of the gospel at this stage. The gospel realities that first listeners comprehend are *not* dependent on the latter events of Jesus's life (crucifixion, resurrection, etc.), nor do listeners need to know that they will take or have taken place in order to "repent and believe in the gospel" (Mark 1:15).

However, the latter events did happen and do come, so Willard, to be a part of the gospel for second-stage listeners. So how does one understand the kingdom in light of the death and resurrection of Jesus?

The Christology of the second stage conceives of Jesus as a mediator between the person and the kingdom of God. But when he is crucified, the disciples again experience nothing more than the sheer loss of their evangelical mediator. They are, in contrast to the first stage, left with a consolation prize. They have the memories of their great spiritual and moral teacher. This is how many "liberal Protestant" accounts of the Christ event end. It is also how other great movements regard the "gospel" of their initial leader. What remains from the Buddha, Plato, Marx, Gandhi, and even Moses is an account of their life and teachings. Apart from a few inspiring thoughts and life events, the first listeners of the crucified Jesus—indeed, the whole world—are on their own.

But when Jesus is resurrected, the crucifixion adds something new to the ministry of Jesus. As we saw, Jesus's teaching ministry is

---

discipleship is the major problem facing it. He comments, "Only a sustained historical process involving many confusions and false motivations could lead to our current situation, in which faith in Jesus is thought to have no natural connection with discipleship to him" (Willard, *Conspiracy*, 367). Gary Black has tried, with mixed results, to recount and embody Willard's social criticism in his work. See Gary Black Jr., *The Theology of Dallas Willard: Discovering Protoevangelical Faith* (Eugene, OR: Pickwick, 2013). See also Michael Stewart Robb, "A Review Article: The Theology of Dallas Willard: Discovering Protoevangelical Faith, Gary Black Jr.," *Evangelical Quarterly* 87, no. 3 (2015): 264–69.

communicated not just through his words but also through his body. This fact was not lost on his first-century listeners, who knew that following Jesus meant following his bodily behavior and deeds. The crucifixion without the resurrection lacks clear meaning for the body. Was this good; was this bad; should we follow?

Through the resurrection, however, the passion, and public crucifixion of Jesus come to play a part, just as the Sermon on the Mount does, in the *content* of Jesus's teaching. They join the curriculum of Jesus and become things that his second-stage listeners, his disciples, can appropriate and emulate. The resurrection validates and extends Jesus's own teachings about mortification and about his own crucifixion.[68] Willard exegetes the Scriptures on this point in a very traditional fashion. The self-sacrifice of Jesus is the impetus and model for the mortification process of Jesus's disciples.[69]

But the multifaceted ministry of Jesus is not merely authenticated by the latter events of his life. His mediatory ministry is enabled to *continue* and is even *increased*. What Willard means by *continuing* should be obvious. He means that Christ enters his heavenly session, for "Christ, being raised from the dead, will never die again" (Rom 6:9).[70] But what Willard means by the *increase* of Jesus's ministry is more complicated. One must first note how he gives John 16:7 ("It is to your advantage that I go away") a christological interpretation. According to him, it is advantageous for the listeners because what Jesus is able to do as a minister while away *is more* than what he could do while physically localizable in Palestine. The metaphysical and theological understandings of this reality are better discussed in the next stage because it connects with the listeners' growing knowledge of Jesus as the king of the kingdom. Let us

---

68. In a way similar to what we saw in the first stage, the resurrection, ascension, and heavenly session expand the second-stage gospel for the listeners, and the same passages from the third chapter of *Disciplines* could be quoted here. The resurrection *confirms* what the listeners already knew about Jesus's transcendent life. It confirms that Jesus's ministry to the kingdom of God, relied upon *before* his death, was a valid ministry. Jesus "has become a priest . . . by the power of an indestructible life" (Heb 7:16).

69. E.g., Willard, "Trust and Death to Self," MP3/cassette.

70. Willard writes that "provision has been made for us to be with Jesus, as one person to another, in our daily life" (*Conspiracy*, 276).

mainly concern ourselves, at the conclusion of the second stage, with the fact that Jesus's ministry was increased.

Willard, in the eighth chapter of *Conspiracy*, includes a footnote to his book *Guidance*. It is not insignificant that the note comes while he is discussing the nature of Jesus's ministry to his disciples *after* the stark separation of his ascension. The significance is that *Guidance* provides a practical and teleological picture of how Jesus's mediation of the kingdom works in light of his bodily absence.[71]

In the 1993 epilogue of *Guidance*, "The Way of the Burning Heart," Willard writes this of Jesus as ascended: "He is with us, and he speaks with us, and we with him. He speaks with us in our heart, which burns from the characteristic impact of his word. His presence with us is, of course, much greater than his words to us. But this presence is turned into *companionship* only by the actual communications between us and him, which frequently are confirmed by external events as life moves on."[72] Then we get the conclusion: "This companionship with Jesus is the form that Christian spirituality takes as practiced through the ages."[73] For Willard, it is the *resurrection* that validates and stabilizes this form of Christian spirituality that had begun in Galilee. But it is the *ascension* that christens its practice beyond spatiotemporal limitations, not because Jesus is now something ontologically different from what he was before the ascension, but because after the ascension, the first listeners finally learned that their carpenter rabbi could continue to personally support their process of spiritual formation without being sense-perceptibly present. This insight makes possible the grander insight that if he so wished, he could be present always and everywhere.

71. Though *Guidance* spells out the "how," we must recognize that discipleship to Jesus is, for Willard, *more* than receiving his guidance. And guidance is, for him, more than discipleship. Hearing Jesus is only a part of how a person receives his ministry to life in the kingdom of God. And hearing Jesus and depending on his guidance would still be a vital reality even if humanity had never sinned and needed discipleship. The overlap between discipleship and guidance is the central reality of "a conversational relationship" with someone who is (now) invisible, hence the footnote.

72. Willard, *Guidance*, 239.

73. Willard, 239.

In this vein, Willard speaks of Jesus's work as intercessor (John 17:16–17), a characteristically second-stage ministry, saying, "It was necessary for him to go away in the form he had here on earth . . . so that he could be more effectively present to multitudes of people, millions of people, billions of people, all around the world and could be the lord of all those people and deal with you and with me and all of them individually."[74] This thought is expanded in a contribution to *The Life with God Bible*: "The death and departure of Jesus and the coming of the Spirit upon the disciples was, in point of fact, a liberation of Christ from the self-imposed limitations of a divine presence in the individual life of a Jewish teacher and healer (Phil. 2:5–8). With this liberation the person of Christ became free to move with the word of the gospel of the kingdom throughout the inner life of the disciples and about the world at large (e.g., Acts 6:7; 19:20; 2 Tim 2:9; John 14:15–26; Col 3:16). But the Gospels do not provide the final and ultimately perfect way God will dwell in his people, as Acts, the Letters and Revelation vividly reveal. History's work is not yet complete."[75] The ascension understood as a "liberation of Christ" needs to be balanced with a right understanding of those "self-imposed limitations," on which Willard in this passage does not elaborate. Quickly put, the limitations were a matter of the Trinity's *gradual revelation* of who Jesus was—that is, the incarnate Son of God. As his humble covering is gradually removed, Jesus is not ontologically but effectively "free to move." The improved perceptions of the first listeners have altered and opened the door for his increased involvement.

The two dimensions of Jesus's liberation—that is, the expansion of his ministry—are clearly named in the quote above. The first is "throughout the inner life of the disciple." Before the ascension, Jesus's ministry to first listeners like Peter was limited in the extent and depth of Jesus's access to Peter's hidden life—that is, his mind, heart, and soul. Jesus is only on the outside, or so Peter thinks. But upon Jesus's bodily

---

74. Dallas Willard, "Overview of Bringing Truth to Life," *Bringing Truth to Life* (Navigators, Colorado Springs, CO, January 2008), MP3, 3:00.
75. Willard, "People of God with Immanuel," 1788–89.

departure, Peter learns that Jesus is both invisible and ever-present. Jesus's *communication* and *communion* with Peter can penetrate deeper and fill Peter's life to an extent that they could not when Peter only knew of Jesus as a being whose personality was focused exclusively through his human body. This *inner* communication and communion is not the same as what Willard with Paul called *union* with Christ. Willard is careful to distinguish these in *Guidance*. Union with Christ is an advanced stage in one's formation. Hearing Jesus is not. However, "practicing the presence of Jesus" could have had little practical meaning for Peter before he witnessed Jesus's death, departure, and subsequent glorification.

The second dimension is Jesus's movement "about the world at large." Before these events, it was believed that Jesus's personal teaching ministry was limited not only to Palestine but to Jesus's physical location within Palestine. The liberation of Christ, christened by the ascension, made possible a form of personal discipleship that was translocal and thus more prevalent in human history.

In both of these dimensions, a more "final and ultimately perfect way" is entered. About this, the Gospels—books written concerning events before the ascension—have little to say. And so we turn to a new stage.

Part IV

THE THIRD STAGE

Jesus came into the world so that we could trust him and follow him into his kingdom. And he went the length of letting himself die for our sins so that we could get over all of the suspicions we have about God.

—Dallas Willard, Valley Vineyard Christian Fellowship, February 9, 1999

Salvation is a matter of being caught up in the life that Jesus is now living on earth.

—Dallas Willard, National Pastors Convention, March 10, 2004

WHAT A FEW JEWS KNEW

> [*Christ* and *Jesus* are] not synonyms, though they refer to the same person. The difference between *Christ* and *Jesus* is the divinely appointed historical mission into human history of an eternal person who in fulfilling that mission is known as *Jesus*. And *Jesus* refers to someone that was known in a different way. And this, by the way, I think, when you look at the way John winds up his gospel, it's a beautiful way of bringing these two together. You see, what these people who lived in Jesus's time had to deal with is Jesus. They looked at Jesus, and they didn't know who he was. But here's John 20:31. He's talking about the things Jesus did and the signs that Jesus performed. The signs . . . testified that he was not just Jesus. John says in verse 31, "These have been written that you may believe that Jesus is the Christ." See, what you have there is two different ways of identifying. . . . It refers to the same thing, but it has a different meaning.
>
> —Dallas Willard, Fuller Theological Seminary, June 10, 2002

TO EAGER LISTENERS in Galilee and Judea, Jesus preached the gospel of the kingdom of God. Though both the kingdom and Jesus himself were a given for his first listeners, it does not follow that they understood either in any depth. Jesus's specific gospel of at-hand-ness was a *new* understanding for the Second Temple Jews, one that called for metanoia, and through Jesus's ongoing manifestation of and teaching about the kingdom, these first listeners would discover many more of the "secrets of the kingdom" (Matt 13:11). The biggest of these secrets was embedded in Jesus's first and main message.

If one is cognizant, as Willard holds Jesus's contemporaries were, of the kingdom of God's existence and of its (albeit limited) at-handness through the ancient covenant ministry, then the first two stages of gospel understanding follow straightforwardly from what Jesus said and did. But as some listeners walk in faith with Jesus as their deliverer and teacher, they come to know not only more of the kingdom of God but also more of Jesus. Though there were still many secrets to be revealed regarding him, he and his extraordinary life had become a mental given for them. And for first- and second-stage believers, it was clear that *he* was a crucial part of what made his gospel a gospel at all.

I have already had occasion to mention that a doctrine of Jesus as teacher and of his gospel as inviting disciples to learn from him to live in the kingdom (the second-stage understanding) is an (or even *the*) aspect of theology Willard most wished to communicate in his day. It is the aspect he felt was most pertinent for our times and most missing from contemporary theological reflection, and his writing and speaking is filled with support for his view. But as a full-time university professor, Willard undoubtedly had enough other work to keep him from developing his theology to the fullest extent possible. And he, by necessity no less than by choice, took a tactical, prophetic approach to theology in which one must, he says, "judge the lay of the land for your times and shoot where the enemy is."[1] So what Willard's theology lacks is proportion, as I have already mentioned.

When we come to what would be the third-stage understanding of the gospel of the kingdom, Willard had a lot less to say. But Willard's third-stage understanding of the gospel, while lacking comprehensiveness, is not lacking in penetrating and provocative insights that call for deeper exploration and display.

In the second chapter, I described two canonically sanctioned ways of viewing the Christ event: in short, the God's eye view and the first listeners' eye view. Having traveled with the first listeners thus far, I am sure that many readers are wondering what Willard will say about the

1. Willard, "Kingdom Living," 18.

gospel when Jesus is finally regarded with the high or "God's-eye" views of him found in the New Testament. After all, this is the mode in which most of us, Willard included, were taught theology and especially soteriology. I confess that readers will have to wait until chapter 12 (two more chapters) before preparations are made to finally "hear that gospel." Before then, a few ontological and christological threads must be pulled.

Hence, in the current chapter, we will look at how Willard handles the first listeners' acknowledgment that Jesus is the Christ and how this fit together in their minds (or did not) with his crucifixion and ascension, which amounted to their Lord's bodily disappearance.

But confessing Jesus as Lord does not necessarily mean one *knows* that he is divine. With the listeners' eye view in mind, we will ask in the next chapter, On what basis did the first listeners conclude that "the Lord Jesus" (Acts 1:21) is, as Willard calls him, "the unique Son of God"?[2] I am not terribly happy with the sources available for handling this question, for there are many biblical, historical, and metaphysical issues that Willard simply does not address. Nevertheless, I will offer a creative reconstruction of Willard's answer to it as well as of what we may wish to regard as Scripture's answer. To be specific, I will speak of *soteriology proper*, a nonincarnational soteriology that is amply attested to in Willard's corpus, and relate it to the question of the divinity of the first listeners' Lord Jesus. As the first listeners gradually recognize the Lord Jesus's intimate involvement in soteriology proper, the conclusion lies at hand that Jesus is God. Or maybe not.

Many first listeners, as well as Willard, confess to know it. Thus, I will attempt in the last major chapter to give Willard's answer to the age-old question of *cur deus homo*, or why God became man. I am tempted to reveal in this little trailer the end of this epic film. Resisting that temptation, I will only share that the conclusion that Jesus is God reveals to the first listeners a hitherto unknown malady of human existence from which we all suffer. This revelation seems to be on a sliding scale: the more one takes the orthodox conclusion seriously, the

2. Willard, *Disciplines*, 5.

more one recognizes this malady and the more one recognizes the provision of salvation announced in Jesus's gospel. The chapter ends, as all stages do, by moving from the listeners' knowledge to faith. The third-stage gospel is just as prone as the others to remain merely on the level of knowledge and not be made effective through the listeners' faith.

With that in mind, let us begin unpacking the third-stage gospel according to Dallas Willard.

A Secret Ontology

THE CHIEF *SECRET* of Jesus's gospel and the foundational step to the third stage is simple to formulate. Sorting through all the metaphysical issues that arise as a result of it is difficult. And once the first listeners held the secret, they still had many years (or so it would seem from our late historical point of view) before they would work out its many metaphysical entailments.[3]

The secret is this: the person Jesus is *the king* of the kingdom of God. The gospel is still that Jesus makes the kingdom of God available *through offering himself as a reality for trusting.* But third-stage listeners know this to be true because *the king* was and is and will be available.

Lest we forget, availability in the earlier stages was also a matter of trust *in Jesus.* But the Jesus in whom one trusted was perceived as an ad hoc deliverer or as a teacher and mediator of kingdom life. Neither perception is false and, therefore, both obtain the salvation they reach out for. But both only perceive Jesus on the *near side* of the kingdom of God, on our subordinate, creaturely side. In both, Jesus stands on our side of the kingdom and helps his trusting listeners successfully interact with it. But in the third stage, the listeners recognize Jesus on the *far side* of the kingdom of God. On the *God* side.

To reiterate, if the first-stage topography has Jesus standing between the kingdom of God and his listener, the second-stage topography has Jesus standing to the side, as it were, pointing to a direct

3. Needless to say, they are still being worked out. Orthodox Christology is a doctrine whose mystery Willard urges we respect. Nevertheless, Willard does have a fairly consistent evangelical and orthodox metaphysics of Jesus.

interaction between the kingdom of God and his listener. If these crude images adequately describe the real ontological relations undergirding the first and second stages, the third-stage topography has Jesus standing *behind* the kingdom of God—behind, as it were, where God is. This topography, as we will see, does not have the effect of putting Jesus out of the listeners' reach. For it dawns on them in the course of their already existent personal relationship with Jesus.

In commenting on the Johannine exclamation of Jesus, "Have I been with you so long, and you still do not know me, Philip?" (John 14:9), Willard explains, "It was not the historical Jesus that Philip did not know (v. 9). Who he was clearly amounted to *much more* than a carpenter of Nazareth who became a famous rabbi and who was crucified and rose again."[4] Philip and other first listeners had a trusting relationship with an extraordinary person. Thus, when this person comes to be known as even more than a Spirit-baptizing and Spirit-resurrected carpenter, as one who stands *behind* the kingdom of God, the relationship previously established continues. But the new topography also brings with it new vistas and benefits. So with the Oriental rhetorical quality of Jesus's communication in mind, let us consider how third-stage ontology is the secret of Jesus's gospel of the kingdom.

In effect, Jesus's main Synoptic announcement is an enthymeme.[5] One of the syllogism's premises is assumed by all present. It is the commonsense judgment that Jesus is at hand. He is obviously physically present, but he is also open for *interpersonal* contact. The syllogism's conclusion is "The kingdom of God is at hand." The other premise is something Jesus's listeners must go looking for in order to complete the argument. But being unstated does not mean it is unintended.

The other premise is the third-stage ontological secret: Jesus is *the king* of the kingdom of God. As Willard writes, "[Jesus] was himself the evidence for the truth of his announcement about the availability of

---

4. Willard, *Knowing*, 185 (emphasis mine).

5. See Dallas Willard, "Jesus the Logician," *Christian Scholar's Review* 28, no. 4 (1999): 605–14, for more on Jesus's use of the enthymeme. As far as I know, Willard never himself argued that Jesus's Synoptic Gospel announcement was enthymematic.

God's kingdom, or governance, to ordinary human existence."[6] Something approaching this perception is *suspected* by Jesus's first audience and by the readers of the Gospels. But only when it is fully grasped by the mind does the opportunity for full-scale third-stage faith in the gospel and the ensuing salvation present itself.

So now here is an important point for understanding Willard and the rest of this stage: having an understanding of the third-stage *ontology* does not entail that the listener has embraced or even heard the third-stage *gospel*. This is a fundamental feature of Willard's theology of salvation, about which I will have more to say in remaining chapters. In terms of understanding the good news of Jesus, we encountered a very similar issue in the first stage. Mildly educated Jews *already knew* about the ancient existence of the kingdom of God. That idea was no gospel in and of itself. Likewise, proclamation of the reality of Jesus *as God's Son* is no gospel in and of itself. One can know it and still not know, much less believe, the gospel. If true, it is merely a metaphysical fact intrinsic to Jesus's gospel, not dissimilar to the eternal existence of the kingdom. The third-stage gospel is the *availability* of the kingdom *by* Jesus, who is now suspected of being much more than a Spirit-baptizing and Spirit-resurrected carpenter.

Turned around, grasping the ontology *is* essential to feeling the existential force of the third-stage gospel. The first chapter of *Conspiracy* has scattered clues to Willard's mind on this matter. The first is the epitaph from Malcolm Muggeridge: "Jesus' good news, then, was that the Kingdom of God had come, and that he, Jesus, was its herald and expounder to men. More than that, in some special, mysterious way, he *was* the Kingdom."[7] Muggeridge's third-stage conclusion is put in a form that Willard himself does not use: Jesus *is* the kingdom. Nevertheless, he does quote others using it. Other than Muggeridge, he footnotes Barth and also P. T. Forsyth, whose formulation was "The Gospel of the

6. Willard, *Conspiracy*, 20.

7. Willard, 1, from Malcolm Muggeridge, *Jesus: The Man Who Lives* (London: Collins, 1975), 61. Willard recommends this book for reflection on the christological title "Son of God." See Willard, "How Can Jesus Be the Son of God?"

Kingdom was Christ in essence; Christ was the Gospel of the Kingdom in power."[8]

Willard's difficulty with such formulations is that they can be misunderstood as identity statements. And these are, to his mind, as incorrect as saying God is the kingdom of God. While they have rhetorical force and are probably not meant to be taken literally, in Willard's own teaching, he aims at more metaphysical precision. Willard's own way of putting it is to say that the kingdom of God had come near *in Jesus's person*.[9] It is not that Jesus and the kingdom are the same but that the kingdom's availability (its nearness, accessibility, etc.) is a function of Jesus's availability. If one grasps that Jesus is the king of the kingdom, then this dependent relationship makes sense. Jesus makes the kingdom, his kingdom, available by being himself available.

But now we are getting ahead of the first listeners' epistemic progression.

The Transcendence of Jesus: "I Am Going Away"

IN REALITY, THE first listeners come to knowledge of this third-stage ontology of the kingdom and of Jesus through fits and starts. The central concept (the secret and the missing part of the syllogism) is grasped by some of Jesus's listeners *before* his passion begins. But a *mature* or, we might say, *orthodox* third-stage understanding of Jesus and the kingdom forms—and Willard stands with the majority of scholars here—in their minds *only after* the climactic latter events of Jesus's life.[10]

---

8. Willard, *Conspiracy*, 402; P. T. Forsyth, *The Person and Place of Jesus Christ* (London: Independent, 1909), 123.

9. E.g., in "Discipleship, a Strategy for Personal Wholeness" (*Jesus' Words of Eternal Life: What Were They?* [Bel Air Presbyterian Church, Los Angeles, CA, May 7, 1989], MP3/cassette, 15:45), Willard says, "He brought the kingdom of God to earth in his own person. He offered it to others in his own person. And he taught his followers to do exactly the same thing." Cf. Willard, *Conspiracy*, 279–80; and Willard, "What Is the Kingdom of God?," 6:30.

10. This historical circumstance has an effect on how the topics on this stage need to be laid out in these chapters in contrast to the other stages. Here we must begin by discussing the earthly end of Jesus's life in order to adequately reconstruct the first listeners' apprehension of third-stage ontology. Since the three stages rest on a loose—that

Willard has in fact expressed his mind as to why God did not make *irresistible* provision for third-stage knowledge to come about before the ascension. This has become a contestable point in contemporary exegesis. It is not because Jesus needed to first *become* the king of the kingdom of God through one of the latter events.[11] Willard's claim is that, given the stakes, third-stage knowledge could be very dangerous to God's cosmic project with humanity (his divine conspiracy) if it is not carefully and gently introduced. "[Jesus] of course understood all this," Willard writes, "and provision was made for a correct understanding to grow, as resurrection, Pentecost and the following years and centuries of the Church unfolded in the book of Acts and continue to unfold today."[12]

The beginning of the fits and starts was in Galilee, where long before anyone knew anything about his passion, resurrection, and ascension, many had an epiphany of Jesus's kingship. But these early epiphanies were riddled with misunderstanding. What the listeners assumed about the world and about God made it difficult to rightly order their epiphany in their belief system. One of the earliest attempts to reconcile Jesus's kingship with their beliefs about their world was, as Willard teaches, to reduce the exercise of the kingdom of God to an earthly sociopolitical kingdom.[13]

---

is, nonrigorous—reconstruction of the first listeners' actual epistemic progression, it is best to start with the time period when this epistemic progression, as it were, *progresses*.

11. Gary Black, despite his sustained efforts to understand Willard, holds this view. Following exegetical theologians N. T. Wright and Scot McKnight, Black (not Willard, we must assume) writes that "Jesus' rule began when he said it began, at the proclamation of his 'Great Commission'" (Gary Black Jr. and Dallas Willard, *The Divine Conspiracy Continued* [San Francisco: HarperOne, 2014], 4). Statements like this suggest either that the kingdom of God is a historical reality with a beginning in or around the life of Jesus (which contradicts Willard's Old Testament theology) or that Jesus was not antecedently involved in God's kingdom and was at some point *installed* as king (which contradicts Willard's theology proper). Since I doubt Black is advocating Arianism, I assume that he either misunderstands Willard's theology of the kingdom or disagrees with it and has slipped his own view into their cowritten book.

12. Willard, "People of God with Immanuel," 6.

13. Confusing the kingdom with a sociopolitical order is not over, so Willard. Cf. Willard, "Kingdom Gospel," 1:00.

The paradigmatic scene for insight into third-stage ontology and its subsequent misunderstanding is Peter's confession. But a less central scene was the confession and subsequent misunderstanding of John the Baptist. In "Jesus as a Logician and Apologist," Willard looks briefly at the pericope of John's skepticism as he sits in prison (Matt 11:1–6). John's doubt exemplifies the earliest attempts to make sense of Jesus's gospel with third-stage ontology:

> *You know what was in John's mind. He had announced the Messiah. "Behold, the Lamb of God who takes away the sins of the world." But Jesus had not exactly done that in the way that John was thinking about it. . . . See, he had a picture of deliverance that the Messiah was going to bring. And you know the background of this, and you know what a powerful force it was. And you know, even in Acts chapter 1, when Jesus is ministering postresurrection, they are still asking the wrong question: "Jesus, at this time are you going to restore the kingdom to Israel?"*[14]

John the Baptist's misunderstanding of the third-stage ontology did not in his case lead to any particular attempt to misuse his relationship to Jesus. Because of his imprisonment, it led in John's case to doubt and a paralysis of John's rational and emotional life. John expected Jesus to come and free him from his sociopolitical marginalization and oppression. When Jesus does not do it, John doubts his epiphany of third-stage ontology. John's powerlessness, his poverty of any leverage by which he could control the course of history, leads him to a deficient third-stage ontology of the kingdom—one characterized by hopelessness.[15]

At a later date in Jesus's earthly ministry, we encounter Peter confessing—that is, owning up to—his newly acquired view that Jesus is "the Christ, the Son of the living God" (Matt 16:16). This third-stage

14. Willard, "Jesus as a Logician," 18:30.

15. Cf. Willard, "Heavens Were Opened," 27:30; and Willard, "Meaning of Pentecost," 42:30.

understanding, says Jesus, was not attained by flesh and blood—that is, by merely human resources.[16] The Father revealed it to Peter. Willard often connects Peter's personal epistemic progression with Paul's general description of confessing that Jesus is Lord, saying *no one* can perform this act except in the Holy Spirit (1 Cor 12:3).[17] But when Peter first acknowledges that he sees third-stage ontology, he, says Willard, proceeds to show that he doesn't know what he is talking about. In *Conspiracy*, Willard writes, "They [referring to people who have the right understanding of something] are like Peter in his truly earth-shaking confession that Jesus was the One anointed to save humanity. He had it right, of course, but had no real idea of what it meant (Matt. 16:16–19, 23)."[18] So Peter rebukes the Christ.

Crucifixion

WHAT PETER'S AND John's ontology of Jesus and the kingdom is missing is, as Willard sees it, *crucifixion*. "Crucifixion" is a curious cipher in Willard's biblical hermeneutic. Obviously, he reads it in Scripture as at times referring to Jesus's physical, historical, teleological suffering and death on a cross. He reads the crucifixion as referring to Jesus and his followers' transformational embrace of self-denial, mortification, and asceticism.[19] But a much less obvious reading of crucifixion presents itself to Willard with reference to *the workings* of God's kingdom. And the character of these workings makes a difference for how Jesus is king of the kingdom—one that John and Peter did not understand.

"Crucified" with respect to the kingdom refers to Jesus's and his Father's transcendence of human instrumentalities. In the Matthew 16 passage, it is parallel to "flesh and blood has not revealed this to you."

16. Willard, "Spiritual Formation as a Natural Part," 52.

17. Willard, 52. See also Dallas Willard, "How We Learn to Do What Jesus Said," *Reigning in Life through One Christ Jesus* (Okoboji Bible Conference, Okoboji, IA, August 6, 2009), MP3, 4:30; Willard, "Kingdom Gospel," 37:30; and Dallas Willard, "The Church and the Children of Light in Your World," *The Magnificence of Ministry—Your Ministry!* (Baylor University / George W. Truett Theological Seminary, Waco, TX, January 29, 2009), MP3, 19:30.

18. Willard, *Conspiracy*, 316.

19. E.g., Willard, *Renovation*, 66–68.

Flesh and blood—that is, human instrumentalities—were not operative in Peter's epistemic progression. The coming to know was "crucified." It took place with genuine intervention from above.

A revealing instance of Willard using this interpretation is in his 2008 talk "The Gospel of the Kingdom":

> *Galatians 3 has just a few words here I think I would like to emphasize because it seems to me that people generally don't really appreciate what is going on here in this third chapter.*
>
> *Now, you know who he is dealing with. Chapter 3, verse 1: "Foolish Galatians, who has bewitched you, before whose eyes Jesus was publically portrayed as crucified?" Did you ever preach on that? What did he mean—"publically portrayed as crucified"? What does that mean? In the context? Did Paul have a little visual aid there? Maybe a cross with a papier mâché man on it? Or what happened? How was Jesus set before their eyes crucified?* By his action *in response to the words of the gospel. Crucified means, simply, without any human instrumentality, Jesus was present.*[20]

He goes on to read the next verses of Galatians 3, summarizing them: "That is, how does the kingdom of God move? You've seen it. It happened to you. Miracles, that's a part of the natural manifestation of the kingdom. We don't have to do a special deal about it. We just have to live in the kingdom of God, let our expectation be on him, and miracles happen."[21] Willard's point is how Jesus, through Paul's rhetorically unpolished preaching of the gospel, acted in a power that was not traceable to human capacities (which Paul did not have) but was unmistakably and identifiably present to the Galatians.

---

20. Dallas Willard, "The Gospel of the Kingdom" (Theological and Cultural Thinkers [TACT], Los Angeles, CA, September 20, 2008), MP3, 1:13:15.

21. Willard, 1:15:00. Importantly, Willard precedes this exegesis with an exegesis of Matt 10, in which he says that the kingdom came nigh unto the Jewish villages "in the persons of the disciples, of the apostles. They brought the action of God with them." This was discussed under "The Baptism of Moses" in chapter 6.

A written example of this interpretation is found in *Conspiracy*: "Paul's policy with regard to the redemptive community simply followed the gospel of the Beatitudes. He refused to base anything on excellence of speech, understanding, and culture *as attainments of human beings*. Rather, in building the work of God he would disregard everything in the new humankind but what came from Jesus in his crucifixion and beyond: 'I resolved to regard nothing in your midst except Jesus Christ and him crucified' (1 Cor. 2:2)."[22]

To repeat, crucifixion in Galatians 3:1 and 1 Corinthians 2:2 refers, by means of the dramatic event of Jesus's cross, to the fact that the working of the kingdom of God is not dependent on human instrumentalities. Thanks to the hard lessons learned in the exile, the "crucified"—or better, *transcendent*—aspect of the kingdom of God was not new for Jesus's first listeners, since it could be found in their prophets. Despite this acknowledgment, they nevertheless understood that *they* were not prophets and that the kingdom of God, though fundamentally independent of human instrumentalities, was best approached *through* the Jewish religious institutions—that is, human instrumentalities.

The potential "stumbling block" (1 Cor 1:23) for the first listeners was not with the transcendent kingdom of God but with the general association of *the promised Messiah* with a human, sociopolitical kingdom—that is, a human instrumentality.[23] As with the Jewish institutions, the always transcendent kingdom of God, or so they thought, would again be *mediated* through the immanent kingdom of Israel and his Messiah. In speaking about the shortcomings of God's dealings with humanity during the preascension period, Willard says,

> *Social conditions shaped expectations in a manner that prevented many people from being able to receive Jesus as*

---

22. Willard, *Conspiracy*, 126. A few of Willard's recorded lectures also exegete this verse similarly, e.g., Dallas Willard, "Exactly Why the Local Church Is the Hope of the World," *Sermon* (Christ Community Evangelical Free Church, Kansas City, MO, October 1, 2006), MP3, 20:00.

23. Willard's analysis bears striking similarity to John Bright's reading of Isa 40–66 and of the prophets in general. See Bright, *Kingdom of God*, 136–53.

> *"Messiah." In the minds of nearly everyone, the Messiah would bring a kind of radical political reform and restoration of national identity that was flatly incompatible with the realities of God's kingdom and the central teachings of Jesus. This prevented a correct understanding and reception of that kingdom, and made the personal presence of Jesus, though extremely powerful and convincing, also confusing and enigmatic even to his closest followers. Neither Jesus' behavior nor his teaching could be understood within the cultural assumptions at the time he lived of the Gospels.*[24]

As the secret begins to enter the minds of the first listeners and Jesus begins to be thought of as "more than a prophet" and as the expected Messiah, he becomes, in their minds, a very honorable figure but something still less than and frankly incompatible with what he was. He becomes the king of the kingdom of Israel and *not*, strictly speaking, of the kingdom of God.

What will help correct these errant conceptions of the Messiah and bring Jesus's kingship into direct association with the ancient and established conception of the kingdom of God, not reducing it to the then burning expectations of the kingdom of Israel, is the application of *a principle of "crucifixion"* or *transcendence.* Crucifixion in this sense is an *eternal* property of the kingdom of God, whose kingdom does not need human or created instrumentalities to have an effect. Again, this is not a particularly new idea to the mildly educated Jews of Jesus's day *as applied to God and his kingdom.* But as applied to God's *anointed one*, it was. These two concepts brought together—"Messiah crucified"—are "a stumbling block to Jews" (1 Cor 1:23).

But for other Jews and Greeks (and this is the good news of the cross that Willard has in mind), the Messiah's crucifixion is "the power of God and the wisdom of God" (1 Cor 1:24). It is God's power and wisdom *because,* despite the killing of the king's body, the King is *still*

---

24. Willard, "People of God with Immanuel," 6.

powerful and wise. In Willard's words, "The new life that had already been present among them in the person of Jesus could not be quenched by killing the body."[25] Again, what Willard sees in crucifixion with respect to the kingship of Jesus is a display of his transcendence of material reality.

Returning to Peter's confession, we see that Peter's third-stage ontology cannot accommodate for a *Messiah* who exercises power without any recourse to the physical or psychological (e.g., rhetorical) powers that belong to him as a human. *God* could, of course, exercise power without human power. But a "crucified" Messiah, with *Messiah* understood according to the standard expectations of the Second Temple belief system, was a contradictory concept. For it to make sense, for crucifixion and transcendence to be fitting of Jesus and his authority in the kingdom of God, Peter would, via metanoia, have to come to a vision of a more glorious Messiah and a more glorious hope for what God was intending to do on the earth through his Messiah.[26] An impressive but less glorious Messiah is what was embedded in Second Temple expectations of "the anointed one" and what was assumed in Peter's and John's "uncrucified" third-stage ontology.[27]

Willard was of the persuasion that the disjunction between the kingdom of God's principle of crucifixion and our human expectations of how God ought to work was not limited to the first-century Jews.

25. Willard, *Disciplines*, 37.

26. Jesus, no doubt, knows this, and hence his transfiguration follows Peter's messianic confession.

27. We can note here that Bright, with the help of J. W. Bowman, makes the case that, though the suffering servant passage of Isa 53 was not *traditionally* considered a messianic text, it *is* a messianic text because its author thought of it that way, as did Jesus and his early followers. This hermeneutical judgment allows Bright to cast Jesus's kingship into a different mold, that of a king who serves and suffers and who serves and suffers precisely because he is king or Messiah: "It is a Kingdom of the meek and lowly in which the leader is he who is willing to be 'last of all and servant of all'" (Bright, *Kingdom of God*, 210). Bright even goes as far as Willard does to say that "[the messianic pattern of the Servant] is a comprehension of the character of Israel's God and the nature of his redemptive purpose" (213). This is what the Isaianic prophet saw when he saw who his God was. We remember that *crucified* for Willard refers at times to something eternal about God.

Even after Jesus's crucifixion and ascension, the temptation *to want* the kingdom of God to be channeled through elite, temporal human beings continues. Willard sees it most prominently in Simon Magnus in Acts 8:9–24. The "Simonizing tendency" is explained in *Conspiracy* as trying "to get a monopoly on God and prove that *we*, after all, are the ones who have 'got it right.'"[28] In his earliest extant lectures on Acts, an extended excursus is given to Simon Magnus and the laying on of hands, the rights to which he tried to buy:[29] "For example, there are traditions in the Christian church which have made exactly the same mistake as Simon Magnus. Simon Magnus thought that the power could, number one, be restricted and, then, made merchandized of. . . . The mistake of Simon Magnus was that you could corner the Holy Spirit and then you could make a market, you can make merchandise of it."[30] Let us concern ourselves here with the restriction of God's power, not the merchandizing of it. Simon's mistake, as Willard admits, is an understandable one and one that repeats in history. He simply misunderstood how God was intending to work, especially in the wake of Jesus's coming. In Jesus, God was beginning to extend access to his kingdom beyond its covenant restriction to the Jewish people and, indeed, beyond all forms of human organization.

The pre- and postexilic "office" of the prophet (and before that, the "office" of the judges) was a precursor to this new sweeping phenomenon of God working apart from Jewish covenant organization. In chapter 6, we saw how the prophets were unhooked from the Jewish institutions and yet hooked into God. "The radical independence of the prophet from the 'establishment'—even from a Jewish establishment" is one key mark

28. Willard, *Conspiracy*, 280.

29. Dallas Willard, "Jewish Persecution Drives the New Community to the Gentiles," *Studies in the Book of Apostolic Acts: Journey in the Spiritual Unknown* (Woodlake Avenue Friends Church, Canoga Park, CA, December 19, 1971), MP3/cassette, 24:00.

30. Willard does not say which specific traditions he has in mind. The two that immediately present themselves to my mind are the Roman Catholic tradition and the Baptist tradition. This would not be an untypical pairing for Willard. In the notes, he writes, "Before we dismiss Simon Magnus out of hand we must understand how totally saturated American Evangelical 'Christianity' is with exactly this mentality" (Willard, "Handout for 'Studies in the Book of Apostolic Acts,'" 11).

of the prophet.[31] But the prophets, and the judges before them, were a rare occurrence. Most of the people of God did not have the freedom to detach themselves from the institutions of Israel. Thus, the change that Jesus brings about is one in which the kingdom of God—that is, the action and power of God—is available *to anyone* apart from human and certainly religious organizations. This is the teaching that is fundamental to Jesus's gospel but that Simon Magnus did not yet grasp.

Ascension

THE DEFICIENT ONTOLOGY of Peter after his confession and of Simon Magnus in his business plans is shown to be deficient not only in its conception of crucifixion but also in the implications of ascension. Jesus's crucifixion was not without a resurrection that restored to the first listeners a physical, though somewhat geographically unpredictable, Jesus. But even after the crucifixion, the disciples, so Willard, were still asking the wrong question, saying, "Will you *at this time* restore the kingdom to Israel?" (Acts 1:6; emphasis mine).[32] In asking this, they reveal their failure to understand the full significance of Jesus's transcendent kingship.

The ascension, however, would make that question seem absurd by forcing the principle of crucifixion (or transcendence) on the first listeners permanently. A long quote will help display how Willard interprets the crucifixion and the ascension together:

> *Jesus was aware that, as long as he was here "in the flesh," as we say, he was an obstruction to the power of the Spirit coming into the lives of the very people he was training. Now, this is a part of the understanding of death and resurrection in Jesus. Death, among other things, was Jesus' way of getting out of the way of the Spirit. Limited to the flesh, he could not be present everywhere he needed to be, as he can now through the Holy Spirit, which brings him everywhere he needs to be. That's the nature of spirit. . . . But he had to get out of the way.*

31. Willard, "People of God in Exile," 1172.
32. Willard, "Jesus as a Logician," 18:30; cf. Willard, "On Acts, Pt. 1," 42:30.

And that is why you can't find his body anywhere. Any of you know another person whose body disappeared? Moses. Anyone else? Elijah. Anyone else? Enoch. Why do you suppose that's true? What would they have done with Moses' body if they had it? You can bet they would have worshipped it. They would have made an idol out of it. They would have fought over it. "Who gets it?"

This is a very deep lesson, now, about bodily existence generally. It's not a bad thing; it's a good thing. But the second of the Ten Commandments warns us carefully about letting any bodily thing on earth, above earth, below earth, be held up as something to look towards and worship. And God knows human beings have this terrible tendency to idolatry anyway. If they can't find a dead body, they'll make one out of something and then they'll worship that. So now the Spirit coming is to allow the presence of God to be personally accessible in ways that an embodied person could never be.[33]

As I will explain below, one reason for Jesus "getting out of the way" is that something else comes more clearly into view. But another reason for "getting out of the way" was due to the destructive tendency of rebellious humans to idolatrize.[34]

The temptation toward idolatry and monopoly seems to be, according to Willard, the deeper reason why God did not fulfill the

---

33. Dallas Willard, "Living through the Power of the Holy Spirit," *National Gathering* (Ecclesia Network, Chevy Chase, MD, February 2010), MP3, 12:00.

34. In the epilogue of *Guidance*, we are told, "The second of the Ten Commandments tries to help us find God by forbidding us to think of him in visual terms (Ex 20:4). This commandment forbids the use of images as representations of the divine. The entire weight of the history of Israel—and then of its extension through Jesus and his people—presses toward the understanding of God as personal, invisible reality. This God invades history to call human beings to the choice of whether they individually will live in covenant relation with him, or put something else, always something visible, in the place of ultimate importance" (236–37). It was common for Willard to associate the second commandment with God's spiritual and transcendent nature and with nonnaturalism.

first-century hopes for a sociopolitical kingdom. Even with lesser lights such as Enoch, Moses, and Elijah, the temptation to worship and monopolize what is visible and generally sense perceptible is great. In *Knowing Christ*, Willard writes, "Human beings are addicted to 'monopoly' in religion. They want to control access to the divine goods."[35] This is with no other "goods" more likely to take place than with the man Jesus, who, as Peter knows, is "the Christ, the Son of the living God." Hence, Jesus's long-term spatiotemporal resting place could not be, as we saw in chapter 6, in reach of humans.[36] He is still in the physical universe, but not anywhere physically accessible to us.

Willard decries attempts to monopolize and idolatrize *Jesus's instrumentalities* even in his ascended distance. This applies to things like the sacraments, the laying on of hands (Simon's mistake), forgiveness, the Bible's original manuscripts,[37] the gifts of the Spirit, and the apostles and their succession.[38] With respect to the Bible, this would also include the right to interpret the Bible by being a member of the magisterium, the academic scholarly guild,[39] or a confessional association of ministers—for example, Willard's own Southern Baptist Convention. All of these groups have their own way of controlling access to the Bible and therefore, so they suppose, to Jesus.

By contrast, as the first and subsequent listeners recognize that Jesus is the king of the kingdom of God, they need to become used to

---

35. Willard, *Knowing*, 183.

36. I currently have no evidence of whether Willard thought that the kingdom would be restored to Israel. He does, however, make references in the 1980s to a millennial reign of Christ on earth. See, e.g., Dallas Willard, "The Blessed Hope," *Things That Accompany Salvation* (Rolling Hills Covenant Church, Rolling Estates, CA, October 19, 1986), MP3/cassette, 50:45.

37. Willard, "Bible, the University," 36.

38. See Willard, "On Acts, Pt. 2," 13:30, where Willard says, "A human arrangement for forgiveness is something that the church very early on offers to human beings and makes them dependent on the human organization. The human organization has control over forgiveness. I hate to take on the old Catholic understanding, but the understanding of the sacraments as being something that the church has charge of to be dispensed through a properly recognized priest and how that enables people to make clear that they have somehow arranged for forgiveness—that's very powerful."

39. Willard, *Conspiracy*, xvi.

the exercise of his kingdom *without* any historical or geographic fixity. A *crucified* king. Or an *ascended* king. Either way, a physically removed king, for both entail a "getting out of the way." And Jesus, a king independent of human instrumentalities, is able to make use of his own instrumentalities in ways that disestablish human attempts to monopolize them *in order to* monopolize him.

The Presence of Jesus: "I Am with You Always"

IN SUM, THE crucifixion principle describes a negative side of the third-stage ontology: King Jesus's *independence from* created instrumentalities. But the vacuum created by the absence of the physical makes, for *some* first listeners, something else more obvious. For this reason, mature third-stage understanding—more mature than Peter's and John's third-stage epiphanies—develops primarily after the crucifixion, when the transcendence of Jesus is more evident.

Of course, the pre- and postresurrection period was a time of fresh teaching about the upcoming change, for *the ascension* would mark a time when Jesus would cease to be sense perceptible and yet would nevertheless be "at hand." As we saw with the gospel in the previous stages, one of the crucial questions for Jesus's listeners is how his gospel of the kingdom, so linked to his person, will be true when he is gone. How will Jesus be "Messiah" and absent? Many of the effects of Jesus's change in geographical position were discussed in chapters 6 and 9. Though distant, he continues to deliver those who call his name, and he continues to speak and to direct his students with respect to a life lived well in the kingdom. In this section, let us look more generally at Willard's view of the transition itself.

Willard gives his fullest exposition of the events of the transition in a few sections from chapter 8 of *Conspiracy.* The first relevant section, "How Are We to Be *with* Him?" treats the teaching of John 14, in which Jesus promises his absence as well as the presence of "another strengthener."[40] Remarkably, Willard names this strengthener not as *the* Holy

40. Willard, 276–77.

Spirit but merely as the "spirit of truth." What's more, Willard pulls back into a discussion of the spiritual nature of the *whole* Godhead: "The spiritual nature of God, here reaffirmed by Jesus with reference to his own personality, was presented to the Jewish people early in their history (we recall Exod. 20:4; Deut. 4:12, 15, etc.)."[41] Though a little unclear, it seems that Willard is associating *the whole Trinity* in this verse with "the spirit of truth." He contrasts the other strengthener with "the visible Jesus as they had known him" but otherwise does not appropriate this to the Spirit.[42] This ambiguity is characteristic of Willard, who, in practice, does not make heavy use of appropriation to divide the Son and the Spirit in the postascension period. As usual, he upholds Augustine's wisdom: *opera Trinitatis ad extra sunt indivisa.*[43]

Another move characteristic of Willard is the heavy association of God's presence with God *speaking*. I will have more to say about this in the next chapter, but the content of his book *Guidance* should be recalled, not the least because Willard footnotes it here. He writes, "[God] can, of course, make himself present to the human mind in any way he chooses. But—for good reasons rooted deeply in the nature of the person and of personal relationships—his preferred way is to *speak*, to communicate: thus the absolute centrality of scripture to our discipleship."[44] The Jewish experience of YHWH—which becomes the New Testament experience of the Triune God—is centered not on seeing and feeling God but on hearing him.

This, for Willard, points to the *spiritual* nature of God as explicitly mentioned here. Manifesting himself to human beings through a voice, God makes it indescribably difficult to worship some creaturely, material form instead of the true uncreated, nonmaterial being behind it all. This and the later reference to idolatry signal that Willard is handling

41. Willard, 277.
42. Willard, 277.
43. "The external works of the Trinity are undivided." Cf. Dallas Willard, "Entering the Spiritual Disciplines," *Where New Life Begins*, MP3/cassette, which may be the source for this section of *Conspiracy*. He says, "The Logos is going to be substituted for by the Spirit" (7:30), and "the spirit of God is God's unseen activity" (8:45).
44. Willard, *Conspiracy*, 277.

the very theme addressed by the "crucified" workings of the kingdom. But in John 14, Jesus affirms the spiritual nature of God "with reference to *his own* personality," says Willard.[45] Soon Jesus will be with them in Spirit only.

Willard's emphasis on Jesus speaking and his spiritual substance continues in a more novel exposition of the postresurrection period in *Conspiracy*'s following section, "Teaching the Transition." Here Willard reads Acts 1 as referring to a time when Jesus alternated between visible and invisible speaking with his listeners. His lead phrase is "given commands *through* the Holy Spirit" (Acts 1:2). What could the prepositional phrase refer to if not to an extraordinary and indeed new form of communication from the familiar Nazarene carpenter? This image of Jesus communicating invisibly is strengthened for him by the next verse, in which Luke speaks univocally of a *sense-perceptible* presence and communication. Willard emphasizes the contrast with the conjunctive και, preferring to translate it as "also." This unassuming conjunction (normally inserted in Greek to begin sentences even without a strong meaning) gains semantic weight through the content of the verses it combines. In the latter verse, Jesus's sense-perceptible, bodily resurrection–validating appearances are explicitly noted. In the former verse, the routine human activity of giving commands is modified by the atypical description "through the Holy Spirit."

Willard strengthens this interpretation psychologically by claiming that the disciples would not have waited in Jerusalem for the promised power unless they had already had prior experience with "the spirit [*sic*]" in the postresurrection days. Hence, the day of Pentecost is not an abrupt, punctiliar change but the high point of a gradual transition. This view of God's work in and around the latter events is consistent with Willard's overall view of God's work in history, which emphasizes the *gentle* and *gradual* shifts into new and superior circumstances.[46]

---

45. Willard, 277 (emphasis mine).

46. In response to the question of why there needed to be a John the Baptist, Willard speaks of the principle of connexity and God's manner gradually leading people along (Willard, "New Community of God," 4:30).

The theme of the section "'Engulfment' in the Spiritual Presence," Willard's view of God giving "power without position," will be addressed below. It adds to the aforementioned aim of teaching the transition insofar as it addresses the question of how the *power* of Jesus will continue to be present in light of the absence of his body, his personal "power pack."[47] Though the listeners had experience with the same power that Jesus had, they were still under the influence of the idea that the kingdom of God's effect in the world would be attached to some localizable thing, some position.[48] If not to Jesus, then to themselves.

For Willard, Pentecost, when compared to the crucifixion, resurrection, and ascension, does not have a universal significance. It is an occasional event suited to God's purposes at that particular time for that particular community. It is repeatable in a way that the crucifixion, resurrection, and ascension are not, for it is one member of a larger class. But the first Pentecost is historically significant because it happened to *the only group that Jesus prepared* to become the only forebears of the worldwide people of God. All Willard's lectures on Acts from the 1970s emphasize this.

Outside of *Conspiracy*, the 1993 epilogue of *Guidance* describes more of Jesus's teaching of the transition. "His main task as their teacher during these days," says Willard, "was to accustom them to hearing him without seeing him."[49] The key pericope exposited here is the resurrection appearance on the road to Emmaus. Willard interprets the scene not as yet another proof of the resurrection but as primarily a pedagogical experience in which two disciples are taught to recognize Jesus in a manner that exceeds the usual sense-perceptible manner. The disciples afterward spoke about the experience: "Did not our hearts burn within us while he talked to us on the road, while he opened to us the Scriptures?" (Luke 24:32).

But this manner of recognizing Jesus through his "heartburn" suggests it is not a new phenomenon for the disciples. Willard's gloss on

47. Willard, "Spirit Is Willing," 232.
48. Willard, *Guidance*, 138–39.
49. Willard, 238.

the verse explains, "What were they saying to each other? They were recalling that his words always affected their 'heart,' their inward life, in a peculiar way and that this had been going on for about three years. No one else had had *that* effect on them. So they were asking, 'Why did we not recognize him from the way his words were impacting us?' The familiar 'Jesus heartburn' had certainly been a subject of discussion among the disciples on many occasions."[50] The property by which Jesus is identified is not even new. What is new is that Jesus makes himself manifest while withholding the other familiar sense-perceptible confirmations, confirmations that he eventually gives.

This "flickering" manner of interacting with his listeners is preparation for a final word and the inauguration of a new arrangement. The final word, in Willard's own paraphrase, is "Look, I am with you every minute, until the job is done" (Matt 28:20).[51] The arrangement is the ascended absence of Jesus's sense-perceptible body. The "flickering" was not an essential property of Jesus's resurrection body. It was a means employed for teaching.[52]

The Power of Jesus: "All Authority in Heaven and on Earth Has Been Given to Me"

IN THE VACUUM of Jesus's crucifixion and ascension, a parallel positive aspect of Jesus's transcendent kingship becomes visible: Jesus's continuing power. If the first positive aspect was the continuing *presence* of Jesus with his listeners, especially through his speech, the second positive aspect is the continuing *power* of Jesus with his listeners. A vocal but impotent Jesus would hardly suggest to the first listeners that the deliverance gospel they trusted while physically with Jesus continued to

---

50. Willard, 238–39.

51. Dallas Willard, introduction to Willard, *Great Omission*, xiii.

52. A similar interpretation of the postresurrection ministry can be found in Leslie Weatherhead, *The Transforming Friendship* (London: Epworth, 1928), which relies often on W. R. Maltby, "Appendix I," in *After Death* (London: Epworth, 1923), which also contains an interpretation of the resurrection that emphasizes the need to prove both his spiritual and material sides. Jesus is teaching the disciples in the postresurrection period. His unusual manner of appearing is a "hands-on" metaphysics lesson in preparation for a lifelong spiritual fellowship and discipleship.

be valid while he was physically absent. For Willard, the paradigmatic awakening to the ongoing validity of his gospel is not Pentecost but the healing at the Beautiful Gate, already treated in the first stage as an extension of Jesus's ad hoc deliverance ministry.

Willard recognizes that some of Jesus's power was transferable to some of his listeners during his earthly ministry. On his command, the apostles and others were empowered to minister in the Jewish villages without his being present. Then, before he left bodily, Jesus had made intimations that his power would continue to be available. Finally, in light of his ascended absence, a purer understanding of his transcendent power takes root.

The two lectures Willard gave on Acts in 2012 are his longest reflections on this pedagogical theme. There Willard argues for the thesis that Acts is about the disciples' gradual recognition of the availability of "a power without visible position."[53] Willard roots the postascension experience in his familiar exegesis of Genesis 1:26–27, wherein the image of God is about being a person like God and having dominion or rule. But this rule was given with the intent that it be a rule under God, *supplemented by his power*. The power made available in Acts is a part of the restoration of humans to that original arrangement. This links Acts with the second-stage gospel that the kingdom is available *to Jesus's listeners* by means of Jesus's ministry to them. Jesus passes his "crucified" power to his listeners as did Elijah to Elisha.

But while this transition is taking place, how does their vision of Jesus and the kingdom grow, and how does this greater vision change what the first listeners hear as the gospel? Beginning with the very public healing in Jesus's name and the interpretation that "there is no other name under heaven given among men by which we must be saved" (Acts 4:12), *the name of Jesus* is recognized as sufficient for continuing

53. Willard, *Conspiracy*, 278. This is the property of the kingdom's transcendence as applied to Jesus's followers. The kingdom power they have is not connected to their being *next to* any created thing. Indeed, the two passages where Willard believes "crucified" refers to the workings of the kingdom (Gal 3:1; 1 Cor 2:2) refer to the working of the kingdom in the manifestly powerful but psychologically weak rhetoric of Paul.

the already familiar "mighty works and wonders and signs that God did through [Jesus]" (Acts 2:22), what Willard sums up with the term *deliverance*. The name *Jesus* was experientially spotted as something that gives "human beings *access* to the kingdom of God and brought that kingdom into play in the course of human deliverance."[54]

In the lectures that would become *Knowing Christ,* Willard reveals the philosophical view—that is, semantic realism—that he believes fits with the scriptural talk of names.[55] Beginning with Matthew 18:20, he says,

> *That's what it means to baptize them in the name of the Father, Son and Holy Spirit [Matt 28:19]. It does not just mean get them wet while you say, "In the name of the Father, the Son and the Holy Spirit." When the Bible talks of names—the biblical talk of names—it's always what is called* semantic realism. *That means the object comes with the name. And that's why you don't want to take the name of God in vain. It's because his name is inseparable from him.*
>
> *And we're learning to act in the name of Jesus. One of the things that will stand out if you sit down someday and just read the whole book of Acts through at one sitting. . . . One thing will strike you is how important acting in his name is. . . . It will be clear to you that that is what they were learning in the book of Acts. And the reason for that was they were acting in a kingdom, and in a kingdom you work*

---

54. Willard, *Knowing,* 187 (emphasis mine).

55. The concept of semantic realism is associated with the work of analytic philosopher Michael Dummett, who describes and, in turn, attacks it. Willard deals with the theory of names in "Lecture 6," *Metaphysics* (University of Southern California, Los Angeles, CA, January 26, 1984), MP3/cassette, 1:03:30. Willard says he holds to the "causal," "baptismal," "historical" theory in which naming is not reducible to a description of the object in general terms. This is because objects are not reducible to their properties. There is also something that the properties are properties of, something that in the history of philosophy has been dealt with under the concept of substance. And this is what names pick out.

through the name of the head of the kingdom. That's what gives you authority and power.[56]

How did their ontology of Jesus and the kingdom change when they were confronted with how Jesus's name worked? Willard's answer is that they started to preach Jesus—that is, the name of Jesus—*as* the gospel: "Now what you see [in Paul's speech in Acts 20] is Jesus and the kingdom are coming together. They're not two things. They are one thing. . . . And Paul and the others in the book of Acts, they're gradually closing that gap."[57]

As the gap between Jesus and the kingdom closes, the question of blasphemy starts to assert itself. This is what the Jewish authorities, it seems, are insinuating when they authorized Saul "to bind all who call on [Jesus's] name" (Acts 9:14). The gospel is the availability of the kingdom *of God*. As Willard asserts in the phenomenology of kingdoms, "In a kingdom you work through the name of the head of the kingdom." Thus, if any name was to be used to give access to the kingdom of God, would not *God's name* be used?

But the apostles are acting with kingdom-of-God-like effects in the name of someone they and everyone else assumed to be subordinate in the kingdom. Jesus of Nazareth lives fully *in* the kingdom of God but is not *over* the kingdom. Whose kingdom is processing the checks? Jesus's or God's? This is a further example of the enthymematic quality of the gospel of Jesus. Premise 1: the king's name gives authority or power in his kingdom. Premise 2: Jesus's name gives authority or power in the kingdom of God. The missing conclusion: Jesus is God incarnate.[58]

---

56. Dallas Willard, "The Mission of Christ's People on Earth and Beyond: Being Ready for Forever," *The Knowledge of Christ in the Contemporary World* (Eidos Christian Center, Newport Beach, CA, June 28, 2003), MP3, 13:45.

57. Willard, "On Acts, Pt. 2," 49:00.

58. Perhaps. There are other possible premises that would complete the syllogism. God has perhaps abdicated to Jesus, a created demigod, his "Son." Or God has put the creature Jesus in charge of deliverance, miracles, and signs and has kept other areas of his kingdom to himself. In short, Jesus could be the vassal of the kingdom of God. Another alternative is a form of subordinationism. God and Jesus are intimately involved coworkers, but Jesus is fundamentally a creature and worthy of less respect than God.

But orthodox Christology is not how Willard concludes his exposition of Acts. The following from that two-part series is more typical: "Jesus was the king. And if we don't preach him as king and teach him as king, we'll never make disciples. Because when you preach him as king, you present him as leading a life now on earth of which you can now be a part of. So here is a version of salvation: salvation is being caught up in the life Jesus is now living on earth."[59] At the end of Acts, the first listeners do not quite yet see Jesus as the uncreated creator, a full member of the Trinitarian community. But he is, for all practical purposes, *king* of the transcendent, spiritual kingdom of God and, as such, the author of their salvation. With respect to the two positive aspects of the kingship of Jesus—(1) the communicative presence of Jesus and (2) the personal power of Jesus—the first listeners know they are caught up in the present life of Jesus and therein find salvation.[60] We will return to this in the next chapter.

The King: One with Authoritative Position in the Kingdom of God

LET US RETURN to the ontology that Willard identifies with the secret of the kingdom, the kingship of Jesus. The fundamental understanding that is forming at the climactic end of Jesus's earthly life and in Acts is the *transcendence* of King Jesus. The name of Jesus *did not* have its powerful effect on the basis of any human or sense-perceptible instrumentality. *Nor* was Jesus present and vocal on any such basis.

With this property of transcendence, Jesus's status in the economy of God is manifested as *beyond the human level.* Jesus reveals himself to be ontologically more than what the first two stages assumed of him, more

59. Willard, "On Acts, Pt. 2," 49:00.

60. "Being caught up in the life Jesus is now living on earth" is, incidentally, how Willard would typically gloss being "raised with Christ," who is "seated at the right hand of God" (Col 3:1), a verse that sums up the theology of Col 1–2, especially 1:13: "He has delivered us from the domain of darkness and transferred us into the kingdom of his beloved Son." Willard writes, "[Colossians 3:1–3] and the following verses are pure spiritual-formation verses. But notice how being risen with Christ beyond death is the assumption of it all. This is the kingdom as it expresses itself in Christ and, above all, in the resurrection" (Willard, "Gospel of the Kingdom," 45).

than a *human* teacher of the kingdom and more than a *human* prophet or saint of the kingdom. The ontological relations that the first listeners thought were applicable to Jesus and the kingdom of God are, though not necessarily inaccurate, *not sufficient* to describe the realities they are now in contact with. A new ontological relation needs to be applied to him. In this sense, and in contrast to the last stages of understanding, the first listeners understand Jesus as unique and incomparable.

But at this point, Willard's *historical* exposition of the first listeners' epistemic progression in the New Testament stops. For New Testament theology as a whole, he claims that "the story of the New Testament is the story of increasing understanding of who Jesus was. . . . Only in the later parts of the New Testament does there emerge the concept of Jesus as in fact a *cosmic* Christ spanning all geographical and ethnic differences but also providing, as we have seen, the 'glue' of the universe."[61] Despite writing this, the biblical and historical details of this "story" as it plays out in the later parts of the New Testament are missing in his corpus. Pieces of the conclusion are there, such as what he calls "the cosmic Christ." But Willard mainly *extracts* this Christology from the testimony of Paul, John, and the author of Hebrews. He does not tell the history of how the Christology emerged. And quite possibly no one is in a position to tell that history.

In conclusion, let me try to summarize the foregoing and describe the ontological relation that characterizes the first listeners' current vision of Jesus and the kingdom of God, the third-stage topography. Willard dates *some* first listeners' step into a third-stage topography to the time *prior* to the crucifixion and to any clear awareness of the principle of transcendence as applied to Jesus. John the Baptist and Peter were two who confessed, albeit in a rudimentary fashion, to Jesus's third-stage ontology.

This chapter raises the question of the function of christological titles in Second Temple Judaism and in the New Testament, and more could be said about Willard's views here. Suffice it to say, many of the titles, on Willard's account—such as "Son of God," "Lord," "Son of

61. Willard, *Guidance*, 132.

Man," "Messiah," "the one who is to come," and perhaps even "the prophet"—can be pulled together under a concept of *one with authoritative position in the kingdom of God.*[62] This composite concept is the first stone in Willard's third-stage ontology and Christology. It does not, I think, beg the question of orthodox Christology.

Instead, it describes an inexact third-stage insight characteristic of some of Jesus's listeners before his crucifixion and for some time afterward—namely, that Jesus was in some manner a *unique* and *central* ruler in God's kingdom. He was not to them another in the long line of prophets with a righteousness characteristic of the kingdom of God and the corresponding special privileges and abilities. He was not to them yet another "teacher of Israel" (John 3:10) who could effectively lead others to a full life in the kingdom of God. Such persons were, like Moses, faithful *servants* in God's household (Heb 3:5). But Jesus is a *son* in God's kingdom, which meant to them he had the *authoritative position* to represent God and to act in the name of God—that is, on behalf of God and with God's resources.

This inexact belief is singled out in John 17, when Jesus prays, "Now they know that everything that you have given me is from you. For I have given them the words that you gave me, and they have received them *and have come to know in truth that I came from you; and they have*

---

62. In a Q and A, Willard says that *Messiah* is hard to translate but suggests it means "the one in charge of everything," citing Matt 28:18 (Dallas Willard, "Q & A 4," *Jesus Way*, MP3, 36:30). See also Dallas Willard, "Our Current Situation and the Four Great Questions of Life," *Bringing Christ to the World of the 21st Century* (Northfield Methodist Church, Benoni, South Africa, July 25, 2000), MP3/cassette, 11:15, where Willard paraphrases Peter's statement "You're the messiah" with "You're the man," or "You're it."

"One with authoritative position in the kingdom of God" is my wording and not something I have found in Willard, though I believe it is in line with how Willard uses all these terms. Willard interprets "Son of Man" in the traditional theological manner, as the archetypal human being, and not in the more currently fashionable manner, as in the "Son of Man" from apocalyptic literature (Dallas Willard, "Jesus as Savior and Teacher," *National Faculty Leadership Conference 2002* [Christian Leadership Ministries, Chicago, IL, June 28, 2002], MP3, 6:00). If he did have some appreciation—of which I am unaware—of the Son of Man in the apocalyptic sense, then it too would fit under this heading of an authoritative position in the kingdom of God. Also, for the concept of authoritative position in the first century, Willard looks to the Greek word ἐξουσια, most notably used in Matt 28:18.

believed that you sent me" (John 17:7–8). Later the belief is repeated with a glimpse of what it entails: "O righteous Father, even though the world does not know you, I know you, *and these know that you have sent me.* I made known to them your name, and I will continue to make it known, that the love with which you have loved me may be in them, and I in them" (John 17:25–26). Believing that Jesus came from the Father is not exactly orthodoxy, but it is sufficient to mark a mental topography distinct from the first and second levels. And though in this third-stage insight Jesus's first listeners do not yet acknowledge him as eternally one and coequal with the Father, it is sufficient in its description of reality to enable them to hear the gospel in a new way. This, I hold, is an even-handed way of reconstructing Willard's view of the earliest claim for Jesus as "Lord and Christ" (Acts 2:36).

But the topography, the kingship of Jesus, is not the gospel or salvation. Willard's vision of the gospel and the Christ event makes a subtle but important distinction here. The kingship of Jesus is the biblical ontology *intrinsic to* the gospel. The gospel is *the availability* of the kingdom.

11

THE KING AND SOTERIOLOGICAL DÉJÀ VU

> If I believe that Jesus is the Son of God, that he was uniquely divine, I relate to him differently than if I related to him just as a nice man who had a historical significance. "We ought to be like him" or something of that sort. . . . Now then we have a different kind of person that we relate to.
>
> —Dallas Willard, Hollywood, California, 2004

EXEGETICAL SCHOLARS FROM Athanasius and the fourth-century Cappadocians to the present day have argued that orthodox theology is very old and well attested in the Scriptures. Granted it *is* there, how does it *come to be* there in the apostolic age? On what basis did Jesus's first listeners or their followers conclude that Jesus, the Christ, is God incarnate?

In 1988, Willard penned a short piece for a Baptist student periodical answering the question, *How Can Jesus Be the Son of God?* His argument is, in summary, that the father-son relationship has three characteristics: origination, resemblance in character, and the son's enabled entry into the adult world of work. Jesus shows signs of having all three with respect to God. Therefore, he can be the Son of God and, concludes Willard, "therefore be divine."[1]

Quoting Hebrews 3:5–6, Willard clearly wants his argument for the sonship of Jesus to distinguish Jesus, the son, from Moses, the servant. Willard also clearly wants to avoid metaphysical theory and

1. Willard, "How Can Jesus Be the Son of God?"

provide a minimalist "definition" of the concepts (by use of intensions and extensions) so that thoughtful readers might make sense of the Scriptures. This is, of course, a little incongruent for a philosopher who was not averse to abstract thinking or metaphysical deep dives. But in theology, Willard picked his battles and was ready to leave to mystery doctrines he did not see the value of probing. And, we must remember, he was writing a seven hundred-word article for a student magazine.

The trouble with Willard's argument is that the three characteristics are not the sort of things that are outside the realm of possibility for any human, especially given the God of the Bible's revealed goals for his creatures. Willard himself teaches that humans are created by God (origination), should increasingly take on the character of God, and can have a future working intimately with God. What's more, the Bible refers to persons other than Jesus as potential "sons of God." Indeed, it refers to some as becoming partakers in the divine nature (2 Pet 1:4). Do such persons gain the same relationship to God as Jesus has?

Perhaps this broader use of "son of God" was intended by Willard. If so, he has Pauline authority behind him, which calls the Son "the firstborn among many brothers" (Rom 8:29). But then it seems Willard has not answered the question that many rightly ask. They are not asking how Jesus can be *a* son of God. They are asking how Jesus can be something or somebody who is *uniquely* divine, a *unique* part of the Godhead, a *unique* member of something called the Trinity. They are asking how one knows it.[2]

The Parable of the King

WILLARD, FOR HIS part, spoke of Jesus as "the unique Son of God."[3] But his extant arguments in print or speech seem to lack a level of detail

2. The next chapter, if one wishes, will deal roughly with Willard's second criteria, resemblance in character, while this chapter deals with Willard's third criteria of sonship, of a son's participation in his father's business. But the details are drawn from various parts of Willard's corpus, and the overall argument was inspired more by Willard's general history of redemption than by any explicit statement of his to the effect that *this* is how the first listeners came to the knowledge of Jesus's unique divinity.

3. E.g., Willard, *Disciplines*, 5.

that would shore up this claim as knowledge. Let us pull back for a moment and consider the type of theological research or religious epistemology Willard thought most promising.

Usually with religious epistemology, one is right in assuming that Willard is what Donald Bloesch calls an evidentialist and not a revelationist.[4] For Willard, the Bible is a book of knowledge that is gradually gained through the "Jewish experience" of God and his kingdom. This would include the Jewish experience of Jesus's apostles. What the biblical authors were inspired to write, they *know* on the basis of intelligent reflection on the evidence at hand.

But Willard's realist form of evidentialism, though strongly opposed to idealism and empiricism, was not opposed to divine revelation. In other words, the evidence that one needs in order to come to a certain theological conclusion may first need to be revealed. Not all realities are inertly lying around for human discovery. In this important respect, personal or spiritual reality differs from material reality. Persons, says Willard, must *want* to be seen in order to be seen.[5] Theories of the divinity and humanity of Jesus are not merely rational investigations of what Aristotle called secondary substance, of man-ness and god-ness. If Jesus is anything like what some first listeners claimed he is, they are investigations concerning a real person alive today. And this person may not *want* us to know him. On the other hand, if this person *does want* us to know him, our knowledge will be dependent on his decision to reveal himself to us.

Such revelationism is, in fact, what we find in Willard's writing. He thought that divine agency was essential to recognition that Jesus is the unique Son of God, though he did somewhat conflate it with the recognition that Jesus is the Christ. Concerning regeneration, he writes, "The first clear manifestation of heavenly life in the individual is recognition, hearty confidence that Jesus really is the Anointed One, Christ, Lord. . . . It is not possible for the unaided human being to arrive at such

4. For these terms, see Donald Bloesch, *A Theology of Word and Spirit* (Downers Grove, IL: InterVarsity, 1992), 21–22.

5. Willard, "Recovering the Gospel," 40:30.

a condition."[6] Peter's rock, Willard interprets, is "the confidence that Jesus is the Son of God," a confidence that Peter only had and confessed by means of inspiration.[7]

Though Willard's evidentialism does not exclude revelation, neither does his revelationism exclude evidence and reason.[8] This opposes his account to theological fideism, which tended to be the default position of revelationists in the twentieth century. For Willard, revelation or inspiration does not relieve humans of the hard work of gathering evidence and exploring necessary connections. Some of these clues that lead to the conclusion that Jesus is God may be things that *have been* revealed and now lie open on the pages of history. Such revealed clues are not of the sort that are perpetually hidden until the moment of personal revelation. Having been revealed, they may be found if one is looking.

How revelation, evidence, and reason come together for Willard in his Christology is, I admit, still a mystery to me. My best educated conjecture is that the historical communication of Jesus's divinity is, for Willard, *parabolic*. He often appeals to the parabolic manner of Jesus's teaching and of God's self-revelation in history.[9] Jesus's parables, on one hand, reveal reality to those who *want* to know reality. But on the other hand, they obscure and do not reveal reality to those who *do not want* to know reality. For those who *want* the resolution of the enthymeme, the elements are there in the parable. The same could be said for evidence of God's presence in the world and in one's life. The signs are there, but the conclusion must be wanted.

---

6. Willard, "Spiritual Formation as a Natural Part," 52.

7. Willard, "Our Current Situation," 12:00; cf. also Willard, "Heavens Were Opened," 27:30.

8. Cf. Dallas Willard, "The Morally Responsible Skeptic," *Indiana University* (Veritas Forum, Bloomington, IN, December 31, 1994), MP3/cassette, 1:15:30.

9. For a long discussion of this, see Dallas Willard, "The Gospel of the Kingdom of God and How It Comes: Why Parables?," *The Parabolic Teaching about Christ's Kingdom by Christ* (Harbor Church, Lomita, CA, March 6, 1983), MP3/cassette. Willard probably takes his title, if not some ideas, from A. B. Bruce's *The Parabolic Teaching of Christ* (London: Hodder & Stoughton, 1882).

So much is clear with Willard: no first listener called Jesus Lord by their own cleverness alone. The Spirit was involved in every listener's ultimate step to third-level ontology. Even so, inspiration did not negate the use of human reason and evidence. Such evidence may not have hit listeners in the face every morning like the sunlight. Yes, God *could* have done it that way, Willard argues, but God's usual way with humanity is *parabolic*. The clues, revealed or not, can be seen and followed by those who want the conclusion. Nobody can be forced to know that Jesus is God. Indeed, no one can be forced to know anything!

Beyond offering these clarities and conjectures, I will not attempt to argue one way or another about Willard's theory of the first listeners' route to Jesus's *unique* divinity. As in the three-stage structure of this book itself, I will follow in this chapter my own structure, a soteriological path of reasoning, for I simply have not been able to locate anything sufficiently robust in Willard's corpus. I will also in this chapter begin to refer to Jesus as the Christ, since we will be discussing listeners who are in on this secret.

Soteriology Proper

HAVING PULLED BACK to look at Willard's religious epistemology, let us slowly move back in. When researching this third stage in Willard's corpus, it stood out to me that Willard spoke of three different activities that could qualify as Jesus's way of saving as the king of the kingdom. What stood out is that *for two* of these "kingly" activities, Willard never spoke of the incarnation and the Christ event as essential. They were the sort of thing that God could have done *and did do* in his transcendent reign from all eternity. Indeed, Willard spoke of God as doing both in the history of ancient Israel. Only the third activity depended on an incarnation and the Christ event. Only the third activity would have been news to biblically immersed or even mildly educated Jews.

Though it isn't Willard's language, let's call these first two activities *soteriology proper*, for in Willard's theology, they represent the salvific work of YHWH or, in other terms, of the whole Godhead (i.e., the subject matter of *theology proper*). Soteriology proper may admit some appropriation to different members of the Trinity.[10] But it is not dependent for its integrity on the incarnation and the Christ event.

Whether Willard is right about this distinction or not, it was this recognition that led me to infer that Jesus's first two activities, other than continuing God's salvific work with humanity, had an important secondary function in Jesus's work—that of helping the first listeners identify God with King Jesus and King Jesus with God. Having made that connection, the first listeners were enabled to grasp the news of the third activity that *was* dependent on an incarnation and the Christ event. As the reader may guess, the third activity will be the topic of the next chapter.

In this chapter, I will cover the first two activities and how they played out not only in ancient Israel but also among Jesus's first listeners. Of necessity, I need to cover a lot of territory quickly. But at the end, the reader should have a vision of the Christ's place in God's greater plan of salvation that does not depend on knowing that he is divine but does constantly point to his divinity. One may ask why a biblical or orthodox person would want such a vision, and the answer is that we are still tracking the Christ event *according to the way Christ looked to his first listeners*. We will find that the relevance of soteriology proper to the first listeners' route to the anointed one's unique divinity is the reciprocal relation between Jesus's participation in soteriology proper and his ontological unity with God. To the degree that the Christ is involved in and even responsible for YHWH's recognized form of salvation in Israel, his ontological inseparability from this God is deeply suspected and, we might be so bold to say, rightly deduced.

This answer to the question of how the first listeners concluded that Jesus is God incarnate is, if you will, my contribution to this chapter's topic. It seems quite plausible to me as an entailment of Willard's thought, though his mind on this matter is obscure. Willard's systematic theology, which he will never write, would necessarily start further

10. Cf. Willard, "Entering the Spiritual Disciplines," 7:00; cf. also Willard, "Handout for 'The Soul's Eternal Anchor,'" and Willard's various analyses of "word" and "spirit" in the Bible.

back and spell out his notion of soteriology proper—that is, of salvation as an act of God's kingdom, an act that began long before Jesus's coming and that, beginning with Abraham, took a clear and recognizable form to the people of God. Willard speaks of this recognizable form, or so it seems to me, in two ways that correspond to two major components of God's creation. God enacts salvation (1) from the *disorder* in the cosmos, and he enacts salvation (2) from the *disorder* within the individual person. This is a little extra systematizing on my part, but I trust when the details in Willard's thought are seen, it will not seem an imposition. Let us turn to those details now.

1. Disorder in the Cosmos and the Cosmic Christ

THE FIRST SIDE of soteriology proper wherein Jesus takes a commanding role in the New Testament is the salvation of individuals and groups from the disruption of their bodily and soulish life in the cosmos.

Creation as the Word of God

TO SET UP this form of soteriology, we must first look briefly at the relationship between the kingdom of God and creation in Willard's eyes. As discussed in chapter 6, the kingdom of God is a metaphysically more fundamental reality than creation. It, unlike creation, is from everlasting to everlasting and is basic to God's nature as a personal being. By revealing himself as a king, God reveals something very profound about his nature and how he stands in relation to his creation. Willard tells his audiences repeatedly, "Kingdoms work by words."[11] One could speak of the extent of a person's kingdom as the extent of their ability to speak and make it happen. When this phenomenology of kingdoms is applied to God and his kingdom, it moves into a discussion of ultimate things.

Willard's most detailed exposition of this verbal theory of personhood is found in chapter 6 of *Guidance*. Two secondary sources, clarifying his thoughts further, are found in a 1985 lecture given at Rolling

11. E.g., Dallas Willard, "What Is the Kingdom of God?," *Denver Cohort—Session One* (Renovaré Institute, Colorado Springs, CO, October 13, 2010), DVD, 40:00; cf. Willard, *Guidance*, 135.

Hills Covenant Church, "Personal Guidance 2," and a 1990 lecture given at First Hollywood Presbyterian Church, "The Power of the Word of the Kingdom."[12] In these sources, he uses a basic distinction between the word of God generally and the word of God in creation, in the Son of God, and in the Bible, taking most of his examples from the word of God in creation.

One of his favorite biblical sources for a word-centered view of the kingdom is the story of the Roman centurion requesting Jesus's help with his servant (Matt 8:5–13; Luke 7:1–10). When Jesus offers to come, the centurion suggests that Jesus might "only say the word" and thus heal his servant. The gentile, Willard comments, understands that Jesus's kingdom (like all kingdoms) works by the authority of his words, and Jesus praises the gentile's faith in Jesus himself as one with authoritative position. Jesus does "say the word," and the servant is healed. Willard comments, "What we see here is *trust* based on *experiential knowledge of the power that words of authorized individuals have.* In a personal universe, the word directs actions and events."[13]

Willard supports this biblical ontology of the kingdom through exegesis of a few other choice Bible passages. His 1985 lecture includes an illuminating metaphysical exegesis of Psalm 147:10–20. About it and similar "creation passages" in the Old Testament, he says, "The experience of the word of God in the Jewish nation was one which laid the foundation for the doctrine of the kingdom of God as it emerged and came to fulfillment and presence in Jesus himself, who is the king and brought the kingdom with him."[14] In particular, this psalm reveals the cause of snow, hoarfrost, ice crystals, and cold and the cause of their undoing. Verse 18 states, "He sends out *his word*, and melts them"

12. Dallas Willard, "Personal Guidance 2," *Guidelines for Life in the Kingdom of God* (Rolling Hills Covenant Church, Rolling Estates, CA, March 24, 1985), MP3/cassette; Dallas Willard, "The Power of the Word of the Kingdom," *A Series on What Jesus Believed and Taught—and Lived* (First Hollywood Presbyterian Church, Hollywood, CA, March 18, 1990), MP3/cassette. See also Willard, "Secret Manner of the Kingdom's Working," MP3/cassette.

13. Willard, *Guidance*, 136.

14. Willard, "Personal Guidance 2," 12:30.

(emphasis mine). Creation's developments in weather phenomena are the effect of God's word: God "only says the word." For Willard, such biblical exegesis is support for a comprehensive metaphysical statement: "The word of God lies at the root of everything that exists." God himself is an obvious, albeit unstated, exception.[15]

Jesus as the Source of Creative Words

A COSMOS THAT is caused and upheld by the word of a personal God is the biblical ontology that Willard thinks is generally available to the mildly educated first-century Jew—that is, to any with general familiarity with the Hebrew Bible. It is on the basis of such a reconstruction of biblical literacy in the first century that Willard can make the following statement that bears upon our theme: "The reason why people concluded that Jesus was God, for all practical purposes (so we won't get into a long discussion about Trinity in this session), was that he could speak to anything and it would obey him."[16] Speaking *to anything* and evoking immediate obedience is a property of *God*, the metaphysical source of everything. Historically, Jesus leaves behind him a string of diverse public moments when his speech (e.g., Willard points out that Jesus rarely prayed before he healed or did a miracle) evoked immediate obedience outside of his own body and mind.

His exegesis of the cursing of the fig tree (Mark 11:12–14, 20–25) in a 1992 lecture is a pregnant example because it ties in other aspects relevant to Jesus's authority in the kingdom of God.[17] In the pericope, Peter wonders aloud that the fig tree has withered, and Jesus gives the suggestion and explanation, "Have the faith of God." Willard, who often read the Greek and multiple translations when studying a text, preferred

---

15. Though more research is required here, this doctrine of the word of God and the kingdom is the fundamental insight of Willard's theory of *substance*. See Dallas Willard, "Disciplines for the Spiritual Life" (*Essentials of Kingdom Living*, MP3/cassette, 41:30), where he says, "The word of God is not only nourishment. It is the only substance that there is. The word of God is what holds real bread together."

16. Dallas Willard, "How People Perish," 40:00.

17. Willard, "Role of Faith." Admittedly, the 1992 lecture is a bit jumbled because the stated topic is faith and prayer, but in addressing these realities, Willard assumes and therefore must explain to the audience his unfamiliar metaphysics of creation.

the nuance of the subjective genitive in this instance. He says, "Here is what the faith *of* God is like. Here is a kind of attitude that God has when he decides to do something. God works by the speaking of his word in his kingdom. He is the ultimate source of everything and in control of everything. And here is how God has faith when he acts through his word."[18] Later on, Willard reiterates, "When God creates, he sees through faith the reality of that which he speaks."[19] Whether altogether successful or not as an exegesis of Mark 11, the notion of a disposition of God with respect to what is yet inexistent is the key concept to have before us, for the upcoming question will be in what respect Jesus also has the disposition.

But first we should note the connection Willard makes between "the faith of God" and the metaphysics of creation in Hebrews 11. Willard references the connection in the 1992 lecture but gives it a clearer exposition in his 1985 lecture "Personal Guidance 2." Willard's exegesis of Hebrews 11 is that the biblical kind of faith (there are other kinds) *under-stands* (Hebrews 11:3) the universe's *sub-stance*—that is, that the universe was created by the word of God.[20] In other words, biblical faith sees that "the word of God lies at the root of everything that exists."[21] In fact, the faith described in Hebrews 11:3 is not just the first case of a long list of "faiths" but the model for them all. This biblical faith "understands" the foundation of all visible existence *and* "of things hoped for" in God's invisible speech. Moses "endured as seeing him who is invisible."[22]

Having called Jesus Lord, third-stage listeners are enabled to recognize about their Lord in their ongoing experience with him that his word has the same immediate effect as God's creational word. Lord Jesus has a disposition of faith different from the faith of Moses and Abraham.

---

18. Willard, 7:00.
19. Willard, 9:00.
20. Willard, "Personal Guidance 2," 19:45, 21:45.
21. Willard, 11:00.
22. Willard, 26:30. See also Dallas Willard, "Those He Justified He Also Glorified," *Romans* (Faith Evangelical Church, Chatsworth, CA, November 20, 1977), MP3/cassette, 29:45.

Jesus has a disposition of faith *like God's*; he is free to create and re-create in the physical cosmos *by his mere word.* This is the report of the Gospels, and the same is continued in Acts in the act of praying in Jesus's name. But this initial realization is fodder for what Willard sees as the later New Testament understanding of Jesus—namely, "the concept of Jesus as in fact a *cosmic* Christ spanning all geographical and ethnic differences but also providing . . . the 'glue' of the universe (Col 1:17), upholding all things by the *Word* of his power (Heb 1:3)."[23]

This is pretty close to orthodox theology, but as mentioned, Willard does not tell us *how* the first listeners move from a recognition that *some* things obey Jesus's word to one that *all* things obey his word.

Bread as the Kingdom of Christ

ONE OF THE first listeners' thought-provoking steps on their way to that conclusion is found by Willard in Paul's 1 Corinthians 10. There Paul tells us that the rock, which Moses was severely punished for striking instead of addressing, *was Christ* (1 Cor 10:4). This is why, Willard comments, Moses was punished for *hitting* the rock rather than addressing it with words. The *personal* kingdom of Christ is what stood under (its *sub-stance*) the rock in the desert: "Rocks . . . are things that well might respond to words spoken with the appropriate authority and vision of faith."[24]

It would be advantageous if more evidence of Willard's exegesis of 1 Corinthians 10 were to be found, because the end of the chapter turns to the Lord's Supper, of which Willard had a unique view relevant to this theme.[25] In the 2007 sermon "Incarnation and Celebration," Willard drops a quick summary of his view:

---

23. Willard, *Guidance*, 132.

24. Willard, 138.

25. There is some discussion of it in "Baptisms." See also Dallas Willard, "Disciplines for the Spiritual Life," *A Series on What Jesus Believed and Taught—and Lived* (First Hollywood Presbyterian Church, Hollywood, CA, April 1, 1990), MP3/cassette, 5:45, where he says, "By the way, when you take the Lord's Supper, don't be a consumer. Don't think of it that way. It was never intended in that way. The sixth chapter of John is the place you want to read to understand the Lord's Supper. The Lord's Supper is a symbol of our active participation in the life of Christ."

> *There are many dimensions of [incarnation]. For example, you remember when he gave us the Lord's Supper, as we call it, he used the language 'This is my body'? And what was he talking about? Bread. Now, when you begin to understand the greatness of incarnation, you may no longer need special explanations of what was going on there. Maybe he just meant* bread. *Maybe he just meant bread when he said this is my body. Now, when you begin to understand the greatness of incarnation—in creation, in redemption— . . . you'll never look at bread the same again, when you do that. If you don't understand that, you're going to have to think up some special way that the bread becomes something it ain't.*[26]

Then after passing off the standard Roman Catholic, Lutheran, and Baptist(!) views of the ceremony, he explains that his view will be admitted "if you understand that this is the Cosmic Christ who is standing here and claiming all of it for himself. All of it. This. Is. My. Body."[27]

Being the launchpad to discuss other views of the Supper, his statement about the bread becoming something it is *not* is the best clue to his own. On his view, all bread *is* in its sub-stance an instance of the word of Jesus. Said differently, all bread is the realm of Jesus's *personal* kingdom that, like any kingdom, "works by words." The bread of the ceremony does not *need* to be transformed into Christ's body because it already *is* Christ's body. It would not exist at all if it were not a part of Christ's body. Recalling 1 Corinthians 10, the ceremony's bread is Christ in the same way that the rock at Meribah was Christ.[28] In other talks, Willard calls attention to 1 Corinthians 11:29: "anyone who eats and drinks without discerning the body." He reads "discern" in the same way that he reads "understand" in Hebrews 11:3. In discerning, one under-stands

26. Dallas Willard, "Incarnation and Celebration 2," *Valley Vineyard Sermons* (Valley Vineyard, Reseda, CA, December 16, 2007), MP3, 43:00.
27. Willard, 44:45.
28. See Willard, *Disciplines*, 88. Here Willard speaks of "certain intriguing reinterpretations of remarkable events of the Old Testament" made possible by the transfiguration and the postresurrection appearances of Christ, giving 1 Cor 10:1–4 as an example.

the sub-stance of the bread and drink—namely, that they are the word or body of Christ.

This understanding of the Lord's Supper fits with how Willard teaches about fasting from food. He will often refer to manna in the desert and explain that manna is "congealed word of God." So, with regard to Jesus's citation of the verse, "Man shall not live by bread alone, but by every word that comes from the mouth of God" (Matt 4:4), Willard clarifies that bread or food is also *a word of God*. But man lives by *every* word of God, not just God's bread-word. Hence, fasting is a way of finding sustenance through *other* words of God.[29]

This collection of references to the body and to the Cosmic Christ give expression to Willard's metaphysics of creation. The created cosmos is under the immediate authority of Christ's word. It is, therefore, akin to our body, which is in part under the immediate authority of *our* word. For example, in *Conspiracy*, we are told, "Now, roughly speaking, *God relates to space as we do to our body*." And later, "The traditional Christian understanding is that every physical object and every natural law is a manifestation of God's willing."[30] Willard seems to be conceiving of Christ's body the way Husserl does in his anthropological insight that the person has immediate "say" over his body.[31] In Christ's case, this, however, extends beyond his biological body to the whole of the created cosmos. It is called his body *because* it immediately obeys his word, just as our bodies immediately obey our word.

The Cosmic Christ as Jesus

References to "the Cosmic Christ" are scattered throughout Willard's corpus. With it, he refers not to Christ and the created cosmos ontologically bound together indistinguishably or inseparably. He refers to Christ with reference to his transcendence and authority *over* the human and nonhuman cosmos. It is Christ, "present throughout creation and history, inextricably 'with' the God of all, throughout time

29. Willard, 166.
30. Willard, *Conspiracy*, 76 (Willard's emphasis).
31. See the discussion of *Walten* in chapter 5, note 38.

and eternity."[32] It is a title he at times uses in contradistinction to the title "Jesus of Nazareth," which is the same person with reference to his incarnation into "the finite form of one human personality."[33] That both could be one person is the "seeming paradox" of the incarnation. But Willard regards arenas in a similar manner. Both are realms of Christ's ruling word. As we saw above, bread, as all of creation, is a *dimension* of the *incarnation* generally.

Willard's liberal use of the term *incarnation* here and elsewhere may be troubling to orthodox theologians, as it may seem to water down God the Son's historical assumption of flesh and its consequences. But Willard's rhetorical freedom here comes not from understanding the Cosmic Christ as *an extension* of the assumption of flesh. On the contrary, it comes from understanding the assumption of flesh as an instance of the Christ's rule over the whole cosmos.

In *Guidance*, after a long discussion of creation as a dimension of the kingdom of God, Willard begins a discussion on "The Word of God as the Son of God" and states, "The *redemptive* entry of God on the human scene was therefore no intrusion into foreign territory, but a move into 'His own'—a focusing into the finite form of one human personality."[34] The chapter's structure begins with a treatment of the ruling word of God in creation followed by a treatment of the *redemptive* ruling word of God in Jesus. Their common center in the kingdom of God seems to help Willard make sense of one of the paradoxes of the incarnation—not that a man can simultaneously be God but that a man can simultaneously be master of the universe.

In this same chapter, Willard affirms the ancient Christology of the church that is now more familiarly called the *extra Calvinisticum*, writing, "[In one human personality] as always, the control panel of the whole universe lay ready at hand." He combines this high Christology with an idiosyncratic version of the so-called kenosis doctrine. Willard continues the sentence: "though by a voluntary 'emptying' himself (Phil 2:7), he

32. Willard, *Knowing*, 177.
33. Willard, *Guidance*, 132.
34. Willard, 132.

refrained from all but a very selective use of it."[35] Willard's position, which comports with his doctrine of God, is not the traditional kenosis doctrine in which the Son divests himself of certain divine properties. It is what might be called *sovereign kenosis*.[36] The Word divested himself not of properties or *the possession* of his divine authority—divine attributes always remained properties of his being—but of *the use* of his authority.[37]

If this calls into question whether Jesus can rightly be said to be God during his incarnation, Willard would respond that the economic Trinity is also free to operate in a "sovereign kenotic" manner. The clearest case is Willard's doctrine of omniscience. God is not omniscient because he constantly at all times knows or observes every last thing; God is omniscient because he *can* know everything. His sovereignty allows that he does not have to know everything if he *chooses* not to. Even the doctrine of omnipotence, Willard argues, is not that God is constantly at all times *doing* every last possible thing. It is that he *can* do everything. He can choose what to do and what to know.[38] Willard expressed the alternative to his version of open theism (a label that Willard, on one occasion, embraced, having had sufficient time to explain his full position) as "a theology that presents God as a great unblinking cosmic stare"—a jarring phrase for an ancient view of an omniscient God.[39] But he thought a more biblical view is of a God who may lay aside his power to know or to act when it is teleologically or aesthetically appropriate.[40]

---

35. Willard, 132.

36. There is a distinct similarity to the kenotic doctrine of P. T. Forsyth, an author whom Willard read (*Conspiracy*, xviii). See Forsyth, *Person and Place*, 293–320. For a word on kenosis, see Dallas Willard, "Q & A," *Jesus: The Smartest Man*, MP3/cassette, 39:30.

37. In "Heavens Were Opened" (23:45), Willard says, in the event of his baptism, "Jesus at this point in his ministry had the heavens opened to him as he had not before." On another occasion, he says, "I'm not claiming that the incarnate Christ was omniscient" (Willard, "Q & A," *Jesus: The Smartest Man*, 5:15).

38. E.g., Dallas Willard, "Man's Blindness to God," *Soul's Eternal Anchor*, MP3/cassette, 27:30.

39. Willard, *Conspiracy*, 244–45.

40. Because of Willard's teachings on prayer in *Conspiracy* and elsewhere, he was often asked questions about his position regarding open theism. See, e.g., Willard, "Q & A: Prayer," 10:00.

Short of agreeing with it, understanding Willard's theology proper is important for understanding his view of the incarnation because it is *this God* who is sovereign enough to give up his immediate control and knowledge of the created cosmos who becomes incarnate. "Christ's infleshment," writes Willard, "*really* was no imposed restriction, but instead was the supreme exercise of the supreme power."[41] The focus of it was not imposed by the stipulations of human nature but chosen. Conversely, the freedom to do miracles or know extraordinary things was an exercise of Christ's inherent, natural control over the universe. It was not a gift of God for his adoptive son but rather an expression of Christ's basic being.

Revelation aside, the primary evidence for this Christology is in the immediacy of Jesus's working. Jesus, when deciding or when asked to do something humanly extraordinary, did not need to ask a higher authority for permission or power. This was the observation of the first listeners. As mentioned before, the first listeners in Acts began praying *to Jesus* just as they would pray to God because they understood that he possessed the speaking power to effect what they asked for.

Jesus as Cosmic Savior

WITH WILLARD'S VIEWS of how God creates by the word of God, how Jesus's word has a similar power to God's, and how rocks and bread are the body or kingdom of Christ before us, let us look briefly at soteriology proper—briefly, for much that falls into this category either has been discussed or can be anticipated.

In a few of his lectures Willard alliterates on the human predicament in the cosmos by speaking about "The deadly D's"—namely, dread, deficiency, deprivation, and death.[42] These conditions are rampant in human life as it stands apart from its God. For Willard, there

41. Willard, *Guidance*, 132.

42. Willard, "Spirit and Spirituality," 1:35:00. See also Dallas Willard, "How Our Hearts and Lives Are Broken and the Promise of Healing," *Healing the Heart and Life by Walking with Jesus Christ Daily* (Valley Vineyard, Reseda, CA, September 30, 2003), MP3, 20:00.

are many things from which humanity needs salvation that cannot be reduced to sin.[43] Willard's criticism of "gospels of sin management" is pertinent here—for such gospels are concerned only with dealing with sin, whether individual or social. The implicit belief is that if it were not for sin, we would have no need for God. "The deadly D's" do not necessarily fall under hamartiology, yet they are part of the misery for which humans need God and to which divine salvation mercifully comes.

In chapter 6, we encountered Willard's general characterization of salvation in the Bible as deliverance. When Jesus arrives on the scene and as he lives continues with the first listeners through and beyond his ascension, he, in a manner quite literal and obvious to the people around him, delivers people, to use a formulation taken from Willard's description of the "social" gospel of the late nineteenth and twentieth century, "from deprivation and suffering in this life."[44] But Jesus's acts of deliverance, though not opposed to political action and advocacy, went beyond them. They were accomplished "by words and deeds whose powers lay beyond, or even set aside, the usual course of life and nature (as well as the effects of evil spirits)."[45] Willard's teaching about Jesus's ministry of healing would fit here, as would his teaching about Jesus's victories over the kingdoms of darkness and finally about a more general category of miracles to alleviate human suffering.[46]

Of course, Jesus's work of deliverance was not new; it picked up on a soteriological tradition that God had already established in Israel. Willard highlights this in his myriad exegeses of Old Testament texts in which he, as far as I recall, always emphasizes the saving action of the kingdom and the grace of God in the original context and never uses typology to elicit a New Testament teaching out of an Old Testament

43. Most of these things are listed in Rom 8:35–39, and Willard has an important three-part series on this chapter titled *Living without Fear* (Rolling Hills Covenant Church, Rolling Estates, CA, July 7–21, 1991, MP3/cassette).

44. Willard, *Conspiracy*, 105.

45. Willard, 288.

46. Though Willard discusses these throughout his corpus, of particular interest is his four-part series *Becoming Transmitters of God's Life and Power* (Kempton Park Methodist Church, Kempton Park, South Africa, August 7–8, 1987), MP3/cassette.

text. Thus it was that Jesus's first listeners knew the stories of how YHWH, their God, came near to save his people from all sorts of suffering. All of their eschatological hopes, as misguided and as overblown as they may have been, were possible because they, as Second Temple Jews, believed that YHWH, the Lord of the cosmos, was able and willing to save people from the disruption of their bodily and soulish life in the cosmos.

This is what I am calling soteriology proper. And the sight of Jesus, both before and after his ascension, participating in it with a power and authority seen only in the creator God himself gave the first listeners occasion to contemplate their risen Lord's ontological relation to God. According to Willard, it seems to have been the basis for the doctrine of the Cosmic Christ that Willard encounters "in the later parts of the New Testament."[47]

The difference between the first stage—wherein listeners recognize Jesus as an intermediary for whom the kingdom of God is available and from whom one can receive deliverance from suffering—and the third stage is that in the latter, Jesus is recognized, mainly through the phenomenon of asking in Jesus's name, as one *by whom* the kingdom is available. He is not observed to be lobbying God for their deliverance; rather, he acts for God to deliver. As this power and the corresponding character of Jesus become more established in their understanding of him, Jesus's perceived closeness to God increases to the point of disappearing, and their Christology becomes centrally involved with their theology and soteriology.[48]

47. Willard, *Guidance*, 132.

48. In the lecture "The Kingdom Gospel," Willard makes the claim that many who have received Jesus do not understand the greatness of what they have (30:00). He then proceeds to explain in a gloss on Eph 3:8 "the unsearchable riches of Christ"—four dimensions of "the greatness of Christ" that, when appropriated in faith, will evoke a euphoric response. The first is that "the physical cosmos belongs to Christ and is totally at his disposal" (41:15). The next three are very similar. Second, Christ is "the master of the moral life." Third, we are told of "the security and glorious future of the individual in Christ." And finally, "the future of the created cosmos" is part of the riches of Christ—that is, "the incredible greatness and beauty of the physical cosmos is something

This providential form of soteriology takes other forms as well. Deliverance from "the deadly D's" and other forms of human suffering is an expression of Christ's kingship on the *imposed, negative, and universal* circumstances of cosmic existence. But Christ's kingship also brings his listeners to salvation with respect to their *free, positive, and special* roles in life.[49] In "The Key to the Keys of the Kingdom," Willard writes the following: "Our confidence in Jesus as the one who 'has say over all things in heaven and in earth' (Matthew 28:18) can develop into practical access to the riches of the Kingdom. These riches, in turn, make it possible for us to do the work we have to do, and to live our lives, in the strength, joy, and peace of Christ. Having the keys is not a matter of controlling access to the Kingdom, as is often thought. Keys do not first mean the right to control access, but the enjoyment of access."[50]

There is more to be said here, for Willard is ultimately laying waste to the lay-clergy distinction with respect to access to the kingdom of God. Along these lines, two positive "graces" one finds in Willard's corpus should be discussed: (1) the "grace" (Eph 3:8) of sacrificially serving God in clerical *or nonclerical* work and (2) the "grace" of lifelong learning from Jesus.[51] In light of Jesus's ontology as the Cosmic Christ, both pursuits are safe and reasonable for his listeners.[52]

And yet, having arrived quite close to orthodox Christology, the listeners have not yet heard, as Willard called it, "The Better New Testament Gospel"—better, that is, than the gospel of the kingdom, which

---

that will never pass away" (1:23:45). All of these dimensions—with the exception of the second, perhaps—are subsumed under the cosmic Christ.

49. See Dallas Willard, "Using the Keys to the Kingdom," *Pausing for a Purpose: A Holy Experience for All the People of God* (Azusa Pacific University, Azusa, CA, October 2001), MP3/cassette.

50. Willard, "Key to the Keys," 33.

51. On the former, consider Willard's vision of our future as judges in, for example, Willard, *Disciplines*, chap. 11; and Willard, "The Desire of All Nations," *Spirituality and Mission*, MP3/cassette.

52. See also the writings of E. Stanley Jones for a presentation of Christ's kingly salvation, which is fundamentally cosmic. The writings of Pierre Teilhard de Chardin also have had some general but unspecifiable influence on Willard's thinking on Christ's relation to the cosmos. See especially Pierre Teilhard de Chardin, *Le Milieu Divin* (New York: Harper Perennial, 1960).

the people of Israel had already known. The knowledge that Jesus the Christ also participates in the God of Israel's ancient will to save people from the disorder of cosmic existence does not ensure the success of God's project. It does not, for example, overcome the personal doubts listeners have about it. Knowing and even believing that Jesus is God is *not* the New Testament gospel for Willard. It is a metaphysical fine point, the knowledge of which does not in and of itself advance the saving faith of the first listeners. The contribution Jesus's historical coming does make to their saving faith will be discussed in the next chapter. For the remainder of this chapter, we'll turn to the other side of soteriology proper.

2. Disorder within the Individual Person and the Mystical Christ

THE SECOND ACTIVITY by which Jesus saves as the king of the kingdom concerns the salvation of individuals from the disorder within their own personality—that is to say, from their depravity and corresponding psychological brokenness.[53] Following the New Testament, Willard recognizes that Jesus also takes a commanding role in this side of soteriology proper.

History of the Psychology of Redemption

READERS SHOULD HAVE the sense that we are entering a topic about which Willard had a lot to say. Two books of Willard's pentalogy, *Disciplines* and *Renovation*, are studies in the condition of psychological brokenness and redemption from it.[54] As studies in *the psychology of redemption*,

53. My use of *psychological* here comports with Willard's own use, which encompasses *all parts* that make up the human person, including the body and not just the soul. Psychological brokenness is not a condition from which a small group of humanity suffers—that is, those with soul-based problems. It is *the* human condition in its rebellion toward God.

54. *Renovation* (2002) is the culmination of Willard's lifelong studies in "Christian psychology"—"Christian" because it is a *biblically informed* analysis of the self in terms of its parts and their relations. *Disciplines* (1988) shows some interest in descriptive Christian psychology, making profound contributions toward a Christian view of the body, but this theme is largely under the surface of the main argument. *Conspiracy*

as Willard called it, the arguments of neither of these books have had much overlap with the main theme of this book—that is, with *the history of redemption*. These two books will not tell us, for example, whether there is any difference between how God expected his people's psychological brokenness to be redeemed in the days of the exile as opposed to the days immediately following Pentecost or as opposed to our own days.

This is noteworthy because Willard's view is that the psychology of redemption (or what is more commonly called spiritual formation and soul care) was a developing science or "body of knowledge" in the people of God. This means that God allows knowledge of it to develop as he does other branches of science but also that God allows it to suffer from setbacks and enter "dark ages." Thus, the task before theologians in every age is to retain and recover the wisdom of the past as well as press forward to new knowledge. An example of the former is Willard's attempt to recover for late twentieth-century Protestants the wisdom of the spiritual disciplines. An example of the latter is Willard's appeal for the development of a descriptive *Christian* psychology, one that would inevitably compete with the currently reigning psychologies.[55]

Now, the difference between progress in a scientific field, such as the psychology of redemption, and progress in the history of redemption is that the latter is an account of *divinely initiated* movements in history—times when God changes how he is dealing with (i.e., redeeming) humanity. A teacher might change how they deal with students because the students have reached a place where they are ready for something else. A doctor might change a treatment plan based on how a patient is progressing. By contrast, if there is progress in the field of the psychology of redemption, it may be merely scientific and thus a matter of theologians discovering after millennia how God was prepared to deal with humanity all along—for example, since the days of Jesus. Nothing

(1998) contains a more substantial preview of the Christian psychology that later appears in *Renovation*. Since Willard expanded and fine-tuned his Christian psychology over the years, *Disciplines* did not benefit from his mature thought in that area.

55. See chapter 6, notes 20 and 21.

would have progressed in the history of redemption, only in human knowledge of it. But in the reverse, a genuine divine movement in the history of redemption (like the coming of Jesus) may require scientists of the psychology of redemption to rewrite their textbooks, so to speak.

This is a crucial distinction for this book on Willard's history of redemption. Can anything be located in Willard's corpus that indicates how, with the coming of Jesus, God might have *changed* how he deals with psychological brokenness? It seems there is. In his lecture "The Better New Testament Gospel," Willard emphasizes how, in Matthew 1:21, Jesus will save his people not from the effects of their sins (or hell) but from "their sins." Summing this up as "the cure of sin," he says that it is "where the Old Testament agreement finally flunked and failed."[56]

But before we try to discern what this change is, we must first consider Willard's general concept of psychological brokenness according to the Scriptures. Though the mode of redemption may change over time, as far as Willard is concerned, the underlying depraved condition has not.

Spiritual Deprivation

IN *DISCIPLINES*, WILLARD describes the depraved and corrupt human state as resulting, in part, from a state of *deprivation*.[57] "There is some pervasive and basic lack in human life," he writes.[58] This fundamental lacuna results in all sorts of other dysfunctions and distortions in human existence. So he asks, "*What* is human life being cut off from to leave it in such a sad and depleted condition?" His answer: "It is the spiritual. Disruption of that higher life wrecks our thinking and valuation, thereby corrupting our entire history and being, down to the most physical of levels. It is this pervasive distortion and disruption of human existence from the top down that the Bible refers to as sin (not

---

56. Willard, "Better New Testament Good News," 0:30.
57. "The light had gone out in their soul," says Willard, among other things, about Adam and Eve in Willard, "Man's Blindness to God."
58. Willard, *Disciplines*, 62.

sins)—the general posture of fallen humankind."[59] "The spiritual," as used here, is a collective term for Willard that refers to God above all but also more generally to the unseen world and all that God is doing in it.[60] The opposite is collectively "the natural"—basically, the spiritually unaided cosmos, including our nonphysical souls (understood in Willard's very specific sense) and bodies. The spiritual dimension of the human (mainly human minds and wills) wavers in the middle, so to speak, and will operate wholly in terms of "the natural" *if* the unseen spiritual world of God is closed off to them.

At work in Willard's assessment of life is a reprisal of the tradition of Aristotle and Aquinas, an attempt to discern within life as a whole a hierarchy of life.[61] With these seminal thinkers, Willard ranks the "souls" of living beings according to their levels of functionality "to relate other things in certain specific ways" and to assimilate them.[62] This is what nonliving things such as washing machines and crystals do not do. In the words of Aquinas, a tulip has a nutritive soul (*anima nutritiva*) but not a sensitive soul (*anima sensitiva*) as a fish does, whose specific soul also encompasses the nutritive function. A human has an intellectual soul (*anima intellectiva*) that encompasses functionalities lacking in the tulip or fish.[63]

At all levels, a living thing is characterized by sensitivity to external realities. A tulip can reach out and assimilate nutrients, whereas a fish's soul is sensitive to the worlds of motion and perception. A kitten, in Willard's poignant example, reaches out and assimilates the realities of play. But backward down the line, each life-form is dead to (in their essence incapable of appreciating) external realities that are nevertheless very real. Kittens do not care about poetry. Though poetry is real, kittens cannot interact with it.

---

59. Willard, 63.

60. This use of "the spiritual" comports with a way in which Willard understood the kingdom of heaven in his earlier thought, most evident in the series *The Kingdom of God* in 1978. I believe this way fades in his mind.

61. Willard, *Disciplines*, 56–58; Willard, *Guidance*, 156–61.

62. Willard, *Disciplines*, 57.

63. Thomas Aquinas, *Summa Theologiae* 1a. 76, 3.

What Willard has in mind with "the spiritual" is another set of very real external realities that a living being *could* be sensitive to—that is, could reach out to and assimilate—or *could* be dead to. Naming the set of external objects is easy. Willard has in mind God and his spiritual, unseen kingdom. These are what a human could be alive to, could reach out to and assimilate. It is our deficiency in these realities that leads to psychological brokenness. However, conceiving of what Willard has in mind with *the power* of humanity that interacts with "the spiritual" genus of things is difficult, mainly because it is difficult to conceive of the will—when you distinguish from it mind, body, and soul—as reaching out and assimilating.

At the time of his writing of *Disciplines* (the mid-1980s), Willard speaks of the spirit as if it were another level of soul functionality (*anima spiritualia*). But Willard's psychology was still developing even after he became a published author. A sermon series, *The Soul*, from 1990 shows that he had an earlier period of believing that the will/heart and the spirit referred to two different functionalities in the person.[64] But by the time he publishes *Conspiracy*, he feels biblically obligated to connect the spirit with the will or heart—the psychology familiar to most readers. Looking backward, Willard's various descriptions of the will do not easily fit into *Disciplines*' description of the spirit—that is, of that in the human person that reaches out and assimilates "the spiritual." Will, says Willard, is self-initiating and *self-sustaining* and indicates the image of God in humanity.[65]

At any rate, will/spirit/heart is not something that dogs and elm trees have or are.[66] In *Renovation*, Willard, let us say, updates the assimilation

---

64. Cf. Dallas Willard, *The Soul* (Valley Vista Christian Community, Sepulveda, CA, August 5–19, 1990), MP3/cassette; esp. "An Introduction to Your Soul," 31:00. This seems to be the psychology out of which *Guidance* and *Disciplines* were written. Willard's change of mind does call into question how we are to understand "the spiritual" in 1984's *Guidance* and 1988's *Disciplines*. See note 60 of this chapter.

65. Willard, *Renovation*, 34.

66. "You have in you an element of the spiritual even if it is dead. See, a dog isn't spiritually dead because it doesn't have a spirit. You have to have a spirit to be spiritually dead" (Willard, "Session 1—Part 2," 24:30). See also Dallas Willard, "Out of the Furnace of Feeling: Escaping the Tyranny of Feeling, Passion & Emotion," *Healing the Heart and*

teaching of *Disciplines*, describing the will as the power that primarily negotiates human contact with "the spiritual"—that is, with God—and he writes, "The God-intended function of the will is to reach out to God in trust. By standing in the correct relation to God through the will we can receive grace that will properly reorder the soul along with the other five components of the self."[67]

This notion of willed dependence on God in trust is given further expression in chapter 4 of *Renovation*, where Willard discusses Calvin and self-denial, death to self, and taking up one's cross. Supplementing this written material in a 2006 sermon, Willard says, "God does not control us mechanically. If you wish, God controls us by invitation. And so, I think, no one understood this better than John Calvin because when you read what he has to say about the spiritual life, you'll see how he recognizes it's opening ourselves to God."[68] That is to say, the deprivation under which a human being suffers and that leads to further corruption in all dimensions can be summarized as an unwillingness to surrender their will to God. This is a colossal theme in the field of the psychology of redemption, and Willard likely has appropriated it from medieval Rhineland mysticism and the nineteenth-century holiness movement just as much as he has from Calvin and the Reformed tradition. The gist is that there is some external reality upon which human life depends and the absence of which causes a state of deprivation and dysfunction.

Original or Unoriginal?

WITH THIS HIERARCHY in mind, let us think briefly about how Willard conceives of the doctrine of sin. Whatever it means for the theory of evolution, Willard has some respect for the traditional theory of a literal Adam and Eve, and he did seem to believe that historically there was a time when humans—that is, Adam and Eve—lived in an integral state:

Life by Walking with Jesus Christ Daily (Valley Vineyard, Reseda, CA, October 14, 2003), MP3, 29:15.

67. Willard, *Renovation*, 40.

68. Dallas Willard, "Cruise Control, Self Control, & God's Control," *Canoga Park Sermons* (Canoga Park Presbyterian Church, Canoga Park, CA, August 6, 2006), MP3, 28:15.

"Human beings once were alive to God. They were created to be responsive to and interactive with him. Adam and Eve lived in a conversational relationship, daily renewed, with their Creator. Their mistrust and disobedience toward God cut them off from the realm of the spirit. . . . Biologically they continued to live, of course. But they ceased to be responsive and interactive in relation to God's kingly cosmic rule."[69] Structurally, we have the first two of Thomas Boston's fourfold state: the integral state and the state of nature.[70] But the fall, or what Willard creatively called "the leap," is not, in its essence, a transgression of God's law, though it is that too. It is a morally reprehensible intention of the human will to depend on something other than God. This chosen disposition cuts Adam and Eve off from "the spiritual," which was meant to be a central external source of their existence, that on which they most depended. The resultant state of being cut off, deprived, is not necessarily sinful (though the initial act was), but it does make psychological brokenness and further sins inevitable. In different language, Willard calls this a state of "vulnerability and the necessity to take care of themselves."[71]

Next, we must wade into more treacherous waters: the effect of Adam and Eve's "leap" on their posterity and the doctrine of *original* sin. Though in Willard's early years he carefully worked through the theology of Charles Finney, he never makes mention, to my knowledge, of the careful distinction (very important to Finney and all New School Calvinist theologians) between physical and moral depravity.[72] Augustine

---

69. Willard, *Guidance*, 156–57. See also Dallas Willard, "Life, Death and Immortality in the New Testament," *How Jesus Abolished Death and Brought Immortality to Light through the Gospel of God's Kingdom* (Rolling Hills Covenant Church, Rolling Estates, CA, February 29, 1984), MP3/cassette, 10:30; and Dallas Willard, "Thinking Good Thoughts about God," *Sermon* (Valley Vista Community Church, Sepulveda, CA, June 25, 1988), MP3/cassette, 27:45.

70. Thomas Boston, *Human Nature in Its Fourfold State* (1720), many editions.

71. Willard, "Life, Death and Immortality in the New Testament," 14:30.

72. Possibly Willard's word for physical depravity is *corruption*. This would imply that the ruin, malformation, and dysfunction of the various dimensions of the self that Willard discusses in *Renovation* are examples of physical depravity. Moral depravity refers, then, to a condition of the will.

is the thinker most associated with the doctrine of physical depravity, as the New School called it. Eighteenth-century New England's Jonathan Edwards, Joseph Bellamy, and Samuel Hopkins and, much more so, their New School successors are associated with calling it into question. These evangelical theologians generally held to a doctrine of *moral* depravity.

The New School position is less familiar in our day, so it deserves a short summary before we continue. New School theologians with and after Edwards accused Augustine and Old School figures like Thomas Boston and even John Wesley of making depravity a matter of basic human nature, a natural or physical inability to love God and neighbor. Just as a quadriplegic is not able to swim because he lacks the basic physiology for it, so in the Old School model an unregenerate sinner is unable to love God and neighbor because that sinner lacks *the basic psychology* for it. Consistent Calvinists, as the New School styled themselves, considered this a theological inconsistency (How could God *justly* require humans to do what is, given their psychology, impossible to do?) and proposed that the unregenerate sinner must have a *natural* ability to love God and neighbor but does not have the *moral* ability. This means that the sinner *can* love God and neighbor but does not *want to*. This is a distinction of which Willard was certainly aware from early on in his adult life. It is impossible to miss if you read much at all of Finney.

To tease out Willard's unique position, we should first take note that his book *Disciplines* seems to situate him in the Augustinian tradition of natural depravity. He commends Augustine's description of human depravity as proceeding from a state of deprivation, a lack of positive good. Natural-born humans lack something that renders them incapable of loving God and neighbor. They must be reinstated before they can act rightly. This basic deprivation leads to their corruption, says Willard: "Humans are not only wrong, they are also *wrung*, twisted out of proper shape and proportion."[73] Such statements would suggest that "physical depravity" is a passable way to describe Willard's

73. Willard, *Disciplines*, 63.

reason for why humans do not love God and neighbor. They simply cannot. Willard's word for physical depravity is, quite possibly, *corruption* along with its synonyms *ruin*, *malformation*, and *dysfunction*. If true, then all of his books, especially *Renovation*, are deeply committed to a version of physical depravity.[74]

But this raises the question of *original* sin. Where did this psychosocial physical depravity come from? We know that Willard read Yale professor George P. Fisher's book *A History of Christian Doctrine*, released shortly after the end of New School theology, which is careful to note, for each theologian discussed, their respective opinion on original sin. Yet with all this before him, Willard does not seem to take over any traditional theory. For example, he shows no signs of considering federalism as an alternative to the Augustinian theory.

In Augustine's familiar theory, it is *corruption itself*, depravity itself, that is passed on to each generation. Hence Anselm, following Augustine's doctrine, feels he must explain Christ's incorruption in light of Christ's biological connection to humanity.[75] For Willard, it is *only deprivation* that continues across the generations. And deprivation is not exactly "passed on" to the next generation like some congenital defect,

---

74. This Augustinianism goes quite far back in Willard's history. Some of the most valuable material on Willard's hamartiology is found in a series he did in 1974 for Woodlake Avenue Friends Church and later at Shepherd of the Valley Lutheran Church. Willard failed to come up with a title for the series, and it was referred to in those days as the series of the "blue sheet" because of the blue paper of the first outline. For years, I was only familiar with this important series in the form of an inexact transcript and two separate outlines and handouts. Recently, some fragmentary recordings have come to light that I, as their curator in the Dallas Willard Research Center, have only cursorily reviewed. The series has since been titled *The Psychology of Redemption*.

Regarding its hamartiology, Willard's first class assignment is that participants study the word *corrupt* in the Bible. Later, working with Romans, he carefully divides between *sins* and *sin*, which he calls a "psycho-social reality" and a "condition" (Dallas Willard, "Some Crucial Concepts for Understanding God's Way to Blessedness: Handout for 'The Psychology of Redemption,'" 1974, Dallas Willard Collection). In exegeting Paul's use of sin in Rom 5:12–14, he says, "Sin here is not an act; it is a state of the soul" (Dallas Willard, "The Condition of Sin," 11:30). Cf. Willard, "Residency Part 2" (4:30), where Willard says *sin* in the singular is a broken soul; it is something that you are.

75. Anselm of Canterbury, *The Virgin Conception*, many editions.

because what humans lack is not a *natural* endowment, something that could be imbued to anyone at natural birth. What is lacked is not something psychological or biological or sociological at all. Rather, postfall humans are cut off from "the spiritual Kingdom of God," as Willard calls it in *Disciplines*—that is, they suffer from an absence of something ontologically external to them but something on which they nevertheless depend for their well-being and full existence.[76]

In one turn of phrase, Willard calls this fallen state "spiritual starvation," and this is enlightening.[77] Food and water are not constituents of the human person, but their absence has a crippling effect on the person. Hence, *natural* inability does not describe the problem of starvation. Famished humans *can* take food; they do not *have* food. The crippling condition is external to the person. One may speak of children born into famine "inheriting" deprivation. But not in the same way that they inherit biological features.

Though being born into a state of spiritual starvation does seem an improvement on directly inheriting corruption, the end result does appear much rosier. Again and again, Willard appears to follow the argument present in Jonathan Edwards's treatise on original sin. Edwards tells us that humans are created with lower and higher principles—the lower sometimes being called flesh and the higher divine nature or spirit.[78] In the fall, God withdraws from the human personality, taking with him the superior principles coherent with his indwelling.[79] With only lower or natural principles to guide them (which Edwards, in contrast to Willard, construes negatively), it was inevitable that humans would become depraved.[80]

On the precise nature of depravity and the individual person's own culpability, it seems that Willard is most aligned with the moral philosophy of Finney, who writes, "Moral depravity, as I use the term,

---

76. Willard, *Disciplines*, 65.
77. Willard, 63.
78. Jonathan Edwards, *Original Sin*: *Works of Jonathan Edwards*, vol. 3 (New Haven, CT: Yale University Press, 1970), 361.
79. Edwards, 362.
80. Edwards, 363.

consists in selfishness; in a state of voluntary committal of the will to self-gratification. It is a spirit of self-seeking, a voluntary and entire consecration to the gratification of self. It is selfish ultimate intention: it is the choice of a wrong end of life; it is moral depravity, because it is a violation of moral law."[81] Willard—in contrast to Finney, we should note—had a graver appreciation for the overall corruption of personality that ensued as a result of this moral depravity.

With a precision lacking in older theologians, Willard takes the doctrine of sin yet further in his theory of human development—that is, of spiritual formation.[82] Our family and social contexts, though not through propagation, do, in fact, contribute strongly to our corruption because they are primarily responsible for our formation. Back in 1974, he said, "You can catch sin and all of us have done it. We caught the condition from those around us who had it."[83] Having not been born alive to "the spiritual," we are susceptible to whatever influences come our way: mostly bad and, mercifully, also some good.[84]

Though I hope there are more to be found, I only know of one reference that clearly indicates Willard's alignment with a non-Augustinian position on how sin is transferred generationally. In an aside in a sermon, he says, "You came out, *I believe* (this is a long discussion in itself), you came out in mint condition, as we say. But pretty soon you came to be bumped up."[85] "Mint condition" is not exactly a traditional theological term, so it is difficult to know where exactly it places Willard. He was not unaware that Eastern Orthodoxy had a long history of being unable to see the worth of Augustine's doctrine of original sin and also that

81. Finney, *Systematic Theology*, lecture 38, 373.
82. Willard, *Renovation*, 19.
83. Willard, "The Condition of Sin," 11:45.
84. In this view, Willard is largely in line with Horace Bushnell's theory of Christian nurture in *Christian Nurture* (1847; repr., New Haven, CT: Yale University Press, 1960).
85. Willard, "Introduction to Your Soul," 26:00. For a reference to "original sin" as the malformation and "bumping up" that we receive from our surroundings before we can make conscious choices, cf. Dallas Willard, "Spiritual Disciplines for Liberation into Eternal Life," *Learning to Live an Eternal Life Now* (Ojai Valley Community Church, Ojai, CA, May 4, 1994), MP3/cassette, 41:30.

others within the Western tradition (such as New School Calvinists) called it into question.

It is an important qualification to Willard's position that the mint condition of our birth does not indicate a reiteration of the integral state of Adam and Eve. Adam and Eve's sin was a historical event that had wide-ranging consequences for the *whole* human race. "Mint condition" indicates how Willard refuses to make corruption something that is given to persons in the same way that their DNA and other natural endowments are given to them in natural birth.[86] Something is "inherited" from Adam and Eve by their posterity, but it is not sin or guilt.

Let us consider original sin from another perspective. Recall how in his exegesis of John 3 Willard takes the phrase "born of water" (John 3:5) to refer to natural birth.[87] For Willard, universal depravity in

86. But can Willard's deprivation solution to original sin resolve the problem that Edwards and his school identify? Is God unjust to require the spiritually unborn to love God and neighbor? Willard's partial answer can be found in his 1987 "Faith, Hope and Love" article, which treats faith, hope, and love as *divine gifts* essential to Christian moral life, precisely the sort of thing newly born humans are deprived of:

> There is surely required some comment on where this leaves the non-Christian. Without the "can" they obviously do not have the "ought." They might seem to be absolved of responsibility for the Christian virtues (though I would prefer to say they are deprived of the opportunity). But we should perhaps say instead that, while they do not have the "can" of indwelling divine love, they nevertheless can obtain it. They have, in Aristotle's language, the potentiality for receiving divine love. Somewhat as a child who cannot do numbers can learn to do them, or the person who cannot drive safely while drunk can (at least in some cases) avoid drinking, and thus drive safely. (Willard, "Faith, Hope and Love")

A fallen human does not lack the psychology to love God and neighbor, but they lack the divine gifts of faith, hope, and love and are responsible for their actions because they *could* avail themselves of those necessary resources through the additional birth. The question then becomes, Is God unjust for making the all-important spiritual birth so contingent on historical accidents and errant humans? But here we find not an exhaustive answer in Willard's corpus but merely the assurance that God in his providence is trying to get as many people into fullness of life in the kingdom of God as possible. God is seeking this end without compromising the one thing that he in his wisdom considers the most important trophy of human history: individuals of inherent dignity and impeccable character.

87. Willard, *Guidance*, 157.

humanity comes not from humans being "born of water" but as a result of their *not* being "born of Spirit."[88] Natural birth does not in and of itself confer spiritual birth or regeneration. Thus, Willard would often call the latter "the *additional* birth"—that is, the birth that is added on to the first.[89] We read, "It was necessary for God to confer an additional level of life on [Adam and Eve] and their children through 'a birth from above' in order for them once again to live unto God, to be able to respond toward and act within the realm of the Spirit."[90] This birth is what is perpetually absent from the human race in natural birth after Adam and Eve. It is the negative fact, the absence of a spiritual birth, that results in "vast positive evils," in the psychological brokenness and universal depravity that we see around us.[91] It results not necessarily in *total* depravity but in "enough depravity," as Willard would wryly say.[92]

This connects well with what Willard has to say about the family, which was already addressed in part when we considered his view of Malachi 4:5–6 in chapter 9. Given the evangelized psychology of the human person, a child quite receptively and trustingly accepts the spoken or unspoken gospels present in their family. Though birthed in "mint condition," the child's naive contact with the *mental* brokenness in human life, primarily in family life, results in the child's *mind* being captured by false gospels and false notions of God and consequently to the child's *heart* not being open to "the spiritual," to God and his invisible kingdom. The result is a child who reincarnates the psychological brokenness of their family and society. This same pattern of contagious corruption is repeated in other dimensions of the self, such as the body and soul. Willard does have the idea that some rare children may

88. "Not born" is effectively the same as "dead," and this is precisely how we find Willard interpreting "dead in trespasses and sins" (Eph 2:5). A person not born into the world of the spiritual, "alive to God," falls very easily into a "life" of trespasses and sins because persons were made to depend on God for their well-being.

89. Willard, *Guidance*, 157.

90. Willard, 157.

91. Willard, 63.

92. Willard, "Spirit and Spirituality," 58:45.

escape much of this destructive cycle by the grace present in an extraordinary family.[93] But Willard maintains, both humorously and seriously, that school recess will, in that case, bring the familiar corrupting effect on the child.[94]

Finishing briefly with *Renovation*, the same teaching about deprivation leading to psychological brokenness and moral depravity is presented, but in a different form. *Renovation*, as referred to above, is much clearer than *Disciplines* on the centrality of *the will* in this process (the latter being focused mainly on the body). In *Renovation*, we encounter two key figures: the human self diagram and the two orders of dominance.[95] The diagram shows the "Word and Spirit of Christ" entering the center of the human person and the ideal result of "Faith in Christ Which Re-establishes Communion with God" coming out. Word and Spirit are a typical way for Willard to parse "grace" (or that which has been absent since the fall) coming into human personality. Again, he writes, "By standing in the correct relation to God through our will we can receive grace that will properly reorder the soul along with the other five components of the self."[96] Deprivation is an absence of this interaction and results in the ruined condition of the whole person.

Likewise, in the other figure, the order of dominance in life away from God places God last in line. Without God, the parts of the person interact according to a different flow with the spiritual dimension of humans taking orders from the more "earthly" dimensions of body and soul. This is, for Willard, Paul's "mind . . . set on the flesh" (Rom 8:6–7). Willard confesses in one talk that he takes these orderings from Augustine, probably from *City of God* XI–XIV.[97]

---

93. Again a position quite in line with Horace Bushnell. I do not think Willard's statements to this effect should be taken as a position that such a child never sins; rather, the gospel of the kingdom is present in their life from time immemorial.

94. Willard, "How Our Hearts and Lives Are Broken," 30:15.

95. Willard, *Renovation*, 38–41.

96. Willard, 40.

97. Dallas Willard, "The Assumptions of Spiritual Direction," *Supervision as Ministry Conference* (Southern Baptist Theological Seminary, Louisville, KY, September 20, 1994), MP3/cassette, 22:45.

In summary, Willard stands in the Augustinian Old School tradition by locating the cause of human evil in the privation of good, especially in the privation of "the spiritual," resulting in a kind of starvation. And this perennial curse of deprivation results in corruption across all the dimensions of the human person, mind, body, soul, and so on and results in people who cannot and indeed do not love God and neighbor. Our family and social contexts add to this corruption thanks to their inevitable involvement in our spiritual formation. But Willard also stands in the Edwardsian New School tradition by not thinking of the sinful human condition in terms of *innate*, *original*, or *socially transmitted* depravity. We are born in "mint condition," whatever that means. But due to our lack of a birth from above and to our formation in our sin-soaked world, we have become selfish in our wills and dependent on ourselves. A doctrine of *original* sin concerns how Adam and Eve's sin and/or guilt is *somehow* universally passed on to their posterity. And for Willard, what is continued (but not exactly passed on) from its origin in Adam is deprivation, not depravity.

Hebrew Mysticism

HAVING BEFORE US the disorder within the individual person that soteriology would heal, we can consider the history of redemption once more. Since Adam and Eve, the basic solution has been a reawakening to "the spiritual," the missing element of human life.[98] Or in other words, regeneration. I touched on this major theme of Willard's thought in chapter 6 and had occasion to speak of its connection to faith and, therefore, of Abraham as regenerate. In this history of redemption and in the coming of Jesus the Christ, nothing changed with the basic biblical solution to the basic human problem. The depraved human personality must be made alive to the spiritual world of God through faith so as to gradually bring the whole person into balance and order, with love of God, self, and neighbor as natural results.

---

98. Willard, *Disciplines*, 65. There Willard calls it "the appropriate relation to the spiritual Kingdom of God."

But regeneration only names the beginning. The middle, as it were, is sustained by even more of the presence and action of God in, on, and around the souls of his people. Let us call the theory of these middle biblical phenomena (or what amounts to the other side of soteriology proper) *Hebrew mysticism.*[99] One may recall from chapter 5 the "baptism of Moses," which refers to God's practice of becoming manifestly present in the midst of the covenant people. This was one of God's ways of sustaining his people in "the spiritual," but it does not exhaust, for Willard, the phenomena described in the Old Testament and continued in the New Testament.

The With-God Life (1)

WILLARD SUMS UP Hebrew mysticism in his proposal for the unity of the Bible. He urges those who would read "the Bible as a whole" to trace the concept of "with God" through the various sacred writings to discover what he calls the Immanuel Principle.[100] In his contribution to the introduction to *The Life with God Bible*, he writes, "Indeed, the unity of the Bible is the development of life 'with God' as a reality on earth, centered in the person of Jesus."[101] This then leads him to say, "The Immanuel Principle is found, after all, to be a *cosmic* principle that has all along guided God in creation and redemption."[102] In his usual exposition of Old Testament literature, he also highlights individuals such as Isaac, of whom it was said, "We see plainly that the Lord has been with you."[103] In some of his recorded lectures, he calls divine presence "the blessing of Abraham," a phrase taken from Galatians 3:14.[104]

---

99. For context for how I am using *mystical* and *mysticism*, I refer readers to one of Willard's favorite books: James Stewart's *A Man in Christ* (London: Hodder and Stoughton, 1935), esp. 160–73.

100. Willard's two plenary contributions to Renovaré's conference "The With-God Life: The Dynamics of Scripture for Christian Spiritual TransFormation" are excellent sources for his view (Renovaré International Conference / Spiritual Formation Forum, Denver, CO, June 20, 2005).

101. Dallas Willard, "Catching the Vision," in Foster et al., *Renovaré Spiritual Formation Bible*, xxvii.

102. Willard, xxviii.

103. Gen 26:28; Willard, *Conspiracy*, 68–69.

104. Willard, "Gospel of the Kingdom," 1:16:00; Willard, "Life in the Spirit," 1:03:00.

This is somewhat a departure from his theology in earlier recordings, in which Willard spoke often of Israel as a social order under the governance of God. In its ideal form, uncorrupted by the political monarchy, true Israel was an instantiation of the kingdom of God on earth. The influence of Bright's conception of the kingdom as centered on the Mosaic covenant or law is evident here.[105] But in later recordings, such as this one from 1997, the following is more characteristic:

> *They [the Jews] have to now understand that Jesus is making a new life available to them. And they don't have to go through the rituals to get it! God had made the kingdom of God available in the people of Israel. . . .*
>
> *We, as Christians, when we look back at Jewish history, we're apt to not realize what an incredible presence there was in the people of Israel. And it never stopped. They thought it, when they tore down the temple and hauled them all off . . . , they thought this was the end of it. And they got up there and found out God was still alive. . . . God does not withdraw. And his presence in the people of Israel, we must always thank God for that; it never ceased.*[106]

105. Bright, *Kingdom of God*, 24–30; Willard, "Presence of the Kingdom," 24:45; Willard, "Kingdom Righteousness," 13:00. See also Willard's old series *The Book of Matthew* (Rolling Hills Covenant Church, Rolling Estates, CA, 1972).

106. Dallas Willard, "Kingdom Living," *Leadership in the Kingdom*, MP3/cassette, 25:00. The difference in Willard's mature view is that the kingdom of God is available *in* and *to* the covenant people but is not identified *with* the covenant people. His mature view—though still captured by transcendent concepts of the people of God such as the remnant, the body of Christ, the church militant, or the continuing incarnation—is more careful about distinguishing the heavenly manifestation of the kingdom on earth from the people of God. Without clearly distinguishing these, Willard's thought falls prey to his own theological criticisms. Though concerned about the two gospels of sin management in early years, from at least 1998, Willard speaks against the gospel of churchmanship. Believing this to be present in Protestant as well as Catholic and Orthodox circles, he perhaps had *his own* earlier teachings in mind. Needless to say, more research into the development of his thought in this area is necessary.

The quote draws attention to the salvific presence of God, "new life," *within* the older arrangement, which included the institutions and rituals. It is a statement of God's corporate and generic presence in Israel, not of its presence to individuals and not of its specific form. More of this has been discussed in previous chapters.

Beyond these grand sweeps, Willard does not finely slice or systematize the presence and action of God in this history of Israel. One could wish for more detailed analysis of the psychology of redemption as the people of God understood it before Jesus. A few glimpses of detail are, however, present in Willard's corpus.

In his lecture "The Old Testament Good News about the Kingdom," Willard draws together the leading individuals Abraham, Moses, and David under the property of "a tender and sensitive heart before God."[107] He, intriguingly, uses circumcision to illustrate this point. In the notes for the lecture, he puts it this way: "This tender relationship is the meaning of circumcision, the mark of the Abrahamic covenant (Gen 17:10–14). As the head of the penis without its foreskin is tender and unprotected, so is the heart of the person who would live from God."[108]

In *Renovation*'s chapter on the soul, Willard draws out the Old Testament testimony to the role of God in the wholeness of the soul: "The book of Psalms is, of course, the great 'soul book' in the Bible, simply because it, more than any other, deals with life in its depths and with our fundamental relationship to the One who is the keeper of our soul (Psalm 121:7)."[109]

Finally, in *Renovation*'s chapter on the mind, Willard turns to worship, a key aspect of the Psalms and no secret to Israel, writing, "Worship is the single most powerful force in completing and sustaining restoration in the whole person."[110] Other examples of Willard's exegeses of Old Testament texts and phenomena could be added here as well—for

107. Willard, "Old Testament Good News," 10:30.

108. Willard, "Handout for 'The Soul's Eternal Anchor.'"

109. Willard, *Renovation*, 207. See also Willard, "People of God in Prayer and Worship," 769–72.

110. Willard, *Renovation*, 107.

example, his teachings on the temple of God and the city of God and on the heavens.

THE HEARING-GOD LIFE (2)

IN ADDITION TO the presence of God and his interaction with the person more generally conceived, Willard highlights a specific aspect of Hebrew mysticism, an aspect that was added for saving individuals from the disorder within them. This is the word of God and especially the law of God.

On one hand, Willard reads in the Scriptures a presentation of the word of God as the sub-stance of creation. On the other hand, he observes the word of God as the source (even the sub-stance) of the "redemptive community," the people of Israel.[111] The with-God life that unifies the biblical books was not a predominantly *quiescent* companionship. God *spoke* to those who were close to him, and his speech made them what they were. Lest it be thought that this was merely professional, contractual communication, Willard recognizes that the word of God for ancient Israel was a *spiritual* entity that had the ability to go to the very core of their selves, to the mind and to the heart.

In *Guidance*, Willard's innumerable references to and examples of the phenomenon of God's speech to individuals in ancient Israel help provide an overwhelming depiction of redeemed human life. *Renovation*'s chapter on the soul includes one of Willard's typical psychological commendations of *the law of God*, which "converts or restores *the soul* of those who seek it and receive it." He adds, "It is a spiritual power in its own right, as is the Word of God generally."[112] One of his favorite verses for illustrating the psychological power of the written law/word

---

111. Willard, *Guidance*, 133.

112. Willard, *Renovation*, 211 (emphasis mine). See also Willard, *Conspiracy*, 136: "Law as God intended it remains forever essential to the kingdom, and Jesus made it clear to his hearers that his aim is to bring those who follow him into fulfillment of the true law. The fulfillment he had in mind was not for the purpose of making them humanly *acceptable*. That is quite another matter. But fulfillment of God's law is important because the law is good. It is right for human life. And the presence of the kingdom brings us all that is right for human life."

of God, especially in connection with memorization, is Joshua 1:8.[113] Commenting on this verse, he writes, "Psalm 1 demonstrates that this [Joshua 1:8] became a part of the recognized practice of spiritual living among the Israelites."[114] This practice was not just a matter of rightful piety; it had a well-established salvific effect on psychological brokenness. This is echoed in verses like Psalm 119:11: "I have stored up your word in my heart that I might not sin against you."[115]

Altogether, the picture Willard paints of soteriology proper in the sense of salvation from the deprivation, the depravity, and the psychological brokenness within the individual is one of *obedient mysticism*. These words are rarely brought together, but they describe, I believe, the type of relationship with God that Willard presents in *Guidance*. Other than in that book, one gets a sense of the sort of obedient mysticism Willard is appealing to by turning to the kingdom theologies of two of Willard's earliest teachers: Charles Finney and E. Stanley Jones.

Finney's vision of God's kingdom is divided into providence and law, with the lectures on providence being located in Finney's unpublished first volume. His two published volumes of *Systematic Theology* focus mainly on law or on what he more familiarly called God's "moral government." His burden in these volumes was to explain how: "Under a gracious dispensation, a return to full obedience to moral law is not dispensed with as a condition of salvation, but this obedience is secured by the indwelling Spirit of Christ received by faith to reign in the heart."[116] In other words, God's moral kingdom is extended into human hearts by inducing obedience to his law *through* the indwelling Spirit. This comports with Willard's own description of the opposing, *un*redeemed situation: "Indeed, the social and political realm, along with the individual

---

113. Willard, "Spiritual Disciplines," 108.

114. Dallas Willard, "Personal Soul Care: For Ministers . . . and Others," in *The Pastor's Guide to Effective Ministry*, ed. William H. Willimon (Kansas City, MO: Beacon Hill, 2002), 126.

115. Willard, "Idaho Springs," 108. See also Dallas Willard, "The Disciplines of Engagement: Study," *Spirituality and Mission*, 9:30; and Willard's word on Ps 19:7–8 in *Renovation*, 106.

116. Finney, *Systematic Theology*, lecture 32, 412.

heart, is the only place in all of creation where the kingdom of God, or his effective will, is currently permitted to be absent."[117]

Jones's doctrine of the kingdom is similar. The presence, especially in Jones's lifetime, of totalitarian systems of government provided the perfect comparison and contrast to the biblical presentation of God's kingdom. In essence, the kingdom of God functioned like a totalitarian government in which the laws of the sovereign penetrated to every aspect of life and were to be obeyed completely. The difference is that God's kingdom is not a man-made "idealist" construct aimed at the betterment of society but "realism." In other words, God's kingdom is the way the universe *is*, not the way it can be remade by human social engineering. The laws of God's kingdom *are* the fabric of the physical world (creation and providence) and of the moral world. To go against them is to fight with what *is*. Jones's picture of the person or group that is not fighting reality is one that has *surrendered* the self's kingdom to God's life-encompassing (totalitarian) kingdom.

Eating Jesus

THE *PRESENCE* OF God (1) with persons—that is, the Immanuel Principle—and the *word* of God (2) to persons are the two aspects that characterize the psychology of redemption, or how God dealt with depravity and psychological brokenness. Since this theology and soteriology is present and well attested in the Scriptures *before* Jesus's coming, it sets the stage for a particular understanding of Jesus and his role in his listeners' psychological redemption.

For the first listeners, there is, first, the recognition that Jesus is centrally involved with the ancient mysticism. Many of the details of Willard's reconstruction of the growing association of Jesus with the Immanuel Principle have already been covered in chapter 10 in the crucifixion principle and on Jesus's continual presence, and these should be recalled here.[118]

---

117. Willard, *Conspiracy*, 25.

118. Notice that the situation pointing to full identification is still enthymematic. Jesus is at hand, and therefore the kingdom of God is at hand. The first premise, representative

But it is the second aspect that stands more prominently for Willard than the first as the one that markedly identifies Jesus with the ancient mysticism and with the Person behind it. This is the phenomenon of Jesus's *speech* leading to his *self-impartation*.[119] Already covered were how words function in creation and how Jesus's words were seen to have the same creational function. A very similar progression is found in the domain of the human personality.

On the first level, Willard notices in Psalm 29 "the unity of the natural order and God's redemptive community under the Word of God."[120] The word of God behind the natural order is the *same* word of God that underlies the redemptive community of Israel. But he goes on to notice that "this same unity is of course exhibited in the life of Jesus." After listing familiar examples of Jesus's word influencing the natural order, Willard comments, "He could also place the Word of God's Kingdom rule into the hearts of men, where it would bring forth fruit, 'some an hundredfold, some sixty, some thirty' (Mt 13:23)."[121] The metaphysical claim is that *the words of Jesus* had for his first listeners a certain quality and effect akin to the quality and effect of the word of God they knew to be present in the ancient redemptive community.

John 6 is perhaps the best text to illumine Willard's reconstruction of the first-century situation. Willard touches on the text in *Guidance*, but in a 2011 sermon, he revisits in greater detail Jesus's provocative, memorable statements that his listeners should eat his flesh and drink his blood.[122] As expected, Willard interprets the teaching as urging a

---

of orthodox theology—that is, that Jesus is the absolute king of the kingdom—is still left unstated.

119. Willard, *Conspiracy*, 277: "[God] can, of course, make himself present to the human mind in any way he chooses. But—for good reasons rooted deeply in the nature of the person and of personal relationships—his preferred way is to *speak*, to communicate: thus the absolute centrality of scripture to our discipleship." In the next note, Willard refers the reader to *Guidance*.

120. Willard, *Guidance*, 133.

121. Willard, 133.

122. Dallas Willard, "Eating the Flesh and Drinking the Blood of Jesus: The Substance of Jesus through His Word," *St. Peter's Sermons* (St. Peter's Anglican Church, Birmingham, AL, August 7, 2011), MP3. See also Willard, *Conspiracy*, 199–200; and Dallas

spiritual, nonphysical form of nourishment. Jesus was speaking "in the most concrete terms" of himself, which he would *impart* to them.[123] In a gloss of John 6:56 ("whoever . . . abides in me and I in him"), Willard says, "What Jesus is actually saying now: You must partake of my life. You must allow me to live in you. And the life that I have is eternal life, and you share that by taking it into you."[124]

Willard goes further to specify the *form* that the impartation of Jesus as spiritual nourishment takes.[125] At the end of the sermon, he says, "You'll see in verse 63 of John 6 the key to the whole passage. He says, 'It is the spirit which gives life. The flesh profits nothing. The words that I speak to you, they are spirit, they are life.'"[126] This key verse is a launching pad in the sermon for his standard teaching about words not being physical realities.[127] In sum, the physical realities sometimes attached to words (sounds, marks, hand gestures) do not contain *the meaning*, which is the only value of words. Hence, "what Jesus is saying [in 6:63 is] you have to move to the meaning, and the meaning is spiritual. And by means of the spiritual reality of the words of Jesus, we consume his substance, we take in his reality."[128]

The spiritual and meaning-full teaching about words communicated in John 6:63 helps his listeners in two ways. In the first instance, they understand that Jesus is *not* talking about eating his flesh and drinking his blood. *That* is not his meaning. Jesus's "literal flesh, when taken apart from his spiritual reality, the personal, would do them absolutely

---

Willard, "Evening Worship 1," *Jesus Christ Is the Same Yesterday, Today and Forever* (Okoboji Bible Conference, Okoboji, IA, August 4, 2009), MP3, 5:00.

123. Willard, *Guidance*, 165.

124. Willard, "Eating the Flesh," 7:00.

125. On his way there, he passes by one view: "We know how through the ages there has been a lot of trouble about [eating his flesh and drinking his blood], hasn't there? And some people have identified eating his flesh and drinking his blood with taking communion. . . . But there is more to taking [*sic*] his flesh and drinking his blood than taking the elements of the communion" (Willard, "Eating the Flesh," 14:00). This sermon does have other statements that help depict Willard's view of "the only ritual Jesus gave us."

126. Willard, "Eating the Flesh," 21:00.

127. E.g., the section on "Words as Spiritual Forces" in Willard, *Guidance*, 124–27.

128. Willard, "Eating the Flesh," 23:00.

no good at all."[129] Rather, "he is talking about the substance of Christ himself that comes through his word to us."[130]

But in the second and more profound instance, they understand how *Jesus's* words function generally. First, they are *spirit*. In *Guidance's* section "Words as Spiritual Forces," Willard points out, "*My* word is not just *a* word. It is me speaking or me writing." He explains this by saying, "What is essential to the word of a person is the meaning given to it by them—that is, what thought, feeling, or action *they* associated with it and hope to convey to others."[131] Meaning (think of that word as a verbal noun, like *running*, or as in the German verbal noun *Meinen*) is something that stems from personal reality. Persons, not words, mean. When Willard says that words are *spiritual* forces, he is saying that words are *person-based* forces. Spirit, according to his definition, is unbodily, *personal* power.

Now, Jesus's words are worthy of consumption not because they are words and have eo ipso spiritual/personal power but because *they* are life. This is the second aspect of how Jesus's words function generally and is an extremely important part of Willard's theological vision. Not everyone's words are life to people. But Jesus's words, and this is the point of John 6, are nourishment for the whole person because they mediate union with the essentially powerful person of Jesus himself and cause the human person to live the eternal kind of life that Jesus has in himself by nature.[132] "Through his words," Willard writes, "he literally imparted himself while he lived and taught among the people of his day."[133]

This is what the listeners in John 6 are invited to test the limits of. In a 2008 lecture, Willard adds an important gloss to Peter's Johannine

---

129. Willard, *Guidance*, 165.

130. Willard, "Eating the Flesh," 24:00.

131. Willard, *Guidance*, 124. In the text, Willard draws quotes from Plato and Augustine to show the broad basis for his view. The same view of words can be found in much more elaborated and argued form in Husserl's sixth logical investigation (Husserl, *Logische Untersuchungen 2. Teil*) and especially in the first chapter of Willard's "Meaning and Universals in Husserl's Logische Untersuchungen."

132. Willard, *Conspiracy*, 14: "the eternal kind of life that was his by nature and becomes available to us through him."

133. Willard, *Guidance*, 165.

confession of Christ wherein he says, "Lord, to whom shall we go? You have words of eternal life" (John 6:68). The Greek, as Willard points out, does not say "the words" but "words." The structure of this confession is that Peter has recognized that Jesus's words were *of a particular character*. Jesus does not have, as some translations suggest, a word *about* eternal life. Jesus's words were not like those of others to whom Peter was not prepared to go. They were eternal-life words. Words that imparted eternal life. Peter is not quite ready to say that the words impart Jesus, but as a member of God's redemptive community, Peter had some limited experience with eternal-life words and recognized that Jesus spoke them.[134]

For Willard, Jesus's bold teaching of John 6 and the first listeners' experiential interaction with the eternal-life words of Jesus prepare them to understand the fine texture of their relationship with Jesus. And they gradually identify this with the ancient mysticism familiar to them from their own limited experience with it and from the Hebrew Scriptures. Thus, we find these words of Willard's: "On the foundation of [Jesus's] words to his followers, the powerful events of Calvary, of the resurrection presence, and of Pentecost brought forth a communion and then a union later expressed by the Apostle Paul as the great mystery of the ages, 'Christ in you, the hope of glory' (Col 1:27)."[135] That is, the climactic events of Jesus's life upheld a new reality—communion and union with him—which *Jesus's words* created and continued to uphold.

---

134. Willard, "Evening Worship 1," 13:45. The talk goes on to examine three words of Jesus, one of which being Jesus's main gospel message, a fact that we will return to presently. See also Willard, "Salvation, Life," 0:30.

135. Willard, *Guidance*, 165. See also Willard's discussion of abiding and indwelling in "The Water of Life and the Healing of the Nations," *How Jesus Abolished Death and Brought Immortality to Light through the Gospel of God's Kingdom* (Rolling Hills Covenant Church, Rolling Estates, CA, April 4, 1984), MP3/cassette, 5:00. Willard says, "In his words he expressed himself, and when his words abide in us, he abides in us. In John 6:63 he says, 'The words I speak unto you they are spirit, they are life.' The way Christ dwells in us is through the truth of his word possessing our lives until we think as he thought, until we feel as he felt, until we will as he willed—naturally in an easy outflow of that inward transformation whereby we have identified with him."

Though Willard does not use any particular phrase parallel to the Cosmic Christ to name this Christology, perhaps one could speak of Christ here as the Mystical Christ.[136] In the previous section, I noted how an antecedent theology and soteriology prepared the way for the Christology of the Cosmic Christ on account of observing how Jesus is intimately involved in that providential form of salvation. In this section, note how the antecedent theology and soteriology of Hebrew mysticism set the stage for the Christology of the Mystical Christ on account of observing how Jesus the anointed one is also intimately involved in that psychological form of salvation.

Let me rehearse the connection of this psychological form of salvation to the doctrine of sin just delineated. God's presence and word are the external realities on which human life depends. The lack of these in the world is the state of deprivation that is passed on from generation to generation. Because of their absence, depravity, learned and chosen, is the inevitable result, working its way through every aspect of human personality. But among the people of Israel, God was active to save individuals from their psychological ruin. The psychology of redemption, if there was a conscious one among the people of Israel, concerned their regeneration by the manifest presence and word of God. It concerned their recontact with the spiritual kingdom of God, and in this new relationship, the faith of Abraham, the recovery of their personality from its depravity, was possible. "Our human life," says Willard, "is not destroyed by God's life but is fulfilled in it and in it alone. The obviously well kept secret of the 'ordinary' is that it is made to be a receptacle of the divine."[137]

Continuity or Transition?

NOW AGAIN TO the question posed at the beginning of this section when we turned to the disorder within the individual person: Can anything be located in Willard's corpus that indicates how, with the coming of Jesus,

136. If this as a word seems troublesome, the reality could just as well be called "the Indwelling Christ" or "the Covenantal Christ."

137. Willard, *Conspiracy*, 14.

God *changed* how he would deal with the depravity and psychological brokenness in humanity? If all one considers is mysticism and the salvific work of the Mystical Christ, the answer, I believe, is no. Willard does not speak of the coming of Jesus as making possible a different form of *regeneration* or of *indwelling interaction* with the presence and action of God or of *union* with God than what was possible before his coming. Hebrew mysticism remains the divine strategy.

On one occasion when speaking of Abraham as regenerate, Willard says, "Now, that doesn't mean fully what we mean by it today because there was no indwelling Christ through the Spirit that came through that."[138] Willard could possibly mean by this that Christ and the Spirit were not a part of Abraham's regeneration. There is some evidence for that interpretation.[139] But I think it is more consistent with Willard's overall view that the whole Trinity was involved in Abraham's and his children's regeneration. Abraham did not know Christ or indeed the Spirit. But neither did Abraham know hydrogen or oxygen, and yet he did know and was alive to water. He could reach out and assimilate H_2O. No doubt his lack of knowledge of the details kept him from interacting with the Trinity or water in all its fullness. This knowledge of the details is what Christ's coming makes possible.

Paul in Colossians speaks of the Mystical Christ or "Christ in us" as "the mystery *hidden for ages and generations* but now revealed to his saints" (Col 1:26).[140] In a gloss of Colossians 1:27 and other New Testament passages, Willard writes, "Human personality in the Christian viewpoint is an incarnate system of mental and physical acts designed to be inhabited by God. We are to be the temple of God, but one that actively understands and cooperates with God's purposes and is inhabited through a willing, clear-eyed identification of ourselves with Jesus Christ, enabled by God himself. It is Christ *in us* that is our hope of glory (Col 1:27)."[141] Often this indwelling is read as a new possibility.

---

138. Willard, "Spirit and Spirituality," 1:08:00.
139. See Willard, "Reigning in Life through One, Christ Jesus," 24:45.
140. For more on the mystery, see Willard, *Conspiracy*, 385–86.
141. Willard, *Guidance*, 51.

But "mystery," Willard writes, "means, in the language of the New Testament, something that had long remained hidden but then came to be known for the first time."[142] In Willard's history of redemption, the mystery of "Christ in you" does not indicate a different metaphysical reality than that by which the ancient Jews were saved from their psychological brokenness. It does indicate a better understanding of that reality. "Christ in you" is a New Testament doctrine, if you will, but an Old Testament reality.

This anticipates one of the objections that Willard may encounter, the objection that the New Testament describes a *closer*, *fuller* personal contact with Christ and the Spirit than was possible before the Christ event, and this is usually expressed by the Greek preposition ἐν. Willard's response would be that it can indeed be closer and fuller but that this is not due to a change in the underlying reality. Relying on the epistemology he learned from Husserl, he would point out that increasingly greater understanding of something always allows for a closer or fuller relationship to it.[143] New possibilities of interaction with water are possible for those who learn that it is H_2O. Likewise, a better understanding of God and the soteriology of "God with us" results in changes in how persons already alive to him may interact with him.

Another objection is a family of teleological arguments that hang the whole reality of communion or union with God on the Christ event. Those partial to these arguments would say that the possibility of mystical participation—"Christ in you, the hope of glory"—is nothing less than the main effect of the incarnation of the Son of God and/or his death on the cross and his resurrection and ascension to glory. There are many ways of spelling this out, but all versions assume that the Christ

142. Willard, *Conspiracy*, 386.

143. See Willard's discussion of progressive fulfillment with respect to a tree in "Ontology of Knowledge: Willard 3," *Ontology of Knowledge* (Biola University, La Mirada, CA, May 29, 1997), MP3/cassette, 48:00. In his theory of distinctions, Willard would call the difference between "Old Testament" and "New Testament" mysticism a distinction of reason. Like the morning star and the evening star, they are different and not meaningless ways of referring to the same thing. One will find Willard using the distinction of reason with various entities, the heart/will/spirit, Jesus/Christ, and most importantly, the kingdom of God.

event initiates and thus makes possible a glorified form of divine-human coexistence that would not have been possible otherwise.

The most traditional of these is the version held up by Athanasius, the Cappadocians, and the Orthodox Church today. In this theological tradition, the incarnation, more so than the incarnate one's death and resurrection, was the event for which God arranged so that humans could become deified and what God always intended them to be. God shares in the whole of our humanity *so that* humans can share in the divine-human union that was God's intent for them from before creation. The details of this view are unimportant because the broad strokes reveal the difference from Willard's view. The claim is that *God required* an incarnation (and to a lesser degree, a death and resurrection) before he could move into mystical union with his creatures. "For that which He has not assumed He has not healed," writes Gregory of Nazianzus.[144] To suggest that this union was the right of ancient Israel is to suggest that the incarnation and the Christ event, the assumption of flesh, are unnecessary.

The non-Orthodox accounts are similar, though they tend to put more emphasis on the death and resurrection of the Son than on his incarnation. John Calvin's view, for example, was that Christ's obedience in life and descent to the cross make possible our participation with him in it and in the benefits thereof. This also makes possible our participation in Christ's glorification (or ascent) through his resurrection and heavenly session and through his outpouring of the Spirit. Because of these events, we are given access to a new form of union with God. Suggesting that the Israelites were capable of the same form of mystical union spoken of in the New Testament documents suggests that the death and resurrection are, again, unnecessary.

These are arguments with the force of tradition behind them. But it should be emphasized that, though Willard may have some specific views of its precise nature, he is not denying the mystical teaching of

---

144. Gregory of Nazianzus, epistle 101, in *Nicene and Post-Nicene Fathers*, 2nd ser., vol. 7, ed. Philip Schaff and Henry Wace (New York: Christian Literature Company, 1894), 440.

the New Testament. But he, or his theology, is calling into question its causal relation to the Christ event. In the history of theology, the overwhelming tendency has been to assume a contingent relationship between *orthodox* Christology and the soteriology of the Christ event. You cannot have the latter without the former. What is usually behind these accounts is a particular doctrine of God that is being worked out teleologically in a doctrine of salvation with a so-called *objective* theory of the atonement. God wants to dwell with and in his people, but *something about him* stops him from doing so, and *somehow* the event of God coming in the flesh, dying, and ascending to the heavens makes it possible for him to do what he otherwise could not have done.[145]

The Gospels, Acts, and even the Epistles, as Willard reads them, throw a wrench into this scheme. If his reconstruction of the first listeners' evangelical progression has any historical truth to it, then *from the perspective of the first listeners*, Jesus's coming was not initially salvific and worthy of great celebration, of proclamation around the world, and even of martyrdom because it concerned a God-man. Willard takes it for granted that only a very forceful, dogmatic reading of the New Testament could argue that the initial positive reactions to Jesus, even well into Acts, were due to a conviction of Chalcedonian Christology. Thanks to their basic familiarity with the theology of their people and their outstanding experiences with Jesus before and after his ascension, the first listeners knew that God was saving his people in Jesus—as prophet, as teacher and as king—long before they had suspicions that he was *vere deus*. Thanks also to their actual experience of ancient forms of divine salvation in the name of Jesus (his presence and providence), they knew in time that Jesus could be nothing less than divine. In their epistemic progression, soteriology never preceded Christology, but it did precede *orthodox* Christology.

---

145. Even though Willard has appreciation for an objective theory of the atonement, he says on one occasion, "If that's all you have, you will have a hard time understanding why Christ waited so long" (Willard, "What Christ Did," 16:30). In other words, there must be some salvific value in God's gradual work with humanity and especially Israel over time. God cannot be conceived of as waiting aimlessly to do the one thing necessary for our rescue.

The counterarguments against Willard all assume that salvation in Christ and the gospel is incomprehensible without a Chalcedonian form of Christology. In other words, Jesus's first listeners could not have known the gospel until they knew that he was divine. Willard does not doubt that Jesus's followers began to contemplate a very high Christology very soon after Jesus ascended. But Jesus's followers certainly did not begin their faith-based following of him at the point of quasi-Chalcedonian Christology.[146] Why would they if the gospel, the news of their salvation, was incomprehensible to them? Either their previous conceptions of Jesus were a complete misunderstanding or there is something to them, and *this* was the reason for their elation with Jesus and their ability to go "from faith to faith" (Rom 1:17, KJV) and comprehend greater ontologies of Christ. The burden of proof that Willard's exegesis lays on this counterargument is to show how devout Jewish listeners concluded that Jesus is God without a genuine (though not complete) understanding of the soteriology of the Christ event.[147]

The Difference Jesus Makes

IF NOT PROVIDENCE or mysticism, what, for Willard, changed with Jesus in the history of redemption? How does Jesus "save his people from their sins" in light of the fact that this is "where the Old Testament agreement finally flunked and failed"?[148] One part of Willard's answer has

146. One of the negative side effects, it seems, of the church having fought tooth and nail for the confession of orthodox theology is the tendency to overargue one's position and hang too much on its reality.

147. The most traditional route to the divinity of Christ has been that of the revelationist and fideist. God revealed to the Jewish apostles and New Testament writers that Christ is divine, and we must either know or trust the authority of their Scriptures (e.g., Augustine) or the church (e.g., Aquinas) or God gives us a more personalized revelation of it (e.g., Barth). From here, theology is an exercise of faith seeking understanding—that is, of turning one kind of thing (faith) into another kind of thing (understanding).

Whatever route we take, we must be careful, first, to not beg any questions. For example, orthodox Christology cannot be a premise before it is a conclusion. And second, we must be careful to not think about it in abstraction from how the Jewish first listeners thought of it. Because, after all, *they* are the ones who told *us* about it and not vice versa.

148. Willard, "Better New Testament Good News," 0:30.

already been discussed in the first- and second-stage understandings of the gospel. Jesus enters human history as one who lives in the kingdom of God to a degree that no other human being has and as one who is ready to take on disciples and teach them how to live in the kingdom of God. Personal discipleship to Jesus then "in the days of his flesh" and now "through the Holy Spirit" is a new reality that was not offered to ancient Israel but contributes mightily to YHWH's ancient plan to enact salvation from the *disorder* within the individual person. What changed in the psychology of redemption such that its scientists must rewrite their textbooks? Discipleship to Jesus.[149]

The other change that the coming of Jesus occasions is no less than the gospel of the third stage. But before we turn to that, let us remember where we came from in this chapter. The question at the beginning was, What did those in on the secret know or come to know in time about this king? Mainly, they learned through their experience of his providence and communicative presence how Jesus participates in and even initiates the two forms of YHWH's salvation recognizable to his covenant people. And by means of this interactive relationship, they learned that Jesus stood in authoritative relationship to the two main divisions within the kingdom of God in the created universe. He is the Cosmic Christ and he is the Mystical Christ. Since these are the ontological relations to the universe in which God himself is known to stand, the first listeners have the evidence, but only parabolically so, to affirm a very high Christology. In this way are Jesus's prayers in John 17 answered: "Glorify your Son that the Son may glorify you" (John 17:1) and "glorify me in your own presence with the glory that I had with you before the world existed" (John 17:5).

---

149. Willard, *Conspiracy*, xvii.

CUR DEUS HOMO?

> In the incarnation he focused his reality in a special way in the body of Jesus. This was so that we might be "enlightened by the knowledge of the glory of God in the face of Jesus Christ" (2 Cor. 4:6).
>
> —Dallas Willard, *The Divine Conspiracy*

> The main point is that God has created us for intimate friendship with himself, both now and forever.
>
> —Dallas Willard, *In Search of Guidance*

IN AN INTERVIEW on his show, the radio host Frank Pastore once asked Dallas Willard, "Why the incarnation?" Willard answered,

> *It's because human beings individually and corporately are stuck down in this hole of trying to manage their lives. And in that hole, they can't see very much, so they need someone to come into that hole—again, I'm speaking corporately and individually—and bring with it the idea of another world. . . . What happens with Jesus is not only does he come into the world, but he comes into the world in such a* way *that he is able to contact any person who is simply willing to look. That's what Christmas and also Easter is about. It's about, if you wish [chuckles], God coming down into our little hole and*

saying, "Hey, how you doing in there? Would you like to see something different?"[1]

Though this is not a systematic or even rehearsed answer, we hear something that was characteristic of Willard's doctrine of salvation. The dire situation that salvation addresses is not necessarily one that human beings will recognize *apart from* the salvific intervention itself. In the dark hole, humans "can't see very much." What human beings take to be dire about their situation may not be their real problem.

In this chapter, we will work from the knowledge, attained by the listeners' experience with Jesus and the kingdom of God, that Jesus is not only the "crucified" Christ but also uniquely divine. In past chapters, we spoke of mildly educated Jews who, on the basis of a certain biblical ontology, could hear the gospel of the kingdom. The same is true here. A certain ontology of Jesus and his union with the God of the kingdom is the basis for hearing the gospel of the third stage.

I admit that there may be some blurs in Willard's reconstruction of the listeners' thought and experience that brought them to that ontology.[2] Indeed, I welcome better attempts to recover his thought. But if I am right that Willard regards Jesus's unique divinity as parabolically communicated to humanity, then a paucity of evidence is precisely what we would expect to find such that the orthodox conclusion is not forced on anyone.

The orthodox conclusion is not forced on anyone, *but* some first listeners conclude it. And that means we are at a point in the first listeners' stages of understanding Jesus and his gospel where we can ask different questions—questions that are more typical of systematic theology, like, Why the incarnation? Or more traditionally, *cur deus homo*? Or in terms more in line with the language of this book, What is the connection between Jesus's ontological association with the God of the kingdom

1. Dallas Willard, "January 2012 Interview," *Frank Pastore Show*, January 6, 2012, MP3, 4:45.
2. For more on blurs, see Willard, "Ontology of Knowledge: Willard 1," 1:45:00.

and Jesus's gospel of the availability of the kingdom of God?[3] In this chapter, though not without forgetting the first listeners' eye view (see chapter 2) that brought us here, we will seek Willard's answer to these God's eye view questions.

True God, True Man: Why Do They Coinhere?

AS IT NOW stands in our reconstruction of the first listeners' epistemic progression, Willard's Christology and his soteriology look rather disjunctive. On one hand, Willard speaks of the work of Christ as *vere homo*—an extraordinary, paradigmatic man. He is a prophet such as the listeners had heard of but greater than any before and any since, for he lives in the kingdom of God better than any. He is also an outstanding mediator who proclaims, manifests, and teaches the kingdom and thereby effectively leads others into life in the kingdom of God, which, he proclaims, is open to them just as it is open to him. He is unable to be contained by the grave, since God has raised him up, and from his position in heaven, he, as *vere homo*, continues the prophetic, mediatory work he began on the earth.

On the other hand, Willard speaks of the work of Christ as *vere deus*, the God of Israel. He is the Word in creation, "the 'glue' of the universe (Col 1:17), upholding all things by the *Word* of his power (Heb 1:3)," and from that position, he delivers his people from the disorder around them—including, above all, death.[4] He is also the Word in God's redemptive community, whom he calls and regenerates "through the living and abiding word of God" (1 Peter 1:23), and from that position he, as *vere deus*, delivers his people from the disorder within them—including, above all, sin.[5]

The disjunction is the following. For the former work, there does not seem to be a need for this prophet and mediator to be divine.

---

3. The questions can also be put in modern theological terms: What is the connection between orthodox Christology and the work of salvation? What is the soteriological significance of the Christ event as an incarnation of a divine person? Did God really have to become human in order to accomplish salvation?

4. Willard, *Guidance*, 132.

5. Willard, 158–65.

Powerful, perfect, and human, yes. But divine, no. For the latter work, there does not seem to be a need for this cosmic, mystical person to be human. Immanent, humble, and divine (or at least fully authorized by God), yes. But human, no.[6] There is nothing about the work of Christ discussed thus far that calls for God becoming man. The only thing binding the human work of Christ together with the divine work of Christ is the listeners' observation in the transition period that the same person who ascended into heaven seems to do both and thus be both *vere deus* and *vere homo*.

Let us begin here with Willard and the first listeners and think anew about the whole fact of Christ. Let us ask why it might be that *vere deus* would deem it necessary to coinhere with *vere homo*. It seems to me in reading Willard that the act of incarnation and the corresponding coinherence set into motion for him two theological inferences.

Self-Blindness

TO BEGIN, THE listeners' knowledge that Jesus's existence as a man is an action of God, enveloping it in the sphere of God's eternal purposes, recasts his human life in terms of what the theological tradition has called the divine missions. This first inference builds upon all that we have discussed in the first and second stages and, therefore, should be fairly easy to understand. By it we learn two things about God's eternal purposes. We learn, first, the importance in human history of Jesus as an *instantiation* of perfect humanity. Willard writes, "Indeed, by taking the title Son of man, he staked his claim to be all that the human being was originally supposed to be—and surely much more."[7] This

6. One could argue here, as some in the Anselmian tradition have argued, that a perfect, powerful human was impossible for God to find after the fall. Who apart from God could perfectly perform the vocation of humanity, both as a testimony to humans and as an offering to God? There is something to that argument given Willard's account of the fall, though it constantly is dogged by the complaint that a divine person had resources available that humans do not have. For Anselm, this is advantageous for his doctrine of salvation because, in offering to God his due, only a being with more hierarchical clout than a mere man could suffice.

7. Willard, *Conspiracy*, 27. See also 254 and Willard, "Jesus as Savior and Teacher," 6:00.

is a brief point in *Conspiracy* but a Christology with a rich theological history.

William Temple's essay "The Divinity of Christ" is quoted by Willard in *Guidance* and *Disciplines* and is recommended elsewhere for further reading in Christology.[8] Consider the salient parts of the passage that Willard quotes from: "We do not know what Humanity really is, or of what achievements it is capable, until Divinity indwells in it. . . . We must ask, 'What is Humanity?' and look at Christ to find the answer. We only know what Matter is when Spirit dwells in it; we only know what Man is when God dwells in him."[9] Willard uses this quote to name his *norm* when discussing the possibilities of human sanctification and glorification. Jesus of Nazareth is an *instance* of the *universal* human being as they should be.[10]

The second thing we learn is similar though far less represented in the history of theology. In a 1979 Sunday school lesson called "What Christ Did to Save Mankind," Willard gave a rare but clear description of the mission of God as a man in which he said the following:

> *Jesus Christ came into this world at the fullness of time in the course of history and established a beachhead in the kingdom of darkness by drawing out a group of people in whom he and his Father could fully dwell. . . . He comes down into this world and he draws around him a group of people—not a large group of people, because size is not really what is required . . .—and he begins to rebuild them. And he carries them through the time of his life with them as he teaches and as he shows forth the kingdom of God and begins to communicate the power of God's kingdom to them also.*

8. Willard, "How Can Jesus Be the Son of God?"
9. Temple, "Divinity of Christ," 211–63.
10. For another historical example, see Jeremy Taylor, "An Exhortation to the Imitation of the Life of Christ," an introductory essay to his *The Great Exemplar* (1649; repr., London: Richard Royston, 1653). Taylor was one of Willard's confessed influences.

> *And then in order to complete his work of redemption, in order to be with them in a new and different and even better way, he dies of all things. He says to his followers, "It is expedient that I go away." Because, you see, he is founding a redemptive kingdom, a redemptive body, which is not anything like the human kingdoms with which we are acquainted, whether we call them religious or otherwise. It is a redemptive group of people through whom the power of God flows and comes out and touches the world and touches one another and nourishes them and restores the connection.*[11]

In the final sentence, one can see remnants of Willard's older notion of the kingdom of God, which is more interchangeable with the church universal or the body of Christ. This aside, what we have here is a description of Jesus's earthly ministry, his "taking students in the master class of life," *as central* to God's eternal purposes in history.[12] It is curious that in the years after 1979, Willard rarely takes this wide-angle view of the ministry of Jesus. One can hear in his corpus the redemptive-historical importance with which he regards, as a book by A. B. Bruce calls it, Jesus's "training of the twelve."[13] But this 1979 quote explains why it was so important. "Discipleship to Jesus," he says in *Conspiracy*, is "the very heart of the gospel."[14]

By looking at Willard's early description of God's purposes with creation, we can piece together why discipleship is the very heart of the gospel. In 1971, Willard writes of "God's Aim in History" as "the creation of an all-inclusive Community of loving persons, with Himself included in that community as its prime sustainer and most glorious inhabitant."[15] Since, as Willard admits, the concept of discipleship is still forming in his mind in the 1970s, this community is apparently formed

11. Willard, "What Christ Did," 21:15.
12. Willard, *Conspiracy*, xvii; cf. 15–16.
13. A. B. Bruce, *The Training of the Twelve* (Edinburgh: T&T Clark, 1871).
14. Willard, xvii.
15. Willard, "Handout for 'Studies in the Book of Apostolic Acts,'" 2.

by things like church attendance, trying harder, and perhaps some revival. But by 1979, for Willard, Jesus's ministry of discipleship has clearly become the means by which God will create this all-inclusive community, a type of thinking that culminates in *Conspiracy*: "The purpose of God with human history is nothing less than to bring out of it . . . an eternal community of those who were once thought to be just 'ordinary human beings.' Because of God's purposes for it, this community will, in its way, pervade the entire created realm and share in the government of it. . . . He will be its prime sustainer and most glorious inhabitant."[16] Notice, again, how this community will not merely be loving but have a responsibility to rule, which apparently requires some training. This is how God's coming in Jesus to take and train disciples to be like himself finds its meaning in the grand purposes of God for creation.

Before moving on to the second inference, George Barker Stevens's book *The Christian Doctrine of Salvation* should be mentioned.[17] Willard did not drop the names of many books that helped him understand a God's eye view of salvation, but this is one he did name a few times, beginning with the 1979 Sunday school lesson.[18] In Stevens's constructive development of the doctrine of salvation, he includes a chapter called "The Personality of the Saviour," which has much overlap with Willard. Stevens says, for example, "I find the gospel, and the whole gospel, in Jesus himself, present with a clarity, a simplicity, a transcendent beauty and matchless power nowhere equalled."[19] On the next

---

16. Willard, *Conspiracy*, 385–86.

17. George Barker Stevens, *The Christian Doctrine of Salvation* (Edinburgh: T&T Clark, 1909).

18. Aaron Preston remembers that Willard recommended the book to him in the early 1990s (Moon, *Becoming Dallas Willard*, 278n22). Willard also distributed pages 239–61 to students for some lectures on atonement in April 2000 ("Letter to Participants in Vineyard Young Leaders Network from Todd Hunter," March 28, 2000, Dallas Willard Collection). In 2003, Willard also recommended the book to help understand the history and biblical presentation of the atonement. He added, "If I recommend a book, that doesn't necessarily mean that I agree with everything it says. But that is an excellent study" (Willard, "Session 2—Part 1," 1:51:15).

19. Stevens, *Christian Doctrine of Salvation*, 293.

page, he speaks of Jesus's "passion to reveal to men their possible sonship to God and to help them to realize it. Accordingly, we find that his life produced the impression that he was the typical, representative, ideal man."[20] If Willard did not learn this way of enveloping the life of Jesus in the sphere of God's eternal purposes from Stevens, then he nevertheless found in him a kindred spirit.

God-Blindness

THE SECOND INFERENCE that the coinherence of *vere deus* and *vere homo* in the person of Christ engenders for Willard requires a much longer explanation. The listener's knowledge that the God of Israel "lived among us as one human being among others" ties this God—not necessarily ontologically but *meaningfully*—to the life of Jesus, and it recasts the life of Jesus in terms of divine revelation.[21]

The significance of the listeners' discovery that the man Jesus channels YHWH's solutions to the disorder in the cosmos and in the human soul and thus is suspected to be YHWH himself can be heard if we rephrase Jesus's gospel announcement. It might read now as "Begin metanoia, for YHWH's mystical presence and special providence is at hand." Why would such an announcement be news to a Jewish audience? It is news, so goes Willard's answer, because, though God's communicative presence and providence were available, they were not altogether *effectively* available.

Before Jesus came, life in the kingdom of God was not the sort of thing that people, even the natural-born covenant people of Israel, easily found their way into. This is a crucial point in Willard's thought, especially concerning the history of redemption. To his mind, what was needed in the history of redemption was not some new functionality in the mechanics of salvation. It is not as if God's providence and presence did not work. It is not as if God were not ready. The "problem" was not the basic engineering of redemption. It was its accessibility. What had made YHWH's providence and mysticism relatively inaccessible to

20. Stevens, 294.

21. Willard, *Conspiracy*, 334.

humanity, as Willard sees it, was primarily humanity's *bad theology*. Or what I called in the section on progressive apprehension in the second chapter *shoddy theology*.

For Willard, bad theology was an ancient and perennial problem in the history of the world and even among the covenant people. By the first century, it is still only provisionally solved. Though we have spoken of the perennial problems of "the deadly D's" and of psychological brokenness in human life, these solutions do not depend on the uniquely divine Son's assumption of flesh. It was a low or false view of God that was the human problem that, according to Willard, the historical incarnation of a divine person was intended to solve.[22]

Dread of God, to give an example, is a result of bad theology. Though the ancient Hebrews knew God, dread of him (not fear of God, which would be positive and righteous) dominated the covenant people for centuries.[23] Because of it, the fullness of salvation that God always offered and longed to offer to them (and to the gentiles) was left on the shelf or, at least, approached with great reservation. Intermediaries like Moses were preferred to direct interaction with a dreadful God and his kingdom.

The human malady here is a skewed view of the character of divinity, a view of a god with whom one can have no peace. Its remedy must not only be fitting but also respect God's greater purposes. Thus, one of Willard's favorite verses for encouraging reflection on this and the historical work of Jesus is 1 John 1:5: "This is the message we have heard from him and proclaim to you." At this point in talks, he usually stops rhetorically, as he does in *Conspiracy*, and asks his readers to complete the sentence based on their own grasp of theology and Jesus's message. The verse continues, "that God is light and in him is no darkness

22. Dallas Willard, "Death and Transfiguration," *Death and Transfiguration* (Rolling Hills Covenant Church, Rolling Estates, CA, February 7, 1982), MP3/cassette, 21:30.
23. For more on Israel being afraid of God, see Dallas Willard, "God's Guidance through Our Conversational Relationship with Him," *In Search of Guidance* (Bedfordview Methodist Church, Bedfordview, South Africa, August 4, 1987), MP3/cassette, 30:30.

at all."[24] For Willard, 1 John 1:5 is a reconstruction of Jesus's "The kingdom of the heavens is at hand." For what kept the kingdom of the heavens at arm's distance was a false theology that there might be darkness in God, something to dread.[25]

The Unknown Malady

HAVING BRIEFLY STATED what Willard regards as the solution (Jesus's representation of God) and the problem (bad theology), let me name his approach. Willard, I have found, follows an evangelical order in approaching this doctrine. That is, he starts with the solution (Jesus as God's representative) before exposing the predicament (bad theology).

As we have often observed in Willard's corpus, some of the ills of humanity were known to the people who inherited the Jewish tradition of knowledge, "the law and the prophets." In *Knowing Christ*, Willard has an important section on Hosea 4:6 and its context where he explains how idolatry in Hosea's day represented the fundamental lack of knowledge about God that was ruining his people.[26] Of course, idolatry in the classic sense of "graven images" of stone and wood was not an inadequate view of God that characterized Jesus's first listeners. Willard does not discuss, to my knowledge, whether Jews ever had a general diagnosis of the predicament of the human situation *as* rooted in bad theology. In the least, he does not lay this diagnosis in the minds of first-century Jews.[27] When Jesus arrived, there was no general cry for

---

24. Willard, *Conspiracy*, 321.

25. In one of his lectures, Willard describes the unredeemed human disposition toward God by speaking of people who say, "I'd like to see God." He comments, "If you tell someone, 'God is in the next room; you go in there and you'll see him,' they will think twice before they go through the door. Because we know that the greatness of God is something that is so devastating. It calls us in such question; it pulls us beyond our depths" (Willard, "Old Testament Good News," 3:00). In another message, he says, "We talk glibly about meeting God, but if you'll notice, the people who meet God in the Bible often wind up in a dead faint. The experience of God is a powerful thing" (Willard, "Man's Blindness to God," 12:15).

26. Willard, *Knowing*, 40–43.

27. Neither does he lay the diagnosis of deprivation, as discussed in the previous chapter, in their minds. The story of Jesus and Nicodemus would have been his main warning against doing this.

a savior who would unveil the God of whom they and the other nations had collectively lost sight.[28]

The gospel for the first listeners starts, rather, with the new fact: Jesus is suspected of being with God from eternity and eo ipso of bringing better knowledge of God. With the solution in hand, a first listener can discern their predicament. That is, only after they make the shift to third-stage topography and only after they suspect Jesus of being God, or at least of being very close, can they appreciate Jesus's *unique* salvific role of bringing knowledge of God.

Of course, as a man, Jesus also taught about God. His teaching about God was for his listeners, as for the whole world, surprising and wonderful. But this prophetic manner of bringing knowledge of God can be adequately accounted for within a second-stage topography and Christology. In the third stage, Jesus brings knowledge of God by merely being who he is, by being God's representative.

Though Willard never makes this second-/third-stage distinction with such clarity as I am making it here, Willard clearly has a pattern of speaking of Jesus as the unique representative or even incarnate Son of God who, *when known as such*, brings knowledge of God to the earth.[29] As God's unique representative, Jesus pushes forward even the best of Israel's accrued knowledge of God. By doing so, he exposes in reverse that Israel, despite its rich history with God, could not fully "get" God. He exposes how pervasive this problem has been in human history, stemming from the oldest account of sin. In this evangelical order, knowledge of sin follows knowledge of salvation.

Recall here Willard's doctrine of progressive apprehension from the second chapter. Willard's solution to the divergence in the biblical

---

28. It seems to me that a case could be made, though not with great historical detail, that this hamartiology was in Israel's tradition—that is, that the prophets recognized not only their people's culpability but also their own in this.

29. This pattern mingles, however, with another clear pattern: speaking of Jesus as a *human* teacher who has extraordinary knowledge of and faith in God. The latter pattern is more dominant in chapter 3 of *Conspiracy*. Willard's original vision for *Conspiracy* was as a book on Jesus's beliefs. As such, it was conceived as a companion volume to *Disciplines*, which was reportedly a book on Jesus's practices. The idea of writing a whole book on Jesus's beliefs (his faith) was on Willard's mind since the late 1970s at least.

record had the advantage of implicating *humanity* for its own shoddy theology. Though Willard will emphasize the gradual progression of Israel's theology from the days of Moses to the days of Daniel and Esther, the progression engendered by the Christ event was a profound step in his mind and, really, the paradigmatic developmental step. For Willard, Jesus not only apprehends God himself and passes that knowledge on (stages 1 and 2); he also, being who he is, reveals God (stage 3) and thus makes possible an even better and clearer apprehension of God for those who apprehend *him*, Jesus.

Deus Absconditus

WILLARD'S MOST SYSTEMATIC presentation of the problem of bad theology is in the first two lectures from 1988's series *The Soul's Eternal Anchor*. In the first, "God Created the Heavens," Willard explains his reason for taking the series title from Hebrews 6:19 and the theology of the "veil" spoken of in that verse: "Which hope we have as an anchor of the soul, both sure and stedfast, and which entereth into that within the veil" (KJV). He explains that the weakness of the veil metaphor is that it suggests a break in the relationship between those on either side. Positively, he explains, "But the veil as used here refers to the hiddenness of the kingdom of God. It is hidden from us, but it is not distant from us. What did Paul say in Acts 17? 'In him we live and move and have our being.' The hiddenness of Jesus, the hiddenness of the throne of grace, is not a matter of distance. It is a matter of our attitudes and our abilities, and sometimes the veil is drawn. When Stephen was dying, he looked up, and the veil was drawn."[30] The language of *drawing* the veil or of the heavens *opening*, which Willard often uses, suggests that God is responsible for keeping the veil in place. This is true in part, and this *positive* side of the doctrine is what Willard sums up with the concept *Deus absconditus*.

In a 2006 article, "The Bible, the University and the God Who Hides," Willard develops his view of Deus absconditus straightforwardly:

30. Dallas Willard, "God Created the Heavens," *Soul's Eternal Anchor*, MP3/cassette, 29:30.

> *Suppose for a moment that there is a God as the Bible reveals: one of unlimited intelligence, power and love, with the highest possible intentions for humanity and creation. How would he be present to a humanity in flight from him? One might at first think:* overwhelmingly! . . . *But would that accomplish what he has in mind for human beings in his cosmos? What would the result be? People intimidated into submission, no doubt. Cringing cinders. Robots. Persons totally dominated by fear, unable to have a vision of good to be accomplished or to take initiative toward it. Not a notably glorious outcome.*[31]

Elsewhere he speaks of the result as the obliteration of human history and, more profoundly, as making impossible God's purposes in his economy. So God, in his wisdom, is responsible in part for not removing the veil so as to be overwhelmingly present. Then, writing more soberly, Willard says,

> God is not obvious, *not even in the Bible, which offers so many opportunities for man to go wrong—as history and contemporary events surely witness. This is an undeniable fact, which is absolutely consistent with the further idea that he can be found, and found in the Bible also. By seeking.* Deus absconditus *is a deep theological principle. Isaiah cries out in amazement from his own experience: "Truly, Thou are a God who hides Himself, O God of Israel, Savior!" (45:15). He reveals himself, and uniquely in the Bible, but in a way that allows him to be hidden to all but those who resolutely seek him (30:20, Job 23:9–10).*[32]

---

31. Willard, "Bible, the University," 34.

32. Willard, 35. This should be a familiar theme from *Conspiracy*, in which the epitaph from Lewis's *Screwtape Letters* interprets the book's presentation. A more direct explanation of this "deep theological principle" can also be found in Dallas Willard, "The Craftiness of Christ: Wisdom of the Hidden God," in Gracia, *Mel Gibson's "Passion,"* 167–78.

As is evident here, Willard has a notion that ancient Hebrews like Isaiah knew the importance of God's hiddenness. It protected them from the uncomfortable situation of meeting God before they were ready.[33] But this *positive* interpretation of the veil is only half of the story. The veil was not God's perfect intention for the world but a stopgap measure.

By contrast, a *negative* interpretation of the veil is developed by Willard in the second lecture from the 1988 series, titled "Man's Blindness to God." Originally, Adam and Eve were created to live without a veil, created to live with a clear view of God and of the heavens where God manifests himself. But in order to disobey God and aspire to be God, Adam and Eve needed to put away knowledge of God and hide from him—that is, try to keep him from knowledge of their activities. The notes for the lecture contain this generalizing statement: "*Heaven is not visible because men do not want to see it, and God in his gentleness co-operates with their wish.* He establishes His continuous witness, and those who seek Him find him. But the blindness of human beings to God is based upon their desire to *be* God, which they could never maintain in the face of God's visible presence. Satan has lured them into his own many-faceted, rebellious delusion (Isa 14:12–14, Gen 3:5)."[34] Though the spoken lecture is far less explicit, this written statement explains Willard's concept of "man's blindness to God" from the lecture's title. Humanity's blindness is a self-inflicted blindness. Unhealed from generation to generation, the self-infliction has had such drastic effects on human character that even if they wanted to, humans could not see heaven and the reality of God. God, "in his gentleness," participates from generation to generation in this choice because he knows the counterproductive effect that his visibility would have on humans in their current condition and thus on the fulfillment of his purposes.

This account of widespread denial (a concept already studied) and avoidance of knowledge is often connected in Willard's thought with Genesis 3's talk of *hiding*—namely, Adam and Eve hiding in the

33. See Willard's description of the tabernacle in "The Eternal Kind of Life Available in Christ," 25:15.
34. Willard, "Handout for 'The Soul's Eternal Anchor.'"

garden. Addressing this in more detail in the lecture, Willard, however, writes briefly in the notes, "God in his mercy lets us hide (Gen 3:9–10), while extending his tender mercies to us in our hiding."[35] Though connected, the two human reactions to sin—denial and hiding—are not the same. Denial is our attempt, only made possible by God's compliance, to restrict our knowledge *of God*. Hiding is our attempt—again, only made possible by God's compliance—to restrict God's knowledge *of us*. Both reactions make wrongdoing a possibility and thus make the formation of character a possibility. Both reactions also contribute to closing the veil.

In the beginning of the lecture, Willard uses an exegesis of Romans 1 to give weight to his account of the role of knowledge in the fall. He reads Paul's Epistle as depicting the depraved condition of humanity as a result of *willingly not knowing*:[36]

> *If you reject that knowledge [of the nature of God], what happens is exactly what you find in the rest of Romans 1. . . . Let me just summarize it. They knew God, verse 21, but they didn't glorify him as God; neither were [they] thankful. See, that's the only appropriate attitude, is to glory in and thank God. . . . Now, the effect of refusing to glorify God in your mind, to dwell upon him to be thankful, is your imagination becomes vain, and your foolish heart is darkened. The light goes out. . . . And because of this, you see, the first thing that goes is the mind; the darkness moves in as the mind moves away from the knowledge of God against all efforts on God's part to come through to be present. And the next thing that goes is the whole character: "God gave them up."*[37]

35. Willard.

36. A similar interpretation can be found in Willard, "Paul's Good News about God as Seen in Romans."

37. Willard, "Man's Blindness to God," 16:30. See also Dallas Willard, "Occupy till I Come," *Faith Evangelical Sermons* (Faith Evangelical Church, Chatsworth, CA, September 17, 1978), MP3/cassette, 33:15.

This, we could say, is the core problem that the solution will address: an erected veil between God and humans that makes human perception and thus knowledge of God impossible and then makes increasing levels of wickedness possible.

Having described the problem, in the third lecture of *The Soul's Eternal Anchor*, Willard puts the ensuing question succinctly: "So how does God come to man? How does he begin to break through the veil in such a way that he will not destroy those who are on the other side?"[38] With this question and this hamartiology in mind, let us consider Willard's interpretation of Romans.

Romans

VERY EARLY ON in his career, Willard taught regularly on Romans. Few of his later audiences seemed to have known this, and because Willard only went to speak where he was invited, after 1980, he never again gave a full series on Romans. Some of his teachings on Romans 6 became chapter 6 of *Disciplines*, and some became chapter 7 of *Renovation*. Occasionally, he incorporates parts of his exegesis into other lectures, and potentially enough has survived to one day reconstruct his whole argument.

One finds in *Conspiracy* this two-line summary of his Romans exegesis: "Indeed, for Paul, the redemptive act of Jesus becomes the key to understanding the very *dikaiosune* of God himself (Rom. 1–8). It is the person of Jesus and his death for us that makes clear what it is about God that makes him 'really good.'"[39] As we unpack this, it may surprise some that Willard does not think that Paul's main argument in Romans is about the atonement. Paul speaks of atonement, uses the fact of atonement as a premise in the epistle's argument, but he is not *explaining* atonement to the Romans. Instead, Willard believes, Paul is explaining how the *whole life of Jesus*—as he calls it in *Conspiracy*, "the

38. Willard, "Old Testament Good News," 5:15.
39. Willard, *Conspiracy*, 146.

redemptive act of Jesus"—is the basis for an advancement in the Jewish (and indeed human) knowledge of God.[40]

In one of the surviving recordings from his Romans teachings, a sermon called "Thus Justified, We Are at Peace with God," Willard begins by talking about the gospel narrative: "We can never stress too often the great difference in the view of God which Jesus Christ presented and the view of God which is present in the world around us. Jesus was a shocking revolutionary. He outraged the people who heard him." Reading from Luke 4:14–30, Willard explains, "[Jesus] began to explain how God loved people and accepted them where they are. He began to present the great and loving heart of God, who accepts all people—without qualification, just accepts them. And in so doing, he claimed to be accepted by God himself. And the response of the people at that time is seen in the twenty-eighth verse of the fourth chapter: 'and all they in the synagogue when they heard these things were filled with wrath.' It made them very angry. It undercut all of their ways of thinking about God upon which they had based their lives."[41] Willard is claiming that Jesus not only preached the embracing love of God; he also manifested it in the way he treated "sinners," those whom Jesus's culture had dismissed as unacceptable to God. Willard is claiming that the sufferings of Christ are not the first indication that God and Jesus, "His servant" (Acts 3:26), love sinners. Jesus's whole life and ministry were directed toward showing acceptance to sinners, and his public crucifixion, which he and his Father planned, was the culmination of it.

Now, this core thrust of the life of Jesus, his revolutionary view of God and his acts of inclusive love in the name of God, was *a fact* in the day of Paul the missionary. Reminding his audience of the old hymn "Christ Receiveth Sinful Men," Willard proclaims, "*That* is the

---

40. Commenting on Rom 1:16–17, Willard says, "What is it that makes God right? You see it in the gospel. And that gospel extends to and essentially includes the person, the death, the resurrection, the present position of Jesus Christ in our lives. That's where you see the righteousness of God" (Willard, "Discipleship, a Strategy for Personal Wholeness," 15:00).

41. Dallas Willard, "Thus Justified, We Are at Peace with God," *Romans* (Faith Evangelical Church, Chatsworth, CA, October 16, 1977), MP3/cassette, 2:45.

offensive message which Jesus brought, and that is the message which Paul is preaching in the book of Romans. He is saying, 'Whosoever will may come, no conditions.' And that's an upsetting message."[42] Because it was such an obvious fact of Jesus's life, Paul does not need to establish it by explaining the mechanics of atonement. What Paul must do is make sense of the fact that "Christ Receiveth Sinful Men." He must, to borrow Willard's description of the ministry of apologetics, lift doubts about the fact *in light of what his audience already knew* (or thought they knew) *about God.*[43]

That Paul has the teaching and, indeed, the whole life of Jesus in mind when he is making his argument to the Romans—and not just the spilling of his blood in death—is hard for some to see. But Willard sees it in Paul's crucial use of πιστις 'Ιησου Χριστου, the faith of Jesus Christ (Rom 3:22), and believes it is implied in most other references to faith.[44] One must recall that Willard reads New Testament faith as something that Jesus, above all, exemplified, being "the founder and perfecter of our faith" (Heb 12:2). It will be recalled that chapter 5 of this book was not only the biblical ontology of ancient Israel but also the core loci of Jesus's *faith*. It will be recalled from chapter 6 that Jesus had an astonishing faith in God that his first listeners initially admired but did not share.

With this in mind, consider how Willard, immediately after commenting on Luke 4, describes the legacy of Jesus that Paul inherits: "The effect of all of the life and death and teaching of Jesus Christ is to show forth *the kind of faith in God which he had* and which enabled him to live as the Son of God, the unique Son of God in this world."[45] One should not fail to notice how the faith of Jesus includes his death but also his

42. Willard, 12:15.
43. It will be remembered that lifting doubts is what Willard held to be the essence of the New Testament ministry of apologetics. See Dallas Willard, "Apologetics as a Fundamental New Testament Ministry," *Apologetics in the Manner of Jesus* (Grace Church, Los Alamitos, CA, April 22, 1990), MP3/cassette.
44. Though this is now a lively debate in Pauline studies, Willard took the subjective genitive route as early as the 1970s. It is unclear to me which source, if anything besides the Greek New Testament, he is following in this interpretation.
45. Willard, "Thus Justified, We Are at Peace," 12:30 (emphasis mine).

life and his teaching. This faith was not only something that "enabled him" to live as he did but also something that he intended "to show" the world and especially his disciples. This, Willard believes, is what Paul calls πιστις Ἰησου Χριστου in Romans and twice in Galatians 2.

The key loci of Jesus's faith that is at issue in Romans is the nature of God. And at issue was not so much God's greatness as his moral character, "what it is about God that makes him 'really good.'"[46] Willard reads most references to δικαιοσύνη θεου as subjective genitives—that is, God's righteousness. Therefore, Willard reads key passages like Romans 1:17 and 3:21–22 as about how God's own righteousness is made manifest in Jesus and in Jesus's gospel and not about how divine righteousness will be transferred to humans.

This will be clearer if we look briefly at what Willard says about δικαιοσύνη θεου in a Romans lecture from 1972, "Paul's Good News about God as Seen in Romans":

> *[Paul] says the gospel is the power of God that really delivers [1:16–17]. Why? Because in the gospel we come at last to really see God as he is. The righteousness, what makes God right, is finally revealed in the gospel. That's why it delivers. See, if you understand who God is and what God is, if you really understand that, your life will be transformed.*
>
> *And that's what Jesus is all about, is to make so clear to people what He's like that they can live as he taught.*[47]

"The gospel" here is not just a proposition that Jesus lays on his audiences. The gospel for Willard is an expression of Jesus's own faith in God. His personal faith in God was on display in his life *and in his death* and in what he proclaimed in words to his listeners. With respect to the argument in Romans, this gospel concerns, above all, God's righteousness, who God really is.

46. Willard, *Conspiracy*, 146.
47. Willard, "Paul's Good News about God as Seen in Romans," 39:15.

Returning to the 1977 sermon "Thus Justified, We Are at Peace with God," we can now understand Willard's next statement: "The mediation of Christ is to bring us into that same faith in the goodness and acceptance of God so that we will have a new righteousness based upon the presence in our hearts of the same kind of love that makes God right."[48] Showing forth in his life and death "the kind of faith in God which he had," Jesus saves his listeners by helping them share *his faith*.[49] The second part of the statement—how those with Jesus's faith will have "a new righteousness"—is the subject, so Willard, of Romans 5–8. In these chapters, Paul turns to the question of the psychology of redemption or "growth in grace" (2 Pet 3:18).[50]

This means that Romans 5:1—the main text for "Thus Justified, We Are at Peace with God"—is, according to Willard, a pivot point in the epistle. The main question preceding Romans 5:1 is how one is to *comprehensively* understand the nature of God in light of two things: (1) Jesus's revolutionary faith in the goodness and acceptance of God and (2) how possession of this same faith puts *anyone* into saving contact with God. This raises the question, Why is God's righteousness at stake in the first place? It is because the historical fact, "Christ Receiveth Sinful Men," upsets how some, both Jews and gentiles, think about God. It confronts bad theology.

It is a peculiarity of Romans that Paul does not argue for the uniqueness of Jesus's life or for his messiahship—that is, his authoritative position in the kingdom of God. He assumes that his readers know of and accept the Son of God's extraordinary life, teachings, death, and resurrection (Rom 1:1–6). Despite this, Jesus's faith is still a stumbling block for some because of how both those "who do not have the law" and

---

48. Willard, "Thus Justified," 12:45.

49. This is the gist of Rom 3:22 and the subject of Willard's previous sermon, the notes for which (in the Dallas Willard Collection) but not the recording is extant.

50. See Willard, *Disciplines*, chap. 7, as well as Willard's use of Romans in his 1974 series *The Psychology of Redemption* (Woodlake Avenue Friends Church, Canoga Park, CA, April 7–June 23, 1974). Rom 5–8 is about atonement only if atonement is understood holistically in the sense of the complete restoration of and reconciliation of a human person to God.

those "under the law" have understood "the very *dikaiosune* of God himself."[51] Paul's attempt to lift doubts about God starts back at his introduction to the letter in Romans 1:16–17 and his digression on sin and the wrath of God in Romans 1:18–3:20. Paul points out that just as the righteousness of God is revealed in Jesus's gospel—that is, in the *right* apprehension of God (Rom 1:17)—so the wrath of God is revealed in false apprehensions of God (Rom 1:18–20).[52] The fallen human condition is one of a "reprobate mind" (Rom 1:28 KJV), "the mind which God rejects."[53] Those who think they know what God is like—the gentiles *and* the Jews—actually do not. And it is obvious they do not because they are "under sin" (Rom 3:9), all living contrary to the revealed law of God.

The Jews may think they have an advantage, and they do (Rom 3:1–2), but it is not what they think. The law reveals their sin, and their sin reveals that they too have a "reprobate mind," a mind that God rejects. Though they are "under the law" (Rom 2:12; 3:19), and God's law is good and holy, the law is only how God *initially* meets the reprobate mind.[54] It is "God's gift for those who will not receive something better."[55] The result is that their minds only know God's rightness according to the law—one who punishes and rewards by deeds. This is, to return to a theme from chapter 7, *the faith of propriety*—the belief that God *always* works according to a principle of propriety.

When a new vision of God's righteousness enters the world in Jesus and is attested by his extraordinary life, it causes consternation for those absorbed in a system of propriety. If Jesus is right, if his gospel is right, God does not appear to be δικαιος (righteous). He appears to be unjust because, as Willard says in a 1979 lecture titled "What Christ Did to Save Mankind," he seems to be too accepting of "all the atrocities that are done by human beings in this world." As Willard continues,

---

51. Willard, *Conspiracy*, 146.

52. Cf. Willard, "Paul's Good News about God as Seen in Romans," 42:00.

53. Dallas Willard, "Dallas Willard's Notes for 'What Did Jesus Do to Save Us,'" 1977, Dallas Willard Collection.

54. Willard.

55. Dallas Willard, "Dallas Willard's Notes for 'God's Wrath Revealed in the Abandonment of Man,'" 1977, Dallas Willard Collection.

"There is a question about God's character which was raised when Jesus came in . . . and he was so forgiving and so friendly with those who are obviously in the wrong. . . . [In Romans 3:23–26,] the same question arises with God: Now how can he be just and a justifier of those who do wrong?"[56] The mind that only knows God's rightness according to the law says, "This cannot be God's true δικαιοσύνη." "There are many people," Willard says, "who feel . . . that the justice of God depends upon his being ready and willing and persisting in punishing."[57]

Sin and wrath, so Willard, points back to and is ultimately rooted in bad theology. This is the upshot of Romans 1:18–32. As Willard goes on to explain, again in "Thus Justified, We Are at Peace with God," "Do you know this world has been at war with God ever since that thought stole into the mind of Eve, which said, 'God is trying to keep something back from you. God is trying to sell you short'? Eve picked up that thought, and from there on, it is war."[58] *This* is the human condition into which God sends "the law and the prophets" but also into which he sends his Son to make peace (Rom 5:1). It is a condition in which, though they presume otherwise, humans do not *really* know God. Hence, when some presume they know what makes God righteous and thus call into question Jesus's gospel of God's embracing love, Paul reminds them that all, they too, are under sin. Boasting is excluded (Rom 3:27).

But the fact of the gospel stands. Through the πιστις Ἰησου Χριστου, a conception of God's righteousness has entered the world that is "apart from the law" and apart from the conceptions of those who, even though they may be "under the law," are "under sin." Paul does not defend this gospel—Jesus's presentation of God—over and against the presentation of "the law and the prophets," though he does point out that "the law and the prophets" also point to a different conception of God's rightness (Rom 3:21).[59]

---

56. Willard, "What Christ Did," 26:00. See also Willard, "Death and Transfiguration," 22:15.
57. Willard, "What Christ Did," 26:00.
58. Willard, "Thus Justified," 14:15.
59. A point Willard makes use of. See Willard, "Dallas Willard's Notes for 'What Did Jesus Do to Save Us.'"

Reasoning up to this gospel is impossible. Humans are blinded by their sin and the mental schemes of Satan. They not only believe God is to be dreaded; they also believe that they know what it is that makes God right. In the midst of this confusion, God entices humans to peace with him (Rom 5:1) by addressing the underlying problem of what humans think they know about him by saying, in effect, "Hey, how you doing in there? Would you like to see something different?"[60]

God's Pursuit of Man

THE THIRD-STAGE GOSPEL of availability solves a real problem, even for the covenant people. Even before Jesus came, life in the kingdom of God was not the sort of thing that people easily found their way into. Human beings' shoddy theology, among other things, erected a veil between God and themselves. In the second lecture from his series *The Soul's Eternal Anchor*, Willard makes a quick sketch of how Christ's coming and his representation of God contribute to the solution, a sketch that is also a summary of how he typically exposits the first four chapters of Romans. Commenting on Romans 1:16, Willard asks why the gospel is the power of God for salvation and answers, "Because in it, 'the righteousness of God is revealed from faith to faith.' The power of the gospel depends upon the effect of the truth about God on the human mind. We preach the gospel, we reveal the nature of God, and Christ coming makes clear that the nature of God is *love* as well as power. And the acceptance of that in the mind begins the transformation of the self. That's the power of God unto salvation."[61] All of Willard's standard exegetical moves in Romans are present. The gospel Paul preaches about Jesus (and that Jesus preaches about the kingdom) saves powerfully because it is a teaching addressed to the human mind about *who God is*. This

---

60. Willard, "January 2012 Interview," 4:45.

61. Willard, "Man's Blindness to God," 9:15. In lesson 5 of Willard, "Handout for 'Studies in the Gospel of Jesus Christ,'" we get another glimpse of how Willard interprets Rom 1–4. Willard writes that righteousness greater than that of the scribes and Pharisees "comes upon us in and through our faith in the goodness of God, the faith which leads us to turn to his Kingdom." See also Willard, "Dallas Willard's Notes for 'What Did Jesus Do to Save Us.'"

"truth about God" is revealed in the historical life of the Christ, God's Son (Rom 1:2; 3:22). Simply by coming and being who he is—that is, the unique Son of God—Christ's nature and life history proclaim to his listeners and to the world that *God's nature* is power and love. This vision of "the righteousness of God" (Rom 1:17; 3:21–22) is gradually "revealed" to each listener of the gospel as they gradually increase in faith. A listener moves "from faith for faith" (Rom 1:17) until, as Willard continues, they "become more sure that God is really what the Bible says he is."[62]

Through Christ alone, knowledge of God (particularly of his righteousness) is restored to those who *want* to know.[63] To this effect, in *Disciplines*, Willard quotes Albert Magnus, the anonymous author of *On Cleaving to God*, who says, we "find God through God Himself; that is, we pass by the Manhood into the Godhood, by the wounds of humanity into the depths of His divinity."[64] Jesus, by virtue of who he is, represents God. This is Willard's answer to the question, *cur deus homo?* This is how he thinks of the gospel of the kingdom and Jesus's role in salvation *given a third-stage topography of Jesus and the kingdom.*

As we have seen in these pages, this high Christology and the gospel that it makes possible has a long gestation period. It begins with a preparation of the Jewish people that goes back centuries, back to God's first contact with Abraham. Building upon that, God comes into the world as an unassuming person—a man, a carpenter—and begins a special preparation of Jewish apprentices. Through inviting fishermen and "housewives" into a trusting relationship with him, he begins to share *his life*, at least as much of it as they can stand. He offers to them his service, his presence, and his spoken word. At first, Jesus's associates

62. Willard, "Man's Blindness to God," 10:15.

63. Willard, "Session 1—Part 2," 25:15. "Jesus Christ comes back into the world, incarnate, to reestablish that confidence in God through what he has done for us and how he presents God to us through him. 'God commends his love towards us in that while we were yet sinners Christ died for us.'"

64. Willard, *Disciplines*, 178. See also Dallas Willard, "Introducing the Spiritual Disciplines as a Dimension of Pastoral Care," *Spiritual Resources for Pastoral Ministry* (Kempton Park Methodist Church, Kempton Park, South Africa, August 13, 1987), MP3/cassette, 18:00.

think they are receiving communication, communion, and union with a man whose kingdom is the standard human one. Gradually, they come to think that his kingdom is a nonstandard one but still a human or at least creaturely one. All the while, Jesus's greatness grows, especially after his resurrection and ascension, and *his* kingdom—not God's per se—is finally recognized to be much, much larger than originally assumed. He is the Cosmic Christ and the Mystical Christ. Only having come through this long process can listeners appreciate an argument like the one Paul presents in Romans about God's righteousness.

The Significance of Acts

LET US NOW see how Willard puts this Pauline and epistolic theology together with the gospel of the kingdom, for as Jesus grows in the minds of his listeners, his basic offer, holds Willard, does not change. As the ascended Lord, he is still offering himself as a reality for trusting. He is still open for personal, trust-based relationship. His gospel is still the *availability* of the kingdom of God through faith in him. Paul is presenting the same gospel as Jesus even though Paul's language is different and he preaches *Jesus*.

The best way to understand this transition in the Scriptures, so Willard, is "to walk through the book of Acts and watch how the gospel of the kingdom and the gospel of Jesus come together." What one will find there he summarizes in one of his pithy, oft-repeated phrases: "You will see them separate at the beginning and together at the end. This was a matter of *putting a face to the kingdom and the kingdom to a face*."[65] What does this phrase mean? It means that for persons like Peter and John, the loving, joyous, peaceful face of Jesus was known (1 John 1:1–2), but it was attached to a kingdom of limited greatness and power. In time, however, they came to a view of the greatness and power of Jesus, which, if not full-blown orthodox Christology, ascribed to Jesus increasingly lofty metaphysical properties. Jesus's kingdom was being united in their minds with God's kingdom: "'Ultimate reality'—to speak

65. Willard, "Kingdom Salvation," 29:15.

grandly—permits itself to be addressed and dealt with through the Son of man, Jesus."[66] In other words, through someone with *the face* of Jesus.

At the same time, the phrase calls attention to a merger of the kingdom and the face progressing in the opposite direction. Experience with God's kingdom—divided, shall we say, into God's providence and communicative presence—was a staple of the Jewish experience of reality. According to Jesus's gospel, it was now available directly to anyone just as it was to him. Individuals like Peter and John participated in expeditions like the sending of the Twelve (Matt 10) and of the seventy-two (Luke 10) and the initial mission in Jerusalem of the nascent community of Jesus (Acts 1–7). They knew the availability of God's kingdom for them (e.g., Luke 10:17) and joined Israel's prophets in that knowledge. "Theirs is the kingdom of God," yes, but with a caveat. That kingdom still belonged to a divine face of dubious character.[67] Could God be fully trusted? Would he judge them according to a principle of propriety and count their trespasses against them?

While still in doubt about God's *face*, they likewise observed how God's *kingdom* "anointed" Jesus (Acts 10:38) and attested him "with mighty works and wonders" (Acts 2:22). They observed how Jesus was "declared to be the Son of God in power according to the Spirit of holiness by his resurrection from the dead" (Rom 1:4). Thus, they dared to believe, as Willard writes, that "all of Jesus' teachings about life in the Kingdom were true."[68] And they dared to believe that Jesus's teachings about God were true, teachings including his statement "Fear not, little flock, for it is your Father's good pleasure to give you the kingdom" (Luke 12:32). Because of Jesus's clear connection with God's kingdom, the sovereign God's face was being conceptually united with Jesus's face to the point that the listeners knew that what they saw in Jesus's face was in actuality the face of Israel's covenant God, the ruler of the universe.

---

66. Willard, *Conspiracy*, 27.

67. Is it in the context that Jesus tells the participants in his ministry that the real cause for rejoicing is that God is a God who cares for them—that is, that "[their] names are written in heaven"? For more on these gospel periscopes, see Willard, *Guidance*, 138–39.

68. Willard, *Disciplines*, 35.

Many attempts to answer the question of the incarnation—the Anselmian question, *cur deus homo?*—focus on a particular moment of the Christ event. For some, it is the metaphysical union, the act of assumption. For others, it is the passion of Christ and especially the moment of death and descent into hell. For still others, it is the resurrection and Christ's triumphant ascension to glory. But the key feature in Willard's incarnational account of salvation, I argue, is Jesus's face. Jesus does many things to accomplish our salvation. These have been discussed in the previous chapters. But as the God-man, the second person of the Trinity's *unique* role in the Triune God's plan of salvation is to be, for human history, the unique face of God.

The appearing of God's face in Jesus was the Trinity's plan to get past the veil, to attack the problem of bad theology, to restore the knowledge of God to humanity, and to do all this in a way that accomplishes God's grand redemptive purposes. Because of what he wants to get out of human history, God could not barge into history and force his face on the world. But why *in Jesus*? Why *in a human creature*? Given what Willard has said about crucifixion and ascension, we know that it is not because humanity needed something sense perceptible in order to know God.[69] This would violate for Willard the gist of the second commandment. Indeed, it is not Jesus's fleshly face that Willard is speaking of.

Jesus's face in these statements refers, rather, to what we might provisionally call his existential persona—that is, not what he looked like but *who he was*. Taken at a glance, *who he was* is what the four canonical Gospels try to capture. They are uninterested in what he looked like, his fleshly face. As Willard says about John 6, "His literal flesh, when taken apart from his spiritual reality, the personal, would do them absolutely no good at all."[70]

How, according to Willard, was Jesus's human existential persona perceived by those who knew him?[71] Here we must return to Willard's

69. Perhaps contrary to Aquinas, *Summa Theologiae* 1a. 76.

70. Willard, *Guidance*, 165. On face, see also Willard, *Conspiracy*, 75-76.

71. That they did perceive him beyond his fleshly appearance was covered in the first- and second-stage Christology sections.

Christian psychology. It is Willard's view that humans have something other than their body that is immediately recognizable about them. For example, in his work as a professor and itinerant speaker, Willard thought that people would quickly forget what he said but not forget who he was.[72] This memorableness is due to the obviousness of the human face—a person's existential persona and what he calls, at times, their "inner life."

On one occasion, Willard makes this comment: "When we talk about the inner life, often we talk about something sort of [like] . . . you're going to disappear now. But the inner life is the most obvious thing about you. That's what everyone knows about you almost immediately is the quality of your inner life."[73]

According to Willard, certain aspects of human personality can be hidden. Humans can and do use their bodies to hide their souls. By contrast, young children and the very old are cherished because they cannot hide, or have given up hiding, their souls. Likewise, our thoughts, as children soon learn, are basically hidden. Feelings, though much harder to hide, are masked with great ability by actors and many in professional roles, such as doctors and clinical psychologists. But our inner life is not hidden and perhaps cannot be hidden. This is why one's inner life is connected, for Willard, with being the light of the world and a city on a hill that cannot be hidden.[74] Similarly, this is why we will recognize one another in the preresurrection afterlife even though we will not have bodies. Our faces will tell those who have known us on earth who we are. For this reason, Jesus on the Mount of Transfiguration did not need to introduce Moses and Elijah, whose fleshly

---

72. Dallas Willard, "Life and Spiritual Life: The Spiritual and the Non-spiritual Person. Spiritual Life from Christ Makes Moral Goodness Easy," *The Knowledge of Christ in the Contemporary World* (Eidos Christian Center, Newport Beach, CA, June 28, 2003), MP3, 29:00.

73. Dallas Willard, "Learning to Walk in the Eternal Kind of Life Now: Who You Are and Why You Are Here," *Journey Inward, Journey Outward* (Association for Christians in Students Development, Santa Barbara, CA, June 7, 1994), MP3/cassette, 11:45. After this comment, Willard relates the idea to Prov 4:23.

74. For more on this, see Willard's concept of witnessing. E.g., Dallas Willard, "The Witness: Giving the Life of Christ," *Death and Transfiguration*, MP3/cassette; and Willard, "Tenure in a Secular University.'"

faces had long been forgotten. Peter, John, and James recognized them by their existential personas.[75] Despite the number of times he makes reference to our nonphysical face, Willard never says, to my knowledge, what our face is in terms of where it fits into his mature Christian psychology. I would argue, therefore, that the face, for Willard, is *seated* in a person's heart—that is, their spirit—and is *expressed* in their conscious actions as well as the unconscious, automatic tendencies of the body.[76] With respect to Jesus, his face is the shape of his heart. It is what those historically and geographically close to him perceived of him and did not quickly forget. It is *who he was*, his inner life.[77] It, of course, was manifested in his interactions with people and in his public ministry of proclaiming, manifesting, and teaching. But it was just as obviously manifested in his coming into flesh, his voluntary public death, and his return to his disciples via resurrection three days later. To listeners who were not given access to Jesus's loving, joyous, peaceful face in private, his public life and death also proclaim his face. Humans cannot hide their faces. In this way, Willard makes the crucifixion essential to the cosmic purposes of God. Only in the righteousness of Jesus's unjust suffering unto death could the face of God be revealed to sinful humanity.

This psychology of face is vital to understanding the incarnation's unique role in the history of redemption. Simply put, *Jesus manifested the Triune God's face to people simply by being present with them in human form while he was on earth.* Humanity suffered from wretched theology,

---

75. Willard, "Residency Part 2," 30:15, and later 32:15. See also Willard, "How People Perish," 30:15. "Did you ever wonder how the apostle knew who Elijah and Moses was [*sic*] on the mount of transfiguration? See, the real person comes through the body. We use our bodies to hide the real person. . . . But God intended our bodies to be a revelation of the real person."

76. See Willard, *Disappearance*, 38–42, for how Willard thinks morality is communicated in the university classroom.

77. Willard's understanding of how God manifested and manifests his inner life, his face, without having a body is a matter that does not need to be explored here. But bodies are not necessary for having or expressing faces, and this gives support to Willard's belief that the inner lives of humans survive the death of the body and can be manifested to others without aid of the human body. For our purposes, it is enough to note Willard's view that humans' inner lives *are* manifested through their bodies.

but in the words of John, "The only God, who is at the Father's side, he has made him known" (John 1:18).

This salvific act and answer to the question, *cur deus homo?* shows up in a few places in *Conspiracy*.[78] Though framed in terms of what we do in response to God's salvific act, the most detailed passage is in chapter 9. There we read that the first primary objective in a curriculum for Christlikeness should be "to bring apprentices to the point where they dearly love and constantly delight in that 'heavenly Father' made real to earth in Jesus and are quite certain that there is no 'catch,' no limit, to the goodness of his intentions or to his power to carry them out."[79] Willard mentions three areas of the knowledge of God that are important for salvation from bad theology, and the second area, "The God of Jesus and His People," focuses on God's entrance into human history and especially into human flesh.

Paul's phrase from 2 Corinthians 4:6, "Knowledge of the Glory of God in the *Face* of Christ," is how Willard titles the subsection I want to focus on.[80] This verse, central to any Christian theology of the face of God and the knowledge thereof, names the central arrangement that underlies Willard's incarnational account of salvation. The section it titles is an exegesis of the verse, one could say, in terms of Jesus's life as a whole. Any ministry that intends to encourage others to contemplate and love God must follow the path God himself has forged. One must look for God's face in the place where he most intensely manifested it on earth.

Notice that Willard uses the classic text of John 14:8–9, "Whoever has seen me has seen the Father," to introduce the arrangement God has made for our knowledge of him.[81] In light of this new fact of human history, the incarnation of God's Son, human ministers are advised to "bring the heart-wrenching goodness of God, his incomprehensible graciousness and generosity, before the mind of disciples by helping them

---

78. See Willard, *Conspiracy*, 11–14, 21.
79. Willard, 321.
80. Willard, 334 (emphasis mine).
81. An important verse for Willard's argument in "What Christ Did."

to see and understand *the person of Jesus*."[82] Because of the arrangement provided in the incarnation, "the key, then, to loving God is to *see Jesus*, to hold him before the mind with as much fullness and clarity as possible."[83] This is, so Willard, what it means for Paul to know God in the face of Christ.

In terms of the specifics of teaching others to "see Jesus," Willard divides the task into four aspects. One could consider these the *four locations of Jesus's face* in human history. The last two, Willard's third- and fourth-mentioned locations, should be oddly familiar. The third location is primarily a function of Jesus's communicative presence with his listeners after his ascension. Jesus's face, so Willard, could be seen by looking at the *ecclesia* gathered in his name, the people who were interacting with him as a resurrected, ascended being. Willard called this "the continuing incarnation," which turns out to be a fairly important concept in Willard's theology.[84] As a location for Jesus's face, his point is that a study of church history (particularly the lives of the saints) and of the local and "nonlocal" church (the "saints" whom we meet in the course of life) will catalyze knowledge of Jesus's face and thus knowledge of God's face. This strategy for seeing Jesus corresponds, so it seems, to Jesus's work as the Mystical Christ and to the church as the body of Christ. It corresponds, that is, to the effect of God's kingdom *upon individual persons*. The fourth location of Jesus's face corresponds to the effect of God's kingdom *upon the physical cosmos*. It corresponds to the Cosmic Christ and to the body of Christ in the bread and wine of the ordinance but also in creation as a whole.

But the first two locations are the most relevant to a third-stage understanding of the gospel and how God saves by means of an incarnation. Willard speaks of Jesus's face revealed, first, in the record of Jesus's life and ministry in the four Gospels and, second, in the record of his

82. Willard, *Conspiracy*, 334 (emphasis mine).
83. Willard, 334.
84. See Willard, *Conspiracy*.

crucifixion, resurrection, and ascension.[85] By contrast, the third and fourth locations are simply *christological* extensions of classic locations of God's face and kingdom—that is, locations known to ancient Israel.[86] In light of the increasing recognition of the divinity of Jesus as the Cosmic Christ and the Mystical Christ, these two traditional locations for showing forth God's face and his kingdom also now show forth *Jesus's face and his kingdom* and, in turn, show forth God's face in greater clarity. However, the first two locations deal with how a face was put to the kingdom in the incarnational existence of *the man Jesus*.[87]

More could be said in particular about how the crucifixion and resurrection show Jesus's face.[88] But on a more general level, consider how God's strategy of revealing his face through Jesus solves humanity's fundamental problem of God-blindness. Again, from the series *The Soul's Eternal Anchor*, we hear Willard say the following: "What Jesus came to do was to break through the veil that we talked about last time. He broke through the veil, and he made the contact, and he taught about the kingdom, and then he let evil do its worst to him and rose beyond it in a resurrection life."[89] Breaking through the veil was not a matter of overcoming some geographical or cosmological barrier between God and man. As already quoted, God and his kingdom are "not distant from us." Breaking through the veil was a matter of making the face of God visible in a way that allowed true knowledge of God to be restored to creatures who were caught in the bondage of bad theology.

---

85. Curiously, Willard omits here the resurrection and ascension despite his belief that the resurrection "validated the reality and the indestructibility of what Jesus had preached and exemplified *before* his death" (Willard, *Disciplines*, 37). We can assume the omission is simply rhetorical.

86. Moses and Elijah were two "saints" whose faces reflected God's face, and Isaiah knew "holy, holy, holy is the Lord of hosts; *the whole earth* is full of his glory" (Isa 6:3; emphasis mine).

87. Willard, "Kingdom Salvation," 29:15.

88. See Willard, *Conspiracy*, 334; Dallas Willard, "What to Do after You Decide to Do What Jesus Said to Do," *Life with God: Celebrating Lifelong Discipleship* (Renovaré, Houston, TX, October 2008), MP3, 17:45; and Willard, "Meaning of the Rule," 46:00.

89. Willard, "Man's Blindness to God," 10:45.

The Shape of the Face

AT ONE POINT in his speaking ministry in the 2000s, Willard began asking his audiences to reflect for a moment and search for one, and only one, word that they could use to describe Jesus.[90] It was an exercise for him of attempting to name *precisely* what the Gospel writers said could be seen in Jesus's face. After a few moments, he would propose a single word to his audience: *relaxed.* He would then use the story of Jesus sleeping in the boat during the storm to illustrate how Jesus's heart was, at bottom, at rest. The exercise with his audiences was primarily a pastoral move with the intended effect of calling attention to something about Jesus's inner life that Willard thought his audiences were apt to miss. But it is a good exercise for trying to name the knowledge of God that, according to the apostles, Jesus brought through the veil.

Faces come in shapes. It should be obvious that Willard's notion of Jesus putting a face to the kingdom is not a matter of some *generic* face being revealed. The whole point is that personal particularity, *a* face or *Jesus's* face, is put to the kingdom and not just generic "face."[91] What, then, is the testimony of those first listeners who witnessed Jesus's inner life, his existential persona, his face? *What face* was put on the kingdom?

Conspiracy, one could say, is Willard's sustained attempt to profoundly sum up the content of Jesus's face. At the beginning of the book, he writes, "He sends among us the Way to himself. That shows what, in his heart of hearts, God is really like—indeed, what *reality* is really like."[92] The word to note is *heart. God's* heart. Jesus came to show God's heart. And immediately following the description of that heart is one of Willard's most repeated phrases: "In its deepest nature and meaning our universe is a community of boundless and totally competent love."[93]

---

90. E.g., Dallas Willard, "Expectation and Engagement," *Following Christ 2002* (InterVarsity, Atlanta, GA, January 1, 2003), MP3, 27:45.

91. In metaphysics, we are dealing with a particular if it cannot be predicated of anything else.

92. Willard, *Conspiracy*, 11.

93. Willard, 11.

Later in the section of chapter 9 discussed above, Willard makes another attempt to specify *God's* inner life. He writes, "[Knowledge of God through his creation] does not begin to make clear the extent to which God loves, and loves human beings in particular. It cannot make clear, to humans as they are, the 'Father heart' of God toward us."[94] "Father heart" becomes a turn of phrase to explain "what God is really like." Later, Willard explains that "Abraham and the tradition of faith that comes down from him through the ages was to be *the publically appointed place in history* where the nature of God's Father heart was to be accessible to all."[95] This historical appointment of Abraham's children, needless to say, climaxes in Jesus, whose life, above all others, shows forth God as fatherly.

Another of Willard's attempts—this time more contentious—to express the shape of the face put on the kingdom is connected with the topic of forgiveness. Regarding the story of Jesus and the harlot of Luke 7, Willard writes that "the woman *saw* Jesus." He then gives us the substance of what she saw: "She knew he was *forgiving and accepting* her before he ever said, 'Your sins are forgiven.' She knew because she had seen a goodness in him that could only be God."[96] Forgiveness and acceptance were evident features of Jesus's existential persona.[97]

The view that God's *forgiving* inner life could be known *without knowing* that Jesus died on the cross (or especially without knowing the terms of any atonement theory or even the right atonement theory) is one reason why Willard stood by his contentious interpretation of the Beatitudes for over forty years: "[The Beatitudes] serve to clarify Jesus' fundamental message: the free availability of God's rule and righteousness to all of humanity through reliance upon Jesus himself, the person

---

94. Willard, 332.

95. Willard, 333 (Willard's emphasis).

96. Willard, 19 (emphasis mine).

97. In a gloss on "For God did not send his Son into the world to condemn the world" (John 3:17), Willard says, "The thing which most stands out in Jesus himself and in the picture of God which he presents is he doesn't condemn" (Dallas Willard, "No Condemnation," *Living without Fear* [Rolling Hills Covenant Church, Rolling Estates, CA, July 7, 1991], MP3/cassette, 34:15).

now loose in the world among us."[98] The Beatitudes for him express *in words* the acceptance and forgiveness of all people that Willard thought lay in Jesus's nonphysical face.[99] The crucifixion of Jesus and his passion as a whole express, then, *in deeds* the acceptance and forgiveness that were embedded in Jesus's will. Regarding crucifixion as the second location of Jesus's face in human history, Willard says, "No one can have an adequate view of the *heart* and purposes of the God of the universe who does not understand that he permitted his son to die on the cross to reach out to all people, even people who hated him. That is who God is."[100]

To these ways of characterizing Jesus's face many more could be added. Though his face is certainly not a Rorschach, the instances of "the knowledge of the glory of God in the face of Christ" (2 Cor 4:6) are numerous for Willard. *Gentleness,* already mentioned, was a feature of Jesus's heart. We are told that Jesus's *humility* is one of the things Paul "got" about him.[101] In the third chapter of *Conspiracy,* Willard uses the word *happy* to describe the inner life of God.

Divine Friend: Φιλαδελφια

AS IMPORTANT AS a restored vision of the "heart-wrenching goodness" of God is, it is not the specific gospel of Jesus. By putting a face to the kingdom, the listeners have only come so far as to describe God's eternal disposition toward them. But Jesus's specific gospel takes a further step. Even in the first stage of their understanding, Jesus's listeners know that Jesus is positively disposed toward them, that his heart is benevolent. Nevertheless, if this is all there is, then there is possibly still something clinical about their relationship. Patients might trust a doctor who is positively disposed toward them, but this does not imply more than a strong professional relationship. For the majority of Jesus's first listeners,

---

98. Willard, *Conspiracy,* 116.

99. It should go without saying that Willard did not believe in a doctrine of limited atonement, the belief that God's forgiveness was only extended to those who entered the blessed afterlife. See Willard, "Heavens Were Opened," 43:45.

100. Willard, *Conspiracy,* 335 (emphasis mine).

101. Willard, "Kingdom Gospel," 37:45.

there was simply no occasion to be more intimate with Jesus than clients of a competent and benevolent man would be.

Among those who stepped into discipleship, the occasion for intimacy increased. Yet few of Jesus's disciples were in close enough proximity to him to, with any justification, relate to him on a more intimate basis than as their "master." After the Twelve and a few others, the rest fade into "the crowd." But proximity is only the basis of a more intimate relationship. This basis, as we have noticed, is extended and expanded by Jesus's resurrection and ascension. It was always his intention that all persons *may be* as proximate to him as Peter was. Even Peter himself experienced an increase in Jesus's proximity to him in light of the resurrection and ascension. But there is more to intimacy than this. A family member or an employee may have copious contact with a person and still be internally distant from that person.

Biblically, the level of care and concern between persons that I am driving at can be found, in part, in John 15:12–15: "This is my commandment, that you love one another as I have loved you. Greater love has no one than this, that someone lay down his life for his friends. You are my friends if you do what I command you. No longer do I call you servants, for the servant does not know what his master is doing; but I have called you friends, for all that I have heard from my Father I have made known to you." This Johannine verse describes a *special* kind of personal relationship that Jesus seeks with his associates. It is predicated on his love for them (v. 12). But it also depends on their love for him, the terms for this love being given in verse 14 ("if you do what I command you") but spelled out in verse 12 ("love one another"). But Jesus is adding something new to the relationship: knowledge of his intentions and his mind (v. 15). Entering into this new relationship does not depend on his associates exemplifying a particularly advanced righteousness. The initiative lies with Jesus, but how far the relationship goes from there depends, in part, on them.

I wish to remind readers yet again that the three stages in the first listeners' understanding of Jesus's gospel are my conceptualization of the process. It is inspired by and based on Willard's thought, but it is not directly his. In systematizing his thought, there are times when premises imply a certain conclusion, but that conclusion is not to be found in any explicit statement of his. This is a place where that is the case. Willard never, to my knowledge, puts the incarnation and Jesus's announcement of the kingdom together.

On Being a Friend

ALLOW ME TO attempt to put the two together for Willard. Let me combine what Willard said about God's incarnational plan for rescuing humanity from its God-blindness with Jesus's news that the kingdom of God is at hand through trust in him.

"Atonement is an eternal fact in the nature of God," Willard says on one occasion.[102] The shape of God's face, seen in Jesus's face, is an eternal reality. Its historical revelation in the life and death of Jesus is not, but its principle is.

On the other hand, Jesus's gospel is not naming an eternal reality; it is an announcement, an invitation to a particular kind of relationship with Jesus, who offers himself as a reality for trusting. In previous stages, I described this reality as, first, a prophet and, second, a teacher or a mediator. But in light of the "Father heart" of God that shined through Jesus's life and death and the ontology in which Jesus is revealed to stand, the best concept for the reality that Jesus presents himself to his listeners as is that of a *friend.* In announcing that his kingdom is at hand, he is saying, "I will be your friend. And you can be mine." This is the form that God's good heart takes when it reaches out in action.

I admit that Willard is in the habit of loosely using "friend" to refer to *anyone* who has a trusting relationship with Jesus—for example,

---

102. "Atonement," he continues, "is not something that was an afterthought; it is the natural expression of who God is—that he would come and die on the cross and experience the depths, the very bottom, that ordinary human beings apart from God experience. And he would come right in there, and then we could be united with him." Willard, "Atonement in the Spiritual Life," 15:15. On another occasion, after an exegesis of 1 John 2:2, he says, "The atonement is Christ himself. Now, that involves everything he did, but it keeps us out of the position that the atonement is something that he did that is detachable from him" (Dallas Willard, "Attention to Christology and Atonement," *Denver Cohort—Session Two* [Renovaré Institute, Allenspark, CO, March 16, 2011], DVD, 1:03:00).

he calls Jesus's disciples his "first friends."[103] But in order to make a point about something important in Willard's theology as a whole, I want to use this concept much more precisely than Willard does. For that reason, "friend" in what follows is much more a heuristic than a strict exegesis of Willard's concept. Despite the vagueness of terms, with the concept of friendship, we are on solid ground in Willard's thought world.

Before we consider examples of divine friendship in Willard's theology, I want to begin with some phenomenological elucidation of the concept. Unlike other descriptions I have used, *friend* is more phenomenologically obscure. Being a friend expresses two things, both of which are intrinsic to Willard's thought.

First and most importantly, *friend* refers to a character trait, a personal quality, the shape of a face. This aspect of being a friend parallels Willard's interpretation of the parable of the Good Samaritan. Willard points out that the question at the end of the parable uses *neighbor* as a character trait. Jesus does not repeat or answer in essence the lawyer's original question, Who is my neighbor? He asks his listeners to identify who in the story had a *neighborly* heart.[104] In common use, *friend* has much more of a virtuous sense than *neighbor* does. *Friend* refers to a person who is friendly and who is friendly to me. *Friend* emphasizes a person's love and care of others. But it also communicates a person's openness to others and attention to their lives or existence. Centrally, a friend is a person whose very being, their personhood, is *available* to another person. We can refer to this character trait in Jesus as his friendliness or biblically as φιλαδελφια—that is, brotherly love.

But *friend* can commonly also express a voluntarily chosen status. As such, it refers to an intentional action or work. Like the neighbor in Jesus's parable, it names an informal position, even an "office"—the sort of thing we actively and consciously pursue. Commonly, we speak of someone befriending someone or being a friend to someone. We

103. Willard, *Conspiracy*, 84.

104. Dallas Willard, "The Good 'Half-Breed' and the Full-Blooded Stinkers: The Neighborliness of the Kingdom," *The Parabolic Teaching about Christ's Kingdom by Christ* (Harbor Church, Lomita, CA, May 29, 1983), MP3/cassette, 16:00.

speak of lifelong friends, trying to be friends, and the choice to remain friends. We speak of a person who is a "good friend" to others—that is, a person we would be blessed to have as a friend. One person can be a better friend to someone who is not as good of a friend in return. As a voluntarily chosen status, the concept assumes the character trait of friendliness. But the reverse is not necessarily true. A person with the character trait of friendliness may, for good reason, *not* actively pursue the position of being a friend to another. Humans, in contrast to God, are limited in their ability to be in relation to others. Though a human is genuinely friendly in character, in their limitation, they may not be capable of being a friend to yet one more person. We can refer to this status of being a friend in Jesus as his offer of friendship or in terms of his specific friendships.

Though *friend* is more my term than Willard's, the reality of *a special kind* of personal relationship with Jesus, as seen in John 15:12–15, is there in Willard's portrayal of Jesus's life and ministry. In *Conspiracy*, Willard gives a reconstruction of how 1 John 1:1–5 happened historically in Galilee. Significantly, it is a reconstruction placed *after* his quick history of the with-God life in the Old Testament records: "Of course, incarnation in the person of Jesus is the most complete case of 'God with us,' or 'Immanuel.' The apostle John, who as a youth was *the closest of companions with Jesus*, marvels in his old age that he and others had with their physical senses—their ears, eyes, and hands—known the very source of life, which was from the beginning of everything (1 John 1:1)."[105] For Willard, the incarnation, as an instance of "God with us," was focused on someone (John) becoming "the closest of companions with Jesus." It describes a concrete effect of Jesus's breaking through the veil. Historically, of course, John did not know as Jesus was first befriending him that *God*, "the very source of life," was befriending him. His friend's face had not yet been put to the kingdom. What he did know with appropriate clarity was the shape of the face. It was the face of a willing companion, the face of a person who welcomed even closer companionship, the face of φιλαδελφια.

105. Willard, *Conspiracy*, 69–70 (Willard's emphasis).

Willard's interpretation of 1 John 1:1–5 is that despite John's assumption of the mere humanness of Jesus's kingdom, the benefits of being friends with God—the resources of God's life—were in the process of being communicated to John.

But the clearest example of this special kind of relationship with Jesus is found, of course, in *Guidance.* Rewriting the introduction for the second edition, Willard writes, "The main point [of the book] is that God has created us for intimate friendship with himself, both now and forever."[106] Though Willard's first book was the only one to be written as a book for laypersons rather than for professional ministers and educated readers, it contains Willard's deepest soteriology—even deeper, I believe, than what is found in *Conspiracy.* Because of the book's lightness, its themes are often more theologically profound than they appear at first glance.

Willard consciously but subtly argues for a position that sets him apart from a few great traditions of the past. In Western theology, it sets him apart from the tradition that sees humanity's greatest good in a passive contemplation of the beatific vision. In Eastern theology, it sets him apart from the tradition that sees humanity's greatest good in theosis insofar as its ideal is a wordless, unconscious, and inactive union of a creature with God's uncreated energies. If one reads *Guidance* with the thought in mind that, while being practical and simple, Willard is arguing for a *specific* vision of our future glorification, these deeper theological moves become clear.

In sum, the pastoral thrust of the book is to move people away from thinking of God's guidance in subservient or oracular terms. Willard's view is that guidance is intended by God to be both (1) a redemptive act that raises up mature, rational beings and also (2) a paradisal act between God and these mature, rational beings who are now equals *of a sort.* On the latter, he writes, "The *ideal* for divine guidance is finally determined by who God is, what kind of beings we are, and what a personal relationship between God and us should be like"—that is, it

106. Willard, *Guidance*, x.

is determined by what it is like in paradisal circumstances.[107] Shortly following, we hear what this paradisal relationship looks like: "The sort of relationship suited to *friends* who are mature personalities in a shared enterprise, no matter how different they may be in other respects."[108] Following this, he makes some of the distinctions already made: "But the Heavenly Father's ideal for his family is clearly something very different from the relation of a boss to subordinates. It was expressed by Jesus in his prayer: 'That they may all be one; even as thou, Father, art in me, and I in thee, that they also may be in us' (Jn 17:21, RSV). The intended relation is one of being in us. *We are to be friends* (2 Chr 20:7; Jn 15:13–15) and fellow workers (1 Cor 3:9) with God."[109] In these texts, Willard lays before us an *advanced* level of intimacy. We should note how Willard's mind quickly turns to a classic text for the doctrine of union with Christ, John 17. We should also note how he combines friendship with *conscious*, *active* participation in another's purposes ("shared enterprise," "fellow workers") and gives classic texts for that teaching. Jesus's friends know his and his Father's purposes and share and support them.

The Unique Representation of the Friendliness of God

WHAT DOES JESUS'S announcement that *his* kingdom is available have to do with being his friend, with this special kind of relationship to him? Recall that in Willard's ontology of persons, all persons have kingdoms, and all kingdoms are personal. Phenomenologically considered, the closer you become to being someone's friend, the more this person's heart and mind and their kingdom (what they have say over) are *available* to you and yours to them. *Kingdom availability* is the currency of friendship. Though friends remain ontologically distinct and separable, a genuine friend lets that over which they have say mesh with that over which another has say *as* their wills and minds come into closer alignment.

107. Willard, 17 (emphasis mine).
108. Willard, 17 (emphasis mine).
109. Willard, 23 (emphasis mine).

Love, especially mutual love, is at the core of friendship and a friend's offer of availability. But this is why the revelation of God's righteousness is not Jesus's specific gospel: love is not as inclusive of friendship as friendship is of love. One may seek the good of a person or creature and still have good reason for not—or at least not yet—extending friendship to them. Regarding these distinctions, Willard observes, "A mere benefactor, however powerful, kind, and thoughtful, is not the same thing as a *friend.* 'But I have called you friends' (Jn 15:15). And: 'Look, I am with you every moment, even to the end of the age!' (Mt 28:20; compare Heb 13:5–6)."[110] There is nothing inconsistent about God loving his creatures without befriending them. This, depending on the creatures and his ends, may be a very wise strategy. Jesus advises not to throw pearls to swine (Matt 7:6).[111] His wise, loving strategy is to wait with his disciples before inviting them into something more and calling them to be his friends. Though he loved and chose them before the foundation of the world, his intent is to be helpful. So God waits until his listeners are mature enough to be invited into his friendship. And in light of his self-revelation in Jesus's life and death, extending friendship is now a wise expression of his love.

This, I think, is where a distinction between the character trait of friendliness and the offer of friendship helps explain the difference between the historical revelation of God's righteousness and Jesus's specific gospel of the kingdom. For Willard, the unique, historical work of God in the advent of Jesus is the representation by Jesus of the *friendly* inner life of God. Concrete friendships certainly also formed in Jesus's historical coming as he befriended specific people. It was not insignificant that when he ascended, he left behind a small group of friends. But this befriending work is not, in Willard's view, *specific* to his sojourn on earth or even to his incarnate nature.[112] Abraham was a friend of God,

---

110. Willard, 10.

111. See Willard's interpretation of this verse in Willard, *Conspiracy*, 228–29.

112. One might consider how this is contrary to Lesslie Newbigin's assessment of the uniqueness of Jesus's life. For Newbigin, it is highly significant that Jesus befriended certain people who became the first link in the long relational chain we know as the church stretched out in history. Though not for the reasons typically emphasized, Newbigin is

as were many of his children, those with "the blessing of Abraham" (Gal 3:14). In the same way, countless persons after Jesus's physical absence can rightly claim to be friends of God.

What's more, in terms of appropriation of the work of salvation within the Trinity, friendship is not appropriated by Willard to the Son. Once a Trinitarian level of understanding of God is reached—the only level at which it is possible to speak of appropriation—Jesus's friendships are understood to be not exclusive to the Son. In a message on the Trinity, Willard says, "That's the call upon us to join that community, to step into the stream of life, to know the power of God that is moving, and to understand the reality of love as a triune structure—where I love you, and you love me, and we love them. Love is always threefold; it's Trinitarian. Love is Trinitarian. Love is never completed without three."[113] When Jesus befriended Peter and John in the first century, it *was* the whole Trinity that befriended them. There is no indication in Willard that a human might be more capable of friendship with the Son than with the Spirit or the Father. A human could, however, not know the metaphysical and personal depths of their friend. For Peter and John, the greater ontological reality of their Friend Jesus was still behind the veil.

So the specific gospel of Jesus in his statement that the kingdom of God is at hand is his concrete offer for one to become a friend of God through becoming a friend of Jesus. In terms of availability, God in Christ makes his kingdom, his personality, available to anyone. In the first stage, Jesus's first listeners understood availability in terms of availability *for* Jesus and the by-product of that relation as their good fortune. In the second stage, they understood availability in terms of availability *through* Jesus—that is, in terms of his mediating work between two parties. In this third stage, where something of the divinity of Jesus is in view, they understand availability in terms of availability *by*

---

interested in claiming apostolic succession, for it helps him connect church fellowship to the gospel, the life of Jesus (see Lesslie Newbigin, *The Gospel in a Pluralist Society* [Grand Rapids, MI: Eerdmans, 1989], 80–88, 92–99).

113. Willard, "Beyond Personality," 43:45.

Jesus. Availability in the third stage is not so much something Jesus does for the kingdom as something Jesus *is* as the kingdom's king.

Third-Stage Faith: Two Types of Biblical Faith

TO CONCLUDE THIS stage, I want to consider once again the human response to this understanding of the gospel, for as wonderful as Jesus's gospel is, it is useless to anyone so long as it remains a theological bullet point. Jesus's third-stage listeners also face a decision—one to be made in a moment or over time. Will they trust King Jesus in his offer of friendship?

In the fourth chapter on faith, I discussed Calvin's emphasis on *evangelical* faith, faith *in the gospel*, as opposed to other notable kinds of biblical faith. It should be clear now that this very emphasis is echoed in Willard.[114] Willard is, however, less inclined than Calvin to restrict regeneration and justification to only those who believe in Jesus and his gospel, Abraham being the prime example.

This difference from Calvin points to the fact that there are *two* important types of faith in Willard's system. The most important type is seminally present in Abraham. It is faith in God and his kingdom. Indeed, it is faith in the Triune God inter alia. But Abraham does not need to have all of orthodox theology in view for his faith in the Person to be real and effectual. Willard is apt to also call this faith "the faith *of* Christ." That is, it was Jesus's own faith in (and knowledge of) God and his kingdom, a faith that enabled *him* to lead a robust life in the kingdom of God. Let us call this *integral faith* because it is the faith that was intended for Adam and Eve in creation and for all persons in the new creation.

The second type of faith in Willard's system is "faith *in* Christ." This faith is Willard's *evangelical faith*. It is the faith that Jesus's public ministry in Galilee first makes possible *as a new means* to a robust life in the kingdom of God. The conditions for its possibility were absent before Jesus's entrance into human history. For millennia, Jesus and his gospel were still "the mystery hidden for ages and generations"

114. See the discussion of Abraham's paradigmatic faith in chapter 6.

(Col 1:26).[115] This second evangelical type of faith is not integral but redemptive, because if humanity had never willfully given up integral faith in the fall, there would be, with some qualification, no need for it.

One might consider this book as a breakdown of Willard's second type of faith, *evangelical faith*, into three stadial instances and an attempt to distinguish these evangelical stages of faith from other genuine instances of faith. In three stages, I have attempted to discern what it meant, according to Willard, for the first listeners to trust in Jesus and his gospel of kingdom availability. Often, the other genuine but not evangelical instances of faith were bona fide aspects of the faith *of* Christ, such as faith in the existence of the kingdom of God or in Jesus's divinity.[116] Because of Willard's view that faith can have myriad iterations, with each iteration producing a different kind of life in the person, the concept of faith can be confusing in Willard's thought. But this is part of the *objectivity* of faith. As Willard says, "Faith is a reality which has its causes and its effects."[117]

Only one type of faith—evangelical faith or "faith *in* Christ"—is the iteration of faith that became possible in Jesus's life, ministry, and death and that gave persons (in contrast to the ancient covenant ministry) *easy* entrance into a robust life in the kingdom of God. If a type of faith that is *not* this New Testament faith is presented to people, it will not have, so Willard, the New Testament effects evident on its pages. It will not lead anyone easily into the faith of Abraham and into the faith *of* Christ with the corresponding effect of a robust life in the kingdom of God.

So how does evangelical faith have this effect?

115. Though Willard speaks of the gospel of the Old Testament, it is different from the better gospel of the New Testament, though the prize is the same.

116. Sometimes they were aspects of the body of *knowledge* Israel learned and passed on. Sometimes they were not faith at all.

117. Willard, "Role of Faith," 30:00.

Through *Faith in Christ* to *Faith in God*

INTEGRAL FAITH AND the biblical phrase "the faith of Christ," says Willard, refer mainly to Jesus's faith *in God*. Jesus, unlike sinful humanity to which he came, believed that God was present, able, and good.[118] And to second-stage listeners, Jesus preached a gospel to the effect that he could be trusted as a teacher about God. This means he made disciples who were learning how to believe in God as he did. This, as we have seen, is one way of moving people from faith in Christ to the faith of Christ.[119]

But it is not unlike what mere humans can do for other people. If this is all there is, Jesus is merely a guru, a religious genius, who inspired the apostles to become gurus themselves. What, then, does the secret of the kingdom, the knowledge that Jesus is Lord, add to this? How does faith in Christ *as divine* lead persons to share in Christ's integral faith in God?

Taking a cue from Calvin in his *Institutes*, let me be clear about what, for Willard, the third-stage object of faith is. What is *the reality* known and presented for trust to third-stage listeners? Generally, it is Jesus the person. But specifically, it is King Jesus *as* personally available. It is not Jesus *as* divine or *as* Messiah or *as* authoritative in the kingdom of God. This is not Jesus "clothed with his gospel," as Calvin would say.[120] The reality the third-stage listeners are invited to trust is King Jesus *as a friend*. And when they do trust in him as such, they eo ipso become his friends.

Having, then, this faith in King Jesus, King Jesus's friends move toward faith in God as a friend by means of Jesus's increasingly unique representation of and increasingly unique relationship to God. Jesus, their friend, gradually reestablishes faith in *God as a friend* as they gradually come to put a kingdom to the face. In other words, third-stage trust in Jesus slowly engrafts the believer into personal trust in God. Third-stage

118. Willard, 35:45.
119. Willard speaks about this way in Willard, *Conspiracy* (319), using 1 Pet 1:21.
120. Calvin, *Institutes* 3.2, 6.

believers trust Jesus as present, able, and good, and that trust is gradually and naturally tied into trust in God as present, able, and good.

The mechanism of this engrafting is the increasing revelation of Jesus's eternal position before God, his metaphysical reality. As Jesus is glorified by his Father in heaven, his friends are brought into greater friendship with God himself. But what is trusted is not the mechanism, not his glorification or his metaphysical reality. What is trusted is Jesus's personal availability. And the revelation of the reality of Jesus's position before God transfers the faith in Jesus as personally available to faith in God as personally available. This final instance of faith is part of Willard's integral faith, "the faith *of* Christ." It is the faith in God that Christ has in God—and indeed that God has in himself.

One example of Willard giving voice to this dynamic is in the teachings that make up *Renovation*. In the lectures that inspired *Renovation*, Willard says,

> *The word of the gospel comes into the mind, accepted into the heart, reestablishes the connection with Christ and, through him, to God.*
>
> *I love old Peter's way of putting that in 1 Peter. . . . "He was foreknown before the foundation of the world but he has appeared in these last times for your sake* who through him are believers in God." . . . *It is not safe to go to God without the redefinition that comes in Jesus. It is not possible to go to God.*[121]

This teaching is sketched in his diagram of the human self in *Renovation*.[122] On one side, we see *the cause*, the "Word and Spirit of Christ Enters." This act of grace has *the effect* of "Evoking Faith in Christ Which Re-establishes Communion with God." For those whose faith in Christ

121. Willard, "Changing the Depth," 40:45 (emphasis mine).

122. Willard, *Renovation*, 38. This book and this diagram, it will be noticed, are constructed with an assumption of orthodox Christology—that is, from the perspective of third-stage listeners. See also Willard, "Residency Part 2."

includes a high Christology, the dynamic present in the cause and effect is an engrafting dynamic. We enter first through faith into communion with Christ, who "loved us and gave himself up for us" (Eph 5:2). And on the heels of our faith in him as personally available, communion with God naturally follows.[123] Thus, faith in Christ *reestablishes* faith in God ("*through him* you are believers in God"). Commenting on 1 Peter 1:21 in 1994, Willard says, "Jesus came into the world. He invites us to trust him. And as we trust him, God raises him from the dead. We see the new life, and our faith and our hope are in God."[124]

Engrafting is also the dynamic evident later in *Renovation* in Willard's interpretation of Romans 5:1. He summarizes his whole exegesis of the passage by calling it "an instructive and inspiring progression from an *initial* faith in God."[125] But in detail, it is faith *in Christ* that starts the process: "The initial faith in Christ gives us 'our introduction by faith into this grace in which we stand' (verses 1) [*sic*]. This is the new birth into Christ's kingdom. It puts an end to the war between me and God that has gone on most of my life and surrounds me with God's gracious actions. Now, because of Christ's death for me and his continuing graces, I know that God is good, and I am thrilled with the hope that God's goodness and greatness will serve as the basis of my own existence as well as of everything else."[126] We come to peace with God and "this grace in which we stand" ("God's gracious actions") through our, as Willard calls it, "initial faith *in Christ*" and "the new birth into *Christ's* kingdom." In the Greek text, Willard seems to be interpreting the two prepositional phrases δια . . . Χριστου and δια ου as referring to all that Christ did to allow us to have faith in him. This faith *in* Christ puts us

---

123. This particular model of regeneration is probably most relevant to non-Jews, who supposedly had no communion with God before the more inclusive gospel of Jesus was offered to them.

124. Willard, "Human Disaster of Unbelief," 21:30. See also Dallas Willard, "Kingdom Living—Part 2," *Kingdom Living: Rediscovering Our Hidden Life in God* (Church of the Open Door, Maple Grove, MN, August 25, 2000), MP3, 0:45. Also in Dallas Willard, "Two Faiths / Two Gospels: Jesus' and Ours," *Talbot Chapel* (Biola University, La Mirada, CA, May 21, 1991), MP3/cassette, 20:45.

125. Willard, *Renovation*, 129.

126. Willard, 130.

in touch not with a theological system but with Christ, who, being the unique Son of God, fuses our faith in him with faith in God.[127]

But there are other occasions in *Renovation* when Willard expresses this movement in reverse—that is, in terms of God's movement to humans—and much as described in his exegesis of Romans. Consider the following from the same chapter of *Renovation*:

> *In such a world [where love is unnatural] God intrudes, gently and in many ways, but especially in the person of Jesus Christ. It is he who stands for love, as no one else has ever done, and pays the price for it. His crucifixion is the all-time high-water mark of love on earth. "While we were still helpless, at the right time Christ died for the ungodly" (Romans 5:6). No other source comes close to what God in Christ shows of love. This is the first "move" of love in the process of redemption. "He first loved us" (1 John 4:19).*[128]

This statement explains God's plan to show forth his love through Jesus's love. This initial divine movement allows for a reverse movement back toward God, what Willard calls "the second movement": "Love is awakened in us by him. We feel its call—and first to love Jesus himself, *and then God*."[129] Though the exchange here is put in terms of love, it is not difficult to see that faith follows the same path, being inseparable from love. We first are drawn into love of Jesus, who makes himself personally

---

127. Another verse Willard uses to teach the same dynamic is John 16:23: "In that day you will ask nothing of me. Truly, truly, I say to you, whatever you ask of the Father in my name, he will give it to you." He says, "See, Jesus came to put us in touch with the Father. And at that point, he is saying their confidence would be so great that they would no longer say, 'Jesus would you please stop the storm.' They wouldn't ask him that; they would now ask the Father in his name. The connection would have been made so that Jesus now is one among many brethren" (Willard, "Water of Life," 9:45). In *Disciplines* (178), Willard speaks of worship as moving from Jesus to God, quoting Albert Magnus per above.

128. Willard, *Renovation*, 131–32.

129. Willard, 132 (emphasis mine).

available to us. And his love and personal availability take us into the love and personal availability of God.

The Life of Faith

WHERE DOES THIS faith in Jesus and then God leave those who possess it? What is the *effect* of having faith at this level of gospel understanding? In brief, it is friendship with God. *Communion* is a more traditional theological word. *Reconciliation*, also a good word, is almost too weak because it can be and has been shrunk down to mere pardoning and thus does not involve the restoration of relationship. The effect of this faith is communion with the whole Trinity.

This communion, since our journey through the epistemic progression of the first listeners has been tedious, may seem to be an advanced spiritual condition. But really it is, in the scope of Willard's thought, merely a starting point and not a conclusion. It is much like becoming a disciple—also a starting point and not a conclusion. Indeed, many of Willard's books begin with the assumption that their readers are already friends with God. This is especially true of *Guidance*, *Disciplines*, and *Renovation*. Introducing one of these books, he writes, "The Spirit of the Disciplines is nothing but the love of Jesus, with its resolute will to be like him whom we love."[130] In a sense, *Guidance* and *Renovation* could have begun with a similar statement, for Willard thought of his readers' application of these books in terms of "the second movement" of love back to God *through Jesus*. These books on the work of sanctification—or what Willard preferred to call growth in grace—are intended to show those who already commune with God through Jesus how to go on to greater heights of knowledge and grace (2 Pet 3:18).

And if friendship, like discipleship, is a starting point, where are the greater heights? Perhaps not where we were expecting. "We were *not*," says Willard, "designed just to live in mystic communion with our Maker, as so often suggested." As Willard understands it, friendship with God is not a *telos* in and of itself. "Rather," Willard continues, "we

130. Willard, xii. In the writing process, this book was called *Exercise unto Godliness: A Practical Theology*. This paragraph was written to accommodate the new title.

were created *to govern the earth* with all its living things—and to that specific end we were made in the divine likeness."[131]

Why the Incarnation?

WHY THE INCARNATION? *Cur deus homo?* Willard's answer centers on Christ's unprecedented and unsurpassed representation of man and of God. But there are other answers. Athanasius, in *De incarnatione*, explains how, on one hand, the original image of God in human creatures and in creation would have sufficed as witnesses of God had humans not fallen. Athanasius explains, on the other hand, how humans, having fallen, are fixated on the sense perceptible. He appeals to both of these facts to explain the need for God to condescend to humanity and take on, through a human body, sense-perceptible qualities, especially visible qualities, in order for them to regain knowledge of him.[132] God's solution to ignorance of himself ("bad theology") has always been to teach, and this "the God Word" does, as Athanasius says, "in manifold ways and through many forms."[133] But not all ways are as effective for creatures "with their eyes held downwards seeking god in creation and things perceptible."[134] For this reason, the God Word "takes to himself a body and dwells as human among humans and draws to himself the perceptible senses of all human beings."[135]

Perhaps the reader can already formulate in their mind why Willard does not go for such a solution. Or why he resists the answers that Anselm gave in his famous treatise.[136] I am conscious that some theologians may be underwhelmed by Willard's own answer to *cur deus homo?* feeling that one on a mission as *true* God and *true* man should have accomplished more. Researching Willard has taught me (if anyone cares to know) how tempting it is for orthodox theologians to overanswer *cur*

131. Willard, *Disciplines*, 48.

132. Athanasius, *De incarnatione* xv; cf. Henry Churchill King, *The Seeming Unreality of the Spiritual Life* (New York: Macmillan, 1908).

133. Athanasius, *De incarnatione* xi.

134. Athanasius, xv.

135. Athanasius, xv.

136. Anselm of Canterbury, *Cur deus homo?*

deus homo? and load too much of the weight of salvation on the mission of a God-man. Willard never seems to doubt the fact, but he is careful to distribute the weight of God's plan for humanity onto more than our feeble attempts to make sense of the metaphysics of the Christ and what that mystery might mean for eternity.

CONCLUSION

It is a part of the "spirit" of phenomenology to *not* approach issues or texts und headings anyway—even the heading "Husserlian" or "phenomenology." . . . One of the ironies of philosophical greatness is how the accumulating interpretations of a great philosopher can lead to the obscuring of his own writings—to what, for example, is "Kantian," but very little of Kant. . . . Having, by now, seen a great deal of work supposedly in the "spirit" of some great philosopher, one might fairly conclude that a little subservient exposition might not be an altogether bad thing. After all, there really are very few philosophical geniuses, and a sedulous working out of their texts might prove to be one of better ways toward genuine philosophical enlightenment—better, even, than imaginative constructions under the banner of a great one.

—Dallas Willard, "Translator's Introduction,"
Philosophy of Arithmetic

13

THE ODD DUCK FOR TWENTY-FIRST CENTURY THEOLOGY

> In these three books there is very little that is new, though much that is forgotten. Indeed, if I thought it were new, I would certainly not advocate it or publish it. To see that it is old, and only very recently forgotten, one need only compare it with the writings of P. T. Forsyth, C. S. Lewis, Frank Laubach, E. Stanley Jones, and George MacDonald, among many others of the quite recent past. Then, if one wishes, go on to the greater postbiblical sources such as Athanasius, Augustine, Anselm, Thomas, Luther, and Calvin—and, finally, to the teachings about the world, the soul, and God that lie richly upon the pages of the Bible itself.
>
> —Dallas Willard, *The Divine Conspiracy*

RESEARCH NEVER PROCEEDS in the orderly fashion in which its findings are published.

In approaching the historical task of researching Willard for this book, I devoted much time to reading authors that Willard had some direct relationship with—authors he demonstrably had read in theology, philosophy, psychology, sociology, and so on. One day, after most of my research and writing for this book had drawn to a close, I, for my own personal enrichment, purchased a few theology volumes. On the same day, I remember buying both a treatment of Aquinas's thought and McLeod

Campbell's book *The Nature of the Atonement.*[1] Both sat on my shelf for a while, and eventually I read the Aquinas volume first. Afterward, I pulled down Campbell and, at first, found it cumbersome, though not unrewarding, reading. I was already aware of Campbell's notion of vicarious repentance and, because that was all I knew, had never thought of Campbell in connection with Willard.

Willard, to my knowledge, never mentioned Campbell publicly, nor did he ever speak of atonement in terms of Christ vicariously dealing with God on behalf of man, confessing and repenting of our sin.[2] Campbell is discussed and criticized in a book that Willard appreciated for its historical treatment, G. B. Stevens's *The Christian Doctrine of Salvation.* I had seen *The Nature of the Atonement* on Willard's shelf near to Stevens's book when I visited his house in 2013, but I had also seen thousands of other books. All that is to say, when I read McLeod Campbell, I did not expect to find Dallas Willard.

Campbell's book was the sort of discovery that, if I had read it before I began researching and writing, this book, *The Kingdom among Us*, might have looked very different. It is, I suppose, the sort of connection that we do theological research to find, to be able to see. In the introduction, I stated that this book is the result of research that began as early as 2004, when I received an email from Willard. Here again is the heart of that email: "Nearly all of my 'influences' are from people long dead. I have arrived at my views by studying the Bible philosophically, if you wish, and by reading widely through the ages, and trying to put it all into practice. It is presumptuous to say, but I believe that God has guided my thinking. Certainly nothing I have is really new or 'my own.'"[3]

---

1. McLeod Campbell, *The Nature of the Atonement* (1856; repr., Edinburgh: Handsel, 1996).

2. I did find a handwritten reference to *The Nature of the Atonement* in some of Willard's notes on atonement. The note reads, "The Practicality of the Atonement, the Cross, pp. 267ff of McLeod." The notes were preparation for an April 2000 meeting of the Vineyard Young Leaders Network hosted by Todd Hunter and including Stanley Grenz, Brian McLaren, and Willard, available in the Dallas Willard Collection. Apparently, Willard gave two talks on atonement of which I have found no recording, though I have spoken with persons present.

3. Dallas Willard, email correspondence with the author, July 3, 2004.

It would take a separate essay to make the case that McLeod Campbell is one of those people who was an "influence" for Willard. Perhaps one day I will write that essay.

But Campbell was not the only long-dead theologian who made an impression on Willard. The long-dead Charles Finney, also from the nineteenth century, was a confessed early influence. Willard said that Finney had taught him, among other things, that Jesus's agony in the Garden of Gethsemane was born not of Jesus's desire to avoid the cross but of his desire to get to the cross.[4] Campbell, however, interprets the agony in the garden as an anticipation of suffering, albeit not of physical suffering. We see in a little example like this how Willard sifts through these influences; he is taking the parts that, to his mind, accord with "the presentation of the kingdom of God in the Bible as a whole" and leaving the rest.[5] For what it's worth, I believe Campbell's own argument would only have been strengthened by interpreting the garden experience as Finney does.

Where Campbell, Finney, and Willard line up is that all see the Christ event as saving those who relate to Christ in faith to an abundant life *now*. Campbell calls this the prospective reference of the atonement—namely, the gift of eternal life. And he interprets eternal life as "a manner of existence" or "a kind of life" with which some are acquainted now as "a life lived in humanity." He writes that John the epistle writer witnessed eternal life's manifestation in Jesus's life on earth and that John sought to share this life with others through his Epistles.[6] Finney equally had in view the prospective reference of the atonement that was a life lived in holiness to the Lord now. This is a life, which Finney makes clear in his *Systematic Theology*, that is wholly dependent on the action of the Holy Spirit, who reveals in faith the living Christ in all of his possible relations to us.[7]

---

4. This fact was related to me by Ryan Harmon, who once spent three hours in the car with Willard on the way to the Minneapolis airport.

5. Willard, "Q & A 4," *The Divine Conspiracy* (e4, Hollywood, CA, July 8, 2004), MP3/video, 43:30.

6. Campbell, *Nature of the Atonement*, 42.

7. Finney, *Systematic Theology*, lecture 62.

Very early on, perhaps earlier than we may ever have evidence for, Willard called into question the soteriology of his fundamentalist, dispensationalist, neoevangelical upbringing that the Christ event was intended to save those with faith (in a theory of the atonement and a few other "fundamentals") from an afterlife spent in hell. Within such soteriology, Willard writes, "getting into heaven after death is the sole *target* of divine and human efforts for salvation."[8] With this he contrasts his own view of salvation's target: "having life from the kingdom of the heavens now—the eternal kind of life." This is a state of being that one may know by acquaintance, if one wishes, and is continuous with the life one may live after death. It is hard not to hear echoes of Willard when Campbell writes, "I do not speak of an unknown future blessedness, in a future state of being, of which conscience can understand nothing; but I speak of life which in itself is one and the same here and hereafter."[9]

Moving On

IN THE END, Willard was not a Campbellite any more than he was a Finneyite. And so it was with many of Willard's long-dead influences; he followed them to a point and moved on. The same could be said of the heavyweights Willard names at the beginning of *The Divine Conspiracy*: Athanasius, Augustine, Anselm, Thomas, Luther, and Calvin.[10] And the same could be said even of American fundamentalism and neoevangelicalism. And though in the latter case, the moving on was significant biographically for Willard, it is important to recall how he retained some respect for the teachers of his fundamentalist youth, dedicating *Conspiracy* to five "giants," as he called them.[11]

Where Willard ended up theologically is not exactly easy to put in a word or a short statement. I find it difficult to even identify one like-minded contemporary. I daresay there are not any. Three of the people

---

8. Willard, *Conspiracy*, 47.
9. Campbell, *Nature of the Atonement*, 42–43.
10. Willard, *Conspiracy*, xviii.
11. Willard, v.

named in *Conspiracy*'s introduction—C. S. Lewis, Frank Laubach, and E. Stanley Jones—were alive while Willard was still in graduate school.[12] To that list one could add James S. Stewart; John Bright; D. Elton Trueblood; A. W. Tozer; Agnes Sanford; his teachers at Baylor, such as Kyle Yates, Leonard Duce, Haywood Shuford Jr., and Jack Kilgore; and even the late Dietrich Bonhoeffer. But all these persons were two generations removed from Willard and do not exactly constitute a school of theology. So one is pressed to look even deeper in the history of theology, and one will find, I believe, that the only school or book Willard did not sift like wheat is the Bible. There is no reliable way to measure it, but friends' and Willard's own personal anecdotes suggest that Willard read and studied the Bible *a lot*, memorizing large portions.

But studying the Bible and having a voracious reading habit do not alone account for his thought or its uniqueness in the twentieth century. We must look to his research in philosophy, which he undertook, let us never forget, mainly in order to be a more capable disciple and minister of Christ. I do not think he set out to be a twentieth-century maverick, but the discoveries he brought from philosophy into theology have been little seen. It is fair to say that Willard was a Husserlian, but in the same sense that I, having had high school geometry, am a Euclidean. I've seen for myself the properties of triangles, and Willard saw for himself, or so he says, the properties of consciousness, of universals, of knowledge, and so on.

These discoveries and others in his philosophical research helped him make sense of the knowledge of God and the soul he was finding in the Bible, in Jesus, and in Jesus's people. For example, in the introduction to *Conspiracy*, he writes, "I assume that they [the writers of the Bible] were quite capable of accurately interpreting their own experience."[13] This statement is influenced by Willard's study of Husserl and phenomenology, which helped Willard understand subjective experience in ways that are not subjective. Whether a theologian as worried about the role of experience as Karl Barth could get behind Willard's approach to

---

12. Willard, xviii.
13. Willard, xvi.

experience for theology I admit I do not know. But I do know there are phenomenological tendencies scattered through the history of theology, not just in Schleiermacher or Wilhelm Herrmann. Though one can see that theologians have always had implicit, nonrigorous, and limited knowledge of phenomenology, it took an Edmund Husserl to push humanity forward to explicit, codified, and extensive knowledge. But there are other philosophical gains for theology in Willard's corpus, and books different from this one will be necessary to bring those to light.

"Just Look at Him"

IN *THE KINGDOM among Us*, I have tried to set forward Dallas Willard's understanding of the gospel, especially Jesus's gospel. In a real sense, Jesus's gospel is not a message but Jesus himself. In evangelizing the earth, he offers himself to the world as a reality for trusting. Jesus's main message, "The kingdom of God is at hand," is eo ipso a revelation of who he is, for his personal reality is one that has real relations to the kingdom of God. And through those real relations to the kingdom of God, Jesus makes a robust life in the kingdom of God possible for his listeners. This is the Christ event, the gospel according to Dallas Willard.

Though in my interpretation of Willard I could have taken a God's eye view of the Christ event, there were many advantages to taking a listeners' eye view, not the least of which is its being an approach the Scriptures themselves take. I think one of the biggest gains is that the conspiratorial nature of Willard's presentation of Jesus comes across better. In a sermon from 1982, Willard says,

> *When I am engaged in a discussion with someone who wishes to argue about the deity of Christ, I normally will not try to haggle about the words with them but simply say, "Just look at him and then you call it whatever you want to. Just look at him. Take the gospels. Take the history of the church. Take the literature and the lives that have been reflective of him through the ages. Just look. And you put whatever name you want to on it. But look. Look at it. Take it in. Absorb it in your mind."*

> *I don't believe it is useful to go on great surges of self-righteousness to try to prove these things and that, in fact, if you do that, you're apt to distract the person who needs it most from the clear look at Christ himself. Christ will carry his case.*[14]

This gentle, conspiratorial, look-for-yourself approach to Jesus is what Willard sees in the Christ event itself. Jesus shows up, he helps people with their real lives, he speaks enthymematically about himself, and he leaves. But for those who seek him, he remains, says Willard—and is more available than ever.

Following that pattern, it was only in the final chapters of this book that this listeners' eye view began to meet a God's eye view, or at least as much of the latter as divine revelation and mundane human experience allow for. The God's eye view, so Willard, is that the personal reality of God entered the world in the man Jesus and by means of his life and message (offering himself as a reality for trusting). "We are invited to make a pilgrimage," Willard writes, "into the heart and life of God."[15] Though "God's desire for us" was always "that we should live in him," through Jesus, God brought his eternal purposes into a new era of fulfillment.[16]

One must not understand the newness of the new era too radically, thinks Willard. There is a great deal of continuity in God's work before Jesus and after Jesus. Above all, the kingdom of God had always been available, though given the depraved state of human life, it had not been as effectively available as God wanted. When Jesus comes and offers to induct everyone who trusts in him into the kingdom, the old ways of inducting people into the kingdom become obsolete. Jesus's ministry to the kingdom of God is simply better. He is a teacher taking apprentices—disciples—who learn from him how to live in the

---

14. Dallas Willard, "The Way of Peace," *Death and Transfiguration*, MP3/cassette, 24:00.
15. Willard, *Conspiracy*, 11.
16. Willard, 11.

kingdom of God as he himself does. This offer is something new in human history.

It is also something new that God reveals himself more fully in Jesus and reveals himself as "light," as one in whom there "is no darkness at all" (1 John 1:5) or, as Willard writes, "a community of boundless and totally competent love."[17] McLeod Campbell calls this aspect of the Christ event "the Son's honouring the Father in the sight of man."[18] This is the gospel of the *availability* of the kingdom, "the message we have heard from him and proclaim to you" (1 John 1:5) with a God's eye view. Willard acknowledges the years of experience with Jesus that the listeners needed before they could reliably identify him with the God of Abraham, Isaac, and Jacob. Only then could they appreciate Jesus's evangelical revelation of God in his life, his message, and his ongoing work at the right hand of the Father.

What has given this book on Jesus and his gospel its particular character as a study of Christology and soteriology is the fact that I have tried to set forward Dallas Willard's understanding of how Jesus's first listeners gradually embraced him and his gospel in knowledge *and* faith. Though knowledge is essential, it is the listeners' faith in Jesus that made them into regenerate children (stage 1), then disciples of Jesus (stage 2), and then friends of God (stage 3). Looking back from stage 3 to stages 1 and 2, I would caution readers to *not* think of these as stages of sanctification as, for example, some church fathers divided between stages of purgation, illumination, and union. Looking back, they are better thought of in Willard's theology as three starting points corresponding to three ontological relations that exist between Jesus and the kingdom of God. Some traditions of sanctification have been better at promoting one over the other. That claim is a historical essay in and of itself. Indeed, I am not even supposing that these three ontological relations systematically exhaust Jesus's ontological relations to the kingdom. What we often need in systematic theology are shelves to unpack our traveling suitcases, if only temporarily, in order to show others how they

17. Willard, 11.
18. Campbell, *Nature of the Atonement*, 133.

may begin to understand biblical ontology for themselves. That too is something that Willard's work in phenomenology could teach theology.

In Lieu of a Eulogy

AFTER PRODUCING A book of this size, it is hard to disguise the fact that I think Willard's thought is worth the attention given to more celebrated theologians. I admit it; I hope that this book will help pull Willard out of the category of an inspirational speaker and spirituality guru with a few books that sold well and show him to be a theologian with a love for the Bible, deep familiarity with intellectual history, and intimidating philosophical muscle. Whether Willard was a theologian in the truest sense of the word—that is, a person with genuine knowledge of God and the soul—is another question and not one I have dealt with directly.

The primary question for this sort of scholarship in our generation is whether we have understood Willard. Even with the contribution of this book, I believe we have only begun. There is the massive work of piecing together his philosophical thought. This will not be as easy as reading Willard's PhD, two monographs, and more than sixty published papers, though that is a good start and not one that I surmise those who dismiss Willard as an uncelebrated minor philosopher have attempted. Fifty million Frenchmen *can* be wrong and so can twentieth century professional societies largely dismissive of philosophical realism.

But I would feel dishonest if I did not point out some of the weaknesses of Willard as a theologian. I appreciate, as mentioned in the first chapter, that Willard did not seek a place to speak or to publish but sought above all to have something to say. But I disagree, as I said, with how Willard conducted himself as an intellectual once he knew he had "something to say." Calling it in *Conspiracy* his "too-great readiness to accept various kinds of commitments," he was simply too free with his calendar to appropriately leverage for good the knowledge he had been given.[19] He left a book on the epistemology of logic and a book on identity and substance unfinished and would have left his book on the

19. Willard, *Conspiracy*, xix.

disappearance of moral knowledge unfinished if not for the eleventh-hour intervention of his former students.[20]

In theology, instead of using the success of his books to create space to more fully research and expound his views, he gave huge amounts of his time to being an itinerant Sunday school teacher. No doubt, he was a very, very good itinerant Sunday school teacher, but in the last fifteen years, the talks and lectures tended to be very similar because he had less time to prepare and because, with ever new audiences, he had to return again and again to the basics. Perhaps he was imitating one of his mentors, Edmund Husserl, who famously thought of himself as "a perpetual beginner." More likely, I believe, he did not manage his time well enough to devote his best time to teaching more advanced topics for more advanced audiences and to writing.

That decision, or lack thereof, had an effect on the quality of sources Willard left. Perhaps there is conspiratorial wisdom in leaving your life's work to the whims of "sound guys" in the back of the room. Jesus, after all, left it all up to the memories of his listeners, and we know Willard took conscious steps to imitate Jesus's approach. But the quality *is* lacking. Even if the difficulty of listening to audio were lightened by the availability of transcriptions (something that we may still hope happens), many of Willard's late messages are merely creatively reassembled versions of other messages.

Even if Willard had structured his last twenty-five years differently, even if he had given his best time in those years to the gospel and had researched and published his theology more straightforwardly, there would still have been gaps in his theological knowledge. His grasp of intellectual history was impressive but was of necessity skewed toward the history of philosophy and the questions typically addressed there. It is true that Willard left very few theological rocks unturned, but he did not study each spot in detail. He told one audience, "I'm not a professional in the history of theology. I have other things to

20. Willard, *Disappearance*, xiv–xv.

do."[21] Take a doctrine like the kingdom of God, which Willard studied for decades. Most likely he could not have given details of how this concept was treated in each of the church fathers or in the latest monographs of biblical scholarship. Whether this would have mattered for his own knowledge of the kingdom is another question.[22] But it was a gap.

These weaknesses acknowledged (and there are more), it is not accurate to regard Willard as a lay theologian—as, for example, we often rightly regard C. S. Lewis. Lewis remained and, at least within his tradition, lived like a layman; Willard, however, felt the gracious responsibility for preaching and teaching the gospel all of his adult life and, notably, for marshaling the best knowledge for that work. In that respect, he was more akin to Dietrich Bonhoeffer, who combined trust in the gospel and a pursuit of the best knowledge with an active and time-consuming concern for the welfare of the church and individuals in his time.

The difference between Bonhoeffer and Willard is in the maturity to which each could develop their thought. Bonhoeffer died at thirty-nine years of age. But Willard, upon turning thirty-nine in 1974, had already spent eighteen years as a minister, ten of those in university posts. Listening to young Willard teach in their small church, Richard J. Foster recalls thinking, "This is what it must have been like to be at Finkenwalde, hearing Bonhoeffer."[23] But unlike Bonhoeffer, Willard would be given almost another thirty-nine years for reading, researching, teaching, and ministering before dying in the year he would turn seventy-eight. These are the thirty-nine years in which he published his first two books, at age forty-nine. These are the thirty-nine years when he entered the spotlight, at age fifty-three. So if Foster's comparison with Bonhoeffer is accurate in 1974, to whom should one then compare a man who had another thirty-nine years to develop his theology? I won't answer that question. I will simply leave it here for readers to ponder.

---

21. Dallas Willard, "The Necessity of Being a Disciple of Jesus," *Restoring Your Spiritual Passion* (First Evangelical Free Church, Wichita, KS, February 24, 1995), MP3/cassette, 53:00.
22. Probably not.
23. Moon, *Becoming Dallas Willard*, 165.

SUBJECT INDEX

NAME INDEX

SCRIPTURE INDEX